The
Craft
of
Argument

Third Edition

Joseph M. Williams
University of Chicago

Gregory G. Colomb
University of Virginia

PEARSON
Longman

New York • San Francisco • Boston
London • Toronto • Sydney • Tokyo • Singapore • Madrid
Mexico City • Munich • Paris • Cape Town • Hong Kong • Montreal

Senior Sponsoring Editor: Virginia L. Blanford
Senior Marketing Manager: Sandra McGuire
Senior Supplements Editor: Donna Campion
Media Supplements Editor: Jenna Egan
Project Coordination, Text Design, and Electronic Page Makeup: Thompson Steele
Senior Cover Design Manager: Nancy Danahy
Cover Designer: Nancy Sacks
Manufacturing Manager: Mary Fischer
Printer and Binder: R.R. Donnelley and Sons
Cover Printer: Phoenix Color Corporation

For permission to use copyrighted material, grateful acknowledgment is made to the copyright holders on page 487, which are hereby made part of this copyright page.

Library of Congress Cataloging-in-Publication Data

Williams, Joseph M.
   The craft of argument / Joseph M. Williams, Gregory G. Colomb.–3rd ed.
     p. cm.
   Includes index.
   ISBN 0-321-45327-1
     1. English language—Rhetoric. 2. Persuasion (Rhetoric). 3. Report
writing. I. Colomb, Gregory G. II. Title.

PE1431.W65 2007
808'.042—dc22

                                                                2006026416

Please visit us at www.ablongman.com

ISBN 0-321-45327-1

1 2 3 4 5 6 7 8 9 10—DOH—09 08 07 06

Brief Contents

PART I: THE NATURE OF ARGUMENT   I

Chapter 1: Argument, Critical Thinking, and Rationality   3

Chapter 2: Argument as Civil Conversation   32

Chapter 3: Motivating Your Argument   72

PART II: DEVELOPING YOUR ARGUMENT   III

Chapter 4: The Core of Your Argument: Finding and Stating a Claim   113

Chapter 5: The Core of Your Argument: Reasons and Evidence   132

Chapter 6: The Core of Your Argument: Reporting Evidence   160

Chapter 7: Your Reader's Role in Your Argument:
Acknowledgments and Responses   185

Chapter 8: The Logic of Your Argument: Warranting Claims and Reasons   203

PART III: THINKING ABOUT THINKING IN ARGUMENTS   233

Chapter 9: The Forms of Reasoning   235

Chapter 10: Arguments About Meanings   246

Chapter 11: Arguments About Causes   274

PART IV: THE LANGUAGES OF ARGUMENT   301

Chapter 12: Clear Language   303

Chapter 13: The Overt and Covert Force of Language   331

CHECKLISTS FOR PLANNING AND REVISING   347

Appendix 1: Avoiding Inadvertent Plagiarism Through Proper Citations   360

Appendix 2: Cognitive Biases and Fallacies   373

PART V: READINGS   383

Detailed Contents

A Topical Contents of the Writing Process Sections   *xv*

Teaching the Craft of Argument   *xix*

A Message to Students   *xxix*

Acknowledgments   *xxxv*

PART I: THE NATURE OF ARGUMENT   1

Chapter I: Argument, Critical Thinking, and Rationality   3

What Is Argument?   3

What Good Is Argument?   5

Arguments Help Us Think Critically   5

Arguments Help Us Sustain Communities   8

Arguments Define Academic and Professional Communities   9

Arguments Enable Democracy   11

What's Not an Argument?   12

Three Forms of Persuasion That Are Not Arguments   12

Arguments and Explanations   13

Arguments and Stories   14

Arguments and Visual Images   15

Writing Process: Argument and Critical Thinking   16

Thinking and Talking   16

Reading and Researching   19

Preparing and Planning   20

Drafting   21

Revising   22

Working Collaboratively   23

Inquiries   24

Reflections   25

Tasks   26

Projects   27

Focus on Writing   28

In a Nutshell   31

Chapter 2: Argument as Civil Conversation   **32**

  The Five Questions of Argument   **32**

  The Roots of Argument in Civil Conversation   **34**

    The Core of Sue's Argument   36

    The Explicitly Dialogic Part of Sue's Argument   38

    The Explicitly Logical Part of Sue's Argument   39

  Review: Modeling an Argument   **41**

    The Core of an Argument: Claim + Reasons + Evidence   41

    Dialogue with Readers: Acknowledgment + Response   44

    Explaining Logic: Warrants   46

  Crafting Written Arguments   **47**

  Thickening Your Argument   **49**

  Writing Process: Argument as Civil Conversation   **50**

    Thinking and Talking   50

    Preparing and Planning   51

    Drafting   58

    Revising   59

  Inquiries   **59**

    Reflections   60

    Tasks   60

    Projects   61

  Focus on Writing   **62**

  In a Nutshell   **69**

Chapter 3: Motivating Your Argument   **72**

  Two Kinds of Problems   **73**

  How Practical and Conceptual Problems Motivate Arguments   **73**

    The Two-Part Structure of Practical Problems   74

    The Two-Part Structure of Conceptual Problems   75

    How to Identify Motivating Costs or Consequences
      by Asking *So What?*   76

  Framing Problems in Introductions   **79**

    The Core of an Introduction: Conditions and Costs   79

    The Outer Frame of an Introduction: Common Ground and Solution   84

  Conclusions   **92**

  Introductions and Conclusions as Ways of Thinking   **93**

Problem-Posing Versus Problem-Solving Arguments   94

Writing Process: Motivating Your Argument   **96**

Reading and Research   96
Preparing and Planning   96
Drafting   100
Revising   100
Working Collaboratively   102

Inquiries   **102**

Reflections   102
Tasks   103
Projects   104

Focus on Writing   **104**

In a Nutshell   **108**

PART II: DEVELOPING YOUR ARGUMENT   **III**

Chapter 4: The Core of Your Argument:
Finding and Stating a Claim   **113**

Exploring Claims Without Rushing to Judgment   **114**

What Kind of Claim Does Your Problem Require?   **115**

Is Your Claim Practical or Conceptual?   115
How Strongly Do You Want Readers to Accept Your Claim?   117

What Counts as a Claim Worth Considering?   **118**

What Does a Thoughtful Claim Look Like?   **120**

Is Your Claim Conceptually Rich?   121
Is Your Claim Logically Rich?   122
Is Your Claim Appropriately Qualified?   123

Writing Process: Finding and Stating Claims   **125**

Drafting   125
Revising   126

Inquiries   **127**

Reflections   127
Tasks   128
Projects   128

Focus on Writing   **128**

In a Nutshell   **130**

Chapter 5: The Core of Your Argument: Reasons and Evidence   132

  Supporting Claims   132

  Reasons and Evidence as Forms of Support   133

  Distinguishing Reasons and Evidence   135

  Distinguishing Evidence and Reports of It   136

  Direct and Reported Evidence   136

  Multiple Reasons   140

  Reasons in Parallel   140

  Reasons in Sequence   141

  The Deep Complexity of Serious Arguments   142

  Using Reasons to Help Readers Understand Evidence   142

  Writing Process: Reasons and Evidence   144

  Preparing and Planning   144

  Drafting   148

  Revising   151

  Inquiries   152

  Reflections   152

  Tasks   153

  Project   153

  Focus on Writing   154

  In a Nutshell   159

Chapter 6: The Core of Your Argument: Reporting Evidence   160

  Weigh Your Burden of Evidence   160

  Make a Plan to Find Evidence   162

  The Four Maxims of Quality   162

  Trustworthy Reports of Evidence   165

  Reports of Memories   165

  Anecdotes   166

  Reports from Authorities   166

  Visual Reports with Photographs, Drawings, and Recordings   167

  Visual Presentations of Quantitative Data   168

  Radical Skepticism   171

  Writing Process: Reporting Evidence   173

  Reading and Research   173

  Working Collaboratively   177

Inquiries   **177**

Reflections   177
Task   178
Projects   178

Focus on Writing   **180**

In a Nutshell   **183**

Chapter 7: Your Reader's Role in Your Argument:
Acknowledgments and Responses   **185**

The Importance of Other Viewpoints   186

Questions About Your Problem and Its Solution   187

Questions About Your Support   188

Questions About Your Consistency   189

Responding with Subordinate Arguments   191

Writing Process: Acknowledgment and Responses   194

Reading and Research   194
Preparing and Planning   194
Drafting   196
Working Collaboratively   198

Inquiries   **200**

Reflections   200
Tasks   200
Projects   200

Focus on Writing   **201**

In a Nutshell   **202**

Chapter 8: The Logic of Your Argument:
Warranting Claims and Reasons   **203**

The Reasoning Behind Reasons   204

What Warrants Look Like   206

How Warrants Work   207

Knowing When to Use Warrants in a Written Argument   209

The Most Common Uses for Warrants   209
Two Special Uses for Warrants   211

How to Test a Warrant   213

Distinguishing Reasons and Warrants   218

Review: A Test Case	**218**
Warranting Evidence	**221**
Arguing by Evidence Versus Arguing by Warrants	**223**
Writing Process: Warrants	**224**
Preparing and Planning	224
Working Collaboratively	227
Inquiries	**227**
Reflections	227
Tasks	228
Project	229
Focus on Writing	**229**
In a Nutshell	**231**

PART III: THINKING ABOUT THINKING IN ARGUMENTS	**233**
Chapter 9: The Forms of Reasoning	**235**
Three Forms of Reasoning	**235**
Inductive Reasoning: From Specifics to a General Conclusion	235
Deductive Reasoning: From a Generalization to a Specific Conclusion	236
Abductive Reasoning: From Problem to Hypothesis to Confirmation	236
Real-Life Barriers to Abductive Critical Thinking	**237**
Don't Rely on Warrants in Place of Evidence	237
Don't Collect Evidence Randomly	239
Guard Against the Biases Common in Abductive Thinking	239
Writing Process: The Forms of Reasoning	**243**
Preparing and Planning	243
Inquiries	**243**
Reflections	243
In a Nutshell	**244**
Chapter 10: Arguments About Meanings	**246**
Some Terminology	**247**
Meanings and Problems	**250**
What Problem Does the Definition of Your Term Solve?	250
Is the Issue of Meaning a Surrogate for a Larger Problem?	250

How to Argue About Meanings   **254**

Do Readers Expect Common or Authorized Meanings?   255
Strategies for Using Common Meanings   256
Strategies for Using Authorized Meanings   258
When to Rely on Authorized Definitions   259
Why Dictionaries Cannot Settle Arguments Over Meaning   260

Writing Process: Arguments About Meanings   **265**

Preparing and Planning   265
Drafting   267

Inquiries   **268**

Reflections   268
Tasks   269
Projects   270

In a Nutshell   **271**

Chapter II: Arguments About Causes   **274**

The Impossible Vastness of Causes   **274**

Finding Relevant Causes   **275**

Everyday Thinking About Causation   275
Thoughtful Thinking About Specific Causation   278

Analyzing Causation Systematically   **280**

The Principle of Similarity and Difference   280
The Principle of Covariation   282
ANOVA as Exploration   282
Four Cautions About Using the Principles   283

Causation and Personal Responsibility   **284**

Who's Responsible?   284
Five Criteria for Assigning Personal Responsibility   286
Attribution Bias   287

Writing Process: Arguments About Causes   **291**

Preparing and Planning   291
Drafting   297

Inquiries   **298**

Reflections   298
Task   299

In a Nutshell   **299**

PART IV: THE LANGUAGES OF ARGUMENT   301

Chapter 12: Clear Language   303

Some Principles of Clear and Direct Writing   304

The Principles in a Nutshell   311

Concision and Vividness   312

How to Be Concise   312
How to Be Vivid   314
Abstract Versus Concrete   315
The System of Imageable Words   316
Deliberate Generality   317

Writing Process: Clear Language   319

Revising   319

Inquiries   321

Reflections   321
Tasks   322

A Guide to Terms   323

In a Nutshell   328

Chapter 13: The Overt and Covert Force of Language   331

Invoking Values, Evoking Feeling   331

Value-Laden Words   331
You Can't Avoid Values   332

When Emotional Language Undermines Sound Thinking   334

Polarizing Language   334
Cynical Language   335

Subjects and Point of View   336

Manipulating Subjects to Assign Responsibility   336
Treating Means as Agents   338

Abstractions as Characters   339

Metaphorical Scenarios   341

Writing Process: The Overt and Covert Force of Language   343

Drafting   343
Revising   343

Inquiries   344

Reflections   344

Tasks   345

In a Nutshell   **345**

| **CHECKLISTS FOR PLANNING AND REVISING** | **347** |

A Checklist for Evaluating Discussion/Paper Questions   347
A Checklist for Argument   348
Ten Steps to a Coherent Paper   348
A Complete List of Questions   351
Storyboarding a Long Paper   356

**Appendix 1: Avoiding Inadvertent Plagiarism
Through Proper Citations**   **360**

Appendix 2: Cognitive Biases and Fallacies   **373**

| **PART V: READINGS** | **383** |

Section 1: Attitudes Toward Teaching and Learning   **385**

**Obstacles to Open Discussion and Critical Thinking:
The Grinnell College Study**   **385**
    Carol Trosset

On the Uses of a Liberal Education   **393**
    Mark Edmundson

Has Student Consumerism Gone Too Far?   **401**
    Michael Pernal

**The Student as Consumer: The Implications and Limitations
of a Metaphor**   **406**
    Jill J. McMillan and George Cheney

Customers and Markets   **420**
    Craig Swenson

Section 2: Bingeing, Risk, and Public Health   **425**

Health and Behavioral Consequences of Binge Drinking in College: **425**

A National Survey of Students at 140 Campuses
    *Henry Wechsler, Andrea Davenport, George Dowdall,
    Barbara Moeykens, and Sonia Castillo*

Purging Bingeing   441
  Ed Carson

"Drinking Age Has Simply Got to Go," Say Campus Riots   446
  Pamela White

Wisdom in a Bottle   449
  Camille Paglia

Binge Drinking as a Substitute for a "Community of Learning"   451
  Kenneth A. Bruffee

Smoking and the Tyranny of Public Health   454
  Jacob Sullum

Turkey Police, Beware   461
  Richard Berman

Section 3: Lying   463

Lying: Moral Choice in Public and Private Life   463
  Sissela Bok

Lies, Damn Lies, and Statistics   476
  Jonathan Rauch

Is It Ever Right to Lie? The Philosophy of Deception   479
  Robert C. Solomon

Yes, Sometimes Lying Is Right Action to Take   483
  Lorraine Dusky

Credits   487

Index   488

A Topical Contents of the Writing Process Sections

	CHAPTER	PAGE
Thinking and Talking		
Tell Your Elevator Story	1	16
Think About Your Readers	1	17
Using the Questions of Argument for Critical Thinking	2	50
Reading and Researching		
Get an Overview	1	19
Use Problem Statements to Focus Your Reading	3	96
Planning Your Hunt for Evidence	6	173
Taking Research Notes	6	176
Use Others' Acknowledgments to Understand Context	7	194
Collect Alternatives as You Read	7	194
Preparing and Planning		
General		
Focus on Your Problem	1	21
Exploring a Topic to Find a Problem	3	96
Guard Against Leaping to a Conclusion	9	243
Anticipate the Biases of Your Readers	9	243
Anticipate Questions About Meaning	10	265
Pick a Strategy for Matching Referents and Meanings	10	265
Outlining		
To Outline or Not to Outline	1	21
Three Strategies for Designing an Argument	2	51
Stock Plans to Avoid	2	51
Sketch a Plan for Your Argument	2	52
Five Narratives Supporting Solutions to a Pragmatic Problem	11	291
Strategic Decisions in Designing Narratives About Causes	11	292

	CHAPTER	PAGE
Planning an Argument Assigning Personal Responsibility	11	296
Reasons and Evidence		
Be Aware What Your Reasons Imply About Your Claim (and You)	5	144
Ordering Multiple Reasons	5	145
Warrants		
Identify Your Key Assumptions	8	224
Locate Warrants Where They Do the Most Good	8	225
Use Analogies as Surrogate Warrants	8	225
Acknowledgment and Response		
Add Acknowledgments After You Draft	7	194
Locate Acknowledgments and Responses Where Readers Are Likely to Think of Them	7	195
Building a Whole Argument Around Alternatives	7	195
Drafting		
General		
When to Begin Drafting	1	22
Styles of Drafting	1	22
When to Stop Planning and Start Drafting	2	58
Drafting a Working Introduction	2	58
The Language of Common Ground	3	100
Creating Room to Redefine Terms	10	267
Introducing Dictionary Definitions	10	267
The Language of Causality	11	297
When to Think About Values	13	343
Claims		
Use Specific Language to State Claims	4	125
Reasons and Evidence		
Quoting and Paraphrasing	5	148
Integrating Quotations into Your Sentences	5	149
Avoiding Inadvertent Plagiarism	5	150

	CHAPTER	PAGE
Acknowledgment and Response		
The Vocabulary of Acknowledgment and Response	7	196
Revising		
Match Your Introduction to Your Conclusion	2	59
Test Your Introduction and Conclusion	3	100
Check for Common Themes in the Body of Your Argument	3	101
Build a Title Out of Your Key Concepts	3	101
Qualify Claims That Are Too Certain	4	126
Balance Reasons and Evidence	5	151
Revising for Style	12	319
Subjects and Point of View	13	343
Working Collaboratively		
Process		
Why Collaborate?	1	23
Setting Up a Writing Group	1	24
Activities		
Ask *So What?*	3	102
Share Plans and Resources	6	177
Test Each Other's Drafts	6	177
Ask Tough Questions	7	198

Teaching the Craft of Argument

Our aim in *The Craft of Argument* is to help students integrate the skills of writing, critical thinking, and arguing so that they can write arguments that are clear, sound, and persuasive. We designed the book to support a variety of writing classes, including those that emphasize academic argument, civic argument, critical thinking, or research.

We discuss argument in ways that are rooted in the rhetorical tradition that began even before Aristotle's *Rhetoric,* but we supplement that tradition with new insights not only about the nature of argument but also about how we reason, make decisions, understand matters like responsibility and causation, respond to written texts, and more. We have integrated these insights into a framework of instruction accessible to students and easy to teach without requiring any expert knowledge outside of writing studies.

In this preface, we outline our ideas about how best to use this book and then explain how this book differs from traditional approaches and current texts on argument.

How to Use This Book

We designed this book to engage students with arguments and critical thinking in multiple ways from multiple perspectives. To that end, its chapters have at least four, and in some cases six parts, each approaching its subject from a different angle.

Each chapter has two main units:

- An opening section, which discusses one aspect of written arguments. This section helps students understand the nature of arguments, their parts, their goals, and their role in shaping what we do and believe.

- A parallel Writing Process section, which revisits the earlier discussion in light of strategies, procedures, checklists, and other tools for using what students have learned. It includes units on planning, research, drafting, revising, and working collaboratively.

We regard this dual perspective as crucial. In the first section, students learn a model of argument that helps them understand its nature and analyze specific arguments, their own and others'. But students seldom write better arguments just because they can name their parts. So the Writing Process sections give students nuts-and-bolts advice about how best to use what they learn about argument to write more complete and convincing ones.

In these sections we maintain another dual perspective: arguments have predictable parts because readers ask predictable questions. Each perspective has its own value. Writers are best served by the analytic model of argument when they step back from the flow of their thinking: for planning, organizing, and outlining and then for analyzing, testing, and revising. The questions of argument serve best to guide brainstorming, reflecting, drafting, and other moments when writers benefit from getting caught up in the flow of their thinking.

We hope you will give as much attention to the Writing Process sections as to the opening discussions and that you focus students as much on the questions of argument as on the model and its parts. In our experience, students not only write better but understand argument better when they connect argument to writing on the one hand and writing to conversation on the other.

Students know a lot about argument and bring to class considerable abilities in interacting with others. They will be better able to draw on those resources if you consistently lead them to connect what they are learning with their experience and intuitions. To that end, we have provided additional resources to prime their thinking.

The first resource is in the separate *Guide to Teaching the Craft of Argument*. It describes a hundred or more activities you can use to engage students' intuitions before and as they learn new ways of thinking about argument. (There are too many for any one class, so pick and choose to suit your students and your style.) These include in-class, take-home, and formal assignments that involve students in discussing issues, identifying questions and problems, generating and testing answers, and developing the elements of argument needed to support them. If students then read each chapter *after* these interactions activate their intuitive understanding of cooperative arguing, the chapter will help them organize, consolidate, and apply what they already know to the challenging new task of producing a formal written argument.

Students benefit in another way from guided classroom experience in making arguments for and with their colleagues. These interactions also help students understand the *point* of producing written arguments in the first place. Talking with one another, they discover and articulate problems or questions that potential *readers* think are worth solving or answering, and the kinds of questions *readers* are likely to ask in response to their claims, reasons, and evidence. Without such genuine interaction, students may well feel that their assigned arguments are pointless exercises in grinding out pages only to satisfy a teacher's formal requirement.

We include two more priming resources in the text itself:

- Most chapters are interlaced with examples of argument, many drawn from the readings. Some illustrate the main discussion, but most raise issues that invite students to pursue directions only hinted at in the main text.

- Each chapter has an Inquiries section that raises new questions, prompts reflection over puzzling facts or events, and suggests activities, all intended to spur further thinking.

We include more examples and inquiries than any student can hope to complete. You can tell your students to ignore them entirely, have them pick one or two to think about, or assign some as topics for papers. A few are even worth a research paper. Some of their issues are so difficult that we expect them merely to pique interest and stimulate thinking. None of them, so far as we know, has just one right answer.

Finally, chapters include some additional resources as well:

- In each chapter, we conclude with a concise summary of both the discussion of argument and the writing process advice.
- In several early chapters, we provide either sample student essays that illustrate the uses and abuses of argument or exercises in analyzing and revising those essays.
- In Chapters 1–8, we provide writing projects, ranging from short informal assignments to formal papers.
- In Chapters 3–8, we outline a guided, staged exercise in preparing, planning, drafting, and revising a longer research paper.
- At the end of Part IV, we include a section of checklists and worksheets for planning, revising, and storyboarding papers.
- A companion Web site (www.ablongman.com/williams) includes additional activities and examples, traditional quizzes and exercises, along with other supporting materials.

With all of that variety, we hope to encourage you to use this book to support but not constrain your teaching.

Finally, we hope that this book can help you do more than show students how to write plausible academic papers based on sound critical thinking. We hope that it encourages students to think about argumentation as a subject in its own right, as something at the heart of their public experience in their neighborhoods and workplaces as well as in larger civic arenas. Since argument is central to what it means to be not just a rational individual but a rational citizen, and since irrational persuasion has never been more widely used, we believe that there are few matters students need to know more about than how to make—and judge—sound, rational arguments. We also believe that those who teach argument year in and year out perform a heroic service, especially when they teach it not as a means to get what you want but as the most demanding and valuable form of critical thinking that any of us can do.

What Distinguishes Craft *from Other Books on Argument*

This book differs from others in several ways, but most important, perhaps, is our insistence that we make arguments not just to gain our readers' agreement but to enlist them in solving a problem. The nature of the problem determines the kind of agreement we seek, which in turn determines the kind of argument we make. So far as we know, no other book, ancient or modern, puts problem finding, framing, and solving at the heart of planning, drafting, and revising written arguments. From beginning to end, we emphasize that only after we understand the problem we address *from our readers' points of view* can we make an argument that they will take seriously.

We also help students new to academic argument overcome the special difficulties they often have with academic problems, which can seem to them merely "theoretical"—too abstract to be relevant to their perceived needs and interests. We show students the differences between *practical* problems, the kind most familiar to them, and *conceptual* problems, the kind that may be less familiar, but that most teachers will expect them to address, find, and formulate on their own. Throughout, we help students address the demands of finding academic, conceptual problems that first of all *they* can care about, but that they can also imagine their readers caring about as well.

Another difference from many other books on argument is our steady emphasis on ethos. We show students how they project an ethos through every element of their argument: by how clearly they write, how baldly they state their claim, how thoroughly they support it with evidence, how candidly they acknowledge and respond to objections. We emphasize that even when their argument fails to achieve agreement, they can still call it a success if readers think that they made it in ways that seem reasonable, thoughtful, and fair. At some point, what readers remember from the ethos of individual arguments adds up to their lasting reputation, an important force of persuasion in its own right.

A third difference is that instead of offering an elaborate account of formal deductive logic, we devote considerable attention to critical thinking based on informal reasoning. And instead of focusing on fallacies as the only way to think about sound thinking, we integrate sound critical thinking into our discussion of argument and writing in every chapter. To that end, we have not segregated advice about reasoning and arguing from advice about writing, because we believe that the skills of writing support and illuminate the skills of reasoning, and vice versa. So in the Writing Process section in each chapter, we show students how the processes of planning, drafting, and revising can help them not only generate the substance of an argument but reflect critically on the thinking it represents.

We have also tried to synthesize two aspects of argument that most books on argument keep distinct: dialectic and rhetoric. Dialectic is commonly defined as a process of two people questioning each other in a search for as-yet undiscovered truth (a claim that they can support), a topic now pursued by those calling their work "pragma-dialectical." In contrast, rhetoric traditionally focuses on one person's finding and arranging support for a known claim in order to persuade another to accept it. In our view, dialectic and rhetoric present two perspectives on the same process. Questioning and being questioned helps students both discover a claim worth making and find the support that gives them and others good reasons to accept it. It is a process students engage in every time they have a conversation with friends about an issue they care about. We show students how they can create sound written arguments from those familiar speech genres by imagining questioning exchanges with readers or their surrogates (a thread that may remind some of the Russian literary theorist M. M. Bakhtin).

We also include some topics new to books on writing arguments:

- In the last twenty-five years, research has flourished on "cognitive biases," habits of mind that systematically undermine our reasoning, but that we can manage through the discipline imposed by careful argument. It is not enough, however, to manage our own thinking. We must also plan arguments to anticipate those same biases in the reasoning of our readers. So far as we know, no other textbook on argument calls attention to dealing with the flawed thinking in *readers*.

- Cognitive scientists have also helped us better understand how we use words to categorize and name experience and reason about cause-and-effect—kinds of thinking crucial to a soundly reasoned argument about definition and causation.

- We have only recently begun to understand how the problem that makes an argument necessary shapes how we design and write it.

As important as those insights are, few have found their way into recent books on argumentation, even though they require no expert knowledge to teach.

How Craft *Participates in the Rhetorical Tradition*

Despite those differences from current books on argument, *Craft* is rooted in the 2500-year-old tradition of rhetoric and argumentation. Our aim is to help students develop a public voice appropriate to written arguments in a variety of civic, professional, and academic forums. We believe that thoughtful readers are likely to assent to a claim only when they see good reasons and evidence, when they understand the logical connections among claims, reasons, and evidence, and when they see their own doubts and questions acknowledged and answered. We believe that at base argument is not a coercive device (though it can be), nor even a product of human rationality (though it is), but the fundamental competence by which rationality is created and shared.

Craft's Roots in Aristotle

We have been struck by how closely (though unintentionally) we tracked Aristotle's *Rhetoric*. As did he, we begin by identifying the problems that occasion different kinds of arguments. He focused on the oral arguments occasioned by civic events—trials, funerals, and political decision-making—the triad that has led to the familiar categories of forensic, epideictic, and deliberative arguments (or fact, value, and policy). We believe, however, that the division of fact, policy, and value obscures a more basic distinction between arguments that want us to *do* something and arguments that want us to *understand* or *believe* something. We do not ignore values; in fact, we emphasize how the values of both readers and writers shape all arguments, whether the aim is action or belief.

As did Aristotle, we address not just invention and arrangement, but two other matters as well: style and the psychology of belief, especially the ways that the thinking processes of readers and writers interact. (Those last two topics claim little or no space in most current books on argument.) As did he, we put aside syllogisms, focusing instead on warranted claims. And like his, our aim is relentlessly focused on "how to," on answering two pragmatic questions:

- What does an audience expect in a sound argument?
- How do we express that argument to meet their expectations?

As did Aristotle, we also focus on the role of feelings, of emotions in making a sound argument. Far from rejecting emotion as an element of an argument, we emphasize its importance in framing the problem that the argument addresses and in choosing the language to express it.

Craft's Revision of Toulmin

Like many recent books on argument, we have profited from one of the most influential works on argument since Aristotle, that of Stephen Toulmin. We are especially indebted to him for these three insights:

- Arguments differ in different fields but share a family structure.
- That common structure is based on a logic of question and answer.
- We understand that structure best not in terms of formal deductive logic, but rather of the informal logic of everyday conversation.

As important as these insights are, we believe that teachers of argument who embrace Toulmin's formal layout make a pedagogical mistake. Recall that he represents an argument in a figure of six elements:

Toulmin formulated this model to support after-the-fact analysis of the logical justification for an argument. Not surprisingly, students and teachers alike have found it difficult to apply that model to the task of producing their own arguments and of analyzing the form and structure of the arguments of others. To make Toulmin's insights more useful to writers at all levels, we have modified his layout in five ways.

1. We removed the arrows.

Toulmin may have wanted to represent the movement of an argument, but what he describes seems closer to an alleged process of *reasoning,* a mental movement from one set of beliefs to another. Forms of reasoning, however, are not forms of argument, which is a written or spoken *event.* Most arguments start not with a statement of grounds but with a problem, followed by a claimed solution, followed by intertwined grounds, warrants, and rebuttals. But even as a model of reasoning, his layout is psychologically unrealistic. When we reason about a *problem,* we do not start with grounds, then think our way to a claim (its solution). We begin with the problem that motivates us to search for a solution in the first place, and find a tentative hypothesis based on the facts then available to us. We then use that hypothesis (C. S. Peirce called it a "hypothesis on probation") to find more data that we hope will confirm or disconfirm it. It's called *abductive* thinking, a kind of reasoning that Toulmin's layout cannot represent.

We do not intend our layout to represent any "real time" process—not of reasoning, drafting, reading, or analyzing an argument. It represents only the five elements required in a complete argument and some formal relationships among them. Nor do we intend the model to represent a template for what words must be put on the page. To guide thinking and drafting, we emphasize instead the questions that are the ultimate source of the parts of argument. We offer the model as a tool for understanding and analyzing arguments, most useful for planning a draft—collecting information, organizing, and outlining—and then for testing and revising.

2. We dropped "backing."

Toulmin needed backing to explain how arguments differ among different fields, but that is not our major concern. Moreover, *backing* refers to the grounds that support a warrant viewed as a claim in its own argument. We can more usefully analyze that arrangement as two distinct arguments, one embedded in the other. So backing is redundant. It is surely important to discuss the support for a warrant, but that support need not be formally represented in the layout of an argument.

3. We dropped "qualifier" as a distinct element.

Qualifications such as *probably, most,* and *may* are crucial not just to the accuracy of an argument, but to our experience of its writer's ethos. But qualifiers are not a singular element of an argument like a claim or a reason; qualifiers color every element—claims, reasons, evidence, warrants, and rebuttals. Far from ignoring qualification, we show its crucial role in projecting a thoughtful ethos in every element of an argument.

4. We divided the single element "grounds" into two, reasons and evidence.

Careful readers accept a claim about a contested issue only when they see two distinct kinds of support: reasons and the evidence on which those reasons rest. This distinction reflects a psychological and social imperative: We consider a contestable claim only when it rests on something more "solid" than the arguer's mere confidence in it; we ask for support, for reasons. But reasons provide only the logical structure of that support; evidence is the basis on which that structure of reasons rests, something brought in from "outside" the argument. An argument consisting only of a claim and reasons can seem unsubstantial, but it would seem opaque if it consisted only of a claim and raw evidence such as numbers or quotations. Readers need reasons to help them understand the logic and organization of an argument; they need evidence to understand the basis of those reasons in something they can think of as "external" reality.

5. We replaced "rebuttal" with "acknowledgment and response."

Many have noted that Toulmin's notion of rebuttals is a problem. He defines rebuttals as limits on the scope of a claim:

> Since Harry was born in Bermuda, he is a British subject, _{claim} **unless he renounced his citizenship, or unless one of his parents was a diplomat, or unless . . .** _{rebuttal}

But in ordinary language, what we call a *rebuttal* responds to objections *of any kind*—not just to the scope of a claim but to the source or sufficiency of its support, to the soundness of logic, to the definition of a problem, to alternative solutions. Rebuttals are essential to every thoughtful argument because they acknowledge and respond to a reader's predictably different beliefs and interests. So as have some others, we expand Toulmin's *rebuttal* to refer to responses to *any* anticipated alternative, objection, or criticism. We believe, however, that the term *rebuttal* can encourage responses that are too aggressive, so we substitute something more amiable and accurate: *acknowledgment and response.* This term encompasses two actions: first we acknowledge readers' views by presenting them fairly; only then do we respond to them, and not always to refute them, since mature arguers concede the force of viable alternatives.

In addition to those five modifications, we fill two gaps in Toulmin's account. First, we explain the dual nature of evidence, which exists both inside and outside an argument. Readers are led by our prototypical image of evidence to want "external" evidence that is concrete, palpable—a smoking gun, fingerprints, bones. But writers must recognize how that differs from the representations they can offer in its stead—a *description* of a smoking gun, an *image* of fingerprints. If students learn to distinguish between the evidence "itself" and the reports of evidence used in arguments, they will be better prepared to read others' reports of evidence critically and, when they write, to report their own evidence so that their readers can know where and how they obtained it. No one asks where anyone found a reason; we must all ask where someone found evidence.

The second gap is in Toulmin's account of warrants. So far as we know, no book on argument has explained how a warrant that is true can nevertheless fail. For example,

> You should eat fish _{claim} because it does not raise your cholesterol. _{reason} As we all know, everyone should eat foods that provide roughage. _{warrant}

Each of those three propositions is arguably true, but the warrant fails as a guarantee of the *relevance* of the reason to the claim. We offer what we think is the first intuitively satisfying explanation of how a warrant soundly establishes the relevance of reasons and evidence to a claim, and of how it can fail.

The Design of This Book

This book has five parts and two appendixes:

- Part I surveys argument and its relationship to problem solving.
- Part II looks at the five elements of an argument in detail.
- Part III discusses reasoning, particularly about meaning and causation.
- Part IV treats the role of language in arguments.
- Part V presents a selection of readings, which include sample arguments that students can analyze and respond to with arguments of their own.

We have tried to make the use of this book as flexible as possible. After Part I, you can teach the other parts in any order. You can also teach the chapters within any part in any order, even assign different chapters to different students who need work on particular issues. So do not assume the order of the parts and of their constituent chapters must determine the structure of your class syllabus.

A Message to Students

What Is Argument?

Our aim is to help you do in writing what you do every day in conversation: Solve a problem by giving others good reason to think or act as you want them to.

You:	Let's catch the Vin Diesel movie. I hear it's pretty wild.
Friend:	There's a party over at Jan's. Let's go there.
You:	Her parties always end up with the cops banging on the door.
Friend:	We'll go just for a while. Besides that only happened twice.
You:	But you said you wanted to see Vin's new movie, and so do I.
Friend:	We can see it tomorrow.
You:	I have to work tomorrow.
Friend:	OK. Maybe I'll go to Jan's later.

Conversations like that are often about trivial matters, but not always:

Friend:	It's dangerous for the government to force search-engine providers to turn over records of what terms people searched and what Web sites they visited. We hardly have any privacy left.
You:	I'm not worried. The government is just going after terrorists and pornographers.
Friend:	Yeah, but they want millions of records, most from ordinary people. And no one knows what *else* the feds might do with them. Do you trust the government not to invade your privacy?
You:	You've got a point. But they can't keep those records forever, can they?
Friend:	None of the reports say they have to give them up. Besides, information is power and no government gives up power unless it's forced to.
You:	They would be forced to if they started using that information to invade the privacy of ordinary citizens. They'd be voted out of office.

Friend: The kind of people who would use those records to spy on us are not elected. It's all those faceless bureaucrats who are the real danger.

You: Maybe so.

The problem can be as trivial as what clothes to wear or as profound as what church to join. Conversations like that help us conduct business, set public policy, decide what to believe, find civil ways to settle disputes, and much more. It is how people in every society spend a good part of their social, professional, and even private lives.

We call that universal activity *argument,* a word that alarms some people because it evokes images of quarreling or worse. But arguments need not be hostile; in fact, fair and amiable arguments strengthen social relationships by helping us all understand better what we believe and why we believe it.

Amiably or belligerently, we make an argument every time we

- offer a claim and grounds to support it
- to someone not inclined to accept our claim at face value
- in order to solve the problem that motivated us to make an argument in the first place

The Role of Argument in Your Classes

If you are reading this book in a first-year writing course, you might be surprised that your teachers, in this class and others, expect you to make arguments in most of your papers. And if you do not understand how they will judge those arguments, you may be more surprised by their comments—and disappointed with your grades. We know, of course, that some of you do have experience making academic arguments and others have written arguments in your workplace. But we also know that of the thousands of first-year students the two of us have taught, few have understood the role of argument in their studies—why teachers value it so, how academic argument differs from other kinds, how you can build on your everyday experience of argument in learning to make written ones.

To gain that perspective, you have to distinguish argument from two other kinds of writing that you have probably been assigned most often, summary and personal opinion.

- In a summary, you report what others have written without adding information, especially not your own ideas.

Most first-year students remember summary and its first-cousin, the research report, from high school. In those papers, they did what's called "knowledge telling," reporting back what they read or heard in class. Many come to college expecting to do more of the same, only about more complicated topics. In fact, college teachers will expect you to do something different. You will be asked to write for many reasons, but rarely just to repeat what you have learned. Most teachers, most of the time, will expect you to make an argument, to develop and support not *their* position but *yours,* to make a claim that *you* believe, and to explain *why* you believe it and they should too. They won't demand that your claim be unique, only that you reached it yourself after thinking through its supporting reasons and evidence and the alternative views of others. Although your argument may include some summary of others' ideas, you will be expected not to parrot them but to develop your own.

- In an opinion paper, you merely state what you think, not why others should think so too.

When pressed to support their position on an issue, many writers new to college object, *That's my opinion, and I'm entitled to it. Why do I have to defend it? I have my opinion and you have yours: Isn't that enough?* In one sense, they are right: We are all entitled to have whatever opinion we want, about any subject, for any reason, or, for that matter, for no reason at all. But once you join a community of learning, you are expected to treat your opinions and those of others not as entitlements but as claims subject to testing through questioning. That means you must be ready to not only answer the hard questions of others, but to ask them of yourself. You will be expected to make arguments in cooperation with others, in a spirit not of antagonistic confrontation, but of civil inquiry searching for good solutions to hard problems. It's how academic communities—and most others—work.

Your teachers will also want your claim to *accomplish* something. You might be asked to find and support a solution that corrects a practical, real-world problem such as how to recruit student volunteers for Habitat for Humanity or how to relieve overcrowding in the library. But more often, you will be asked to find and support an answer to a question not to show what you know or to change the world, but to help readers understand something better.

Unfortunately, many students see the questions they are asked to address as mere puzzles, with no connection to any problem in the real world: *Can chimps count? Where did weaving originate in the ancient world? How did the social structure of the South contribute to causes of the Civil War?* If these questions seem no more than puzzles, their answers will seem useless speculation—which they can be, if you do not know how to turn those questions into academic *problems.* That's why we discuss in detail what we call "conceptual problems," the kind you will be expected to find, pose, and solve as you travel through your academic career.

You will not understand how the academic world works until you understand academic argument—why such questions are important to your teachers and why they expect you to support your answers with sound reasons and evidence. In addition, we hope you will understand some other things important to your academic success:

- how and why arguments differ in different fields
- how you can use what you learn about making arguments to understand those you read
- how your arguments shape your *ethos,* your reputation as a thinker

You can use this book as a kind of primer to academic thinking that you may not get elsewhere.

What Experienced Writers Know About Making Arguments

To achieve all that, we will explain how experienced writers think about and make written arguments.

- They know that the point of an argument is not to win but to address a problem that can be solved only with the agreement of others.
- They know they cannot coerce others into agreement, but must consider their questions and objections and respond to them fairly. And if those others are not there to ask questions, experienced writers know that they must imagine those questions on their readers' behalf.
- They know that good arguments and sound thinking go hand-in-hand, that the harder they work on drafting and revising their argument, the better they think about its logic and substance, and vice versa.
- They know they cannot invent a new form of argument every time they write, that readers expect to see familiar forms, and that they can use those forms not just to organize their arguments but to guide their thinking in researching and planning them.
- Finally, they know that even when they do not "win" an argument, they can still gain something almost as important. If they can write arguments that seem reasonable and thoughtful, they earn the reputation of someone with those qualities. And that means readers who know their reputation will take their next argument more seriously.

When we show you how experienced writers put together their arguments, we will give you charts, diagrams, and what look like formulas to follow. But we will also explain the thinking behind the formula. We present our advice in that way because that is what works for most of the writers we have worked with, both experienced and not. Some of you may fear that the charts and formulas will stifle your creativity and make your writing mechanical: *I want my writing to be mine, not the product of your formulas.* Others will think *Great! Just tell me what to do and I'll do it.* We trust that you will discover both that our advice enables rather than limits your creativity and that you cannot follow it mindlessly, even if you want to.

We hope that you will learn to use our models when you need to and to put them aside as soon as you can. You have already done that if you have learned a sport such as golf or tennis or a performance art such as dance or music. You didn't practice a whole skill all at once, but a part at a time: Plant your feet this way, hold your hand that way, move like this. When you first put the parts together, you seem to move by the numbers, more clunky than creative. But once you learn the parts well enough to forget them, there comes a moment when you can go with the flow, assembling the moves into a seamless performance.

At first, you may feel that you are writing arguments by the numbers, especially if you have some experience making good ones. But as you master the parts, the formulas will disappear into the flow of drafting, you will focus on the conversation you are having with your imagined readers, and your arguments will seem more natural and organic. It is then that you can be as creative as you wish. With rare exceptions, creative people start working within boundaries and forms that they first master and then *knowingly* adapt or even break. Shakespeare was the most creative writer in English, but he started working within the dramatic and poetic conventions of his time; he became creative when he broke them knowingly.

We hope you learn the forms of argument well enough to use them creatively. But when you struggle because time is short or the issue complex, formulas give you something that you can fall back on, to help you find and assemble the parts of an argument in a way that puts your ideas—and you—in the best light.

How to Use This Book

We planned this book so that you can adapt it to your own unique needs. While we hope you will find our ideas so interesting and useful that you'll read every page, we also know that everyone is busy and days are short. So on the chance that you don't find argument as fascinating as we do, we have tried to make this book easy to use when you search for particular information or advice. To help you do that, we have organized this book into five parts:

- In Part I, we present an overview of the nature of argument. Try to work through these chapters quickly, because they will help you write complete arguments from the start.

- In Part II, we discuss the five elements of an argument in detail. Your teacher may ask you to work through these chapters in sequence, or to look at individual ones as specific issues arise in your writing.

- In Part III, we focus on reasoning about meaning and causation, two issues that almost every argument has to address. These are the most demanding chapters in the book.

- In Part IV, we show you how to write clearly and vividly and how to use language in deliberately persuasive ways.

- In Part V, we present a selection of readings, which include sample arguments that you can analyze to see how the elements of argument work in practice and that you can use as springboards for your own arguments.

Each chapter has two main units that work together:

- The first unit explains the parts of an argument and how they work.
- The second unit offers nuts-and-bolts advice about writing your argument, about planning, research, drafting, and revising.

We believe that these two sides of argument work together: The better you understand the thinking that goes into a sound argument, the better you will write it; the better you understand the process of writing complete arguments, the more soundly you will think about its substance.

Like every complex but important task, making arguments is not easy, but the satisfaction of making good ones is hard to beat, even when someone says, "Well, I don't agree, but I see your point." Maybe especially then.

Acknowledgments

As we say repeatedly, every writer needs a reader's help because readers know one thing that we never can: they know what it's like to be our readers. We two have been immeasurably helped by those readers who reviewed this book during its development. They told us things that we could never have known on our own (and sometimes did not want to hear). But they read our work better than we ever could, and we have been grateful for their always helpful comments, even when they stung.

Students who profit from this book can thank the following reviewers, as do we: Jonathan Ayres, University of Texas; R. Michael Barrett, University of Wisconsin, River Falls; David Blakesley, Southern Illinois University, Carbondale; Stuart C. Brown, New Mexico State University; Karin Burns, Pierce College; Jami L. Carlacio, University of Wisconsin, Milwaukee; William J. Carpenter, University of Kansas; Peter Dorman, Central Virginia Community College; Tracy Duckart, Humboldt State University; Ellen Burton Harrington, Tulane University; Gina Hochhalter, Clovis Community College; Eleanor Latham, Central Oregon Community College; Carol A. Lowe, McLennan Community College; Margaret P. Morgan, University of North Carolina, Charlotte; B. Keith Murphy, Fort Valley State University; Twila Yates Papay, Rollins College; Velvet Pearson, Long Beach City College; CarolAnn H. Posey, Virginia Wesleyan College; Barbara Presnell, University of North Carolina; Deborah F. Rossen-Knoll, Philadelphia College of Textiles and Science; Mary Sauer, Indiana University Purdue University Indianapolis; Gary Thompson, Saginaw Valley State University; Laura Wendorff, University of Wisconsin, Platteville; Mary Wright, Christopher Newport University.

We are especially grateful to those who taught versions of this book in its formative stages and to their students, who provided invaluable feedback: Thomas Fischer, Paula McQuade, Dev Parikh, Peter Sattler, Bryan Wagner, and Carol Williams.

We would also like to thank Brandon Hight and Virginia Blanford for seeing this manuscript to its present state, and Alec MacDonald for his reliable work tracking down sources and helping assemble the index.

And finally, those closest to us.

There is no way to say how much the growing family has meant to me. The best days are when we're together—Christopher and Ingrid; Oliver and Michele; Megan, Phil, and Lily; Patty, Dave, Owen and Matilde; Christine, Joe, Katherine, and Nicholas. And of course Joan, she who for so many years has put up with my "Just one more minute." Her deep well of patience and good humor still flows more generously than I deserve.

—JMW

I was born to a clan of arguers, and my daughters have inherited the tradition. But what they learned along with their love of argument was that good argument never threatens love. Robin, Karen, and Lauren have kept me on my toes, my arguments well-tested, and my heart full. This last they got from their mother, my companion for almost forty years. Sandra has always been the heart of it all.

—GGC

PART I

The Nature of Argument

In this first part, we discuss what an argument is and does, the kind of think-ing you must do to create a convincing one, and the kind of relationship to others you must create to do that kind of thinking.

- In Chapter 1, we examine how people use arguments, both in their own thinking and in their social, professional, and civic lives—not just to get their way, but to think critically about others' ideas and plans as well as their own. Although these arguments sometimes become belligerent confrontations intended to coerce others into agreement, we offer what we believe is a deeper truth: that argument is a crucial tool for coopera-tive, critical thinking whenever people must find a shared solution to a shared problem. And in that use, the most effective argument is usually a civil one.

- In Chapter 2, we explain the five questions whose answers form the substance of every argument, questions you must answer when you converse with those whose opinion you value. We then show you how to use those five questions both to plan your own written arguments and to judge the arguments of others.

- In Chapter 3, we discuss why people make arguments at all—to solve problems. We explain two kinds of problems that occasion written arguments: (1) pragmatic problems, which we solve by getting others to act or at least support an action, and (2) conceptual problems, which we solve by helping others understand something better. We then explain how to frame an argument by framing your problem in a way that moti-vates readers to learn more about your solution.

CHAPTER I

Argument, Critical Thinking, and Rationality

Critical thinking is simply good problem solving. We can practice it silently, in our minds, as we size up a problem and try to solve it. But often, we must do more than analyze a problem and figure out how to solve it; we must then explain to others why we think our solution is worth their consideration. To that end, we have to make a case for our views, a case that we call an argument. Many of us think of argument as a hostile exchange between two people, each trying to coerce agreement from the other. But at its best, argument is a way to cooperate with others in finding and agreeing on good solutions to tough problems—call it cooperative critical thinking. Even when our arguments fail to achieve that agreement, they succeed if they help us know why we and others differ, in a way that creates mutual understanding and respect.

What Is Argument?

How many arguments have you heard or read today? Probably more than you noticed, perhaps more than you wanted. Television and talk radio have made nasty argument a national sport, and civic discourse seems to have been hijacked by those who shrilly advocate narrow causes in ways that sacrifice not only civility but truth and good sense. Meanwhile, advertisers make arguments that pander to our emotions with slick images and exaggerated claims to support their implied demand, "Buy this!" Hostile or pandering, such arguments might make a thoughtful person wonder whether argument hasn't become too repugnant for good people to engage in at all.

But that's argument at its worst. In an age that increasingly depends on sorting out good ideas from bad, we need good arguments more than ever. On the job, employers increasingly complain that they cannot find good thinkers who can judge others' claims critically and, more importantly, communicate their own conclusions clearly and persuasively. In the civic arena, we have seen in recent debates about ensuring our national security how much our democracy depends on officials and citizens who can judge not just claims but the quality of their supporting evidence. Many states now even require colleges to teach students how to think critically by analyzing the arguments of others and making sound ones of their own.

At their best, arguments are civil, even amiable ways to reach sound decisions. But even when they do become heated, good arguments differ from other forms of persuasion by both their process and their goal. When we engage one another *cooperatively* in arguments, we aim not to coerce or seduce others into mindless agreement, but to enlist them in helping us to find the best, most reasonable solution to a shared problem. We do not attack or pander; we exchange and test claims, assessing the reasons and supporting facts on all sides of the issue.

In this sense, argument isn't always about issues as momentous as national security. We all make countless little ones every day:

- Your friend says she doesn't want to eat Japanese, but you want vegetarian, so you talk it over and compromise on Indian.
- Your teacher rejects a claim that apes can count because it is based on flawed data.
- You complain to your boss that the new software she wants you to use can't generate up-to-date sales reports.
- You tell your friend that he cannot turn in a paper he copied-and-pasted from Web sites because it is unfair to everyone who did the work for themselves.

Even if you spent the day alone reading, you probably had silent arguments with your authors. You read "TV has degraded the quality of public argument" and think, *Wait a minute. What about PBS? I wonder what they would say about the arguments on "The News Hour."* You may even have argued with yourself when you tried to work through a personal issue in your mind: *So what do I do about my chem class? I have no shot at med school if I don't get a B. But can I? It would mean no social life. But do I really want to be a doctor. . . ?*

So as you think about argument, put aside the nasty exchanges, the political battles, and pandering ads, at least for now. Forget that we often talk about argument as though it were a form of close combat: *advancing* our claims, *marshalling* our evidence, *undermining* others' positions and *attacking* their claims, while we *defend* ours from *counterattack*. Forget that even the best of us sometimes argue as though we belong on *Jerry Springer*. Try to think not of *having* arguments with enemies but of *making* them with allies in order to find the best solution to a problem you all share.

The Origin of the Word *Argument*

Occasionally, we'll discuss the original meaning of an important term, because earlier meanings can illuminate current ones. The original meaning of argument, for example, was to "make clear." The Latin word for silver, *argentum*, comes from the same root: what is clear often shines.

What Good Is Argument?

Argument so pervades our thinking that it would be impossible to identify all of its uses, but two stand out:

- to convince others to think or do as we say
- to decide for ourselves what we should think or do

We usually think of argument as primarily a way to convince others. But the best, most critical thinkers also use argument to develop and test their own thinking by questioning their own ideas as severely as they do those of others. Through argument, we are able to make our thinking not only reflect our own experiences and beliefs but respond to those of others as well.

Arguments Help Us Think Critically

Philosophers have long celebrated rational thinking as our crowning human achievement, as one thing that distinguishes us from other creatures. But it is easier to say what rationality is not than what it is. It is not knowing lots of facts or rules of logic. It does not require formal education. It doesn't even mean knowing the truth, because we can rationally believe what we later find is false. For thousands of years it was rational to think the world is flat, because that's what the best evidence of our senses told us. Only when we had more facts and a larger perspective to reason from did we prove ourselves wrong.

We start to become rational thinkers almost from birth, when we first begin to interact with others. Toddlers show signs of rationality when they ask why they should do or think as others tell them to and, soon after, give reasons for what they want from others. We learn early not to accept others' claims and reasons blindly, but to question them in light of our experience and beliefs. But it takes some maturity before we learn to question our own thinking, our own reasons for believing what we do. As our critical judgment matures, we learn that just as others will not accept our claims and reasons without testing them, neither should we.

To make those mature judgments, we have to adopt an intellectual stance that questions what we want to believe, a stance that encourages us to pause before we leap to a conclusion just because we like it. To do that, we have to develop the self-control to slow down our thinking, so that we can not only examine our reasons for our beliefs but also investigate whether we have good evidence to accept them. In that pause, we can exercise other rational competencies:

- the patience to gather all the information that the situation allows— from remembered experience, direct observation, or active research
- the skepticism not to accept that information at face value, but instead to question whether it is factual
- the logical ability to use those facts as evidence in reasoning step-by-step to a conclusion

But that is not yet the crowning achievement of full rationality. To be fully rational, we must be able not only to reason to a conclusion but to reflect on and test the quality of that reasoning. For that, we must learn to

- seek out facts that might **contradict** our conclusions
- change our minds when the facts weigh against our beliefs
- imagine alternative ways of thinking about the problem, the facts, our conclusions
- recognize and question assumptions, inconsistencies, and contradictions

These last steps can challenge even the most careful thinkers, especially when we have reached a conclusion that we *want* to be true. That's when a sound argument is most helpful. The best help is a complete argument that we spell out in writing:

1. *Writing slows us down, giving us time to consider and reconsider.* What we think in an instant takes time to say; and what feels clear and compelling in a private thought often proves murky and uncertain in the public light of words.

2 *It gives us a mental checklist of matters we must consider.* The parts of argument lead us to question our own thinking: Are my reasons really backed up by facts? Are there facts that contradict them? Is my logic sound?

3 *It gives us the benefit of interacting with other minds.* Two heads may not always be better than one, but we usually think better when we consider all available ideas, not just our own. Even if we create it in our own minds, only for ourselves, an argument helps us think as critically as we do when we share our ideas with others who need good reasons before they agree. We have to ask questions about what those others might think, which leads us to consider facts, reasons, beliefs, and other views that we might ignore without the discipline of making an explicit argument.

The Origin of the Word *Critic* and the Spirit of Critical Thinking

Some students and teachers are put off by the term *critical thinking*, because it sounds mean-spirited. As one young man put it, "First you tell us to make nice by writing arguments that are cooperative rather than hostile and then you tell us to be critical. They don't go together." But just as those who abuse argument have given it an undeserved bad name, so has criticism gotten a bad name from those who use it only negatively.

The word *critic* comes from the Greek *kritikos,* someone able to make judgments; that noun comes from the verb *krinein,* to separate or decide. And that's what good critical thinking does: it helps us judge an idea by separating out all the reasons and evidence that support or contradict it from all the feelings, hopes, and self-interest we attach to it.

That's why the most important tool of critical thinking is to ask good questions, including the five questions of argument. To be sure, when we ask questions, we can make people uncomfortable who *don't* want to examine their own ideas. And it can irritate those in power. After all, one of the earliest critical thinkers was Socrates, and we know what happened to him when he asked those in power more questions than they wanted to answer.

But in our world, not only do we have the right to ask questions and think for ourselves; we have an obligation to do so. That means not only asking lots of critical questions of others, but also answering theirs. And if that sounds difficult to you, that's all the more reason for you to learn to question and answer in ways that are civil, amiable, and constructive—which is to say, in service of finding the answers that everyone agrees are sound.

How Argument Supports Critical Thinking

When you use argument to think critically, you test old ideas and develop new ones in three "stages" or "levels." They involve increasingly difficult questions, not just about *what* you think but about your *basis* for thinking it. Since we normally judge others' ideas more critically than our own, we'll start with the kinds of questions you ask others (they are the same ones your readers will ask you). They are also the questions you must eventually learn to ask yourself before you submit your argument to others.

Level 1:   *Is your idea or plan **supportable**? Or is it just opinion, insight, intuition, or some other quick response whose basis you can't really explain? Can you support it with reasons and facts showing that, all things considered, you can make a good case for your claims?*

Level 2:   *Is your belief in your idea or plan **defensible**? Will others think that it is rational to believe it? Have you subjected your supporting reasons and facts to the scrutiny of others? Might someone know other reasons or facts that would contradict it? Have you considered all relevant possibilities?*

Level 3:   *Is your belief in your idea or plan **logical**? Do you base it on principles of reasoning that are valid? Can you explain how the reasons and facts support your belief?*

When the ideas you are testing are your own, the questions are harder to answer: *Can I support my ideas with reasons and facts? Can I show that I have considered all other relevant views and alternatives? Can I explain my principles of reasoning?* Not only do these questions force you to consider new possibilities, but they can be disturbing when they upset familiar ways of thinking or challenge ideas that you *want* to be true.

By learning to make good arguments, you develop an attitude, a frame of mind that is always ready to listen to or can imagine another questioning voice that helps you separate out your ideas and reasons for believing them from the buzzing complexity of your mind and state them clearly. It's easiest when others ask those questions, but when they don't, you have to imagine an inner voice murmuring insistently, *But wait. How good is your evidence? Is it from a reliable source? Do you think your conclusion is right because you want it to be? What would you say to someone who said. . . ?* Once you learn to question yourself and think critically about your own ideas, you'll also learn to welcome the inevitable questions of others.

How Common Are Critical Thinkers?

When one researcher investigated how well people critically reflect on their beliefs, she found that few were able to. She questioned 160 people about problems such as unemployment and school dropouts. They ranged from ninth graders to college graduates to experts in the problems she posed. When someone offered a cause of the problem, she asked questions like these:

- How do you know that is the cause? What evidence would you offer?
- How might someone disagree with you? What evidence might he offer?
- What would you say to that person to show he was wrong?
- Can you imagine evidence that would show your own view to be wrong?
- Could more than one point of view be right?

Fewer than half could think of any evidence to support their views. Though two out of three could think of an alternative view, fewer than half could think of an argument that might support it, and when offered a counterargument, fewer than half could think of an answer to it. In other words, most of those questioned could not imagine another point of view based on sound reasoning, or think of any good evidence to support their own! Even college graduates were not consistently good critical thinkers

Source: Deanna Kuhn, *The Skills of Argument* (New York: Cambridge University Press, 1991).

Arguments Help Us Sustain Communities

Because rational thinking is inherently social, arguments are crucial for living and working with others whose views may differ from your own. So if you hope to be a member of a community of critical thinkers, you must be able not only to *think* critically about your own ideas and plans, but to *explain* your thinking, to give others reason to believe that your views deserve if not their agreement, then at least their respect. In fact, it's when we cannot agree that rational communities need cooperative arguments most—so that in the face of our differences, we can *understand* why others believe as they do, without dismissing their ideas as mere opinion or, worse, nonsense.

Rational argument is especially difficult, but also especially important, when communities include people from different cultures. Claims and reasons that seem reasonable to those of one background can seem wholly irrational to others, not because they disagree about the facts but because they base their claims on incompatible values and principles of reasoning. When we disagree over fundamental values, we often struggle to get beyond simply trading dogmatic claims. In those moments, arguments can become combative rather than cooperative, disrupting rather than supporting rational thinking.

Does that mean that people of different cultures can never agree? On some issues, perhaps not, especially when values are so deeply buried that they have to be excavated before they can even be identified, much less understood (see p. 210). But if cooperative arguments can't settle such issues, they can at least help us understand why not—so long as we can reach the second and third stages of critical thinking that explicitly put our ideas in dialogue with those of others. To succeed, a society of diverse values like ours needs more than good-will and tolerance. We need amiable, civil ways to explain why we hold the values we do and to understand why others hold theirs. Argument is an essential tool for maintaining the fabric of a culturally diverse society.

In the Readings . . .

The Variety of Arguments

On pages 383–86 you'll find brief readings that we will use as examples and you can use for some of your writing projects. From time to time, we'll include a box about the readings or experiences that the two of us have had, pointing out how aspects of argument work in practice.

Some first-year students who read this book in manuscript wondered whether people really have to make arguments as often as we claim. One said, "Since I'm going to be an architectural engineer, I'll just do what my clients ask, so what does this have to do with me? I don't want to argue with my client." He got an answer from a practicing architect (Colomb's brother), who started by recalling all the arguments he had to make as part of a bridge restoration project for the city of Chicago. When he got to about twenty, we asked, "And how many had to be in writing?" He answered by pulling out a two-inch file of proposals, reports, letters, memos, and so on—all written arguments.

Arguments Define Academic and Professional Communities

Thoughtful and civil arguments are also the lifeblood of academic and professional communities. Scientists, engineers, agricultural agents, college professors, and countless others—they all make arguments to find and support solutions to the problems in their fields. They formulate those arguments first in their own minds, then in conversations with colleagues, then often in writing for their wider community.

Most professional communities make arguments to address problems that can be solved only if someone *does* something:

Problem: Binge drinking in college has become a health problem.

Solution: We should devote time in orientation week discussing its dangers.

We call these *practical* problems, problems that, left unsolved, have tangible costs that we can't tolerate. To eliminate those costs, we propose a plan to *do* something.

In academic communities, on the other hand, researchers more often dig into a problem not to fix it directly, but to help us better *understand* something about it:

Problem: We do not understand the psychological factors that cause students to binge.

Solution: An important one is an attraction to risky behavior.

Academic researchers call an issue like this a *problem,* but it is a special kind of problem—it is a *conceptual* problem that we can phrase as a question: *How big is the universe? Do birds really descend from dinosaurs? What causes students to binge?*

Conceptual problems concern the world, but their solutions tell us not how to change it, but how to understand it better. Of course, before we can solve some practical problems, we have to understand them better. And academic researchers believe that the more we learn about the world, the better we can deal with all of its problems. But in the short run, the aim of most academic research is simply better understanding. (We'll discuss the two kinds of problems in more detail in Chapter 3.)

Whether a writer poses a practical or conceptual problem, however, she has to support her solution with an argument so that others in her community can reflect on it, test it, and maybe improve it before they accept it. Both require all the skills of sound critical thinking.

Questions and Answers in Your Education

Researchers have found that many new college students differ from teachers in how they value questions and answers. Some students think their goal is to answer questions by reporting facts they have learned. But most teachers want not those pat answers but more questions—critical thinking about what their students hear and read, a willingness to test claims against alternatives and evidence. That difference confuses many first year students. Here is a test to find out how closely your thinking matches that of your teachers. Do you agree with the following?

1. Once you have the facts, most questions have only one right answer.
2. The best thing about science is that problems have only one right answer.

3. It wastes time to work on problems with no clear-cut answer.
4. Educators should know whether lecture or discussion is the better teaching method.
5. A good teacher keeps students from wandering off the right track.
6. If professors stuck to facts and theorized less, I'd get more out of college.

If you mostly agree, your educational values conflict with those of most of your teachers, and you may be puzzled why they ask you so many questions and give you so few answers. The theme in most of these questions concerns a critical cast of mind, one that emphasizes not settled facts but open questions, not rote knowledge but skeptical inquiry.

Source: M. P. Ryan, "Monitoring Text Comprehension: Individual Differences in Epistemological Standards," *Journal of Educational Psychology* 76 (1984): 250.

Arguments Enable Democracy

Critical thinking and good arguments are also at the heart of this messy way of governing ourselves that we call *democracy*. Dictators do not have to make arguments, because no one dares question their claims, much less their reasons. But in a democracy, those who govern us are, at least in theory, obliged to answer our questions.

In fact, we elect representatives to ask questions, make arguments, and analyze others' arguments on our behalf; and we pay journalists and political analysts to test the arguments and actions of those in power. Our designated questioners might not ask the questions we want them to; often we don't even know what questions they should ask. But democracy is served whenever an official is questioned on our behalf. One of the greatest risks to democracy is for officials to think that they can have their way without giving us sound reasons supported by reliable facts.

Of course, even the best arguments don't always succeed, especially when they threaten the interests of the powerful. Some even claim that rational argument is futile because what counts in politics is not logic and evidence but power and influence. But that view ignores occasions when good arguments have prevailed and, worse, excuses those who exercise power from having to justify its arbitrary use. Even if those in power sometimes get their way without our consent, we at least hold them to the principle that our critical assent is the source of that power.

Developing Democracy Means More Arguments

Here's a news report about democracy in Thailand:

Sumalee Limpaovart thought she was simply a mother protecting her child. But she found herself a warrior in the front lines of a struggle for democratic

(continued on next page)

(continued from previous page)

openness that is being fought today in Thailand and across East Asia. When her six-year-old daughter was rejected by an exclusive government school earlier this year, Mrs. Sumalee did something that would have been unthinkable here only a few years ago: She challenged the decision, using a new freedom of information law to demand the test scores of the other children. In the end, Mrs. Sumalee found what she had suspected: One-third of the students admitted had failed the entrance exam but had been accepted because of their families' status or gifts to the school.

It was just one of the many small, sharp battles that have multiplied in recent years as a bolder, better-educated middle class begins to rise up against the paternalistic order of the past. As they do so, a society built on harmony and civility is becoming increasingly argumentative, confrontational, and noisy.[a]

The historian Robert Conquest makes the same point on a larger scale. He describes the suppression of critical thinking by all three twentieth-century totalitarian regimes—communism, fascism, and nazism:

"Scientific" totalitarianism, which appears to be the rational, ordered form [of society], contains greater elements of irrationality than does the civic culture . . . [because civic culture] contains the element of debate and argument. . . . The totalitarian state contains within itself all of the elements of a more extreme irrationality: the elimination of real debate and criticism.[b]

[a] *New York Times,* August 10, 1999
[b] Robert Conquest, *Reflections on a Ravaged Century* (New York: Norton, 2001): 83–84.

What's Not an Argument?

Three Forms of Persuasion That Are Not Arguments

Argument is often equated with persuasion, especially by those who think that they have to win an argument to succeed. But argument and persuasion are not the same. Not only can one make a successful argument without fully persuading readers, but there are forms of persuasion that are not arguments. Here are three kinds of persuasion that look like arguments but lack a key quality of sound and fair ones: (1) negotiation, (2) propaganda, and (3) coercion.

Negotiation feels like argument when you and another person trade claims and reasons about, say, the price of a car. But when you *negotiate,* you can offer any reason you want, even one you would not accept for yourself, so long as you reach an outcome that both sides can live with. You ought not lie, but you are not obliged (or even expected) to be candid—or complete. So you are not unethical when you do not reveal the highest price you are willing to pay. But when you make an argument, you are obligated to be candid and as informative as possible, and that includes *not* omitting information relevant to your claims or offering reasons you think are bogus.

Propaganda sometimes resembles argument when it offers claims and reasons, but propagandists don't care whether their reasons are any good, only whether they work, usually by exploiting the emotions of their audience. Nor do they care what others think, except to know what beliefs they have to defeat. Least of all do they care whether another point of view should change their own. A fair argument offers only good reasons and is obligated to acknowledge and respond to the beliefs of others.

Coercion solves problems by threat, by making the cost of rejecting a claim intolerable: *Agree or suffer!* Though we think of coercion as a stick, a carrot can also coerce when it's a bribe: *Agree and I will reward you.* Those who present themselves as authorities seek to coerce if they argue *Agree because I know better than you do.* So do those who try to shame us into agreement: When Princess Leia of *Star Wars* pleads, *Help me Obi-Wan Kenobi, you're my only hope,* he must either help or betray his deepest values.

Negotiation, propaganda, and coercion are not always irrational, or even unethical. When we coerce, propagandize, and negotiate with children, we call it parenting. Nor would anyone be irrational to threaten or negotiate with terrorists holding hostage a school bus full of students. Our challenge is to know what form of discourse best serves the cause of a civil and just community. That's usually a fair and candid argument.

Arguments Persuade with Reasons

When Colomb was a boy, his school had a vice principal called the "Prefect of Discipline" who had a paddle called "The Persuader." It influenced Colomb's thinking and occasionally his actions, but getting paddled was not a form of argument, any more than are the insults of those who shout others into silence.

Arguments and Explanations

Some sets of claims and reasons look like arguments but are not:

> Tanya: I have to go home. _{claim} I'm so tired I'm making mistakes. _{reason}

In her first sentence, Tanya makes a claim and in the second offers a reason, but we cannot know whether they constitute an argument until we know Tanya's intention:

> Ron: Leaving? About time. You've been working for hours.
>
> Tanya: I have to go home. _{claim} I'm so tired I'm making mistakes. _{reason}

Tanya offers Ron a reason not to *convince* him that she should go home (he seems to think she should), but to *explain* why she must. Contrast this:

> Ron: You're not leaving, are you? We need you!
>
> Tanya: I have to go home. _{claim} I'm so tired I'm making mistakes. _{reason}

Tanya offers the same claim and reason, but now to *convince* Ron to accept a claim that he will not accept just because she says it. That's not an explanation; it's an argument.

For an exchange to be an argument, it must meet two criteria:

- The first concerns its form. An argument consists of a claim (a statement saying what you want someone to believe or do), and at least one reason (a statement giving that person a basis for agreeing).

- The second concerns the intention of its participants. To make an argument, you must think that the other person will accept your claim *only if* you give her good reason to do so.

For an exchange to be a *thoughtful* argument, one based on all three stages of critical thinking, it has to be more than a one-sided offer of reasons:

- You make an argument that is both sound and fair when you also acknowledge and respond to views that might qualify or contradict your own. Tanya should respond to Ron if he said, "But you promised to stay!"

We use explanations and arguments for different ends, but we usually weave them together. You might argue that the campus bookstore should not sell clothing made in third world sweatshops, but in doing that, you would also have to explain that country's economic conditions.

Arguments and Stories

Stories are as old as arguments, probably older. They often seem like arguments, but they appeal to a kind of reasoning that is not always compatible with sound critical thinking, indeed that sometimes contradicts it.

- Told well, a story can make listeners feel awe, fear, pleasure, disgust. A good argument may give them a sense of intellectual pleasure, but that's less viscerally compelling than anger or delight.

- A vivid story seems to describe what "really" happened so that its truth seems self-evident to the mind's eye. An argument offers patterns of abstract reasons and evidence that lead to the truth more reliably, but much less vividly.

- When you tell a story, you hope listeners will, at least for a time, suspend their critical judgment so that they will not think, *Wait a minute, that can't be!* but instead wonder only *What happened next?* In fact, we seem offensive when we question a story told as a personal experience, because we seem to doubt the story teller's truthfulness. When we write a thoughtful argument, however, we invite a critical response. We should want readers to question our reasons, our evidence, our logic, even the need for an argument at all.

When we tell stories, we want readers to suspend disbelief so that they can *experience* our words; when we make arguments, we welcome readers' doubts so that they *think about* our words.

Inexperienced writers sometimes think that a good story is enough to make a good argument. And some great stories do imply a point so clearly that we can infer their implicit claim. But a story alone can never itself offer a claim or even a reason. That's why so many moral tales end with a message like, *Be careful what you wish for.* Used as evidence, however, good stories can support a reason or claim with great power.

Arguments and Visual Images

Arguments require words, but they can also harness the power of images. With new digital tools, you have more ways than ever to create images that make your evidence, and so your argument, come alive for your readers. (For more on the visual presentation of evidence, see Chapter 6.) New digital tools have even made it possible to create arguments that blend the power of words with the power of moving images. When you can present evidence as a visual story, you can harness its vividness and emotional power to make your argument very persuasive.

But just as a story does not make an argument, neither does a visual image alone: arguments always need words that state at least a claim and supporting reasons. We cannot help but be moved when we see a TV commercial or print advertisement showing starving children. The image seems to cry out for us to do something. But what? Join the Peace Corps? Tell Congress to forgive third world debts? Stop globalization? Send money?—to whom? We know *what* this image wants us to do only when a text or voice-over tells us—Send money to Feed the Children (claim), because we can feed these children for pennies a day (reason).

Logic, Character, Emotion / Logos, Ethos, Pathos

Rational argument is not an exercise in pure logic. Some philosophers exclude emotion from reasoning, but cognitive science has proved that feelings are crucial to human rationality. No rational person could write an argument about the Holocaust or slavery and be unmoved. And we have all acted on conclusions that seemed logical but felt wrong, then regretted ignoring our feelings.

But we cannot support a claim based on feelings alone. We can't justify a claim simply by saying how strongly we feel about it. We have to explain our claims—and our feelings—in ways that seem rational. And that means with reasons and evidence.

Those who write about arguments distinguish three kinds of force in them:

- When we appeal to our readers' logic, we rely on a force we call *logos*—the topic of most of this book.

(continued on next page)

(continued from previous page)

But two other kinds of force depend on the ability to elicit feelings in readers:

- When we appeal directly to their feelings of pity, anger, fear, and so on, we appeal to their *pathos*. (We discuss this issue mainly in Part 4.)
- When we project a trustful, open-minded character, we hope readers will be moved by our *ethos*. (We discuss that force throughout this book.)

We can separate these appeals for analysis, but in practice they are so intertwined that to distinguish them is often just splitting hairs.

WRITING PROCESS

Argument and Critical Thinking

It is crucial to learn to write sound arguments, but the habits of many inexperienced writers hinder them from doing that. Once they have a claim to make, they plunge into drafting and go where chance takes them. Others plan in painful detail, then write up their argument exactly according to plan, ignoring opportunities to discover something new. Experienced writers know they have to think and plan before they draft, but also that they are likely to change their minds as they draft and revise.

That is a habit of mind that takes practice. To start you on that learning curve, in each chapter we discuss strategies that experienced writers use to produce effective arguments in a reasonable time. We organize this advice into six categories: (1) thinking and talking, (2) reading and researching, (3) preparing and planning, (4) drafting, (5) revising, and (6) working collaboratively. Those look like sequential stages, but don't try to follow them step-by-step. Be ready to loop back and forth.

We also include a section that will lead you through the more demanding process of writing a research report, a paper that depends on supporting a claim with published sources.

THINKING AND TALKING

Your mind begins working on an argument long before you write anything. And if you let it, your unconscious mind will keep working on it even when you're thinking about other things. In this section, we show you how to work on your argument even when you're not reading or writing, from the moment you get an assignment until you turn it in.

Tell Your Elevator Story

Expert writers know that the more and the sooner they talk about what they plan to write, the better that first plan will be. Student writers, on the other hand, often keep their developing ideas to themselves, because they are afraid to look foolish by sharing unformed ones. To help yourself start talking about your ideas right away, you can do what professionals do: tell your elevator story. Imagine that as you step into an elevator headed to the fifth floor, you run into your teacher who says, "So, tell me what are you going to write in your paper." You don't have long, so you need to say what's interesting about your argument in just a few sentences.

Of course, you won't have much to say if you are still looking for a problem to write about. (To develop one, see "Exploring a Topic to Find a Problem," pp. 96–100.) For an elevator story, you must already have a general idea about an issue you want to address, either because it was assigned or is important to you. But that's how just about every argument begins, with a rough sense that you believe something that others don't and that you have some reasons to support your claim. Once you have that, an elevator story will help you develop that rough sense into a responsible and plausible argument.

A good elevator story has four elements, each of which is only one or two sentences long:

1. the question or problem your argument will address
   I'm writing about the question/problem of. . . .

2. why that problem or question is important or interesting
   I chose that question or problem because. . . .

3. your current best guess at an answer, if you have one; otherwise, your best guess about where one can be found
   I think the answer/solution is. . . .
   I think the answer/solution has something to do with. . . .

4. where you expect to find evidence to support your answer
   I think the best evidence is. . . .

A good elevator story includes all four elements:

> I'm writing about the question of how actual families differed from the way they were depicted in 1950s sitcoms, because I think those depictions created expectations that a lot of people thought they should live up to, but couldn't. I think I can show that TV families were idealized and that actual families were much more varied. I can find evidence about TV families in the video-tape collection of the media studies library, and there is a government database with statistics on actual families.

For now, just describe each element as best you can. In Chapter 3 we'll explain a better way to state your question and why it is important.

Don't put off formulating your elevator story until you have all the answers. Create one as soon as you can, and practice it as often as your friends will listen. Your story—and your ideas—will get better each time you tell it.

Think About Your Readers

As you tell your elevator story, keep in mind that what you count as an important problem others might not, and what you think are good reasons and evidence, others might reject. You might think there's a problem with rising college tuition, but a recent graduate might not care one bit. So once you understand what problem or question you want your argument to address, you must try to imagine how your readers will react to it. (We'll discuss these issues in Chapter 3.)

When you think about readers, don't imagine yourself behind a podium reading your argument to a faceless crowd in a dark auditorium; imagine your readers as amiable but feisty friends sitting across the kitchen table, interrupting you with hard questions, objections, and their own views. In that situation, you have to respond to their questions and objections, especially questions like *So what? Why should I care?*

Real Versus Stipulated Readers

You may face a challenge if your teacher tells you to address readers different from the ones who will actually read your paper—a teacher, grader, or classmate: *You are a researcher at Ace Advertising, working on the new V-Sport Vehicle account, and your manager wants an analysis of how Ford and Chrysler ads appeal to consumers under twenty-five.* No ad manager will read your paper, but your writing teacher will judge it as if she were one. So you have an actual reader (your teacher) and a stipulated reader (the imagined manager). If you know about ad managers, you may be able to anticipate their questions. If not, all you can do is imagine yourself in their shoes, then decide whether your real reader will imagine the same thing.

If your assignment stipulates that your reader is "the general public," you have an even bigger challenge because there is no such reader. But if that's your assignment, assume (though it is not true) that this "general public" reads publications such as the *New York Times, National Review,* or *Scientific American.* Alternatively, assume that the "general public" is someone like yourself. They have read what you have but have not discussed it and want to hear more.

Talk to Readers If You Can

The best way to learn about readers is to talk to them. It's what experts do.

- Before an architect draws up a proposal, she finds out everything she can about her clients, from their finances to their living habits.
- Before a lawyer drafts a pleading, he checks out the judge who will hear the case by reading her decisions and asking other lawyers about her.

You might not be able to do that kind of detailed research, but it is a good idea to find out what your readers know and believe.

- Suppose Elena is preparing a proposal for a Center for English Language Studies to help students whose first language is not English. She could visit administrators to find out what they know about ESL students, whether they have dealt with the issue before, who will have a say in approving her proposal, and so on.

It's also wise to find out how readers react to your argument before you write it:

> • Once Elena has a proposal, she could visit readers to gauge their reactions to it. Do they think there is a problem? Do they think resources should be invested in other services? Do they have a cheaper alternative? Readers often judge an argument more generously when they are familiar with it before they read it.

Of course, for most students, talking to readers means talking to their teacher. But that's not a bad thing. Not only will it help you anticipate your teacher's responses, but it will prepare her to read your argument more generously by giving her a stake in seeing it succeed. When you can't talk to readers directly, imagine someone who is smart, amiable, and open-minded, but inclined to disagree with you; write to that person.

READING AND RESEARCHING

Only rarely will you be able to make a sound and complete argument without finding new information, usually by reading published and online sources. In this section, we show you how to find and use sources to develop your argument. Since most of what you read will also be arguments, you can use what you learn about writing them to help you read them more effectively. The best way to understand an argument you read is to write about it as you go. Mark it up: underline, highlight, comment in the margins, talk back to the writer by writing out questions or reservations.

Get an Overview

Start by skimming to create a framework for more careful reading. Ask these questions of your authors:

- • What problem do you solve? What question do you answer?
- • What is the solution to your problem, the answer to your question?
- • Do you want me just to think something or to do something?
- • What reasons support your claim?
- • What evidence supports your reasons?

Why not just read straight through? Because once you have a framework, you can read faster, understand better, and remember longer. Here is a procedure for skimming to create that informed framework:

Articles
1. Locate where the introduction stops and the body begins. That may be marked with a heading, extra space, or another typographical signal.

2. Skim the introduction, focusing on its end. You are most likely to find there a statement of the problem or question that the author addresses. Highlight it. You may also find the main point, the answer to the question, the solution to the problem. If so, highlight it too.

3. Skim the conclusion. If the main point was not at the end of the introduction, you should find it here. Highlight it.

4. Look through the body for headings that reveal its organization and sequence of topics.

5. Skim just the first paragraph or two of each main section.

Books

1. Read the table of contents and the opening section that contains an overview. It might be called "Introduction," "Preface," or "Chapter 1."

2. Focus on the beginning and conclusion of the overview, looking for a statement of the issue, problem, or question the book addresses.

3. Read the conclusion, noticing how it relates to the overview. Look for the main point. Highlight or summarize it.

4. Skim the first and last few paragraphs of each chapter.

Web Sites Many texts posted on the Internet have the same structure as published articles, and you can use the approach above. Otherwise, do this:

1. Look for an overview or introduction. It might be on the home page or a page of its own.

2. Look for a site map to see how it is organized into topics and sections. If you find no map, read through the major links on the home page.

Once you have a general sense of a text, question it as you read. Jot down disagreements, questions, alternative points of view. This is a useful habit, because it helps you imagine your readers doing the same with you.

When you've finished reading a section, write—or at least mentally rehearse—a brief summary. Think of it as the elevator story for that text. It will help you fix in your memory a clearer image of what you understand.

PREPARING AND PLANNING

Expert writers plan an argument in many ways, but they know that the more they plan, the faster they write and the better the argument they make. In time, you'll discover what rituals of preparing and planning work best for you—what you have to write out, what you can do in your head, and what you don't even have to think about. Nothing replaces experience, but what you practice now mechanically, you'll do automatically later.

Focus on Your Problem

Start planning your argument by deciding what you want it to achieve. What do you gain if readers agree with your solution? What do you lose if they don't? Do you propose ways to improve the world or just ways to understand it better?

- Your problem is *conceptual* if you solve it by getting readers simply to *understand* something better. What do you want readers to *understand* about Super-Kmart and Wal-Mart?

  Mega stores force small family stores out of business, replacing the intimate spaces of small stores where neighbors could meet with huge impersonal barns where everyone is a stranger, thereby eroding community values.

- Your problem is *practical* if you solve it by getting readers to *do* something or to support an *action* by others. What do you want readers to *do* about mega stores?

  Because large mega stores erode the quality of community life, this county should pass zoning laws to keep mega stores out of small towns.

Even if you are not yet certain what specific question or problem you will address, decide as soon as you can whether you want to make a claim about what your readers should think or what they should do. In most cases, your teacher will expect you to address a conceptual problem, since that is what most academic writing does and there are few serious practical problems you can solve in a few pages. So even if you feel that it's important to *do* something about those mega stores, consider building your argument around a question whose answer might be one step toward that goal.

To Outline or Not to Outline

Experienced writers have mixed feelings about outlines. When the two of us left high school, we were glad to be shut of formal outlines with their roman numerals and letters, an "ii" for every "i." We no longer make elaborate outlines, but we do depend on sketchy ones for the general shape of our arguments. If you like formal outlines, use them, but don't reject a scratch outline because you reject a formal one. Find the kind of outline that works best for you, even if it is only a list of topics. Whatever it is, don't start a serious first draft without one. (We'll discuss plans in more detail in Chapters 5 through 8.)

DRAFTING

You may not yet be drafting an argument, but when you start, think of doing it in two overlapping stages: drafting and revising. We all revise as we draft, but it's useful to reserve time after you've finished a first draft to look at it fresh. We are all amazed at how much less convincing an argument seems the day after we wrote it. You'll write better and faster if you draft first and revise later. So as you write, try not to be too self-critical.

When to Begin Drafting

It might seem logical to begin drafting only after you're dead certain of the solution to your problem, but that can be a mistake, because one way of discovering a solution is to do some writing to help you explore your problem. Start by formulating a few tentative solutions—call them *hypotheses*. You don't have to be 100 percent sure you are on the right track; think of this early writing as an opportunity to "audition" claims. (One student compared this process to dating: no commitment, just interest.) Once you can state even a tentative claim, list reasons that would encourage a critical reader to take it seriously. That list can become your scratch outline *after* you arrange those reasons into an order that readers can recognize.

Styles of Drafting

Some writers draft slowly and carefully, others as quickly as they can. Most experienced writers are closer to quick than to careful, but you should draft in whatever way works for you. There is no best way, and both involve trade-offs:

- *Careful drafters* have to finish one sentence before they begin the next, get each paragraph right before they move on to another. Slow and careful drafters need meticulous plans, but even small changes can cascade, each requiring another, finally forcing changes bigger than the original plan allows. If you draft slowly, plan carefully.

- *Quick drafters* expect to revise, so they don't stop to find exactly the right phrase. When they get on a roll, they leave out quotations, data, even whole paragraphs that they know they can fill in later. When they bog down, they jump ahead or go back to parts they skipped, edit for grammar and spelling, or look for that right word. Quick drafters know they risk rambling, so they leave lots of time to reorganize and rethink their argument. If you draft fast, start early.

REVISING

Experienced writers know that once they figure out what to say, they still have to say it in ways that meet their readers' needs and expectations. In fact, many experienced writers spend more time revising than drafting.

Your biggest obstacle in revising will not be too little time, but too much memory. None of us can read our own writing as our readers will, because we remember too well what we wanted to mean when we wrote it. So we read into our writing what we want readers to get out of it. Our readers, however, have to depend on what they see on the page.

Given that problem, you have to get distance on your draft. Set it aside until it is no longer fresh in your memory, or ask someone to read it back to you, out loud. But the best strategy is to revise your draft in a way that deliberately sidesteps your too-good understanding of it, a process we'll explain in every chapter that follows.

WORKING COLLABORATIVELY

Why Collaborate?

Making an argument ends not when you finish it but when your readers respond to it (and not even then if you respond to their responses). So create imaginary readers or enlist real ones to help you anticipate their responses. Your teacher knows how this works: she has worked with reviewers, editors, and colleagues on almost everything she has published. Some students fear that working together is dishonest, but it doesn't have to be if you don't depend on those others to draft your paper. Instead use them to get feedback on your outlines and drafts. Revise for yourself on the basis of their responses. You should also let your teacher know what you are doing.

You benefit from working with others in many ways:

1. Since you can't read your own work as your readers will, you see your work more objectively.

2. Since you must make arguments in dialogue with others, you learn how to anticipate their questions and objections. You learn to listen and respond to other points of view.

3. By practicing the skills of civil disagreement, you learn to ask hard questions in an amiable way and then to listen to answers.

4. You learn to interact with others in ways that project a credible character, what we've called your ethos. You project an ethos in many ways, but none more directly than in how you respond to questions and objections.

5. You learn to critique the arguments of others. As you advance in your studies, you will have to think critically about what you read. And in the workplace, where collaboration is the norm, you are likely to be responsible for responding critically *and helpfully* to the work of colleagues and eventually to the writing of those who work for you. That may seem distant, but you can prepare yourself for that task by practicing thoughtful, generous, and helpful criticism now.

Our Many Collaborators

We got lots of help writing this book. Early drafts were critiqued by more than a dozen readers. We also got help from teachers who listened to our ideas at conferences and workshops or used the manuscript in classes. Some of their students wrote us responses, even e-mailed us their questions.

At times the process was painful. Early reviewers said things like "I'm afraid to say that unless [this book is] revised extensively, it will prove to be a great disappointment to many who [use] it." But even after we revised for years, some reviewers were still

(continued on next page)

> *(continued from previous page)*
>
> not satisfied: "The text seems in a very early stage of completion. . . . It feels as if the authors were more concerned with being done than with complete coverage. . . . I hope that these [problems] are indeed [be]cause of the youth of the manuscript." We took no pleasure in comments like that, but they helped.

Setting Up a Writing Group

The best way to help one another is to create a writing group. You have to invest time organizing it, but it is an efficient way to improve your writing. Find three or four people you can disagree with amiably and who can meet at an agreeable time—not at eleven the night before a paper is due. You will need to exchange work to review ahead of meetings. Unless everyone is at the earliest stages of preparing, group members should circulate something for each meeting—a draft, an outline, even just a list of ideas. The group should also respond to one another's work in writing: lists of comments, marked up drafts, and so on.

Groups work best with a *facilitator* and a *recorder* (pass the jobs around):

- The facilitator keeps the group on task, makes sure everyone participates, and deflects debate when it gets prickly. At the end of the meeting, she has the group set an agenda for the next one.
- The recorder records what each person agrees to do for the next meeting and if possible, reminds everyone by e-mail.

The most delicate task is keeping everyone working productively. There are some predictable problems of group behavior:

- One or two people dominate the conversation or remain silent.
- One or two become the "experts" on whom the others rely.
- One or two are regularly discounted.

In each case, the problem is as much with the group as with the person. Someone can dominate or be silent only if the group allows it. You guard against that by giving everyone a specific task. If everyone has a task, the group will not suffer from some members' not pulling their weight.

INQUIRIES

These inquiries offer a wide range of questions, puzzles, things to do, suggestions for class discussions, short papers, and even research papers, all intended to help you understand the nature and uses of argument. There are three kinds of inquiries: A **Reflection** asks you to think. A **Task** asks you to do something and discuss it. A **Project** asks you to engage in active research. Most chapters have too many inquiries for anyone to complete, so don't try to do them all. Pick those that interest you, especially if your teacher asks you to prepare some for class discussion.

REFLECTIONS

1. Imagine that someone discovers a group of people isolated in some part of the world and claims that they are "completely irrational." Can you explain what would count as evidence that a whole society is completely irrational? Could an irrational society survive?

2. How is it possible for two rational people who agree on the facts to come to diametrically opposite conclusions? Is it impossible for this to happen?

3. Have you ever been in a conversation where you thought you were simply explaining something while the other person thought you were making an argument? What caused this confusion?

4. Must we know the truth about something before we can think about it rationally?

5. How often do you argue because you want someone to do something rather than believe something? Why does anyone bother to argue over "mere" beliefs? What difference does it make whether we agree on ideas? When was the last time you changed what you did on the basis of changing what you believed? What was the most important time?

6. We can only speculate on how rationality evolved, much less why. Here is a fable about its origins:

> At first, our forebears solved problems like the disputed ownership of a rock by hooting at or beating on each other until one retreated. The first advance in the technology of dispute resolution occurred when one of them found he could effectively claim ownership of the rock by clubbing the other with it. It was a pivotal moment: No longer was size or strength the only means of persuasion; humankind had developed the intelligence to make tools, especially those we call weapons. But the greatest change in our means of persuasion occurred when our ancestors replaced stones with words. Imagine that it might have happened like this: Once, when one of our forebears wanted to settle the question of who owned a useful rock, he uttered the equivalent of "Mine!" The other one in the confrontation might have just lunged at the one claiming the rock, but instead did something that must have amazed the other. She (or he) asked something like "Why?"—an act that transformed a physical confrontation into a verbal one. Then the first one did something more amazing yet. Instead of ignoring the question and just whacking the other with the rock, he (or she) offered the other a reason: "I found it." But the most amazing moment of all came when the other agreed: "OK, your rock." When they settled the issue not with blows but with good reasons, they together created the kind of talk we call argument and marked the beginnings of shared rationality, the ability to share our beliefs and the reasons that make us hold them, in the hope that others will agree.

In that story, humans began to offer claims and reasons to avoid violence. Can you imagine other ways that argument could have originated? (One of us [JMW] thinks this story must have a nub of truth; the other [GGC] thinks it unlikely.) Since we can never know for sure, you can be as fanciful as you like. Is the idea of an "origin" even possible to speculate about? Does the fact that our metaphors for argument are so predictably drawn from images of combat offer any assistance here?

7. What metaphors do we use when we talk about reasoning? Are they as misleading as those we use for argument? Here is an example:

   I tried to resist the force of her logic, but it was so overwhelming that I could not stand up to it. I was simply compelled to accept her reasoning.

8. What metaphors do we use when we talk about expressing an opinion? (You might look up the original meaning of *express*.) Are they misleading? Here is a pair of passages that depend on different metaphors:

   It is important for me to *express* my ideas *honestly*, so I *lay out* my thoughts on the page as directly as I can. When I just *let it flow*, when I can *pour* my ideas out without any interference, I write most sincerely.

   It is important for me to *share* my ideas in a way that makes them *attractive* to readers. I try to *dress them up* with good reasons, to *show* them to *best advantage* and *hide* any weaknesses or rough spots.

   If those two speakers argued in the way their metaphors suggest, how would their arguments differ?

9. What metaphors other than combat might describe arguments? Try out these: game, exploration, love affair. Imagine how arguments would work if we talked about them in those terms. Now invent a new metaphor. Could these new ways of describing an argument change how you understand arguments and how they might work? Are there any advantages to keeping the metaphor of argument as combat?

TASKS

10. Sketch supporting reasons for a position on one of these issues: (a) Computers seem to behave in ways that we would never call irrational, but should we call them rational? (b) How about animals? What would count as rational or irrational behavior in a dog? A chimp? A spider?

11. List the sorts of occasions in which public figures at least seem to listen to questions and answer them. How do they most commonly duck their responsibility to the questioner?

12. We've suggested that people make arguments to solve problems. Are there arguments that we have just for the sake of having them, regardless of whether the outcome resolves an issue? List some occasions when you have participated in or witnessed such an argument. Was it appropriate in the circumstances?

13. In your experience, are children more likely to argue just for fun than adults? Boys more than girls? Men more than women? People at home more than people at work? Why?

14. Recall an occasion when someone spoke or acted in ways that you judged irrational. What factors led you to think so?

15. Is it rational always to be completely rational? If not, list some occasions when you think that it is better not to be rational. Why would it be wrong to be rational on those occasions? Compare your list with those of your classmates. If you have items on your list that they do not, what reasons can you offer for adding those items to their lists? Or for deleting them?

16. Are arguments good for anything other than getting someone to accept your opinion or grant your request? Find an example of an argument (a) that succeeds but does not achieve agreement; (b) that achieves agreement but does not solve the problem that occasioned it; (c) that gets another to say *I don't agree, but I see your point.* What good is this last response? Has the argument failed?

PROJECTS

17. Keep a diary for a day (or at least a few hours) in which you record how often you felt you had to give reasons to someone before that person would do or believe something you wanted that person to. Which occurred more often, arguments over what to think or what to do?

18. At what age do children begin to offer reasons for their claims? At what age do they understand the question, *Why do you think that?* How would we know whether they understood the question but couldn't answer it, or just didn't understand the question? At what point are we ready to say that a child becomes rational? If you can observe children interacting, watch how they make arguments. Do they negotiate? Coerce? Propagandize?

19. Watch some cable talk shows that feature pundits debating each other. Rarely do the participants end up agreeing on anything. Why do they argue then? Why does anyone watch?

20. Some inexperienced writers are surprised that they are expected to convince a teacher of something. They wonder, *Isn't my job just to show my teacher what I know?* Survey five or six students to find out what they thought their goals were when they wrote in high school. Was it to show the teacher what they had learned? To give back what the teacher said in class? To express an opinion? To support a claim that the teacher might not be inclined to agree with? To practice making good arguments? Now survey some teachers in your current classes. Ask them what they want students to achieve in their papers. How much agreement is there? Pool your answers. What do you conclude?

FOCUS ON WRITING

$$\boxed{1}$$

Context.   What follows are scenarios in which you have been asked to participate in a discussion group, by someone who wants you to think about a problem that you can help solve.

Task.   In each scenario, you are not asked to prepare a formal report, only to think and take some notes. To help you do that, you've been given an outline of points to make notes on. You can be assured that everything you say will be kept confidential. Pick one scenario. Read the request and write out a page or two of notes that will help you discuss the issues in question but that are also clear enough for you to share. Bring your notes to class, one copy for yourself and one to turn in.

Scenario 1.   From your high school: *We hope you are off to a good start in college and feel prepared for your work. Your Old High School has received a grant of money to improve teaching. To decide how to use these funds, we want to find out how you judge the teaching you experienced. What qualities did you admire most in your best teachers? What qualities did you like least in those who helped you the least? In other words, what can your best teachers teach other teachers? To make the best use of your time, here is a list of topics you might think about. Thanks for your help.*

1. What qualities in your best teachers did you admire most?
2. What qualities distinguished the teachers who helped you least?
3. What larger problem can you see arising if we don't help our weakest teachers improve?
4. Can you suggest two or three specific ways to solve this problem?
5. What do you think will be the biggest obstacles to solving it?
6. Can you give us a story about the best and worst teaching you had?
7. If someone questioned your analysis, what is the strongest "hard evidence" that you could offer to back up what you say?

Scenario 2.   From your college: *We are conducting a self-study to determine how to improve the quality of student life. We hope your experience has been good, but we know that in every complex process, there are glitches. We invite you to a discussion with a few classmates to help us find out how to fix those glitches. To make the best use of your time, here is a list of topics you might think about. Thanks for your help.*

With respect to your daily life as a student,

1. What do we do best right now?
2. What problem do you think we should focus on?

3. If we do not solve this problem, what larger problem do you think might arise?

4. Can you suggest two or three specific ways to solve this problem?

5. What do you think will be the biggest obstacles to fixing it?

6. Can you describe in detail an example of this problem?

7. If someone questioned your analysis, what is the strongest "hard evidence" that you could offer to back up what you say?

8. Can you cite others who feel the same way, not by name but by recounting their experiences?

Scenario 3.   From a former employer: *We here at [your former employer] have embarked on a self-study to find out how we can become a better company. We are asking former employees how we could improve our operations, from our treatment of customers to employee relations. To make the best use of your time, here is a list of topics you might think about. Thanks for your help.*

With respect to our day-to-day operations,

1. What do we do best right now?

2. What problem do you think we should focus on?

3. If we do not solve this problem, what larger problem do you think might arise?

4. Can you suggest two or three specific ways to solve this problem?

5. What do you think will be the biggest obstacles to fixing it?

6. Can you describe in detail an example of this problem?

7. If someone questioned your analysis, what is the strongest "hard evidence" that you could offer to back up what you say?

8. Can you cite others who feel the same way, not by name but by recounting their experiences?

Scenario 4.   From any other organization you have been a member of, such as a church or civic group, a sports or hobby club, and so on: *We here at [organization] have embarked on a self-study to find out how we can achieve our mission more effectively. We are asking members how we could do our work better. To make the best use of your time, here is a list of topics you might consider. Thanks for your help.*

With respect to our day-to-day operations,

1. What do we do best right now?

2. What problem do you think we should focus on?

3. If we do not solve this problem, what larger problem do you think might arise?

4. Can you suggest two or three specific ways to solve this problem?

5. What do you think will be the biggest obstacles to fixing it?
6. Can you describe in detail an example of this problem?
7. If someone questioned your analysis, what is the strongest "hard evidence" that you could offer to back up what you say?
8. Can you cite others who feel the same way, not by name but by recounting their experiences?

2

Context.   A common charge against advertising is that it appeals to our basest emotions—insecurity, pride, greed, lust, and so on. If that were true, advertising would be a dangerous influence on us, like pornography. But is that a fair charge? Is it true of all ads?

Scenario.   One of your classmates has attacked advertising as morally degrading, and when you tried to respond in class, you realized you hadn't thought through the issues. Alternatively, someone has defended advertising as decent and useful, and you think it is dangerous. The topic will come up again in the next class, and this time you want to be prepared.

Task.   Find three print ads that you think appeal more to your rational powers than to your emotions. Photocopy the ads and prepare notes that would let you respond to someone charging that advertising is intellectually corrupt. Try to find a second ad for a similar product that does appeal to base emotions, so that you can make your point by contrasting the two. Or prepare the opposite case. (*Note:* Do not defend or attack advertising as commercially necessary, as a way to communicate news about a product to the public. Focus on advertising strictly in terms of its moral, ethical, and intellectual qualities.)

3

Task.   Select one of the Tasks or Projects (or even a Reflection) from pages 25–27 on which you can take a strong position. Work up notes for an argument that might support that position.

4

Task.   If you have a recent paper, work up notes on an argument someone could make to support a position different from yours. Do this only if you can make a case for that position.

5

Scenario.   Your class is reading a variety of articles about student life, with each student reading different articles. You have been assigned the article by Carol Trosset, "Obstacles to Open Discussion and Critical Thinking: The Grinnell College Study" (pp. 385–392). Your teacher has asked you to focus on this question: *Does this article reflect your own experience?* You will have to summarize and respond to the article in class, confirming, contradicting, or qualifying the author's claim.

Task. Write detailed notes outlining the argument of the article along with a possible response, agreeing or disagreeing.

IN A NUTSHELL

About Your Argument . . .

We do not define an argument by its abrasive tone, the belligerent attitudes of arguers, or by the desire to coerce an audience into accepting a claim. Instead, we define an argument by two criteria:

- Two (or more) people want to solve a problem but don't agree on a solution.
- They exchange reasons and evidence that they think support their respective solutions and respond to one another's questions, objections, and alternatives.

You make an argument not just to settle a disagreement. Good arguments help you explore questions and explain your beliefs, so that even when you and your readers can't agree, you can at least understand why.

. . . and About Writing It

Your first task in writing an argument is to understand the problem that occasions it. Why (other than the fact that your teacher assigned it) are you writing it? What do you want it to achieve?

- Do you want your readers just to understand something, with no expectation that they will act? If so, why is that understanding important?
- Do you want your readers to act? If so, what do you expect them to accomplish? What problem will that action solve?

Once you understand your problem, try out a few solutions, pick one that seems promising, then list reasons that would encourage readers to agree. You can use that list as a scratch outline or, if you wish, expand it into a formal one.

Draft in whatever way feels comfortable: quick and messy, or slow and careful. If you are quick, start early and leave time to revise. If you are slow, plan carefully and get it right the first time, because you may not have time to fix it.

CHAPTER 2

Argument as Civil Conversation

In this chapter, we show you how to build an argument out of the answers to just five simple questions, questions that we ask one another every day. Then we show you how to use those questions to have a conversation with yourself to develop a written argument that your readers will judge to be thoughtful and persuasive. The same questions are also the key to critical thinking: you use them to test not only others' ideas but your own as well.

The Five Questions of Argument

You make arguments so often that you probably never reflect on how you do it, but it is something you must understand if you are first to create written arguments that you trust to be sound and then to explain to others why they should trust them too.

To make successful arguments, you have to do at least three things:

- Offer the kinds of support that careful readers expect.
- Demonstrate the qualities of critical thinking that encourage readers to trust you.
- Incorporate readers' views by imagining their questions or objections and then by answering them in your argument.

It's easier to earn that trust in conversation than in writing, because you don't have to guess what questions a reader might ask; someone is right there asking them.

It's more difficult to earn that trust when you're "conversing" on a pad of paper or computer screen, because you must imagine readers' questions before you can answer them, a skill that's hard to learn.

Fortunately, there are only five kinds of questions, and you've asked and answered them countless times. The first two we have no trouble asking others and are happy to answer when asked of us:

1. *What's your point? What are you **claiming** that I should do or believe?*

2. *Why should I agree? What **reasons** can you offer to support your claim?*

The third question seems a bit more confrontational, since it implies that others may not take you at your word:

3. *How do I know those are good reasons? On what facts do you base them? What **evidence** do you have to back them up?*

When you can answer those three questions, you create the **core** of your argument: claim-reasons-evidence.

The next question is harder, since it requires that you imagine how a good critical thinker would analyze your argument and question it:

4. *But have you considered. . . ? But what would you say to someone who said/ objected/argued/claimed. . . ? Do you **acknowledge** this alternative to your position, and how would you **respond**?*

When you acknowledge and respond to these last kinds of questions, you create a new level of **dialogue** with your readers. In the core of an argument, you answer readers' questions, but those questions are about what *you* think. Now you open a dialogue with readers in which you explicitly include their views and their voices. This part is crucial to your image as a thoughtful advocate who is more committed to finding the right answer than to defending the one you want. It is also the part that we most often leave out because we prefer to avoid raising the possibility that we might be wrong.

But even if you feel challenged by these questions, you must at least try to ask and answer them because they are essential to your reputation not only as a fair advocate but as a critical thinker as well. In fact, good critical thinking is defined partly by how well you can ask these questions not just about the arguments of others, but about your own.

The final question is hardest of all. It asks you to demonstrate the logical *soundness* of your argument:

5. *What's your logic? What principle makes your reasons relevant to your claim?* (We'll call that principle a **warrant**.)

When you explain your reasoning in response to this last set of questions, you create the explicitly **logical** part of your argument.

Of course, all of an argument must be logical, but that logic is mostly implicit, assumed. If you explicitly explained each logical step, you would overwhelm your readers. So we spell out the logic of an argument rarely, only when we imagine that readers will ask us to explain it. And that's what makes that question about relevance the most challenging of all. First, we don't want readers to ask it, because we feel almost offended when someone questions our logic. Second, we can't easily imagine when readers might ask it, since nothing seems more obvious to us than the logic of our own thinking.

This step may feel too much like an exercise in Logic 101. But try to take it anyway, because it distinguishes the best thinkers and you will need it when you make arguments addressed to those with different views, experiences, and cultures.

When you can ask and answer all five kinds of questions, you can generate the substance for each element of a sound argument:

In this chapter, we first look at those questions in conversations. Then we discuss how to assemble their answers into a written argument that readers will at best accept and at least consider thoughtful, judicious, and fair.

The Roots of Argument in Civil Conversation

Here is a conversation among Sue and Raj, two friends home on spring break from different colleges, and Ann, one of their high school teachers. After chatting about Raj's school, Ann asks Sue about hers:

Ann:	So what's new at your school?
Sue:	I've been tied up with a student government committee working on something we're calling a "Student Bill of Rights."
Ann:	What's that?
Sue:	Well, it's a plan to improve life on campus and in class.
Ann:	What's the problem?
Sue:	We think our school is taking us for granted, not giving us the services we need to get a good education.
Raj:	What's your solution?
Sue:	We think the university should stop treating us only as students and start treating us like customers.
Ann:	Why customers? What's behind that?
Sue:	Well, we pay a lot of money for our education, but we don't get near the attention customers do.
Ann:	How's that?

Sue:	For one thing, we can hardly see teachers outside of class. Last week I counted office hours posted on office doors on the first floor of the Arts and Sciences building. [She reads from a piece of paper.] They average less than an hour a week, most of them in the late afternoon when a lot of us work. I have the numbers right here.
Ann:	Can I see?
Sue:	Sure. [She hands the paper over.]
Ann:	[reading] Well, you're right about that one floor in that one building. What do you think a bigger sample would show?
Sue:	I don't know.
Raj:	I agree about office hours. We have the same problem at my college. But I want to go back to something you said before. I don't see how paying tuition makes us customers. What's the connection?
Sue:	Well, when you pay for a service, you buy it, right? And when you buy something you're a customer. We pay tuition for our education, so that means we're customers and should be treated like one.
Ann:	But an education isn't a service. At least it's not like hiring a plumber. Doctors get paid for services, but patients aren't customers.
Raj:	Does your idea mean that we just buy a degree? And what about the saying, *The customer is always right?* My test answers aren't always right.
Sue:	I'm not saying that we're exactly like customers in all respects. We just want to be treated reasonably, like better bus service from off-campus dorms and the library to be open if we need to study late. And most of all, we want teachers to be more available. A lot of us work when we're not in class. Why should we have to take off work to see them?
Raj:	You're right about teachers. I've had trouble seeing my psych prof.
Ann:	How about students as clients? When you go to a lawyer, he doesn't tell you what makes you happy just because you pay him. And good lawyers worry how you feel, so maybe it should be the same with a college. Maybe it should treat students like clients.
Sue:	"Students as clients." Doesn't sound as catchy as students as customers, but it's worth talking about. Thanks for the idea. I'll bring it up.

Sue, Ann, and Raj didn't settle any of their questions once and for all; no one's mind was completely changed. But they now understand one another's views better and can think about those issues more clearly. Sue offered a claim about students as customers that Raj and Ann helped her test and develop by asking her just five kinds of questions. Let's look at that conversation from that point of view, as an exercise in critical thinking and developing an argument.

The Core of Sue's Argument

A Question About What Sue Thinks

When Ann asks Sue about what's new at her school, Sue raises the problem that motivates the rest of the discussion:

Ann:	So what's new at your school?
Sue:	I've been tied up with a student government committee working on something we're calling a "Student Bill of Rights."
Ann:	What's that?
Sue:	Well, it's a plan to improve life on campus and in class.
Ann:	What's the problem?
Sue:	We think our school is taking us for granted, not giving us the services we need to get a good education.

Raj then asks a question that elicits the gist of Sue's claim.

•Question 1: *What are you claiming?*

Raj:	What's your solution?
Sue:	We think the university should stop treating us only as students and start treating us like customers. _{claim}

Two Questions About Why Sue Thinks She's Right

Most of us welcome the first question, because it invites us to share what we think. Ann then asks another welcome question that invites Sue to expand on what she thinks by explaining why she thinks it.

•Question 2: *What are your reasons?*

Ann:	Why customers? What's behind that?
Sue:	Well, we pay a lot of money for our education, but we don't get near the attention customers do. _{reason}

If at this point, Ann and Raj agreed with Sue, they could move to another topic. Or if Ann felt defensive about criticism of other teachers, she could counterattack: *That's silly!* But that would be neither friendly nor thoughtful. Ann accepts that Sue may have a problem worth understanding, but she isn't ready to accept Sue's claim and reason, so she asks for facts. This question sounds more challenging, but Ann asks it not to prove Sue wrong, but to understand why Sue thinks she's right and to decide for herself whether she should think so too.

•**Question 3: *What evidence supports that reason?***

Sue: Well, we pay a lot of money for our education, but we don't get near the attention customers do. _{reason}

Ann: How's that? *[What facts show that you don't get enough attention?]*

Sue: For one thing, we can hardly see teachers outside of class. Last week I counted office hours posted on office doors on the first floor of the Arts and Sciences building. [She reads from a piece of paper.] They average less than an hour a week, most of them in the late afternoon when a lot of us work. I have the numbers right here. _{report of evidence}

Although Ann doesn't dispute Sue's summary report of her evidence, she wants something more reliable, something closer to the actual evidence. So she asks another challenging question about Ann's record of the numbers:

Ann: Can I see? *[Can you show me something closer to the hard evidence?]*

By asking to see the numbers, Ann verges on challenging Sue's reliability. But she's not *disagreeing* with Sue's evidence, only assuring that Sue has a good basis for it. When Sue hands over the paper with her data, she brings Ann as close as she can to seeing the evidence for herself. Unless Ann wants to check the office hours personally, she has to settle for Sue's report of them.

In their questions, Ann and Raj helped Sue complete the first stage of critical thinking: they did not just accept her idea because it sounded good or because they wanted to support their friend or because they wanted to be agreeable. Instead, they paused to reflect on her idea, asking questions until Sue gave them not only a good reason to accept it but also reliable facts to support it.

In her answers to her friends' questions, Sue now has all three elements in the core of an argument: a claim based on a good reason based on reliable evidence. We can picture the core as a pyramid, with a claim resting on a base of reasons, resting on a wider base of evidence:

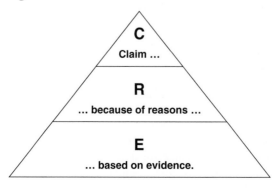

Although Ann and Raj may have put Sue on the spot with their critical questions, they were not attacking her or even disagreeing with her claim; they just wanted to understand it better—and in doing so helped Sue think better about it. In fact, without Ann and Raj to help with their questions, Sue would have had to imagine those questions on her own.

The Explicitly Dialogic Part of Sue's Argument

Challenging Questions About What Sue Hasn't Thought About

The answers to the first three questions helped Sue develop the core of her argument: a claim supported by a reason based on evidence. But that's not enough for Ann and Raj, because those questions have explored only what Sue thinks. Ann and Raj have ideas of their own, and until Sue can address them as well, her argument will be neither complete nor convincing. So Ann and Raj ask another kind of question:

> •**Question 4:** *What do you say about this evidence / complication / principle / perspective / etc.?*

Because they have many ideas, Ann and Raj have many questions about matters that seem to them relevant to the issue but that Sue has not yet considered, not all of which Sue answered. Here are some of those questions.

- • Ann questioned the quality of Sue's evidence about office hours:

  Well, you're right about that one floor in that one building. What do you think a bigger sample would show?

- • Raj points out a cost of accepting Sue's claim, one perhaps greater than the cost of the existing problem:

  Does your idea mean that we just buy a degree? And what about the saying, *The customer is always right?* My test answers aren't always right.

- • Ann offers an alternative solution and a bit of an argument of her own:

  How about students as clients? When you go to a lawyer, he doesn't tell you what makes you happy just because you pay him.

Raj and Ann could have asked Sue more questions:

> What do you mean by "enough" office hours?
>
> Do you have other reasons to think you aren't being treated well?
>
> What do you think teachers would say about that? Or parents? Or state legislators?
>
> Do you think you could actually get the school to adopt that policy?

But each of those questions is just a variation on one of the other four: *What do you mean by. . . ?* asks Sue to state her claim, reason, or evidence more clearly; *Do you have any other reasons/evidence. . . ?* asks for more support; *What do you think teachers would say. . . ?* raises another objection.

With these questions, Ann and Raj shift the ground of Sue's argument from exploring what Sue thinks to exploring how Sue's ideas interact with their own.

From the answers to these questions about *other* ways of thinking, Sue can create the second, **dialogic** part of her argument, where she gives readers their say.

This part of argument is easier to create if you have good friends like Ann and Raj to ask the questions and raise the alternatives you must acknowledge and respond to. Otherwise, you must *imagine* readers who will raise questions, objections, and alternative views. You must create a voice in the back of your mind, insistently asking, *But what about. . . ? But what would you say to someone who argued. . . ?* If you can't imagine questions to respond to, you will seem unwilling or unable to examine your own ideas critically, and readers will judge the quality of your mind accordingly. It may seem paradoxical, but readers will trust your argument more when you acknowledge their objections to it.

Moreover, when you fail to acknowledge the ideas of others you don't weaken just your ethos: you also weaken your argument itself. When you address a serious problem, it's in your best interest to find its best solution, regardless of the solution you prefer. And you are not likely to find the best solution if you consider only your own ideas. So by acknowledging views that might seem to contradict the core of your argument (claim, reasons, evidence), you in fact improve and protect it. That's why this part of argument reflects perhaps the most important stage of critical thinking: evaluating each claim and its support in light of all the alternative and contradictory information you can find.

The Explicitly Logical Part of Sue's Argument

A Most Challenging Question About Sue's Reasoning

Every argument must be anchored in evidence that readers accept as fact. But it needs a second anchor in logic. Each step in an argument must be logical, but writers almost never lay out that logic explicitly because they assume that readers will follow the connections among their claims, reasons, and evidence. And usually, they are right: They rarely have to spell out their logic. But they do when they think readers might question those connections.

> •**Question 5: *What principle connects that reason to that claim [or that evidence to that reason]?***

Raj: I agree about office hours. We have the same problem at my college. But I want to go back to something you said before. I don't see how paying tuition makes us customers. What's the connection between paying tuition and making someone a customer? I don't see it.

Sue may be correct about her facts: Students do pay good money for their education, but Raj doesn't see how that fact is *relevant* to her claim that they are *therefore* customers. He doesn't see the *logic* of the connection.

When Raj asks *how* Sue's reason supports her claim, he seems to challenge her even more sharply than when Ann questioned her evidence, because he now asks about something more fundamental and more difficult to explain: the logic *behind* her reasoning. To answer, Sue has to analyze her own thinking; she must find a general principle that explains why she thinks her reason is relevant to her claim. Sue rises to the challenge, answering,

> Sue: Well, when you pay for a service, you buy it, right? And when you buy something you're a customer. general principle We pay tuition for our education, reason so that means we're customers and should be treated like one. claim

There are different technical terms for the principle that connects a reason to a claim. Logicians sometimes call it a *premise,* others an *assumption.* When that premise is explicitly stated in a written argument, we call it a *warrant.* Like all warrants, Sue's has two parts:

1. a general circumstance, which lets us draw
2. a general conclusion

Graphically, a warrant looks like this:

(1) General Circumstance   — lets us draw→   (2) General Conclusion

The two parts of the warrant correspond to claim and reason:

(1) Specific Circumstance_reason —lets us draw→ (2) Specific Conclusion claim

Sue offers this general warrant:

(1) When a person pays for a service reason   (2) that person is a customer. claim

If Raj and Ann believe Sue's warrant, Sue can apply it to her specific circumstance and draw her specific claim:

Circumstance	Conclusion
When a person pays for a service,	that person is a customer. warrant
Because we pay for our education, reason	we are customers. claim

Warrants connect a reason to a claim. They explain logical connections not by laying out every step of your reasoning but by telling readers what general principles should guide their reasoning.

We should alert you that almost everyone finds warrants hard to understand, including the two of us. That's why this part of an argument represents the third and most difficult stage of critical thinking. It is one thing to have to consider evidence you didn't know about or perspectives you don't share. But nothing is more challenging—or more valuable—to developing your powers of critical thinking than to identify and explain those places where someone might doubt your principles of reasoning. We will return to warrants to explain them in more detail.

Review: Modeling an Argument

You might better grasp how those five questions work if you see how their answers combine into the structure of a complete argument, the way atoms combine into molecules. Since some of us understand a structure better when we can picture it, we'll include diagrams showing how the elements of argument work together.

The Core of an Argument: Claim + Reasons + Evidence

In its simplest form, an argument is just a claim and its support:

> Because major college sports have degenerated into a money-making sideshow that erodes the real mission of higher education, _{reason} they must be reformed. _{claim}

We can represent the relationship between a claim and its support like this:

> **Support ... therefore ... Claim**

That diagram does not represent the only order of those elements. We could reverse them:

> **Claim ... because of ... Support**

> Major college sports must be reformed, _{claim} because they have degenerated into a money-making sideshow that erodes the real mission of higher education. _{reason}

To keep things simple, we'll regularly put the claim on the left and its supporting reason on the right. In real arguments, they can occur in either order.

Distinguishing Claims and Reasons

Some students puzzle over the difference between claims and reasons, pointing out that reasons also make claims. They're right; those terms can be confusing. In fact, every sentence we write makes a claim in some sense of the word. But in order to keep the parts of argument distinct, we'll use *claim* and *reason* not in their loose, ordinary sense but as technical terms:

- We'll use *main claim* to refer to the one claim that states the point of the *whole* argument. It's the statement the rest of the argument supports (some call it a *thesis*).

- We'll use the term *reason* to refer to a statement that supports a main claim.

But here's where the complications arise. A reason that supports a main claim is itself a subordinate claim, since it states a judgment that is more than just plain fact.

- We'll use the term *reason* also to refer to a statement that supports a reason, a subordinate claim that supports a larger claim.

All that means is that before you can decide whether to call a particular statement a claim or a reason, you have to know how it's used, where it fits into the core of an argument. Here is a sentence used as a claim:

Children who watch violent entertainment tend to become violent adults, claim because they lose their ability to distinguish between reality and fiction. reason

And here is that same sentence used as a reason:

Violence on television and in video games should be moderated claim because **children who watch violent entertainment tend to become violent adults.** reason

There is another complication: A statement can be used as both a reason and a claim *at the same time* if it supports some larger claim but is also supported by its own reason. Here is that sentence used as both at the same time:

Violence on television and in video games should be reduced claim 1 because **children who watch lots of violent entertainment tend to become violent adults.** reason 1 supporting claim 1 / claim 2 supported by reason 2 They become so used to constant images of casual violence that they assume it's just part of daily life

reason 2 supporting reason 1

This can get confusing when you try to analyze a complex argument down to its smallest parts. But when you're dealing with your own arguments, you have to remember only that reasons support claims and claims are supported by reasons.

Anchoring Reasons in Evidence

In casual conversation, we might support a claim with just a reason:

Larry: We'd better stop for gas here. claim

Curly: What reason do you have for saying that?

Moe: Because we're almost empty. reason

This is so trivial a matter that Curly is unlikely to respond, *How do you know we're almost empty? What evidence do you base that reason on?* But when an issue is important or a reason is not obvious, readers want to know why you think that your reason is *true*. Not only will they ask a question about your claim, they'll ask a question about your reason as well. The answer to that question is your *evidence*, facts that support that reason and claim:

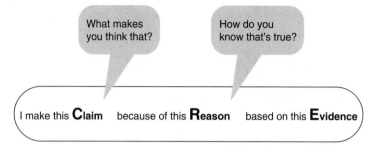

In the following argument, the issue is important and the reason is not obvious, so readers expect to see evidence supporting the claim:

> We have tried to make our undergraduate education second to none _{claim} by asking our best researchers to teach first-year students. _{reason} **For example, Professor Kinahan, a recent Nobel Prize winner in physics, has taught physics 101 for more than fifteen years.** _{evidence}

To emphasize the difference between reasons and evidence, we distinguish them in diagramming the core of an argument. When you think of the *order* of elements in an argument, picture them like this:

But if you want to emphasize their logical relationships, picture them like this:

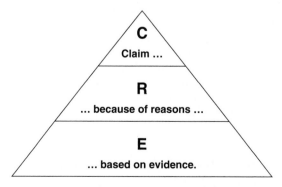

Think of evidence as anchoring your argument in facts.

At times, reasons and evidence might seem to be just different words for the same thing, but they are not:

- We think up reasons.
- We don't "think up" evidence; it must seem to come from "out there" in the world, something we can point out to our readers.

For example, we couldn't point to athletics degenerating into a sideshow, but we could point to someone handing athletes money or exempting them from academic requirements. (We discuss the difference between reasons and evidence in more detail in Chapters 5 and 6.)

Origins of the Words *Reason* and *Evidence*

The original meanings of *reason* and *evidence* illuminate their different meanings:

- *Reason* is related to *rational*. It comes from the Latin *ratio*, "to calculate or think." We seem to construct reasons in our minds.

- Evidence is related to *vision* and *evident*, as in *self-evident*. It comes from *e-videre*, "to see." We seem to see evidence out there in the world.

IN THE READINGS . . .

Reasons and Evidence

In "Lies, Damn Lies, and Statistics," Jonathan Rauch defines the "strange but common animal, the policy lie" with a story of how President Clinton's drug czar, Barry McCaffrey used evidence (pp. 476–78). When the Dutch challenged McCaffrey's claim that their liberal drug policy was an "unmitigated disaster," he offered as a reason that the Dutch murder rate was double that of the U.S. When challenged again, he reported as evidence Interpol statistics that he acknowledged might not be accurate: "We have said if we are wrong, speak to Interpol—it's not our statistics, it's (their) reporting." (If this seems to make no sense, remember that he is a politician.) In exposing McCaffrey's "policy lie," Rauch reports several kinds of evidence to show that the Netherlands is in fact safer than the United States. Read the passage, picking out those places where Rauch reports evidence. How does he make his evidence seem more credible than McCaffrey's? Does he persuade you that it's better?

Dialogue with Readers: Acknowledgment + Response

Readers learn your solution to your (and you hope their) problem in the core of your argument. But thoughtful readers are likely to have alternative views that they expect you to address. So to the largely one-sided dialogue in the core of your argument you have to add another dialogue that includes those other views. Imagine your reader asking questions, not about what you think but about what others might think:

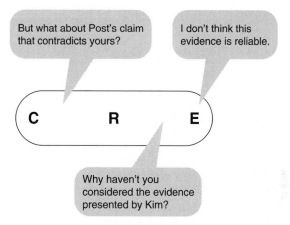

Once you imagine these questions, you have to acknowledge and respond to them in your text.

For example, someone familiar with college teaching might argue that famous researchers don't always make good teachers, a view that a skilled writer ought to anticipate:

> We have tried to make our undergraduate education second to none _{claim} by asking our best researchers to teach first-year students. _{reason} For example, Professor Kinahan, a recent Nobel Prize winner in physics, is now teaching physics 101. _{evidence} **To be sure, not every researcher teaches well,** _{acknowledgment} **but recent teaching evaluations show that teachers such as Kinahan are highly respected by our students.** _{response} **Of the last twenty recipients of the college teaching award, sixteen have been full professors with distinguished records of research.** _{further evidence}

You can't imagine a question for every aspect of your argument. You add them only in those places where you think readers might raise a question serious enough to acknowledge and respond to:

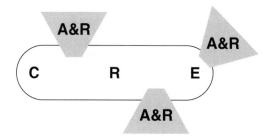

When you picture the role of acknowledgment and response in an argument, think of it as an additional dialogue that brings readers into your argument, surrounding the core with their questions:

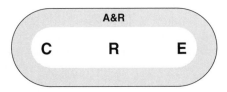

Explaining Logic: Warrants

Readers may agree that you based a reason on good evidence and adequately addressed their views but *still* think that you have not supported your claim *logically*. Even if readers accept that your reason is *true*, they may not accept that it is *relevant* to its claim. If so, your reason doesn't "count" as a reason: *I accept that some of the best researchers are successful teachers, but I don't see why that means the college puts its educational mission first. Why does that claim follow from that reason?*

If you think readers might ask that question, you have to state the principle of reasoning that connects that reason to that claim, what we've called a *warrant*. For example, the first sentence in this next little argument lays out a warrant, a general principle of reasoning that the writer will use to connect her reason to her claim.

> **When an institution has its most eminent faculty teach undergraduate classes, it can justly claim that it puts its educational mission first.** _{warrant} We have tried to make our undergraduate education second to none _{claim} by asking our best researchers to teach first-year students. _{reason} For example, Professor Kinahan, a recent Nobel Prize winner in physics, is now teaching physics 101. _{evidence} To be sure, not every researcher teaches well, _{acknowledgment} but recent teaching evaluations show that teachers such as Kinahan are highly respected by our students. _{response} Of the last twenty recipients of the college teaching award, sixteen have been full professors with distinguished records of research. _{further evidence}

Here is a formal way to check whether a warrant does connect a claim to its reason. State the warrant in two parts, the first stating the general circumstance beginning with *whenever* and the second stating the general inference beginning with *then we can claim*. Next list the reason and the claim underneath in a "warrant matrix." If the reason is a good instance of the *whenever* half of the warrant and the claim is a good instance of the *then we can claim* half of the warrant, the warrant justifies the logical connection between the reason and claim:

WARRANT MATRIX	
Whenever an institution has its most eminent faculty teach undergraduate courses,	then we can claim that it puts its educational mission first. _{warrant}
Because we ask our best researchers to teach undergraduates, _{reason}	we have tried to make our under graduate education second to none. _{Claim}

If your evidence anchors a reason in the reality of facts, then your warrant anchors it in the soundness of your logic.

Like acknowledgment and response, warrants show readers how your argument is based in part on their ideas. They explain how your logic rests not on what you alone believe but on *general* principles that a community of thinkers accepts as true. Since they too connect the core of your argument to others' ideas, we include them as the outer layer in the diagram:

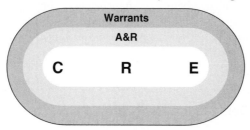

Crafting Written Arguments

In casual conversation, we can't organize our answers to the five questions of argument, because we and our partners just go where the conversation takes us, rarely in a straight line to a conclusion. We manage well enough, though, because the back-and-forth helps us clarify points, elaborate on difficult concepts, even figure out what claim we can plausibly support. But when we write, we have to decide on our own what to say and in what order, with no second chances.

Although you can vary the order of elements in a written argument, you can also rely on some standard orders: The default order for the three core elements is Claim + Reason + Evidence. Since you will rarely support any serious claim with only one reason, you arrange core elements by simply adding more Reason + Evidence pairs. You sandwich those elements between an introduction that states the problem and its solution (your main claim), and a conclusion that restates that claim:

Default Plan for the Core of An Argument

Introduction
   A: Problem   What problem motivates this argument?
   B: Claim/Solution: What is its solution?
Body
   Reason 1:   What reason do you offer in support?
   Evidence 1:   What evidence do you base that reason on?
   Reason 2:   What reason do you offer in support?
   Evidence 2:   What evidence do you base that reason on?
   [Additional Reason + Evidence pairs]
Conclusion
   Restatement: What are your problem and solution again?

We can't tell you exactly where to put acknowledgments and responses or warrants, except to put them where readers are likely to ask the questions they answer.

- Locate acknowledgments and responses where you suspect readers will think of objections and questions. Alternatively, put them all after the core of your argument.

- Locate warrants just before or after the claim they apply to, so that readers understand how your reason connects to your claim. (We know warrants are still murky; we promise they will become clearer.)

Here we add the two surrounding elements to the default plan:

Default Plan for a Complete Argument

Introduction

A: Problem	What problem motivates this argument?
B: Claim/Solution:	What is its solution?

Body

Warrant 1	What principle justifies the logical connection of your reason to your claim?
Reason 1:	What reason do you offer in support?
Evidence 1:	What evidence do you base that reason on?
[Additional Reason + Evidence pairs]	
Reason X:	What reason do you offer in support?
Evidence X:	What evidence do you base that reason on?
A & R X:	But what about this way of interpreting that evidence?
General A & R:	But what about this additional evidence?

Conclusion

Restatement:	What are your problem and solution again?

Sue could organize a written argument following that plan. In a one-paragraph introduction, she states her problem and solution:

> Recently, student government has been studying complaints about life at Midwest U. Some are minor, such as the bursar's office closing at 2 P.M. But others are major, such as teachers not keeping enough office hours. These problems suggests that the university cares little about our needs, apparently thinking of us only as transients, paying to be here but deserving little consideration. If the administration ignores this issue, we risk gaining the reputation of a "student unfriendly" place that will gradually erode our reputation and ultimately threaten the quality of our education. problem We believe the university should think of us not just as students, but also as customers vital to its success. solution / claim

Then she lays out the body of her argument, starting with a warrant:

When someone pays for a service, she deserves to be treated as a business treats its customers. _{warrant} Students pay for the services of teachers. _{reason 1} According to the Academic Senate, student tuition represents more than 60% of the funds used for faculty salaries. _{report of evidence} But we don't get the consideration that customers do. _{reason 2} For one thing, many faculty don't keep enough office hours. _{reason 2.1 supporting reason 2} In a survey of the first floor of Arts Sciences Hall, office hours averaged less than an hour a week. _{report of evidence} No business would survive if it treated customers like that. _{reason 3, not supported by evidence} Of course, this is only a small sample of many university services, _{acknowledgment of anticipated objection} but it indicates the wider problem. _{response}

Admittedly, we can't push the analogy too far—the university can't educate us if it treats us like customers in all respects, especially in class. _{acknowledgment of alternative} Still, if thinking of us as customers leads the university to make our experience more productive, then we think the principle of "student as customer" is worth considering. _{response / restatement of claim}

In that example, Sue made every sentence mechanically answer one of the five questions, but you probably won't match every sentence in your arguments to one of the questions. In an argument about a complex issue, you usually have to explain some matters beyond the five questions. For example, if you argue that gasoline additives cost more than their environmental benefits, you might have to explain the chemistry of carbon-based combustion. If you do explain background concepts, wait until you need them in your argument. Some writers explain everything first in a background section, but that's risky. Readers don't remember background information when they don't yet know why it's relevant, and they may get impatient for the meat of your argument.

Thickening Your Argument

If you support your claim with as little as Sue does, you're unlikely to earn assent to the solution of a problem as complex as whether a college takes its students seriously. Experienced writers know that readers reject arguments that seem "thin," "undeveloped," or worst of all, "simplistic." When they find those faults, they implicitly think something like this:

- *You offer only one reason for treating you like a customer. I need more than that.*

- *You offer some evidence, but I need more as well as assurance that it's sound. You say teachers keep too few office hours, but you surveyed only one floor in one building.*

- *You offer a warrant but not an argument that it's true. Why do you think that just because someone pays for something, that person is a customer? I can't agree.*

- *You acknowledge that you have little evidence about office hours, but you claim that it still shows there's a problem. I need an argument before I accept that.*

You build a nuclear argument out of the answers to the five questions, but you typically have to treat each statement of a reason, warrant, and response *as a subclaim in its own argument* with its *own* reasons, evidence, warrants, and responses. In so doing, you "thicken," "broaden," and "deepen" your main argument. Readers judge an argument to be more complete—and the mind of its maker to be thoughtful and thorough—when they see simple nuclear arguments assembled into complex ones.

In Chapters 4 through 8, we look in detail at each of those elements.

WRITING PROCESS

Argument as Civil Conversation

THINKING AND TALKING

Using the Questions of Argument for Critical Thinking

You can get your mind working on your argument long before you start to write, maybe even before you start to plan. Unless your question requires research on an issue new to you, you'll have plenty of ideas relevant to your argument. And as you think about them, you'll notice many more relevant ideas of others, in what you read, hear, and remember. But many of those ideas will not be as precise and specific as you'll need them to be. So before you decide to use them, put them to the test of your critical thinking. The easiest way is to test those ideas (or of those who propose them) using the five questions of argument.

1. What does this idea *claim*?

   What specifically does it require me to think or do? What are the consequences if I think or do it? What other ideas or plans does it imply?

2. What *reason* do I have for accepting this claim?

   Do I know at least one but preferably more lesser claims that I believe are true and that lead me to this claim?

3. What *evidence* do I have for thinking those reasons are true?

   Do I know or can I find reliable facts support those reasons? Do I know or can I find facts that contradict or qualify them?

4. What *alternatives* and *objections* can I think of?

   Can I think of a different perspective on this issue? A different interpretation of the facts? Can I think of someone who might draw a different conclusion?

5. What general principle of reasoning do I have to believe before I can accept that this evidence and reason lead to this claim?

   What general principles does this argument assume? Can I restate the reason and claim more generally in a sentence of the form, "Whenever . . . then we can conclude . . ."? If so, do I believe that the more general sentence is true? Always and everywhere?

If you have an idea or hear one that cannot pass the test of your own questions, it is not likely to pass the test of your best, most critical readers. Before you use the idea, invest the time to create a mini-argument to support it. If you can't, look elsewhere for ideas you *can* stand behind.

PREPARING AND PLANNING

Three Strategies for Designing an Argument

There are three strategies for planning your argument:

1. Let the argument fall out of your head onto the page as it will. Some writers do that successfully; most can't.

2. Follow a stock plan you get from teachers or textbook writers like us. The problem is that while some stock plans are reliable, many are not—and you have to know which one is right for your situation.

3. Create a new plan for every argument. This strategy has two problems: first, to do this well, you have to know a lot about your particular readers; second, you never gain the benefit of experience.

We suggest combining the second and third strategies. The set of common plans is a fairly small one that experienced writers improvise on, the way a pianist vamps on a tune or a basketball player varies the moves of a set play. Start with one of our stock plans, but don't let it tyrannize your thinking. Treat it as scaffolding that supports your argument as you construct it, but that lets you improvise the details to suit your readers.

Stock Plans to Avoid

Before we offer some reliable plans, we should mention four stock plans that you should avoid:

• The five-paragraph essay: These essays follow an all-too-predictable form:

¶1. *Introduction:* There are three reasons why you should floss your teeth.

  ¶2. The first reason is . . .

  ¶3. The second reason is . . .

  ¶4. The third reason is . . .

¶5. *Conclusion:* So we see there are three reasons to floss.

That may have worked in high school, but it reminds college teachers of high school thinking.

• A narrative of your thinking: A blow-by-blow account of how you thought your way from a problem to its solution will engage those interested in the workings of your mind, but most readers care more about its product. A single unrevised draft usually records only the history of your struggle to write it.

- A summary of your sources: When you make an argument based on what you read, avoid a summary that tracks the order of its ideas. You will seem only to rehash them, with nothing new from you.

- Thing one and thing two: If you write about two (or more) objects, such as people, books, or places, avoid dividing your argument into two parts, the first based on Thing One, the second on Thing Two. In comparing *Romeo and Juliet* to *West Side Story,* for example, don't devote part one to *Romeo and Juliet* and part two to *West Side Story.* Instead, organize your argument around aspects of the two works, such as their themes, actions, emotional impact, and so on. If you can't avoid the obvious two-part organization, at least use phrases in the second part that recall and connect it to the first: *In comparison to Romeo and Juliet. . . , In contrast to Romeo and Juliet. . . , West Side Story shares with Romeo and Juliet. . . .* Otherwise, your argument will read like two unconnected summaries.

Sketching a Plan for Your Argument

Before you draft, make an outline, no matter how sketchy. As you gain experience, you may get by with just a scratch outline—even one you don't have to write down. But in your early papers, you're likely to need all the help you can get. We recommend that you create a storyboard: it's a low-cost way not only to plan a paper but to manage the process of writing it.

Stage 1: Prepare Your Materials

1. **On one page, sketch the problem or question you're addressing and a plausible solution or answer.**

   Don't wait to plan your paper until you are sure about your main claim. As soon as you know what problem you hope to address, make your best guess about its solution even if it only suggests a general direction for further thought (see Chapter 4).

   Binge drinking is out of control. ₚₚₒblem

   Don't punish all students just because some drink too much. ₛₒₗᵤₜᵢₒₙ

As you develop your argument, return to this page to revise your solution in light of what you have learned.

   Binge drinking is out of control. ₚₚₒblem

   Rather than ban drinking, we have to do a better job of identifying students likely to binge dangerously so that they can be counseled. ₛₒₗᵤₜᵢₒₙ

2. **At the top of *separate* pages, write the main reasons that would encourage readers to agree.**

   Assume that you need more than one reason. If you think of more than five, pick only the most persuasive ones.

R1:   Only a few students are the real problem drinkers.

R2:   When rules can be ignored without penalty, all students disrespect the administration.

R3:   Blanket prohibition deprives responsible students of a right.

R4:   Regardless of prohibitions, students will drink.

R5:   When the reckless drinkers are identified, they can be counseled.

3. **Under each reason, list the evidence (data, facts) or the additional reasons that support that main reason.**

This is hard. You can think up reasons, but you have to hunt down evidence.

R: Only a few students are the real problem drinkers.

E1:   A study in the *Journal of the American Medical Association* says that fewer than one in five student drinkers cause most of the problems.

E2:   The Dean of Student reports that of the students cited by university police for excessive drinking three in four are repeat offenders.

If you can't think of any evidence, list the kind of evidence you hope you might find so that you at least know what to look for.

R: Only a few students are the real problem drinkers.

E1:   Look up statistics about student drinking.

4. **At the bottom third of each page, list objections and alternatives that your readers might raise; then sketch responses to them.**

A1:   It has been claimed that bingers can't be controlled through education.

R1:   Researchers at the University of Washington have found otherwise. In their study, . . .

A1:   It's true the administration has a legal responsibility to set rules to protect students.

R1:   A rule that can't be enforced protects no one. We have seen this happen before in the case of. . . .

5. **On another page, sketch a conclusion.**

Don't just repeat the main claim from your introduction. You can restate it in more detail, but also add something to indicate the value of your solution.

Banning drinking will only encourage contempt for rules. It did not work during Prohibition, and it won't work now. Instead we have to help students make better decisions for themselves. If we can identify students most at risk for bingeing dangerously, the university can counsel them before they develop a pattern of bingeing. In that way, the university can do what it does best, educate, and avoid the kind of intrusion into students' lives that poisons students' attitudes and doesn't work anyway.

Stage 2: Organize and Arrange Your Materials
  1. **Decide where to locate your main claim (the solution to your problem).**

If you follow the steps above, you will write your main claim on your storyboard twice, once on your introduction page and again on the conclusion page. But for your paper you actually have two choices that imply different "social contracts" with your reader.

  • State your main claim twice, once at the end of the introduction and again in the conclusion.

When you do that, you in effect say to readers at the end of your introduction, *You know my problem and its solution, so you're in control of your reading. You know the most important things I have to say, so you can stop, read on, skim, or skip around.*

  • Save your main claim for the conclusion.

When you make readers wait until your conclusion to read your main claim, you in effect say to them, *I am in control, so follow me as I reveal my reasoning, and in the end I will reveal the solution you've waited for.*

Readers occasionally agree to that second contract with pleasurable anticipation, but only if they enjoy following the twists and turns of an intellectual journey. Some teachers, especially in the humanities, prefer an argument that unfolds like a mystery story. Most readers, though, want to control their own time. So they prefer to learn your main claim early, at the end of your introduction. That sounds cut-and-dried, but few readers have the leisure to see how a mystery argument turns out.

Some students hold back their main claim, fearing that if they "give it away" too soon, readers will lose interest and stop reading. That's a mistake. If you pose a problem important to readers, they will read on, even if they see its solution in the introduction. Conversely, no one is motivated to read about a trivial question just because you make them play hide-and-seek with its answer.

Other students think that if a reader might resist their main claim, they should sneak up on it. Only a skilled writer can lure readers toward an unwelcome conclusion that they don't see coming a long way off. And even if you do pull it off, readers may feel you've tricked them. Your best chance to win over hostile readers is not by manipulating them but by acknowledging differences from the start. If they are so set against your claim that they refuse even to consider your argument, you won't persuade them in any event. But if you approach them as readers who give a fair hearing even to positions they don't like, they may not accept your claim, but they will at least grant that you have good reason for believing it, which is not a small success.

Neither social contract, point-first or point-last, is intrinsically better. They're just different, each implying a different relationship among the writer, reader, text, and circumstances. Most of us, though, most of the time prefer to see a point early because that puts us in control of our own reading.

If you do hold off your main claim until the conclusion, you should give readers some guidance about what to expect: End your introduction with a sentence that anticipates your main claim by introducing the key concepts that you will use to develop it in the body of your argument. For now, add a sentence like that at the bottom of the first page of your storyboard, below your problem and proposed solution. If you can, make that sentence more rather than less complex by adding all of the most important ideas in your reasons. Compare the following two ways of setting up an argument about binge drinking:

> **Times** have **changed**, and universities have to **understand** how they have if they are to address **drinking** effectively.

> The **traditional role** of a university, **in loco parentis**, is more **complex** now than a generation ago, because it involves issues of **civil rights**, **privacy**, and **student autonomy**. Not until it **understands** where it **stands**, **legally, pragmatically**, and **morally**, can this university formulate workable **policies** to address the problem of **binge drinking**.

The boldfaced words in the second state more key themes that you can use to develop your argument. Make these sentence as full as you can, even if it seems overly complex: You can always pare it down once you begin to revise.

2. Decide where to put the reason and evidence in each section.

Just as you have to decide where to state the main claim of your whole argument, early or late, so you have to decide where to put each reason in its own section. Since each reason is the point of its section, you can put it at the end of the introduction to that section or in its conclusion. Here too, the default choice is to state the reason early, at the end of the introduction to that section. If you decide to save a reason for the end of its section, add to your storyboard a set-up sentence that announces the key concepts of that section.

If you put the reason in the introduction of its section, the evidence must follow. If you decide to save the reason for the end, then you must start with evidence. Readers can easily manage short sequences of EVIDENCE + REASON, but if a section opens with lots of evidence, readers may struggle because they can't tell what that evidence supports. So if you save the reason for the end of a section and present its evidence first, introduce the section with a sentence or two suggesting what the evidence relates to. That sentence should also introduce the key concepts you will develop in the section. For example, the following sentence might set up the evidence supporting a reason claiming that a blanket prohibition unfairly deprives responsible students of their rights.

Some colleges have instituted **blanket prohibitions** against all drinking on campus without any regard for how such an **indiscriminate** policy affects the **rights** of **responsible** students or for the **invasions of privacy** required to **enforce** such policies.

Add a set-up sentence to the top of each reasons page in your storyboard.

3. Decide how to order the sections.

The challenge now is to shuffle the separate reason pages into a sequence that will make sense to readers. First, group reasons on the same topic. For example, how would you group the five reasons to counsel students rather than ban drinking?

R1:   Only a few students are the real problem drinkers.

R2:   When rules can be ignored without penalty, all students disrespect the administration.

R3:   Blanket prohibition deprives responsible students of a right.

R4:   Regardless of prohibitions, students will drink.

R5:   When the reckless drinkers are identified, they can be counseled.

You might group those reasons into those involving all students and those involving just irresponsible ones:

R1.1:   Blanket prohibition deprives responsible students of a right.

R1.2:   When rules can be ignored without penalty, all students disrespect the administration.

R1.3:   Regardless of prohibitions, students will drink.

R2.1:   Only a few students are the real problem drinkers.

R2.2:   When the reckless drinkers are identified, they can be counseled.

Next choose a standard order for those grouped reasons: more important to less important (or vice versa), more familiar to less familiar, less complex to more complex. If readers can't see how you've ordered your reasons, they are likely to think your argument incoherent. So state up front the principle you are following, or introduce each section (*not* each sentence) with transitional words such as *More important, therefore,* and *on the other hand.* (To learn more about ordering reasons, see pp. 145–47.)

4. Decide where to put acknowledgments and responses.

Ideally, you should acknowledge and respond to questions or objections the moment readers will think of them. Unfortunately, few of us are smart enough to predict when that will be. But just by acknowledging *some* objections and responding to them *anywhere,* you show readers you're aware of some alternative views, if not theirs in particular.

5. Decide where to put warrants.

This is the hardest choice, because you have to decide whether to state warrants at all. You almost always omit them when your readers share your values, assumptions, definitions, and so on. If they don't, you may have to state them as warrants, typically before the reasons they apply to, and maybe even support them with their own reasons and evidence. For example, after reading the following argument, we could reject the claim at the end by objecting that what children watch is irrelevant to their psychological development:

> Every day, children are bombarded by TV violence. reason The average child sees almost twelve acts of violence a day, most more graphic than necessary, few causing permanent damage, and even fewer condemned or punished (Smith 1992). report of evidence When that kind of violence becomes a pervasive part of their experience, restatement of reason it's likely to damage their psychological development. claim

On the other hand, if the writer can first get us to agree to a general principle about the influence of example on child development, then she is more likely to get agreement later that her reason (violent TV) in fact supports her claim about children being damaged:

> **Most of us believe that when children enjoy stories about admirable actions, they are more likely to become healthy adults.** warrant 1 **Isn't it likely, then, that when they see degrading behavior, they will be hurt by it?** warrant 2 Every day, children are bombarded by TV violence. reason The average child sees . . . evidence · · · [Watching TV violence] is likely to damage their psychological development. claim

The argument now opens with two warrants, followed by a reason, evidence, and claim. We may be more inclined to think that the reason supports the claim if we first accept the general principle (*when children see degrading behavior, they are hurt by it*). Of course, if we rejected those warrants, the writer would have to back them with their own supporting arguments.

If your warrants apply to the argument as a whole, put them on a separate storyboard page, usually right after the introduction. But if they apply to a specific reason or evidence, add them to the corresponding reasons page.

6. Decide what you have to explain.

Are there concepts, definitions, processes, background, history that readers need in order to understand your reasons and evidence? Add them to your storyboard, on a separate page if necessary but preferably on an appropriate reasons page.

This kind of storyboard will follow the stock plan we sketched earlier (imagine explanations being distributed throughout):

INTRODUCTION: Problem + Claim/Solution
BODY
   Warrants for Main Claim
   Reason 1
   Evidence 1

   [Additional Reason + Evidence pairs]

   Reason X
   Evidence X
   A & R X?

  General A & R

  CONCLUSION: Restatement of problem and solution

We know that plans like these seem formulaic, but think of them not as detailed blueprints but as rough sketches that you modify and develop. As you gain experience making arguments, you'll know when to forget these plans and go with your intuition. Even then, it's still a good idea to have *some* plan before you start.

DRAFTING

When to Stop Planning and Start Drafting

It's so much easier to keep reading than to start writing that many of us just go on researching in order to put off the tougher job of drafting. Resist that trap: Set a deadline to start drafting by back-planning from your due date. Decide how much time you need to draft. If you draft quickly, add another 20 percent for drafting and 20 percent more for revision; if you draft slowly and carefully, add even more. Then leave time to proofread.

Drafting a Working Introduction

You may have been told to write introductions last, after you've drafted something to introduce. That's a good idea, but you should also sketch a working introduction to focus your thinking as you draft. Try this plan:

1. **Start with a sentence or two of shared context for your problem.**

   For centuries, drinking has been a part of college life. For some students, it's almost a rite of passage. But it has become deadly.

2. **Add a sentence or two that articulate the problem.**

   To control the risk, the university wants to pass regulations banning alcohol at all student events, even fraternity and sorority parties.

3. **In a sentence or two, state the consequences of the problem, what it does or will cost readers.**

Students ignore these rules, which encourages contempt for university authority. And if the rules are enforced, responsible students will be deprived of a legal right.

4. End your introduction with the gist of your solution to the problem.

Student Government must join the Greek Council in opposing these rules and support instead educational programs.

REVISING

Matching Your Introduction to Your Conclusion

Leave time to revise, but when time runs out, here is a quick fix to ensure that your introduction and conclusion at least don't contradict each other.

1. **Draw a line after the introduction and before the conclusion.** Readers are confused when they can't see those boundaries. If you can't find them easily, your readers may not find them at all. Always start a new paragraph after your introduction and at your conclusion.

2. **Highlight the main claim.**
   - If you stated the main claim at the end of the introduction, highlight it there and again in the conclusion.
   - If you stated the main claim for the first time in the conclusion, highlight it there but also highlight the last sentence or two of the introduction.
   - If you put your main claim anywhere else, revise so that it's either first or last.

3. **Compare the highlighted sentences in your introduction and conclusion.**
   - If they don't agree, revise the one in the introduction to match the one in the conclusion, because what you wrote last probably reflects your best thinking. If you repeat the main claim in both places, don't make them identical, but they should seem closely related.

4. **If you have time, repeat this process for each section longer than a page.**
   - In its introduction and conclusion, highlight the reason/claim that is the point of that section.
   - Put that point at the end of its introduction, or at least in its conclusion.
   - If it's in the introduction, be sure it harmonizes with the conclusion.

INQUIRIES

Remember that these inquiries offer a wide range of questions, puzzles, and other things to do. Most chapters have too many for you to complete, so pick and choose the ones that catch your interest.

REFLECTIONS

1. Some reject rationality as a means to enlightenment: Mystics and spiritualists seek understanding from spheres of experience other than the merely intellectual or physical; subjectivists depend on feeling, impressions, intuition, and so on. How would a mystic or a subjectivist defend, justify, or explain mysticism or subjectivism? Would they be able to think critically about their mysticism or subjectivism? How would a mystic or subjectivist show another mystic or subjectivist that he had reached a mistaken conclusion? Does that question even make sense?

2. Here is an example of the most common way that one partner in a dialogue deliberately derails a conversation. What is it?

   Myles: You've claimed that if you are elected, you will balance the budget by cutting waste. Can you tell us what you will cut?

   Kwan: Unless we resolve to take some tough actions, this state will be bankrupt in five years. We can't just go on spending, spending, spending. We've got to stop it somewhere.

3. Some say that ethos and reputation work best in the dark: They have the most effect on those who know least about the issue being debated. They believe that the more you know about the person (as opposed to just an image) and the more you know about the facts of the case, the less you should be influenced by ethos or reputation. Do you agree that if an argument is strong enough, the character of the person making it should not matter? What if two people make equally strong arguments, but one seems trustworthy and the other doesn't? Why do ethos and reputation matter to you, if they do?

4. When is a written argument more appropriate than a conversation? When is a conversation more appropriate than a written argument?

TASKS

5. The first question asked in the Bible is in Genesis 3.9: "Adam, where are you?" Read the whole passage. Why is the first question in human history (according to the Bible) asked not by Adam or Eve but by God? Why would God ask a question at all? Don't we ask questions to find out something we don't know? Where is the next question in the Bible? What do you make of it? Who asks it? Why?

6. How much are you influenced by reputation? Identify people whose judgment you trust, including public figures and people you know personally. List the features in their *manner* of arguing. Are they passionate or reserved? Do they qualify their statements or speak with unqualified certainty? Do they acknowledge the contributions of others? Do

they use statistics? Anecdotes? What is their tone? Is there a pattern in the attributes of arguers you trust? If so, what does that say about you?

7. Are there questions other than the five listed in this chapter that you *must* imagine yourself answering before your listener or reader would understand your argument? How about these?

How do you feel about that?

How sure are you?

What is the source of your evidence?

Can you define. . . ?

8. The five questions underlying argument can be asked in relatively explicit ways or with just "Umm" or "Oh?" Observe two or three conversations in which people make arguments. Notice how many different ways they ask others to expand and explain their arguments. Are their questions explicit or implicit? How often do people push far enough to get the hard evidence on which someone bases a claim?

9. The next time you disagree with someone, spend a few minutes asking the other person questions to help you understand what that person's argument *is*. Ask about general principles. Offer alternatives in the form of questions: *How would you answer someone who said. . . .* Do some questions elicit more heated responses than others? How do you feel about asking them?

10. If you subscribe to an e-mail discussion list, choose a series of postings that make arguments. How many participants seem to you critical thinkers? What features of their arguments make you say that? How many seem to think more critically about others' ideas than their own?

11. Are arguments at work different from arguments in school? If you have a job, notice how people make arguments with those above them, below them, and on the same level. Do they offer as much evidence as academic writers do? Do they acknowledge alternatives? What would explain the differences?

12. Ask your writing group or roommate to ask you the five questions. Which questions are hardest to answer? When do you find yourself feeling a bit annoyed? When are you *very* annoyed? Can you explain why some questions are more vexing than others?

PROJECTS

13. Many teachers and departments keep model essays of the kind of writing you are expected to do. (Your writing center may also keep models.) Work with classmates to analyze model papers. If you are in a first-year writing class, concentrate on introductory courses in a variety of disciplines. Once

you have some models, group them in terms of how they seem to you now. Then try again after you have studied the parts of an argument.

14. Collect some papers you have written. (Hold on to them because you will be asked to analyze them over the next few chapters.) Select the shortest, least developed one. How would you thicken its argument?

15. Are advertisements arguments? Few say explicitly, *Buy this car!* or *See this movie!*, but they still try to get you to do something specific. Most of them give reasons, and the photograph or drawing of the product seems to count as something like evidence, something you can see with your own eyes. Try analyzing them as arguments. What difference does it make whether we call them arguments or not? Look for advertisements that seek to persuade by means other than reasons and evidence. Can you find an ad that acknowledges another point of view?

 # FOCUS ON WRITING

1

Task. Organize the notes you assembled for the Writing Projects in Chapter 1 under headings that you can turn into a storyboard of an argument addressed to those who asked you to help solve their problem. Then, if your teacher asks you, turn the storyboard into a full written argument. Before you assemble an argument, work your way through the questions listed below for Project 2.

2

Scenario. You have been asked to contribute to a "Forum" on the issue of "Students as Customers," published by the student newspaper in response to a statement approved by [Choose one: Student Government, the Faculty Senate, a dean of your school, the state legislature]. Your argument is one of several, and not the first in the series. Assume that the statement takes a position opposite to yours.

Task. Read the material on "Students as Customers," and decide where you stand: Should students be treated as customers? Outline an argument to support your stand. Before you do, work your way through the questions below.

QUESTIONS

1. What position do you take, exactly?
2. What do you think is at stake here? What difference does it make whether your group's problem is solved, whether we think of advertis-

ing as irrational, or whether the university thinks of you as a customer, student, or client?

3. Why do you take that position? What reasons do you have for wanting others to think or do that?

4. That's too few reasons. Can you think of at least one or two more?

5. What hard evidence do you have to go on? What facts and data can you offer to back up your reasons?

6. If you had to imagine how your readers will state their position, what would they say? What reasons do they have for believing their claims?

7. How do you respond to those reasons? Why do you not accept them?

8. What experiences might they have had that are relevant to their reasons?

9. What objections do you think they will make to your position?

10. What are your basic assumptions? Is your position a specific example of a more general principle?

11. What principles might your readers have that differ from yours?

Context. The issue of lying became a topic of national concern when President Clinton admitted he lied about his private affairs. The responses ranged from, *Oh, everyone lies about sex* to *Any lie is grounds for impeachment!* The issue arose again with the second President Bush, this time concerning his use of flawed evidence to support his arguments for the war in Iraq. In fact, lying has been a matter of moral concern for thousands of years, with philosophers of all schools examining different kinds of lies in different situations. The readings on lying (pp. 463–86) lay out some of the issues.

Scenario 1. You are a candidate for office in student government. At a public meeting, someone asks you about your position:

> We all tell little lies very day. We tell a friend not to fear the worst about a test, when we know he has probably failed it. We know government officials sometimes lie. The Secretary of State says she is on vacation when she is really in secret negotiations. No one expects anyone to be 100 percent truthful 100 percent of the time. But we have a right to expect that as a student government official, you won't lie to us all the time. Can you give us a sense of how you decide when a public figure can legitimately tell a lie? I'd like to hear some specific examples of when you'd lie and when you wouldn't, and the general principles by which you'd decide those cases.

Task 1. Write a two- or three-page answer to that question. To help yourself think through the issues, answer—or better, discuss with someone else—the questions on pages 62–63. Use the answers to build your argument.

Scenario 2.   You are being interviewed for a job with considerable responsibility and the salary to go with it. The interviewer makes this statement:

> Our company has a reputation for integrity, so we try to hire people with high personal standards. Now we know that we all tell each other little white lies. But we can't afford to lose our reputation as people of integrity, because our business depends on trust. I'd like a sense of where you draw the line between white lies and serious lies. For example, suppose you're doing business with one of our best customers who happens to be anti-gay or pro-gay, pro-life or pro-choice, and she asks you where you stand. If you knew your position opposed hers and you suspected she might take her business elsewhere if she knew what you thought, would you lie? I'm interested in how you make decisions in tough cases. Do you have any general principles about when to tell the truth and when not?

Task 2.   Write up two or three pages laying out your position. Write it as if you were proposing a company-wide policy. And don't use that example about the customer. Find new ones. To help yourself think through the issues, answer—or better, discuss with someone else—the questions on pages 62–63. Use the answers to build your argument.

Scenario 3.   Your best friend is in a class whose instructor suspects students have been buying term papers off the Internet. Your friend did not but knows who did, and her teacher asks her for the names. If she doesn't give him the names, he will try to get her disciplined in some way. She asks you whether she should refuse to answer or to lie and say she doesn't know who plagiarized. You tell her she should follow her conscience. She decides to lie and say she doesn't know. But the plagiarists are caught and reveal that in fact, your friend did know. She tells the administration that you told her to follow her conscience. Now you are in trouble, because you knew that someone knew about plagiarism and you did not turn that person in.

Task 3(a).   Write a defense of your own action in a letter to the Disciplinary Committee. To help yourself think through the issues, answer—or better, discuss with someone else—the questions below. Use the answers to build your argument.

Task 3(b).   Write a defense of your friend's action in a letter to the Disciplinary Committee. Even if you don't ultimately approve of her action, make the best case for it that you can. To help yourself think through the issues, answer—or better, discuss with someone else—the questions below. Use the answers to build your argument.

Scenario 4.   Your school is considering an honor code that obligates everyone to turn in not only known cheaters and plagiarists, but anyone who knows about cheaters and plagiarists but does not turn them in.

Task 4.   Write a paper supporting or opposing that proposal. To help yourself think through the issues, answer—or better, discuss with someone else—the questions below. Use the answers to build your argument.

Scenario 5. Your workplace is suffering from internal theft. Your employer proposes that not just the thieves but anyone who knows of theft and does not report it will be fired. You are on a union committee negotiating with the company about that policy.

Task 5. Write a position paper for your committee on that issue. To help yourself think through the issues, answer—or better, discuss with someone else—the questions below. Use the answers to build your argument.

QUESTIONS

1. What is the problem? What is at stake in whether readers agree or not?
2. What position do you take? That is, what are you claiming?
3. What reasons do you have for taking the position you do?
4. What hard evidence do you have to back up your reasons?
5. How will your readers state a position different from yours?
6. What reasons do they have for believing their position?
7. How do you respond to those reasons? Do they have a point? Why do you reject them?
8. Those who disagree may have had experiences relevant to their reasons. Can you imagine what they might be?
9. What objections might they make to your reasons and evidence?
10. Can you say what your basic assumptions are?

$$\boxed{4}$$

Context. The most common objection to all lying is the "slippery slope" argument: If you tell a little lie, you inevitably go on to tell a bigger one, and then a bigger one yet, and pretty soon, you're lying whenever it's convenient.

Scenario. For a workshop on morality in public life, you have been asked to read the materials on lying and respond to the question of whether one lie always leads to ever bigger ones. Take whatever position you want on this issue; the audience consists of people exactly like those in your class.

Task. Write your statement.

SAMPLE ESSAYS

Here are two essays on binge drinking. They respond to a proposal that a university should notify parents when students under twenty-one are caught drinking by university officials, even if no charges are filed. Most students and some faculty oppose it. To help you focus on the substantive elements of these arguments, we have selected essays that won't distract you with complex language or grammatical errors. So don't get caught up in *how* these essays make their points (we'll come back to that later); focus on their substance. Read both, then look at the two tasks that follow.

Student Privacy and Drinking

1   University President, Albert Tanaki, recently proposed that the university should notify parents whenever a student is caught drinking before the age of twenty-one. Tanaki says this will help prevent students from binge drinking. This is wrong because students have rights to privacy and the university should
5   respect them. Tanaki also fails to realize that present-day student life is surrounded by alcohol.

The first aspect in which I feel that Tanaki's proposal is wrong is when he suggests that the university owes it to parents to tell them that their son or daughter is drinking in school. This suggestion clearly violates students' rights to
10   privacy. Young people who do not go to college do not have anyone calling their parents when they get caught drinking before twenty-one. When students are home for the summer, they do not have parents following them around and looking over their shoulder constantly to see whether they are drinking. Parents realize that their children have privacy rights and do not interfere with their social
15   lives. Besides most parents don't care whether their college-age children drink. But even if they don't care themselves about our drinking, parents will get upset with us if they get a notice from the university that we were caught drinking.

Another way in which Tanaki's proposal is wrong is that students will think of the university as the enemy if it does not respect their rights to privacy. The
20   university should not act like a high school and "rat" on students every time they have a problem. It doesn't have parent-teacher conferences, so why should it notify parents about drinking?

University students do not even like it when the university mails grades home to parents. (Other schools mail grades only to the students because they
25   know that grades are a student's private property that she can decide for herself to share with her parents or not.) If the university becomes a tattle-tale, students will have a bad attitude toward it, which would cause them to participate less in university social activities and look for social life away from campustown, where there will be even more drinking. Besides their bad attitude will spill over and
30   harm their studies.

This brings me to my next point that no matter what the university does about student drinking, students are still susceptible to drinking in any environ-ment they live in. It is obvious that Tanaki is looking to eliminate student drinking and protect students from harm by violating their rights to privacy, but Tanaki is
35   totally ignorant of the era in which we live. Life is not as it used to be in the past and drinking is an obvious part of everyday college life; therefore, I feel that getting students in trouble with their parents may not influence whether they drink as much as Tanaki thinks. We live in a time in which young people feel it is necessary to drink in order to fit in with the crowd. Their parents drink, their
40   friends drink, and even their teachers drink. President Tanaki may say that it is wrong for students to drink, but he has lots of alcohol at the faculty parties at his house on Marrs Hill, right in the middle of the campus.

Furthermore, you can't go to any kind of student party that does not have drinking around you. It is not just the Greek parties that have liquor everywhere.
45　Most dorm parties, even in the first year dorms, have alcohol that anyone can drink. Students bring alcohol and other drugs as well to concerts at University Hall. When there is not a concert, students have to go to campustown bars to hear live music since first-year students cannot keep a car at their dorms. The city says it is legal for students under twenty-one but over eighteen to go into
50　bars for the music, and it is obvious that they would then be around people drinking. It is a mistake if anyone thinks that students can live in an environment in which they are surrounded by alcohol and never have it pass their lips. As Billy Joel says, "We didn't start the fire." It was our parents and people like President Tanaki who put us in an alcohol environment.
55　　In conclusion, I would like to state that Tanaki's proposal is a complete infringement of the privacy rights of students and won't work anyway. I also feel that instead of trying to tattle on students to their parents, he should do something to make the social life of first-year students better so that they do not have to drink because there is nothing better to do at night. It is obvious that the
60　university needs a better solution to the problem of binge drinking than invading the privacy of every student who takes one drink.

Binge Drinking and Parental Notification: Students' Rights to Privacy or Parents' Right to Know?

1　　When University President Albert Tanaki announced that he wanted to notify parents when students under twenty-one were caught drinking by university police, there was an uproar among students and faculty. The Student Council passed a resolution the next day stating that "any invasion of student privacy is
5　wrong." Council Chair Susan Ford wrote in the *Student Daily,* "This is morally wrong, legally wrong, and besides it won't work." It is understandable why students have gotten so upset over Tanaki's proposal. But by thinking only about how the proposal impacts on their rights, students and the faculty who have come out in support of them have forgotten about the rights of their parents.
10　　The first thing most people have said against the proposal is that it treats students like children instead of adults who have a right to privacy. Well, students do not live in the world of adults. Adults work to pay for their food, housing, phones, computers, and transportation. Students get them free. They even get free condoms. It is true that some students work part time, but that
15　barely covers their spending money in most cases. That is not the world of adults. It is obvious that if you do not have the responsibilities of adults then you cannot expect to get the rights of adults.

On the other hand, students who say they have a right to privacy are not entirely wrong. Most students had privacy rights when they still lived at home.
20　Five of the six people living in my dorm suite had the right to keep our parents out of our bedrooms. Most high schools cannot go into a student's locker unless the police are looking for drugs or guns. Students should not have less right to privacy at college than they did when they were younger. That does not necessarily mean, however, that students get all the privacy of adults just because
25　they are in college.

In addition to the question of whether students deserve all the rights of adults, we have to consider how much privacy adults get. Privacy invasions exist on a continuum. There is a huge difference between sneaking pictures of someone through their bathroom window and telling parents when you break the law
30   by doing something that could harm you forever. What if you overheard your best friend talking about suicide when he was having a private phone conversation? Would you protect his privacy? Or would you tell someone who can help him? Which is the greater evil, to violate someone's privacy or to let them harm themselves? Telling parents about a student's drinking may be an invasion of
35   their privacy and treating them like a child, but it is also doing something to keep them from harming themselves. There is not a huge difference between telling someone to stop a student from killing themselves and telling parents about a student doing something as stupid and dangerous as getting drunk enough to get caught by university police.
40   The one point that no one has considered, however, is the rights of parents. They are the ones who finance our academic joy ride. They pay for our tuition, board, books, and just about everything else we take for granted. They don't pay for these things just so that we don't have to work like adults. They pay because we are their dependents and they are investing in our future by paying for our
45   education. But when people make investments, don't they watch where their money goes? Silicon Valley investors keep track of what the companies they invest in do with the money they give them. As investors in a start-up company (us), our parents have a right to know what we are doing with the money they give the university for us. As their dependents, we should not forget that
50   beggars cannot be choosers.
Just because the student opposition to the proposal looks at things from a self-interested perspective and does not consider the rights of parents, that does not mean that the proposal is a good one in every way. I think the proposal is on the right track and is generally a good idea if the university only notifies
55   parents when a student is seriously drunk and not just sneaking one beer. But both President Tanaki and the opposition act as though all university students live in dorms and do their drinking on campus or in campustown so that university police might catch them. What about students who have moved out of the dorms and live in apartments? There are hardly any juniors or seniors in my
60   dorm. What about students who live at home? About one-third of university students never live on campus. According to the figures on the registrar's Web page, 36 percent of this year's first-year students do not live in dorms. Besides, students who are over twenty-one can have drinking problems as much as those under twenty-one can. The student who died from binge drinking last year
65   was a senior and so probably over 21. The registrar does not give figures for this, but my first-year classes have lots of students who are older and probably have a family of their own. What about them?
When you consider all of the factors, President Tanaki's proposal may not be perfect but it does not look like an evil invasion of privacy as the opposition says
70   it is. It is an invasion of students' privacy, but for a good cause. It also protects the rights of parents, who as long as they are paying have the right to know what we are up to. Most of all, it lets parents do something to help their troubled children who risk their lives when they engage in binge drinking. I believe that rather than selfishly oppose the proposal, students should work with President

75 Tanaki to create one that can help deal with the problem without invading
students privacy rights any more than is necessary.

Task 1.   Identify the elements of argument in each essay. Make a copy
and mark it up with different colored highlighters, or use line numbers to identify specific sentences. Indicate in which sentence or sentences the writer does
the following:

1. States the **main claim** or point of the essay. Is that claim repeated elsewhere in the essay?

2. States the **main point** of each body paragraph (ignore the introduction
   and conclusion). These points should be major **reasons** supporting the
   main claim and will themselves be claims that the rest of the paragraph
   supports.

3. Presents information that you regard as hard **evidence,** or as close to
   hard evidence as you can reasonably expect the writer to get.

4. **Acknowledges** an objection or alternative point of view. Indicate next
   to each one whether the writer seems to respect the alternative (R), is
   neutral toward it (N), or is disrespectful (D).

5. **Responds** to an objection or alternative point of view. Indicate next to
   each one whether the writer seems to respect the alternative (R), is
   neutral toward it (N), or is disrespectful (D).

6. States a general principle or **warrant** that explains why a reason
   supports a claim.

Task 2.   Write a brief answer to the question below. Don't get caught up
in whether you agree or not; focus on *how* the writers make their case. Use the
results of your analysis in Task 1 as evidence to support the claims you make in
your answers.

> Which essay seems more like an amiable conversation in which the writer
> answers the five questions and considers the views of others? Why?

IN A NUTSHELL

About Your Argument . . .

We build arguments out of answers to just five kinds of questions we ask one
another every day:

- What are you claiming?
- What reasons do you have for believing that claim?
- What evidence do you base those reasons on?
- What principle makes your reasons relevant to you claims?
- But what about. . . ?

In conversation, someone asks us those questions, but when we write, we have to imagine those questions on our readers' behalf.

You anchor your argument on two of those answers: evidence and warrants. If your readers don't accept those elements, you can't make an argument at all. You must report evidence explicitly; you leave most warrants implicit, if you and your readers share assumptions. But you usually have to state them when you address contested issues. Most of us assume, however, that we and our readers share more than we actually do, so it's wise to be more explicit than you think you have to be.

Those five elements constitute the core of a simple argument, but you may have to treat each reason, warrant, and response to a different point of view as the claim of another, subordinate argument. That's how you "thicken" your argument.

. . . and About Writing It

As we said at the end of the last chapter, you have four initial tasks:

- Understand the problem that occasions your argument.
- Formulate hypotheses that are plausible candidates for a solution.
- Pick the best candidate.
- List the reasons that encourage your reader to agree with your solution.

Avoid these stock plans:

- the five paragraph essay
- a narrative of your research and thinking
- a summary of your sources
- organizing parts around things rather than ideas and concepts
- organizing the argument into two obvious parts

Once you have reasons to support your claim, think about evidence to back up those reasons. Then imagine someone asking *But what about. . . ?*

Here is a plan for drafting your argument:

- Sketch the problem and its solution.
- List reasons that you think your readers would accept as sound.
- Articulate the evidence on which you think those reasons rest.
- Order those reasons in a way that will make sense to your reader.
- Imagine objections and respond to them.

Draft a working introduction:

- Start with a sentence or two of shared context for your problem.
- Add a sentence or two that articulates the problem.

• State what the problem costs readers.

• Finish with a sentence that sketches the gist of a solution.

Set off your introduction and conclusion from the body of your paper, then compare the last sentence or two in your introduction to the most important claim in your conclusion. If they don't complement each other, change them so they do. (You will more likely have to change the one in the introduction.)

If you can, do the same in each major section: Set off its introduction and (if it has one) conclusion and compare them. The main point in each section should probably appear at the end of the introduction to its section.

CHAPTER 3

Motivating Your Argument

A good critical thinker knows that an argument is intended to resolve a problem of some kind. She also knows that if she fails to define the problem, she is unlikely to solve it. And if she does not frame the problem clearly and persuasively for readers, she is unlikely to motivate them to take the time to consider her solution. In this chapter we discuss how to define problems and then to write introductions and conclusions that frame an argument in ways that help readers understand it.

You can occasionally choose whether to make an argument face-to-face or in writing, but often you have no choice. You have to argue in person when you have no time to write or need a personal touch. You have to write when you can't meet readers in person or need time to plan and test your argument before sending it off, or your audience wants time to study it.

But writing has drawbacks. If you don't know what your readers are like—cooperative or prickly, generous or difficult—you might not know the right tone to take. Worse, if you don't know what your readers think, you can't correct their misunderstandings or respond to surprising questions. You could just guess about readers and hope for the best. Or you can use the five questions of argument to think about readers critically and systematically, so that you can anticipate and answer their questions before readers become more focused on the issues you do not consider than on those you do.

But a written argument must overcome an even bigger disadvantage that again calls for the skills of critical thinking. When you make an argument face-to-face, others respond to your predicament because they respond to *you*. They are drawn in by your look, voice, and body language. If, for example, you ran into the dean of students after a bad day at the health service, your angry look and edgy voice would communicate your distress. And the dean would probably feel your distress more intently than if he were alone in his office reading your angry letter. Human presence engages us as words on a page rarely can.

When you make an argument in writing, you must therefore overcome the handicap of your absence by offering readers good reasons to engage your argument at all. The most devastating response you can get to your argument isn't *I don't agree* but *I don't care.* But to find good reasons for readers to care, you have to think critically and systematically about both the problem your argument solves and how that problem affects not you, *but your readers.*

In this chapter, we show you how to motivate readers to care about your argument by showing them that, whether they know it or not, they have a problem that you can solve.

Two Kinds of Problems

As we said in Chapter 1, problems are of two kinds, depending on what readers must do to solve them:

- One kind can be solved only if readers take (or at least support) an overt action that will change their situation. We call that kind of problem *practical.*

A practical problem is a bad situation that you want to eliminate, like discrimination, AIDS, genocide, sagging profits, rising tuition, a loud radio—any situation that makes you angry, sad, disgusted, frightened, pained, guilty, embarrassed, ashamed, discouraged, or even just annoyed, for yourself or empathetically for others. Your argument solves a practical problem only if it leads someone to *do* something that breaks the chain of causes and effects that makes you and your reader unhappy (or to *stop* doing something, such as not wasting energy).

- The other kind of problem can be solved only if readers believe or understand something differently. We call that kind of problem *conceptual.*

A conceptual problem is something we can state as a question: *How old is the universe? Why don't chimps cry? What did Thomas Jefferson really think about slavery?* An unsolved conceptual problem rarely causes sadness, anger, or pain, but it does frustrate our fundamental human desire to know more about the world, even about things as trivial as why the biggest nuts in a can end up on top. Your argument solves a conceptual problem only if it leads people to *believe* something that improves their understanding of the world (or to *stop* believing something, such as that AIDS was created by the CIA).

How Practical and Conceptual Problems Motivate Arguments

In your academic career, you will be asked to address both kinds of problems, but you will have to write different arguments supporting their solutions. So you must first understand how they differ in structure and motivation.

The Two-Part Structure of Practical Problems

Here is an example of a practical problem that you would never write about but makes our point: Imagine you're driving to a final exam that you must pass to graduate. You partied last night, then slept through the alarm. You'll probably be late, but even if you make it on time, you'll probably fail, because you didn't study. You hit a traffic jam; now you *know* you won't make it. Do you have a problem?

Your situation seems to have the makings of a problem, not because of the traffic jam itself but because of what the jam leads to, which will make you very unhappy indeed:

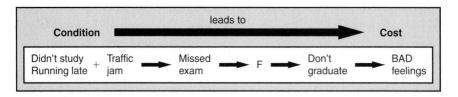

Then you see your instructor in the car next to you and realize you no longer have a problem. In fact, that traffic jam is your solution! The exam will be put off, and you'll even have more time to study:

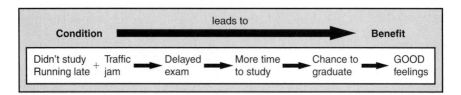

No cost, all benefit, no problem.

Here's the point: Every practical problem has two parts:

- **Part 1:** An event, condition, or circumstance unsettles your world. We'll call this part of a problem its **destabilizing condition.**

We usually name a practical problem by stating just its condition: *alcoholism, racism, cancer, AIDS.*

But the condition alone is not the problem: every problem must have a second part:

- **Part 2:** That destabilizing condition must have an effect that you believe will make you—or someone you care about—feel bad. We'll call this part of a problem its *cost.*

By this definition, a situation that at first seems to be a very bad problem may not be one at all if it exacts no cost: a painless disease that will kill you tomorrow is no problem for you today if an asteroid is going to kill everyone on earth tonight.

With rare exceptions, people are motivated to act on a practical problem because they want to avoid the bad feelings that define its costs. So when you argue for a solution to a practical problem, you must make readers see its two-part structure, especially the costs *to them* if it's not solved. So you must see the problem as your readers do. No matter how bad the costs may seem to you, what matters is how your readers feel about them.

Sometimes, you don't have to state the cost of a problem because it seems obvious—we all know the cost of AIDS, homelessness, or genocide. More often, though, you do have to state the costs your solution will address because they are so often not at all obvious *to the reader*. For example, you might write to the administration arguing that your student health service should have separate waiting areas for men and women. But until you can point out specific *costs* that *administrators* now pay and that your solution will reduce, they are unlikely to see any problem at all, or at least not the one you do.

The Two-Part Structure of Conceptual Problems

A conceptual problem also has a destabilizing condition and a resulting cost, but they differ from those in practical problems. In a practical problem, the destabilizing condition is *any* situation that a reader finds intolerable: If winning the lottery made you unhappy, it would be a practical problem for you. But in a conceptual problem, the destabilizing condition always has the same form:

- **Part 1:** In a conceptual problem, the ***destabilizing condition*** is always something you don't know or understand but want to: a puzzle, a gap in understanding, a discrepancy or contradiction between a new fact and old ones—anything that leaves you uncertain, confused, or even just so curious that you want to resolve it.

You can always express the destabilizing condition of a conceptual problem as a question, because a question implies something you do not know.

How many stars are in the sky?
How do children respond to the fragmented structure of TV programs?

Conceptual problems also differ from practical ones in their costs, in the effects of their destabilizing conditions.

- The cost of a practical problem is some kind of tangible unhappiness, pain, and so on.
- The cost of a conceptual problem is *another and more significant* gap in knowledge or understanding.

That result is so intangible, however, that instead of calling it a *cost* we'll call it a *consequence*.

- **Part 2:** In a conceptual problem, the ***consequence*** of its destabilizing condition is something *else* that you don't know, another question whose answer is *more* significant than the answer to the first. In other words, the consequence of a conceptual problem is a puzzle.

Therefore, a conceptual problem consists of not *one* question, one thing you don't know, but *two*.

That is less confusing than it first seems. It works like this:

- You have the first part of a conceptual problem, its condition, when there is something you don't know but need to. You can phrase that condition as a question.

How many stars are in the sky?

- You have the second part of a conceptual problem, its consequences, when you can say why you want to find out the answer to the first part. You can also phrase that second part as a question.

If we can't answer the question of how many stars are in the sky, _{condition / first} _{question} then we can't answer a more important question: Does the universe have enough mass for gravity to hold it together? _{consequence / larger question}

How to Identify Motivating Costs or Consequences by Asking *So What?*

Since readers are motivated to read by the significance of a problem's costs to *them*, you must imagine your problem from their point of view. To do that, imagine them repeatedly asking *So what?* until one of your answers makes them say, *Oh, that's important to know!* That's when you know that your reader wants to hear your answer and its supporting argument.

Finding Costs of Pragmatic Problems

Because a pragmatic problem has tangible costs, they are generally easier to find. Here's an example:

> Industries are releasing chemicals that are creating a hole in the ozone layer.
> *So what?*
> Less ozone means more ultraviolet light.
> *So what?*
> Too much ultraviolet light causes skin cancer.

If your reader again asks *So what?*, you might question her moral rationality, but if you still needed to motivate her to care, you'd have to try again:

> More skin cancer means higher health care costs and many deaths.

If, however improbably, she again asks *So what?,* you've failed to state your problem in a way that makes her to see it as hers. You can only shrug, baffled at her values. Only when she says *What do we do?* will you know that you have identified costs that motivate her to read about your solution to her problem.

Finding Consequences of Conceptual Problems

Because the immediate consequences of a conceptual problem involve not tangible harm but some larger question, they can be harder to find. You do it, however, with the same process of asking *So what?* until you reach a question that will motivate your readers. Here's that example about stars in the sky:

> We do not know how many stars are in the sky.
>
> *So what?*
>
> Then we can't answer a more important question: Does the universe have enough mass for gravity to hold it together?.

If your readers want to learn an answer to that second question, then you've stated a consequence that makes them think your first question is worth asking too. So they will want to read an argument supporting its answer.

But what if your reader might again ask *So what?*

> So what if you don't know whether the universe has enough mass to hold it together?

At that point, you'd have to pose a yet larger question whose answer is *even more* significant to his understanding:

> If we can't answer the question whether the universe has enough mass for gravity to hold it together, _{second question} then we can't answer a more important one: Will the universe one day cease to exist? _{consequence / larger question}

If that person asked *So what?* yet again, you could only shrug and think, *Wrong audience.*

Students new to a field usually struggle to find consequences that matter to their readers. Experienced researchers like your teachers already know what questions interest others in their field, so they can know when a question they want to answer might lead to a bigger one. But you can't know that if you're just starting out in a field or haven't even chosen one. You will have to rely on teachers, colleagues, and lots of reading to help you discover what questions are *worth* asking.

Before you look elsewhere, though, the first and most important step is to find an issue that *you* want to pursue, even if it interests only you. Once you find that first question, keep asking *So what if I answer it?* If you're engaged in a long research project, you may not find the best—or even a good—answer until you're near its end. Don't be discouraged: that happens to everyone. But don't wait until the end of a project to start asking *So what?* The sooner you can state the larger question that your specific question helps you answer, the better you will understand your problem and the more easily you will answer it.

Practical Costs Versus Conceptual Consequences

Some first-year students struggle with conceptual problems for another reason: they are interested mainly in the practical uses of their education. *How,* they ask, *will knowing more about ancient Greeks help me be a better engineer or accountant?* We could make the case that knowing history can make someone a better professional of any kind, but we'll only repeat what engineers and accountants now on the job commonly say about their education: They regret that they did not take more courses to broaden their understanding of history, culture, communication, psychology, philosophy, and so on, where questions are answered not to solve the world's immediate problems but to understand that world better.

Some very practical-minded people, especially politicians, think we waste money trying to solve purely conceptual problems: *Who cares,* they ask, *why the biggest nuts end up on top? How will that improve the world? Why should our taxes support the search for an answer?* Scholars defend "pure" research of this kind by arguing that all knowledge is valuable, because we need to understand every part of the world. That was the defense of a University of Chicago professor who, puzzled by the mixed nuts phenomenon, spent a lot of time figuring it out. (As it happens, his answer helps shipping companies pack granular materials more efficiently, construction companies build tougher roads, and drug companies make better pills.)

Pure Research and Larger Questions

A "pure" historical question has recently come closer to an answer that will not change our world, but might help us understand some of its history better:

Did Thomas Jefferson have children with his slave Sally Hemings?

DNA evidence suggests that he could have, but so what if we never find out? *Well,* the historians answer, *until we know, we can't answer bigger questions.*

Until we know for sure, we can't know whether his actions contradicted his claims about equality and morality.

But so what if you don't know?

Until we know that, we can't evaluate his moral values.

But so what if you can't?

Until we can, we won't understand the author of some of our key political principles.

Some might still ask, *So what? Who cares?* In fact, many historians care. And now so do a few others who need the answer to solve a practical problem unique to them: Only blood relatives are entitled to lie in the family cemetery at Monticello, a right recently claimed by Sally Hemings' African-American descendants. (When Jefferson's white descendants met to decide whether to let them in, they voted to create a separate cemetery for them.)

The Wider Coherence of Conceptual Problems

Those new to academic research face yet another challenge with conceptual problems: Not only must they answer their question, but they must make that answer fit with the larger body of knowledge and beliefs shared by those in the field, from basic facts to political and ideological values. We accept a solution to a conceptual problem only if it fits our entire mental landscape.

For example, here's a question with a new answer that has upset people because it conflicts with some larger ideological positions: *Why did the mammoth, camel, and other large mammals disappear from North America about 12,000 years ago?* Researchers used to think those creatures died out because of disease or climatic change; now some claim they were hunted to extinction by the earliest Native Americans. That claim is heatedly opposed by those who believe that those first peoples lived in harmony with nature, and so *in principle* they could not have wiped out whole species, as Europeans almost wiped out the bison. So even if some evidence suggests otherwise, they resist an answer that would make them revise so much of what they believe.

Is this a failure of critical thinking? It is too early to tell. Good critical thinkers never cling to an idea when the evidence against it is too strong; on the other hand, they do not jettison a well-established idea at the first sign of contradictory evidence. The trick is to know when the attachment to an old idea has become irrational and uncritical. That's why those who make a living solving conceptual problems rarely embrace any answer wholeheartedly. We can be certain of a claim only when we are certain that no new evidence can contradict it. But new evidence always turns up.

When you are new to a field, you can't know all the facts, principles, theories, and political views that your claims must harmonize with. That's another way your teacher can help you overcome inexperience. But ultimately, the only fix is knowledge based on experience.

Framing Problems in Introductions

Readers understand your argument better and remember it longer when you motivate them to read it closely. You do that best when you state your problem in a way that helps readers see *their* stake in your solution, its costs or consequences to *them*. Most introductions have three parts: (1) an opening segment we will call *common ground,* (2) the statement of your problem, and (3) its solution. We'll start in the middle, with the core of every introduction, its problem.

The Core of an Introduction: Conditions and Costs

To state a problem explicitly, you must state the situation or condition that leads to a cost and then spell out that cost, whether practical or conceptual. We will call that condition the "destabilizing" condition because it upsets some settled situation.

Some costs may seem too obvious to state, and some may seem too distressing for anyone not to care. But it's risky to assume that your readers will understand the costs as you do. So you have to step back from your own view of the problem to think critically and systematically about the costs your readers will see and care about.

To identify the costs that will motivate your particular readers, do this:

1. List all the costs you can think of, even minor or speculative ones.
2. Arrange your costs by your *readers'* priority, from most to least important.
3. If you have readers who will respond differently from one another, make a priority list for each.

Because you may need different solutions to remove different costs, do this:

4. Create a second list, matching each cost to the solution most likely to remove it.
5. Arrange your solutions by how acceptable they will be to *readers,* from most to least.
6. If you have readers who will respond differently, make an acceptability list for each.

You can then use the lists to decide which solution(s) you must argue for and so which cost(s) to raise in your introduction.

For example, binge drinking among college students is a problem with obvious costs, but different readers may see different ones:

1. It threatens the lives of drinkers and those around them.
2. It encourages moral weakness.
3. It tarnishes the image of the university.
4. It exposes the university to legal action for its damages.

When you state each cost as something worth caring about, you imply that you and your readers share certain values: cost (1) implies that you both feel anguish over injury and death; cost (2) that you condemn moral weakness; cost (3) that you fear loss of the university's prestige; and cost (4) that you fear loss of the university's money. Each cost also implies that the problem can be solved in a different way:

1. Since bingeing threatens lives, prohibit students from drinking.
2. Since it erodes morality, teach moral values.
3. Since it makes the university look bad, launch a public relations campaign.
4. Since it exposes the university to lawsuits, limit the university's liability.

Those different costs would encourage us to write different introductions. Contrast how these next three introductions describe the problem:

1. When students drink, many "binge," consuming large amounts of alcohol at one sitting until they pass out. destabilizing condition We cannot end bingeing, but we must control it. promise of solution

That introduction implies that binge drinking is a problem, but names no costs; it fails to answer the question *So what?* These next two introductions state costs, but they address different readers with different values and therefore call for different solutions.

2. When students drink, many "binge," consuming large amounts of alcohol at one sitting until they pass out. _{destabilizing condition} Bingeing is, tragically, far from harmless. In the last six months, it has been cited in three deaths from alcohol poisoning, two from falls, and one in a car crash. It crosses the line from fun to reckless behavior that, if uncontrolled, kills and injures not just drinkers but those around them. _{costs} We cannot end bingeing, but we can control its worst costs by educating first-year students how to manage its risks. _{promise of solution}

3. When students drink, many "binge," consuming large amounts of alcohol at one sitting until they pass out. _{destabilizing condition} This behavior not only tarnishes our image, but exposes us to liability if a student injures himself or others. Until this problem is solved, we risk criticism from the state legislature, with possible cuts in our budget, and increased insurance costs, either of which will delay faculty salary increases. _{costs} We cannot end bingeing, but we can control its damage by educating the public and the legislature that the problem is caused by lax parenting. _{promise of solution}

If you have readers who will respond to different costs, your best strategy is to find the solution that eliminates the cause of the problem, thereby removing all of its costs. But if you can't, you may have to offer multiple solutions that appeal to different readers in different ways.

Removing Causes Versus Ameliorating Costs

This book will not teach you to be an expert problem solver, but to make effective arguments you should know some things about solving problems well. One is to know whether your solution to a practical problem fixes its *causes* or merely eases its *symptoms*. If a solution removes the root causes, it eliminates the problem entirely; otherwise, it can only lessen the costs. For example, no one can cure AIDS, but physicians can control its costs by removing some of its devastating symptoms and postponing death. People can thus be infected with HIV (the condition), but live with the problem, if its symptoms (costs) are ameliorated.

Suppose Sue convinces administrators at her school that students need more access to teachers outside of class, and they imagine two solutions. One would eliminate a root cause and so the problem: require teachers to have more office hours. The other would ameliorate the costs, thus making the problem smaller: make teachers available online. They might also find a solution that simply changes how students feel about the costs: Give each student a $500 budget to spend on office hours at $50 an hour and tell them they can keep what they don't spend. That last solution is tongue-in-cheek, but it would give at least some students (not all, we would hope) reason to be happy about not meeting with teachers.

You can solve a problem in two ways: Remove its cause or ameliorate its costs. The problem with ameliorating costs is that root causes have a way of sprouting new costs in unexpected places.

An Alternative Way to State Practical Costs

You can state the costs of a problem more positively if you rephrase them as potential benefits of a solution. This introduction focuses on costs:

> When students drink, many "binge," consuming large amounts of alcohol at one sitting until they pass out. destabilizing condition **Bingeing is, tragically, far from harmless. In the last six months, it has been cited in three deaths from alcohol poisoning, two from falls, and one in a car crash.** costs We can reduce bingeing through better education. solution

This one focuses on benefits:

> When students drink, many "binge," consuming large amounts of alcohol at one sitting until they pass out. destabilizing condition **Had certain universities reduced bingeing, they might have saved the lives of the six students who died in the last six months as a result of bingeing.** benefits We can reduce bingeing through better education. solution

You might think that this is just a stylistic choice, but psychologists have shown that most people fear a loss more than they are attracted to a gain, even when those costs are objectively identical. For example, the cost of a hole in the ozone is the same, whether we say its solution might *save* 10,000 lives or leaving it unsolved might *cost* 10,000 deaths. But we seem to react more keenly to the risk of 10,000 dead than to the chance of saving an equal number of lives.

So if you want to cite benefits but still frame your problem most strongly, state the negative costs when you first introduce the problem and add the positive benefits after you state the solution:

> When students drink, many "binge," consuming large amounts of alcohol at one sitting until they pass out. destabilizing condition **Bingeing is, tragically, far from harmless. In the last six months, it has been cited in three deaths from alcohol poisoning, two from falls, and one in a car crash.** costs We can reduce bingeing through better education, solution **and thereby not only save those who binge from injury or death, but mitigate the damage they do to those around them.** costs restated as benefits

Stating the Conditions and Consequences of a Conceptual Problem

Conditions. In a conceptual problem, the destabilizing condition is something your readers do not know but should want to. You can articulate that condition in different ways. You can tell readers that they or others have been just plain wrong:

> Many educators proclaim that online classes will usher in a new era of education. [relevant quotations] **But the facts have contradicted these promises of a golden age. Few students are motivated to learn. . . .**

You can also tell readers that others have erred in some method of research (something academics love to point out):

> Critics of American education rightly argue that our high school students trail those in other countries in math and science. **But a study of the populations of students tested suggests sampling errors that put those criticisms in doubt.**

Or, more politely, you can tell readers that their knowledge and understanding are merely incomplete:

> Problem solving is a well-investigated aspect of cognitive behavior. [review of research.] Despite this extensive research in problem solving, **cognitive science knows little about the issue of problem finding. . . .**

Or, more politely still, you can tell readers that questions they can answer point to others they cannot:

> One of the oldest questions in the criticism of Flannery O'Connor's is how her religious beliefs shaped her fiction. One of the newest has been O'Connor's response to racism. Both issues have been studied thoroughly. [summary of criticism.] **But no one has yet asked how religion has shaped O'Connor's view of racism. . . .**

Although you can always phrase the condition of a conceptual problem as a question—*How did O'Connor's religion shape her view of racism?*— most writers phrase it as a statement that something is not known or fully understood.

Consequences. It is harder to express the consequences of that gap in understanding, the "why readers should want to know" part. We too easily assume that if we just say what is not known or understood, readers will think finding out is worth their time to read our argument. For example:

> When some critics charge that Flannery O'Connor does not appreciate the evil of racism, they ignore her religious beliefs. _{destabilizing condition} Her stories show that her treatment of racism as a spiritual crisis is sympathetic to equality and suggests an understanding of racism that sets her apart from liberals of her time. _{answer / main claim}

If you're among those who criticize O'Connor or are fascinated with everything about her, you might read on to find out why this writer thinks her critics are wrong. But if you haven't thought much about O'Connor, you're likely to ask not *Why do you think that?* but *Why should I care that you do?*

In short, you can't count on readers to see the consequences of a conceptual problem, so you must state them explicitly: If you do not answer the specific question, what larger question remains unanswered? Just as with a practical problem, you can state consequences of a conceptual problem twice, once as a negative consequence of not knowing, and again as the positive benefit of having the knowledge. For example:

> When some critics charge that Flannery O'Connor does not appreciate the evil of racism, they ignore her religious beliefs. _{destabilizing condition} **If we fail to recognize that O'Connor saw racism as a symptom of a larger spiritual and religious crisis, we risk overlooking her insights into sources of racism that are deeper and more harmful than mere social or cultural causes**. _{consequence} Her stories show that her treatment of racism is more sympathetic to equality than is apparent and suggests an understanding of racism that sets her apart from liberals of her time. _{answer / main claim} **Once we recognize the spiritual basis of her thinking, we see that O'Connor's exploration of Southern culture is far more penetrating than her critics ever understood.** _{consequence restated as benefit}

By stating the consequences of understanding O'Connor's ideas on race *twice* in detail, the writer casts a much broader net: She makes a claim on many readers' interest, not just those concerned with those specific ideas but also anyone who cares about O'Connor, her stories, Southern culture, sources of racism, the role of religion in culture, and so on. She gives a rich and detailed answer to the question, *So what?*

Now the fact is, not every one of your teachers is likely to be as interested in your problem as you are. That's just a fact of life. But what they will be interested in is whether you can use the strategic "moves" that experienced writers do, because they are looking ahead to when you will be writing as a member of a specialized community. Right now, that time may seem a long way off, but that gives you time to practice.

Consequences and Costs in Framing Applied Conceptual Problems

We call a conceptual problem *applied* when we can trace its consequences to some ultimate tangible cost. But the immediate consequence of an applied conceptual problem is still something that we do not know.

Some students feel that tangible costs are more motivating than conceptual consequences. So when they state a problem, they jump right to those tangible costs:

If we can't answer the question of how children respond to the fragmented structure of network TV programs, _{condition / first question} then we risk stunting their intellectual growth by letting them watch it. _{cost / tangible harm}

But that way of thinking about a problem jumps over the link between a conceptual condition and an ultimate practical cost: *What must we understand before we know what to do?* To state an applied problem clearly, you have to state not just the conceptual condition and its ultimate practical cost, but also the chain of conceptual consequences that connect them:

If we can't answer the question of how children respond to the fragmented structure of network TV programs, _{condition / first question} then we can't answer a more important one: Does network TV affect children's ability to concentrate? _{consequence / larger question} If we can't answer that question, then we can't answer a more important one: Do we stunt children's intellectual growth by letting them watch network TV? _{cost / tangible harm}

So if you address an applied problem, clearly explain why we cannot know what to do until we understand some specific aspect of the problem.

The Outer Frame of an Introduction: Common Ground and Solution

Thus far, we've described the core of an introduction, the statement of a problem. Schematically, it looks like this:

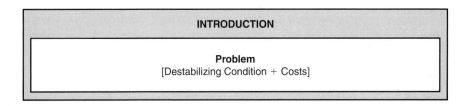

Most introductions, however, have two more parts that give readers a framework for understanding the problem.

- Before they read about a problem, readers expect an introductory contextualizing element that we'll call **common ground.**
- After they read about the problem, they look for its **solution,** your main claim (or at least a gesture toward it).

Thus a full introduction consists of these elements:

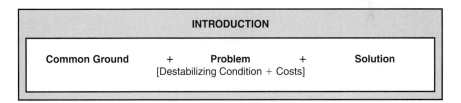

We'll discuss the solution first, then common ground.

The Solution

After you pose your problem, readers usually look to the end of your introduction to find the gist of your solution. The solution of a practical problem calls for or implies an action; the solution of a conceptual problem answers a question. For example, this introduction to the practical problem of bingeing calls for an action—educate students:

> . . . Bingeing crosses the line from fun to reckless behavior that, if uncontrolled, will kill and injure still more students. _{costs} We will never end bingeing entirely, but **colleges must start educating students how to manage its risks, just as we now educate them about sexual harassment and other social problems.** _{solution / main claim}

Though it is a bit of a cliché, a rhetorical question can achieve the same end:

> We will never end bingeing entirely, but **is it possible to educate students in how to manage its risks, just as we now educate them about sexual harassment and other social problems?** _{solution / main claim}

Some writers only hint at a solution, implying that they will not state it explicitly until their conclusion:

> . . . Bingeing crosses the line from good times to reckless behavior that, if uncontrolled, will kill and injure still more students. _{costs} **We will never end**

bingeing entirely, but it is a problem we cannot ignore. The solution isn't obvious, but finding one must be part of our educational mission. _{promise of solution}

Notice, however, that while that last sentence only promises a solution, it introduces concepts—*part of our educational mission*—that suggest ideas that the writer will develop in the body of his argument.

Think twice, however, before you decide only to promise a solution in your introduction. Readers may suspect you're hiding a solution they won't like, or that you don't have a solution at all. If you have reason to withhold a solution to a practical problem but you want to avoid seeming to conceal it, express your problem so precisely that readers can infer its solution.

For example, we can infer a solution to the problem of binge drinking from this introduction, because its states the destabilizing condition so explicitly:

> Increasingly, except for driving under the influence, college students are unaware of the risks of excessive alcohol consumption. First-year students in particular gravely underestimate the risks they face. Fewer than 40 percent even know about the toxic effects of alcohol, and most of them think it affects only long-term drinkers. Yet the university does nothing either during orientation or later to alert students to those risks and how to manage them. _{destabilizing condition} As a consequence, many students "binge," until they pass out or worse, injure or even kill themselves. In the last six months, bingeing has been cited in three deaths from alcohol poisoning, two from falls, and one in a car crash. Bingeing injures not only drinkers but those around them. _{costs} We may never eliminate bingeing, but finding a way to lessen its risks must be part of our educational mission. _{promise of solution to come}

We can predict that the solution will involve educating first-year students about the risks of drinking, probably during orientation week. So if you think you must withhold your main claim until the end of your argument, try to state your problem so clearly that it implies its solution.

You can't do that with a conceptual problem, however, no matter how specifically you state it:

> Although excessive drinking has always been part of college life, we do not know why particular students engage in dangerous bingeing, whether they binge because of a psychological condition, or because of response to peer pressure. _{destabilizing condition} Lacking that knowledge, we do not know what kind of programs would. . . _{consequence}

We know what gap in understanding is at stake in answering that question, but not at all what the answer will look like. In conceptual problems, you can help readers anticipate your answer only if you explicitly state or strongly imply it:

> Lacking that knowledge, we do not know what kind of programs would. . . . _{consequence} **We believe, however, that at least some bingeing is associated with a personality type that is attracted to risk taking.** . . . _{solution}

◆ EXAMPLE

A Problem That Forecasts Its Solution

Here is the skeleton of an argument about doing research on the Internet. Notice that at the end of the introduction, the writer does not specify a solution because it is so obvious.

Does the Internet help college students learn? Enthusiasts proclaim it has made a world of information available to any freshman with a computer. Skeptics warn that cyberspace is so full of junk that research in it will never amount to anything more than garbage collecting. . . . I concede that the skeptics have a case. _{common ground} But the problem with doing research on the Internet isn't about garbage. It's that, by doing all their homework on the Internet, _{destabilizing condition} students may develop a misunderstanding of research itself and even of the subjects they are studying. _{cost} [end of introduction]

Historical research takes place in libraries and archives, but it isn't a straightforward process of retrieving information. _{reason 1} You may open a box of manuscripts . . . but . . . every document . . . must be read between the lines and related to all the surrounding documents. . . .

Moreover, most documents never make it into. . . . _{reason 2}

[Moreover] . . . no digitized text can duplicate the original—its handwriting or typography, its layout, its. . . . _{reason 3}

[Finally d]igitizers often dump texts onto the Internet without considering their quality as sources, and students often fail to read those texts critically. . . .

_{reason 4} [end of body of argument]

Such thoughts touch off Luddite fantasies: smash all the computers and leave the Internet to drown in the ocean of its own junk. But that way madness lies, and my students have taught me that, if handled with care, the Internet can be an effective tool. . . . Instead of turning our backs on cyberspace, we need to take control of it—to set standards, develop quality controls, and direct traffic. Our students will learn to navigate the Internet successfully if we set up warning signals and teach them to obey: Proceed with caution. Danger lies ahead. _{solution / main claim}

Source: From Robert Darnton, "No Computer Can Hold the Past," *New York Times,* June 12, 1999.

IN THE READINGS . . .

A Helpful Introduction?

The introduction to Carol Trosset's "Obstacles to Open Discussion and Critical Thinking" (p. 385) is a very brief synopsis of her article. Compare the information in the introduction to what you find in the rest of the article. Does the introduction do justice to what's interesting and important in the article? Pick out her problem statement. Does it clearly indicate who should care about the problem her article solves? Does it state consequences that indicate specifically why they—or anyone—should care?

Compare the introduction to the last four paragraphs of the article (p. 392). Does Trosset say things there that make it clear whose problem she is addressing? Would some of those things make her intended audience sit up and take notice?

Finally, identify the main point of the article, the main claim that the argument supports. Is it easy to find? Is it in the introduction?

Clearly Trosset's introduction may not help some readers get through the rest of the article easily, with clear expectations that the article fulfills. Sketch out a new plan for an introduction that states her problem clearly, indicating both who should care and why, and that follows the problem with the gist of her solution. That's the kind of introduction that your readers will hope you offer them.

Common Ground

As we've seen, experienced writers motivate readers to read by describing the costs of a problem so that readers want to see it solved. But before they do that, writers often use another device to encourage readers to take their problem seriously. They open with a statement of what we call *common ground,* the general context of their problem that most readers aren't surprised by. Then they immediately upset it, something we did in opening this paragraph.

In that first sentence, we stated something we hoped you would accept as unproblematic because you already heard us say it:

> As we've seen, experienced writers motivate readers to read by describing the costs of a problem so that readers want to see it solved.

That was our common ground. In the next sentence we strongly qualified it with something we thought you did *not* know, implying that your knowledge was at least incomplete.

> As we've seen, experienced writers motivate readers to read by describing the costs of a problem so that readers want to see it solved. _{common ground} **But before they do that, writers often use another device to encourage readers to take their problem seriously.**

In that second sentence, we destabilized what we hoped you had taken as settled. To make sure you noticed, we opened it with **But** *before they do that.* In other words, we began with stable common ground just so that we could upset it.

Common Ground in Practical Problems. In practical problems, you can use anything as common ground, so long as it can be upset by the condition of your problem. Here is a fact about drinking that most of us know:

Drinking has been part of American college life for more than three centuries, and it has been accepted, even celebrated as part of growing up.

If you accept that as common knowledge, we can upset it by stating that something has changed. We signal that destabilization with a *but, however,* or other term warning that we're about to qualify what we just said:

Drinking has been part of American college life for more than three centuries, and it has been accepted, even celebrated as part of growing up. _{common ground} **But recently,** a new, dangerous kind of drinking known as "binge" drinking has become increasingly widespread. _{destabilizing condition}

When writers address a well-known problem, they often omit common ground, beginning directly with the problem:

The recent rise in college fatalities and injuries _{cost} caused by binge drinking _{destabilizing condition} has convinced many administrators that they must address the problem directly. Some have instituted rules regulating drinking on college property, one of which is claimed to work: ban alcohol entirely. _{solution}

If a writer simply wanted to echo that solution, she could go from there to her main claim:

. . . one of which is claimed to work: ban alcohol entirely. _{solution} We support that position, for several reasons. _{main claim}

But if she disagreed, she could turn *all* of that into common ground with a *but* or *however* that introduces the real problem:

. . . one of which is claimed to work: ban alcohol entirely. _{common ground} Such a blanket prohibition, **however,** will do more harm than good. _{destabilizing condition} It will cause students to. . . . _{costs} Therefore, we must seek. . . . _{solution}

In other words, in a practical problem you can use *anything* as common ground, if readers accept it and you can upset it with your destabilizing condition.

Common Ground in Conceptual Problems. Academic writers usually create common ground for a conceptual problem by sketching current knowledge that they will claim is incomplete or wrong. Skilled writers also use this statement to highlight those themes that the writer will take issue with. For example, the following introduction uses common ground to sketch what critics believe about Flannery O'Connor's views on Southern racism. In it, the writer introduces three themes that she develops thereafter: southern culture, attitudes toward race, and religious beliefs (those themes are capitalized, bold faced, and italicized):

> *"I write the way I do because . . . I am a Catholic*
> *peculiarly possessed of the modern consciousness."*

Although Flannery O'Connor's stories give us deep insights into Southern culture, some have criticized her attitude toward **race,** calling it the product of "an imperfectly developed sensibility" and claiming that "large SOCIAL ISSUES as such were never the subject of her writing." _{common ground} But that criticism ignores her *religious beliefs*. _{destabilizing condition} If we fail to see that O'Connor treated **racism** as a symptom of a larger *spiritual* crisis, we risk overlooking her insight that the sources of **racism** run deeper than mere SOCIAL OR CULTURAL CAUSES. _{consequence} Her stories show that her treatment of **racism** as a *spiritual* crisis is more sympathetic to **equality** than is apparent and suggests an understanding of **racism** that sets her apart from liberals of her time. _{answer / main claim} Once we recognize the *spiritual basis* of her thinking, we see that O'Connor's exploration of SOUTHERN SOCIETY AND CULTURE is even more penetrating than her critics assumed. _{consequence restated as benefit}

Literature Review as Common Ground. If you write a research paper for an advanced class, you will typically use as common ground a "literature review," a survey of research on the topic. But you'll simply irritate your readers if you offer an endless list of every bit of published research remotely connected to the problem. Limit a literature review to work directly relevant to your problem. Cite only those articles whose claims you intend to extend or correct.

The most familiar common ground in academic writing is something widely believed by those in a field, a statement of prior research or "truth" that the destabilizing condition will disrupt and put into question. But the common ground that most academic readers find most interesting isn't a statement of truth that turns out to be wrong, but a statement of a problem that turns out to be the wrong problem. This problem statement offers only the problem it will solve:

> The majority of Americans now support plans to administer regular achievement testing, end social promotions, and hold teachers and schools responsible for the performance of their students. _{statement of fact as common ground} **But more testing will be ineffective if school boards don't provide enough money to make it work.** _{destabilizing condition}

But this one offers as common ground a mistaken view of the problem.

> The American public school system has been the foundation of this country's political and economic successes. But for decades, American students have scored lower than those in almost all the world's economic and political powers, largely because we have stopped holding all students to the standards of our best. _{statement of fact as common ground} The American people now seem to agree that we can stop this decline by administering regular achievement testing, ending social promotions, and holding teachers and schools responsible for the performance of their students. _{mistaken problem as common ground} **However, the real solutions won't be found in testing because the real problems are rooted not in our children's classrooms but in their living rooms and bedrooms, not in their teachers' lack of ability or commitment, but in their parents' lack of involvement.** _{destabilizing condition}

Because academic readers value questions more than answers, they prefer problems that raise new questions to those that contradict old answers.

Prelude

There is one more element that writers use to introduce all these elements, particularly in popular journalism. You may recall being told to "catch your readers' attention" by opening with an interesting anecdote, fact, or quotation. What better catches our attention is an interesting problem in need of a solution. But a catchy opening works when it vividly introduces key concepts related to the problem. To name this device, we've borrowed a musical term: *prelude.*

Here are three preludes you could use to open an argument about bingeing.

1. A startling fact:

   A recent study reports that at most colleges three out of four students "binged" at least once in the previous thirty days, drinking more than five drinks at a sitting. Almost half binge once a week, and those who binge most are not just members of fraternities, but their officers.

2. A quotation, familiar or not:

   "If you're old enough to die for your country, you're old enough to drink to it." How often have you heard that justification for allowing 18-year-olds to drink?

3. An illustrative anecdote:

   When Jim Shay, president of Omega Alpha, accepted a dare from his fraternity brothers to down a pint of whiskey in one long swallow, he didn't plan to become this year's eighth college fatality from alcohol poisoning.

We can combine all three:

"If you're old enough to die for your country, you're old enough to drink to it." _{quotation} Tragically, Jim Shay, president of Omega Alpha, won't have a chance to do either. When he accepted a dare from his fraternity brothers to down a pint of whiskey in one long swallow, he didn't expect to become this year's eighth college fatality from alcohol poisoning. But he did. _{anecdote} According to a recent study, at most colleges, three out of four students have, like Shay, drunk five drinks at a sitting in the last thirty days. And those who drink the most are not just members of fraternities, but, like Shay, officers. _{striking fact} Drinking, of course, has been a part of American college life since the first college opened. . . . _{common ground} But in recent years. . . . _{destabilizing condition}

Writers in the natural and social sciences use preludes rarely. They are more common in the humanities and most common in writing for the general public. You use a prelude best when it introduces key themes that your argument will pursue, particularly when it represents your problem in a vivid and concrete example.

Here now is the structure of the fullest introduction:

INTRODUCTION				
Prelude	**Common Ground**	+	**Problem** [Destabilizing Condition + Costs]	+	**Solution** or **Promise of Solution**

You don't need all five elements in every introduction. The only one you always need is a destabilizing condition (if its cost is obvious). For a long argument, though, you can expand each element to a paragraph or more, creating an introduction several pages long.

IN THE READINGS . . .

Common Ground, Prelude, and Coda

In "On the Uses of a Liberal Education" (pp. 393–400), Mark Edmundson offers as common ground a popular view of what ails the academic world "Current critics tend to think. . . ." But before that, he opens with a long description of "evaluation day," with plenty of concrete details about his students' behavior and his responses to it, a description he echoes in the coda at the very end. Why do you think Edmundson chose to open his essay with that prelude and common ground? What themes do they establish that he pursues through the rest of his argument?

Edmunson's essay appears in a general circulation magazine whose readers include many people familiar with current university culture and many who are not. With such a varied readership, the long prelude is likely to prepare different readers in different ways. What does it do for readers who recognize his account as a familiar aspect of a world they know? For readers who are not familiar with this aspect of university life? For readers who know about universities but who do not recognize Edmundson's experience as typical of what they see?

Conclusions

Conclusions vary more than introductions, but in a pinch, you can map their parts onto the parts of your introduction. Just reverse their order:

1. Open your conclusion by stating (or restating) the gist of your main claim.
2. Explain its significance by answering *So what?*, in a new way if you can, but if not, restate what you offered in the introduction, now as a benefit.
3. Suggest a further question or problem to be resolved, something still not known. Answer not *So what?* but *Now what?*
4. End with an anecdote, quotation, or fact that echoes your prelude. We'll call this the *coda*.

For example, here is a paraphrase of the introduction to that Flannery O'Connor paper on pages 89–90.

1. "I write the way I do because . . . I am a Catholic peculiarly possessed of the modern consciousness." _{prelude}
2. Critics say O'Connor had no social conscience. _{common ground}
3. But she viewed racism not as a social issue but as a spiritual crisis. _{destabilizing condition} (*So what?*)
4. If we ignore this, we miss her insights into the true sources of racism. _{consequence}
5. Her treatment of racism is more sympathetic to equality than is apparent. _{answer / main claim}

To create a conclusion, the writer could first restate her main claim, then add a new consequence, raise a new question to pursue, and close with a coda in the form of another quotation from O'Connor that echoes the opening prelude:

> So those who claim that O'Connor was indifferent to racism fail to see how she saw past the surface of social conflict to a deeper crisis of faith—our failure to recognize the healing knowledge that comes from suffering. _{main claim restated} Indeed, these insights put her among a select few Southern writers who saw the failure of the modern world to deal with human differences not just as an economic or social problem but as a spiritual one. For example, . . . _{new consequence / significance} Seen in this light, a rereading of her private correspondence might reveal. . . . _{new questions to pursue} As she said in one letter (May 4, 1955), "What I had in mind to suggest [in that story] was the redemptive quality of the Negro's suffering for us all . . . . I meant [a character in the story] in an almost physical way to suggest the mystery of existence." _{coda}

There are other plans for conclusions, but this one works when nothing better comes to mind.

Introductions and Conclusions as Ways of Thinking

Some think schematic plans like these cramp creativity and fresh critical thinking; in fact, they encourage both:

- Preludes and codas force you to think about key concepts and how to encapsulate your problem in vivid language.
- Common ground forces you to think about what your readers believe that your problem will unsettle.
- A destabilizing condition forces you to think about the part of a troubling situation your solution will change.
- The question *So what?* forces you to think about costs that your readers are unwilling to pay and larger questions they want answered.

Some students fear that this pattern will become boring, but you can vary it so much that readers notice it only when they look for it.

IN THE READINGS . . .

Introductions

You can see in the readings that writers follow the pattern for introductions in so many ways that we notice the pattern only when we look for it. Here is an outline of the very long introduction to Pamela White's "'Drinking Age Has Simply Got to Go,' Say Campus Riots" (p. 446). The numbers refer to paragraphs.

[1] The young are always the first to recognize hypocrisy. . . . So it's no wonder that Boulder's young adults are incensed over the state's drinking laws. _{prelude}

[2] Last weekend marked the first anniversary of the University Hill "beer" riots. . . .

[3] Old people, like me, have responded . . . with scorn. . . .

[4] Our disgust with the violence and its emotional and financial costs is well-justified. Violence can only be justified in cases of self-defense, and, even then, it is a tragedy. Rioting should never be condoned. _{common ground}

[5] But when we casually dismiss the root of these young people's anger, we are missing the point. _{destabilizing condition} Their frustration has less to do with a desire to drink booze and more to do [with] social justice. _{consequence}

Paragraphs 6 through 12 elaborate the consequences.

[13] I suppose the nation could choose to. . . . _{rejected solution}

[14] It might also be a good idea to. . . . _{rejected solution}

[15] Still, the best solution might be the most difficult . . . we should abolish the drinking age completely. _{solution}

Problem-Posing Versus Problem-Solving Arguments

There is a kind of argument common in newspapers and magazines that addresses a problem not to solve it but only to show readers that a problem exists. Instead of building the introduction around a full statement of a destabilizing condition and costs, concluding a solution, the writer describes only the condition, making that the main claim. For example:

> Colleges are aware of the risks of binge drinking and its costs, _{common ground} but there has recently appeared a new threat, one that seems more benign, but could be worse. _{destabilizing condition} It is a drug called *Ecstasy*. Users report that it induces a sense of serenity and connection to others, but its long-term damage is only now beginning to emerge. _{end of introduction}
>
> First, . . . _{cost 1}

In the body of the argument, the writer goes on to prove the existence of the problem by describing its costs, turning each into a reason; he does not argue for a particular solution, only that some solution must be found.

These two outlines contrast the structure of problem-solving and problem-posing arguments.

<table>
<tr><td>

Problem-Solving Argument

Introduction
  (Prelude)
  (Common ground)
  Destabilizing condition
  Costs
  Gist of solution / **Claim**

Body
  (Warrants)
  Reasons supporting solution
  Acknowledgment / Response

Conclusion
  Solution / Claim restated

</td><td>

Problem-Posing Argument

Introduction
  (Prelude)
  (Common ground)
  Destabilizing condition / **Claim**

Body
  (Warrants)
  Costs as reasons supporting claim
  Acknowledgment / Response

Conclusion
  (Gesture toward a solution)

</td></tr>
</table>

◆ EXAMPLE

A Problem-Posing Argument

In this essay, the writer works harder to pose a problem than to solve it. He opens with common ground that he destabilizes by claiming that final papers he recently received were worse than those in past years because students did their research on the Internet.

Sometimes I look forward to the end-of-semester rush, when students' final papers come streaming into my office and mailbox. I could have hundreds of pages of original thought to read and evaluate. Once in a while, it is truly exciting, and brilliant words are typed across a page in response to a question I've asked the class to discuss. _{common ground}

But this past semester was different. I noticed a disturbing decline in both the quality of the writing and the originality of the thoughts expressed. What had happened since last fall? Did I ask worse questions? Were my students unusually lazy? No. My class had fallen victim to the latest easy way of writing a paper: doing their research on the World Wide Web. _{destabilizing condition}

[Author specifies the costs of that destabilizing condition, how they were worse.]

It's easy to spot a research paper that is based primarily on information collected from the Web. First, the bibliography cites no books, just articles or pointers to places in that virtual land somewhere off any map: http://www. _{reason 1} Then a strange preponderance of material in the bibliography is curiously out of date. . . . _{reason 2} Another clue is the beautiful pictures and graphs that are inserted neatly into the body of the student's text. They look impressive . . . but actually they often bear little relation to the precise subject of the paper. _{reason 3}

[Author gestures toward a solution at the end, but nothing in his argument supports it, so it is just a way to bring his argument to a close.]

I'd like [my students] to . . . ponder what it means to live in a world where some things get easier and easier so rapidly that we can hardly keep track of how easy they're getting, while other tasks remain as hard as ever—such as doing research and writing a good paper that teaches the writer something in the process. Knowledge does not emerge in a vacuum, but we do need silence and space for sustained thought. Next semester, I'm going to urge my students to turn off their glowing boxes and think, if only once in a while.

Source: From David Rothenberg, "How the Web Destroys the Quality of Students' Research Papers," *Chronicle of Higher Education,* August 15, 1997.

◆◆◆

WRITING PROCESS

Motivating Your Argument

READING AND RESEARCH

Use Problem Statements to Focus Your Reading

Read introductions carefully; they tell you what a writer thinks is important.

- The common ground provides context. What other writers does he respond to? What views does he claim his will replace? Literature reviews are particularly useful as bibliography for future reference.
- In a practical problem, the destabilizing condition states what the solution will change; in a conceptual one, the gap in knowledge or understanding that the answer will close.
- The costs or consequences tell you why the writer thinks the problem is important.
- The solution tells you how to read what follows.

If you don't find a problem in the introduction, look for it in the conclusion.

PREPARING AND PLANNING

Exploring a Topic to Find a Problem

Most classroom arguments are based on assigned readings, but when you have to write a research paper from scratch, you must find a problem on your own. Here are four steps to help you do that: (1) find a topic, (2) narrow it, (3) question it, (4) turn the best questions into a problem.

Step 1: Find a Topic That Interests You
If your assignment doesn't specify a topic, look for one that interests you. Worry later whether it will interest others.

For General Topics

1. If you are free to explore any interest, what would you like to know more about? Think about its history, economics, politics, and controversies.

2. What are politicians *not* talking about that they should? If your governor were to speak on campus, what issues should she address?

3. What public issues make you angry? Finish this sentence: *What bugs me about politics / teaching / movies / radio / TV / advertising is.* . . .

4. Browse a big magazine rack for a title that grabs your interest. Skim the article to see if you'd like to know more.

5. Join an e-mail group or visit a Web site on a subject that interests you. Look for debates, questions, archived messages, and related sites.

6. What courses will you take next term? If you can find a topic related to one of them, you get a head start on your work.

For Topics in a Particular Field of Study

1. Ask your teacher which issues discussed in class are hotly contested.

2. Browse through a recent encyclopedia in the field you are studying, looking for open questions.

3. Do an online search for course guides and syllabi for classes at other schools. What issues do they raise? Do they mention controversies you can pursue?

4. Ask a teacher or librarian for journals that review the year's work in your field.

We cannot exaggerate how important it is to find a topic that will hold your interest. If it bores you, you will surely bore your reader.

Step 2: Turn Your General Topic into a Specific One

A general topic is like an entry in an encyclopedia:

AIDS	Balance of trade	Jefferson-Hemings debate
Homelessness	Evolution of birds	Campaign finance reform

Too often, inexperienced writers think that when they find a topic, they've found a problem. Not so. To find a problem, they must first turn their general topic into a specific one by adding relationships, connections, and qualities:

SIMPLE TOPIC	SPECIFIC TOPIC
Territorial behavior in ground squirrels	The **acquisition** of **territorial protection behavior** in young ground squirrels and its similarity to behavior of **human children**

SIMPLE TOPIC	SPECIFIC TOPIC
Calvinism in Lincoln's Gettysburg Address and other speeches	The **influence** of **Lincoln's Calvinist beliefs** about **destiny** on his **justification** for the need for **political and personal sacrifice** in the Gettysburg Address and other speeches

We realize you might be puzzled after reading these suggestions: *How can I add relationships and connections until I know something about the topic?* In truth, you can't. That's why it is hard to write a research paper in a course with no specialized content. You have to find a topic and read a lot about it, maybe aimlessly, before you can narrow it, much less find a question to answer.

Step 3: Question Your Topic

Once you narrow your topic, ask five kinds of questions about it. The first two break your topic into its parts so that you can see how it functions as a self-contained system of parts that relate to one another in different ways.

1. Identify the component concepts that constitute your specific topic. What are their parts and how do they relate to one another?

   What are the elements of Lincoln's Calvinist beliefs about destiny? Did one of them in particular cause him to believe sacrifice was necessary? How did the element of destiny relate to the elements of punishment? What are the elements of punishment? Of sacrifice?

2. Turn your topic into a narrative of a process. How did it begin and how does it end? What are its historical stages, its evolution?

   How did Lincoln's ideas about fate, punishment, and sacrifice change? How does the Gettysburg Address relate to earlier and later addresses? How did Calvin's ideas reach Lincoln? How does Lincoln relate his ideas to those of the founding fathers? How were his speeches influenced by traditional patterns of oratory?

The next two questions ask you to look at your topic as a part of a larger whole, related to other parts:

3. Every thing is part of some larger thing. Put your topic into a larger system. How does it relate to other parts of the system?

   Were Lincoln's beliefs part of a larger philosophy? Were his calls for sacrifice similar to those of others? How did his understanding of destiny fit into a general religious outlook?

4. Everything has a larger history. What came before? What comes after?

   What did those before Lincoln think about destiny? How have those after him thought about it? How have they thought about his ideas?

The final question evaluates qualitative aspects of your topic:

5. Everything has qualities. What are the qualities of your topic?

   Is Lincoln's use of these ideas effective? Traditional? Innovative? Mistaken? Cruel? Wise?

After you ask lots of questions, ignore the ones you can answer easily, because they are probably not worth pursuing. Focus on those that both interest and perplex you. Now ask each of those questions, and imagine someone asking in return *So what? What if you never answer that question? What would you do with the answer? If you can answer that question, what bigger question can you answer?* It will be a frustrating but invaluable exercise because it will help you focus on the significance of your question, and it's the significance of a question that determines its potential for turning into a good research problem.

Step 4: Turn Questions into a Problem

The more you know about a topic, the better you can turn your best questions into a problem. Here is a formula to help you do that. Fill in the blanks in each of the following three steps. These steps help you develop a practical problem:

1. I am working on the problem of . . .
2. in order to find out how to change . . .
   [So what if you don't?]
3. so that you / we / someone can avoid the cost / get the benefit from. . . .

For example:

1. **I am working on the problem of** traffic congestion after football games,
2. **in order to find out how to** move traffic more quickly,
   [So what if you don't?]
3. **so that** businesses will not suffer from traffic gridlock.

For a conceptual problem, you depend even more on questions, because they define what you do not know. *Why* and *how* questions are most useful:

1. I am working on the issue of . . .
2. in order to find out why / how / when / what . . .
   [So what if you don't find out?]
3. so that I can understand better why / how / what. . . .

For example:

1. **I am working on** the appeal that the Taj Mahal has in the West,
2. **because I want to find out why** Europeans think of it as the only master-piece of Indian architecture,
   [So what? What if you never find out?]
3. **so that I can understand better why** we misunderstand the art of other cultures by focusing on a few notable but not representative works.

Some of us cannot do that last step (. . . *so that I can understand better why* . . .) until we are close to the end of our work. If you are in the early stages of a research project, don't spend a lot of time trying to figure out what larger question you can answer. Work on the first question (. . . *in order to find out why* . . .). Have faith that once you answer that first question, you will discover how to answer the second one. It is usually late in the game that any of us sees the full significance of our work.

DRAFTING

The Language of Common Ground

If you have a problem imagining common ground, use one of these phrases to get you going:

> Most / many / some people have thought / believed. . . .
> At first glance, it might appear / seem that. . . .
> It is widely believed / reported / claimed / said. . . .
> X (some authority) has claimed / asserted / stated. . . .

Finish the sentence, then begin a new one with *but, however, in fact,* or some other signal that you will qualify what you just wrote. Or try this: Recall what *you* thought about your topic before you started your research. How has your thinking changed? Describe your original, uninformed beliefs in your common ground. Start with something like *It is easy to think. . . ,* complete it with what you thought before, then go on with a *but* or *however* to destabilize it with what you know now. You can develop a repertoire of moves to state common ground by regularly skimming the first few paragraphs of editorials and articles in magazines, journals, and newspapers.

REVISING

Test Your Introduction and Conclusion

Once you finish a first draft, revisit your introduction to make sure it fully states your problem and accurately predicts the key concepts in your argument. Ask these questions:

1. If you have a prelude, does it introduce themes that you develop through the rest of the argument?
2. Does your common ground mention those themes? Does it state something readers believe and that you can correct?
3. Does the destabilizing condition contradict or qualify that common ground?
4. Do your costs or consequences answer the question *So what?*
5. (a) Does your introduction conclude with the solution to your problem or the answer to your question? That is, does it conclude with your main claim?

   (b) If you withhold your main claim until the conclusion, does your introduction end with a sentence that uses its key concepts?

Now check your conclusion:

1. Does the main claim there restate, complement, or at least not contradict the end of your introduction?
2. Have you suggested the significance of your main claim? In a pinch, restate the costs from the introduction as benefits.

Check for Common Themes in the Body of Your Argument

Once you are sure that the concepts in your introduction and conclusions cohere, test whether you have kept your readers on track by repeating those concepts through the body of your argument:

1. Find the sentences at the end of the introduction and beginning of your conclusion that promise, state, or restate your main claim. Circle three or four main concepts in them, especially those that you contributed, that were not in the language of your assignment.
2. In the body of your argument, circle words you circled in (1).
3. Underline words in the body that closely relate to those you circled.

Now scan your argument:

1. If you have neither circled nor underlined many words in the body, you may have gotten off track.
2. If in the body you circled few words but underlined many different ones, change some of the underlined words to words you circled.
3. If words appear frequently in the body but not in the introduction or conclusion, revise your introduction and conclusion so that they do.

The point is to ensure that readers think your argument hangs together around a few key concepts announced in your introduction, developed in your body, and tied up in your conclusion.

Build a Title Out of Your Key Concepts

Your title should preview the key concepts in your argument, so build it from words that you circled in your introduction and conclusion. We suggest a title consisting of two parts, separated by a colon. Such titles may feel stiff, but they give you two chances to tell your reader what to expect. For example, the *least* useful title for that Flannery O'Connor paper (pp. 89–90), would be this:

Flannery O'Connor's Attitudes toward Race

Readers would get more from a title built out of key words:

Flannery O'Connor's Critique of Our Modern Spiritual Crisis:
Racial Suffering as Spiritual Redemption

If you are working in a field that encourages section headings, create one-line headings for each section based on words in the main point of that section.

WORKING COLLABORATIVELY

Ask *So What?*

Besides providing a fresh eye for one another's papers, your group should routinely work through the checklists in the Writing Process sections. The most important question to keep asking is *So what? What is the significance of your problem? Why should readers care about your answer? What are the consequences to them of answering it? What cost do they pay if you don't? How do they benefit if you do?* At first you may feel rude asking such questions, and you may be annoyed when asked them. But if you ask early, often, and amiably, you'll get used to it.

INQUIRIES

REFLECTIONS

1. Pure researchers defend their work by arguing that without it we would still be in the Dark Ages. Does that seem a reasonable defense? Without tangible consequences to judge by, how do you know when pure research is pointless and wasteful or worth the effort? For example, one researcher dug up the body of Jesse James to see whether he was actually shot in the back, as legends say. Is it worth disturbing the dead to find that out? Can you think of any good reason to dig up someone who died a century ago?

2. The question of whose children are whose is but one of many historical questions that can now be answered with scientific tests. In the Sally Hemings–Thomas Jefferson case, the test was performed on tissue from Hemings's youngest son, Eston, and five acknowledged descendants of Jefferson. But what if it would have been necessary to exhume Jefferson's body to conduct the test? If the decision was yours, would you give permission to exhume Jefferson to obtain a sample for scientific testing? Should his heirs have a say? What if Jefferson were not a national hero, but an ordinary person?

3. A skeleton was found in Washington State that may predate even the Native Americans who settled in the area and is said to have features of Caucasians. Native Americans in the area want to rebury the skeleton as one of their ancestors just as it is; the National Park Service wants to test the skeleton, claiming it might not be a Native American ancestor and, under any circumstances, is so unusual that it deserves further study. How should we settle this kind of question? On the one side are the religious beliefs of Native Americans, on the other scientific interest in a skeleton that could rewrite the prehistory of America. Native Americans frame this

matter as a practical problem, the National Park Service as a conceptual one. How would you decide what kind of problem it should be?

4. Some scholars argue that all knowledge is worth having, no matter how esoteric. Here are two things you do not know: (a) How many hairs were on Abraham Lincoln's head when he was assassinated? (b) What was John Wilkes Booth thinking about the moment he shot him? If you could know only one or the other, which would you choose? How would you justify your choice? What would you say to someone who said they are equally unimportant, so it really doesn't matter?

5. Some cultures avoid questioning established knowledge and beliefs. What do you make of a society that does not value new knowledge? Is it appropriate to make a value judgment about such societies? Is it possible to want to know too much? Are there some things we should not know?

6. We talked about ways to motivate readers to care about your problem by getting them to care about its costs. But every cost can be restated as an opportunity to gain a benefit:

    Bingeing crosses the line from good times to reckless behavior. If it cannot be controlled, it will kill and injure still more students. _{cost}

    Bingeing crosses the line from good times to reckless behavior. If it can be controlled, we can save the lives of many students. _{benefit}

    What difference does it make whether you state consequences as a cost or as a possible benefit? Which do you think motivates readers more? (Try a thought experiment: When would you be more likely to risk going into a busy street to retrieve a twenty dollar bill—when the bill happens to blow past you or when it falls out of your pocket?)

TASKS

7. Pick a practical problem that affects you right now—crowding in the dorms, difficulties registering for classes, over-large classes, lack of Internet access, etc. List everyone who could conceivably help you solve it—friends, roommates, parents, teachers, school officials, etc. Then list the costs that might motivate each of them to act to solve the problem. Don't focus on the costs your problem exacts on you, but on those it exacts on them.

8. The film *Contact* is, among other things, a parable written by a scientist about the value of pure research. Watch the film with friends, if possible. How do you respond to its defense of pure research? What do your friends think? Is it reasonable for the movie to portray the National Science Advisor who is skeptical of pure research as a villain? What do you think of the way the movie uses the romance between the two main characters to contrast the scientist's faith in research with the religious leader's faith in God? What about the industrialist's claim that he funds pure research to "give something back" to humanity?

9. Here are two introductions that address the same issue. Explain why one poses a problem and the other doesn't.

   A. In the last few years, children have been taught to read by two methods. Some have been taught to read by the phonics method, in which children sound out words they don't know, letter by letter, until they can pronounce the word. Then if they don't know the meaning, they look it up in a dictionary. Others have been taught to read by the "whole word" method, in which they guess at the meaning of a word from its context. These two methods are common today, and each has its adherents.

   B. School boards have been debating whether to teach reading by the phonics method, in which children sound out letters, or by the "whole word" method, in which they try to understand the meaning of a word from its context. Each side has accused the other not only of failing to teach children to read effectively, but of inculcating children with their ideological beliefs. The phonics side claims that "whole word" teachers undermine mental discipline in favor of sloppy guessing, while the "whole word" side accuses the phonics teachers of suppressing children's intellectual and imaginative powers. If our schools make the wrong choice, we can expect that our children will suffer in ways that go beyond reading ability. The best method, though, is as we might expect: some of both.

10. Look over papers you have written in other classes. Did they address practical or conceptual problems? Look especially at papers written in your humanities classes. Did you have a problem at all?

PROJECTS

11. You probably think of poetry, drama, and fiction as being far from argument. Nevertheless, pick a favorite poem, story, novel, or play, and imagine that the author wrote it as the solution to a conceptual problem. Write an argument claiming that your poem, story, or play solves that problem. (This is easier with satire and other forms that seek to teach readers lessons.) Be sure not to confuse the problem that the characters in the story have with the problem that the author wanted the story to solve in the real world.

12. Look at the introductions to three editorials or editorial columns in your local newspaper and analyze how they formulate problems and motivate readers.

 FOCUS ON WRITING

1

Context.   Today, politicians increasingly depend on consultants and pollsters to decide what positions to take on controversial issues. Rather than rely on their own sense of right and wrong, they want to know how the voters will react to one decision or another.

Scenario.   You have an internship in the campaign office of a local candidate for Congress. Your candidate intends to position himself as a new kind of politician who listens to the people rather than to the pollsters and political consultants. Your boss has just read an editorial in the student newspaper complaining that politicians always talk about the same problems but never address the ones that matter most to people. Since his district includes the university, he wants you to talk to some of your classmates and identify problems that students think politicians should talk about but do not.

Task 1.   Survey students to find out what problems they think politicians, especially local ones, should talk about but do not. When you have a list of ten or so items, group them into three or four categories. Write a report to your boss, briefly outlining the four or five kinds of problems students think are important. Be sure to explain why they count as problems and what costs students think they are paying. Your class might pool its results.

Task 2.   Form two-partner teams in which one person lives on campus and one lives at home. The on-campus partner should survey students on campus (as in Task 1). The off-campus partner should survey people in his or her neighborhood. When each of you has listed ten or so problems, group them into four or five categories. Write a brief report to your boss outlining the difference between students' perceptions of important problems and those of the local community. Be sure to focus on costs. Again, your class might pool its results.

Task 3.   Decide what you think is the most important problem your candidate should address. Write a report in which you identify the problem and explain why it is important, why the voting public will care about it, and why your boss will benefit by talking about it. Be sure to focus on costs.

$$\boxed{2}$$

Context.   Some students object to required courses that have no obvious relevance to their careers. Colleges praise the value of a "liberal education," preparing students to think critically, to expand intellectual horizons, and so on, but many students look upon this as propaganda. What would count as evidence that such courses do what supporters claim they do? One kind of evidence might be self-reports of those now working in a profession. How do they feel about the liberal arts courses they took? If they did not take any such courses, do they regret it?

Scenario.   You have been asked to write a feature article for your school newspaper that argues for or against requiring students to take liberal arts courses.

Task.   Interview a few people who graduated from college at least three years ago. Choose those whose judgment you trust. Report their views about taking courses that had no direct relevance to their work today. Do they wish they had taken more? Do they wish they had not bothered with any? This is a project where collaborative work will be particularly useful, because if each member of the group can talk to one or two people, the whole group can share the evidence.

$$\boxed{3}$$

Context.   Some critics think we are becoming a "nanny state" where the federal government wants to guard us from every risk of modern life. And so we have laws banning smoking, requiring motorcycle helmets and seat belts, and so on. Some also claim that people are becoming interested in extreme sports such as skateboarding, rock climbing, and mountain biking because they reject the risk-free world that the nanny state seems to create. Those who court risk argue that it gives life an edge that humdrum existence lacks, and it is no one's business but their own whether they risk their own lives. Others say people can do what they want, only as long as they alone pay the price if the worst happens. This means that you can bike without a helmet as long as no one else pays when you are injured—no rescue teams or paramedics supported by tax dollars, no disability, no insurance. If we all have to share in the costs associated with your risky behavior, then you do not have a right to take those risks. Why should we (they say) pay for the consequences of your recklessness?

Scenario.   You have an internship in the Washington office of your local member of the House. Congress is considering a law regulating rock climbing, hang gliding, mountain biking, skateboarding, roller blading, sky diving, and all other "sports involving inordinate risk" on federal property or sponsored by organizations receiving federal funds. According to the proposed law, you must get a license to do any of those things, and to get a license you must demonstrate that you have taken a certified safety course, that you own and use appropriate safety equipment, and that you are insured against injury and death.

Task.   Your boss wants a "position paper" that summarizes the issues raised by this law. She doesn't want you to tell her how to vote. In fact, she is the kind of person who gets bent out of shape when anyone tells her what to think. So you have to lay out the problem in a way that she sees as entirely objective and neutral. All she wants is three or four pages to help her understand the problem.

RESEARCH PROJECT

For the next five chapters, we will include writing assignments for an ongoing research project. Each step in the project will show you how to use the material in that chapter to produce a substantial research paper. If you have one due at the end of the semester, start now; you'll do a better job if you don't rush. If you have only a few weeks to devote to your project, follow these steps but more quickly. We assume that during these weeks you are researching your topic.

Scenario.   You have just begun a class on a subject you have always wanted to study: the anthropology of the South Seas, the sociology of sport, the history of the blues, the economics of the fashion industry, the automobile in American popular culture—whatever strikes your fancy. Your teacher conducts the class as a seminar: each student selects an aspect of the topic, researches it, and presents a research paper to the class. Everyone is as interested in the topic as you are, so assume that your imagined classmates can't read enough about it.

Task 1.   Your first task is to interest your teacher and classmates in your problem. Using the four steps presented in "Exploring a Topic to Find a Problem," (p. 96), select a general topic, and then narrow it to a specific problem. Focus on *how* and *why* questions; avoid those that ask for simple yes / no answers. Write a one-page proposal that states your research question / problem and explains how it relates to the general topic of your imagined class and why your classmates should care about it. If the subject matter is new to you, you will have to do some reading to discover why others are (or should be) interested in it and what information is available.

Task 2.   Exchange preliminary proposals with two or three classmates. Make brief written notes on your reactions, comments, and suggestions; give the notes to the writer, but also explain them in person. After reading your classmates' notes, sketch a preliminary introduction and conclusion for your proposed paper. At this point, you can only guess how you will answer your question, but you should be able to sketch a working version of the common ground, destabilizing condition, and consequences.

SAMPLE ESSAYS

Here are the introductions to the two essays presented in Chapter 2 (you can review the essays on pp. 66–69):

Student Privacy and Drinking

1   University President, Albert Tanaki, recently proposed that the university should notify parents whenever a student is caught drinking before the age of twenty-one. Tanaki says this will help prevent students from binge drinking. This is wrong because students have rights to privacy and the university should
5   respect them. Tanaki also fails to realize that present-day student life is surrounded by alcohol.

Binge Drinking and Parental Notification: Students' Rights to Privacy or Parents' Right to Know?

1   When University President Albert Tanaki announced that he wanted to notify parents when students under twenty-one were caught drinking by university

police, there was an uproar among students and faculty. The Student Council passed a resolution the next day stating that "any invasion of student privacy is
5 wrong." Council Chair Susan Ford wrote in the *Student Daily*, " This is morally wrong, legally wrong, and besides it won't work." It is understandable why students have gotten so upset over Tanaki's proposal. But by thinking only about how the proposal impacts on their rights, students and the faculty who have
10 come out in support of them have forgotten about the rights of their parents.

Task 1. Pick out the elements of each introduction. In which sentences does the writer state the following:

- Common ground
- Destabilizing condition
- Costs or consequences
- Solution or promise of solution

If you can't find a sentence that explicitly states one of the elements, indicate which sentence comes closest to stating it. Then try to formulate an explicit statement of it for yourself.

Task 2. Review both essays (pp. 66–69). Identify the main claim in each. Is it a solution to the problem? Is it a viable solution?

Task 3. Using your own words, reformulate the problem for each essay. Restate the problem or find a new one so that you state a problem that is solved by the main claim of the paper. State each part of the problem separately:

Destabilizing condition:
Cost or consequences:
Solution / main claim:

Task 4. Write a new introduction for one or both essays. Your introduction should include all four elements: prelude, common ground, problem, claim. It should also give readers a rich cognitive framework for the essay. Make sure that your statement of the problem and solution introduce the main themes repeated through the rest of the essay.

IN A NUTSHELL

About Your Argument . . .

We make arguments to solve two kinds of problems, practical and conceptual. Both kinds of problems have the same structure:

> **Problem = Destabilizing condition + Cost/Consequence**

But what goes into that structure is different. For a practical problem:

- The destabilizing condition can be, literally, any situation, condition, event at all, so long as it has a cost.
- The cost answers the question *So what?* The answer always points to some form of unhappiness, pain, loss, distress—something that you and your readers want to avoid.

For a purely conceptual problem:

- The destabilizing condition is always some gap in knowledge or lack of understanding.
- The consequence of that gap answers the question *So what?* The answer always points to another gap in knowledge or lack of understanding, but one that is more significant, more consequential than the first.

Introductions to conceptual and practical problems have up to five elements:

- An opening prelude that offers an anecdote, fact, or quotation that forecasts or encapsulates the problem.
- Common ground or some belief or idea that your audience holds that is not quite right, or is at least incomplete.
- Your problem, which consists of two parts:

Part 1: A destabilizing condition

Part 2: A cost or consequence of that condition.

- The gist of your solution, or at least a sentence introducing some of the key concepts that the rest of the argument will use in getting to the solution.

Many introductions do not have all of these elements. Preludes are more common in journalistic or popular writing, less so in academic or professional writing. If the problem is well-known and on readers' minds, you don't need common ground. In some cases, the cost of the problem is so obvious that it's not necessary to state it.

You can map your conclusion onto your introduction:

- Recapitulate your main claim (or express it for the first time).
- Describe why your claim is significant.
- Add what is yet to be done, how your argument is incomplete.
- Close with a coda that echoes the prelude.

. . . and About Writing It

Your first job is to transform your topic into a problem.

- Narrow your topic by adding to it as many qualifiers and modifiers as you can.

- Ask questions about its relations to other things, about its own history, about its role in a larger history, and about its qualities.
- Focus on your problem by running through the following formula every so often.

For a practical problem:

1. I am working on the problem of . . .
2. in order to find out how to change . . .
   [So what if you don't?]
3. so that you / we / someone can avoid / get the cost / benefit from. . . .

For a conceptual problem:

1. I am working on the issue of . . .
2. in order to find out why / how / when /what . . .
   [So what if you don't find out?]
3. so that I can understand better why / how / what. . . .

Be sure that throughout your introduction, but particularly in the last couple of sentences, you use concepts central to the rest of your argument. Do this:

- Circle the key words in your introduction and conclusion.
- In the body of your argument, underline those words or words related to them. Look for both synonyms and homonyms.

If you underline only a few words in the body of your argument, you may have gotten off track. Even if you haven't, your readers will think so. Insert those circled words and words related to them. If you can't do that easily, you have to start over. Now do the same thing for each major section.

Finally, create a title out of the most important words you have circled.

PART II

Developing Your Argument

In Part II, we explain in detail the five elements that make up the substance of an argument and the kind of thinking you need to create them.

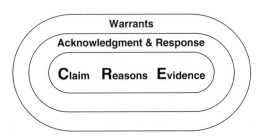

In Chapters 4 through 6, we analyze the core of every argument: its claim and support, in the form of reasons backed by evidence. Since you cannot create an effective argument if you do not think critically about your own ideas, in these chapters we show you how to use your readers' questions, both real and imagined, to ensure that you do in fact have sound reasons and reliable evidence to support your claim.

- In Chapter 4, we discuss what readers will count as a reasonable and thoughtful claim. We show you how to formulate a claim that your readers will judge to be significant, thoughtfully complex, and critically tested.

- In Chapter 5, we show you how to support a claim with reasons and evidence. We distinguish between reasons and evidence and then make a finer distinction between evidence "itself" and what we actually offer in most arguments, which is not evidence at all, but reports of it.

- In Chapter 6, we explain how to report evidence so that readers can recognize not only why they should accept the evidence as reliable but also how that evidence supports its reason.

In Chapters 7 and 8, we turn to the parts of argument that bring your ideas into connection with those of your readers. Although you create the core of an argument out of your answers to readers' questions, those answers do not explicitly address your readers' own views and ideas. So in these chapters we show you how to bring readers more directly into your argument its the last two parts: (1) acknowledgment and response and (2) warrants.

- In Chapter 7, we discuss how to acknowledge and respond to your readers' points of view. We show why you must imagine your readers asking questions, raising objections, and offering alternatives and why you must respond to them.

- In Chapter 8, we discuss an element that has vexed students of argumentation for millennia. Some call it a *premise* or *assumption;* we call it a *warrant.* Warrants state the principles of reasoning that you and your readers must share for them to accept your argument as logical.

CHAPTER 4

The Core of Your Argument: Finding and Stating a Claim

In this chapter, we look in detail at your main claim, the solution to your problem, the point that your argument supports. We show you how to develop a claim that readers will judge to be thoughtful and that can guide you through the process of drafting the rest of your argument.

At the heart of every argument is its main claim, the point you want to support, the solution to the problem that caused you to make an argument in the first place (some teachers call it your *thesis*). *Claim*, though, has two meanings: When you claim *that* something is so, you also make a claim *on* your readers' time to consider what you've written in support of it. You justify that second claim only when you offer them something in return for their reading. That's why we stress that a claim is not just a statement that you want readers to agree with, but a plausible solution to a problem that you think they should care about.

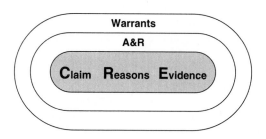

The tough part, of course, can be finding that solution. Sometimes you don't have to search far. If you believe human cloning is wrong, you know where you stand on the issue. But on other issues, you may have no ready answer: Should insurers do genetic screening for a tendency toward alcoholism? How have TV sitcoms changed our attitudes toward families in the last fifty years? We can't answer such questions for you, but we can tell you how to search for answers as experienced problem solvers and careful, critical thinkers do. We will also suggest ways to express the answers you find in a way that readers judge to be thoughtful.

Exploring Claims Without Rushing to Judgment

Whatever strategies you follow to solve your problem, you cannot wait until you have looked at all the evidence before you come up with a solution to test. Experienced problem solvers don't wait. They size up a problem quickly, then spin off a few tentative solutions that roughly fit the data they started with. Then they let those tentative solutions guide their search for more data, using those new data to test each hypothesis and, if one fits, to support it. Without those initial hypotheses, they would not know what evidence to look for or how to evaluate what they found.

But the most expert problem solvers know better than to accept their first ideas uncritically. They treat their initial hypotheses as merely "working hypotheses," *and they hold them lightly*. They do not give up their deepest convictions and beliefs easily, but neither do they embrace them so closely that they cannot step back to examine them critically, perhaps even to see past them to new, still deeper truths.

Uncritical problem solvers also jump to a quick solution, but then they cling to it, so that their first thought becomes their last. They may use that idea to guide further research, but only to confirm what they already believe. For them, research does not open up thinking but shuts it down. They don't make that mistake intentionally; it's just that all our human minds are built to make quick judgments that reflect what we want to be true, usually what we already believe. It's a habit of mind that, in the short run, helps us manage crises. But it's risky when a lot rides on making the right decision for the long run.

Think, for example, of those who propose the same solution to every problem. The next time gun-toting students shoot up a school, no matter what the facts are, some will instantly point to the too easy availability of guns, others to poor family values, still others to violent movies and video games. The business world has a maxim about such people: *To a person with a hammer, every problem is a nail*. If profits are falling, the ad manager thinks the solution is more advertising; the operations manager thinks it is to modernize the plant; the personnel manager wants to invest in recruiting and training. Each might be partly right, but when they insist on their pet solution to the exclusion of others, they risk missing the best one, because all they see is the nail that fits their particular hammer.

Admittedly, our advice to think critically about your own ideas is hard to follow, but here it is: Formulate a few tentative solutions to a problem sooner rather than later, but hold them lightly as you critically test them against the evidence. Resist what most uncritical thinkers do: Jump to a simple conclusion that they cannot give up. You cannot change human nature, but you can guard against a tendency toward hasty, superficial judgments by stepping back to think critically: Ask the toughest questions you can imagine others might ask; consider *all* the evidence you can find, especially what doesn't fit your ideas; reason through all the steps of your logic; and especially talk things over with others who disagree. In short, be as critical of your own ideas as you are about the ideas of others.

What Kind of Claim Does Your Problem Require?

In the previous chapter, we discussed how a well-framed problem motivates readers to read. You motivate them further when you state at the end of your introduction a solution that is not self-evidently true, but seems clear, plausible, and thoughtful. As we said, we can't help you find the best claim; that requires research and testing, and every field has its own way of doing that. But we can suggest ways to evaluate, develop, and state your best claim so that your readers will at least give it a fair hearing.

Is Your Claim Practical or Conceptual?

Above all, you need to decide early whether you can solve your problem by getting readers to understand or to act, because we make arguments about conceptual and practical problems differently. The solution to a conceptual problem asks readers only to *understand* or *believe* something, as this claim does:

> Not only do students whose first language is not English do better in class when they receive tutorial help, but in the long run they require less faculty time.

The solution to a practical problem asks readers not only to understand but to *do* something (or endorse an action). Such claims are typically built on a *should* or *must*:

> State U. should increase the budget for tutorial help for students whose first language is not English.

If you trust readers to read between the lines, you can hope they will infer your solution, as we can from this claim:

> Since students whose first language is not English require less faculty time when they also receive tutorial help, State U. could save money by increasing the budget for tutors.

Most of us, though, think readers are able to infer more than they actually do. So when in doubt, *explicitly* state what you expect of them: to understand something, with no intent that they act, or to perform (or at least support) an action.

When you can, state your claims affirmatively. For practical problems especially, a negative solution does not suggest a plan of action; a positive one does. Compare:

> The university should stop using its teaching evaluation form because it does not reveal students' feelings about learning.

> The university should develop a new teaching evaluation form that tells faculty whether their students think they are learning useful skills.

If you cannot find a plausible solution and your assignment allows it, redefine the problem: break the problem into parts, one of which you might be able to solve, or at least clarify. Suppose you start with the conceptual problem of how TV sitcom families have changed in the last fifty years, but decide that question is too large for you to answer in a short paper. You can narrow it: How have the families changed in the highest-rated sitcoms in the first year of every decade since 1950? Or, suppose Elena thinks she cannot solve the problem of the university's failure to provide international students with enough help in English. She might instead address a smaller problem: international students do not know where to find the help that is available. You can also redefine a practical problem as a conceptual one by identifying questions whose answers will eventually help solve the practical problem.

Values Claims

Claims that assert something is right or wrong, good or bad, are often called "values" claims. Some so-called values claims are covert practical claims. They imply that readers should do something to be on the side of what they say is right or good, without stating exactly what. For example, in a *Washington Times* newspaper column, restaurant owner Richard Berman complains about extremist food recommendations, such as replacing the Thanksgiving turkey with turkey-shaped tofu. His main point states values that he implies readers should act on:

> In an effort to change American eating habits to conform to their puritanical vision, groups such as the Center for Science in the Public Interest, the Vegetarian Society, and People for the Ethical Treatment of Animals are perverting the way Americans look at food.[a]

By not saying what we should do about those arguments—ignore extreme claims, cook a traditional Thanksgiving turkey, or eat in a restaurant—he relieves himself of the obligation to defend any solution.

On the other hand, a values claim is conceptual when it implies only that we should approve or disapprove, and nothing more:

> As president, John Kennedy was inspirational, but as a person, he was sexually corrupt.

That claim asks us only to disapprove of Kennedy's character. While it might imply, *Don't be like him!*, we don't have to act to solve the conceptual problem posed by the writer: *You might be wrong about what you think of John Kennedy and therefore about the role of models in political life.* That problem is solved by our negative judgment alone.

Whether you assert a values claim that is practical or conceptual, you still have to make a supporting argument with reasons, based on evidence, governed by warrants. You still have to acknowledge and respond to other views. Values claims can be tricky, however, because they assume beliefs, definitions, and values that transcend the particular issue. We will agree that Kennedy was corrupt only if we already hold moral principles that a writer can appeal to. If not, a writer would have to state those principles, and then convince us that they are true.

[a] *Source:* "Turkey Police, Beware," *Washington Times,* November 26, 1998, p. A19.

How Strongly Do You Want Readers to Accept Your Claim?

Some writers think that the agreement their arguments deserve is all-or-nothing, win-or-lose, agree-or-die. But that's shortsighted. You might not need readers to accept a big claim about a big problem if you can persuade them to accept a modest one about part of it. For example, Elena might think her college devotes too few resources to helping international students with their English, but she also knows it is unlikely to spend lots of money on a new language center. If, however, she can get some administrator just to *consider* increasing the budget for language tutors, she will achieve something valuable, even if it is only a small step toward her larger goal. Partial success is rarely total failure.

So as you formulate a claim, think how you want readers to take it. What do you want them to do?

- **Respect** your reasons for making your claim and, by extension, respect you.
- **Approve** of your claim and the argument supporting it.
- **Publicly endorse** your claim as worth consideration.
- **Believe** in your claim and in your argument supporting it.
- **Act** as you propose, or support someone else's action.

Only the last two count as complete success for those who see argument as a win-or-lose proposition. But those who do must fail more often than they succeed, because few arguments completely convince anybody of anything. Your argument is a total failure only when your readers scoff not only at it, but at you, rejecting both as not worth their time, much less their respect.

Giving Readers an Alternative Solution

If you fear your readers might reject a too-costly solution, offer the solution to part of the problem that readers can implement. One good strategy is to make the too-costly solution your main claim, but mention the alternative solution in an acknowledgment and response: acknowledge the value of the lesser solution, but respond that your solution is better. As you explicitly support your preferred solution, you implicitly support the alternative:

> Although more English language tutors would provide some immediate help, _{acknowledgement / implicitly supported alternative solution} only a Center for English Language Instruction will solve the problem entirely. _{response / explicitly supported solution} More tutors would help students with assignments and reduce faculty time spent on minor issues of grammar. But without an infrastructure to support them, international students will not improve their English enough to do well without help from tutors. _{support for response}

Explicitly, this is an argument for building a language center; implicitly it shows the value of increasing the number of tutors.

What Counts as a Claim Worth Considering?

A claim will motivate readers to read the argument supporting it only if it seems on its face worth considering. For example, it makes little sense to make an argument supporting a claim either that the earth is round or that it's flat. Since no one questions the shape of the earth, no one would bother to read an argument for either claim. So once you have a claim you think is worth your time supporting, ask three questions to determine whether your readers will think it worth their time reading.

1. Can Your Claim Be Contested?

Even if they have no settled beliefs about a topic, critical readers will—or should—adopt an amiably skeptical attitude: *Well, that's interesting, but let's see your support.* You are in trouble if instead they think, *That's obvious!* A claim is worth considering only if readers might *contest* it. You have no good reason to ask for their time to read your supporting argument if they already believe your claim or are indifferent to it. For example, how would readers respond to claims like these?

> 1a. Education is important to our society.
>
> 2a. We should not ridicule how people look.
>
> 3a. I will summarize current views on the disappearance of frogs.

Can you imagine a reader thinking, *If that's true, I'll have to change my mind about education/ridicule/frogs?* Not likely. Those claims don't need an argument, because no one would contest them.

Here's a quick way to assess whether a claim is contestable (another way of saying significant): Revise it into its negative form (or revise a negative claim into its affirmative). Then assess whether it still seems plausible or significant.

> 1b. Education is **not** important to our society.
>
> 2b. We **should** ridicule how people look.
>
> 3b. I will **not** summarize current views on the disappearance of frogs.

Most readers would judge claims (1b) and (2b) to be self-evidently implausible, so those claims fail the test. No one will question a claim if no one believes its opposite. The negative claim (3b), on the other hand, seems trivial. If the negative is trivial, then most readers would judge the affirmative to be trivial too. In none of these cases is the claim worth supporting, because no one would contest any of them.

We must note, however, that human thought has been revolutionized when someone has proved false a claim that at the time seemed self-evidently true:

> The sun does **not** go around the earth.
>
> We do **not** consist of solid matter.

We cannot rule out as forever false the claim that education is not important (some groups in fact believe it). You would make your reputation if you could convince us of that, but it would take a powerful argument to do so.

2. Can Your Claim Be Proved Wrong?

At least in principle, state your claims so that they can be proved wrong (the technical term is *disconfirmed*). That may seem odd. Don't we make claims we can prove, not ones our readers can *disprove*? In fact, careful arguers make claims only when they believe that *at least in principle* someone might find evidence that would prove a claim right or wrong and are willing to consider that evidence.

For example, suppose a person wants to argue that ghosts exist. Imagine someone asks that person,

> What would it take to convince you that they don't?

And that person responds,

> There is no evidence that could prove they exist one way or the other, so no conceivable argument or evidence could convince me that ghosts do not exist, because I just know in my heart they do and *nothing* can prove that souls do not survive death.

Both parties might learn something about the other from an exchange of views, but there can be no rational argument if a claim is not subject to evidence. If an arguer believes that no evidence can disprove his claim, not even in principle, then he gives us no role in his argument—not only can we not participate by engaging our own views, but we cannot even be rational judges of what he says. We can simply take him at his word, or, more likely, not.

We make arguments most productively when both parties embrace an essential characteristic of a critical thinking: they can both imagine being wrong; both see the issue in question as contingent, not settled, always open to question if new evidence comes along. That means all parties in an argument should agree to a first principle in the social contract of cooperative arguments: *Both reader and writer must be able to imagine that there could be evidence that might change their minds.*

Now that principle does not disparage belief in ghosts or anything else we can't prove. We are entitled to believe whatever we please, for any reason, good or bad, or for no reason at all (we might not be thinking critically, but that would be a private matter).

But when we make *public* claims about a private belief in order to answer some significant question or solve some difficult problem that we want others to take seriously, and we ask readers to *agree* with our claim, we must open our own minds to their arguments *against* our beliefs as much as we ask them to open their minds to our arguments for them.

3. Is Your Claim Reasonable on Its Face?

Once you have a claim that readers can contest and at least in principle disprove, you must start listening to that critical voice in the back of your mind asking questions your readers are likely to ask, questions like these:

- Is your solution **feasible?**

  Tanya is unlikely to get a hearing from the dean if she suggests that the problem of weak teaching could be solved by shifting half the athletic budget to a Teaching Resource Center. But the dean might listen if she suggested a small tax on research grants to subsidize one.

- Is your solution **ethical** (or **legal, proper, fair,** etc.)?

  Tanya would be instantly rejected if she proposed that the administration secretly monitor classes, but she might get a hearing if she suggested that faculty be encouraged to observe one another's teaching.

- Is your solution **prudent?** Might it create a problem worse than the one it solves?

  Tanya would have no chance of getting the dean to cut the salary of faculty with poor teaching evaluations because they would rebel. But he might consider merit raises to reward good teaching.

What Does a Thoughtful Claim Look Like?

At some point—sooner better than later—you have to get a hypothesis out of the dark comfort of your mind into the cold light of print. Only then can you ask, *Will this claim encourage readers to judge it—and me—as thoughtful?* Sad to say, we cannot teach you how to be thoughtful. We can only describe what encourages readers to think you might be. Compare these claims:

TV makes crime seem a bigger problem than it is.

Though violent crime has declined around the country, many believe it has increased in their own neighborhoods because night after night their local TV news shows open with graphic reports of murder and mayhem, making it seem that violence happens every day just outside their front door.

The second claim seems more interesting, because its verbal complexity reflects the complex situation it describes (and indirectly the mind that made it).

Now we are *not* asserting that a wordy claim must be better than a short concise one. Too many words can obscure issues, and a few well-chosen words can focus readers on what's important. But inexperienced writers commonly make claims that are too thin rather than too thick. So in what follows we will go overboard in encouraging you to make claims as detailed as you can, even too detailed. You can always revise them later. So take what follows as an exercise in exploratory thinking, not as a plan for drafting what you will actually submit to your readers.

Is Your Claim Conceptually Rich?

When your claims include more concepts, you give your readers and yourself more to work with. Compare these three claims:

> The **effects** of the Civil War are still **felt** today.
>
> The Civil War lives on in the **sunbelt axis** of the **federalist question.**
>
> The **ideological and social divisions** of the Civil War still **exert a historical influence** today on the **political discourse** of **North** and **South** (and the **West**), reflected in their **antithetical political theories** about the **relative scope** of **state** and **federal powers** and the **proper authority of government** over **free individuals.**

The first feels both thin and vague. It mentions unspecified *effects* that are *felt* in some general way. The second is specific, but still feels thin for readers unable to unpack the technical terms *sunbelt axis* and *federalist question.* The third expresses a richer set of concepts—in fact, too many for one claim, but remember we are exploring and developing claims, not writing final drafts yet.

A claim rich in concepts helps readers see the full implications of what you ask them to do or believe. A conceptually rich claim also helps you improve your argument in two ways:

- It obligates you to develop those concepts named in your argument.
- When readers see you return to them in the body of your argument, they are more likely to think your argument is coherent (it might help to review p. 101).

So when you think you have the makings of a good claim, add more concepts than you think necessary. (We show you steps for doing that in the Writing Process section below.) If you add too many, apply the Goldilocks rule to find a happy medium (not too many, not too few, but just right):

The **ideological divisions** of the Civil War still **shape** the **political discourse of North and South** today, reflected in their **antithetical theories** about **state** and **federal powers** and the **authority of government** over **individuals.**

Is Your Claim Logically Rich?

At the core of most claims is a simple proposition like this:

State U. should do something about rising tuition. _{claim}

That claim borders on simplistic: What does *do something* mean? We can make its language richer:

State U. should limit tuition increases to the rate of inflation. _{claim}

But we can also elaborate its logic in two ways:

1. Add a reason-clause beginning with *because* or *if,* or a phrase beginning with *by* or *in order to.*

Compare these two claims:

State U. should slow tuition increases to the rate of inflation. _{claim}

State U. could slow tuition increases to the rate of inflation _{claim} **if it reduced its administrative costs to the level of comparable universities,** _{reason 1} **and its faculty taught as much as faculty do at other state schools.** _{reason 2}

The first claim states a proposition that is logically thin. In the second, readers can see the gist of a solution in the *if*-clause and can thereby better anticipate the rest of the argument.

Note: Be aware that if the problem concerns not what is wrong but what causes it, your main claim may be in a *because*-clause. If the writer and reader agree State U should slow tuition increases, the main claim would involve the two causes for high tuition. You can avoid confusing readers by revising so that the two causes appear in a main clause:

State U. must slow tuition increases to the rate of inflation. **Its administrative costs are significantly higher than comparable universities,** _{claim 1} **and its faculty teaches less than other state schools.** _{claim 2}

2. Add a concession-clause beginning with *although, while,* or *even though* or a phrase beginning with *despite, regardless of,* or *notwithstanding.*

When you open with an *although*-clause, you acknowledge an alternative point of view. There are three common options:

• An alternative point of view contradicts your claim:

Although some argue that we must raise tuition to meet the rising costs of maintaining State U.'s physical plant and updating research facilities, _{acknowledgment of alternative conclusion} State U. could slow tuition increases to the rate of inflation because its administrative costs are significantly higher than comparable universities and its faculty teaches less than professors at other state schools.

• There is evidence that argues against your claim:

Although State U.'s administrative costs have not risen faster than inflation and it has hired no new faculty in three years, _{acknowledgment of contradictory evidence} State U. could slow tuition increases to the rate of inflation because its administrative costs are still significantly higher than comparable universities and its faculty teaches less than professors at other state schools.

• Something limits the scope of your claim:

Although college costs will always rise to reflect inflation, _{acknowledgment of limited scope of claim} State U. could slow tuition increases to the rate of inflation because its administrative costs are significantly higher than comparable universities and its faculty teaches less than professors at other state schools.

If your claim grows too long, divide it. Put a period after the *although-*clause and delete the *although*. Then begin the main claim with *but, however, even so, nevertheless,* etc. (It is *not* a grammatical error to begin a sentence with *but* or *however*.)

The costs of maintaining State U.'s physical plant are rising, and scientific advances require it to update research facilities continually. **However,** State U. could slow tuition to the rate of inflation because its administrative costs are significantly higher than comparable universities and its faculty teaches less than professors at other state schools.

Is Your Claim Appropriately Qualified?

Critical thinkers can be confident in their judgment, because they put their own ideas to the test. But even so, they know that few things in this world are 100 percent certain, unqualifiedly true. And so they rarely make claims with flat-footed certainty, and they distrust those who do. So when you state your main claim, make it judiciously modest, unlike this one:

State U. would stop tuition increases if it eliminated administrative waste and required faculty to teach more classes.

Thoughtful readers will wonder, *How can you be so sure? How can the problem be so simple?* Contrast that flat-footed certainty with this more modest, more nuanced claim:

State U. **might be able** to **slow** its rates of tuition increases, if it **could reduce** administrative costs and get **more** of its faculty to teach **more** classes.

(You can find vocabulary for qualifying in the Writing Process section below.)

Of course, if you overqualify, you give readers reason to doubt your confidence. It's a balancing act. Compare these claims:

1. Research proves that people with a gun at home **will** use it to kill themselves or a family member rather than to protect themselves from intruders.

2. **Some recent** research **seems** to **suggest** there **may** be a **possible risk** that **some** people with a gun at home **could** be **more prone** to use it to kill

themselves or a family member rather than to protect themselves from **potential** intruders.

3. **Recent** research **suggests** that people with a gun at home **more often** use it to kill themselves or a family member than to protect themselves from intruders.

Most academic and professional readers would reject (1) as too absolute and (2) as wishy-washy, but find (3) closer to the confidently temperate stance they trust. Of course, it comes closest to that Goldilocks rule: not too certain, not too uncertain, maybe not just right, but closer than the first two.

Certainty in Eighteenth-Century Politics and Twentieth-Century Science

Those who think that hedging is mealymouthed might note Benjamin Franklin's account of how he deliberately created his ethos of judicious moderation by speaking

> . . . in terms of modest diffidence, never using when I advance anything that may possibly be disputed, the words *certainly, undoubtedly,* or any others that gave the air of positiveness to an opinion; but rather say, *I conceive,* or *I apprehend a Thing to be so* or *so It appears as to me,* or *I should think it so* or *so for such and such Reasons,* or *I imagine it to be so,* or *it is so if I am not mistaken.* This habit I believe has been of great advantage to me . . . To this habit (after my character of integrity) I think it principally owing that I had early so much weight with my fellow citizens when I proposed new institutions or alterations in the old, and so much influence in public councils when I became a member.

That advice is relevant today. Among those who make arguments for a living, scientists may distrust certainty the most because they know how fast scientific truths can change. You see this not only in the way they test claims, but in the language they use to make them. Here, a science journalist describes how scientists typically comment on published research:

> Notice the qualifiers on belief: "pretty much," "more or less," "don't particularly disbelieve." Scientists are great suspenders of belief. They know that their measurements often have large margins of error, their experimental devices are often relatively inadequate, and their own understanding incomplete. They know that the world is complex, interconnected, subtle and extremely easy to get wrong. Geologists once believed that the Sudbury mineral complex in Ontario, the source of most of the world's nickel, precipitated out of a melt formed when the liquid in the earth's middle rose up through the crust. But after finding shattered rock, microscopic mineral grains subjected to intense pressure, and other signs of a great impact, they now believe the nickel formed when a 6-mile-wide meteorite hit the Earth so hard that the crust melted. . . . Geologists will mostly believe that until more evidence comes along.

Source: From Ann Finkbeiner, "In Science, Seeing Is Not Believing," *USA Today,* October 21, 1997.

WRITING PROCESS

Finding and Stating Claims

DRAFTING

Use Specific Language to State Claims

When you state a claim using specific words, readers can understand it better and then use it to help them anticipate how you will support it. Before you draft a claim, either your main claim or major subclaims, do the following:

1. **List additional specific terms that might fit your claim.** Concentrate on nouns and verbs; you'll have to ask different questions about each. For example, for the claim *The divisive effects of the Civil War are still felt today,* ask these two questions:

   - For nouns, ask *What kind of?* Then ask it again for each term in your answer. Add all the terms that might apply to your list.

     For example, for the term *effects,* ask, *What kind of **effects?**—political rivalry, regional prejudice, economic competition, ideological differences.* Then for the term *ideological differences,* ask, *What kind of **differences?**— theories of government, states' rights, individual freedom, right to work laws, Bible belt fundamentalism.*

   - For verbs, ask *How?* Add all the terms that might apply to your list.

     For example, *How are effects **felt?**—by the regions mistrusting one another, by the South voting as a political bloc, by the South seeing federal efforts toward desegregation as an imposition from the North, by old divisions influencing new attitudes, by the politicians of each region advancing different theories of government.*

Once you have a list of specific terms relevant to your claim, look for related words that might express your ideas more precisely.

   - For each term, ask the question *as opposed to?* If a new term expresses your ideas better than the old one, replace the old one.

     For example, **Differences** as opposed to *divisions, disruptions, disagreements.* **States' rights** as opposed to *federalism, the power of the federal government, the freedom of states to govern themselves.* **Influence** as opposed to *determine, shape.*

2. **Write the claim using the most appropriate words on the list.** Review your lists, picking out three or four terms that best express the key ideas of your claim (in bold). Then write a claim using those terms and any others that fit (in italics):

Relevant Kinds of Effects

ideological divisions, political rivalry, **theories of government,** *state vs. federal power, individual freedom*

Relevant Ways They Are Felt

old divisions shape new attitudes, bloc voting in the South, *politicians of each region advance different theories of government*

The **ideological divisions** of the Civil War still **shape** the *political discourse* of North and South today, reflected in their **antithetical theories** about *state and federal powers* and the *authority of government over individuals.*

REVISING

Qualify Claims That Are Too Certain

Readers distrust claims (and their makers) that express arrogant, unquestioning certainty, preferring claims that show the kind of civil diffidence that communicates a critical thinker's cautious confidence: *I have tested this claim in all the ways I know, but of course we never know what new evidence might turn up.* When you review the sentences in a completed draft, check the language of your main claim and major subclaims for too much certainty.

Watch for sentences that overstate the scope of your claim by suggesting that something is *certainly* true *always* and *for everyone*:

- **Probability:** If you find *certainly, absolutely, without question,* etc., consider writing *probably, normally, likely, tend to, inclined to,* etc. If you find *impossible, inconceivable,* etc., consider writing *unlikely, improbable,* etc.

- **Frequency:** If you find *always, every time, without fail,* etc., consider writing *usually, frequently, predictably, habitually, almost always,* etc. If you find *never, not once,* etc., consider writing *seldom, rarely, infrequently, almost never,* etc.

- **Quantity:** If you find *all, every, each,* etc., consider writing *many, most, some, a majority, almost all,* etc. If you find *none, not one,* etc., consider writing *few, hardly any,* etc.

Remember that a claim may seem too certain even without any of these words. If you write the claim, "Readers distrust writers who are certain," readers may assume that you mean *"All* readers *always* distrust *all* writers who are certain."

At the same time, don't overqualify. You would seem wishy-washy if you wrote "Some readers are occasionally somewhat inclined to distrust writers who are certain." Usually, one qualification is enough: "Readers *are likely to* distrust. . . ," "Readers *often* distrust. . . ," "*Many* readers distrust . . ."

Even more than they distrust writers who make unqualified claims, readers distrust those who assert those claims too strongly. When you claim that your reasons or evidence support a claim, be moderate in asserting how strong your case really is:

• **Level of proof:** Unless you have the strongest possible evidence, avoid phrases like *X proves Y, X settles the question, Y is beyond question, without a doubt,* etc. If you find X *demonstrates, establishes,* or *shows* Y, consider writing X *suggests, points to, argues for, leads us to believe, indicates,* etc.

Here too, you don't want to diminish the real strength of your argument, but readers are likely to be suspicious if you exaggerate the level of your proof.

IN THE READINGS . . .

Comparative Hedging

We have said that one aspect of your ethos is how boldly or modestly you state your claims. Compare how hedges communicate different degrees of certainty in "On the Uses of a Liberal Education" by Mark Edmundson (p. 393) and "Has Student Consumerism Gone Too Far?" by Michael Pernal (p. 401). Read both essays without stopping to analyze specific passages. Which writer comes across as more certain of himself? Which one comes across as more trustworthy?

Now look for specific hedges. Starting from the beginning, read until you have identified five places where each writer hedges an important claim or a report of evidence. Now do the same, starting from the end. Which one had more explicit hedges per page? Does that coincide with your general impression of how certain they are? How does it affect your judgment of their credibility?

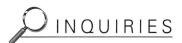

INQUIRIES

REFLECTIONS

1. Are those who make conceptual arguments responsible for what others do with their claims? Is a scientist who discovers something that someone uses to create new weapons responsible for their consequences? Should a geneticist get credit when his discoveries help doctors save lives? If so, should he be blamed if those same discoveries are used in immoral ways? What about a political scientist whose ideas about limiting the power of government inspire someone to bomb a federal building? What principle might we use to make distinctions among these cases? Could you make a case that some claims should never be made? What about a discovery that makes it possible for anyone to build an atomic bomb in his kitchen? What might be the unintended consequences if researchers kept secret discoveries that they thought might be potentially dangerous?

TASKS

2. Suppose you have been asked for suggestions about recreational facilities, intramural sports, cultural activities, or some other part of your college life. Make a snap judgment about what you think is a problem and offer a quick and easy solution. Now approach the same problem by following all three stages of critical thinking (see p. 7). Assume that quick, unreflective judgments are usually wrong. Did you identify the real problem the first time?

3. Try the negation test (pp. 118–19) on the claims in some of your old papers. What does it tell you about the significance of your claims?

4. What kinds of claims have you made most often in your papers, calls for action or claims that something is true? Try revising each claim that explicitly calls for an action into a claim that only implies one, and vice versa.

PROJECTS

5. Suppose you are a leader in a national student organization dedicated to reducing the costs of a college education. Sketch a plan of action for asking college presidents to support a policy that will lower tuition. What role would negotiation or mediation have in your plan? What about propaganda (advertising, public relations, etc.)? Coercion (demonstrations, civil disobedience, lobbying legislators, etc.)? How would argument fit into your plans?

6. Look in your old papers for the qualities of good claims (pp. 118–23). Look especially for signals of cause and effect (*because, so, in order to,* etc.) and reservation (*despite, although, while,* etc.). If your claims seem thin, elaborate them in ways we've suggested (pp. 125–26).

 FOCUS ON WRITING

Context.   In the fairest arguments, writers present the positions of those with whom they differ in a way that their "opponents" would accept as accurate. But nothing is more common than for writers of opinion pieces in newspapers and magazines to distort the positions of those they oppose. For instance, it is likely that the three organizations named by Richard Berman in "Turkey Police, Beware" (p. 461) would reject his characterization of their beliefs. You can find information about the organizations and their positions in the library and on the Web (www.cspinet.org; www.vegsoc.org; www.cyberveg.org; and www .peta-online.org).

Scenario 1. You have an internship with one of three organizations [choose one]: Center for Science in the Public Interest, Vegetarian Society, or PETA. Your job is to monitor the press for mentions of the organization.

Task 1(a). Berman's essay has landed on your desk. Your job is to draft a letter to the editor of the *Washington Times* correcting Berman's characterization of your organization and its position.

Task 1(b). Berman's essay has landed on your desk. Your job is to draft an opinion piece that counters Berman's essay without responding to it directly.

Scenario 2. You have an internship with the Guest Choice Network, the restaurant association founded by Berman.

Task 2(a). Berman has been notified by the *Washington Times* that it has received a response from one of the three organizations [choose one], accusing him of misrepresenting them. The paper would like to have a letter from Berman responding to their letter (nothing sells papers like controversy). Your job is to draft a letter proving that the organization is as extreme as he said it was.

Task 2(b). Berman reads in the *Washington Times* a response from one of the three organizations [choose one], accusing him of misrepresenting them. He wants you to draft another essay, this time focusing on just the one organization, arguing that it takes extremist positions concerning food.

RESEARCH PROJECT

Scenario. In Chapter 3 you shared your problem statement for the Research Project with your teacher and classmates. They agree that your problem has promise, but your teacher wants to be sure that you can answer the question that you propose.

Task. Write a formal proposal for a research paper in which you do the following:

- State your research question/problem.
- Explain how your question/problem relates to the topic of your real or imagined class.
- State its consequences explicitly, what is not now known that your readers should want to know.
- Offer some speculative answers.
- Explain what kind of support you might find to back up your answer(s).

You can make each of these items a separate section with its own heading. You might also decide to reorder items. As you speculate about answers, avoid rushing to judgment. Append to your proposal a revised version of your preliminary introduction and conclusion.

IN A NUTSHELL

About Your Argument . . .

Claims are at the heart of every argument. They are your main point, the solution to your problem. Though you should try to formulate a tentative claim or hypothesis as soon as you can, you must also work hard to keep your mind open to giving it up in favor of a better one. That's why it's important to imagine a number of hypotheses and hold them all in mind as you work your way toward a best one.

Useful claims have these qualities:

• Your claim should be clearly **conceptual** or **practical.** It should assert what readers should know or what they should do.

• Your claim should be something that readers will not accept without seeing your good reasons. It should be **contestable.**

• Your claim should in principle be capable of being proved wrong, because you can imagine evidence that would make you give it up. It should be **disconfirmable.**

• Your claim should be feasible, ethical, and prudent. It should be **reasonable.**

Be clear to yourself the degree of assent you seek. What do you want your readers to do?

• **Respect** your reasons for making your claim?

• **Approve** of your claim and the argument supporting it?

• **Publicly endorse** your claim as worth serious consideration?

• **Believe** in your claim and in the argument supporting it?

• **Act** as you propose, or support someone else's action?

When you make a plan to gather evidence, think about these questions:

• What kind of evidence do readers expect you to report?

• Will the cost of searching for specific evidence be greater than the benefit of finding it?

• Where are you most likely to find the evidence you need? Libraries? The Internet? Personal interview? Observation?

When you gather evidence, follow these steps:

• Start by sampling the evidence from a source to see whether it is relevant and sufficient.

• Periodically take stock of the evidence as it mounts.

• Don't wait to get every shred of evidence before you start writing.

. . . and About Writing It

Work toward a claim that has these qualities:

- Its language is explicit and specific. It previews the central concepts that you will develop in the rest of the argument.
- It is elaborated with clauses beginning with *although, because,* and *unless.* If you think that makes the claim too long and complex, then break it into shorter sentences.
- It is hedged with appropriate qualifiers such as *many, most, often, usually, probably,* and *unlikely* instead of *all, always,* and *certainly*.

CHAPTER 5

The Core of Your Argument: Reasons and Evidence

In this chapter, we focus on the support that makes a claim seem credible and convincing. We distinguish three kinds of support you need to keep straight: reasons, evidence, and reports of evidence. We also show you how to arrange reasons into an order that is useful to readers.

The heart of your argument is your claim; its main substance is what you offer to support that claim, reasons and evidence. Reasons and evidence work in tandem to support a claim, but they are also different, in their form, in how you find them, and in how you use them. In this chapter, we examine those differences so that you can know how best to use both reasons and evidence to support your claim.

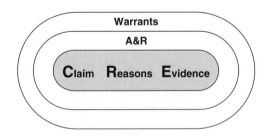

Supporting Claims

Those who make a flat claim, expecting us to agree just because they say so, risk seeming arrogant. We expect writers to approach us as critical thinkers who judge for ourselves, and so we look for both support for a claim and some qualification. Compare these examples:

TV's obsession with sexuality damages the social and emotional development of our preteens. _{claim}

Though the TV networks have improved children's daytime programming, _{acknowledgment} their prime-time obsession with sexuality **may** be damaging the social and emotional development of many preteens _{claim} **because they model their behavior on what they see others do.** _{reason}

The second version seems more thoughtful and respectful. It treats us as critical thinkers who want at least one good reason before we accept the claim, and it acknowledges that the issue is not cut-and-dried, but complicated enough that the claim is not unqualifiedly true.

But most critical thinkers expect more. A thoughtful reader will think that reason (children model their behavior on others) supports that claim (obsession with sexuality may be damaging) only if it is based on more than the writer's opinion, only if the writer offers *evidence* demonstrating that preteens *in fact* base their behavior on TV.

Reasons and Evidence as Forms of Support

As we saw in Chapter 1, the language we use about *having* an argument pictures it as combat. But when we describe *making* one, we sound less like combatants than builders. We *build support* for a claim by adding reasons that *rest on a firm base* of *hard* evidence. That *grounding* should create a *solid footing* so *unshakable* that critics cannot *topple* our argument by *undermining* its *foundation.* Such language visualizes an argument not as a linear sequence of elements but as a vertical structure of logical relationships something like this:

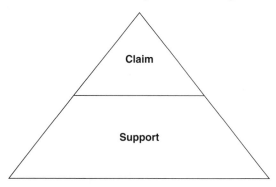

Those building metaphors are useful, but to understand how we actually plan and draft arguments, we need five terms with more literal meanings: *fact, data, exhibits, evidence,* and *reasons:*

- A *fact* is a statement in words or symbols that readers accept as true, or at least don't contest: *The capital of Ohio is Columbus; 2 + 2 = 4.*
- *Data* (the singular is *datum*) are sets of facts. Data can be any information you have gathered, but we often think of data as numbers. We can

summarize numerical data in words: *In 1985, Abco's market share was 19.4%; by 1995, it slipped to 11.7%; but it has now grown to 22%.* But more often, we present data in tables, graphs, and charts:

ABCO MARKET SHARE (%)

1985	1995	2005
19.4	11.7	22.0

- *Exhibits* are concrete examples of your object of study. They might be copies of the texts you analyze (including quotations); reproductions of paintings or other images; photographs or drawings of buildings, objects, landscapes, cloud formations, or bugs, and so on.

By themselves, however, facts data, and exhibits are just inert information. Only when you bring them into your argument do they become *evidence*.

- *Evidence* includes facts, data, and exhibits that support a reason. They become evidence when you show that they have a logical connection to the reason, when readers look at the evidence and think, *If this evidence is reliable, then this reason must be true.*

- *Reasons* are statements that generalize on the evidence to show how it backs up your claim.

Here is a brief argument with data as evidence:

Although television has improved after-school programming, its prime-time shows may be undermining the social and emotional development of many preteens _{claim} by exposing them to sexually explicit behavior that encourages them to engage in sex play before they understand its consequences. _{reason} In his report on the relationship between TV watching and sexual experimentation, **Kahn (1996) studied children ages 10–13 who regularly (three times in four weeks) watch sexually oriented television shows (more than five references to or images of sexual conduct). He found they are 40% more likely to engage in sexual play than those who do not watch such programs at all.** _{evidence}

That passage presents the core of an argument in a standard form: Claim resting on Reasons resting on Evidence.

Distinguishing Reasons and Evidence

The difference between reasons and evidence seems intuitively obvious, but is more complex than it seems. We occasionally use those terms interchangeably:

> What reasons can you offer to support your claim?
> What evidence can you offer to support your claim?

But we also distinguish them in sentences like these:

> We need to think up *reasons* to support our request.
> We need to think up *evidence* to support our request.
>
> Before I accept your *reasons,* I have to see the *evidence* they rest on.
> Before I accept your *evidence,* I have to see the *reasons* it rests on.

Most of us find the first sentence in each pair natural, the second a bit odd.

One source of the difference is the images we associate with reasons and evidence. To describe evidence, we use metaphors like *solid* or *hard* that incline us to think that we can see evidence out in the world, "outside" our subjective experience. We feel that reasons, on the other hand, metaphorically come from "inside" our minds. We believe we could check your evidence by looking for ourselves, if you told us where to look; we don't ask where to search for your reasons.

Since we assume evidence is at least in principle *public* and *sharable,* readers ask some predictable questions about it:

- Where did you find your evidence? What are your sources? Are they reliable?
- How did you collect it? What methods and devices did you use? Could I see it for myself?
- What are its limitations? Is it reliable? What problems did you have collecting it?

Recall Sue's conversation with Ann and Raj: When Sue claimed that her school treated students badly, she offered a reason: teachers kept too few office hours. When asked what she based that reason on, she reported the actual hours posted: *Prof. X, Monday, 4–5 P.M., Prof. Y, Friday 4–4:30 P.M.,* etc. Those names and numbers were not her reasons, not her judgments or opinions, but what she hoped her friends would accept as *evidence,* as facts independent of her belief that teachers kept too few office hours, but supporting it.

Figuratively, Sue's argument looked like this, with the parts she has constructed in her mind, her claim and reasons, resting on a solid foundation of external evidence:

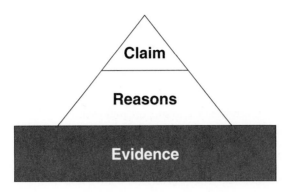

We judge reasons that we think lack a foundation of evidence as "mere opinion," and mere opinion is, to continue the construction metaphor, "too flimsy" to support "sound" claims about "weighty" problems.

Distinguishing Evidence and Reports of It

You can use that construction image as a loose way to think about the core of an argument, but when you examine it closely, it turns out to be a bit misleading. In what follows, we make a distinction that may seem like academic hairsplitting, but it is crucial to understanding how arguments really work. You need to understand the distinction because what people call evidence rarely is.

Direct and Reported Evidence

As unsettling as it may seem, what we call evidence is almost always just a *report* of it, or even a report of a report. Most direct evidence cannot be "in" an argument, if we define direct evidence in the metaphorical language that we so often use for it, as that objective stuff we could find out in the world, if we just went to look for it.

- In a murder trial, the direct evidence might be a bloody glove that a prosecutor can hold up for the jury to see, but in a written argument, she can only state facts that describe the glove or show a photograph of it as an exhibit.

- An economist making an argument about unemployment could physically point to a few actual individuals with no jobs, but in a written argument, he could only refer to the millions of unemployed in words or numbers.

- In an argument about the nature of matter, a physicist can't even point to the smallest particles he investigates. He can refer to them only in mathematical terms or reproduce photographs of the traces they leave on his detectors.

What we offer as evidence is almost never direct evidence, but only a *report* that describes, pictures, represents, refers to, or enumerates actual gloves, people, and particles.

Even when you've seen "real" evidence directly with your own eyes, you can bring it into your written argument only by representing it in words, numbers, images, or sounds. For the purposes of your argument, you have to ignore a multitude of details, because it is impossible to represent them all. When you report evidence, you also smooth it out, tidy it up, make it more coherent, more regular than the "stuff out there" really is. So what you ask readers to go on is not evidence, but only your selective and reshaping report of it.

Representations as Evidence

Some students wonder about quoted words. Aren't they "the evidence itself"? Even when words are quoted correctly (which is often not the case), they are only an exhibit—selected, taken out of context, used for a new purpose, all leading us to experience them in ways that their context may contradict.

What about photographs? Even when we reproduce a photograph as exactly as possible, it is still seen on a different paper, in a different context, with a different purpose.

Try to report evidence as directly as possible, but when you read reports of it in the arguments of others, remember that just as a picture of an apple is not an apple, so a report of evidence is not the evidence.

We belabor this distinction because the word *evidence* carries so much authority and seems so weighty and objective. When someone offers what it claimed to be "hard" evidence, we are likely to be half convinced that it has an objective reality that we should not question. But evidence described in a report is neither objective nor real. What we call evidence is almost always a report of it shaped to fit an argument.

Once you grasp that distinction, you can see why critical readers want to be sure that your reports of evidence are reliable and from a good source, and why they expect you to tell them where you found the evidence or, if you rely on others' reports, who gathered and reported it. They want to know how much it's been shaped even before you found it. That's why readers look for citations to assure them that they could, if they wanted, track your reports back as close as they can get to the direct evidence "itself." Evidence is only as sound as the chain of reports leading to it, and in your argument, the last link in that chain is always you.

Recall again that in the discussion among Sue, Ann, and Raj, the question of evidence turned on that very issue:

Sue: Well, we pay a lot of money for our education, but we don't get near the attention customers do.

Ann: How's that?

Sue: For one thing, we can hardly see teachers outside of class. Last week I counted office hours posted on office doors on the first floor of the Arts and Sciences building. [She reads from a piece of paper.] They average less than an hour a week, most of them in the late afternoon when a lot of us work. I have the numbers right here.

Ann: Can I see?

Sue: Sure. [She hands the paper over.]

But when Ann looked at the numbers, she was still not looking directly at the evidence "itself": that was attached to doors. Ann must assume that Sue copied those hours accurately and reported them fairly. (But see also Inquiry 1 on p. 152.)

If the distinction between evidence and reports reflects how most arguments really work, then Sue's argument is not *directly* grounded on external reality, as in this diagram:

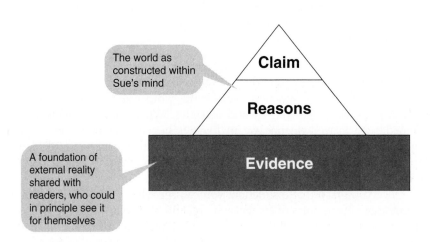

Instead, her argument—including the evidence she *refers to and describes*—is all her construction. She may rest her *report* of evidence on a ground of external, direct evidence, but that external ground cannot be a part of the argument itself:

What Sue can offer as evidence *inside* her argument is only a report that she hopes Ann and Raj accept as reliably grounded on direct evidence *outside* the argument. But Ann and Raj won't go look at the direct evidence, at the hours posted on actual doors; so from their point of view, Sue's reports of evidence are all the ground they have.

They have to trust that she got the numbers right. And that's why you must develop a reputation for reporting evidence accurately, without obviously self-interested spin, because the last person in the chain of trust is you. Betray that trust, and you lose credibility, not just for your current argument, but possibly for the next one and the ones after that.

On the Evidence of Dinosaurs

Even when it seems we can hold direct evidence in our hands, we may be holding only nature's report of it. Not long ago, paleontologists announced that they had uncovered the heart of a dinosaur, the first ever found. After examination, they decided that it had two chambers—evidence, they said, that the dinosaur it came from may have been warm-blooded. The evidence they could point to, however, was not the actual heart of that dinosaur; it was a fossil stone casting created by natural processes—nature's "report" of the evidence. Moreover, what the scientists pointed to as evidence was not even the fossil casting but a series of two-dimensional CAT scans of its internal structure that they assembled into a three-dimensional model. Their evidence that dinosaurs might have been warm-blooded is a three-dimensional model that reports on a series of two-dimensional images that report on a stone fossil that reports on an organ that no longer exists. The hard question is how much each of those reports distorts that once-beating heart (if it is in fact a heart, which some paleontologists doubt).

At this point you may have an uneasy feeling that reasons and reports of evidence are a lot alike, because both are the products of a subjective mind. They are a lot alike, but here's one way to sort them out: Think of reasons as the *outline* of an argument, its logical structure. Think of reports of evidence as what readers *accept* as true to support the points in that outline. Think of direct evidence as something a reader would have get up out of her chair to go look at.

Multiple Reasons

Even when you base a reason on reliable (reports) of evidence, readers may not accept just one reason as sufficient support for a significant claim. So you usually have to offer more reasons that relate to your claim in two ways:

- You can offer parallel reasons, each one supporting a claim directly.
- You can offer "stacked" reasons, each one resting on the one before, the first one directly supporting your claim, the last one resting on evidence (or a report of it).

Reasons in Parallel

Until now, we have lumped reasons in our discussions and diagrams. But when you create an argument with parallel reasons, you need to keep them separate in your mind, on your storyboard, and in your report. That calls for a somewhat more complex picture:

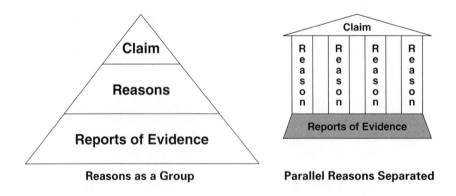

With parallel reasons, each one stands independently of the others. Take one away and the claim might slump, but the other reasons might be sufficient to prop it up. Take away more, and it might collapse.

Three reasons in parallel is the standard plan for the five-paragraph essay many of us learned in high school:

¶1 There are three reasons why we should curb binge drinking. _{claim}

¶2 First, it gives the campus a bad image. _{reason 1} For example, . . . _{report of evidence}

¶3 It also creates legal liability. _{reason 2} Four cases have been . . . _{report of evidence}

¶4 Finally, it causes injury and even death. _{reason 3} Last month, . . . _{report of evidence}

¶5 Therefore, we can see that bingeing has become, . . . _{repeated claim}

Some good arguments actually have only three reasons, but so many bad ones have been forced into that form that the five-paragraph, three-reason essay has an amateurish image at the college level. So avoid three if you can.

Reasons in Sequence

You can also arrange reasons not separately in parallel, but "stacked," each reason resting on another, the first directly supporting the claim, the last resting on reports of evidence:

(You can also imagine these reasons sideways, as links in chain or a series of steps.)

For example, in the following argument, the writer bases a main claim on three stacked reasons resting on a report of evidence:

Congress should pass a law requiring colleges and universities to measure the skills that their students learn during their undergraduate careers. _{claim}

R1:   We must sure that our college graduates are learning what they will need to meet the challenge of global competition. _{reason 1 supporting claim}

R2:   We know that India and China are graduating students who one day could surpass our leadership in science, technology, and business,
_{reason 2 supporting reason 1}

R3:   because they are graduating many more students than we are, most of whom demonstrate high levels of skills in math, science, and communication. _{reason 3 supporting reason 2}

E: The *Journal of International Education,* for example, reports that following numbers: Every year, we graduate ... while China and India graduate ... _{report of evidence supporting reason 3}

Only Congress can ensure that our colleges and universities are graduating students who can meet the challenges of an increasingly globalized world. _{claim restated}

Experienced writers create arguments like these by laying deeper and deeper foundations for their claims (another of those construction metaphors), thereby thickening their arguments. The risk of such an argument is that if readers miss just one intermediate step, they lose track of the logic, and the argument collapses.

The Deep Complexity of Serious Arguments

When we address an issue that requires more than two or three pages of argument, we build them out of multiple reasons in parallel, each of which rests on multiple reasons in sequence, all of them based on evidence. In so doing, we create an argument of considerable complexity. Yet as complex as it might seem in writing, we create that kind of complex argument in conversation every day whenever we engage in a lot of back-and-forth about a serious issue. Your task in writing an equally complex argument is simply to plan patiently, organizing reasons in parallel and in series, all based on evidence.

Using Reasons to Help Readers Understand Evidence

If evidence anchors an argument, why bother with reasons at all? Why not just base a claim directly on reports of evidence? Sometimes we do, especially when we offer simple numbers. But reasons help readers understand and interpret complex evidence. Consider this sentence and the data that support its claim:

> Most predictions about average gasoline consumption have proved wrong. claim

TABLE 5.1   MILEAGE AND GASOLINE CONSUMPTION

	1970	1980	1990	2000
Annual miles (000)	9.5	10.3	10.5	11.7
Annual consumption (gal.)	760	760	520	533 reported evidence

A diligent reader could figure out how the numbers support the claim—mileage has gone up but gas consumption has gone down. But we would understand all that more easily if the writer added a sentence explaining how the numbers relate to the claim, a more informative title, and visual help that focuses us on what to see:

> Gasoline consumption has not grown as many have predicted. claim Even though Americans drove 23 percent more miles in 2000 than in 1970, they used 30 percent less fuel. reason

TABLE 5.2 PER CAPITA MILEAGE AND GASOLINE CONSUMPTION, 1970–2000

	1970	1980	1990	2000
Annual miles (000)	9.5	10.3	10.5	11.7
(% change vs. 1970)		8.4%	10.5%	23.1%
Annual consumption (gal.)	760	760	520	533
(% change vs. 1970)			(31.6%)	(29.7%)

reported evidence

Some writers fear that they insult readers when they spell out in a reason what readers can figure out for themselves. And it is true that no one wants to read the obvious. But all writers, experienced and inexperienced alike, overestimate what readers will figure out on their own. So you usually do them a service when you add a reason that points out what is important in a report of evidence, making clear how it supports your claim.

Readers need the same help when the evidence is a quotation. Here is a claim about Hamlet that rests directly on the evidence of a quotation:

> As Hamlet stands behind his stepfather Claudius while he is at prayer, he demonstrates a cool and logical mind. _{claim}
>
> Now might I do it [kill him] pat, now he is praying:
> And now I'll do't; and so he goes to heaven;
> And so am I reveng'd. . . . [Hamlet pauses to think]
> [But this] villain kills my father; and for that,
> I, his sole son, do this same villain send to heaven[?]
> Why, this is hire and salary, not revenge. _{report of evidence}

Many readers find that argument a bit hard to follow. Nothing in the quotation seems obviously to support a claim about Hamlet's cool reason. By omitting a reason, the writer forces us to figure it out on our own. Compare this version:

> As Hamlet stands behind his stepfather Claudius while he is at prayer, he demonstrates a cool and logical mind. _{claim} **At first he impulsively wants to kill Claudius on the spot, but he pauses to reflect. If he kills Claudius while praying, he sends his soul to heaven. But Hamlet wants him damned to hell forever. So he coolly decides to kill him later:** _{reason}
>
> Now might I do it [kill him] pat, now he is praying:
>
> And now I'll do't; and so . . . _{report of evidence}

That reason tells us what to see in the quotation that relates it to the claim.

A detailed report of evidence seldom speaks for itself. Without a reason to speak for it, readers often struggle to understand what it signifies. They work less hard when you add a reason that both supports the claim *and* explains the evidence. Visually, it looks like this:

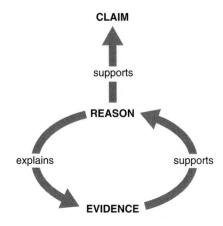

So when you offer evidence in the form of quotations, images, or data in tables and charts, don't just attach it to a claim. Add a reason that tells your readers what to see in the evidence.

WRITING PROCESS

Reasons and Evidence

PREPARING AND PLANNING

Be Aware What Your Reasons Imply About Your Claim (and You)

Once you assemble your reasons, consider what they imply about both you and your readers. Since every reason implies a principle of reasoning (warrant), each one tells readers something about your values and what you think of theirs. Even if a reason is true and supports your claim, it could poison your argument and your ethos if readers reject the values it rests on.

Suppose Jorge claims that plagiarism from the Internet should be curbed, offering these reasons:

R1:   Plagiarism prevents good students from standing out.

R2:   It erodes the foundations of trust that a community depends on.

R3:   If the public learns about it, it will make the university look bad.

R4:   It makes students think they can get something for nothing.

Each reason casts a different light on both Jorge and on the kind of person he imagines his reader to be. Most of us would rather be identified with preserving the social foundations of trust rather than protecting the university from bad press.

Once you have a list of reasons, test each for what it implies about your ethos and your image of your reader. If you can't tell, ask someone.

Ordering Multiple Reasons

Once you have a list of reasons, decide how to order them. Too many writers put their reasons in the order they thought of them, which is rarely the best order.

Parallel Reasons

If you have parallel reasons supporting a claim, arrange them in an order that creates the best impact and that readers will think is coherent.

Ordering Parallel Reasons by Their Substance You might find a principle of order based on the ideas or things the reasons refer to. The most obvious choice is to group them based on who or what the reasons are mostly about. For example, in these three reasons supporting the claim that even small "social" lies should be avoided, two are about liars and one is about the person lied to:

R1: Once you get used to little lies, you tell bigger ones more easily.

R2: The person you lie to suffers from not knowing the truth.

R3: You eventually lose credibility.

So on the face of it, we should probably put (1) and (3) together, either before or after (2).

You can also order reasons on the basis of their relation to some preexisting order, either standard orders such as chronology and geography, or one specific to your particular claim, such as least-to-most controllable cause. For example, to explain the causes of the Holocaust someone might offer these five parallel reasons:

R1: Allied leaders did not try to stop the Holocaust for political reasons.

R2: Germany had a long history of anti-Semitism.

R3: Many societies have practiced other versions of ethnic cleansing.

R4: Hitler and those around him were uniquely evil.

R5: Jews did not resist soon enough.

It's hard to see any principle in that order. An order based on chronology would be clearer: 3 and 2 (distant and recent history), 4 (Hitler's evil), 5 (weak resistance), 1 (failure of Allies). But if you wanted to emphasize the difference between social causes and personal ones, that principle would give you this order: 3 (human culture), 2 (immediate society), 5 (collective response), 1 (lack of courage), 4 (personal evil).

Ordering Parallel Reasons by Readers' Responses   A better way to order parallel reasons is by how you want readers to respond to them. One principle of order is relative **strength.** For example, the reasons for the Holocaust might be ordered from what readers would take to be weakest to strongest, or vice versa, depending on whether we want to make a quick impact or to build toward a climax. (Of course, readers differ in which reasons they judge strong or weak.)

A second principle of order based on readers' responses is relative **acceptability.** Even when readers think a reason is strong, they may still not like hearing it. For example, it is likely that Jews, Germans, and those associated with the Allies would resist most strongly the reason that assigns responsibility to each of them. Each group would probably want to see other causes acknowledged before considering their own responsibility.

Another principle of readers' order is relative **complexity.** Readers grasp simpler reasons more easily than complex ones. (What is easier or more difficult, of course, depends on what they know.) For example, to argue that our ability to learn language is not like our ability to learn chess or algebra but is based on a genetically determined competence, we could offer three reasons:

R1:   All human languages share the same complex principles of grammatical organization.

R2:   Children all over the world learn to talk at about the same age.

R3:   Chimpanzees can't learn the grammatical structures that two-year olds master easily.

The first reason is very difficult to grasp; the second easier; and the third easiest of all. If so, we would understand the argument better if those reasons were in reverse order, because that would allow us to build some "momentum" in understanding the argument.

Finally, reasons can be ordered by **familiarity.** (This too depends on particular readers.) Readers understand familiar reasons more readily than unfamiliar ones. For example, of the three reasons about learning language, the first is least familiar to most of us, the second most familiar for those of us who have been around children. So for them, the best order is 2–3–1.

If these principles of order conflict, the simplest principle is to put your strongest reasons last, if you are sure your reader will read to the end of your argument. If you fear your reader may not reach the end, put your strongest reason first.

Under any circumstances, choose *some* principle of order and make clear to your readers what it is.

Reasons in Series

When you offer a series of reasons, each one not supporting the claim directly, but linked to the one before and after it, you have to use different principles of order, but you have only two choices: first to last or last to first. Jumping around guarantees confusion.

Process Orders   If your reasons reflect some external process, you can order them to reflect its sequence. Begin at the beginning of the process and move to its outcome, like this:

> When buyers are satisfied with the quality of a product and the quality of service when it breaks down, $_{step\ 1}$ they are likely to become loyal customers. $_{step\ 2}$ Loyal customers are important, because they don't need advertising or a high-powered sales force to buy that product again. $_{step\ 3}$ So the more loyal users a product has, the more profits a company can expect. $_{claim}$

Or you can begin with the outcome and move back to its beginning, like this:

> Manufacturers increase profits and sales $_{step\ 3}$ when they create loyal customers who buy their product once and return to buy it a second time, $_{step\ 2}$ without the need of advertising or a high-powered sales force. Customers become loyal when they are satisfied with the quality of service they get on the product when it breaks down, but more importantly with the product's intrinsic quality. $_{step\ 1}$ Therefore, while manufacturers should focus on both service and product quality, they should emphasize the product quality. $_{claim}$

Both orders make sense. Which you choose depends on how you want readers to think about the process. The step they read last is the one they will focus on.

Reasoning Orders   You can order sequential reasons to follow not an external process but the internal process of your readers' logic. In the next example, the writer reports Thomas Jefferson's order of reasoning. The second reason depends on the logical principle stated in the first, and the third reason depends on the second (and the writer bases it all on the reported evidence of Jefferson's words):

> When Jefferson wrote "all men are created equal" with "certain inalienable rights," $_{evidence}$ he laid down the first principle of civil society—we all have intrinsic rights that cannot be taken away. $_{reason\ 1}$ To protect those rights, we establish government, $_{reason\ 2}$ but when government tries to take those rights away, we have the duty to replace it with one that will protect us. $_{reason\ 3}$ In a democracy, we do that by the vote. But when a government is a ruthless tyranny, we have the duty to throw off its rule by force, if necessary. $_{claim}$

The reverse order is possible, but harder to follow.

We can't tell you how to choose among these orders: that depends on your argument, on your situation, but most of all on your readers. So find surrogate readers on whom to try different orders. Under any circumstances, though, always question an order that you did not *choose*. Assume that the order in which you happened to write down your reasons is probably *not* the order that best helps readers grasp them.

IN THE READINGS . . .

Ordering Reasons

In "The Student as Consumer: The Implications and Limitations of a Metaphor" (p. 406), Jill J. McMillan and George Cheney list four reasons against using the metaphor and three recommendations for counteracting its effects. What principle of order do they follow in laying out these reasons and recommendations? Do they forecast the order so that readers know what to expect? Can you think of a better order?

DRAFTING

Quoting and Paraphrasing

When you report written evidence, you have to quote directly, paraphrase, or summarize. The difference is not one of degree:

- When you quote directly, you reproduce the original text word-for-word, punctuation-for-punctuation.

- When you paraphrase, you substitute your words for the authors' in order to make a statement clearer or to fit its context better. A paraphrase is usually shorter than the original, but it need not be. Readers should be able to say, "This sentence parallels the one on page X."

- When you summarize, you reword and condense the original text to less than its original length. Readers should not be able to say, "This sentence matches the one on page X."

Paraphrasing or Summarizing in Disciplines That Focus on Data

In the natural sciences and the "harder" social sciences, writers draw on sources for one or more of three reasons:

- to review previous work in the common ground,

- to acknowledge alternative positions, or

- to use the source's findings (main claim) or data to support their own claims and reasons.

In these cases, readers care more about results than the exact words reporting them, so writers seldom quote sources directly; instead, they paraphrase or summarize.

When you paraphrase a source, use the citation form expected in your field. Include the author's name in your paraphrase if the source is important; otherwise, put the name in a citation:

> Several processes have been suggested as causes of the associative-priming effect. For instance, in their seminal study Meyer and Schvaneveldt (1971, p. 232) suggested two, automatic (attention-free) spreading activation in long-

term memory and location-shifting. Neely (1976) similarly distinguished between a process of automatic-spreading activation in memory and a process that depletes the resources of the attentional mechanism. More recently, a further associative-priming process has been studied (de Groot, 1984).

The writer thought that Meyer and Schvaneveldt as well as Neely were important enough to name in her sentences, but cited de Groot only as a minor reference.

Quoting in Disciplines That Focus on Words

In the humanities, writers both quote and paraphrase. Use direct quotations to

- cite the work of others as primary evidence
- focus on the specific words of a source because
  - they have been important in other arguments
  - they are especially vivid or significant
  - you want to focus on exactly how a source says something
  - you will dispute the source and want to avoid seeming to create a straw man

Paraphrase or summarize

- when you are more interested in the substance of reasons and evidence than in how they are expressed, and
- when you can say the same thing more clearly.

Don't quote just because it's easier or because you don't trust yourself to report a source fairly.

Integrating Quotations into Your Sentences

When you offer quotations as evidence, follow the conventions in your field. They differ, but here are some common ones:

- Introduce a quotation with a colon or introductory phrase:

  Plumber describes the accident that took Princess Diana's life in terms that reflect the cost of too little government regulation: "People like Diana believe they are immune from ordinary dangers and so don't bother with things like seat-belts. But everyone who died was not belted, and the one who survived was" (343).

- Weave the quotation into your own sentence (be sure grammar of the quotation fits into yours):

  Plumber speaks in terms that remind us of the cost of too little government regulation when he points out that "everyone who died [in that crash] was not belted, and the one who survived was" (343).

(Note that when this writer changed the original, she used square brackets to indicate the change.)

- Set off quotations of three or more lines in an indented "block quote":

After Oldenberg's balloon crashed into the ocean on his fifth failed attempt to circumnavigate the globe, his wife began to suspect there was more to his obsession than the "desire to achieve." She thought she found an answer in evolutionary biology:

> The brain of the human male evolved under circumstances where caution was essential because risk was ever-present. When civilization reduced the risk, men began to feel that their natural, evolved impulse toward caution made them weak and unmanly. When men create situations of extreme risk, it's not the risk they crave but a worthy reason to exercise their caution. (Idlewild, 135)

Avoiding Inadvertent Plagiarism

You know that you must cite any passages, distinctive words, or ideas that you use from a written source (see Appendix 1). But in addition to citing what you take from a source, you must also reproduce that material appropriately.

Quotations

Any time you use more than a few words from a source, you must (1) quote the words exactly as they appeared in the original, (2) indicate omissions with ellipses and changes with square brackets, and (3) show which words are quoted by putting them within quotation marks or setting them off in a block quote. You have no decision to make here: *always* set off as quotations *all* passages you take from a source. If you don't, you risk being charged with plagiarism. That's why it's so important to take good notes by copying quotations exactly and putting any quoted words in a different font or different color and surrounding them with extra-large quotation marks.

But if you use only a few words, you have a decision to make. Because you are writing on the same topic as your sources, you will inevitably use many of the same words and phrases, because they are what *anyone* might use to talk about that particular subject. Those words you should not put in quotation marks. But if you use words or phrase that are distinctive to that source, then you must indicate that they are quotations.

For example, here is a passage from a book about technology:

> Because technology begets more technology, the importance of an invention's diffusion potentially exceeds the importance of the original invention. Technology's history exemplifies what is termed an autocatalytic process: that is, one that speeds up at a rate that increases with time, because the process catalyzes itself (Diamond 1998, 301).

If you were reporting Diamond's ideas, you would not use quotation marks for a phrase like *original invention,* because those are words anyone might use. But two of his phrases are distinctive and reflect his original thought and expression: *technology begets more technology* and *autocatalytic process.* Those words you should put in quotation marks the first time you use them; after that, you can repeat them without the marks.

Paraphrase

If you paraphrase rather than reproduce the exact words of a source, you do not need quotation marks or a block quote. But you also must not paraphrase so closely that you seem to follow a source word for word. For example, the following paraphrase would plagiarize this paragraph:

> If you paraphrase, avoid language so similar to the source that your words correspond to its words, For instance, this plagiarizes what you just read.

To avoid inadvertent plagiarism, read the original; sit back and think what it means; then express it in your own words without looking back. You are too close to the original if you can run your finger along a paraphrase and recognize the same sequence of concepts (not words). The following would not be plagiarism of this paragraph:

> Williams and Colomb suggest that to keep from plagiarizing, digest the meaning of a passage, summarize it in your own words, then compare the sequence of ideas in your summary with the source (164).

Our advice applies to most fields in the humanities, but practice differs in different fields. In the law, for example, writers regularly use the exact words of a judge's ruling without quotation marks. In some social sciences, researchers closely paraphrase the main finding of an experiment. Find and follow the practice in your field.

REVISING

Balance Reasons and Evidence

Beware the data dump. Readers want reliable reports of relevant evidence, not all the data you can find. If you can find the best evidence to support a reason, don't confuse the issue with less relevant evidence. If your evidence is less than best, you'll need more, but no careful reader will be convinced by tons of undigested data and quotations.

Beware as well the opinion piece. Readers want your reasons, but they expect you to back them up with evidence. If you can't find reliable evidence to support a reason, find another reason you can support. If you can't support most of your reasons with evidence, then your claim is not provable and so not suitable for argument.

To diagnose whether you have done either, highlight every quotation and statement of data:

- If you highlight more than two-thirds of your paper, you may have a data dump.

- If you highlight less than one-third, you may not have enough evidence to support your reasons.

INQUIRIES

REFLECTIONS

1. Sue copied the office hours from the schedules posted on professors' doors. But are the actual, physical pieces of paper listing office hours the "hard evidence" that "proves" that on average teachers are in their offices for less than an hour a week?

2. Here is something that some people might take to be a "fact" and therefore usable as evidence in favor of allowing people to carry concealed weapons:

   According to an NRA press release, states that have passed laws allowing citizens to carry concealed weapons in public have experienced on average a 4.6 percent drop in daylight assaults and robbery.

   How many removes from the primary evidence itself would you estimate that report of evidence is?

3. How close to the primary evidence itself are these: (a) a musical score; (b) musical recordings made from that score; (c) color reproductions of oil paintings in art history books; (d) full-size exact reproductions of etchings in art books; (e) a videotape of an automobile accident; (f) a tape recording of a meeting; (g) a transcription of that tape recording; (h) a drawing of a witness in a courtroom; (i) a photograph of a witness in a courtroom.

4. What counts as evidence for being in love? For sexual fidelity? For God directly telling someone to do something? For pain that disables someone from working?

5. Which of the following statements is closer to the truth? Does it matter?

   Most of the important questions in the world are those for which we have no good evidence to decide either way.

   Most of the important questions in the world are those for which we have no good reasons to decide either way.

6. When Jefferson says "We hold these truths to be self-evident," what does he base that on?

7. Consider these three statements:

   a. The comments on my history paper did not provide specific advice about improving the next paper.

   b. The comments on my history paper averaged about six words, and all of the comments expressed only approval or disapproval.

   c. The comments on my history paper were very brief and uninformative.

   All might be true, but which seems closest to representing what's "out there," independent of anyone's judgment? Can you order them as a claim supported by a reason supported by evidence: "X because Y because Z"?

8. Some people refuse to judge any reason good or bad, because any reason is a good one for the person offering it. If so, then all reasons are equally good. They are in effect just opinions, and everyone's opinion is as good as anyone else's. Do you agree that all opinions are equally good? If you do, then some philosophers would claim that you have contradicted yourself. Have you?

TASKS

9. Pull out those old papers you've been working with. Select one that has the most evidence. Identify each report of evidence and grade it on a four-point scale:

   4 As close to primary evidence as anyone could get

   3 Your own report of primary evidence that you directly collected or experienced

   2 Your secondhand report of what is reported by the person who directly collected or experienced the primary evidence

   1 Your third- or fourth-hand report of what someone else reported that someone else reported

   What is your average score? Could you have raised it if you had done more research?

10. This exercise asks you to see how arguers can gain your trust by exploiting your bias to think of evidence as "out there in the world." Find a textbook that relies on complex data (experimental psychology, physics, economics). Pick out reports of evidence offered as factually true, beyond question (look for tables and graphs). Do you understand that evidence? Does it seem to you self-evident, obvious in the external world? What would you have to believe to accept this evidence as "given"? Now find the same thing in a newspaper or newsmagazine, then in a television newscast.

11. The next serious disagreement you get into, try to establish what you and the other person are willing to accept as evidence. How hard is it to do that? Is there any disagreement about what to count as evidence?

PROJECT

12. Select one of your old papers, and imagine that you intended it for a reader who does not trust you and will question your reported evidence. What would you need to bolster each of the reports of evidence in your paper? Do some research to see whether you can get it. (You may not be able to put your hands on the evidence now, but you should be able to find out whether it is at least out there.) For quotations, imagine that your reader suspects that you quoted out of context. How could you show that you did not?

 FOCUS ON WRITING

$$\boxed{1}$$

Context.   One good way to develop an argument is to adapt a related argument that you or your readers find convincing. For example, in literature classes students often develop arguments about a book not discussed in class by applying to it the general structure of argument and some of the evidence used to discuss a related book that was assigned for class. This is also a common practice among professionals, such as management consultants. When they investigate the case of one client, they often make arguments similar to those they have previously made for other clients. This is not plagiarism, as long as you acknowledge your source and no one is fooled into thinking that you built the argument from scratch.

Scenario.   You work part-time in the office of the Dean of Students. Your boss, the dean, has been pressured by parents and the surrounding community to curb binge drinking among students. She has resisted because she believes that antidrinking measures infringe students' rights and hamper their growth as adults. She asked you to research the issue, and you provided her with a number of articles, including Camille Paglia's "Wisdom in a Bottle: 'Binge Drinking' and the New Campus Nannyism" and Jacob Sullum's "Smoking and the Tyranny of Public Health." The dean likes Paglia's piece and has been echoing its argument in her own statements. You have told her that you think Sullum's argument is more appropriate.

Task 1.   Your boss sends you the following e-mail: "I've been thinking about your concerns about using Paglia's argument, and you may have a point. I'm going to be visiting high schools for the next few days, but I'll check my e-mail. Send me a brief summary about the problems you see in Paglia's case and why you think I should use Sullum's instead." Write an e-mail memo to send to your boss.

Task 2.   Your boss wants a quick-and-dirty outline of an argument about drinking parallel to Sullum's argument about smoking. Outline Sullum's main reasons. Create a new outline by adapting, replacing, or deleting specific reasons so that the argument now applies to binge drinking.

Task 3.   Your boss wants a more detailed outline that she can use as "talking points" when she speaks around campus and in the community. Add evidence to support each reason. You can borrow Sullum's evidence when it applies; when it doesn't, find evidence focused on drinking rather than smoking.

Task 4.   Your boss wants you to ghostwrite an essay for the student newspaper. She will rewrite your argument to make it suit her style, but she wants a complete and polished draft from you.

RESEARCH PROJECT

Scenario.   Your proposal for a research paper has been accepted and you will be working on it for weeks. Your teacher wants to keep up with your progress by seeing your work along the way. You have two options: create a detailed outline by following steps 1, 2, and 3(a) (best for slow and careful drafters), or create a scratch outline and begin drafting by following steps 1, 2, and 3(b) (best for quick and dirty drafters).

Task.   Follow these steps:

- **Step 1:** Determine the major sections of your paper. After selecting the most promising answer to your research question, list the major reasons in support of that claim in an order that will help your readers understand it. Try several stock orders (familiar to unfamiliar, simple to complex, less to more controversial, etc.) as well as others that come to mind. You now have a rough outline of the major sections in your paper to share with your classmates.

- **Step 2:** Sketch a brief introduction to each section that states what part of the main question/problem you address in that section. End it with the reason that will be the main claim/point of that section.

- **Step 3a** (for slow and careful drafters): Create a detailed outline for the section using the procedures in Step 1. Under each reason, indicate what evidence you offer to support it. If you already have evidence, summarize it. If not, summarize the kind of evidence you expect to collect and how you expect to get it.

- **Step 3b** (for quick and dirty drafters): Draft each section including evidence you have collected. Otherwise indicate the kind of evidence you will look for. If you think that you can find a particular kind of evidence, summarize it. Indicate clearly that you have not yet checked your sources. (You can start these paragraphs with a note to yourself, *Although I have not yet looked, I expect that* [SOURCE] *will show that. . . .*)

SAMPLE ESSAY

The essay that follows uses evidence gathered from sources. You may not yet be writing papers as fully researched as this one, but even a shorter essay has to use its sources well. Read the essay and do the following:

Task 1.   Pick out the reasons and evidence in the essay. This will be easiest if you make a copy and mark it up with different colored highlighters. Otherwise, use line numbers to identify specific sentences. (Save your marked up copies; you'll need them again.)

1. How many reasons are supported with specific evidence? How many have no evidence at all?

2. On average, how many items of evidence does the writer present in support of each of the major reasons? (You can estimate this.)

3. Estimate the following: (a) What percentage of the evidence in this paper is reported primary evidence (one step away from the evidence itself; that is, the writer observed or collected it directly)? (b) What percentage is secondary evidence (two steps away from the evidence itself; that is, the writer reports on evidence reported by someone who observed or collected it)? (c) What percentage is tertiary evidence (three or more steps away)?

Task 2. Answer the following questions, using your analysis in Task 1 as evidence for your claims.

1. In general, does the evidence in this essay support its reasons?

2. Assuming that you accept those reasons, how well do they support the claim "that guns were not popular in America until after the Civil War, and that the reasons people began to buy guns had more to do with money than with patriotism"?

3. How well do they support the claim that "People should not be duped into thinking that supporting gun control laws is unpatriotic or un-American"?

4. Does the presentation of evidence in this essay make the writer seem more or less credible? Why?

Guns in America

1   If you listen to the NRA, owning a gun is the ultimate symbol of American freedom and democracy. So most people believe them when they say that gun ownership has been a part of America since the Revolution and that it is a violation of basic American beliefs when the government tries to take away the
5   people's guns. But this is just propaganda. The claim that for our forefathers owning guns was a patriotic duty is erroneous. History shows that guns were not popular in America until after the Civil War, and that the reasons people began to buy guns had more to do with money than with patriotism. People should not be duped into thinking that supporting gun control laws is unpatriotic
10   or un-American.

It is true that in colonial days many Americans owned guns, but they faced many dangers, and there was no police force to protect you. The rule was, defend yourself or die. But later, when the country became more civilized, people stopped owning guns. According to historian Michael Bellesiles, "It
15   would appear that at no time prior to 1850 did more than a tenth of the people own guns" (1966). This conclusion is based on surveys done by the states to see how many people owned guns so that they could serve in state militias. The state of Massachusetts counted all the guns owned by private citizens, and in

every survey until 1840 it found that less than 11 percent of the people owned
20 guns. "At the start of the War of 1812, the state had more spears than firearms
in its arsenal" (*Economist,* 1999). Also, guns were not the sort of thing people
bought for a hobby, as they do today. The first magazine devoted to guns was
not published until 1843.

One example of heroic gun owners that gun supporters talk about is the
25 Minutemen of Massachusetts. These were farmers who, on a minute's notice,
formed an army to defeat the British at Lexington and Concord, supposedly
shooting the British soldiers from behind fences and hedges because they were
great marksmen. But they were really a minority. Bellesiles did a study in which
he checked wills and "probate inventories" (records of personal possesses
30 when people died) between 1765 and 1790, and he found that less than 15
percent of all households had guns, and that more than half of the guns were
broken (Bellesiles, 1966). So by the time of the Revolution most Americans had
already stopped owning guns. In 1793, less than twenty years after the
Revolution, Congress passed a law to buy 7,000 muskets because it was
35 worried that so few people owned guns that the country would not be able to
defend itself (there was still no army). But the people didn't want the guns.
From 1808 to 1839, the government had a program to give a gun to every white
male who belonged to a state militia, but only half the militias bothered to ask
for them (*Economist,* 1999). This was not because the militia members already
40 owned guns, but because they didn't care about owning guns. In the 1830s, the
general sent down by the federal government to lead the Florida militia in a war
against the Seminoles, Winfield Scott, complained that the militia had almost no
guns.

The militias are another example of heroic gun owners held up by gun
45 supporters. But they were mostly a joke. Militia members were mostly "town
paupers, idlers, vagrants, foreigners, itinerants, drunkards and the outcasts of
society," according to the adjutant general of Massachusetts (*Economist,* 1999).
It was even more of a joke to think of them as marksmen like the Minutemen. In
Pennsylvania, one militia held a shooting contest, but no one hit the target and
50 the winner was the one who came closest. According to the newspaper, "The
size of the target is known accurately, having been carefully measured. It was
precisely the size and shape of a barn door" (Bellesiles, 1998). Most militias
stopped having shooting practice because it was embarrassing how badly they
shot. In 1839, the Secretary of War complained that militias were "armed with
55 walking canes, fowling pieces or unserviceable muskets" (*Economist,* 1999).

If you go by the movies, everyone had a gun in the Wild West. But Robert
Dykstra says that it was more peaceful in cattle towns like Tombstone, Arizona,
or Dodge City, Kansas, than in the cities in the east. It is true that most cowboys
carried rifles on the trail (mostly for hunting) and some of them carried pistols.
60 But when they came to a town, they did not have to defend themselves against
the dangers of the trail, so they left their guns behind because most cattle
towns had strict anti-gun laws and the Sheriff would take them away. "During
its most celebrated decade as a tough cattle town, only 15 persons died
violently in Dodge City, 1876–1885, for an average of just 1.5 killings per cowboy
65 season" (Dykstra, 1968). Living in these towns was more like *The Little House
on the Prairie* than the *Wild Bunch.* Maybe the movies have so many guns in

Westerns because gunfights are exciting and add to the action, or maybe they are just trying to support the myth that America is the land of the free and home of the brave because it is the home of the gun.

70   Why did most Americans not own a gun before the Civil War? There were two reasons. First, they didn't need them. It is a myth that violence has always been a part of American life. In the early years of the country, nine Americans out of ten did not feel that they needed a gun to protect themselves. Second, guns were expensive. A gun would cost a farmer a whole year's income

75 (*Economist,* 1999).

Why did more Americans own guns after the Civil War? There was one reason: money. When the war started, the Union government owned 327,000 muskets and rifles and the Confederate government owned 150,000. By the end of the war, the Union army had given out 4 million weapons to its soldiers.

80 Of course it also trained those soldiers to shoot. The Union army had 1.5 million soldiers and the Confederate army had 1 million. When the war was over and the soldiers went home, the army let them keep their guns. Now there were many more Americans with guns they got for free (Bellesiles, 1999).

The war also made guns less expensive. In the few years of the war, gun

85 manufacturers made more guns to supply the war than they had made in the entire history of the country (*Economist,* 1999). The gun manufacturers had to learn how to mass produce guns to supply the army with so many guns so quickly, which meant that not only did they have many more factories but that the guns were much cheaper. When the government stopped buying guns for

90 the war, the manufacturers had to sell more guns or close down the new factories, but they were saved because the war had created many new customers who owned guns and had learned to shoot in the war.

So you can see that it is a myth that guns have always been a part of American life and that without people owning guns America would not have

95 been able to protect its freedom. Gun supporters say people buy guns to protect themselves, but according to the statistics the only people likely to be shot by their guns are themselves or a member of their family. People say they buy guns to defend America's freedom, but who do they think they will defend it from? Those who believe in the myth of a nation of Minutemen may be sincere, but all

100 they guard is the profits of the gun manufacturers who have blood on their hands.

WORKS CITED

Bellesiles, Michael. "The Origins of Gun Culture in the United States, 1760–1865." *Journal of American History.* 83 (1966): 425–455.

Bellesiles, Michael. "Gun Laws in Early America." *Law and History Review.* 16 (1998): 567–589.

Bellesiles, Michael. *Lethal Imagination.* New York University Press: 1999.

Davidson, Osha Gray. *Under Fire.* University of Iowa Press: 1998.

Dykstra, Richard. *The Cattle Towns.* Knopf: 1968.

Economist Staff, "Guns in America." *Economist.* July 3, 1999.

National Rifle Association *NRA-ILA Research and Information Page.* The National Rifle Association Institute for Legislative Action. http://www.nraila.org/research/.

IN A NUTSHELL

About Your Argument . . .

You rest claims on reasons and rest reasons on reports of evidence. When you report evidence that you yourself observed or that someone else has reported, report it accurately and cite your sources so that readers can check it for themselves.

Since readers usually need more than one reason before they will agree to a claim, don't be satisfied with only one.

Except for the simplest, most obvious cases, don't cite reports of evidence without also stating a reason that connects those reports to the claim. Reasons not only support claims, they also interpret evidence. The reason should tell readers what to see in the evidence that is relevant to your claim.

. . . and About Writing It

When you have multiple reasons, select an order that helps readers:

- If reasons are parallel, order them on the basis of strength, acceptability, complexity, or familiarity.
- If your reasons are linked, decide whether you want them to follow some external process or an internal process of reasoning.

Keep a balance between reasons and reports of evidence:

- Beware the argument that is made up mostly of quotations or data.
- Conversely, be certain that you have at least tried to find evidence for every reason.

CHAPTER 6

The Core of Your Argument: Reporting Evidence

In this chapter, we discuss different kinds of evidence, with a special focus on how to evaluate what you have and decide what more you need.

In many ways, evidence is the substance of an argument: It distinguishes a well-founded claim from mere opinion or rigid dogmatism and is the largest part of most written arguments. Critical readers judge your argument and your ethos on the basis of your evidence, whether it is sufficient, of the right kind, gathered from sources they consider reliable, and reported—and cited—fully and accurately. In this chapter we show you how to find evidence, evaluate what you find, and then report it so that you readers will trust it and you.

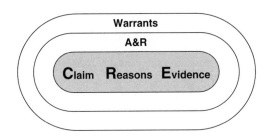

Weigh Your Burden of Evidence

In every argument, readers expect enough quality evidence to overcome their doubts. In conversation, you know you have met that burden of evidence when the other person doesn't ask for more. But when you write, you don't have readers there to tell you when they have seen enough or when they want more. You have to judge each case individually, but the following three questions will help you decide what kind of evidence you need, how much, and how good it has to be. (From here on, we use the term *evidence* to refer to both the evidence itself and your reports of it. When we have to distinguish them, we will.)

1. What kind of evidence will your readers expect? Readers in different academic or professional communities require different kinds of evidence. An environmental science teacher will expect you to draw toxicology data about a local lake from technical reports, not a newspaper; a history teacher will expect you to work with primary documents, not textbook accounts of them. Disciplines vary too much to give you a general rule other than this: When you write in a new community, ask an experienced member what counts as acceptable evidence in that field.

The first question to ask is whether your readers will want empirical evidence (numbers, controlled observations, etc.) or will they want "softer" forms of evidence (personal narratives, eyewitness reports, etc.). You also have to match the kind of evidence you report to the kind of problem you address. In an argument about binge drinking, for example, you would need one kind of evidence to argue that it is caused by the psychology of late adolescence, another by our culture of addiction, and another yet by a genetic predisposition to risk taking.

Each new argument presents new demands that you have to puzzle out case-by-case. Don't assume that the evidence you need is the evidence you can get most easily. Resist the temptation to rely only on what you happen to have experienced—the striking event you witnessed, the memorable person you knew, that one time you talked with a binge drinker. A "for instance" is not proof.

If your problem requires personal evidence or if that's all you can get, don't settle for anecdotes you have told and retold: Search the details of your own memory, and when you can, seek corroboration from records or other participants. Memory is a poor witness; it needs all the help you can give it.

2. How strongly will readers resist your claim? The more readers resist a claim, the more evidence they want. Assume your readers will want more evidence when you ask them to

- Accept a claim that contradicts what they deeply believe.
- Do something that costs them time or effort.
- Do or think something that creates new problems, such as the loss of something they like or the disapproval of others.

In these situations, their feelings matter as much as your logic. Suppose you found evidence that a famous political figure knowingly included false stories in a book that made her famous. Her political opponents will snap up any evidence against her, while her admirers will demand more and better evidence before they agree that she is a fraud, because in accepting that claim, they have to give up more than a belief. (See the case of Rigoberta Menchú in Inquiry 10 on p. 179.)

3. How fully do you want your readers to accept your claim? If you ask readers to accept a strong claim wholeheartedly, they will expect your best reports of the best evidence. But they may be satisfied with less if you ask less of them—for example, to approve a claim rather than act on it, or only to understand and respect your reasons for making it. If Harry asks the dean to extend library hours to accommodate students with day jobs, the dean will want more than anecdotal evidence about dissatisfied students. But she may be receptive to a few good stories if Harry wants her only to have an assistant find out whether students have a reasonable complaint.

Make a Plan to Find Evidence

We risk misleading ourselves when we speak of "gathering" evidence, as if it were scattered around, waiting to be picked up. Getting evidence is closer to hunting down a specific quarry. Colomb spent five years, on and off, hunting for the address of a doctor who practiced in London at the end of the seventeenth century. You probably can't spend weeks, much less months or even years, hunting for evidence, but you'll still need to do some sleuthing to meet your burden of evidence.

Your hunting is not likely to be successful if you don't know what you're looking for or where to look. Before you fire up a search engine, invest some time to decide first what kind of evidence your readers will expect and then how you can best get it. For one plan, see the Writing Process section (pp.173–75).

The Four Maxims of Quality

Once you find evidence, you have to evaluate it as your readers are likely to. Doing that will be hard, for it is a sad but true comment on the human mind that we all tend to seize on evidence that confirms what we want to believe; and worse, we ignore, reject, or even distort evidence that contradicts it. So to meet your burden of evidence, you have to anticipate the questions readers may ask, which means seeing your evidence through their eyes.

Once you think you can meet your readers' expectations with sufficient evidence of the right kind, evaluate its quality, but again from their point of view. Readers judge evidence by four criteria: (1) accuracy, (2) precision, (3) representativeness, and (4) reliability. How severely they apply those criteria depends on their stake in your claim. For instance, for a claim that some natural herb improves Alzheimer's symptoms, FDA researchers responsible for testing such cures will demand multiple studies that meet all four criteria; family members caring for an Alzheimer's sufferer are likely to accept a lower threshold of evidence; and the producers of the herb a lower one yet. Imagine your readers asking the following questions about your evidence:

1. Is your report of evidence accurate? This is the prime maxim. Get one fact wrong and readers may distrust everything else you say—and you, as well.

2. Is your report of evidence precise enough? It is 100 percent accurate to say that the population of Ohio is between a million and a billion, but not precise enough for most purposes. What counts as precise, though, differs by both use and field. A physicist measures the life of a particle in millionths of a second; a paleontologist might be happy to date the appearance of a new species give or take half a million years. Reports of evidence can be too precise. A historian would seem foolhardy to date the collapse of the Soviet Union at "2:11 P.M. on August 18, 1991, because it was at that moment that Gorbachev...." When you write "many" or "some," critical readers will want to know how many is many and how few are some.

3. Is the evidence you report representative? This depends on your kind of problem. If you generalize about how people get off welfare, you need a huge sample to cover all the reasons. But if you are studying a new chemical compound, you can make big generalizations from tiny samples. Human populations vary a lot; samples of a chemical compound little or not at all. These days, representative sampling depends on statistical methods whose principles every educated person should understand.

4. Are your reports of evidence from reliable sources? The problem of reliable sources turns on four issues: currency, reputation, disinterestedness, and level of source.

- **Currency:**
  Is your source up-to-date? Again, this varies by field. In computer science, a year-old research report is probably out-of-date; in philosophy, ancient authorities are always relevant. In general, look for the most recent work in a field.

- **Reputation:**
  Readers are more likely to trust evidence from people with good reputations, strong credentials, important positions, and name recognition. They will be suspicious at best of data that you pull from the Web site of someone neither you nor they have ever heard of. But even expert credentials do not ensure reliability: Linus Pauling won a Nobel Prize in chemistry, but he was judged to be a flake when he moved out of his field to tout vitamin C as a cure for most ills known to medicine.

  Be aware that some journals have better reputations for publishing sound research than others. Find out which journals are most (and least) respected before you cite evidence from one. If you find journal articles online, be sure that whoever posted them is also reliable: You can trust one posted by the journal itself, by the author, or in your library's online databases.

- **Disinterestedness:**
  Will readers be confident that, however expert your sources, they are not tainted by self-interest? Not long ago, a government study of the safety of silicone breast implants was almost wholly discredited when it was discovered that one scientist on the panel had received research funds from a company making implants. Even if that scientist had been utterly objective, the critics were right to charge that the mere appearance of a conflict of interest was enough to undermine the image of integrity of the whole panel. The best sources of evidence are those who have something to lose in offering it. For a claim that trigger locks make guns safer, the CEO of gun manufacturer Smith and Wesson is a weightier source than Oprah.

• Level of source:
Generally, you should get as close as you can to the evidence itself. Primary sources are closest. If you are studying texts, primary sources are the original books, letters, diaries, and so on. For textual evidence, use a recent edition by a reputable publisher. If you are studying physical phenomena, primary sources are the notebooks of those who directly observed and collected the evidence "itself," along with their first-hand reports based on their notes. For physical evidence, use the original article (not just the abstract or, worse, someone's report of it).

If you can't find primary sources, look for reliable secondary sources— scholarly journals and books that report on primary sources. Tertiary sources report work found in secondary sources; they include textbooks, articles in encyclopedias, and mass publications like *Reader's Digest*. If these are the only sources available, so be it, but assume that careful readers will not accept them as authoritative. They know that a report of a report of a report is too far from the evidence itself to be trusted.

In the Readings...

Evidence, Ethos, and Credibility

It can be tricky deciding what readers will count as acceptable evidence, and how their decision affects your credibility. In "Purging Bingeing" (p. 441), Ed Carson argues that bingeing is not the problem many say it is. He questions the credibility of those who say it is a problem by questioning one use of unrepresentative evidence:

> So last year, when the Center on Addiction and Substance Abuse at Columbia University (CASA) claimed the percentage of college women drinking to get drunk had more than tripled during the previous 15 years, the news media were quick to hype the finding that drinking on campus had reached "epidemic proportions." But as Kathy McNamara-Meis revealed in the Winter 1995 Forbes MediaCritic, CASA's conclusions were based on a misleading comparison of results from a 1977 survey of all college women and a 1992 survey of freshman women. Since freshmen drink more than any other class, such a comparison would suggest an increase in drunkenness even if nothing had changed.

In response, Carson offers not a report of evidence but a report of a claim by someone presented as an authority by virtue of his credentials:

> In fact, says David Hanson, a professor of sociology at the State University of New York at Potsdam who has studied alcohol use on campus for more than 20 years, "the evidence shows that the actual trend is as flat as your little sister's chest."

If Carson is right that the CASA based its claim on unrepresentative evidence, does that disprove its claims that bingeing is on the rise? How credible does Carson's authority seem? Does Carson affect his own credibility and ethos by quoting that tasteless comparison?

Trustworthy Reports of Evidence

We've emphasized that what you offer as evidence is more likely to be a report of it, and that a report predictably shapes evidence to suit a writer's own goals and interests. So when you gather evidence from the reports of others, be aware that your source has already shaped it, and that you will again. Even when you report your own observations of the evidence "itself," you cannot avoid giving it some "spin." To report evidence responsibly, you have to understand its different kinds, what to use each kind for, how we predictably distort it, and what are the best ways to present it.

Reports of Memories

As you read these words, you can feel the heft of this book, the texture of its pages. You can close the book and hear it snap; you can sniff it, even nibble at a page to taste it. Your nerve endings are reporting on the data from "out there," data that support your belief that this book exists. Now put the book down for a moment and look away. [_____] The instant you did that, the "self"-evidence of this book vanished, leaving you with nothing but mental traces—a lingering taste, perhaps; a visual or tactile memory. At that moment your memory was reconstructing those sense data, reporting the reports of your senses.

Memories often feel like trustworthy evidence, a record of our "direct" experience through our senses. But in fact, memory is one of the least reliable forms of evidence. When we construct a memory of an event, our minds unconsciously give it a form easy to store and recall. We shape it into a coherent story, eliminating some details, enhancing others, even inventing elements to it flesh out. And the more impressive the event, the more our memories are likely to change it. Even if we strive to avoid consciously embellishing a memory when we report it, our mind has already reshaped it for us. So use evidence from memory cautiously and corroborate it with other evidence whenever you can.

Never Trust Eyewitnesses

In one study, people recalling a videotape of a car accident estimated the speed of the cars differently, depending on whether they were asked how fast the cars were going when they either "bumped" or "smashed" into each other. Depending on the wording of the question, the subjects even "remembered" different amounts of broken glass, though the videotape showed none at all!

Source: Elizabeth F. Loftus and John C. Palmer, "Reconstruction of Automobile Destruction: An Example of the Interaction Between Language and Memory," *Journal of Verbal Learning and Verbal Behavior* 13 (1974): 585–589.

Anecdotes

An anecdote is a report of memory designed for public consumption. Even if we try to stick only to known facts (and many of us don't), we reshape our already storylike memory into an even better story, adding and deleting still more details, reorganizing them to make the story funnier, more dramatic, more pointed to support whatever reason we had for telling the story in the first place. After we tell it a few times, we have turned that anecdote into a finely honed short story with a beginning, middle, and end—likely to have a distant relationship to the event it reports.

That's why illustrative anecdotes can be so persuasive, especially when we use one to dress up "objective" numerical data. When readers see pallid statistics enlivened by a vivid anecdote, the numbers take on the quality of evidence from "out there" because we seem to experience what they represent in our mind's eye. Compare these:

> Fifty-three percent of Americans over the age of 65 have an annual income above $30,000, but 15 percent have incomes of less than $7,000 a year.

> Around 9 A.M., the cabin attendant on UA flight 1643 to San Francisco asked Oliver and Sarah Peters whether they wanted the western omelet or the fruit plate for breakfast. Recently retired, they were on their way to visit their children and grandchildren in San Diego, happy to be escaping the below-zero windchill in Chicago. At about the same time, 85-year-old Amanda Wilson was sitting at her kitchen table on Chicago's south side, staring at two five-dollar bills, a quarter, and a dime, trying to figure out one more time how to get through the next two weeks on 85¢ a day. She lives on $565 a month Social Security, most of which goes for heat, light, and rent on her one-room apartment. She had a daughter once, but . . .

The anecdote is a good illustration, but bad evidence.

Some writers claim that personal experience is truer than cold, objective data. But it is not the kind of public, shared truth that readers want as a basis for a contestable claim. So be aware that if you do use a personal anecdote as evidence, readers may be too polite to question it openly, but will silently dismiss it as they think to themselves, "Anecdotal." You can anticipate that response by acknowledging the limits of personal evidence, "This is only my experience, but . . ." More importantly, look for other evidence that will corroborate it and bring it alive.

Reports from Authorities

Some students think they offer evidence when they quote an authority. But what they usually offer is only that authority's own report of evidence, or more often, just their own reason restated in someone else's more authoritative voice. For example, Mai might think she is supporting her claim with evidence in the form of a quotation, but here she only restates her reason in words more authoritative than her own:

> Teachers should be required to respond to their teaching evaluations _{claim} because those who read them are more likely to improve their teaching than

those who don't. _{reason} According to J. Wills, for example, teachers who study their evaluations "profit from their openness to criticism" (*The Art of Teaching*, 330). _{reason restated}

Mai may be right that the teachers are more likely to improve, but the quoted words only restate her own reason: they are evidence only that Wills has said the same thing. Mai could strengthen her claim if she reported not just Wills's claim but his evidence as well:

Teachers should be required to respond to their teaching evaluations _{claim} because those who read them are more likely to improve their teaching than those who don't. _{reason} According to J. Wills, for example, teachers who study their evaluations "profit from their openness to criticism" (*The Art of Teaching*, 330). _{reason restated} He studied 200 teachers who spent at least an hour reviewing their evaluations. The next term, they achieved 15 percent higher evaluations than those who circulated teaching evaluations but did not read them (*The Art of Teaching*, 333–335). _{reported evidence}

When you quote authorities, you do two useful things:

- If your authority is credible, you make your own position more credible.

- If your authority gathered evidence you report, you bring readers as close as they can get, short of reading the authority itself.

Of course, you still have to show that the authority has based her reasons on sound evidence.

Why Question Others' Reports?

If you need reason to suspect the reports of evidence that you find in your sources, consider some research by Robert P. Newman and Keith R. Sanders. They studied the transcripts of a National College Debate Tournament to identify every instance where a debater cited specific testimony (quotations, numbers, etc.). They then compared each citation with its source to determine how accurately the debaters reported it. They found that more than half of the reports of reports of evidence were wrong! (Of course, we have to trust that Newman and Sanders collected their evidence accurately.)

Source: "A Study in the Integrity of Evidence," *Journal of the American Forensic Association* 2 (1965): 7–13.

Visual Reports with Photographs, Drawings, and Recordings

"Ocular proof" is compelling, because it makes us feel we can see what really happened. Like stories, visual images bring data to life by letting us experience them more directly than through words. For example, it is only when we see images of starving refugees and massacred civilians that we translate abstract claims about moral imperatives into vivid, concrete experience. And recall the power of those videos and photographs of the twin towers coming down on 9/11.

We might think that videotapes, photographs, and recordings are more reliable than memories, but as we all know, images and recordings of all kinds can be fabricated so convincingly that even experts cannot distinguish fakes from the real thing. (Always distrust images on the Web whose sources are not rock-solid reliable.) But even when they are not doctored, images and recordings reshape what they record. That's why you must tell your readers who took the pictures or made any recording you offer as evidence, and under what circumstances.

Visual Presentations of Quantitative Data

For some readers, numbers are the most compelling evidence, in fact the only acceptable evidence, partly because numbers seem most objective, partly because they are recorded by exacting types like scientists and accountants. If any evidence feels as though it is "out there" in the world, it is what we can count, and what we can count we can objectively quantify.

But just like any other report of evidence, numbers are shaped by the aims and interests of those who record them. When researchers gather data for an argument about the safety of air bags, the counters have to decide what to count—traffic fatalities, serious injuries (what counts as serious?), people brought to hospitals, those who make insurance claims, etc. They also have to decide how to organize the numbers—total fatalities, fatalities per year, fatalities per thousand, fatalities per miles driven, fatalities per trip, etc., each of which affects the impact that the numbers have on readers.

For example, imagine you are deciding whether to invest in one of two companies, Abco or Zorax. Look at the three ways shown here to represent the same "facts." Which way of representing the data helps you make the best decision?

TABLE 1   INCOME, ABCO AND ZORAX

	1996		1997	
	Gross Income	Net Income	Gross Income	Net Income
Abco	145,979,000	32,473,000	164,892,000	32,526,000
Zorax	134,670,000	25,467,000	136,798,000	39,769,000

We could also represent these data in words, but words spin the data even more than visual images do. How attractive are Zorax and Abco in these two accounts?

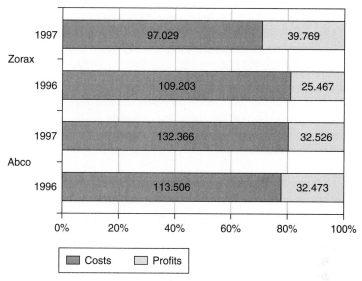

FIGURE 1 PROFIT AS A PERCENTAGE OF INCOME, ABCO AND ZORAX

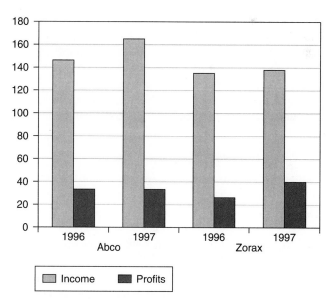

FIGURE 2 INCOME AND PROFITS, ABCO AND ZORAX

Zorax improved its net profits in 1997 from 1996 by more than 50 percent despite relatively level sales. In contrast, Abco failed to increase its net profits significantly despite substantially higher sales.

In comparison to Zorax's increased sales and profits, Abco increased its profits and significantly increased its gross 1997 income over 1996.

We might think that a table of numbers is most "objective," but that apparent objectivity is itself a rhetorical choice. While these reports offer the same factual data, we are affected by them in different ways. The right choice depends partly on the kind of evidence your readers expect, but also on how you want them to respond.

Our Misplaced Trust in Numbers

Numbers are useful as evidence because most readers trust them more than they should. Here are one expert's reasons why you should not put too much trust in numbers:

What do you mean when you say in your book that facts don't speak for themselves?

We all talk about facts as though they're rocks you pick up and they have an independent existence, and they don't. When you hear a statistic, someone has created that. You cannot take that number and assume that is a pure reflection of reality.

Take me through the process of how an accurate number gets transformed into an inaccurate one.

An article appears in the newsletter for the American Anorexia/Bulimia Association, and they quote a physician who says perhaps 150,000 people have anorexia, it's very serious and some people die. This was transformed, I think, first in a scholarly book, where someone said 150,000 people die from anorexia every year. You can see how this happens, maybe sloppy note-taking. Once the figure is out there, it's very hard to take back.

What's the biggest trap people fall into when hearing a number?

I think the biggest error is that we hear a number, and we automatically assume we know what is being counted. When we hear an estimate for the number of missing children, we imagine these are children abducted by strangers; we hear numbers for child abuse, and what pops into our mind is the worst possible case, and I think what people don't understand is how broadly these phenomena are being defined in order to generate these big numbers.

Source: Interview with Joel Best, author of *Damned Lies and Statistics: Untangling Numbers from the Media, Politicians, and Activists* (2001), in the *New York Times*, May 26, 2001, p. A17.

IN THE READINGS . . .

Kinds of Evidence

In "Obstacles to Open Discussion and Critical Thinking" (p. 385), Carol Trosset offers as evidence both quotations and statistics. Why present both? Select three quotations that she presents as evidence. What does each one do for her argument that the numbers cannot do? What do her numbers do for her argument that her quotations cannot? If you had to choose between the numbers and the quotations, which do you think would help you understand her claim better? Which would be more important to you in deciding whether to accept her claim?

Radical Skepticism

When we treat evidence and reports of evidence as matters of agreement, we seem close to giving up the metaphor of an argument resting on a solid foundation of factual evidence. And in fact, we do. Some philosophers object to that, arguing that if we base our reasoning on anything less than utterly certain, objective fact, we surrender to relativity and subvert not just the quest for truth, but the very idea that it exists. How can we be sure of anything if we define evidence merely as what we agree to?

But this definition of evidence should not threaten us if we agree to base our beliefs on the best arguments we can make, based on the best reports of the best evidence we can find. We could, for example, agree that the world is flat, and base our claim on the evidence of our senses. But to keep believing that, we would have to ignore reliable reports of other intractable, undeniably better evidence that should lead us to believe that the world is round. That makes "truth" less a matter of capricious agreement and more a matter of thoughtful inquiry and argument.

To be sure, if readers want to be difficult, they can stubbornly refuse to agree to any evidence. It is a standard trick for derailing arguments. When critics charged that New Jersey state police stopped African American drivers almost five times as often as they did whites, one participant in the debate kept questioning the data because, as he said, "everyone knows you can twist statistics to mean anything you want." In so doing, he refused to engage in a good faith argument because he denied even the possibility of reliable evidence.

So what do you say to someone who never accepts anything as uncontested but just keeps asking, What is that based on? Can you show me more? Nothing. Such a person has refused your offer to engage in a collaborative search for the truth.

Turtles All the Way Down

There is a story told by the anthropologist Clifford Geertz of an Englishman in India, who, upon being told that the world rests on the back of an elephant, asked "On what does the elephant stand?" "On the back of a turtle," he was told. "And on what does the turtle stand?" he asked. "On the back of another turtle." "And on what" the Englishman asked again, "does *that* turtle stand?" "Ah, Sahib," replied the Indian, "after that, it is turtles all the way down!"

Arguments are a bit like that. Our claim is the world that rests on the elephant of our reasons; that elephant stands on the back of a turtle of evidence. But when someone asks what that turtle rests on, we realize that our argument is potentially turtles all the way down. We can only hope that at some point readers stop asking about the next one.

IN THE READINGS...

Trusting Authorities

In the sample essay, "Guns in America" (pp. 156–58), the writer relies heavily on the work of historian Michael Bellesiles, which is based on extensive archival research. At the time the essay was written in 2001, Bellesiles's work was highly respected, had even won awards. He had critics, but most were gun advocates who complained more about his conclusions than about his research. But by early 2002, his work was criticized by scholars who questioned his research methods. When they asked to see some of his raw data, he had to confess that some of his notes were lost when his office flooded. The criticisms concerned only a part of his archival research, but they were serious enough that historians devoted an entire issue of a journal to questioning his research and his university convened a committee to investigate charges of academic fraud. Although the committee stopped short of finding him guilty of fraud, it concluded that his documentation of his evidence was "skimpy" and "sloppy," and that he was guilty of unfairly presenting his evidence because his research was "superficial" and "thesis-driven."[a] Professor Bellesiles has since resigned.

Presumably, it was fair for the writer of "Guns in America" to rely on Bellesiles before the questions about his research became widely known. Would it be fair to rely on him now, if you knew these questions had been raised? What if the writer discovered the questions only after her paper was virtually complete and the deadline was near? Should a first-year student be responsible for checking out the reputation of apparently reliable authorities whose work she uses? Should a fourth-year student in an honors seminar be responsible for checking the reputations of sources? Does this mean you should never rely on authorities?

[a] "Report of the Investigative Committee in the matter of Professor Michael Bellesiles," July 10, 2002, http://www.news.emory.edu/Releases/Final_Report.pdf.

WRITING PROCESS

Reporting Evidence

READING AND RESEARCH

Planning Your Hunt for Evidence

Research is like diamond mining: You have to know what you are looking for and where to look; then you must process lots of dross to find a few gems; and even then your best finds need polishing. In the same way, when you address a problem that requires more than casual research, you need a systematic plan to guide your search for evidence. If you have only a topic to guide you, you may have to read widely before you find a problem worth pursuing. But as soon as you find that problem and you generate one or more hypotheses for a tentative solution, you can plan your research systematically.

Once you select a tentative claim, focus your reading or other data collecting on the evidence you'll need to test and support it. You'll waste a lot of time if you collect information randomly. Instead, invest some time to imagine the best possible evidence and use it to plan your search.

1. Decide what kind of evidence readers expect in support of your claim.

Your reasons must be relevant to your claim, and your evidence must be relevant to your reasons. But your evidence must also be the *kind* of evidence that readers expect in support of your particular *kind* of claim. You have to step back to think critically about what you should look for—not just the kind of evidence that will convince yourself that your claim is sound, but the kind that will convince your readers. For example, what evidence would convince your particular reader that extrasensory perception exists? Striking anecdotes? Objective data generated by controlled experiments? Testimony from someone they trust? Only their own personal experience of it? Imagine that evidence, and then use what you imagine both to guide your search and to test what you find.

2. Weigh the cost of the search against the value of the evidence.

You want the evidence that best tests and supports your claim, but second-best evidence is better than none. Decide how long it will take to find the best evidence. Is there a risk that you will find none? If the best evidence may be too hard to find, limit your risk by gathering the most readily available evidence first. For example, if Elena had only a few weeks to prepare her argument supporting a Center for English Language Studies, she could not survey every college with a center. She would have to settle for a less reliable phone survey of a few she knew about. But she would then also have to acknowledge that her evidence is less than the best (more about that in Chapter 7).

3. Decide on the most likely source of evidence.

You have many options:

- **Libraries:** A college library will provide most of the data you need. The trick is knowing how to find them. Every library has a tour, and most librarians are eager to help. An hour or two invested in learning how to find resources in different fields will pay off in time saved later.

- **The Internet:** The Internet is an increasingly important source of information, but it is still like an undiscriminating library without librarians. Most of the Internet has no gatekeepers to screen information for quality: some is reliable, some not. So it is a case of "browser beware." At least be sure you know who stands behind the information in a site. You can trust some sites: the site of a print journal; a peer reviewed online journal (if the site doesn't say, ask your teacher); an e-text site at a university you've heard of; the Gutenberg project; the site of a scholarly or professional organization. Otherwise, use the Net for the following purposes, cautiously:

  - *To get a quick overview:* You can use Google Scholar to get a quick sense of what's been published on your question. (Just don't trust it to be as complete as a good library's online catalogue.) Also, Wikipedia and other online references can give you an overview with additional references you can check. (But go to the primary sources; don't cite any wiki as your source.)

  - *To access your library's collection:* Most libraries have online catalogues and offer electronic access to articles, abstracts, and databases. If yours doesn't, try to get access to the library of a state university or go to the Library of Congress at www.loc.gov.

  - *To get public materials:* Most major newspapers and magazines maintain Web sites with information on recent articles, sometimes the articles themselves. You can purchase reprints of articles in the *New York Times* and other major newspapers.

  - *To find information too recent to be found in libraries:* Many government reports are released first on the Web, then in print.

  - *To supplement information you find in libraries:* Some journals conduct Net-based discussions among readers and authors. Others use the Web to archive data not included in printed texts.

  - *To find information that libraries don't collect:* For example, a student interested in steel pan music found that many steel bands have their own Web pages.

- **People:** You may need support beyond the written word. When you use people as sources, plan carefully to avoid wasting not just your time, but theirs.

  - Prepare questions and bring them to the interview. Use them to avoid wasting time, but don't read them like a script.

- Record all identifying information—including the exact spelling of your source's full name. Record the date and place of the interview.

- Tape-record the interview if you can. If you can't, try to get the exact words.

- If you transcribe from a tape recorder, delete the *umm's* and *you know's,* but don't change anything else.

• **Direct observation:** Many questions can be answered only through field studies or controlled experiments conducted in ways a discipline requires. In a writing class, you're unlikely to be assigned a problem that requires such evidence, but you might construct a problem that needs it: How do instructors in different departments mark their papers? Do some bars encourage binge drinking more than others?

- Before you start observing, record the date and place of the observations and relevant circumstantial details. If the location is relevant, take a digital photo or sketch a map.

- If you record quantitative data, create a blank data table or chart before you start; record data precisely, right then, not later from memory.

- In your argument, use only the data that your *records* support, not what you recall after you realize you failed to record information you should have. Be sure to tell readers how you collected the data. And if you have data that call your claim into question, you are obliged to report them as well.

• **"I search":** In some classes, teachers expect students to gather most of their evidence from personal reflection: not *research* but *I search.* If your assignment calls for this kind of evidence, guard against the deceptions of memory: We are all prone to remember what we think ought to have happened rather than what did. And never treat this kind of evidence as an objective "outside" source.

4. Sample the evidence.

Don't waste time looking for evidence that a source can't provide; sample sources first to determine their value. For a survey, test your questions in a trial run or focus group. For books or articles, skim a few introductions and abstracts to see whether they look promising. For direct observation, make a quick visit to the site to see what it offers.

5. Take stock as the evidence mounts.

Some students turn off their judgment when they start gathering evidence, reading book after book, taking endless notes before they realize that most of what they have is irrelevant to any claim they might make. So from time to time, pause to consider the value of what you have collected. Avoid the common mistake of assuming that you have done your job when you have found any evidence at all. Teachers more often complain that students offer too little evidence than too much.

Taking Research Notes

When you assemble an argument based on sources, your most important preparation is taking notes. You'll need bibliographic information so that you don't have to look up a source again to cite it properly. You'll need to copy quotations accurately to avoid errors that might damage your credibility and clearly distinguish quoted words from your own so that you don't inadvertently plagiarize. When you take notes, keep several things in mind:

Notes from Written Sources

- Record all bibliographic information:

  For a book, record the full title, author, and publication date, plus the name of the publisher and city. If you photocopy the title page, write down the year of publication from the back side of the title page. Include the library call number, because you may need your source again.

  For a journal article, record the author, full title, volume number, and page numbers. Record the call number of the journal.

  For an Internet source, record the URL (uniform resource locator) and any information you can find about the author of the text and the date it was posted and last changed. For a site that changes quickly, also record the date you accessed it. If you can, save a copy of any pages you cite onto your computer.

- Summarize and paraphrase when the information is important, but its particular form of expression is not.

- Quote the exact words when they are striking or complex. If a passage or data table is long, photocopy it.

In your notes, distinguish what you quote directly from what you summarize or paraphrase, and without fail distinguish what you paraphrase from your own thinking. (Use different colored ink or cards; on a computer, different fonts.) A week later, it is easy to think that what you took as notes are your own ideas in your own words, when in fact they belong to someone else.

- Record the context. Note whether the quote is a main point, a minor aside, a concession, etc. It is unfair to your source and reader to treat what a writer says in passing as something she would stand behind.

Notes from Interviews

- Record all identifying information—including the exact spelling of your source's name. Record the date and place of the interview.

- Tape-record the interview if you can. If you can't, try to get the exact words. If you transcribe from a tape recorder, edit out the *umms* and *you knows*, but don't change anything else to make it sound better.

- Prepare your questions and bring them to the interview. Don't read them like a script, but use them to avoid wasting the time of the person you are interviewing. Before you leave, glance over your questions to see if you have missed any important ones.

Notes from Observation

- Record the date and place of the observations and any relevant circumstantial detail before you start. If the location is relevant, take a photo or sketch a map.
- Record data precisely. If you record quantitative data, create a data table or chart before you start.

WORKING COLLABORATIVELY

Share Plans and Resources

Of all the jobs in assembling an argument, gathering evidence is one that your teacher may be happiest to see you share. If your teacher approves, work with others to formulate a plan for gathering evidence. As you all search for evidence, you are likely to find evidence helpful to one another.

Test Each Other's Drafts

Since evidence is what readers do not question at the time, your colleagues can help you anticipate what readers will accept. Once you have a draft, try this:

- Ask two colleagues to highlight the most and least reliable reports of evidence in your paper. If they disagree, ask them to explain.
- Ask other members of the group to evaluate how well your reports of evidence meet the four maxims of quality (pp. 162–64).

When someone questions a report of evidence as not close enough to a primary or secondary source, you must accept that judgment as appropriate for that reader. If that person is responding in good faith, there is no point debating whether he or she should have questions. If several colleagues have questions, assume your readers will too.

 INQUIRIES

REFLECTIONS

1. How many removes from "the evidence itself" are the following?

   Fourteen notices of office hours posted in Blaine Hall were as follows: 3 hours: 1; 2 hours: 2; 1 hour: 9; 30 minutes: 2.

   Faculty in Blaine Hall keep inadequate office hours.

   The average number of office hours per week that faculty in Blaine Hall keep is about one.

2. Invent three or four plausible scenarios in which others will feel you are being rude to ask them to justify a report of evidence they have just offered. What makes your question impolite?

3. In the early history of science, an experimenter invited other scientists to witness an experiment so that they could testify to the accuracy of the data gathered. Would it seem reasonable today for a scientist to insist on watching data being collected before she accepted it as sound? Why not? How then do we today get "testimony" concerning the reliability of reports of research?

4. Should reproductions count as primary evidence? How about a videotape of an event? An audiotape of a speech? A photograph? Would you trust a tape or photo more or less if you knew the person who offered it were technologically naïve? What if that person were a technological whiz? Why should that matter? Would it help to have witnesses who could testify about the circumstances in which the tape or photo was produced?

5. Are there situations in our everyday lives when we expect each other to be as hard-nosed about evidence as juries and scientists should be? Are there situations when we should not be hard-nosed about seeing the evidence for ourselves? How do you distinguish the two kinds of situations?

6. Some people think that just as there is no disputing taste, it is pointless to argue about values. Others say that we can argue about values, but that we have to use a different kind of evidence. Consider an argument about disputed values, such as whether it is morally wrong to help someone with a terminal illness commit suicide. What would count as evidence supporting reasons for or against such a position? What sources would be more authoritative than others? How do they derive their authority? Is there in fact a difference in the kind of evidence we use in arguments about values? Is there a difference in how we use it?

TASK

7. Return to the old papers that we asked you to work on. Highlight in a dark color reports of evidence that you think no reader would have questioned. Then highlight in a lighter color reports of evidence that some readers might have questioned. How "weighty" is the evidence in your argument? If you have highlighted more than two-thirds of your paper, it is probably too weighty. What would you add: more reasons, warrants, acknowledgments, and responses? If, you have highlighted less than one-fourth of your paper, it is not weighty enough. How easily could you get more evidence?

PROJECTS

8. Analyze a magazine ad as an argument. (Select one that's half a page or larger.) Assume that the main claim is an unexpressed *Therefore you*

should buy this product. What does the ad offer as reasons for buying the product? What does it offer as a report of the evidence? If it is a picture, how did the ad "spin" that report?

9. Look at the advertising in four or five magazines that appeal to people with different demographic profiles. For example, a teen magazine, a techie magazine, an intellectual magazine, a sports magazine, a woman's magazine, etc. How do they differ in the ways advertisers try to get their particular readers to buy products? Do the ads in the same publication use similar kinds of reasons and evidence? Do ads for similar products use similar kinds of evidence even for different readers?

10. A book that uses stories as evidence is *I, Rigoberta Menchú,* a searing account of atrocities allegedly committed by the Guatemalan army. Written by Rigoberta Menchú Tum, the human rights activist and winner of the Nobel Peace Prize, the book became highly controversial required reading on hundreds of campuses because it sparked a debate over the "higher value" of falsehood over truth. The controversy began when prestigious schools like Stanford required the book in general education courses, in some cases replacing writers like Shakespeare. Then in 1998, David Stoll, a specialist in Mayan history, showed that Menchú had fabricated some of her most sensational stories:

   • She described herself as a child working in near-slave conditions, unable to speak Spanish until adulthood, but she had actually attended Catholic boarding schools.

   • She describes acts of violence as though she witnessed them; in fact, she was away at school most of the time.

   • She says she watched the Guatemalan military burn her brother alive, but she wasn't there when it happened and the military probably did not do it.

   • She says another brother starved to death, but she had no such brother.

   • She says that her family lands were confiscated by wealthy landowners; in fact, they were lost to her father's in-laws.

   Menchú at first denied that she had committed "purposeful inaccuracies," adding, "I didn't find anything in these reports that changes the fact that my people are dead. And that is my truth" (*New York Times,* January 21, 1999). Later, she admitted some inaccuracies, but has yet to recant her story.

   Her critics were severe: one nominated her for the "Nobel Prize for Lying." Most of her supporters echoed her defense that she told a "larger truth." Some attacked Stoll for valuing mere fact over a "higher" truth. Others suggested that facts don't even matter: "Menchú made it clear from the outset that [she] had a political purpose, . . . to expose the atrocities committed by the Guatemalan army. This was not the fruit of some judicial investigation striving to be fair" (*Guardian*, December 16, 1998). But even before Stoll had exposed her, her admirers had argued that an oppressed person has an authenticity that lets her speak for all her people; that what matters is not truth, but personal, ethical, and economic motives that break the "silence of the oppressed."

Suppose that Menchú's critics are right: What she says she saw, she did not. In fact, some of the things she said happened never happened at all. But also suppose that in a sense she is right: things like those she described did happen to people like her and her family. Should she have described her work as a work of fiction? Would it have had the same impact? Would it have been effective to add incidents that happened to others without pretending they happened to her? List reasons for accepting or rejecting her "larger truth" defense. Which weigh more with you?

11. Given what you learned about lying in the readings, do you think Rigoberta Menchú lied? If so, was it an acceptable lie? List your reasons for saying so. What general principle (warrant) would you offer to explain why you make that judgment?

12. The Greek philosopher Aristotle argued that fiction describes events more truthfully than a history. A history, he said, has to stick to the facts, whereas fiction can describe things more plausibly—as they should have occurred, not just as they happened to. Can you think of a way to defend Menchú's book based on Aristotle's idea of truthfulness? Sketch the major steps in such an argument. Would *you* accept such a defense?

 # FOCUS ON WRITING

1

Context.   It is an old belief that "factual" or "scientific" truth (the kind we establish by arguments based on evidence) is not the only truth. But in recent years, some postmodern theorists have argued that it should not be the only kind of truth we accept in fields such as law or history. It is an act of political oppression, they say, to require just the facts.

Scenario.   In 1999, six Nobel Peace Prize winners gathered for a conference on the future of human rights and social justice. The event was such a success that several colleges in your state are jointly sponsoring a similar conference at the state capitol. Among the speakers will be Rigoberta Menchú, but local political groups are trying to get her removed from the conference because of the controversy over her book (see Inquiry 10). As the student representative from your school on the organizing committee, you have been appointed to the subcommittee assigned to respond to those who oppose Menchú's participation.

Task 1.   Your subcommittee has asked you to write a brief summary of the controversy. (You can find a list of articles, including abstracts, in the newspaper databases available in most libraries.) Be sure not to represent the controversy as a simple for-or-against debate.

Task 2.   The subcommittee has decided to respond to what it sees as an unfairly one-sided presentation of the issue by the opponents. Your assignment is to draft an essay describing the controversy, which will be published in the student newspapers of all participating colleges. Above all, the committee wants you to represent the different positions fairly, including the support for the claims.

Task 3.   The subcommittee wants to make the entire Menchú episode a learning experience for those who attend the conference. It will include in the conference program a collection of essays on the issue of factual evidence versus larger truths. Your assignment is to write an essay taking a stand on the issue. Since the subcommittee wants these essays to be models of fair argument, be sure that your argument acknowledges the strengths of the other positions.

RESEARCH PROJECT

Scenario.   Your teacher has made it clear that he will focus on the quality of the evidence in your research paper.

Task.   For each report of evidence, summarize why you think it is (1) accurate, (2) precise, (3) representative, and (4) reliable.

SAMPLE ESSAY

Task 1.   Return to your marked-up pages evaluating the evidence in "Guns in America" (pp. 156–58). Select the four most important items of evidence. Evaluate each in terms of the four maxims of quality (pp. 162–63).

Task 2.   Compare the evidence offered in support of the first major reason, "guns were not popular in America until after the Civil War," with the evidence offered in support of the second, "the reasons people began to buy guns had more to do with money than with patriotism." Which evidence is stronger? Why? Should the writer have downplayed the reason with the weaker evidence? Why or why not? What other options might the writer have for acknowledging this disparity in the evidence?

Task 3.   Here again is the introduction to "Guns in America." Identify its elements by picking out the common ground, destabilizing condition, cost or consequences, and solution or promise of solution.

Guns in America

If you listen to the NRA, owning a gun is the ultimate symbol of American freedom and democracy. So most people believe them when they say that gun ownership has been a part of America since the Revolution and that it is a violation of basic American beliefs when the government tries to take away the people's guns. But this is just propaganda. The claim that for our forefathers owning guns was a patriotic duty is erroneous. History shows that guns were not popular in America until after the Civil War, and that the reasons people began to buy guns had more to do with money than with patriotism. People should not be duped into thinking that supporting gun control laws is unpatriotic or un-American.

Now read this revised introduction with the new title, "The Minuteman Myth: The True Story of Guns in America." Identify its elements by picking out the common ground, destabilizing condition, cost or consequences, and solution or promise of solution.

The Minuteman Myth: The True Story of Guns in America

1   When the English colonists sailed to America, they brought to this continent many ideas that made America what it is today: religious freedom, dedication to liberty, and the belief that people should govern themselves. Did they also bring over the American love of guns? One of the first laws passed in Jamestown,
5   Virginia, required every man to own a gun for defending the settlement. By the Revolution, most of the colonies had laws requiring citizens to own guns (Davidson, 1998), and after the Revolution, since the federal government had no army, local governments were required to have a militia made up of gun-owning citizens (*Economist,* 1999). Also, the Bill of Rights included the idea that the
10   safety of the country depended on people owning guns: "A well-regulated militia being necessary to the security of a free State, the right of the people to keep and bear Arms shall not be infringed."

Today the government passes laws, not to require citizens to own guns, but to restrict them from owning guns the government thinks are dangerous, such
15   as assault rifles. Supporters of gun control say we need laws because of all the crazies and criminals who get their hands on guns: Lee Harvey Oswald, John Hinkley, the Columbine killers, drug pushers, and many others. Opponents of gun control like the NRA try to offset this by talking about gun-owning American heroes from history, such as the Minutemen of the Revolution and Daniel Boone
20   (NRA, 1999). They say that even if bad people get guns, good people need them too for the same reason that the colonists and the other historical heroes needed them—namely, to defend themselves and their families. Besides, owning a gun is presented as the ultimate symbol of American freedom and democracy. So most people believe them when they say that gun ownership
25   has been a part of America since the Revolution and that it is a violation of basic American beliefs when the government tries to take away the people's guns.

But this is just propaganda. People should not be duped into thinking that supporting gun control laws is unpatriotic or un-American. The gun control oppo-

nents' claim about Americans always owning guns because we believed that
30 owning guns was a patriotic duty is erroneous. History shows that guns were
not popular in America until after the Civil War, and that the reasons people
began to buy guns had more to do with money than with patriotism.

1. Which introduction makes the writer seem more knowledgeable? More evenhanded?

2. How does the inclusion of evidence affect your response to the "Minuteman" introduction?

3. How does the new title better prepare readers for the rest of the essay?

4. How does the expanded common ground better prepare readers?

5. How do the new title and expanded common ground change your perception of the writer's ethos?

IN A NUTSHELL

About Your Argument . . .

No skill is more useful than distinguishing reasons, evidence, and reports of evidence from your readers' point of view. You need more and better evidence when you want readers to change important beliefs, to do something costly or difficult, or to accept a solution that may create new problems. Your biggest challenge will be to find enough evidence to satisfy your readers, because we all tend to be satisfied with less evidence than our readers want.

Once you think you have enough evidence, evaluate it: Is it accurate, precise, representative, and authoritative? Use each kind of evidence only in the ways it is most reliable:

- Memories are always unreliable, because our minds shape them into a storylike structure influenced by what we believe or want to be true. Always try to find corroborating evidence.

- Anecdotes are even less reliable, because we impose on them an even more shapely story structure. Anecdotes can be good illustrations, but they are never the best evidence.

- Reports from authorities may be evidence only of what they believe. Distinguish what they offer as reasons from the evidence they report.

- Photographs and recordings are never objective. Even when they haven't been doctored, they depict just a slice of what they seem to represent.

- Quantitative data can be represented in different ways, and each gives it a "spin."

Remember that you ask readers to accept reports of evidence in lieu of the evidence itself, so they must be confident that you report it accurately. Along with warrants, evidence is one of the two anchors that readers must agree on before you can even make an argument.

. . . and About Writing It

When you report what a written source says, ask whether your readers expect the exact words or a paraphrase. In general, those in the humanities are more likely to expect the exact words; those in other fields will accept close paraphrases.

When you copy notes into your argument, be aware of how easy it is to forget that what you copy is not your own words, but those of your sources. You can avoid that by scrupulously distinguishing in your notes your own words and those from a source. If you take notes on a computer, use a distinctive font; if you write them out, use colored ink or cards—whatever will help you distinguish your own words from those of your sources. You can afford to be wrong; you cannot afford to be accused of plagiarism.

CHAPTER 7

Your Reader's Role in Your Argument: Acknowledgments and Responses

In this chapter we discuss the kinds of questions, reservations, and objections that you can expect critical readers to raise about your arguments. We show you how to anticipate them and decide which to acknowledge and how to respond to them. When you acknowledge and amiably respond to your readers' questions, you demonstrate a level of critical thinking that will lead readers to trust your arguments and you.

Y ou can build the core of an argument by answering just three of argument's five questions:

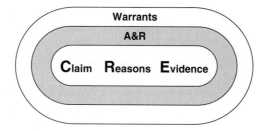

What are you **claiming?**
What are your **reasons** on which you base your claim?
What is your **evidence** on which you base your reasons?

Occasionally, that alone will convince a reader. But just the core of an argument is rarely enough when your readers are thoughtful and critical or you address complex and contested issues. In that case, if you fail to bring your readers' views into your argument, you can seem ignorant of them or, worse, arrogantly indifferent; or worst of all, you can seem to be a dogmatic, narrow thinker who sees things only one way and expects everyone else to do the same. None of that adds to your credibility.

You will seem more cooperative, more open to discussion and debate when you add to the core of your argument another layer, one that acknowledges and responds to the differences between you and your readers. When you do that, you show readers that you arrived at your claim not by jumping to a conclusion but by carefully considering all relevant factors, including their beliefs. In short, you demonstrate that you are a reliable critical thinker. But that kind of critical thinking also requires an act of critical imagination. To acknowledge readers' views, you must first be able to imagine the questions critical readers are likely to ask:

> But what about these alternatives, reservations, and objections? How would you respond to someone who said. . . ?

Imagining and answering the questions of others can be hard if you don't like to acknowledge that you might be less than entirely right. Faced with such questions, some of us go into a combative stance, counterattacking any objections. But when you can imagine and then amiably answer such questions, not just once but throughout your argument, you do more than improve your thinking and deepen and broaden your argument. You also project the ethos of a judicious, careful thinker, someone willing to scrutinize your own ideas as rigorously as you do those of others. Over time, that attitude creates an ethos that becomes your reputation.

The Importance of Other Viewpoints

When we say, *There are two sides to every question,* we underestimate how complex most issues are—the sides are more often three or four, and they differ not just over claims but what counts as reasons, evidence, warrants, even the existence of a problem at all. How many sides are there on the question of whether Congress should apologize for slavery? How many ways do different people judge the quality of American education?

In conversation, those who offer endless alternatives and objections seem willfully obstructive—and sometimes they are. But in arguments about serious issues, you serve others badly if, to avoid seeming obstructive, you offer only mindless agreement or, worse, silent dissent. All parties to an argument have a duty to air alternatives and raise objections in a spirit not of contention but collaboration, to create the soundest and most thoughtful argument possible.

But even those who speak up to question others' arguments often struggle to think as critically about their own. Most of us find it hard to engage alternatives and objections for four reasons. Two have to do with the limits of our knowledge and critical imagination:

- We are ignorant of others' contrary views because we overlook them or never seek them out.

- We can't imagine that there could be other views to consider. Recall the research we reported on page 8, showing that few people could think of even one argument as an alternative to their own.

But two have to do with our fear of losing:

- Even when we know or can imagine other views, we feel defensive about acknowledging that we might be wrong, or at least not entirely right.
- Some of us fear that we undermine our own argument when we acknowledge any uncertainty in it or any strength in the arguments of others.

But in most cases, the truth is the opposite: We should fear losing less than we fear seeming ignorant or arrogant. Thoughtful readers who take a cooperative stance tend to distrust those who lack the knowledge—or confidence—to acknowledge that others might think differently.

Regardless of age, education, intelligence, and even experience, we all have to resist the most common flaw in human thinking: We hold tight to our own beliefs, seeking only evidence that supports them, ignoring contradictory evidence, or twisting what we do find until it supports our position. We don't do it knowingly. It's just what we are all are inclined to do.

You can compensate for that bias if you actively seek out views that contradict your own and study them until you understand why someone could believe them. If you are making an argument about an issue without well-known contradictory views, imagine a skeptical but helpful friend questioning two aspects of your argument, its intrinsic quality and its failure to consider all factors:

- If she challenges the intrinsic soundness of your argument, she will object that your claims, reasons, evidence, or warrants are wrong or unjustified, that you have too little evidence or too few reasons.
- If she acknowledges that your argument is not intrinsically flawed but thinks it incomplete, she will offer alternatives that complicate or qualify it: other claims, reasons, evidence, or warrants or other interpretations of your evidence and warrants.

To help you imagine that friend raising objections or alternatives, we offer a checklist of questions in the next sections.

Questions About Your Problem and Its Solution

At the most general level, readers may question how you frame your problem and solution, even whether there is a problem at all. Recall the conversation about students as customers among Sue, Ann, and Raj (pp. 34–35). If Sue raised the lack of convenient office hours with her dean, the dean might ask some blunt questions (most questioners would be more tactful):

1. **What makes you think there is a problem?** *How many students in fact can't see their instructors when they have to?*

2. **Why have you posed the problem that way?** *Could the problem be not office hours but the willingness of students to make an effort to see teachers?*

3. **Exactly what kind of solution are you asking me to accept?** *How should we treat you like customers? What exactly should we do?*

4. **Have you considered limits on your claim?** *Are you saying that every instructor in every department should treat you as a client? Most? Some?*

5. **Why do you think your solution is better than the alternatives?** *What's wrong with the student as client model?*

Most important, though, are two objections that every solution to a pragmatic problem must overcome:

6. **How do you know your solution won't cost more to implement than the problem costs?** *To treat you like customers, we'll have to retrain everyone, which will take resources from current programs.*

7. **How do you know your solution won't make things worse by creating a bigger problem?** *If we treat you like customers, we will erode the teacher-student relationship that a sound education depends on.*

Questions About Your Support

After your readers question your problem and solution, they are likely to question its support. They will probably start by questioning whether you have enough evidence. Imagine the dean responding to Sue's charges:

1. **Your evidence is not sufficient.** *You gathered office hours from a single floor in one building. That can't be more than twenty offices. I need more evidence to take your claims seriously.*

Next are challenges to the quality of her (reports of) evidence:

2. **Your evidence is not accurate.** *I looked at those offices, and you counted three faculty who are on leave.*

3. **Your evidence is not precise.** *You said faculty average "about" an office hour a week. What's the exact figure?*

4. **Your evidence is not current.** *Are those hours from this semester or the last one?*

5. **Your evidence is not representative.** *You looked at offices from the same department. What about other departments? Are they all about the same or do most faculty keep more with only a few keeping much less?*

6. **Your evidence is not authoritative.** *How do you know the posted hours are the only times teachers see students? Have you asked the teachers?*

Finally, there are possible objections concerning warrants (see Chapter 8):

7. **Your warrant is not true.** *You say someone who pays money for something is a customer. Why should I believe that?*

8. **Your warrant is too sweeping.** *You say that anyone who pays money for something is a customer, but that's too broad. Employers pay employees.*

9. **Your warrant does not apply.** *What students pay for is nothing like what a customer buys. An education is not a stove, so paying tuition is not like buying appliances.*

10. **Your warrant is inappropriate.** *The idea of applying the principle of buying and selling in higher education is simply unacceptable.*

We have phrased these responses bluntly, not to make Sue's dean seem antagonistic, but to encourage you to be honest with yourself. Face-to-face, most people would raise their objections more amiably: *I wonder whether these office hours represent all office hours. Do you suppose that there might be cases where people pay money for something but aren't customers?* But readers are likely to ask their questions and make their objections very directly in the privacy of their minds. In whatever spirit they ask them, though, they are meeting a responsibility we must all accept: the duty to engage actively to find the best solution to a problem, and that always means asking questions that most of us don't much like answering.

Questions About Your Consistency

Readers will look for one other weakness in your argument—that you contradict yourself or have failed to consider obvious counterexamples.

> Senator, how can you condemn me for accepting contributions from the National Rifle Association when you accept contributions from the Ban Handguns Alliance?

> How can you say that children's moral growth is harmed by sexually explicit movies when you also say that it is not harmed by violence on TV?

Readers will think you contradict yourself when you seem to apply a warrant selectively, using it when it suits your purposes and ignoring it when it does not. For example, if you claim that children are harmed by sex in the movies, readers will infer that the claim is based on a general principle of reasoning something like this:

> Whenever children experience vivid representations of glorified behavior, they are more likely to approve of and imitate it.

But that warrant does not distinguish between sex in the movies and violence on TV. If we believe one is harmful, then we must believe that the other is as well, unless you can show that a more narrow warrant applies—perhaps that older children are *more* influenced by representations of sex than of violence because their awakening sexuality makes them respond to sexual images more intensely. But, of course, you would have to state that narrow warrant explicitly and, since it is not obvious, support it.

If a critic can show that a claim in one case contradicts a claim in another or that you have ignored an obvious counterexample, you will seem to be guilty of intellectual inconsistency—a charge profoundly damaging to your ethos, especially when the inconsistency seems self-interested:

- In a practical argument about what to do, you will seem *unfair* if you expect others to follow a principle that you ignore.

- In a conceptual argument about what to believe, you will seem *intellectually dishonest* (or at least careless) if you apply a principle selectively to get an answer you want.

So in planning your argument, ask whether your readers can apply the principle behind the case at hand to all similar cases. If not, you have to formulate a more narrow principle that distinguishes your case from the others.

◆ EXAMPLE

How to Use a Response to Restate Your Argument

The excerpt below is from an argument claiming that undergraduate majors should be abolished because students do not benefit from specialized studies and need more general education. The writer acknowledges and responds to possible objections while simultaneously restating both the gist of his main claim and its support. Here, in outline, are the steps he follows:

1. He imagines that those who raise the objection already accept part of his claim, *Students need more general education,* thus reinforcing it.

2. He states the objection as an alternative solution, but one that partially agrees with his proposed action: *Majors should be, not abolished, but reduced.*

3. In response to that alternative, he indirectly restates the remaining part of his claim: *Specialization does not benefit students.*

4. Then, to support that response/claim, he restates his three reasons why specialization is not a benefit.

5. Finally, he acknowledges a qualification to his claim, Some students might benefit from specialization, but then restates his claim again. Other students should not be forced to specialize.

Here's the passage:

Another objection I anticipate [to my argument that majors should be abolished] is from people who would agree that the basic liberal arts learning students get today is inadequate, and who would buy into the idea of an expanded general education program _{restatement of part of main claim} · · · [but who would still argue for] a minimally sized major. Students could have the best of both worlds: the advantages of specialism along with the advantages of generalism. _{alternative solution}

Certainly a curriculum like this would be preferable to what we have now; more, it would be a great improvement. _{benefits of alternative solution} But there is still a difficulty. It is still assumed that having a specialization, regardless of its size, is truly an advantage for students. And that is precisely what I am throwing into question. _{response / restatement of part of main claim} I have suggested that there is no more rigor in forcing the mind toward the greater depth of a major than there is in forcing it toward the lesser but significant depths of several different fields. _{restatement of reason 1 supporting response / main claim} And I have suggested that the way in which a major fine-tunes the mind may end up as a limitation more than an asset—inclining a student to see things from the narrows of one perspective alone. _{restatement of reason 2} Add to this the fact that many students' interests aren't strongly enough defined to make a commitment to a major, and the fact that many others don't need one for the vocational preparation they desire since they will be getting that in graduate school. _{restatement of reason 3} These are all telling reasons for questioning the practice of requiring students to have a major, and together they form a powerful and sensible rationale.

All of this isn't to say that no student should have a major. _{acknowledgment of limitation} But it is to say that we should not require it of all students. _{restatement of main claim} Those in fields like engineering and architecture, those who have an obvious and strong inclinations in other fields, should take majors . . . [But] for other students, there is no good reason for forcing them to specialize.

Source: Reprinted by permission of Transaction Publishers, "Do College Students Need a Major?" by William Casement, *Academic Questions,* Summer 1998. Copyright © 1998 by Transaction; all rights reserved.

◆◆◆

Responding with Subordinate Arguments

When you explicitly acknowledge views different from your own, you signal readers that you welcome and respect their views. But you show readers you are even more thoughtful and respectful when you respond to their views not with bald restatements of your own but with additional reasons and evidence that show why you respond as you do.

For example, here is part of an argument claiming that a university should invest more resources in course evaluations beyond simple in-class surveys:

> . . . Faculty can continue to improve if they get as much information as we can give them about our responses to their teaching.
>
> Some students may ask "If faculty aren't interested enough to improve their teaching on their own, why would they respond to our criticisms?" _{acknowledgment of objection} We think that view is cynical and that most teachers do care about our education. _{partial rebuttal of objection} But even if they have a point, _{partial concession to objection} the new information we propose to gather will include more

than just student gripes. Once the information is part of the record, teachers will not ignore it. ₛₑₛₚₒₙₛₑ / claim This happens in many professions. When doctors, airlines, or car manufacturers learn about problems with their products or services, they try to improve. ᵣₑₐₛₒₙ For example, when data about the quality of the university hospital were made public, hospital officials tried to do better because they were concerned about loss of business. Now the hospital advertises its standings in surveys on TV. ᵣₑₚₒᵣₜ ₒf ₑᵥᵢₑₑₙcₑ When the shortcomings of a profession become public, they take action to improve. warrant

This writer imagines and acknowledges a possible objection from colleagues, conceding they might be partly right. But she then responds to that objection with reasons, evidence, and a warrant to show why it would not apply in this case.

The writer might anticipate, however, that her readers will in turn question her response. For example, she might imagine that her most demanding readers would reject the comparison between teachers and airlines:

> But teachers are not like airlines; they have tenure and can't be fired, and colleges are not out to make money, so your analogy doesn't hold.

If she imagines that objection, she must respond to it with yet another argument:

> Of course, tenured professors differ from doctors and airlines because they don't need the approval of customers to stay in business. acknowledgment of limitation But most professors are responsible professionals who understand that colleges have to attract students. ₛₑₛₚₒₙₛₑ / claim Even state universities depend on tuition, especially higher out-of-state tuition. ᵣₑₐₛₒₙ Last year, out-of-state students saved us from a deficit that threatened faculty raises. report of evidence Students have many choices and can shop around. ᵣₑₐₛₒₙ When they research schools, they consider the quality of teaching in deciding where to go. warrant

We can imagine someone criticizing that response too, but at some point enough is enough. Life and papers are too short to answer every objection. But you don't have to answer every one to show that you have been thoughtful enough to consider some.

What if you can't answer a question? Our recommendation may seem naïve, but it is realistic: If you believe your argument has flaws but none so serious as to defeat it, concede them. Then assert that the balance of your argument compensates for its imperfections:

> We must admit that not every teacher will take these evaluations seriously. But even so, if we can get a substantial number to . . .

Conceding what cannot be denied is how thoughtful arguers respond to legitimate uncertainty.

Nothing reveals more clearly the kind of mind you have, indeed the kind of *person* you are, than your ability to imagine and then respond calmly to alternatives, objections, and reservations. You cannot be a true critical thinker without that kind of critical imagination.

To be sure, few of us consistently do it well. But when you exercise your own critical imagination even occasionally, not only will your argument gain credibility, so will you, particularly when you acknowledge objections and reservations that are not simply wrong, but not well thought out—and then respond by presenting readers your more thoughtful account.

IN THE READINGS . . .

Acknowledgments and Combativeness

We have emphasized the value of thinking of argument not as combat but as collaboration, and we have shown you how to respond to questions your readers will ask so that you can create a collaborative relationship with them. But you won't find much friendly collaboration in one of the most entertaining readings, Camille Paglia's "Wisdom in a Bottle" (p. 449). In this ultra-hip article from the online journal *Salon*, Paglia reinforces her reputation as a pugnacious gadfly, responding to the question of binge drinking by redefining the problem: *It's not binge drinking that's the problem—it's the banality and mediocrity of American higher education.*

Nowhere does she acknowledge views other than her own, much less respond to them. But she does characterize those who disagree. Would they accept her characterizations as fair? Would she want them too? If there is such a thing as combative argument for the fun and sport of it, this is an example. But would Paglia's opponents share her fun? Would her article persuade them to redefine the problem? Do you think she cares? A final point: Notice that the question from "Shaken, not Stirred" begins with an acknowledgment and response. Does that give her or him an ethos different from Paglia's? Why or why not?

Acknowledgments and Collaboration

Like Paglia, Craig Swenson knows that most of his readers will resist his argument in "Customers and Markets" (p. 420). But unlike her, he uses acknowledgment and response liberally to diffuse their resistance to his moderate claim that educators can "balanc[e] the goals of a liberal education with those of a practical education without diminishing the worth of either" (p. 424).

Pick out three or four places where Swenson explicitly acknowledges the contrary views of others and three or four where he does so only implicitly. What does he do to win over readers who hold those contrary views? Do his responses imply that those views are wrong? Silly? Self-interested? Or otherwise embarrassing to those who hold them? If not, how does he contradict those views without characterizing them too negatively?

WRITING PROCESS

Acknowledgment and Responses

READING AND RESEARCH

Use Others' Acknowledgments to Understand Context

When you read an argument in a new field, you may not see what is at stake in every part of it. But you can infer some of that from the common ground, especially if the writer reviews research leading up to her question. You can find more context in the objections and alternatives that she acknowledges and responds to. She defines the limits of debate in her field in what she acknowledges or dismisses and defines what she thinks is relevant to her position in what she concedes or responds to at length.

Collect Alternatives as You Read

When it is hard to imagine alternatives, start by making a list of pros and cons and add to it as you prepare your argument, especially cons. But if you have to do research to gather evidence, you'll find lots of alternatives you might acknowledge in your sources.

- Take notes on positions your sources respond to. If you disagree with the source, those objections may support your own position and suggest further reading. If you agree with it, you can acknowledge and respond to some of those alternatives and objections (after you look at them for yourself, of course).

- Don't record only claims that support your position; also record those that contradict it, along with the reasons and evidence offered in support. If you decide to acknowledge and respond to it, you will need a full argument to respond well.

- When you collect evidence to support your reasons, keep track of what might limit or contradict them. You may decide not to acknowledge those reservations, but they might help you imagine others.

PREPARING AND PLANNING

Add Acknowledgments After You Draft

When you sketch an outline or create a storyboard, don't focus on the alternatives or objections you intend to acknowledge, but on your own core argument. When you draft, focus on imagining all the possible forms of support for your position, not every possible objection. That invites writer's block. Then *after* you draft your core argument, work through it point by point, imagining questions readers might ask.

You might even include objections that you can imagine but that readers might not. They don't want to follow you down every blind alley, but they benefit when you share alternatives you pursued but ultimately rejected. They will also respect your candor. We know this advice seems disingenuous—being candid about failure as a rhetorical strategy to ensure success. Nevertheless, readers judge your ethos by how open you are to alternatives, and they will know that only if you show them which ones you considered.

Locate Acknowledgments and Responses Where Readers Are Likely to Think of Them

Once you identify alternatives to acknowledge, think of a response, outline it, and decide where to put it. Acknowledge alternatives early if they are well established and relate to your whole argument:

- If your whole argument directly counters another, acknowledge that other argument in the common ground of your introduction and again early in the body of your argument.

- If your whole argument relates to another but you want to drop the other one quickly, acknowledge it only in the common ground:

    Many teachers believe that the most important skill they can teach is the ability to solve problems. _{acknowledgment / common ground} But as important as that skill is, it is less important than the ability to discover, then articulate a problem clearly. As Einstein said, "A problem well put is half solved."
    _{response / destabilizing condition}

- If your whole argument relates to another that will occur to readers once they see your problem and solution, acknowledge it right after your introduction, as background:

    . . . The most valuable skill for students is the ability to discover and then articulate problems clearly. _{claim}

    The issue of problem formulation, however, has received little attention from teachers. Their traditional focus has been on teaching students to analyze problems in order to . . . _{acknowledgment}

- Respond to incidental alternatives as they become relevant:

    There is a Web site that rates colleges based on students' reports of their experience. That may not be a reliable source, _{acknowledgment} but it is one that students check. _{response / claim} For example, . . .

Building a Whole Argument Around Alternatives

If you know that readers will think of more than one alternative to your solution, you can organize your argument by sequentially eliminating those alternatives, leaving your solution as the last one standing.

    How then should we respond to global warming? It has been suggested that we just ignore it. [explanation] But that won't work because . . .

It has also been suggested that we exploit it by adapting our lives and agriculture to warmer conditions. [explanation] But that won't work either because . . .

At the other extreme, some argue that we should end all atmosphere emissions immediately. [explanation] But that idea is impractical because . . .

None of these responses addresses the problem in a responsible way. The only reasonable way to deal with global warming is . . .

DRAFTING

The Vocabulary of Acknowledgment and Response

Writers fail to acknowledge and respond to alternatives usually for three reasons. First, they don't know and cannot imagine any. Second, they think that by acknowledging them, they weaken their argument. But a third reason is more mundane and more easily solved: They simply don't know the expressions experienced writers use to introduce alternatives and responses.

We offer here that lexicon of words and phrases. To be sure (there is one of them right there), your first efforts may feel clumsy (*may* is common in acknowledgments), _{acknowledgment} *but* (a response usually begins with *but* or *however*) as you use them, they will come to seem more natural. _{response / claim}

Acknowledging

When you respond to an anticipated question or objection, give it the weight that readers do. You can mention and dismiss it, or address it at length. We order these expressions roughly in that order, from most dismissive to most respectful.

1. You can downplay an objection or alternative by summarizing it briefly in a short phrase introduced with *despite, regardless of,* or *notwithstanding:*

    Despite Congress' claims that it wants to cut taxes, _{acknowledgment} the public believes that . . . _{response}

    Regardless of problems in Hong Kong, _{acknowledgment} Southeast Asia remains a strong . . . _{response}

    Notwithstanding declining crime rates, _{acknowledgment} there is still a need for vigorous enforcement of . . . _{response}

    You can use *although,* and *while,* and *even though* in the same way:

    Although Congress claims it wants to cut taxes, _{acknowledgment} the public believes that . . . _{response}

    While there are problems in Hong Kong, _{acknowledgment} Southeast Asia remains a strong . . . _{response}

    Even though crime has declined, _{acknowledgment} there is still a need for vigorous enforcement of . . . _{response}

2. You can indirectly signal an objection or alternative with *seem* or *appear,* or with a qualifying adverb, such as *plausibly, justifiably, reasonably, accurately, understandably, surprisingly, foolishly,* or even *certainly.*

In his letters, Lincoln expresses what *seems* to be depression. _{acknowledgment} But those who observed him . . . _{response}

Smith's data *appear* to support these claims. _{acknowledgment} However, on closer examination . . . _{response}

This proposal *may* have some merit, _{acknowledgment} but we . . . _{response}

Liberals have made a *plausible* case that the arts ought to be supported by taxes. _{acknowledgment} But they ignore the moral objections of . . . _{response}

3. You can acknowledge alternatives by attributing them to unnamed sources or to no source at all. This kind of acknowledgment gives a little weight to the objection. In these examples, brackets and slashes indicate choices:

   It is easy to [*think / imagine / say / claim / argue*] that taxes should . . .

   There is [*another / alternative / possible / standard*] [*explanation / line of argument / account / possibility*] . . .

   Some evidence [*might / may / can / could / would / does*] [*suggest / indicate / point to / lead some to think*] that we should . . .

4. You can acknowledge an alternative by attributing it to a more or less specific source. This construction gives more weight to the position you acknowledge:

   There are some [*many / few*] who [*might / may / could / would*] [*say / think / argue / claim / charge / object*] that Cuba is not . . .

   [*Most / Many / Some / A few*] knowledgeable college administrators [*say / think / argue / claim / charge / object*] that researchers . . .

   One advocate of collaboration, Ken Bruffee, [*says / thinks / argues / claims / charges / objects*] that students . . .

5. You can acknowledge an alternative in your own voice or with a passive verb or concessive adverb such as *admittedly, granted, to be sure,* and so on. You concede the alternative has some validity, but by changing the words, you can qualify how much validity you acknowledge.

   I [*understand / know / realize / appreciate*] that liberals believe in . . .

   It is [*true / possible / likely / certain*] that no good evidence proves that coffee causes cancer . . .

   It [*must / should / can*] be [*admitted / acknowledged / noted / conceded*] that no good evidence proves that coffee causes cancer . . .

   [*Granted / admittedly / true / to be sure / certainly / of course*], Adams stated . . .

   We [*could / can / might / may / would*] [*say / argue / claim / think*] that spending on the arts supports pornographic . . .

   We have to [*consider / raise*] the [*question / possibility / probability*] that further study [*could / might / will*] show crime has not . . .

   We cannot [*overlook/ ignore / dismiss / reject*] the fact that Cuba was . . .

   What X [*says / states / writes / claims / asserts / argues / suggests / shows*] may [*be true / have merit / make sense / be a good point*]: Perhaps Lincoln did suffer . . .

Responding

You signal a response with *but, however,* or *on the other hand.* Remember that after you state your response, readers may expect reasons and evidence supporting it, because they will take that response to be a claim needing its own support. You can respond in ways that range from tactfully indirect to blunt:

1. You can state that *you* don't entirely understand:

   But I do not quite understand . . . / I find it difficult to see how . . . / It is not clear to me that . . .

2. You can state that there are unsettled issues:

   But there are other issues . . . / There remains the problem of . . .

3. You can respond more bluntly by claiming the acknowledged position is irrelevant or unreliable:

   But as insightful as that point may be, it [*ignores / is irrelevant to / does not bear on / was formulated for other situations than*] the issue at hand.

   But the evidence is [*unreliable / shaky / thin / not the best available*].

   But the argument is [*untenable / wrong / weak / confused / simplistic*].

   But that view [*overlooks / ignores / misses*] key factors . . .

   But that position is based on [*unreliable / faulty / weak / confused*] [*reasoning / thinking / evidence*].

Addressing Logical Error

When you differ with a reader because you are reasonably sure the reader has not thought through the issues as carefully as you, you need a few phrases to introduce your point of view civilly. Here are a few:

> That evidence is certainly important, but we have to look at all the evidence available.

> That explains some of the problem, but it is so complex that no single explanation is enough.

> That principle does hold in many cases, but we must also consider exceptions.

You get the idea: Acknowledge the value of a particular view, but suggest that there is more to consider.

WORKING COLLABORATIVELY

Ask Tough Questions

It is hard to imagine alternatives on your own, but you can help one another do that by asking tough questions. For each argument you review, find enough weak points and strong alternatives to make the argument seem questionable. Of course, your real aim is to identify just the two or three key alternatives or objections that each writer should acknowledge. Try this in a spirit of goodwill (someone should record what follows):

- Ask the writer of the argument to raise the most severe objections.
- Have each person in turn add objections.
- When the group runs out of ideas, rank the objections from most to least serious and alternatives from most to least viable.

From these two ranked lists, each writer can decide what to acknowledge.

If the group has trouble getting into the spirit of this game, run down the following list of comments and questions. Remember to smile when you offer them.

Problem

1. This is not a problem. Everyone knows that . . .
2. The real problem is not this, but the fact that . . .

Solution

1. I can think of three exceptions to your claim: First . . . , second . . . , and third, . . .
2. I can think of two better solutions/answers: First . . . , and second. . . .
3. This solution will cost too much. It will cost . . .
4. This solution will create several new and bigger problems: First, it will . . .

Reasons

1. I can think of two reasons not to accept your claim: First . . .
2. I can think of three exceptions to your reason: First . . .
3. Why haven't you included this other reason?

Evidence

1. There is better evidence. Why didn't you include it?
2. That evidence is from an untrustworthy source. Why do you believe it?
3. That evidence is not entirely representative. Why should we trust it?
4. That evidence is vague/imprecise. What makes it good enough for the purpose?
5. I doubt your evidence is accurate. How do you know it is?

Warrants

1. You seem to assume that when X is true we can infer Y, but I think that when X is true we must infer Z.
2. That reason/claim does not seem to be a good example of the reason/claim side of the warrant.
3. I can think of three exceptions to that warrant: First . . .

INQUIRIES

REFLECTIONS

1. In most academic and professional situations, we make arguments stronger by acknowledging their limitations. But different standards apply in some professional situations—a lawyer defending a client in court, for example. Can you think of other circumstances in which you should not acknowledge any weakness in your argument? How do those circumstances differ from those that you normally find in academic and professional arguments?

2. Suppose that just before you turn in a paper for a class, you discover an objection to your argument that substantially weakens it. You cannot think how to counter the objection. In fact, you now think your argument is wrong. What should you do? This question is both ethical and practical. Are you ethically obligated to reveal this objection? Why or why not? Practically speaking, would it be wise to tell your teacher that you recognized the objection, but it was too late to do anything about it? Or should you just keep quiet and hope your teacher doesn't notice? Which response do you think will project the best ethos?

TASKS

3. In Chapter 6 we asked you to highlight the evidence in some old papers. Return to those marked-up copies and question the evidence in as many ways as seem appropriate. Do you see weaknesses in your argument now that you did not see then? How would you acknowledge and respond to them?

4. Look at the editorial and op-ed pages of your local newspaper. Identify all the acknowledgments and responses. Which pieces use them best? Do these acknowledgments make the arguments persuasive? Do the same with some TV talk shows. Do the participants acknowledge and respond to other points of view as often? If not, why not?

PROJECTS

5. Spend an hour or so with the editorial and op-ed page of your local newspaper. Identify the parts of argument in each, and then formulate reasonable questions that raise objections or alternatives for each. Finally, sketch how you would answer those questions if you were the author.

6. Return to the old papers you used for Task 3. Add more acknowledgments and responses than you really need, then eliminate those that don't make your argument more presuasive. How far short of this optimum did your original paper fall?

FOCUS ON WRITING

1

Context.   Pamela White's column, "'Drinking Age Has Simply Got to Go,' Say Campus Riots," appeared in several student newspapers. As you can see, the last paragraph suggests that her college student readers should not just believe something, but act on their beliefs by writing letters urging state legislators to abolish the drinking age.

Scenario and Task.   Choose one:

A. The Greek Council has voted to encourage students to write letters about lowering the drinking age on the basis of the argument in this article. You have been chosen to compose a model letter for others to use in writing theirs.

B. You are a member of a student political organization that wants students to write letters about lowering the drinking age but thinks there are better arguments than those in the article. You have been chosen to develop that better argument and compose a model letter.

C. You are a member of a student organization that opposes lowering the drinking age. You have been chosen to make the argument and compose a model letter .

2

Return to any of the papers you wrote in the first weeks of the class. Revise its scenario so that before your readers encounter your argument they believe a position different from the one you have argued. Rewrite the paper, adding acknowledgments and responses supported by subordinate arguments.

RESEARCH PROJECT

Scenario.   Your teacher has asked the class to review each other's drafts before presenting them.

Task.   Find one or two people who will review your draft not to make editorial suggestions but to share their responses: *Where are they confused? Where do they want more evidence? More reliable evidence? Where do they have objections or want to add important qualifications?* If they are confused about your logic, add warrants. If they want more or better evidence, add it. If you can't, acknowledge the problem and respond as best you can. If they raise objections or qualifications, acknowledge and respond to them. Using those responses, produce a final draft. Be sure, as a last step, to revise your prose in accord with the procedures in Writing Processes 12 and 13.

IN A NUTSHELL

About Your Argument . . .

You communicate the quality of your critical thinking by how candidly you acknowledge and respond to views different from your own. Admittedly, nothing is harder than finding those views, so you need a list of questions to ask yourself on behalf of your readers. Anticipate questions and objections about two aspects of your argument:

- Readers question the quality of your claims, reasons, evidence, or warrants. They assert that you are just wrong.
- They find nothing wrong with your argument per se, but think of alternative claims, reasons, and evidence, even ways to frame the issue.

Readers may also question how you frame the problem:

1. Why do you think your problem is a serious one?
2. Why did you pose the problem this way rather than that?
3. Exactly what claim are you asking me to accept?
4. Have you considered these exceptions to your claim?
5. Why do you think your solution is better than an alternative one?
6. How do you know your solution won't cost more than the problem?
7. How do you know your solution won't create a new problems?

Readers also question evidence: They question whether it is sufficient, current, accurate, precise, representative, and authoritative. They might also question whether your warrants are true, too broad, inapplicable to your reasons and claims, or inappropriate for your readers.

. . . and About Writing It

When you acknowledge and respond to an imagined objection or question, you can follow a well-established formula:

- Begin with a phrase such as *to be sure, admittedly, some have claimed,* etc. Then state the acknowledgment.
- Follow with *but, however, on the other hand,* etc. Then state your response.

When you respond to these kinds of objections and alternatives, you have an opportunity to thicken your argument by supporting your response with reasons, evidence, warrants, and yet more acknowledgments and responses to your response.

CHAPTER 8

The Logic of Your Argument: Warranting Claims and Reasons

In this chapter we address the task of deciding whether you have connected reasons and claims soundly. Even when reasons are true and based on reliable evidence, readers have to believe that each one logically supports its claim. When the logical connection between a reason and its claim might be in question, you show its relevance through warrants.

You create your most effective arguments when you answer your readers' questions before they are asked. Readers first want to know what *you* think: what you are claiming, why you believe it, and the evidence on which you base your reasoning. You enter into a more critical dialogue with readers when you imagine them asking more questions about what *they* think, questions that reflect their disagreements, objections, and different points of view. Indeed, by asking those questions *on your readers' behalf,* you draw them into your argument, joining their voices with yours. You may find such questions and objections vexing, but you can also use them as opportunities not just to connect with your readers but to test your own thinking and create a more compelling argument.

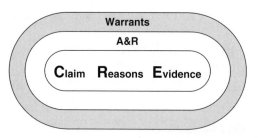

There is, however, one kind of critical question that is especially difficult to ask and answer because it questions not the substance of your argument but the quality of your thinking. The problem is that we are usually so unaware of our own processes of reasoning that we are surprised when someone questions them. But if readers cannot tell how we reach a conclusion even after they understand our reasons, evidence, and responses to their views, then we have failed to establish the most important relationship our readers need from us: a sense of shared logic and assumptions.

For example, recall Sue's argument about tuition and services:

> Sue: We think the university should stop treating us only as students and start treating us like customers. . . . We pay a lot of money for our education, but we don't get near the attention customers do.

Raj agreed with Sue on a lot of points, but he asked one question indicating that on that matter he couldn't follow Sue's logic, her line of reasoning.

> Raj: . . . I don't see how tuition makes us customers. What's the connection?

That kind of question goes to the heart of Sue's thinking, but she was able to answer it:

> Sue: Well, when you pay for a service, you buy it, right? And when you buy something you're a customer. We pay tuition for our education, so that means we're customers and should be treated like one.

Sue answered Raj's question by offering him an explicit statement of the general logical principle that governs her line of reasoning. With that general statement, she explains how her specific reason (*we pay tuition*) connects to her specific claim (*we are therefore customers*). We call that kind of explicit statement of a general logical principle by many terms: a *premise,* an *assumption,* a *general principle.* Those who study arguments have a technical term for it. They call it a *warrant.*

Now imagine that Sue were writing her argument and that Raj had not been there to ask that question. Sue probably would have thought that everyone could see the connection between tuition and customers. But if her readers were like Raj, then at least one of them would have thought, "Wait a minute. I don't see the connection. I don't follow that thinking." And when that happens, an argument fails.

Your arguments can succeed only if your readers can follow you from evidence to a reason to a claim. To do that, they must see—or hear from you— the logical principles that make those connections.

The Reasoning Behind Reasons

Here is an example of public argument that actually failed because the public could not see the logical connection between a reason and a claim. When diet sodas first became popular in the 1960s, some scientists warned that the sweetener in them, cyclamate, increased the risk of cancer:

> We believe that people who drink diet sodas sweetened with cyclamate increase their risk of cancer _{claim} because laboratory rats fed large doses of cyclamate show an increased rate of cancer. _{reason} That relationship is based on these data. . . . _{evidence}

Most diet soda drinkers did not believe that claim. No one disputed the fact that rats got more cancer when they consumed cyclamates, but most people did not see any logical connection between the rats' health and their own. What does one have to do with the other?

The scientists responded by stating a general principle to connect their reason (*rats getting cancer*) with their claim (*diet soda drinkers more likely to get cancer*), a principle that most people in their field accepted (boldfaced):

> Based on many studies, we know this: **When large doses of a substance cause cancer in laboratory rats, we can conclude that small doses of that substance will cause some cancer in humans.**

Today, almost everyone accepts this principle: when scientists show us that something is bad for animals, we believe it is also bad for us. At that time, however, few people believed that principle and the scientists did not explain it well enough, so the public thought the argument made no sense, rejected its claim, and drank more diet soda than ever.

Those scientists were not being *illogical*: their argument made good sense to experts who already believed the general principle. Their problem was that, like most of us, they did not think anyone else would question their reasoning. They assumed that everyone would think as they did, so that the public would share even their unspoken assumptions. It is a problem that we all have to guard against.

You cannot assume that you and your readers think alike. You always have to consider the possibility that readers might look at your reasons and think, as did Raj and those who heard about the dangers of cyclamates, "Your reason may be factually true, but I don't see how it supports your claim. How do the two connect?"

If you can imagine that your readers might ask that question, you have to give them a general principle stated as a warrant that makes the connection explicit. And if, as in the case of the cyclamate warnings, they do not understand or believe the general principle that the warrant states, then you also have to make an argument to explain the principle or show them that your warrant is true.

This chapter will show you how warrants work, how to know when you need one, and how to construct one your readers will accept—not because you need one in every argument, but because your arguments will fail when you do need a warrant but you don't know how one works.

What Warrants Look Like

Warrants come in all shapes and sizes, but they always have or imply two parts. One part names a general circumstance:

Winter roads are slippery. part 1: a general condition

The second part states a general conclusion that we can infer from that circumstance:

You need four-wheel drive. part 2: a general consequence

Put together, the two parts explicitly state a general principle of reasoning that a certain general condition leads to a certain general consequence:

When winter roads are slippery, general condition you need four-wheel drive. general consequence

We can also state that warrant in ways that only imply the connection between the parts:

Winter roads condition require a four-wheel drive. consequence

We can also reverse the order

You need a four-wheel drive consequence on winter roads. condition

There is no one right way to state a warrant, but for our purposes we will state them in the same way every time, not because that's how you should too, but because it is the clearest way for us to explain how they work. We will follow this formula:

Whenever X, condition Y. consequence

Sometimes, we might choose other introductory words: *if, when, if and only if.* But *whenever* is useful because it encourages you to consider how widely you can apply a warrant. *Whenever* implies that a warrant is true under all circumstances, something that is rarely the case. So the *whenever* form will help you think of limits or qualifications to your warrants.

Warrants are most familiar to us as proverbs:

When the cat's away, the mice will play.

Schematically, we can represent that warrant like this:

The authority is absent—[so we infer]→ those under that authority will slack off.

If you believe that *general* principle, then you can link a *specific* instance of authority being absent to a *specific* instance of those under that authority slacking off. Schematically, the link looks like this:

WARRANT		
General Circumstance	*predictably allows*	General Conclusion
When the cat's away		the mice will play.
✔		✔
Coach can't supervise practice _{reason}	*therefore*	the team will probably goof off. _{claim}
Specific Circumstance	*lets us infer*	Specific Conclusion
	CORE OF ARGUMENT	

The check marks indicate that we think the specific circumstance qualifies as a valid instance of the general circumstance in the warrant, and the specific conclusion qualifies as a valid instance of the warrant's general conclusion. (Later, we'll see cases where they don't.) In most cases, readers connect claims and reasons on their own, but when you think they may not, warrants show them how.

How Warrants Work

Suppose Leah is telling Tariq about the new place she rented:

Leah: I'm so lucky. I found a place to rent on Carter's Mountain that feels like it's miles away from civilization. I've always wanted to live deep in the woods.

Tariq: Good for you, but you'll have to trade in your car for something with four-wheel drive. _{claim} In winter the roads are too steep and slippery for a car. _{reason}

Leah: That makes sense. Thanks for the good advice.

Any time we make or accept a claim based on a reason, we connect that claim and reason by a general principle of reasoning. In this case, the principle is based on our experience of the world: *when you live on a bad road, you need a vehicle that can handle it,* a principle that Leah believes. Since she also believes that Tariq's reason is true, she thinks his claim follows from his reason. As she says, the connection "makes sense."

But sometimes, we don't see the connection, and the claim doesn't make sense. In that case, we ask a question: *Why does that specific reason lead to that specific claim?*

Tariq: If you're going to live alone in the woods, _{reason} you should also buy a gun. _{claim}

Leah: I don't like guns. Why does living alone mean I should buy one?

This time Leah does not see how living in the woods is a reason for owning a gun. To show her, Tariq has to offer a general principle that explains it:

Tariq: When you live alone in an isolated place, you need protection. _{warrant}

Before Leah accepts Tariq's claim that she should own gun, she has to accept two more claims: that the general principle is true and that it applies to her circumstances.

Here's how that works in detail. (*Warning:* What follows may sound like Logic 101.) First Leah must believe that the warrant is true: That is, if you live alone in an isolated place, then it is true that you need protection. But it is not enough that Leah believe the principle. She must also believe that it *applies* to Tariq's specific reason and specific claim:

- The specific reason (*you live all alone in the woods*) must be for her a valid instance of the general condition (*you live alone in an isolated place*). Since she lives alone and the woods is an isolated place, that connection between the general condition and the specific instance seems evident enough.

- The specific claim (*you should buy a gun*) must be for her a valid instance of the general condition (*you need protection*). Since a gun is a form of protection, that connection between the general and specific also seems plausible.

If Leah accepts the principle and believes it applies to her situation, then Tariq has shown her why his claim follows from his reason. We can diagram that outcome like this:

WARRANT		
General Circumstance	*predictably allows*	General Conclusion
When someone lives in an isolated place		that person needs protection.
✔		✔
You will live alone in the woods_{claim}	*therefore*	you should buy a gun._{reason}
Specific Circumstance	*lets us infer*	Specific Conclusion
CORE OF ARGUMENT		

But what if Leah thinks that a gun is not an *acceptable* form of protection? Then she would object:

Leah: Maybe I need some form of protection. But for me a gun is not good protection. A gun is more likely to harm its owner than anyone else. Besides, I could never shoot a gun.

In other words, for Leah Tariq's claim is not a valid instance of the general conclusion because even though a gun may be a form of protection for someone else, it is not suitable protection for her. We can diagram that outcome like this:

WARRANT		
General Circumstance	*predictably allows*	General Conclusion
When someone lives in an isolated place ✔		that person needs protection. ✘
You will live alone in the woods*claim*	*therefore*	you should buy a gun.*reason*
Specific Circumstance	*lets us infer*	Specific Conclusion
CORE OF ARGUMENT		

Now Tariq has two choices. He can offer Leah an alternative that she *will* see as a valid instance of protection:

Tariq: If you won't get a gun, at least have an alarm installed.

Or he can defend his principle by making an argument that a gun is the best form of protection, even if Leah doesn't like them. And in doing so, he'll have to make two more arguments: one against Leah's counterprinciple that guns are dangerous for their owners and another against her claim that she could never use one. Now we begin to see why it is so hard to reach agreement on vitally contested issues.

Knowing When to Use Warrants in a Written Argument

We use warrants less often than other elements of an argument because readers usually accept the connection between a claim and its reason without even thinking that they need a principle to connect them. And we would bore or even insult readers if we explained the obvious. So to use warrants successfully, we have to identify those few occasions when readers need them.

That's seldom a problem in conversation, because others usually tell us when they need a warrant: They object, ask questions (as Leah did), frown, or in some way show that they don't see the connection between a reason and a claim. But when we write, we have to anticipate those occasions on our own.

The problem is that you cannot know when readers will need a warrant just by reading your draft, because nothing seems more obvious to you than your own way of thinking. Sometimes you can find out when you need a warrant from surrogate readers (such as a writing group), who will read your argument and tell you when connections between reasons and claims are a problem. But usually, you'll have to *imagine* readers asking a question—an exercise more challenging for warrants than for any other element of an argument.

The Most Common Uses for Warrants

You can anticipate that readers will need warrants when your experience and knowledge are very different from theirs. One common case is when specialists write for nonspecialist readers (as in the cyclamate example). All specialized fields rely on principles of reasoning not widely shared outside the field—that's part of what makes a field hard for outsiders to understand. So a specialized argument is likely to fail with ordinary readers unless its writer uses warrants to explain those principles.

For example, here is an argument that may puzzle you:

> The words *pork* and *beef* refer to meat that we eat at table, ~reason~ so we can assume that they were borrowed from French into the English language after 1066. ~claim~ The words *swine* and *cow* refer to the animals that pork and beef come from, ~reason~ so we can assume they are probably native English words.
> ~claim~

Linguists see that argument as perfectly logical because they know the principle of reasoning behind it, which they could, if asked, state like this:

> When an English word names a kind of meat that has been prepared for eating, ~condition~ that word was probably borrowed from the French after 1066. ~consequence~ When a word names the animal the meat comes from, ~condition~ that word is probably a native English word. ~consequence~

That principle is familiar to anyone who knows the history of the English language: After the Norman conquest in 1066, English servants used French names for food they prepared for their French masters, while field hands kept using their native words. Specialists are unlikely to realize that ordinary readers would need them to explain that principle in a warrant: It is so deeply embedded in their thinking that for them it goes without saying—unless they are forced to say it because of a reader's question or the useful habit of imagining such questions on their reader's behalf.

Another occasion that commonly calls for warrants is when you write for readers with different backgrounds, values, or cultures. Most principles of reasoning are based on experiences so much a part of our way of life that they feel not learned but natural. So when we write for people who do not share our experiences, what seems natural to us may seem foreign, alien, inexplicable, even abhorrent to them.

For example, in our culture most of us immediately see the connection between this reason and claim:

> The editor of the school newspaper believes that the university has ignored racial tensions on campus, ~reason~ so he has the right to express that concern in an editorial. ~claim~

We take for granted the principle that connects the reason to the claim, a principle that we could express in a warrant like this:

> When an editor of a newspaper has an opinion, he or she has the right to print it.

In other parts of the world, however, that argument would be considered ridiculous and the warrant dangerous.

You may have to state and defend many warrants for readers who don't share your experience, values, or culture. But don't defend your principles by arguing that theirs are wrong—you will not convince them to change deeply held values and beliefs. Instead, state your principle, explain how it works, and acknowledge that others might see things differently. You probably won't convince anyone to change their way of thinking, but you can convince them to respect your specific principles and to consider the conclusions you draw from them.

Warrants as Expressions of Cultural Codes

Warrants help us understand why people of different cultures struggle to make good arguments together. We all reason alike, but different cultures start from different assumptions. Those assumptions are not just static beliefs, but dynamic principles that tell us how to reason about specific facts. We often express them in proverbs that reveal much about how we think and what we value. For example, suppose we say of a child *She really stands out from the crowd because she thinks for herself and says what she thinks.* We might then conclude, *When she grows up, she'll get her way,* because we have a cultural assumption reflected in a familiar proverb:

The squeaky wheel gets the grease.

But the Japanese have a proverb that warns people not to stand out:

The nail that sticks up gets hammered down.

In other words, when someone stands out from the crowd, that person will be—rightly—forced to conform. So we agree on the same fact, a child standing out from the rest, but our different communities justify different conclusions from it because they reason from different assumptions. Such differences cause many cultural conflicts. Expressing them clearly as warrants is difficult, but it lets us, if not always resolve, at least understand the source of our differences.

Two Special Uses for Warrants

We normally state warrants when we think readers will not readily connect our reason and our claim, because they do not know or do not accept our principle of reasoning. But we use warrants in two other ways, both of which are easier to manage because we do not have to know or imagine what our readers might be thinking. We also use warrants to emphasize a key point or to build consensus for a controversial one.

Using Warrants for Emphasis

Readers generally dislike explanations for obvious connections. But you can state an obvious principle for emphasis *after* presenting the reason and evidence it covers. Recall, for example the argument from Chapter 2 that tries to prove that a college is committed to undergraduate education:

> We have tried to make our commitment to undergraduate education second to none _{claim} by asking our best researchers to teach first-year students. _{reason}

> For example, Professor Kinahan, a recent Nobel Prize winner in physics, is now teaching physics 101. _{evidence} To be sure, not every researcher teaches well, _{acknowledgment} but recent teaching evaluations show that teachers such as Kinahan are highly respected by our students. _{response} Of the last twenty recipients of the college teaching award, sixteen have been full professors with distinguished records of research. _{further evidence}

The writer assumes that her readers can recognize the principle that connects that claim and reason:

> When an educational institution commits its best faculty to an activity, it shows that it gives that activity its highest priority. _{warrant}

If the writer imagined that her readers might not know or accept that principle, she would state it as a warrant, usually before presenting the claim and reason. To use that principle for emphasis, she would state the warrant in abbreviated form at the end of this mini-argument:

> We have tried to make our commitment to undergraduate education second to none _{claim} by. . . . Of the last twenty recipients of the college teaching award, sixteen have been full professors with distinguished records of research. _{further evidence} **Given this record, it's clear that we back up our commitment to teaching with our resources.** _{warrant}

Warrants used for emphasis are more common in public, business, or informal contexts than in academic ones, where some readers consider them too obvious.

Using Warrants to Build Consensus

When you ask readers to accept a difficult or unwelcome claim, they sometimes feel that you are being pushy because you are encouraging—forcing—them to consider evidence and reasons that lead to a result they do not like. You can both soften the blow and increase the chance that readers will follow your argument, if you start out with warrants that remind readers that they do in fact believe in your principles, even if they don't like where they lead.

Perhaps the most famous example of this strategy is that part of the Declaration of Independence that so many of us have memorized:

> We hold these truths to be self-evident . . . when a long train of abuses and usurpations, pursuing invariably the same Object evinces a design to reduce them under absolute Despotism, _{general condition side of the warrant} it is their right, it is their duty, to throw off such Government, and to provide new Guards for their future security. _{general consequence side of the warrant} Such has been the patient sufferance of these Colonies [i.e., a long train of abuses in this specific case]; _{specific condition / reason} and such is now the necessity which constrains them to alter their former Systems of government [i.e., the duty to throw off such government in this specific case]. _{specific consequence / claim}

Here's how the same strategy would work in the example about teaching:

> As Dean, I am proud of the education we offer our students. But I am also keenly aware of how much students and their families sacrifice to afford that education. And I cannot deny that, in order to keep costs down, we have

increased the size of the student body, which has led to more large lecture classes and fewer small classes with more students in them. ~problem~ But we all know that the most valuable resource of any school is its faculty. And while smaller classes are desirable, it is the quality of teaching that is most responsible for a quality learning experience. **There is no better way for any institution to ensure the quality of its undergraduate education than to see that students learn from its very best minds.** ~warrant~ We continue to make our commitment to undergraduate education second to none ~claim~ by asking our best researchers to teach first-year students. ~reason~ For example, Professor Kinahan. . . .

How to Test a Warrant

Since you will use at most a few warrants in any argument, you have time to test each one to make sure that you need it and correctly state it. To decide whether a warrant is necessary, ask yourself this question:

> Will readers question whether that reason clearly and unequivocally supports your claim?

Most cases fall somewhere between, leaving you to decide case-by-case which principles to state and which not. To do that, you have to anticipate when readers either cannot imagine any principle for connecting your reason and claim or might imagine one different from yours. Consider this little argument:

> Our school needs more writing tutors ~claim~ because we are unsure our education is worth our rising tuition costs. ~reason 1~ Tuition has gone up faster than inflation. ~reason 2~ In 1997, inflation was 2.4%, but tuition rose 5.1%; in 1998, inflation was 2.1%, but tuition rose 6.7%. ~evidence~

The dean might respond:

> True, tuition has gone up faster than inflation. You may even be right that we need more writing tutors. But why do you think we need them *because* you are not sure you are getting your money's worth? Why does your reason—you're not sure you're getting your money's worth—*have anything to do with* your claim—that we need more tutors? I don't see the connection.

That is a hard question. The dean is not saying that she rejects either the reason or the claim, but that she cannot imagine any principle that would make the claim follow from the reason.

WARRANT		
General Circumstance	*predictably allows*	General Conclusion
?????????????????		????????????????.
?		**?**
Not sure getting money's worth ~reason~	*therefore*	need writing tutors. ~claim~
Specific Circumstance	*lets us infer*	Specific Conclusion
CORE OF ARGUMENT		

If you cannot think of a principle connecting a reason to your main claim, your readers probably cannot either. In that case, you need to state one explicitly. Here is a way to do that.

1. Replace the specific terms in your reason and claim with general ones:

   We are not sure we are getting our **money's worth** from our **tuition**, so we need more **writing tutors.**

money's worth —> value equal to our cost	**writing tutors —> services**

   We are not sure we are getting a **value equal to our cost,** so we are entitled to more **services.**

2. Rephrase the general version with a *whenever:*

   Whenever we are uncertain that we are getting value equal to our cost, we are entitled to more services.

You can know whether your readers will accept a warrant only after you state it for yourself. But that one seems dubious: Why should uncertainty about value for cost entitle a person to demand more? If you offer a warrant, you must therefore ask yourself three more questions:

- Will readers think your warrant is true?
- Will they think that it applies to the reason and claim?
- Will they think it is appropriate to their community?

1. Is Your Warrant True?

A warrant fails when readers reject it as false. Here is an argument about gangsta rap:

The lyrics of gangsta rap are so vulgar toward women ₍reason₎ that the FCC should ban them from the radio. ₍claim₎ Whenever language is degrading to any group of people, we should not allow it to circulate over public airwaves.
₍warrant₎

We can rephrase that warrant into our standard form, *Whenever X, Y:*

WARRANT		
General Circumstance	*predictably allows*	General Conclusion
Whenever language is degrading, to any group of people,		we should not allow it to circulate over public airwaves.
✔		✔
Gangsta rap lyrics are vulgar toward women ₍reason₎	*therefore*	the FCC sould ban them from radio. ₍claim₎
Specific Circumstance	*lets us infer*	Specific Conclusion
CORE OF ARGUMENT		

If we accept the warrant and reason, then the claim follows. But a reader might believe that the principle is not true because another warrant trumps it:

> I can't agree. Whenever we express our ideas, the Constitution bars the government from interfering with that right. _{competing warrant} According to the Supreme Court, the First Amendment protects sexually explicit movies that are degrading to women. So even though you may not like the degrading language in gangsta rap, it has the same constitutional protection as those movies or any other free expression of ideas.

If the counterargument is relevant, it contradicts the original warrant and replaces it with another one.

Schematically, the counterargument looks like this:

WARRANT		
General Circumstance	*predictably allows*	General Conclusion
Whenever people express their ideas,		the Constitution bars the government from interfering with them.
✔		✔
Rap lyrics express ideas_{reason}	*therefore*	the FCC cannot ban them from radio._{claim}
Specific Circumstance	*lets us infer*	Specific Conclusion
CORE OF ARGUMENT		

Now the question of banning such lyrics turns into a question of which warrant is more important in our system of beliefs. To settle that, the person making that argument would have to make another argument treating those dueling warrants as claims needing their own reasons, evidence, and yet more warrants. At this point, we can understand why some arguments never get settled: The participants cannot agree on first principles.

Overreaching Warrants

We might accept some warrants as true *in general* but not when people try to use them to justify extreme cases. What about the following argument?

> I helped you wash your car two years ago, _{reason} so you should help me paint my house. _{claim} After all, one good turn deserves another. _{warrant}

If your friend did help you wash your car, you might feel you owed him something, but not as much as he asks:

> You did help me wash my car, and in general one good turn deserves another, but only when the magnitude of the returned favor is proportional to the original one.

In other words, the warrant is generally true, but it has limits. And once you think of one limit, you can think of more:

. . . and so long as I am capable of doing it, and so long as the favor is requested reasonably close in time to the first good turn, and so long as . . .

When we state a warrant like *One good turn deserves another,* we rarely, if ever, add the obvious limitations: *Of course you can do only what you are able to; of course you expect that a returned favor won't be asked for thirty years later.* All that goes without saying, so we don't say it. What's tricky about using warrants is not just that we usually take them for granted; even when we do state them, we take for granted their default limitations, as well.

2. Will Readers Think Your Warrant Applies to the Reason and Claim?

This next problem with warrants is the most difficult to grasp. Consider this argument:

> I helped you wash your car, ₍reason₎ so you should help me cheat on my test. ₍claim₎
> After all, one good turn deserves another. ₍warrant₎

Represented graphically, it looks like this:

WARRANT		
General Circumstance	*predictably allows*	General Conclusion
When someone does you a good turn,		you should do one in return.
✔		?
I helped you wash your car ₍reason₎	*therefore*	you should help me cheat. ₍claim₎
Specific Circumstance	*lets us infer*	Specific Conclusion
CORE OF ARGUMENT		

The warrant is true, and helping you wash your car is a valid instance of doing a good turn. So if your friend did help you wash your car, how could you refuse to help him cheat? You might say,

> True, one good turn deserves another, but in this case, helping you cheat on a test *does not count as* a legitimate example of "a good turn." In fact, it would be a bad turn. So your reason is not relevant to your claim.

The warrant does not apply to the claim, because the claim is not a valid instance of the conclusion part of the warrant.

3. Will Readers Think Your Warrant Is Appropriate to Their Community?

Warrants can fail in one more way, having less to do with truth or reasoning, than with their appropriateness. Some warrants are shared by most of us:

> When people tell many lies, we eventually distrust what they say.

Other warrants reflect the beliefs of different historical times. A change between these two warrants marked a change from one period in European history to another:

> When evidence contradicts traditional beliefs and authorities, ignore the evidence.
>
> When evidence contradicts traditional authority, question the authority.

The second characterizes what some call the modern skeptical mind.

There are also beliefs shared by most of us in the United States, but not by all societies:

> When an action is protected by a Constitution, government may not interfere with it.

As communities become smaller, they share increasingly specialized warrants. For example, first-year law students often have a hard time "thinking like a lawyer." Like most of us, they start law school holding beliefs based on common sense. We can state one of those common sense beliefs as a warrant:

> When someone does another an injustice, courts should correct it.

Seems reasonable. But part of the painful education of law students is learning that common sense warrants do not always apply in the law, because other warrants may trump them. For example,

> When people fail to meet legal obligations, even inadvertently, they must suffer the consequences.

More specifically,

> When old people forget to pay real estate taxes, others can buy their house for back taxes and evict them.

That warrant justifies common sense injustice, but if buyers obey the law, they can argue that the house is theirs. Against their most decent instincts, law students have to learn that justice is not what most of us think it should be, but what courts say the rule of law must be.

When you write as one member of a community to others, you have to be sure not only that your warrant is true and applicable, but that it also seems appropriate to that community. On the other hand, when you write as a member of a community to outsiders, you not only have to state the warrants that are unique to your community but also to explain how and why they apply as they do.

But when you are a newcomer trying to sound like a member, you have the hardest task of all. You want to be able to write the way those you read do, but professionals writing to professionals leave only glimpses of their assumptions, enough for other experts, but not for newcomers. None of us can avoid moments in our education when we feel baffled because those at home in a community we are just entering do not feel obligated to justify their reasoning to newcomers. We learn those unstated ways of reasoning only from experience.

Distinguishing Reasons and Warrants

At first glance a warrant seems a lot like a reason, and so it's easy to confuse them. Consider this argument:

> Though Franklin Roosevelt would not appear in public in his wheelchair or be photographed in it, his federal monument should depict him in his chair. _{claim} He overcame a great disability to become a great leader, _{statement of support 1} and a great leader should be remembered as much for the challenges he overcame as for his achievements. _{statement of support 2}

Those two supporting statements both feel like reasons. In fact, in ordinary conversation, that is what we might call them both:

> The Federal monument dedicated to Franklin Roosevelt should depict him in his wheelchair. _{claim} The first reason is that he overcame a great disability to become a great leader. _{statement of support 1} The second reason is that any great leader should be remembered as much for the challenges he overcame as for his achievements. _{statement of support 2}

But those two statements support the claim in such different ways that to understand how arguments work we have to use different terms to name them.

- The first statement refers specifically to Roosevelt and to Roosevelt alone. It is a *specific* reason to support the *specific* claim that a monument should depict Roosevelt in his wheelchair.

- The second statement has nothing specifically to do with Roosevelt or his monument. It is a *general* principle stating that we should remember *any* great leader for overcoming a challenge *of any kind.* If we believe that Roosevelt was a great leader who overcame great obstacles, then he is covered by that generalization we call a warrant.

Warrants Versus Reasons

In ordinary talk, it does no harm to call a warrant a reason. Warrants are, after all, reasons for connecting a reason and a claim. One of our students called warrants extended reasons. And in fact, that captures a bit of what a warrant does: it "extends" over a specific reason and claim, holding them together. Other students have asked us, *Doesn't a warrant just say the same thing as the reason and claim, but in a different way?* Not quite. A warrant covers a conceptual territory similar to the reason and claim, but a much broader one that includes an indefinite number of other reasons and claims, involving not only leaders and challenges we know of, but countless others we don't, even those still to be born.

Review: A Test Case

Warrants are easier to understand in practice than in an abstract analysis, so here is one more example that can serve as a review. (If you think you understand warrants, skip to p. 221.)

Phil: A lot of people condemn gangsta rap, but I think it should be accepted as legitimate artistic expression _{claim} because it reflects the experience of many who listen to it. _{reason}

Mary: It may reflect the experience of many who listen to it. But why does that count as a reason for accepting it as legitimate artistic expression? I don't get it.

Mary can't see how Phil's reason is relevant to his claim, so she asks him to explain his reasoning. He might offer this warrant:

> When an artistic work reflects the experiences of those who enjoy it, it should not be censored or condemned.

Now that Mary knows the warrant, she might ask three more questions.

1. Is your warrant true?

Mary might reject Phil's warrant entirely: *That's just not so.* Or she can acknowledge that the warrant is sometimes true, but deny that it applies to *all* artistic expression, no matter how vile:

> You say that when an artistic work reflects the experiences of those who enjoy it, it should not be censored or condemned. But would you say that about lyrics that described sexually abusing and killing children? Some people might enjoy that because the lyrics reflect their evil behavior, but would you really allow music like that?

Or she can offer a warrant that contradicts Phil's original one:

> Any music should be censored and condemned if it degrades human dignity. When art degrades human dignity, it should be kept out of public circulation. _{counterwarrant} That is more important than complete freedom of expression.

Phil has three options: (1) He can limit the scope of his original warrant to make it more acceptable; (2) he can find an entirely new warrant; or (3) he can make an argument to convince Mary that his original warrant is true.

2. Is your specific reason a valid instance of the first part of your warrant?

Will a reader think that the specific circumstance counts as a good example of the general circumstance side of the warrant? That is, does the warrant "cover" the reason?

WARRANT		
General Circumstance	*predictably allows*	General Conclusion
When a work of artistic expression reflects the experience of those who enjoy it,		it should not be condemned or censored.
?		
Gangsta rap reflects the real experience of those who enjoy it_{reason}		
Specific Circumstance	*lets us infer*	Specific Conclusion
	CORE OF ARGUMENT	

Mary might accept Phil's warrant as true—we should not ban artistic expression that reflects the experiences of those who enjoy it, even when it degrades others. But she might still think that gangsta rap *does not qualify* as an example of "artistic expression," and therefore Phil's warrant does not cover his reason.

If so, Phil has two options. He can make an argument to convince Mary that gangsta rap is a form of artistic expression. Or, if Phil decides he cannot make that argument to Mary's satisfaction, he could revise his warrant to accommodate his reason:

WARRANT		
General Circumstance	*predictably allows*	General Conclusion
When a **popular** form of expression reflects the experience of those who enjoy it,		it should not be condemned or censored.
?		
Gangsta rap reflects the real experience of those who enjoy it*reason*		
Specific Circumstance	*lets us infer*	Specific Conclusion
CORE OF ARGUMENT		

Now the warrant fits the reason (but only if we believe gangsta rap is a popular form of expression). But is this warrant still true for Mary? She might defend serious artistic expression from censorship but not what she considers to be merely popular drivel.

3. Is your specific claim a valid instance of the second part of your warrant?

Assume that Mary accepts Phil's warrant and reason. She *still* might reject his argument if she thinks his claim does not match the conclusion side of his warrant:

WARRANT		
General Circumstance	*predictably allows*	General Conclusion
When a **popular** form of expression reflects the experience of those who enjoy it,		it should not be condemned or censored.
?		**?**
Gangsta rap reflects the real experience of those who enjoy it*reason*	*therefore*	it should be accepted as legitimate artistic expression.*claim*
Specific Circumstance	*lets us infer*	Specific Conclusion
CORE OF ARGUMENT		

She might argue that the claim *accepting lyrics as legitimate artistic expression* is not a valid instance of *not censoring or condemning* them because the warrant requires only that we *tolerate* such music, not *embrace* it as in Phil's claim.

If so, Phil has three options: (1) He can change his warrant to make it stronger: *popular expression should be accepted as art*; (2) he can weaken his claim: *gangsta rap should be tolerated*; (3) he can make an argument to convince Mary that not to condemn offensive art is to accept it as legitimate.

Information Overload?

If you are reacting as have many students using this book, you may be feeling overwhelmed with detail. We've given you a lot to think about and, what's harder, to put into practice. So don't be discouraged if you are feeling like the student who e-mailed us this question:

> Why do I feel less in control of making arguments as I read more about them? I feel like I'm writing worse, not better.

What we told him may encourage you: Several years ago some researchers tested new medical students to learn how well they could read X-rays for lung cancer. They found something odd. New med students quickly learned to do it pretty well, but as they gained more experience, they got worse. Then they got better at it again. The researchers concluded that at first, medical students saw exactly what they were told to see. But as they learned more about lungs, chests, and everything else that casts an X-ray shadow, they got confused: The more they learned, the less able they were to sort it out. But once they did learn to sort it out, they could see what was relevant and got better at reading X-rays again.

That's probably what's making you feel less in control of making arguments. You have more to think about than you did a few weeks ago. But it's not just that: you are probably demanding more of yourself, because you see more clearly what you must do. So as paradoxical as it may seem, your temporary confusion is a sign of progress. Or as the saying goes, if you're not confused, you haven't been paying attention.

Warranting Evidence

Readers expect evidence to connect to reasons in the same way that they expect reasons to connect to claims. And for the most part, you warrant that connection in the same way:

> People condemn gangsta rap but I think it should be accepted as legitimate artistic expression $_{\text{claim}}$ because it reflects the experience of many who listen to it. $_{\text{reason}}$ Every teen-ager I know has at some time felt anger and rage against authorities. $_{\text{report of evidence}}$ When a lot of people share an emotion, then whatever expresses that emotion reflects their experience. $_{\text{warrant}}$

What gets tricky is warranting a body of evidence consisting of numerical data, quotations, pictures, and drawings as relevant to some reason. For example,

> As Hamlet stands behind his stepfather Claudius while he is at prayer, he demonstrates a cool and rational mind. $_{\text{claim}}$ He impulsively wants to kill

Claudius on the spot, but he pauses to reflect. If he kills Claudius while pray-ing, he sends his soul to heaven. But Hamlet wants him damned to hell forever. So he coolly decides to kill him later: _{reason}

Now might I do it [kill him] pat, now he is praying:
And now I'll do't; and so he goes to heaven;
And so am I reveng'd....[Hamlet pauses to think]
[But this] villain kills my father; and for that,
I, his sole son, do this same villain send to heaven[?]
Why, this is hire and salary, not revenge. _{report of evidence}

Someone might question the relevance of that report of evidence to the reason:

I don't see how those words show that Hamlet coolly decides to kill his father later.

If so, we'd have to describe the quotation in words that make its evidence match the evidence side of the warrant:

Here, Hamlet carefully considers the consequences of killing Claudius step-by-step. That is a sign of a man who has put aside passion, at least temporar-ily, in favor of cool reason _{warrant}.

The same is true with tables, charts, graphs, pictures, musical scores, and so on: Describe what you see in the evidence that matches the evidence side of your warrant.

◆ EXAMPLE

The History of a Warrant

In this passage, Suzanna Sherry explains the history of a cherished, but contested warrant: our constitutional guarantee of free speech. She shows how the Supreme Court expanded that warrant by narrowing one of its exceptions: The warrant now covers more kinds of supposedly dangerous speech because the court changed the "dangerous speech exception" to cover fewer instances.

Legislatures have . . . frequently attempted to restrict speech because they believed it to be dangerous. Just before the Civil War, many southern states put abolitionists in prison for publishing their views. During World War I, the government jailed bolshevist sympathizers . . . because they urged men to resist the draft. The McCarthy era saw nationwide crackdowns on anyone with leftist beliefs. . . . And during the war in Vietnam, the government tried to prevent publication of the infamous Pentagon Papers.

The justification for these limits on speech is always the same: Especially in times of crisis, we cannot allow speech that will incite lawlessness or endanger lives. It was not until the 1960s that the courts began to reject that justification [that is, warrant]. Recognizing that all speech is an incitement designed to persuade the listener to action, the Supreme Court, in 1969, specified very narrow circumstances under which a speaker can be liable for the harm that results from his speech: only when the speech is intended to produce, and is likely to produce, imminent lawless action. In other words, we can blame the speaker for the actions of others only when "the evil apprehended is so imminent that it may befall before there is an opportunity for full discussion." Why? Because to do otherwise is to forge a link between speech and action—a link that might be found in any unpleasant speech.

Source: Suzanna Sherry, "I Hate What They Say,
but I Won't Stop Them," *Washington Post*, February 14, 1999.

◆◆◆

Arguing by Evidence Versus Arguing by Warrants

We make most arguments in one of two ways: We support reasons with evidence or we derive claims from warrants. Most academics and professionals base their arguments on evidence, which puts a premium on fact; some civic and many personal arguments rest on warrants, which puts a premium on principle.

For example, suppose a sociologist opposed a needle-exchange program by making this argument based on evidence:

> We should abolish the Southport needle-exchange program. claim It has made the drug problem worse reason 1 because it encourages people to use more drugs. reason 2 A study of those who have participated in it shows that 70% have increased their use of drugs; the average rate has grown from 5.7 to 9.2 injections per week. evidence

Someone who disagreed might question the source or soundness of the evidence, but she would not question its connection to the reason because it seems obvious: *of course* we should abolish a program that increases drug use.

But suppose a politician made this argument opposing the same program:

> We all know that when you make risky behavior safer, you encourage more people to engage in it. warrant Since the Southport needle-exchange program makes drug use safer, reason 1 it encourages people to use more drugs. reason 2 We should therefore abolish the program. claim

That is an argument whose claim is derived from a *principle expressed as a warrant.* When we make that kind of argument, we feel no need to offer any evidence at all if we can show that our general principle applies to the specific case. In fact, this one is an all-purpose argument that could be used against *any* program intended to reduce the cost of *any form of risky behavior,* from automobile seat belts and antilock brakes to the distribution of condoms in schools.

Most thoughtful readers are skeptical of arguments from principle because they ask us to accept a claim based only on doctrinal or ideological truths rather than on the facts of the matter. The danger in making such claims is that your entire argument falls if readers either reject the principle or deny that it applies.

WRITING PROCESS

Warrants

PREPARING AND PLANNING

Identify Your Key Assumptions

When you plan an argument, don't focus only on your key points; you also have to understand the assumptions that you can't imagine questioning, but that your reader might: *What do I believe that my readers must also believe (but may not) before they will think that my reasons are relevant to my claims?*

Suppose you want to argue that the drinking age should be lowered to eighteen because eighteen-year-olds are subject to the draft: What general principle must your readers *already* believe before they will accept that argument?

> When you're old enough to vote, marry, or die for your country, you're old enough to drink.

But is that true? If so, it is perhaps because you believe a more general warrant:

> When a person is old enough to assume basic civic responsibilities, then that person is old enough to engage in all adult activities.

But is that true? Why do you think so?

Before they agree that eighteen-year-olds should be allowed to drink, some readers would also have to hold other beliefs unconnected to drinking in particular but still relevant to the issue:

> When we determine maturity of judgment, we cannot decide on the basis of age alone.

> When we want to prevent bad consequences of overindulging in an activity, we should not ban the activity but try to prevent excess.

> When we criminalize behavior that many people approve of, we do not prevent that behavior, we just make it more attractive.

None of those beliefs directly concerns drinking, but if you are against drinking by eighteen-year-olds based on those assumptions, you have to hope that your readers would not reject them out of hand. Or if you think they would, then you have to make an argument supporting them. You must also think about their limits: Are those principles true under any and all circumstances? You might finally decide not to state any of these principles as warrants in your argument, but you benefit from the discipline of trying to figure out what they are.

Locate Warrants Where They Do the Most Good

Finding the best place for warrants is tricky, but here are two generally reliable principles:

1. Lay out important warrants before you offer specific claims and reasons. If you think readers might reject them, make an argument supporting them.

For example, suppose you want to argue that schools should teach not facts but skills. Rather than jumping straight into the reasons and evidence, you might lay down some general principles that you intend to argue from:

> **When we educate young people in a democracy, our first job is to help them become productive citizens who can make the good decisions necessary for living in a dynamic democratic system.** _{warrant} [Add reasons and evidence supporting this assertion.] Given that responsibility, _{reason} our schools should focus on more than transmitting facts; they should develop children's ability to analyze those facts critically. _{claim}

2. State warrants that readers are unlikely to contest as a logical flourish after you've offered a specific claim and supporting reasons, like a punch line that leaves readers with a sense that the conclusion was inevitable.

> We can no longer be objective about Senator Z's private behavior. _{claim} There are too many reports of unsavory incidents to think that he is innocent of everything he's been charged with. _{reason} **After all, where there's smoke, there's fire.** _{warrant}

Use Analogies as Surrogate Warrants

You can imply a warrant using analogies. The following claim is based on a warrant:

> Don't worry if you begin to feel less in control of making arguments as this book goes on. _{claim} **When people learn a difficult skill requiring complex knowledge, they almost always perform worse when they first learn that knowledge but improve as they gain experience using it.** _{warrant} So you'll have a period of confusion before you master the craft of argument. _{reason}

We can base the same claim on an analogy:

> Don't worry if you begin to feel less in control of making arguments as this book goes on. Just as medical students predictably get worse at reading X-rays before they became experts, so you'll have a period of confusion before you master the craft of argument. _{analogy}

The analogy implies that an unstated warrant covers both cases and connects a claim known to be true (the *just as* part) to a claim in question (the *so* part).

And, of course, you can combine them:

> Don't worry if you begin to feel less in control of making arguments as this book goes on. _{claim} When people learn a difficult skill requiring complex knowledge, they almost always perform worse when they first learn that knowledge but improve as they gain experience using it. _{warrant} Just as medical students predictably get worse at reading X-rays before they became experts,

so you'll have a period of confusion before you fully master the craft of argument. _{analogy}

Readers judge analogies as they do warrants. They must first believe that your point of comparison (the *just as* part) is true—med students do in fact read X-rays worse as they first gain experience but then get better. Then they must believe that your analogy matches the claim and reason you are trying to connect—that *getting worse at reading X-rays* matches *being confused about arguments* and that *becoming expert at reading X-rays* matches *mastering the craft of argument.*

Use analogies

- when you think readers will respond better to a vivid concrete example than to a general statement of a principle
- when you can't think of a way to state the warrant convincingly
- when you have stated several warrants and don't want to overdo it

Avoid analogies

- when readers might question your comparison
- when they might not see how the comparison applies to the reason and claim
- when they might infer a warrant different from yours

◆ EXAMPLE

Analogy

In this passage, the movie critic Michael Medved uses analogy to defend a proposal to require age identification before young people can see movies rated PG-13 and R.

Skeptics raise substantive objections to nearly all the current reform proposals. In today's multiplexes, a resourceful kid might easily buy a ticket to "Tarzan," but then quietly slip into the theater that's showing "The Matrix." Serious new policies might also give rise to a flourishing new market for fake ID's. Meanwhile, the "forbidden fruit" effect may well kick in. By making adult material more difficult to see, we may succeed only in making it seem more alluring and desirable.

Such arguments might also be deployed, however, against long-standing age-based restrictions on the purchase of tobacco and alcohol. Yet no one doubts that these restrictions reduce the levels of youthful indulgence. We don't let twelve-year-olds legally buy cigarettes even though some of them are wily enough to circumvent the rules.

Source: Michael Medved, "Hollywood Murdered Innocence," *Wall Street Journal,* June 16, 1999.

◆◆◆

WORKING COLLABORATIVELY

Most of the people we know share most of our beliefs and values, so we seldom think about warrants at all. That's why even experienced writers have to work hard to figure out which warrants their readers need to see. This is another instance where a group can help by offering an outside point of view. As you read one another's drafts, look for places where the logic seems a bit off:

- You can't think of anything in particular to disagree with, but you just don't like the argument. It doesn't seem to "hang together."

- You don't agree with the claim, but you can't put your finger on anything in the argument that explains why. The reasons offered just don't seem like good ones.

These are often signs that you want the writer to state an explicit warrant.

If the group is tough-minded about pursuing such points of uncertainty, it will force you to explain your logic by stating your warrants.

INQUIRIES

REFLECTIONS

1. Any warrant can be made broader or narrower. Here is a fairly broad one:

    When a form of expression encourages brutality, it must be rejected as a legitimate form of artistic expression.

    You can broaden this warrant by replacing "form of expression" with the more general "symbolic behavior" or narrow it with "song lyrics." When you change its range, do you change the conditions under which it is true?

2. Suppose you offered this objection to the claim that gangsta rap should be accepted as legitimate art:

    Ordinarily we should accept legitimate artistic expression enjoyed by those who create it, but not when it encourages brutal behavior. In other words, when a form of expression encourages brutality, it should be condemned under any and all circumstances.

    Someone responds,

    What about "Onward Christian Soldiers, onward as to war"? Do you condemn that hymn?

    Where do you go from there?

3. Is it possible for two people to agree that some reason supports some claim, even though they are relying on completely different warrants? For example, here's a reason and claim that two people might agree on:

    Grades should be assigned on a curve $_{claim}$ because then we would know who are the most deserving students. $_{reason}$

But here are two different warrants that would "cover" that claim and reason:

When society wants to identify its future elite, it should do so in a way that makes sharp distinctions in quality of performance.

Whenever you want to make teachers objectively identify the hardest-working students, you should force them to rely on the statistically sound assignment of grades.

Imagine two people who accepted the claim, but each on the basis of a different warrant. Would they stop agreeing if they learned about the other's warrant? In other words, are some agreements too shallow to survive shared knowledge?

4. Suppose two people agree to the following:

Whenever you want to make teachers objectively identify the hardest-working students, you should force them to rely on statistically sound assignment of grades. _{warrant} Grades should therefore be assigned on a curve. _{claim}

Can we conclude that the two people have deeper agreement because they agree on a shared warrant? Suppose they had these two reasons:

We need to prevent teachers from judging students on superficial matters of personality, _{reason} so grades should be assigned on a curve. _{claim}

We need to make sure teachers identify students who do not work hard, _{reason} so grades should be assigned on a curve. _{claim}

Both reasons would count as valid instances of the reason side of the warrant. But do these two people really agree? Would they feel that they agreed? Maybe when we agree, we do not agree as much as we think. Are there times when we should be satisfied with superficial agreement? Are there times when we should not?

5. We have discussed principles of reasoning as if they were always in our minds even when they are not stated as warrants and we do not think about them. But when you connect a reason to a claim but do not state a warrant, must there always be a principle "in the back of your mind"? In other words, when people connect reasons to claims, do they always have a principle available to justify the connection? Or do they just connect a reason to a claim because nothing seems to contradict it? How would we find out?

TASKS

6. Here is a middle-sized warrant that many people believe:

When a tourist encounters a local custom characteristic of the country she visits, she should participate in that custom.

That warrant might remind you of the proverb, *When in Rome, do as the Romans do.* Is the proverb broader or narrower than its explicit statement as a warrant? Select two more proverbs that express principles you believe.

Restate them as middle-sized warrants like the one above. Then make each broader and narrower. Do you still accept the principle after you broadened it? If not, why not? If so, broaden it again. Do you accept it now?

7. The warrant about good turns is one that we might describe as signaling obligation: "When X is the case, we should do Y." Here are some popular proverbs. Turn them into "When, then" warrants, then decide what kind of relationship they signal. Is it cause-effect, effect-cause, appearance-reality, etc.?

Where there's smoke there's fire.

One rotten apple spoils the barrel.

You can't tell a book by its cover.

Look before you leap.

If you've seen one, you've seen them all.

What sorts of limitations apply to these?

PROJECT

8. From a dictionary of proverbs, select a dozen or so that you find odd, puzzling, untrue. For each one, try to construct a little story in which someone follows the proverb. For example,

Alana wanted to go dancing on Saturday with her friend Tanya, who already had a date. So Tanya tells Alana, "There's a guy in my chem lab this afternoon who would love to go with you. Want me to talk to him?" "Maybe," says Alana, "but first I want to come by the lab." "Why?" asks Tanya. Replies Alana, "Look before you leap."

Do you find it hard to invent stories in which people would follow a puzzling or untrue proverb? What does that tell you about your ability to understand the warrants of others? Can you imagine yourself acting in the way the characters in your stories do? What does that tell you about your ability to accept the warrants of others?

 FOCUS ON WRITING

1

Context. Proverbs offer insights into different cultures. For example, here is a Japanese saying we mentioned earlier:

The nail that sticks up gets hammered down.

This means that if you are different from everyone else, you will be forced into conformity, and (according to Japanese thinking) that is a good thing. Here is another Japanese proverb:

If you love your child, send him on a journey.

That means that if you want your child to become part of the larger community, send him out on his own where he will be cared for by strangers and learn the ways of the community. Are there corresponding proverbs in English? If not, what does that mean?

Task.   This project will require collaborative activity. It will lead, not to a paper but to more informal writing. Spend some time with students from other cultures, asking them for proverbs in their culture. Distinguish those that have parallels in English from those that do not. Then read some proverbs in English to those foreign students and ask if they have any parallels. The group should then share its findings. Once you see the similarities and differences, try to imagine some situations where we and someone from another culture would reason about a circumstance differently.

Here are some English proverbs you might read to people from other cultures. Notice that all of these have to do with different attitudes toward being cautious versus being bold.

The early bird gets the worm.

Nothing ventured nothing gained.

A rolling stone gathers no moss.

Look before you leap.

Don't count your chickens before they're hatched.

Strike while the iron is hot.

Once burned, twice shy.

Better safe than sorry.

He who hesitates is lost.

No guts, no glory.

A bird in the hand is worth two in the bush.

Do *not* assume that there are no differences between cultures if every proverb you hear corresponds to one in English and if every proverb you offer corresponds to one in that other language. It probably means that you haven't found unique ones yet.

RESEARCH PROJECT

Scenario.   You have worked on this project so long that you fear you cannot see your draft from your reader's point of view.

Task.   Complete your first draft. For each major reason in each major section, list the warrants that connect it to the main claim. Also list the warrants that connect it to its own reasons and evidence. State them using the formula, *Whenever X, then Y.* Use the following list to test your draft:

- Are the warrants true? Do they apply? Do they need to be qualified?
- Will readers need you actually to state them in your text?
- Will readers accept them, or must you include an argument to support them?

IN A NUTSHELL

About Your Argument . . .

A warrant is a general statement that explicitly or implicitly relates a set of general conditions to a set of general consequences. We've expressed warrants in this regular way:

> When children behave in violent ways, it is because they have been influenced by violent movies, TV, and computer games.

But they can be expressed in a less explicit way:

> Violent movies, TV, and computer games cause violent children.

However we express a warrant, it serves to link a reason to a claim:

> More children are playing Mortal Kombat than ever before. _{reason} Since violent movies, TV, and computer games cause violent children, _{warrant} we will see more children attacking other children. _{claim}

If we believe the warrant and the reason, we have to believe the claim.

. . . and About Writing It

You might have problems with warrants in five ways:

- Readers do not see your warrant.
- They think it is not true.
- They think that it is true, but needs to be limited.
- They think the warrant does not "cover" the reason or the claim.
- They think the warrant is not be appropriate to your audience.

When you address highly contested issues, step back and ask yourself what you think your readers must believe *in general* about your issue *before* they will accept your specific reasons as relevant to your specific claims. If you think that your readers do not share those warrants, then you have to make them the center of their own argument, treating the warrants as claims that need their own reasons, evidence, and warrants.

PART III

Thinking About Thinking in Arguments

In this section, we discuss the quality of thinking that goes into an intellectually sound argument and how we make that thinking apparent to careful readers, especially in arguments about words and their meanings or causes and effects. We focus on the qualities of sound thinking and on the pitfalls that even experienced writers can fall into.

- In Chapter 9, we discuss three kinds of thinking—*inductive, deductive,* and what has been called *abductive*—and the typical blunders critical thinkers guard against.
- In Chapter 10, we discuss the kind of thinking you need to do in arguments about the meanings of words.
- In Chapter 11, we discuss the kind of thinking you do in arguments about causes and their effects, including those in which you hold someone responsible for the consequences of an action.

CHAPTER 9

The Forms of Reasoning

In this chapter, we discuss three forms of reasoning: inductive, deductive, and abductive. We show you how these kinds of reasoning are distorted by "cognitive biases," predictable habits of mind that keep us from thinking as well as we can. Finally, we discuss the strategies that critical thinkers use to avoid them.

We've told you how to plan sound arguments and how you can use the parts and questions of argument as tools for critical thinking. But we haven't said much about the quality of reasoning that has to go into those processes. In this chapter, we explain three forms of reasoning—inductive, deductive, and abductive—and the flaws that can afflict them. As you prepare your argument, you must not only recognize those flaws in your own thinking and writing but guard against them in the writing of others.

Three Forms of Reasoning

If you have read anything about reasoning, you probably know about two kinds: *inductive* and *deductive*. Philosophers have distinguished them for about 2500 years, but neither one represents how most of us really think. The more common kind of reasoning is called *abductive*.

Inductive Reasoning: From Specifics to a General Conclusion

You reason inductively when you begin with specific observations and then draw a general conclusion about them. Imagine that over the years Professor Stein records which students wrote papers on desktop computers or laptops, because she is studying trends in computer usage. One day as she looks over her records, she notices that those who used laptops tended to get higher grades than those who used desktops. In reaching that conclusion, she reasoned *inductively,* from a lot of specific instances to a general claim that she did not have in mind until the moment it occurred to her. That's pure induction: from specifics to an *unanticipated* general conclusion.

Deductive Reasoning: From a Generalization to a Specific Conclusion

We call reasoning *deductive* when we start not with specifics, but with a general principle that we apply to specific observations and that we then use to draw a conclusion (which must be more specific than the principle). Imagine that the day after Professor Stein has her inductive insight about grades and laptops, she meets Professor Chen. She tells him about her insight: Students who wrote on laptops tend to get higher grades than those who do not. He thinks, *I know that this year as opposed to last year, more of my students write on laptops, so it looks like I'll be giving higher grades.*

Professor Chen began with Professor's Stein generalization (*students who write on laptops get better grades*), added to it a specific observation (*more of his students write on laptops*), and drew a conclusion; that's pure deductive reasoning (*he's going to give higher grades*).

(We should note that most philosophers define *inductive* and *deductive* somewhat differently. For them, deductive reasoning leads to a conclusion that *must* be true; inductive reasoning leads to a conclusion that is only *probably* true.)

Abductive Reasoning: From Problem to Hypothesis to Confirmation

Those examples, however, are misleading because we invented two implausible stories in which conclusions seemed to jump out of the blue. In fact, we rarely reason like that, especially when we plan an argument. Almost always, we begin thinking about claims not because we happen to have either a lot of random data or generalizations rattling around in our heads waiting for an insight. We usually *start* with a tentative claim because we have a problem that needs a solution, a question that needs an answer, and we have at least an inkling about what that answer *might* be.

When we engage in that kind of thinking—problem-solving-answer-seeking thinking—we typically start with a hunch. We imagine possible solutions until we find one—call it a probationary *hypothesis*—that might plausibly solve the problem. Then we look for data to test that hypothesis. If what we find supports our favored hunch/hypothesis better than any competing one *and* (this is important) we find no data that contradicts our hypothesis, we accept it as the best available solution to our problem, at least at that moment.

For example, imagine that after noticing that most of her students who wrote on laptops got better grades than those who did not, Professor Stein asks this question (that is, she poses a problem): *Could it be that writing on laptops* **causes** *better grades?* To test that hypothesis, she collects more data about students in other classes and discovers that most of those who wrote on laptops also got higher grades. So she tentatively accepts that as a working hypothesis—writing on laptops is a cause of better grades.

But she also thinks of some alternative explanations: Maybe those who choose to write on laptops are somehow more diligent students. Or maybe those who can afford laptops have more time to study because they come from richer families and do not need to work at part-time jobs. If either alternative is true, then using a laptop does not *cause* better grades; using laptops is instead *caused by something else* that also causes better grades: greater diligence or additional time.

So she now poses an even more challenging problem: If her school provided laptops to *all* students for writing their papers, would they all, or least more of them, get better grades? To test her hypotheses that writing on laptops *causes* better grades, she collects yet more data about students in other classes and other schools, including those who are required to use laptops, those who choose to use them, those who choose not to, and, most important, those who have no choice but to write on desktop computers.

Assume her new data support her working hypothesis: Writing on laptops is indeed a significant factor in getting higher grades. If so, she has strengthened (but not totally confirmed) her hypothesis *abductively*. She began with a problem that motivated a hypothesis that accounted for the data she had; she used that hypothesis to look for more data; then she used those data to test and strengthen her hypothesis.

There is, however, one thing she can never do. She can never *prove* her hypothesis/claim true, once and for all. She knows that tomorrow someone might come up with new data that prove her claim wrong. And that is true of every abductive claim: They are only more or less probably true. Even if every bird ever seen by the human eye has had feathers, it is only probably true that all birds have feathers, because somewhere there may be a featherless bird (and, in fact, there is). You never know. Biologists once believed that mammals never lay eggs, until someone discovered the platypus.

Real-Life Barriers to Abductive Critical Thinking

Sad to say, real thinking about real problems is rarely so simple. You take an important step toward good critical thinking when you reason abductively— that is, when you state your problem carefully but as quickly as you can and then formulate a few tentative hypotheses to guide your thinking toward its solution. But even abductive thinking is vulnerable to a set of inherited habits of mind that lead our thinking astray, habits called *cognitive biases*. These biases do not reflect age, intelligence, education, or expertise. They are chronic and incurable, but once you know them, you can use the discipline of sound critical thinking to guard against them, not just in your own thinking but in the thinking of others. What follows are some ways you can do that.

Don't Rely on Warrants in Place of Evidence

It is easy to think we have more support for our hypothesis than we really do, especially when it is a claim that we think is true mostly because we *want* it to be true, because we already believe it, or both. We can fool ourselves in several ways. A common one is to think that we have "proof" when all we have to back our claim is yet another firmly held belief that we use as a warrant.

Recall the argument about DNA evidence proving that someone in Thomas Jefferson's bloodline fathered a child by his slave Sally Hemings (p. 78). Some historians tested their hypothesis against a lot of individual bits of evidence:

- DNA evidence showed that someone in Jefferson's family fathered a son by Hemings.
- The son in question looked like Jefferson.
- Jefferson took Hemings with him when he went to Paris as ambassador.
- Some contemporaries publicly accused him of having children by Hemings.
- Stories about Hemings and Jefferson were passed down in her family for 200 years.
- Hemings's children were the only slaves Jefferson freed in his lifetime.

None of these bits of evidence proves that Jefferson had a child by Hemings, but collectively they led many historians to conclude that he probably did (and keep in mind that someone might ask for the evidence behind *these* so-called bits of evidence).

Historians on the other side dismissed that evidence and the unwelcome conclusion it led to, because they based their claim not on evidence, but on a warrant and reason that they believed made evidence irrelevant:

> When a person devotes his life to freedom and equality, that person's character makes it impossible to do something as immoral as having sex with a slave. warrant Jefferson devoted his life to freedom and equality, reason so he could not have had sex with his slave, Hemings. claim / conclusion

Those historians ignored the evidence about Jefferson and Hemings because they put greater trust in beliefs they already held, which they used as a warrant and a reason.

Good critical thinkers usually reason from lots of evidence to a claim, not from a single principle to a claim that they want to be true. Even when they do reason from a principle, they think about the limitations and provisos that are left unstated. For example, the anti-Hemings historians have to acknowledge that their warrant has limits:

> People do not act against their fundamental character *unless they are under great stress, or they face great temptation, or they are coerced, etc.*

Even the staunchest Jeffersonian would have to acknowledge at least the possibility that after his wife died, he might have been drawn to Hemings, who was her half-sister.

How do critical thinkers resist an unjustified adherence to the One True Principle? They engage with others to seek out different points of view, in person and in their imagination. They question their own principles and encourage that voice in the back (or front) of their mind to keep asking *But what would you say to someone who asked. . . ?*

If you suspect your readers hold fast to One True Principle, you are unlikely to dislodge them. But you might be able to lessen their certainty, if you can show that the matter is more complex than it seems and that your case shows the limits of their general rule.

Don't Collect Evidence Randomly

You are not thinking abductively just because you collect data on a topic. It is not abductive thinking unless you collect those data to test a hypothesis. If you start by randomly gathering data on a topic, hoping a problem and maybe even a solution will turn up, you depend too much on luck and not enough on critical thinking.

Imagine that Professor Stein decided to collect all kinds of data to see whether any other variable correlated with the quality of student writing. So she recorded the grades of students, then randomly categorized them by whether they pierced their noses, wore all black, drove SUVs, were born west of the Mississippi, and so on. That is not as bad as purely inductive thinking, since she at least restricted herself to the topic of writing and sorted grades by *some* categories of evidence. But it would lead her to collect a mound of data with no idea whether it might be relevant to anything.

Abductive thinking begins with a plausible hypothesis to test. Only then can you know what specific data to collect and how to evaluate it.

Guard Against the Biases Common in Abductive Thinking

Even when we do begin with a hypothesis and collect data to test it, we can still fall prey to the most treacherous bias and biggest obstacle to sound critical thinking: We hit on a quick hypothesis, then hunker down on it, usually because it is what we *want* to be true. Once we have our answer, we anchor our thinking to it, even if the best evidence tells us we should let it go.

A good recent example may be the war in Iraq. Those who have studied how that war began say that the Bush administration fell prey to that bias in evaluating the hypothesis that Iraq had weapons of mass destruction. (Some say the administration lied, but biased thinking is the more likely explanation.) The administration believed that Iraq had the weapons; they also wanted to have good reasons to give the UN for supporting the war. So they looked only for facts that supported that hypothesis. When they found ambiguous facts, they interpreted them as unambiguously supporting their position. Then they rejected or ignored any facts that cast doubt on it and derided the UN inspectors who expressed those doubts. In hindsight, it is easy to see where they went wrong. But at the time, they were so wedded to what they wanted to be true, that they stopped thinking critically and saw evidence that made it true everywhere they looked.

We all need to start with a plausible working hypothesis; but instead of trying to poke holes in it, too many of us harden our thinking around it, until it ossifies into an impregnable truth. Here are some strategies that critical thinkers use to avoid that kind of anchoring.

Deliberately Seek Disconfirming Evidence

Once a belief is anchored, we are more likely to seek evidence that supports it than evidence that contradicts it. For example, here is a disconcerting finding about the way many doctors diagnose illnesses. When a patient describes symptoms, doctors are likely to make a quick diagnosis, then order tests to prove that they are *right*. If the results are uncertain, they order more tests that they hope will confirm their diagnosis, and if those don't, still more. But as studies show, doctors seem less inclined to order tests that would *prove their first diagnosis wrong*, even though that would test their judgment more efficiently.

Once you think you have a solid claim, stop and think: What data could disprove it? Then look for those data. No intellectual exercise is more difficult or more valuable. Nothing defines critical thinking more than this one question: *What might prove me wrong?*

What Automobile Ads Do You Read?

What car ads are you most likely to read—those for your own car or for another make? Market studies show that most of us read more ads about our own car because we don't want to see evidence that another car might be better. None of us likes to think we might have bought the wrong car.

Source: Stuart Sutherland, *Irrationality: Why We Don't Think Straight!* New Brunswick, NJ: Rutgers University Press, 1992, p. 141.

Interpret Evidence Objectively

Even when we try to gather evidence on both sides, we tend to reshape what we find to fit our hypothesis. A good example is reported by Stephen J. Gould in *The Mismeasure of Man* (New York: Norton, 1981). Gould writes about Samuel Morton, an early nineteenth-century scientist with a good reputation for gathering objective data, who set out to prove that Caucasians were smarter than other races because they had bigger brains. To measure the size of brains, he filled skulls from different races with mustard seeds, then weighed the seeds, assuming their weight would correlate with the volume of the skull and therefore the size of the brain. He found that, indeed, the seeds that filled Caucasian skulls weighed more than those from non-Caucasian skulls, and so he concluded that Caucasians have larger skulls and therefore larger brains (and therefore greater intelligence—a lot of unsupported *therefores*, of course).

He later repeated his work with lead shot, because it gave more consistent measurements. But when he did, he found—to his surprise—much less difference in the sizes of the skulls. Morton himself reported the puzzle, so he was trying to be objective.

What apparently happened was this: To fill a skull completely with the small, light mustard seeds, he had to pat them down, and he seems to have unconsciously patted down the seeds in the skulls of Caucasians more tightly than he did in others. He thereby increased their density and total weight, thereby biasing his evidence to support the conclusion he wanted to reach: greater volume for Caucasian skulls.

As hard as it is, you must consider what you would do if you were paid to prove that your hypothesis is wrong. Ask yourself, *Could I find more reliable evidence than what I have? How could I interpret the evidence I do have so that it went against rather then for my claim? Is the evidence itself biased?*

Don't Dismiss Contrary Evidence

Not only do we tend to gather and interpret evidence in ways that fit our hypothesis; we also tend to resist evidence that undermines it. In one study, researchers assembled two groups of students with opposing views on the death penalty and established how strongly they held those views. Each group then read two articles, one in favor of the death penalty, the other against. We might expect that after reading an argument opposing their respective beliefs, both sides would moderate their views and end up closer together.

In fact, the opposite occurred. After reading the articles, the two sides were further apart than before. Apparently, both sides put more weight on the article that supported their views and rejected the one that refuted them, entrenching themselves in their prior beliefs even more firmly.

Again, imagine that you are being paid to *disprove* your own argument: *What evidence have I dismissed that works against my claim?*

The Power of a Settled Belief

How strongly do we hold a belief, even when we have evidence we are wrong? More than we should. Researchers gave students invented suicide notes, saying that some were fake and some were real, and asked them to pick out the real ones. As they did so, some students were told they were doing a good job, others that they were not. At the end, the students were told all the notes were fake. Then they were asked how well they thought they would do with a set of real notes. Those who had been told (falsely) that they had done well tended to be more confident that they could pick out real notes than those told (also falsely) that they had done badly, even though all of them knew they had been lied to.

Source: L. Ross, M. R. Lepper, and M. Hubbard, "Perseverance in Self-Perception and Social Perception: Biased Attributional Processes in the Debriefing Paradigm," *Journal of Personality and Social Psychology* 32 (1975): 880–892.

Don't Be So Sure of Yourself

Another reason we hunker down on a claim is overconfidence. For example, do you think you are an above average, average, or below average driver? More than 90 percent of those tested think they are above average, but that cannot be, because by definition half the drivers are below average. Our overconfidence is not a sign of stupidity or immaturity. If we lightly changed our beliefs at the first hint of contrary evidence, we would fail to see the deeper regularities in our physical and social worlds. We need settled beliefs to live settled lives. But the cost of that confidence is becoming so entrenched in a belief that we do not change it when we should. It is behavior that is cost-effective in the short run, which is, after all, where most of us live. In the academic and professional world, however, we are expected to take a longer view.

So be modest in your certainty. As difficult as it will be, think to yourself *I could be wrong,* even when in your heart of hearts you are sure you are right.

The Cautious Language of Good Problem Solvers

A researcher who studied the language of good and bad problem solvers found that weaker problem solvers tend to use words that express certainty and totality: *constantly, every time, all, without exception, absolutely, entirely, completely, totally, unequivocally, undeniably, without question, certainly, solely, only, neither-nor, must, have to.* Better problem solvers more often use words that express uncertainty and qualification: *now and then, in general, sometimes, often, ordinarily, a bit, in particular, somewhat, to a degree, perhaps, conceivable, questionable, among other things, on the other hand, may, can.*

Source: From Dietrich Doerner, *The Logic of Failure: Recognizing and Avoiding Error in Complex Situations,* New York: Addison-Wesley, 1997.

Beware of Insufficient Evidence

Our most common bias in reasoning is jumping to a conclusion from too little evidence. Starting with the hypothesis that global warming is a myth, someone seizes on a record cold January as proof (or a proponent of warming seizes on a record hot August). Critical thinkers will judge your reasoning sound only when they think you have considered *more* than enough data.

The problem, however, is not just to know what your readers will think is enough. You must also know whether *they* hold contrary beliefs based on *their own* insufficient, unrepresentative, imprecise, or even inaccurate evidence. If so, acknowledge that they may have some evidence for their belief, but suggest, carefully, that there is more out there than they know.

WRITING PROCESS

The Forms of Reasoning

PREPARING AND PLANNING

Guard Against Leaping to a Conclusion

Do what critical thinkers do:

1. Consider all the solutions you can think of.

2. Imagine data that would disconfirm your hypothesis, then look for them.

3. If you can't imagine disconfirming evidence that you can find quickly, watch for it as you do your research.

4. Gather data objectively. Ask, *What would I see in this if I opposed my solution/claim?*

5. Interpret data objectively. Ask, *How would I interpret this evidence if I opposed this solution/claim?*

6. Gather more evidence than you think you need.

Follow steps 2–6 even if you begin with a solution/claim that you fully intend to support. You may not change your mind (though you should stay open to that possibility), but you will better anticipate readers' objections.

Anticipate the Biases of Your Readers

To make a good argument, you must do more than think critically. You must also anticipate that your readers might not because they are in the grip of their own cognitive biases. How will they receive evidence that contradicts their beliefs? What kinds of overgeneralizations have they made? What will it take to dislodge them from their favorite explanations and principles? Since it is unlikely that you will be able to shake them loose from their deepest and most staunchly defended beliefs, even ones that seem to you to be self-evidently wrong, you must find ways to help them see that their beliefs are less than 100 percent true in all contexts at all times. You must acknowledge their beliefs and perhaps even allow that they are generally sound, but then show that there may be limits, room for exceptions.

INQUIRIES

REFLECTIONS

1. Think of a public figure you admire—a politician, writer, sports figure, etc. Now suppose you saw seemingly reliable evidence of a flaw in that

person's character: he or she embezzled money, gambles uncontrollably, engages in sordid sex, or any other disturbing behavior. What would be your first impulse: To defend the person? To change your opinion? To feel betrayed? To reserve judgment? Which response do you think would be the most rational? Which would be the most common?

2. Imagine the scenario above involving not a public figure but a close friend or family member. Now what would be your first impulse? Would that response be a rational one? Would a rational response be best?

IN A NUTSHELL

About Your Argument . . .

Traditional philosophers identify two kinds of reasoning:

- *Inductive* reasoning from specifics to a general conclusion about all of them: *Many samples of ocean water are salty, so ocean water must be salty (but there could be exceptions).*

- *Deductive* reasoning from a general warrant and reason to a specific claim: *Ocean water is always salty; this water is from the ocean, so it must be salty.*

But the more common kind of reasoning is *abductive*—reasoning that begins with a hypothesis that might explain the data in question.

When we reason abductively, we test that hypothesis using whatever reasoning seems appropriate. Abductive reasoning is problem-driven, a kind of reasoning that begins with a hypothesis that is the tentative solution to a problem.

Each kind of reasoning is vulnerable to cognitive biases.

- When you think inductively, you risk basing a conclusion on too few instances. You avoid that risk by gathering more evidence than you think you need and by learning something about statistical sampling and analysis.

- When you think deductively, you risk formulaic thinking, applying a rote warrant to every situation.

- When you think abductively, you risk fixating on the first hypothesis that springs to mind. Guard against that by holding your earliest hypotheses lightly, by imagining more than one, and by deliberately seeking out evidence that disconfirms your favorite one.

. . . and About Writing It

The time to protect against bias in your thinking is before you start a first draft. From the time you first select a hypothesis until you have collected all of your evidence, review this checklist to be sure that you have thought critically about your own developing ideas:

1. Consider all the solutions you can think of.
2. Imagine data that would disconfirm your hypothesis, then look for them.
3. If you can't imagine disconfirming evidence, watch for it as you do your research.
4. Gather data objectively.
5. Interpret data objectively.
6. Gather more evidence than you think you need.

CHAPTER 10

Arguments About Meanings

In this chapter, we discuss issues in thinking about the relationship between words and meanings. We show you how to make an argument based on meanings by defining terms in a way that encourages readers at least to consider seeing things as you want them to.

In most arguments, we address issues involving words and their meanings or causes and their effects, and sometimes both, because what we think something is shapes what we think we should do about it. For example, several years ago some members of Congress thought they knew what they should do when they learned that a federal agency, the National Endowment for the Arts, had funded a museum exhibit of photographs by Robert Mapplethorpe, whose images are so sexually explicit that many consider them pornographic. Those critics argued that Congress should abolish the NEA because it promoted pornography.

To support their claim, the critics had to make four arguments. Two were about terms and their meanings:

- What is the meaning of *pornography*?
- What is it about Mapplethorpe's images that puts them in that category?

Two more were about causes and their effects:

- How does the NEA encourage to the dissemination of those images?
- How would closing the NEA discourage pornography?

The critics thought that if they could get everyone to label Mapplethorpe's images *pornographic*, they would then have a better chance of gaining support for *doing* something about them—abolish the NEA.

We base many professional and civic arguments on this relationship between words and deeds:

If civilian militia are *patriots*, _{definition} we should support them as defenders of freedom. _{practical claim}

If competitive ballroom dancing is a *sport*, _{definition} we should make it an Olympic event. _{practical claim}

In the academic world, on the other hand, researchers often make arguments about definitions not to get us to *do* anything, but to help us *understand* something:

> The term *language* is used loosely to mean communicating information through behavior or signs. So it is said that bees use a "language of dancing" to communicate information about how to find pollen. But human language does more than that. It communicates not just predictable and narrowly defined bits of information, but desires, feelings, and ideas unique to the moment. _{definition} Many think such uses of language make us unique in the animal kingdom. But chimpanzees can be taught to do something like it in sign language or by touching symbols on a computer screen. As rudimentary as their communication is, they demonstrate an ability to use language in ways that resemble what humans do. _{application of definition} Their ability demonstrates intellectual powers so much greater than we have suspected _{reason} that **we can no longer think of ourselves as cognitively unique in the animal kingdom.** _{conceptual claim}

If we accept that definition of *language* and agree that what chimps do exemplifies it (it would take a lot of evidence), then we have reason to accept the *conceptual* claim that we can no longer think of ourselves as unique in the animal kingdom. Those making that argument might also be preparing a *practical* claim: they might want us to *do* something, to *act* differently—for instance, to stop using chimps in medical experiments. But their basic aim is to convince us to *think* differently about our place in the animal kingdom.

In this chapter, we discuss how good critical thinkers manage arguments that focus on words, their meanings, and the consequences of choosing one term over another. But first we have to explain some terms of our own.

Some Terminology

To explain how to make arguments about meaning, we use six words that you know—*category, term, feature, meaning, criteria,* and *definition*—but we'll start with one that you may not—*referent:*

- We use words or phrases to talk about something—a person, object, event, concept, idea, and so on. What we talk about can be either out in the world (the Eiffel Tower) or in our minds (the square root of 5). We'll call the thing that we talk about or refer to when we use a term the **referent** of that term.

It is easiest to grasp the idea of a referent when we talk about particular things. If someone asked, *When you said* Sue's cat, *what were you referring to?* You could pick up or point to that specific cat, the referent you had in mind. You would have a harder time showing what referent you had in mind if someone asked, *When you talked about* pet cats, *what were you referring to?* You couldn't pick up all the pet cats in the world; you could only point to individual examples of them. And you would have a harder time yet explaining the referent of *cat* in a sentence like *The cat has been a household pet for thousands of years,* because there *cat* refers to the abstract category of cats. So a referent can be an individual thing in the world, a concept that categorizes many things in the world, or an abstract concept that exists in our minds.

- When we think of sets of things as alike, we group them into mental **categories.** We create categories ranging from very large to very small: *things, creatures, animals, mammals, felines, cats, Persians, Sue's Persian cat.*

We create some categories to match what seem to be natural categories in the world: *tree, dog, water, dinosaur;* other categories we create and then impose on the world: *duty, spice, animals bigger than a breadbox,* even the term *category* itself. (It is a puzzling question whether categories such as "natural kinds" really exist in nature or whether all categories are human impositions, but we'll leave that debate to philosophers.)

- When we talk about categories, we usually name them by **terms.** (We use *term* rather than *word,* because some terms are not single words but phrases.) The terms *animal, mammal, feline, cat,* and *Persian* all name both categories and individual referents in them. We gain and lose terms all the time: *DVD* is a new one; *gramophone* is almost gone. And we invent phrases to name categories for which we have no single word: *creatures that fly.*

- When we distinguish referents in one category from those in another, we talk about their shared and distinguishing **features.** The distinguishing features of Persian cats are that they are fluffy, have pug noses, and meow; the features of Siamese cats are that they are smooth, have pointed noses, and yowl. The problem with distinguishing features is that there may be no one feature that all members of a category share. Some people think that categories are like rigid containers, with referents being either in or out. As we'll see in a moment, that's a mistake.

- We assign **meaning** to a category based on the features that distinguish it from others, but also on the associations, values, and other ideas we have about it. We then attach some of that meaning to the term that names the category. So when we think about the meaning of *cat,* we call up a mixture of images, concepts, feelings, and so on. Like categories, meanings do not have sharp boundaries.

- Psychologists argue convincingly that we experience "meaning" more as a holistic entity than as the sum of individual parts. But when we *talk* about a meaning, we have to break it into elements that we'll call **criteria** of meaning. For example, when someone asks us what the word *friable* means, we say, *It means sort of dry and crumbly and easily broken into little pieces.* Among the criteria for the meaning of *friable* are "dry," "crumbly," "easily breaks into little pieces." Criteria often blend into each other.

- We create a **definition** when we state in words some criteria of meaning of a term that names a category, usually by listing the unique features that all the members of that category share. Most definitions consist of a word that names a general category, which we then modify with more words that narrow its meaning.

To understand arguments about meaning, you have to keep three things in mind:

- We make up definitions. They do not exist in nature. Meaning is something that just happens. It is imposed on us by the way we and others use words.
- The meaning of a term is infinitely more complex than its definition.
- Most importantly, we cannot use the definition of a term to settle questions of meaning, particularly whether we should apply any particular term to any particular referent.

When we decide what to call something, we focus on different features of the referent, but depending on the situation and our ability to think critically, we also focus on many other things as well, including the problem we want to solve. We define *water* as the chemical compound consisting of two parts hydrogen and one part oxygen. But the meaning of *water* includes many facts about it, including that it covers the earth, is necessary for life, and washes away dirt. We don't call H_2O *water* if it is ice or steam because we use those terms so differently: We don't ask for ice or steam, much less H_2O, when the problem is to wash our hands.

We invent new terms when we want to group things into a new category. For example, a few years ago people noticed that some drivers referents were displaying hostile behavior. common feature They drove aggressively and used nasty language or made angry gestures toward other drivers, and so on. common features When people wanted to treat instances of this behavior as part of a pattern, they created a category that had no settled term attached to it. At first, they referred to the category with various terms: *aggressive driving, hostility behind the wheel,* and so on. Eventually one term with a memorable sound stuck to the category, *road rage.* Now when a driver cuts us off, yelling and shaking his fist, we can say, *There's another case of road rage.* If someone asks what we mean, we can point to a specific example, describe a typical case, or give a definition: *driving* (general category) *in ways that seem aggressive, angry, and hostile* (narrowing terms).

If definitions were as clear-cut as that example seems, we would not have to make arguments about terms or their meanings. But within general limits, we all use words and define their meanings in different ways at different times for different purposes to solve different problems. As a consequence, we do not all agree all the time about what words mean, about what referents they name, or about how we should use them.

For example, suppose your friend made a dinner for you that included a dish you thought was awful. You ate it anyway and then told him it tasted great. You have knowingly told an untruth. But would you call that untruth an *out and out lie?* If you told it to be kind to your friend, you might call it a *white lie* or maybe a *fib.* Most of us would be reluctant to call it an *outright lie* even though it might "technically" be one. In other words, we choose one term rather than another in order to solve a social problem: We do not want to be guilty of lying, so we call our untruth a *fib.*

On the other hand, suppose you said the dish was good, hoping that your friend would prepare it again for his (and your) boss, get fired, and you'd get his job. You said the same words (*Great dinner!*) referring to the same referent (an awful dinner), but with a different intention. Now do we call that same untrue statement *a fib, a white lie,* or a *real lie?* Probably the last.

Good critical thinkers know that meaning is, to mix metaphors, slippery and fuzzy at the same time, and it's that quality that challenges us when we craft arguments about terms and their meanings.

Meanings and Problems

What Problem Does the Definition of Your Term Solve?

As with any argument, you plan one about meaning by first asking what problem motivates you to make it and whether it is conceptual or practical:

- In a conceptual argument, you create a definition to help readers understand something important about a larger issue or question.

- In a practical argument, you discuss meaning so that readers will see why an action is necessary.

For example, in Part I we defined *argument* in a way that we thought would help you write good arguments. We focused on a practical outcome and ways to reach it. If that definition worked for you, then together we solved a practical problem: You will write better arguments. If, however, we had been writing a scholarly historical analysis of argument, we would have defined that term differently, because our aim would have been not to help you *do* something about argument (write better ones), but to help you *understand* how the meaning of that term has changed and what it tells us about the social history of reasoning and communication.

So before anything else, you have to understand what specific problem motivates your argument and whether you want readers only to *understand* something or to *do* something.

Is the Issue of Meaning a Surrogate for a Larger Problem?

Sometimes we are not clear about the kind of problem we want to solve because we unknowingly get bogged down in a *surrogate argument.* A surrogate argument is one that stands in for another, usually one we want to avoid because its problem is too large or too contentious for us to solve directly. Surrogate arguments about meaning typically lead us astray in one of two ways: an apparently conceptual problem about definitions masks an underlying practical problem, or a question about meaning masks a conflict over values and feelings.

Don't Confuse Words, Definitions, and Deeds

When you and your readers disagree about terms, good critical thinkers don't assume that they will get anywhere by arguing about definitions. If the terms affect a larger practical problem, that practical problem may be what is really at issue.

Here is an example. Thelma and Louise are debating whether two people of the same sex can have a ceremony we call a *wedding*:

Thelma: I had an interesting weekend. I went to the wedding of two women friends of my aunt.

Louise: Well, maybe it was a ceremony, but it wasn't a wedding because *wedding* means joining a man and woman in marriage. You can't have a marriage between two women, so they can't have had a wedding.

Thelma: Who says you can't have a wedding between any two people when they publicly commit themselves to each other? Who says they can't be the same sex?

Louise: Look at how the word's been used for thousands of years. A wedding has always meant creating a marriage bond between a man and a woman.

Thelma: Words change their meaning to suit new realities.

Louise: Maybe some do, but you can't invent new meanings just because it suits your purpose. For most people, *wedding* still means a marriage ceremony between a man and a woman. That's just what it means.

Thelma and Louise risk endlessly debating the meaning of *wedding* and *marriage* until they agree on what they want their definitions to *do,* what kind of problem they want it to solve. They could conceivably be debating a conceptual problem of linguistic change: *Can we change the meaning of terms when it suits our purposes?* But more likely they are really concerned about different practical problems that can be solved only if society *does* something:

• Thelma may think that same-sex couples like her aunt's friends are often deprived of the social, personal, and economic benefits of traditional marriage. It is for her a problem of social injustice. To solve it, she wants to put same-sex couples in the same category as different-sex couples, an aim she could further by getting Louise to call their ceremony a *wedding* and their relationship a *marriage*.

- Louise may think that if society condones same-sex relationships by calling them *marriages,* it implicitly condones what she believes is immoral behavior. It is for her a problem of morality. To avoid that moral problem, she wants to keep same-sex couples in a different category from different-sex couples, an aim furthered by not calling their ceremony a *wedding* and their relationship a *marriage*.

If it is those underlying practical problems that really motivate Thelma and Louise to debate the meaning of *wedding* and *marriage,* they are stuck in an unproductive surrogate argument. They are unlikely to agree so long as they debate definitions and meanings while they really care about something else.

Here's what to watch for: If you think you have to make a conceptual argument that turns on the meaning and definition of a key term, ask yourself whether your seemingly conceptual argument might be a surrogate for a practical one. If you find yourself going round and round about the "real" meaning of a term, step back and look for a practical problem that motivated you to define the term in the first place. Ask what *consequences* flow from using one term or another to describe its referents. What *follows* from the choice?

If you decide your argument might be a surrogate for a larger problem, try to define that problem and confront it directly. If the real problem is too big or too sensitive to address directly, try addressing an aspect of the larger problem. Otherwise, you risk trapping yourself and your readers in an aimless debate that misses the point.

IN THE READINGS . . .

Definition or Action?

In "Smoking and the Tyranny of Public Health," (p. 454), Jacob Sullum discusses the dangers of surrogate arguments, using the example of obesity, which public health officials define as a "disease" and an "epidemic": "For the most part, Americans are dying of things you can't catch: cancer, heart disease, trauma. Accordingly, the public health establishment is focusing on those factors and causes underlying them. Having vanquished most true epidemics, it has turned its attention to metaphorical epidemics of unhealthy behavior." By defining unhealthy behavior as a disease, health officials hope the public will allow them to attack the behavior with the same kind of coercive authority that let them quarantine infected persons and force parents to inoculate children.

Don't Confuse Definitions and Values

You can also create a surrogate argument if you fail to recognize that what you really want is for your readers to evaluate something as you do, and thereby to feel about it in the same way. Consider this exchange:

Maude: I think *Titanic* is a masterpiece of film art _{claim} that movingly dramatizes the tragedy of an epic event from an intimately human point of view, celebrating human courage and self-sacrifice for another. _{reasons}

Harold: I think it's commercial exploitation _{claim} that crassly appeals to our emotions by cynically denigrating the rich as selfish and cowardly and shamelessly flattering the lower classes as selfless and brave, thereby pandering to class resentments for a bigger box office. _{reasons}

Maude and Harold seem to be concerned with a problem of categorizing *Titanic* and finding terms to name it: Does *Titanic* fit into the category called *masterpiece of film art* or the one called *commercial exploitation?* They could try to find criteria for each category, match them to the features of the movie, and agree which it is—perhaps that it is a bit of both. But their value-laden language suggests that something is at stake beyond mere naming. They use strong words that invoke strong values and strong feelings: *movingly, tragedy, epic, celebrating* vs. *crassly, cynically, shamelessly, pandering.*

If Harold and Maude are talking about *Titanic* to express their values or vent their feelings (two sides of the same coin), then they are arguing not about what *Titanic* "really" is, but about how they feel about it and how each wants the other to. If so, neither is likely to change how the other feels by arguing over definitions. Suppose Harold carefully matched features of the film to criteria for the category *commercial exploitation,* but Maude still responded, *Of course it's commercial exploitation, but so what? It's still a great movie. I love it.* Harold would have won an empty victory in a debate he was finally bound to lose.

Here's what to watch for: Don't debate definitions when you want others to like or dislike, approve or disapprove of something. You won't persuade them by defining terms that someone is *thrifty* rather than *stingy* or *plain speaking* rather than *opinionated.* When a term implies approval or disapproval, we attach to its meaning evaluations and feelings *we already have.* We use evaluative terms *after* we approve or disapprove.

When you find yourself in an argument that seems to go round and round over definitions, do what good critical thinkers do: Step back and ask whether you are having a surrogate argument that you cannot settle until you settle another one. If so, you have the uphill task of matching features to criteria, hoping to overwhelm the other person with detail. (On a personal note, GGC and JMW can testify that it has never worked with their wives or children, or with each other.)

IN THE READINGS . . .

Naming

In "The Student as Consumer: The Implications and Limitations of a Metaphor" (p. 406) Jill J. McMillan and George Cheney claim that "student as customer" is a metaphor and argue that it is misleading. In "Has Student Consumerism Gone Too Far?" (p. 401) Michael Pernal agrees that we should not think of students as customers, but he claims that "student as customer" is not a metaphor, but just the wrong category for students. What difference does it make whether we treat the "student as customer" as a misleading metaphor or as a mistaken category? Is there one "truth" of the matter? If not, how would we decide which is the better approach? If McMillan, Cheney, and Pernal all agree on the main point that schools should not treat students as customers, then why would they care about choosing between thinking of it as a metaphor or a category mistake?

How to Argue About Meanings

When you make an argument that turns on meaning, you usually have a relatively straightforward aim: You want readers to think of a referent in a certain way, so you give them reasons to call it by a certain term. If they do call it by that term, they put it in the category named by the term, and that leads them to think of the referent as you want them to.

Let's say you want to argue that certain photographs _{referents} are not *pornography* _{term 1} but are instead *erotic art.* _{term 2} You therefore have to build an argument in which you do two things:

- You have to give readers reason to accept certain criteria of meaning for your key terms. So you first have to get them to agree with your definitions of *pornography* and *erotic art.* These are, in effect, warrants: When something has features X, Y, and Z, we call it *pornography.* When something has features A, B, C, we call it *erotic art.*

- You also have to give them reason to see that features of the referents, the photos, don't match the criteria of *pornography* but do match the criteria of *erotic art.*

You may have a hard time doing that, because meanings are not as fixed and certain as many think, or wish. Some philosophers treat a category as a rigid container filled with meaning defined by an "essence" that distinguishes that meaning and that category from all others. They claim we can always know whether a particular referent is in or out of a category, because if we just think hard enough, we can discover the fixed, essential criteria that define the category and decide whether a referent has the essential features that match them.

But as much as philosophers might wish we would use words and meanings in such fixed and predictable ways, that is not how we do it in real life, especially in arguments. Categories are not prefabricated containers, and referents are not predetermined to fit into them, the way a round peg fits a round hole. In real-life arguments, we shave pegs and stretch holes to fit each other.

Do Readers Expect Common or Authorized Meanings?

To determine how much freedom you have to stretch a meaning, you have to decide what kind of meaning readers expect you to rely on, *common* or *authorized*.

- A *common meaning* is our everyday, nontechnical understanding of a term, like our ordinary meaning of *dog*. In casual conversation, most of us think a coyote is a "kind of" dog, and for most of us urban dwellers, so is a wolf. When we see hyenas on TV, a lot of us think of them as really ugly dogs (even though they are more closely related to cats and most closely to the mongoose).

- An *authorized meaning*, on the other hand, is a technical "officially" defined meaning, such as the meaning a biologist would associate with *dog* when writing a scientific article about the evolutionary relationships among dogs, wolves, and coyotes. For a biologist, a hyena is no more a dog than a cat is.

If your readers expect you to use a word according to its common meaning, you are free, within limits, to shape your definition to achieve your aim. If you are offended by some sexually explicit images, you can call them *pornographic* and we will all know what you mean. If, however, readers expect you to use a term with its authorized legal meaning, they will hold you within its four corners.

The Supreme Court, for example, has stipulated that for a referent to be "technically" (that is, legally) pornographic, its features must match three criteria of authorized legal meaning. Their definition is in *Black's Law Dictionary*:

> Material is pornographic or obscene [1] if the average person, applying contemporary community standards, would find that the work taken as a whole appeals to the prurient interest and [2] if it depicts in a patently offensive way sexual conduct and [3] if the work taken as a whole lacks serious literary, artistic, political, or scientific value (*Miller v. California*, 413 U.S. 15, 24-25, 93 S.Ct. 2607, 2615, 37 L. Ed. 2d 419).

In court, critics of the National Endowment for the Arts would have to work inside the boundaries of that authorized definition of *pornography* to argue that objectionable photos are legally pornographic. But in a speech to the PTA back home, they could rely on common meanings to create their own "loose" definition: *These images are pornographic because they degrade human dignity by reducing sex to animal behavior.*

Just a Theory?

No word causes more misunderstanding between science and the public than the word *theory*. Scientists use the word in its well-defined authorized sense to mean a clearly stated, well-supported explanation of a phenomenon. So when a scientist talks about quantum *theory* or the *theory* of relativity, she doesn't mean speculation or unsupported belief about electrons or the speed of light, but an explanation that enjoys wide acceptance in the community of scientists. Among a large part of the general public, however, *theory* has a common meaning that is almost the opposite: mere speculation, a hunch or guess. And so when some attack Darwin's theory of evolution specifically because it is called a *theory*, they give the word its common meaning, which is at odds with the biologist's authorized meaning. There may be reason to argue about evolution, but the fact that it is called a *theory* is not one of them.

Strategies for Using Common Meanings

Even though you have some freedom to stretch a meaning and shape a referent to fit it, you have to stay within common sense limits. The more readers use a term and the more they know about a referent, the more likely they will accept only definitions and descriptions that match their sense of things. You could call the Oklahoma City bomber Timothy McVeigh a true patriot, but most of us have a definition of *patriot* that will not stretch that far. But however fuzzily bounded a meaning is, you have to give readers good reason to apply it to a particular referent. Here are three strategies for doing that.

1. Shape criteria of meaning and features of referents to match each other.

If you are not bound to an authorized meaning but can work with a common one, you can shape a referent to fit the meaning *at the same time* you shape the meaning to fit the referent. It is like shaving a peg to fit a hole at the same time you shave the hole to accept the peg.

For example, imagine someone wants us to reject a Constitutional amendment that criminalizes burning the American flag. To do so, she decides to use the term *patriotic* to describe those who burn the flag to protest immoral actions by our government. She reasons that if she can get people to think of flag-burners as patriots, then they may agree that the Constitution should not ban flag-burning but protect it. Since there are no authorized criteria for *patriotic,* she has room to develop its common meaning in ways that help her achieve her aim:

> Those who support a Constitutional amendment criminalizing flag-burning appeal first to our patriotism. Many of them define *patriotism* as honoring the flag: waving it, saluting it, standing at attention as it passes by. They see the flag as synonymous with our country itself: damage it, and you damage America. _{acknowledgment of alternative definition} But for those who see more deeply, real patriotism is loyalty not to symbols, but to the principles those symbols represent, including the idea that when a government violates them, truly patriotic citizens must

protest. Real patriotism calls attention to such wrongs, even if it takes burning the flag to do it. _{criteria for the meaning of patriot} If such symbolic expression is made a crime, _{destabilizing condition of problem} we will threaten our values more than any flag-burner could. _{cost of problem} Congress should reject such an amendment. _{solution / claim}

This writer picks out features of flag-burners that she thinks make them admirable, but at the same time, she crafts criteria for the meaning of *patriot* to match their features: *A true patriot is someone with the courage to enrage others in order to preserve the highest values of our nation. Flag-burners have that courage.*

She is, of course, constrained by how much our beliefs limit the common-sense criteria we will accept for the meaning of *patriot*. She cannot succeed if we think all civil protest is wrong, even in defense of "the principles this country stands for." So you are free to shape features and criteria only to the degree that you do not violate your readers' strongly held assumptions.

2. Match the referent to a model.

We commonly talk about meaning in terms of discrete criteria, but psychologists have shown that we probably think about most meanings and categories differently: When we apply a term to a referent, we do not test the referent against a checklist of criteria of meaning. We compare it holistically to what we think of as the best or most typical instance of the category (what psychologists call a *prototype* but we call a *model*). It is a bit like showing readers that your peg is so much like a model peg that it will obviously fit the hole.

For example, the following passage describes a familiar instance of a patriot, the Minutemen of 1775. If the reader accepts a Minuteman as typical, the writer can try to show that a civilian militia member of today matches that historical model:

> Critics of citizen militias forget that it was civilians with their own guns who won our freedoms 200 years ago. The Minutemen of 1775 were patriots who defended their homes and families by grabbing their rifles from over their fireplaces and joining others in common defense against a tyrannical government, _{model} just as the freedom lover who joins a militia today leaves his home to prepare to defend our freedoms. _{referent} As we honor those patriots who won our freedom then, so should we respect those who defend it now.

Readers will accept a meaning based on a model only when they accept the model as typical of the category *and* they think a referent closely resembles it.

The more vividly you portray the model and the referent, the more persuasive your argument. Of course, you still have to use terms to describe the model, and they all have criteria of meaning. So in a sense, even when you create a model and match your referent to it, you are still matching features to criteria, but less as a checklist than as a word picture.

3. Combine matching and modeling.

You can always combine feature matching with modeling:

> Those who condemn citizen militias as paranoid gun nuts ignore their deep love for the principles that this country was founded on. _{criterion 1} Civilian militias are ready to join with others to rise up against unjust tyranny, relying on

force, if necessary; _{criterion 2} and they are ready to lay down their lives to preserve their freedom and yours. _{criterion 3} They are the true patriots of our time, no different from the Minutemen of 1775, who defended their homes and families by grabbing their rifles from over their fireplaces and joining others in common defense against a tyrannical government. _{model} In the same way, civilian militia keep their guns ready to resist a tyranny that wants to deprive us of our freedom to use them. _{referent} If we honor the patriots of 1775, so should we respect those of today. _{claim}

Our language imposes limits on meanings that we violate at our peril. But within those limits, we are free to craft descriptions of referents, criteria of meaning, and models in ways that solve our problem.

Strategies for Using Authorized Meanings

When readers expect you to use an authorized meaning, you have less freedom. You usually have to accept the stipulated criteria and describe the features of the referent in a way that matches them. For example, the diagnostic manual of the American Psychiatric Association breaks the common term *alcoholism* into several specific conditions and stipulates criteria for each. The most serious condition is *alcohol dependence*. A person is alcohol dependent if he or she meets at least two of four criteria:

1. *Tolerance:* The body's cells adapt to high levels of alcohol so that it has less effect on them.

2. *Dyscontrol* (psychological dependence): The person drinks to relieve bodily or emotional pain, but does not control when, where, or how he or she drinks.

3. *Medical Complications:* The person suffers physical damage from alcohol.

4. *Withdrawal:* When the person abstains from drinking, he or she suffers convulsions, hallucinations, or delirium.

A clinical psychologist arguing in a professional setting must observe that definition, because it is enforced by canons of professional ethics and peer pressure. So if she makes a case that someone is alcohol dependent, she will describe the features of that person to fit the criteria:

> Mr. Jones shows a high tolerance with no visible effects until his blood alcohol level reaches 0.2, twice what should make a man his size intoxicated. Although he has no medical complications, he does exhibit psychological dependence. He begins drinking every morning, usually alone, and continues even after he knows he should stop. Since Mr. Jones drinks every day, we cannot say whether he suffers withdrawal, but it is likely he would if he stopped drinking.

When an authority and its backing institution set out criteria of meaning, you have to match the features of the referent to them. It's a one-way fit, like fitting a wooden peg into a rigid hole: You can't change the hole, but you can shape the peg to fit it, within limits.

When to Rely on Authorized Definitions

When readers in a field read its professional prose, they expect to see writers use terms in their authorized sense. For example, the terms *tragedy* and *comedy* have common meanings that we use freely in everyday conversation. But literary critics have given them technical definitions. So students in a drama class seem more authoritative when they use those terms in their technical sense. In fact, when aspiring professionals use the common meanings of terms that have technical definitions, they seem ignorant and naive.

On the other hand, if your readers understand only the common meaning of a term but you use an authorized one, you risk confusing them and damaging your ethos. Don't try to override their understanding with an authorized, technical meaning: They will only resist, as we see in the debate over the meaning of "theory."

For example, medical and environmental scientists have long failed to educate the public about the "true" risks of nuclear waste, toxic dumps, or trace metals in drinking water. Only recently have they realized why: We define *risk* differently from the way they do. Experts use an authorized, statistical definition of risk roughly like this:

$$\text{Risk} = \text{Probability of occurrence} \times \text{Cost}$$

Risk is the probability that something will happen (over a certain period of time and level of exposure) multiplied by its cost (death, injury, or illness). So a scientist might say that if you lived for 30 years within two miles of an atomic power plant, your risk of cancer from that plant would be .000001, a risk lower than stepping into your bathtub. But for years, risk communication experts could not understand why ordinary folks would not buy their assurances.

It took a long time for social psychologists to figure it out, but now they understand that most of us do not define risk statistically (even when we understand the math), but psychologically, in terms of our own common definition. We judge risk by summing at least these four factors:

1. *Size of the cost:* If the worst happens, will a lot of people be hurt?
2. *Immediacy of the cost:* If the worst happens, will people be harmed all at once or over a long period of time?
3. *Control over the risk:* Does our risk depend on what we do or on what someone else does?
4. *Choice of the risk:* Is the risk one that we choose to run?

There are a few other criteria we use to define risk, but those are the important ones:

$$\text{Risk} = \text{Magnitude} + \text{Immediacy} + \text{Lack of control} + \text{Lack of choice}$$

So long as risk experts talked to us only in terms of their authorized, statistical definition, they had no chance of persuading the rest of us that trucking atomic waste through town posed an "insignificant" risk. But now that they know how to explain risk using our common definition, they are better able to help us make sound judgments.

Here are two things to watch for when using terms with authorized meanings:

- When you use a term that might have a specialized meaning for your readers, look it up in a specialized reference work. You would seem foolish writing to experts in risk communication if you did not acknowledge their authorized definition.

- When you write for ordinary readers, do not expect to override their common definitions with your authorized ones. You may think that your technical terms carry an authority that *should* persuade readers, but they rarely do. You have to adapt your terms to their understanding.

IN THE READINGS . . .

An Argument of Definitions

The argument in Ed Carson's "Purging Bingeing" (p. 441) turns on definitions in three ways:

- The common ground contrasts college students' common definition of bingeing with the authorized one of the "public health establishment."
- The problem is stated as a problem of what to call things: "But this is not a drinking problem; it is a drinking behavior problem."
- And his solution rests on his definition of a new term, *responsible drinking*.

To top things off, he ends his essay with a coda based on a joke about the definition of moderation.

Why Dictionaries Cannot Settle Arguments Over Meaning

When we said that no authority stipulates the criteria for the meaning of ordinary words like *patriotism* and *athlete,* some of you surely thought of dictionaries. Even the Supreme Court relies on them to settle disputes over the meaning of a term as simple as *carry.* (If you have a gun locked up in the trunk of your car as you commit a crime, are you "carrying" a weapon while committing that crime? Based on a dictionary definition, the court said yes.) But good critical thinkers know that even the most authoritative dictionaries cannot capture the full complexity of any meaning, and few readers let a dictionary definition outweigh their sense of what a term "really" means.

The Role of Criteria in Dictionary Definitions

Consider this conversation between Erin and her friend Ethan:

> Erin: If ice dancing is an Olympic sport, and ice dancers are athletes, why shouldn't competitive ballroom dancing also be a sporting event and competitive dancers be considered athletes?
>
> Ethan: I can't buy that. Dancing is entertainment, like the ballet.
>
> Erin: So what? The Olympics are entertainment, and rhythmic gymnastics is like ballet, and so is synchronized swimming, but both are still considered sports.
>
> Ethan: You just don't get the real meaning of *sport* and *athlete*. Let's look them up in Webster's.

Ethan would find that those dictionary definitions have two parts:

1. A word or phrase that names a general category (some call it the *genus*).
2. More words or phrases that narrow the general category to a specific one (some call them the terms that define the *species*).

   athlete: a person _{general category} who competes in contests requiring strength, stamina, or physical agility. _{specific criteria}

   sport: an athletic activity _{general category} requiring skill or physical prowess. _{specific criteria}

A dictionary definition succeeds if it helps us distinguish the meaning of that word from every other one. Some might think we can then know whether the word correctly names any referent. But if Ethan believes that, he is led to a conclusion as unwelcome as it is logical:

> Ethan: Well, it says here that athletes are "persons," and they "compete in contests requiring strength, stamina, or physical agility," so I guess ballroom dancers fit the criteria for athletes. And then it says that a sport is an "activity" that is "athletic," and "requires skill or physical prowess," and competitive dancing does that. So I guess you're right: The tango should be an Olympic event.

He has come to a logical conclusion, but one few readers would accept.

The Limitations of Dictionary Criteria for Common Meanings

Here are two facts about dictionary definitions:

- Dictionary definitions list just enough criteria to distinguish a word from every other word, *but no more.*

Meanings, however, are infinitely more complex than definitions. A dictionary definition is to meaning as a map of Paris drawn on a napkin is to Paris. A lot gets lost.

- The dictionary definition of a term cannot tell you whether a particular referent does or does not belong in the particular category the term names.

When we decide what to call a referent, we use many features of the referent that do not appear in dictionaries as criteria of meaning.

For example, when we decide whether to call an activity a sport, one relevant feature is its history—something no dictionary definition cites. Ice dancing became an Olympic event in 1976, partly because it was related to figure skating (already an Olympic sport), which was linked to speed skating (a model sport). Speakers widened the category named by *sport* by dropping out particular criteria of meaning: Now, if you do anything on skates that takes skill and strength, it is a sport. Maybe one day you can be in the Olympics if you do something that takes a lot of skill and strength not just on skates, but in special footwear of any kind, like snowshoeing, roller blading, pole-climbing, or even stilt-dancing.

Had Ethan thought critically, he could have seen the limits of dictionaries by testing their sparse criteria for *athlete* and *sport* on borderline referents. If an athlete is *anyone* who competes in a contest requiring strength, stamina, *or* physical agility, then Miss America contestants are athletes, along with violin players, lumberjacks, and even cooks. But that contradicts our common sense *use* of the term *athlete,* which is based more on our mental model of a "real" athlete than on criteria listed in a dictionary.

The Limitations of Dictionary Criteria for Authorized Meanings

You might think that officially sanctioned dictionaries that include only authorized definitions escape the limits of standard dictionaries, but their authorized criteria ultimately suffer from the same problem that common definitions do.

For example, those critics who wanted to shut down the NEA because it supported pornography might have used the authorized criteria for the legal definition of *pornography* as listed in *Black's Law Dictionary:*

- The average person, applying contemporary community standards, would find that the work appeals to the prurient interest.

- It depicts sexual conduct in a patently offensive way.

- It lacks serious literary, artistic, political, or scientific value.

Relying on those criteria, the critics could have made a standard, criteria-matching argument claiming that certain photographs are pornographic.

But that is deceptively simple, because they might have been challenged to define the terms naming the criteria. What criteria define the criterion named *prurient?* We could look in *Black's Dictionary* for its authorized definition:

prurient: A shameful or morbid interest in nudity, sex, or excretion . . . having lustful ideas or desires . . . an obsessive interest in immoral and lascivious matters.

But what criteria define the criteria named *shameful, morbid, immoral,* and *lascivious?* Here's *Black's* authorized definition of *lascivious:*

lascivious: Tending to excite lust; lewd; indecent; obscene; sexual impurity; tending to deprave the morals in respect to sexual relations; licentious. [cites]. . . . See *lewd; obscene*.

But now what does that criterion *lewd* mean? Here's part of its definition:

lewd: Obscene, lustful, indecent, lascivious, lecherous.

We have a problem: The criteria for *lascivious* told us to see *lewd*, but the criteria for *lewd* direct us back to *lascivious*.

That's why, ultimately, good critical thinkers do not mechanically base their arguments on criteria-based definitions of any kind. Legislators and scientists can stipulate criteria for the meaning of *pornography* or *planet*, but that just shifts the question one step down: What terms name the criteria, and what criteria define those terms? And what names for what criteria define *those* terms, and then . . . You get the idea. And at some point, the criteria loop back on themselves: *lascivious* means *lewd*, but *lewd* means *lascivious*. Ultimately, all these criteria depend on our agreeing to some meanings *without* criteria or arguments to support them.

Definitions ultimately rest only on our agreement. But that's not a problem; it's an opportunity. It frees us from the rigidity of *all* dictionary definitions (well, at least it gives us some wiggle-room). By defining criteria, we can, within limits, develop our own meanings. Even the court-authorized legal definition of *pornography* ultimately depends on the criteria for terms like *average person, community,* and *serious artistic value,* all terms that depend on common meanings.

As we learned from that Indian sage who explained about the world resting on the back of an elephant standing on the back of a turtle (p. 172): after that, it's turtles all the way down. We just have to stop asking about meanings or turtles at some point, because the meaning of each turtle depends on the next one down.

The Pluto Problem

Not much seems at stake in whether we call Pluto a planet or a big blob of ice, which it resembles more than it does other planets. Yet after years of debate, the International Astronomical Union decided in 2006 that Pluto could not be a planet because it did not meet the authorized criteria that it "has cleared the neighbourhood around its orbit." So instead, the IAU created a new category of "dwarf planets" for which Pluto is a prototype. These scientists demoted Pluto from a planet to a dwarf planet not just because of what they wanted people to understand about Pluto itself, but because of how they wanted people to understand planets in general. They settled the conceptual problem of what to call Pluto by creating definitions that preserved the greatest degree of intellectual consistency (though see Inquiry 3 on p. 268).

If you are not yet immersed in an advanced field of study, this issue of intellectual consistency may seem remote, even hairsplitting. But once you are in a specialized field, you will find that your conceptual arguments will be tested not just by whether a definition you propose solves your local conceptual problem, but by whether it is consistent with the whole body of knowledge, principles, facts, and beliefs that constitute your field.

◆ EXAMPLE

A Definition that Challenged Beliefs

When we define terms in a conceptual argument, we normally observe the rule of consistency. Some writers, however, offer definitions so new but so compelling that they change widely accepted beliefs. We call them geniuses. Isaac Newton was one: He redefined the term *gravity* in ways that revolutionized not only physics but common sense, until Einstein redefined it again. Another was Charles Darwin, whose term *natural selection* challenged common beliefs about science, history, religion, and society—challenges we still debate today. In the following passage, Darwin reflects on the difficulties his term caused. As revolutionary as that term was, he works hard to make his definition fit rather than contradict the common meaning of *natural* and *selection*. Note how he tries to "naturalize" natural selection by finding familiar analogies that match his criteria. (Note as well his deft use of acknowledgment and response.)

Several writers have misapprehended or objected to the term *Natural Selection.* Some have even imagined that natural selection induces variability, whereas it implies only the preservation of such variations as arise and are beneficial to the being under its conditions of life. No one objects to agriculturists speaking of the potent effects of man's selection; and in this case the individual differences given by nature, which man for some object selects, must of necessity first occur. Others have objected that the term *selection* implies conscious choice in the animals, which become modified; and it had even been urged that, as plants have no volition, natural selection is not applicable to them! In the literal sense of the word, no doubt, *natural selection* is a false term; but who ever objected to chemists speaking of the elective affinities of the various elements?—and yet an acid cannot strictly be said to elect the base with which it in preference combines. It has been said that I speak of natural selection as an active power of Deity, but who objects to an author speaking of the attraction of gravity as ruling the movements of the planets? Everyone knows what is meant and is implied by such metaphorical expressions; and they are almost necessary for brevity. So again it is difficult to avoid personifying the word Nature; but I mean by Nature, only the aggregate action and product of many natural laws, and by laws the sequence of events as ascertained by us. With a little familiarity such superficial objections will be forgotten.

Source: Charles Darwin, *Origin of Species,* ch. 4.

◆◆◆

WRITING PROCESS

Arguments About Meanings

PREPARING AND PLANNING

Anticipate Questions About Meaning

No question about a contestable claim is more common than *But doesn't it depend on what you mean by. . . ?* Anticipate that question by identifying your key terms, then imagine readers asking *But what do you mean by. . . ?* If your argument in fact depends on a meaning that may be in doubt, you have to define and illustrate it. *A patriot is someone who. . . , such as . . .*

Pick a Strategy for Matching Referents and Meanings

When you make an argument about meaning, you can create a model to use as a benchmark for your referent, match features to criteria (and vice versa), or both.

Develop Models

To build a model of a category, close your dictionary and crank up your imagination. Imagine a "real" example of, say, a *patriot,* and then bring that image to life in a way that matches your referent. The problem is that we all have somewhat different images, both of a model instance of the category and of the referent you want to apply it to. So to base an argument on a model, you have to determine how closely you can make your model and your image of the referent resemble those of your readers.

For example, to argue that militia members are (or are not) patriots, you would start by comparing your model of a patriot with that of your readers:

- What image first comes to mind when *you* think of an example of *patriotic?* Is it an action, like waving the flag and singing the national anthem, or sacrifice, or protesting laws? Or is it an attitude, a feeling?

- What image do you think first comes to your readers' minds when they think of a prototypical example of patriotism? If you don't know, find out.

If you are a good critical thinker, you will also compare your image of your referent with that of your readers:

- What is your image of a militia member? Is it a potbellied middle-aged gun nut in a camouflage costume running around playing soldier? Or is it a survivalist able to live in the wild while resisting unjust government?

- What do your *readers* think of as a prototypical militia member? If you don't know, find out.

If your images of a patriot and a militia member match theirs, good; if not, you've got a problem. Acknowledge the difference, and try to bring your models in line with those of your readers. If that won't work, find a way to make your argument without relying on models.

Find Analogies

Analogies give you more leeway than models, because you don't need a proto-typical instance of the category, just an unambiguous one.

Analogies appeal to intellectual consistency:

1. Referent$_1$ is like referent$_2$.
2. We say referent$_2$ belongs in category C, so we call it by term T.
3. Therefore, logical consistency allows us to call referent$_1$ by term T as well.

For example, those debating whether alcoholism is a disabling illness or a character flaw analogize it to other mental illnesses or to other character flaws:

> Alcoholism $_{referent\ 1}$ is a *weakness of character,* $_{term\ T}$ like sloth or self-indulgence, $_{referent\ 2}$ because if alcoholics wanted to recover, they could, just as lazy people can get up and go to work if they want to. $_{distinctive\ feature}$ Do we start supporting lazy people? $_{appeal\ to\ intellectual\ consistency}$

> Alcoholism $_{referent\ 1}$ is an *illness* $_{term\ T}$ like depression, $_{referent\ 2}$ because it is as difficult to overcome as depression and just as debilitating. $_{distinctive\ feature}$ If we do not help alcoholics overcome their condition, then do we stop supporting all mental illnesses such as schizophrenia and depression? $_{appeal\ to\ intellectual\ consistency}$

For an analogy to work, you have to persuade readers to accept two claims:

- The referents are alike in relevant ways.
- They should apply the principle of logical consistency.

The problem is, as these examples show, we can find analogies on both sides of most questions.

Appeal to History

You can also appeal to intellectual consistency by arguing that readers should use a term as others have in the past, the argument Thelma made about *wedding.* There is, for example, a debate about the term *holocaust.* Some Jewish historians want to restrict it to what Nazis did to Jews. But some African Americans want to use it to refer to the forced ocean trip from Africa to the Americas that killed countless slaves; and some Cambodians want to use it to refer to the killing by the Khmer Rouge of millions of their own people. To argue their cases, African Americans and Cambodians can point out that *holocaust* was used as early as 1671 to refer to an immense loss of life from fire, and thereafter to any immense loss of life. But that wouldn't settle the issue, because a debate about the use of the term *holocaust* is almost certainly a surro-gate argument.

Duck the Definition Entirely

Do this when you think that readers may never accept your definition, model, analogy, or historical appeal. Focus instead on what is at stake in the problem and what will solve it. For example, a conceptual argument about what alcoholism *is* may be a surrogate for the larger pragmatic problem of what we should *do* about it:

- Many see alcoholism as a character flaw because they believe that if we call it an illness, we undermine personal responsibility and encourage alcoholics to see themselves as helpless victims.

- Many see alcoholism as an illness because they believe that if we call it a character flaw, we encourage people to ignore their human duty to care for those unable to overcome disabling afflictions.

Those on either side of the issue can endlessly debate criteria for *character flaw* and *illness,* but the more productive strategy might be to ignore definitions and focus instead on what good and bad will actually happen, what costs and benefits will actually follow, depending on what we *do* about alcoholics.

DRAFTING

Creating Room to Redefine Terms

There are words and phrases that give you room to define terms and build models to suit your purpose. For example, the writer who wanted to call flagburners *patriots* gave herself some leeway by starting with a standard definition of *patriotism,* waving the flag and so on; she then contrasted it with what she called *real* patriotism. When you need to argue against a standard definition, characterize your definition of a word as defining the *real, true,* or *genuine* thing. When you want to reject someone else's definition, describe theirs with terms like *broadly, loosely, technically,* or *strictly speaking; narrowly* or *broadly defined.*

> *Broadly speaking,* anyone devoted to his country is a patriot, but a true patriot is . . .

> *Technically,* risk is a mathematical probability, but it is *actually* a feeling that . . .

Introducing Dictionary Definitions

Since dictionary definitions settle few issues, you should generally avoid using them. Any term whose common meaning is important enough to define is too complex for a dictionary definition. But if you feel you need help from a dictionary, don't simply quote it:

> According to *Webster,* a *patriot* is "a person who loves his country, zealously supporting it and its interests."

That is amateurish at best. Instead, paraphrase the definition and introduce it as a common meaning:

Most of us think of a patriot as someone who loves his country and zealously acts to support and defend it.

If you want to invoke the authority of a dictionary, cite it in a footnote.

When you need to introduce an authorized meaning in a formal way, paraphrase; don't quote the definition or mention a dictionary in your main text. Mention instead the authority that stands behind it:

> Most experts in risk communication define *risk* as . . .
>
> The legal meaning of *pornography* depends on three features that the Supreme Court stipulated . . .
>
> According to the APA, alcoholism is . . .

Document the definition in a citation.

 INQUIRIES

REFLECTIONS

1. If all art that arouses sexual urges is pornographic, does that mean *erotica* and *pornography* are the same thing? Does it matter? Think in terms of what problem one or the other word might help you solve.

2. Are there meanings for which there are no words? Why? Are there words for which there are no meanings? If not why not?

3. When the International Astronomical Union announced that Pluto would no longer be a planet, many people hated the idea. Do an Internet search to find ten negative responses to the IAU announcement. How many of them raised conceptual problems? How many were practical? How did the conceptual and practical complaints differ?

4. For a long time, the diagnostic manual of the American Psychiatric Association categorized homosexuality as a mental illness. Then in 1980, psychiatrists voted to remove it from the list. Were they mistaken before about homosexuality being an illness? Lay out the considerations that a search for an answer would involve. Start, as always, by thinking about the problem. Is the debate really about whether homosexuality is an illness, a choice, or an inherited disposition, or is that just a surrogate argument?

5. Here is another contemporary example of competing definitions: Is nicotine an addictive drug? What are the competing definitions? Is this argument "really" about the definitions? What is actually at stake here? Is this another surrogate argument?

6. Typically we think of truth and lying as opposed. But is that a genuine opposition? Can you not tell the truth but not lie? Can you tell the truth and still lie? Does it matter how you answer these questions?

7. What might be at stake in deciding whether something should be called by the following:

art vs. craft   pet vs. livestock   athlete vs. competitor
sport vs. game   addiction vs. habit   housewife vs. homemaker
eccentric vs. mentally ill   hate speech vs. free speech
economic stagnation vs. slump vs. recession vs. depression

8. Read or do Task 9 and Project 13; if you only read them, spend a moment imagining how you would perform them. Did they elicit stronger feelings than other tasks or projects you have tried? If not, do you know people for whom they would? What does that say about the nature of the task? What does it say about what is at stake in the legal names of things?

TASKS

9. In recent years, our society has renamed many things. When the two of us were young, someone in a wheelchair would be called a cripple; later, *cripple* was replaced by *handicapped,* which has been replaced by *disabled, differently abled,* or *physically challenged.* Although some people complain that we have gone too far and bristle at terms ending in *-challenged* (one of your authors is vertically challenged, the other horizontally), there are often good reasons for proposing such changes. Think of a pair of terms, one that was once common but would now be judged offensive and one that is a politically correct alternative: *crippled–disabled, drunk–alcoholic, retarded–mentally challenged, old–elderly,* etc. For each term (1) list your criteria of meaning and (2) sketch a verbal portrait of a model instance of each category. Do your criteria change when the word changes? Does your model? What does this say about the value of changing terms for sensitive categories?

10. The word *marriage* has so many social, religious, and moral connotations that its use in a phrase like *legalizing homosexual marriage* raises endless problems. Is there any difference between calling the event a *wedding* and calling it by some combination of these words?

celebration   ritual   ceremony   union   covenant
bonding   contract   pledge   fidelity   commitment

That is, how does "a celebration of our covenant of bonding" differ from "wedding," and how does the result of that celebration of a covenant of bonding differ from what we call *marriage?* Create three or four combinations that could serve as a term for the event in which same-sex partners agree to live together in what others call "marriage." The terms should be ones that you think would satisfy those who want to use the term *marriage* but who might be willing to compromise on another, less contentious term. Then imagine the objections of those who would reject your argument.

11. Search the Internet to find Web sites that concern addiction. How many different conditions do people include in the category *addiction?* List five that seem to you either not "real" addictions or borderline cases. What disqualifies or makes them borderline? What does that tell you about how you understand the term? Why do the writers of the sites want to call them addictions?

12. The meanings of some words seem relatively distinct from other words: *triangle* vs. *circle, odd number* vs. *even number,* and so on. The meanings of other words, however, are more relativistic. What is the difference between a very high hill and a very low mountain? Between a very narrow road and a very wide path? We sometimes can't sharply distinguish such oppositions out there in the world, but that does not mean there are no such things as hills and mountains, roads and paths. Imagine an occasion where you have to decide between calling something an unusually high hill or an unusually small mountain. What is the *first* question you would ask?

PROJECTS

13. This project picks up on Task 9. Pick the term that you think most likely to be accepted by those who want same-sex unions to be legally recognized. Suppose that term has been proposed as the one your state will use for legal purposes, such as qualifying for health benefits, state income taxes, and so on. List reasons for or against the use of that term, including issues such as what it says about the state's attitudes toward its referents. Assume this is for a public argument in which you must avoid offending people unnecessarily. (Don't be deflected to the issue of whether it is *right* to legally recognize same-sex unions. Stay with the question of what to call them.)

14. In 1990, a 22-member panel authorized a new definition of *alcoholism* that they hoped would be (1) scientifically valid, (2) clinically useful, and (3) understandable to the public. Their work was sponsored by the National Council on Alcohol and Drug Dependence and the American Society of Addictive Medicine, an organization dedicated to effective medical and social treatment of those suffering from addictions. Their aim was not to change how specialists diagnosed alcoholism but to give the public signs to watch for so that people could intervene sooner. How do the goals of these organizations influence them to define *alcoholism* differently from that of the APA? What parts of the 1990 definition are most related to the larger goal of securing fair treatment for those who suffer from addictions? Do they make it less objective than the APA definition? Less scientific?

Here is the NCADD definition, including definitions for each of the major criteria:

Alcoholism is a primary, chronic disease with genetic, psychosocial, and environmental factors influencing its development and manifestations. The disease is often progressive and fatal. It is characterized by continuous or periodic: impaired control over drinking, preoccupation with the drug alcohol, use of alcohol despite adverse consequences, and distortions in thinking, most notably denial.

Primary . . . suggests that alcoholism, as an addiction, is not a symptom of an underlying disease state. **Disease** means an involuntary disability. It represents the sum of the abnormal phenomena displayed by a group of individuals. These phenomena are associated with a specified common set of characteristics . . . which place them at a disadvantage. **Often progressive and fatal** means that the disease persists over time and that physical, emotional, and social changes are often cumulative. . . . **Impaired control** means the inability to limit alcohol use or to consistently limit . . . the duration of the episode, the quantity consumed, and/or the behavioral consequences of drinking. **Preoccupation** . . . indicates excessive, focused attention given to the drug alcohol, its effects, and/or its use. The relative value thus assigned to alcohol by the individual often leads to a diversion of energies away from important life concerns. **Adverse consequences** are alcohol-related problems or impairments in such areas as: physical health . . . psychological functioning . . . interpersonal functioning . . . occupational functioning . . . and legal, financial, or spiritual problems. **Denial** is used here . . . broadly to include a range of psychological maneuvers designed to reduce awareness of the fact that alcohol use is the cause of an individual's problems rather than a solution to those problems. Denial becomes an integral part of the disease and a major obstacle to recovery.

IN A NUTSHELL

About Your Argument . . .

We typically make arguments about meaning when we want readers to understand what something *is*—in practical arguments, because we believe that what it *is* justifies *doing* something about it; in conceptual ones, because we believe that understanding what it *is* helps us understand a larger issue.

An argument about meaning almost always addresses two issues:

• What criteria of meaning define the term in question?
• What features of the referent qualify it to be named by that term?

Your problem is to match the features to the criteria, in one of three ways:

• When you work with an *authorized meaning* whose criteria are stipulated by some authority, you have to accept those criteria and describe the referent so that its features match them. For example, the criteria for *U.S. citizen* are relatively fixed; so you have little latitude to modify them and can only adapt the features of a referent to match them.

- When you work with a *common meaning,* you can shape both its criteria and the features of the referent, so long as you remain within your readers' common sense understanding of the term and referent. The common meaning of *good American* is flexible enough to let you shape it to fit very different referents.

- When you work with a *model of a common meaning,* you are free to portray any model that your readers will accept as within the common sense meaning of the term and to describe your referent to fit the model. Readers know many model Americans, and you can choose whichever ones suit your referent and your purposes.

In a practical argument, readers focus on the pragmatic consequences of using one term or another to refer to a referent. The Branch Davidians who died at Waco were called either a *religious sect* or *cult,* depending on how people thought the government should deal with them. In a conceptual argument, readers expect definitions to be consistent with everything else they know. Whether Pluto is a planet or an especially large chunk of space rubble depends less on Pluto than on our whole system of understanding and belief about planets and space rubble.

You can go astray in arguments based on meaning in two ways:

- You unknowingly use an argument about meaning as a surrogate for other issues, either a practical problem or a question of feelings and values.

You are most likely to fall into a surrogate argument when the larger problem behind the question of meaning involves values and has consequences that you would rather not deal with directly.

- You use dictionary definitions as though they carried more authority than they do. A dictionary alone will never settle a question of meaning.

Anticipate the kind of definition your readers expect you to use. If they are experts, use their terms according to the criteria authorized by their field. If, however, you are the expert and writing to those who are not, you cannot assume that your readers will accept your authorized definition, no matter how much academic or technical weight it carries.

. . . and About Writing It

As you plan your argument, list every key word that you think you will use. If you are confident that your readers understand those words as you do, don't define them, especially not from a standard desk dictionary: You'll make yourself seem uncertain. If your readers might not understand those words as you do but won't question your meaning, define them in passing, as in this definition of *themes:*

No question about an argument is more common than *But what do you mean by* _____*?*, especially about your key themes, those terms that you will mention in your main claim and repeat often in the body. If you expect readers to disagree about their meaning, define them explicitly.

When you make an argument about meaning, state the meaning, describe the referent, and show how they match so that readers accept all three.

• When you argue about an authorized meaning, do this:

- State your criteria so readers recognize them as authoritative, stipulated ones. Cite a technical reference work if you want to be sure that they do.

- Describe your referent one feature at a time, so that readers see how each feature fits the stipulated criteria.

If the fit is not obvious, make a small argument to support it—thus thickening your larger argument.

• When you argue about common meaning using criteria, do this:

- State your criteria to match features of the referent, but remain within the bounds of readers' common sense understanding.

- Describe your referent one feature at a time, so that readers see how each feature fits your criteria.

If readers might question your criteria or the fit, you can make a small argument to support them.

• When you argue about common meaning using a model, do this:

- Describe the model so that readers recognize it as typical of their common sense understanding of the term.

- Describe your referent so that it is as close to the model as is consistent with your readers' common sense understanding of it.

If readers might question the match, make an argument supporting it; but if your readers reject your model, do not try to make an argument that they should accept it: that is not how models work. Models are so deeply entrenched in our social and cultural understanding that they are the equivalent of visual warrants.

CHAPTER 11

Arguments About Causes

In this chapter, we discuss arguments claiming that one event or condition causes or will cause another. We discuss the nature of causation, how good critical thinkers decide what causes to focus on, and why we so often think about causation less carefully than we should. Then we show you how to design arguments about causation.

We spend a good part of our lives figuring out why things happen as they do or how to make them happen as we want. We tackle problems ranging from the trivial—why the car won't start—to ones that require complex written arguments: Why do young people engage in destructive binge drinking and how do we keep them from doing it? To understand an issue that complex, good critical thinkers expect more than a narrative of one event after another; they want reasons to believe that one event in fact causes the next. Then if we're addressing a practical problem, they also want reason to believe that our solution will change things as we say it will. Our desire to understand and control causes is a uniquely human trait.

The Impossible Vastness of Causes

Causation itself seems simple enough. The classic example is a cue stick hitting a billiard ball, causing it to move and hit another. To explain the causes of a more complex event like binge drinking, it might seem that we just have to track more balls on a bigger table. But philosophers have shown how little we actually understand causation and how often we explain it badly.

First, causation is not something we see. We say that the cue hitting a ball "causes" it to move, but that is only shorthand for saying that when we see the stick touch the ball, we see the ball move, as we expect it to. What we call *causation* is only a predictable relationship between two or more events or conditions.

274

Moreover, we cannot, even in principle, account for more than a fraction of all the events and conditions that cause the ball to move when the cue strikes it:

- *Every cause is part of an endless chain.* The immediate cause of the ball's moving is the cue's hitting it, but the cue is caused to move by an arm, which is caused to move by muscles, which are caused to contract by a thought, which . . . How far back must we trace the chain of causes? To an earlier thought? To the beginning of time? We cannot describe them all, so how do we decide where to begin?

- *Every "link" in a chain of causes consists of countless smaller ones.* A contracting muscle moves the arm, but that contraction involves events in countless muscle cells, each one of which involves countless electro-chemical events, each of which. . . . You get the idea. We cannot describe them all, so how do we decide how finely to describe the links in the chain?

- *A cause has an effect only when enabled by countless contextual conditions.* The arm has to be strong enough to move the cue, the cue straight enough to hit the ball, the ball light enough to roll. We cannot describe every condition, so how do we decide which ones to ignore?

- *Every cause depends on the absence of disabling conditions.* The arm can move only because it was *not* paralyzed by a stroke a moment before. And what about a plane that did *not* crash into the building, because a part did *not* fail, because. . . ? The events and conditions that did *not* happen are effectively infinite, so how do we decide which ones to select as relevant?

Finding Relevant Causes

The causes and conditions that contribute to any effect are so vast that we can never name them all. So when we argue about causes, we must select only relevant ones. We do that in two ways. The first is our unreflective, everyday way of thinking about causes; it is easy, and as a consequence, typically superficial and simplistic, often misleading. If, however, we are good critical thinkers, we choose another way, one that forces us to be more focused, more self-conscious, and in the long run, is more reliable and productive. But since the first kind of thinking is so pervasive, it is useful to understand why we cannot rely on it.

Everyday Thinking About Causation

When we think about causes, we tend to mislead ourselves systematically, because, as hundreds of studies show, our minds are tuned to focus on certain causes and to ignore others. For example, binge drinking has become more common among college students, causing increasing numbers of injuries and even deaths. To solve that problem, we have to change something, but before we can know what, we first have to understand why some students binge and others do not. Two possibilities leap to mind, usually in this order:

- Bingeing is caused by something in a binger's personality: immaturity, insecurity, recklessness.
- It is caused by something in a binger's circumstances: bad friends, peer pressure, easy availability of alcohol.

If we knew which was the "real" cause (maybe both are), we could do something about it. But there are many other possible causes that don't occur to most of us, at least not at first. Here are two:

- Occasional drinkers underestimate the risks of drinking lots of alcohol in a short time.
- Schools fail to educate first-year students about those risks.

Most of us overlook those causes, because we tend to focus on causes that are present and immediate, not on ones that are absent and remote. It's not that we're stupid or careless; it's just how we humans tend to think.

So before you plan an argument about causes, do what good critical thinkers do: Be aware of the tendencies that predictably undermine sound thinking about them, tendencies called *cognitive biases*. There are five common ones, and they all lead to the same problem: a causal explanation that is too simple to explain a complex effect convincingly.

1. We tend to assign causality to an event that occurs immediately before an effect.

We call such causes "proximate" or "immediate." For example, when someone sinks a two-point basket at the buzzer, winning the game by one point, we are more likely to think that shot won the game than a three-pointer a minute earlier, even though the shot at the buzzer would have made no difference without the earlier three-pointer—*and every other made shot*. In the same way, when we think about binge drinking, we think first of its immediate causes: *It's Friday night, finals just ended, there's a party, . . .* We are less inclined to think of a remote cause, such as the person was *not* told a year *earlier* about the risks of bingeing. So when you think about causes, consider immediate ones, but systematically look for more remote ones as well, especially if you think your readers are likely to leap to the seemingly obvious conclusion.

2. We tend to assign causality to events that occur rather than events that do not.

Imagine you are driving along and your passenger asks you to slow down, causing you to catch a red light. You stop, and get rear-ended. You might think, *If he hadn't asked me to slow down, I wouldn't have stopped at that moment.* You are less likely to think, *I stopped at that light at that moment because my friend did* not *ask me to slow down five minutes ago.* We are more likely to see what did happen as a relevant cause than what did not, even though both contributed to an outcome. As for why a student binges dangerously, we are not inclined to think about what does not happen, like a friend *not* intervening, much less that remote negative cause—the lack of education a year earlier. When you think about causes, consider what did happen before an effect, but think as well about what did not and thereby contributed to that effect by its absence.

3. We tend to assign causality to surprising events, not routine ones.

Imagine your teacher always announces a test before he gives it. Then he pops a quiz and you get a zero. You are more likely to think that you got the zero because your teacher *unpredictably* did not announce the quiz than because you *routinely* did not prepare until warned. Similarly, bartenders predictably serve drinks, so we do not identify that ordinary action as a cause of someone's dying from bingeing. But imagine that the bartender offers a "lucky fan" all the free drinks she can down in five minutes, someone takes the offer, and she dies. That offer is unusual, so we'd focus on it as a relevant cause, not on the fact that bartenders routinely serve drinks. When you think about causes, note unpredictable, unexpected ones, but think as well about those that are so routine that they escape notice.

4. We tend to find causes that confirm our assumptions.

Some claim that childhood violence results from the erosion of family values, a cause that they think explains most ills of American life—crime, divorce, drugs, and so on. So when a child shoots a classmate, they offer their standard explanation: *No family values.* We all tend to fit facts to our beliefs rather than change our beliefs to fit the facts. In regard to bingeing, many of us hold assumptions that we can state as one of these two common warrants:

> Those who behave self-destructively have a weak character.

> Those who behave self-destructively are victims of bad influences.

When you think about causes, don't jump to a favorite account. Explore other possibilities, such as that self-destructive behavior is caused by complex, unpredictable interactions of many factors, including chance. And then think hard about what kind of explanation your readers are likely to lean toward.

5. We look for causes whose magnitude is proportional to their effect.

When several years ago TWA flight 800 exploded over Long Island, many looked for a cause that would morally and emotionally balance the enormity of the disaster. They rejected what proved to be the most likely cause, static electricity in a fuel tank, because a random spark seemed too trivial to cause such an awful effect. So they blamed terrorists or the U.S. military, because only a massively evil cause could balance so large a tragedy. When you explore an effect as emotionally "big" as a student drinking herself to death, look for causes large enough to bear the blame, like recklessness or the irresponsible encouragement of friends, but think as well about the little causes that otherwise escape not just your attention, but your readers', as well.

The Aesthetics of Causation

The historian William Manchester explains why people still can't accept that Lee Harvey Oswald acted alone when he shot President John F. Kennedy:

> In the wake of that dreadful Oliver Stone movie [about the assassination], I read that some 70 percent of the American people believed that Kennedy was the victim of a conspiracy. I think I understand why they feel that way. And I think, in a curious way, there is an aesthetic principle involved. If you take the murder of six million Jews in Europe and you put that at one end of a scale, at the other end you can put the Nazis, the greatest gang of criminals ever to seize control of a modern government. So there is a rough balance. Greatest crime, greatest criminals.
>
> But if you put the murder of the President of the United States at one end of the scale, and you put Oswald on the other end, it just doesn't balance. And you want to put something on Oswald's side to make it balance. A conspiracy would do that beautifully.

Source: Bob Herbert, "In America: A Historian's View," *New York Times,* June 4, 1997.

The sum of these biases is typically the One True Cause story and the Silver Bullet Solution: *If we could just get parents to spend more time with their children, . . .* As you develop your argument, consciously monitor your own thinking. Remind yourself that no one cause is responsible for any complex problem and no one action is likely to solve it. But as you draft, keep in mind that your readers will be just as attracted as you to their own One True Cause and Silver Bullet Solution. You may have to acknowledge what seems to them to be the most obvious cause and then show what led you to move beyond it.

Thoughtful Thinking About Specific Causation

Other ways of finding relevant causes are harder but more reliable. The first step is to decide which *specific* causes might be relevant to solving your *particular* problem. For example, how would we choose just the most relevant one from among the infinity of causes that contribute to the cue stick's moving the billiard ball? We would first have to know why we want to talk about the movement of the cue ball at all: What problem does explaining its movement solve? If we want to improve someone's game, we'll look at certain causes having to do with muscles, eyesight, and so on; if we want to explain the ballistics of round objects, we'll look at others such as the surface of the ball, its weight, the momentum of the cue stick; and if we want to explain free will, we'll look at others yet, such as our thoughts and desires. In other words, the nature of the problem limits and defines the kinds of causes we consider.

Of course, we define relevance differently for practical and conceptual problems. If we propose a solution that calls on someone to act, we will focus on some causes; if we propose a solution that calls on someone only to *understand*, we almost certainly would focus on others.

Causation in Practical Problems

In solving a practical problem, we look for causes that we can change or remove to eliminate the costs that make it a problem. We'll call such causes *practically relevant*. For example, when your car won't start, you might hypothesize that the practically relevant cause is a dead battery, because that's a cause you can do something about. You might suspect it's dead because someone left the lights on all night, but while that remote cause might be *conceptually* relevant in helping you *understand* why the battery is dead right now, it is not *practically* relevant to solving the immediate problem of starting the car (though it might be relevant to making sure it doesn't happen again). Use your problem to focus your thinking on the point in the chain of causes and effects where you—or someone—can intervene to eliminate its costs and thereby solve the problem.

Causation in Conceptual Problems

It is harder to define relevant causes in conceptual problems, because every cause of an event, no matter how small, is potentially relevant to understanding it. For example, those trying to end the strife in the Middle East have a practical problem: Where do they intervene in the chain of causes and effects that lead those of different religions, sects, and ethnic groups to attack each other? But a historian trying to solve the conceptual problem of explaining those causes would in theory have to consider every cause that has ever contributed to the current troubles, including centuries of conflict over religion, politics, economics, ethnicity, and social class. And there is no limit to how finely he could decompose those causes into constituent ones. Even a fleeting thought a century ago could be relevant to explaining an event today. When understanding is at stake, everything is potentially relevant.

So where do we start? That decision is usually made for us by our personal background, academic training, and other interests that point us toward some issues and away from others. A historian trained as an economist, for example, is more likely to study how religion affects income than how it affects attitudes toward violence, because she is trained to look at economic causes.

That explains why those new to an academic field often struggle to find conceptual problems to write about. They typically do not yet have special academic interests that focus their attention on specific issues, and so they feel overwhelmed by the possibilities. It is a problem only experience can solve.

Analyzing Causation Systematically

Once you identify causes that might be relevant to your problem, you must then evaluate them to be sure they are in fact causes. When you do advanced work, you will learn how to analyze causes in the specific ways appropriate to your field. In basic classes, you evaluate causes more informally, but that doesn't mean superficially. To be sure you have analyzed causation thoughtfully, you can use two principles formulated by a nineteenth-century philosopher, John Stuart Mill: the principle of similarity and difference and the principle of covariation. These principles will not help you discover causes to test, but they will help you demonstrate that those you propose are worth your readers' consideration.

The Principle of Similarity and Difference

When researchers try to decide whether something is a plausible candidate for a cause, they try to determine how regularly it "correlates" with its alleged effect: Does the effect occur more often when the proposed cause is present than when it is absent?

For example, when researchers study why some first-year students get better grades than others in writing classes, they try to discover factors shared by students who do well (their similarity) that are not shared by students who do worse (their difference). Researchers might argue that those who get better grades compose on laptops (the similarity). But they would also have to show that those who do less well do *not* compose on laptops (the difference).

To use this principle of similarity and difference systematically, some researchers use a 2 × 2 grid that forces them to consider all combinations of cause and effect, both present and absent. It looks like this:

TABLE 11.1   SAMPLE ANALYSIS OF VARIANCE

	Effect occurs	Effect does not occur
Cause present	_____%	_____%
Cause absent	_____%	_____%

Down the left, list a proposed cause as present and absent; across the top, list whether a proposed effect does or does not occur. In the boxes, put the *percentages* (not raw numbers) of the correlations between the presence or absence of a cause and the presence or absence of an effect. (The percentages in the horizontal rows must add up to 100.) Social scientists call this an *analysis of variance,* or *ANOVA,* for short.

Here's a simple case: An astronomer wants to prove that massive objects bend light. He assembles his data and finds this:

TABLE 11.2   BENDING OF LIGHT NEAR MASSIVE OBJECTS

	Light bends	Light does not bend
Massive object	100%	0%
No massive object	0%	100%

According to these data, light bends always when an object is present, never when an object is absent. The researcher can therefore tentatively argue that massive objects cause light to bend (unless bent light causes the presence of an object or a third cause both bends light and causes the object's presence, both unlikely but conceivable).

Natural scientists hope for such unambiguous all-or-nothing results, but social scientists cannot. They have to settle for "more or less." For example, those looking at writing by first-year students might find these numbers:

TABLE 11.3   LAPTOP USE AND GRADES IN PROFESSOR STEIN'S CLASS

	Upper half	Lower half
Always use laptops	72.1%	27.9%
Never use laptops	34.5%	65.5%

The correlation is not perfect, but on the basis of the numbers, we can tentatively infer that students who always compose on laptops are more likely to be in the upper half of their group than those who never do.

The more the numbers differ vertically, the more likely you can convince readers that you have found a possible causal relationship. But if the numbers are close vertically, as in the next table, you can claim a causal relationship (and only a slight one, at that) only if you have counted very large numbers of students.

TABLE 11.4   LAPTOP USE AND GRADES IN PROFESSOR CHEN'S CLASS

	Upper half	Lower half
Always use laptops	72.1%	27.9%
Never use laptops	65.5%	34.5%

To know how large the difference must be for you to claim that it is significant, you have to use complex statistical computations that everyone who expects to make a living in the twenty-first century ought to learn. Good critical thinking depends on knowledge as well as training and practice.

Be aware that, if the percentages are less than 100 percent, as they almost always are outside the physical sciences, you can support a claim of only partial, *contributory* causation. In Table 11.3, for example, some students who *do* use laptops are in the *lower* half of their class and some who do *not* use laptops are in the *upper* half. We must therefore assume that other causes also contribute to students' grades. We *can* claim that the cause we have tested is a *relevant* one, perhaps even the one that points to the best solution to the problem of improving student writing. But we *cannot* claim that it is a *sufficient* cause, able to bring about the effect in question by itself. As we said before, good critical thinkers know that complex events never have a single cause. (You also have to check whether your analysis has reversed cause and effect: Maybe students who write better choose to write on laptops.)

The Principle of Covariation

Researchers are most confident about causes when the magnitude of a possible cause varies with the magnitude of a proposed effect. For example, *Do students who have composed on laptops for many years write better than those who have written on laptops for fewer years?* If so, then the use of laptops is a highly plausible cause of better writing. To test for covariation, we add additional cells for different magnitudes:

TABLE 11.5   YEARS OF LAPTOP USE AND GRADES

Laptop Use	Upper Third	Middle Third	Bottom Third
6 years	62.2%	21.9%	15.9%
4 years	41.3%	39.0%	19.7%
2 years	32.5%	45.6%	21.9%
0 years	25.3%	32.8%	41.9%

Results are rarely so neat, but it is what researchers hope for.

ANOVA as Exploration

You do not need a lot of data to use an ANOVA table if you are using it simply as a device to force yourself to think more critically than you might have otherwise. For example, some have claimed that students binge because they are attracted to risk. We might imagine this table:

TABLE 11.6   STUDENTS' ATTRACTION TO RISK AND BINGE DRINKING

	+ Binge	– Binge
Attracted to risk	?%	?%
Not attracted to risk	?%	?%

Simply by imagining this table, you force yourself to consider four correlations:

1. How many students attracted to risk *do* binge?
2. How many students attracted to risk *do not* binge?
3. How many students *not* attracted to risk *do* binge?
4. How many students *not* attracted to risk *do not* binge?

If you cannot imagine a 100 percent correlation between bingeing and risk taking, then you know bingeing is too complicated for a One True Cause explanation.

The Dog that Didn't Bark

Of course, sometimes there is one cause. In one case, Sherlock Holmes noticed that a dog did not bark when the person who committed a crime must have walked by it. What Holmes found significant was the *not* barking. In effect, he created a mental ANOVA table like this:

	+ Bark	– Bark
Stranger walks by dog	100%	0%
Master walks by dog	0%	100%

Holmes concluded that since the dog did not bark, his master must have committed the crime.

Four Cautions About Using the Principles

To think critically about causes, do this:

1. Imagine and test as many causes as you can.

These principles help you test causes but do not help you find causes to test. If all your hypotheses are wrong, these tests show you only that—a useful result, though not always one to celebrate. Years ago, for example, malaria was a mystery until someone thought to investigate mosquitoes. Today, researchers face the same problem with Alzheimer's. They have tested every cause they can think of, but all have failed the tests.

2. Create contrasting groups.

Once you hypothesize a cause, you have to create contrasting groups, one exposed to a possible cause, the other not. Some researchers can directly create those groups, as when a biologist plants two fields of corn and treats only one with a new fertilizer. Often, though, researchers have to assemble contrasting groups by retrospective sampling. That's how smoking was discovered as a cause of cancer. The problem is that retrospectively created groups can always differ in some unexpected way that turns out to be crucial. In fact, cigarette manufacturers once argued that the urge to smoke and cancer might both be caused by some third thing.

3. Be wary of oversimplification.

When we find that an effect covaries with a suspected cause, we tend to think *Aha, I've figured it out. We can get students to write better if we make them write on laptops.* But complex effects have complex causes. Maybe students who can afford to buy a laptop come from wealthy neighborhoods with better schools. And be aware that you may be reversing cause and effect. Maybe those who write better choose to write on a laptop.

4. Don't ignore interactions.

Even when you think you have found a cause, consider the complex ways that causes and effects may interact:

- *Shared cause:* Sometimes two *effects* correlate not because one causes the other but because both are caused by a third thing: Chronic unemployment and crime correlate, but both may be effects caused by long-term poverty.

- *Mutual cause:* Some causes and effects influence each other. Poverty correlates with poor education, poor education with crime, and crime with poverty, and they probably all cause one another.

- *Compounded effects:* A recent study reported that the mentally ill are no more likely to commit a crime than well people, while drug addicts are four times as likely. But when the mentally ill are on drugs, they are *seven* times more likely to commit a crime. The effect of combined causes may be more than the sum of their individual effects.

A last caution: we can't easily use this kind of analysis to account for the cause of a unique event, such as the Civil War or the explosion of TWA 800. For singular events, we have to reason by analogy from a set of similar cases or closely trace the specific chain of events that resulted in the event we are explaining (see pp. 293–94).

Causation and Personal Responsibility

Sometimes we face problems that we can solve only by convincing readers to hold a specific person or institution responsible for specific consequences of their actions. These are occasions for praise and blame. In such cases, we have to think about causation differently from the way we do when we conduct scholarly, objective research. In these matters, it is important to evaluate cause and effect as objectively as we can, but even the best critical thinkers cannot avoid some subjectivity when faced with a problem of assigning personal responsibility, especially for purposes of meting out praise or blame.

Who's Responsible?

A few years ago, some preschool children on an outing at a riverfront park let go of a hand line used to keep them together, and they fell in the water. They were saved when a bystander jumped in after them. Everyone agreed on the facts, but made different claims about who was responsible for the accident:

- The media blamed the teachers, because they did not watch the kids as they should have.

- The children's lawyers who wanted to sue someone blamed the teachers, but also the Park Department, because it had not built a protective railing along the river.

They also differed on who was responsible for saving the children:

- The mayor and the media praised the rescuer for his heroism.
- The Red Cross praised its life-saving course, which the rescuer had taken.
- A psychologist said that the rescuer's actions were caused by an instinct to aid the helpless, reinforced by cultural training from TV, movies, and books.

We can explain two of the claims about responsibility easily enough:

- The teachers were a responsible cause of the accident, because they were there and did not do what they were expected to do: They did not watch the children.
- The person who jumped in to save them was a responsible cause of their surviving, because they would have drowned but for his extraordinary action.

Even though the next two explanations seem a bit of a stretch, they solved the problems of those who proposed them, because they had different stakes in whom to praise and blame:

- The Red Cross solved the problem of publicizing its programs and getting more income by saying it, in the form of its lifesaving course, was a responsible cause of the rescue, remote to be sure, yet nevertheless relevant because but for its course, the rescuer might not have jumped in.
- The lawyers for the children had the problem of finding someone to sue who had more money than the teachers. Those missing railings pointed to a solution: The lawyers said the city was a responsible cause because it failed to build railings along the wharf.

But why didn't anyone focus on other obvious causes?

- No one held the children or their parents responsible, even though the children let go of the ropes and their parents sent them to that school.
- Nor did anyone give credit for the rescue to a bystander who threw a rope in the water and pulled the rescuer ashore.
- Nor did anyone blame gravity as a cause, even though but for it, no one falls into anything.
- Nor did anyone blame geography for the presence of the river.

None of these factors met anyone's criteria for naming plausible responsible causes. Except for the psychologist, who had no stake in assigning praise or blame, the parties involved could solve their respective pragmatic problems only by identifying *someone* to hold responsible. You can't praise, blame, or sue gravity.

Five Criteria for Assigning Personal Responsibility

When we can solve a practical problem only by making someone a *responsible* cause, we have to address more questions than we do for a conceptual problem involving "pure" causation. After we determine what events and actions actually caused an outcome, we have to answer two more questions: *What was the state of mind of the persons involved?* and *How did external circumstances affect their actions?*

To infer a person's state of mind, we ask three questions:

1. Did the person *choose* to perform the action that led to the effect in question? Or did someone or something force that person to act?
2. Could the person have *foreseen* the consequences of the action, both its benefits and its risks?
3. Were the person's *motives* appropriate or questionable?

Then we ask two more questions about circumstances:

4. How commonly do similar people in similar circumstances act in that way?
5. Did circumstances create an obstacle to the action or enable it?

Those criteria suggest why people assigned responsibility for the riverfront accident as they did:

- Though the children were the immediate cause of their accident, no one held them responsible because they could not foresee what would happen if they let go of the rope.
- Nor did anyone hold the parents responsible, because parents commonly send children to day care and they could not have foreseen that the teachers would be inattentive.
- Everyone held the teachers responsible because (1) they should have foreseen the consequences of not paying attention to the children, (2) most other teachers do pay attention to children they are responsible for, and (3) nothing kept them from doing so.
- The lawyers held the city responsible because it should have foreseen the risks of not having railings along the river and nothing prevented it from building railings (though many other cities do not build railings along public walkways by rivers).
- The media praised the rescuer because he seemed to perform his action freely, foreseeing the benefit to the children and the risk to himself, and because few people would have done the same.

• The Red Cross made itself a responsible actor, because it did something with foreseeable benefits that few other agencies do—train people in life saving.

But the psychologist did not seem to make the rescuer "responsible" at all. He seemed to say that the rescuer acted impulsively, without conscious choice. And that is why his explanation is so different from the others. Instead of framing the problem as one of assigning responsibility, as others did, he framed it as a problem in the social sciences, as a purely conceptual problem of objective causation: What causes people to act impulsively?

So when you make an argument that someone is responsible for an outcome, be clear why you do so: Do you want only to explain the outcome? Or do you want to convince readers to praise or blame the person who brought it about?

Explain or Judge?

In a 1999 interview, Hillary Clinton suggested that a factor in her husband's infidelity was conflict in his childhood. Critics charged that she was trying to excuse him of responsibility for his actions. One commentator saw in this a lesson about how we tend to think:

> [There is a] tendency of modern Americans to either misunderstand or fail to recognize the distinction between *explaining* a person's or group's actions and *justifying* them. . . . [I]t is the one error committed by both conservatives and liberals, although usually for opposing reasons. Conservative Americans are so committed to the principle of personal responsibility that they either deny or are hostile to any explanation of human action in sociological or psychological terms, fearing—incorrectly—that this implies people are not answerable for their actions. Many liberals fall in the opposite trap: an oversocialized view of people, so sensitive to the social forces conditioning us that they are unable or unwilling to hold those who fail responsible for their actions. What each side misses is that it is possible to both explain a person and hold that person responsible for his or her actions. The failure to make this distinction between explanation and justification bedevils human relationships and public policy.

Source: Orlando Patterson, "The Lost Distinction Between 'Explain' and 'Justify,'" *New York Times*, August 8, 1999.

Attribution Bias

To solve a problem involving personal responsibility, we must infer the thoughts, feelings, and motivations of others. If we apply the five criteria on page 286 thoughtfully, we can limit, though not entirely avoid, the subjective element in making that calculation. But we do not think well about causation when we fall into a common cognitive bias that psychologists call *attribution bias*.

When we decide a question of personal responsibility by explaining why someone has taken an action, we typically do not refer to a complex array of causes. Instead, we tend to oversimplify by attributing the cause of the action either to that person's personal qualities or to the immediate external circumstances, a decision that we seldom make objectively.

For example, why did Barry Bonds, Mark McGuire, and Sammy Sosa hit so many home runs? Is it their personal qualities—talent and hard work—or their circumstances—weaker pitchers, livelier baseballs, and steroids? If we like them and are inclined to give them credit for their achievements, we emphasize the personal causes; if not, we emphasize circumstantial ones. A more objective observer would have to say that all were perhaps relevant causes, and many others as well.

We might think we can find the "right" explanation if we approach the question objectively. But as many studies have shown, we all seem to be biased toward thinking that the right explanation is usually the personal one. When we explain why others act as they do, we systematically overvalue the influence of personal qualities, motives, and psychological dispositions and systematically undervalue the force of external circumstances. But how much we succumb to that tendency depends on our own subjective dispositions and ability to think critically.

So as you develop an argument assigning personal responsibility, be aware of your own disposition to make that assignment subjectively. But even more than that, be aware that *your readers* are subject to the same biases and that *their* biases might or might not be the same as yours. Here are four variables to watch for: (1) knowledge, (2) personal investment, (3) ideology and politics, and (4) culture.

Knowledge

The less we know about a person and the circumstances of her actions, the more likely we are to attribute the cause of her actions to her character and motives. For example, those who know few gays and lesbians are more likely to attribute their orientation to choice; those who know many are more inclined to attribute the cause of their actions to circumstances—genetic predisposition, for example. It is a consistent (but by no means universal) pattern of causal attribution.

If you have to argue why someone behaved as she did and you know relatively little about her or her situation, be aware that you are likely to overvalue her motives and character as causes of her actions. So you should carefully consider her circumstances as well.

But you must also think about your readers. If they know more than you do about the situation, they will be inclined to make the opposite interpretation: They are more likely to assign responsibility to her circumstances than to her personal qualities. (Of course, the situation may be reversed; you may know more than your readers do.)

So assess not only your own bias but whether it matches that of your readers. You do not want to risk unknowingly making an argument that your readers are predisposed to reject. (A harder ethical question is whether you should knowingly appeal to their biases.)

Personal Investment

A second variable concerns how we feel about a person and the results of a particular action. For example, when someone we like does something we admire, like winning an award, we tend to attribute the achievement to her intelligence, hard work, and so on: we say she *earned* her award. But if she loses, we are more likely to say circumstances conspired against her. On the other hand, if someone we dislike wins, we are more likely to attribute her success to luck or other circumstances; if she fails, we tend to attribute it to personal weakness.

It is familiar behavior. To his supporters, the president is responsible for everything good that happens during his administration but is a victim of circumstances in regard to the bad. To his detractors, he is personally responsible for all the bad and not responsible for any of the good. We do not all make decisions along these lines all the time; it's only a tendency. But it is a tendency worth reflecting on when you have to make any argument assigning praise or blame.

When you feel personally invested in someone, either positively or negatively, be aware that your judgment about personal responsibility may be biased. And depending on how your readers relate to that same issue, you may be working with or against the grain of their judgmental tendencies.

Ideology and Politics

A third variable is our politics. Stereotypical liberals argue, *Circumstances deprive those on welfare of opportunities to escape poverty;* stereotypical conservatives argue, *They don't want to work.* Knee-jerk liberals justify gun control by arguing, *Our high murder rate is due to the easy availability of guns;* knee-jerk conservatives respond, *Guns don't kill. People do.* In other words, extreme conservatives *tend* to locate responsibility in individual will; extreme liberals *tend* to emphasize circumstances.

But we cannot apply this distinction too broadly. When there was a controversy in Los Angeles over racial profiling by police, liberals who distrusted police attributed it to their racist disposition; conservatives who trusted police attributed it to the dangerous circumstances of urban life. In this case, personal investment trumped ideology and politics.

Culture

Anthropologists point out that unlike other world cultures, Westerners in general and Americans in particular are inclined to believe that people control their own actions. In contrast, researchers have found that in many other cultures people tend to think personal actions are due more to social context than to individual choice. So when you have to make an argument with someone from a culture different from yours, keep in mind that you may judge personal responsibility much differently from the way the other person does.

Those four factors strongly influence how you will think about explaining causation. But when you construct your argument, you must also consider how *your readers* are likely to think about It. If you argue for a circumstantial explanation of someone's actions, think whether your readers might have a personalistic one (or vice versa). If so, you have a tough job ahead of you, because you will then have to do more than offer lots of reasons and evidence in support of your argument. You will also have to overcome a deeply entrenched *way of thinking* about causation.

Blame in Two Cultures

A study comparing Japanese and American newspaper reports of financial scandals found that American writers tended to focus more than twice as often on personal motives while Japanese newspapers tended to focus on circumstances:

> One [*New York Times*] article described Mozer as "Salomon's [a financial firm] errant cowboy": who "attacked his work as aggressively as he hit tennis balls." Another implied Hamanaka's lack of shrewdness in stating that he "was known more for the volume of his trades than his aptness." Whereas the lack of organizational controls was a minor theme of Americans in the *NYT,* it was a major theme of Japanese reporters . . . [They] commented that "somebody in Sumitomo [a financial firm] should have recognized the fictitious trading since documents are checked every day," and that Daiwa [another firm] "is embarrassed that its internal controls and procedures were not sufficient to prevent the case."

Source: Tanya Morris et al., "Culture and the Construal of Agency: Attribution to Individual Versus Group Dispositions," *Journal of Personality and Social Psychology* (1999).

The Fallacy of One True Cause

Above all, think hard before you attribute the cause of an effect *entirely* to someone's motives or *entirely* to his circumstances. Imagine readers asking either of two questions:

> Are you saying X was *entirely* responsible for his actions, that circumstances played no role at all?

> Are you saying X was *entirely* a victim of circumstances, that he bears no responsibility at all for his actions?

Knowledgeable critical thinkers are suspicious of explanations that are that simplistic, but especially when they exclude circumstances as a relevant cause.

WRITING PROCESS

Arguments About Causes

PREPARING AND PLANNING

Five Narratives Supporting Solutions to a Practical Problem

As you outline a cause-and-effect argument addressing a practical problem, you have to plan not just one narrative about causes and effects, but at least two and maybe up to five. These narratives support the solutions to five conceptual problems that you have to solve before you can solve the practical one. We can express those five problems as questions.

1. What causes this problem?

Readers trust a solution only when they know the story of what causes the problem. (Imagine each step expanded as a claim at the heart of its own argument.)

> Administrators don't know about new research in evaluating teaching, $_{cause\ 1}$ . . . so they use flawed evaluations. $_{effect\ 1\ /\ cause\ 2}$ . . . As a result, they don't know why students don't learn effectively, $_{effect\ 2\ /\ cause\ 3}$ . . . and that deprives students of better opportunities to learn. $_{effect\ 3}$

2. How will the action you propose solve the problem?

When you propose a solution, you must construct a second narrative about the future. It must explain how intervening in the chain of causes and effects will eliminate the cost of the problem. (Each of these steps could also be fleshed out.)

> We can improve teaching through a better evaluation form. $_{cause\ 1}$ . . . to help teachers better understand what confuses their students and how to avoid doing so, $_{effect\ 1\ /\ cause\ 2}$ . . . giving students better opportunities to learn. $_{effect\ 2\ /}$ $_{elimination\ of\ cost}$

Even if readers accept your account of the problem and solution, you may have to construct three more narratives to respond to objections and reservations. These narratives would be about the future.

3. How will your solution be implemented?

If readers might think your solution is not feasible, you have to answer that doubt by explaining how the solution can be implemented:

> To create a new teaching evaluation, the administration can appoint a student committee to develop it, $_{step\ 1}$ . . . and then with the help of consultants $_{step\ 2}$ show faculty how to use and learn from it. $_{step\ 3}$

4. Will your solution cost more than the problem?

If readers might think that your solution could cost more than the problem, you have to tell another story to show them that it will not:

A new evaluation may require resources, ~acknowledgment~ · · · but the benefits will outweigh the costs. ~response~ First, we are likely to attract more students as we become known for good teaching ~reason 1~ · · · Second, · · · ~narrative of costs and benefits~ Some fear that teachers might feel coerced into grading more leniently or giving less work. ~acknowledgment~ But that risk is slight, because . . . ~response~

5. Why is your solution better than alternatives?

Every problem has more than one solution, so you may have to show that yours is best, or at least can work with others:

> Some have suggested that instead of revising evaluations, we should institute seminars for faculty. Such seminars would be a valuable resource, ~acknowledgment~ but if we must choose between them and new evaluations, the evaluations would be a better choice. ~response / claim~ First, the cost of bringing in consultants will exceed the cost of revising the evaluations ~reason 1~ · · · Second, it will be hard to offer seminars to every faculty member. ~reason 2~ · · · third, seminars are a one-time event; better teaching evaluations will occur every semester ~reason 3~ · · ·

When you compare solutions, avoid an *either-or* argument.

> We can improve teaching in lots of ways, including *both* seminars and better evaluations.

Strategic Decisions in Designing Narratives About Causes

Once you have a plan, answer a few more questions:

- How far back on the chain of causes and effects do you start? Do your readers need to know the most remote causes of bingeing?

- How much detail do they need? Must they understand the minute psychological processes that compel people to binge?

- How much must you "thicken" your narrative by arguing that event A really does cause B? How do you know that in fact people attracted to risk are most likely to binge?

Where Do You Start Narrating the Problem?

We cannot give you a rule for where to start in the chain of causes and effects. For practical problems, readers need enough context to understand the causes you finally focus on. Start at least a step or two before the point where you propose intervening with a solution:

> For more than 500 years, college life has been so associated with drinking that getting drunk is now a tradition. ~remote cause~ Of course, many students began drinking in high school, often with their parents' tacit approval. ~middle cause~ But they lose even that loose supervision just when they join a community that seems to encourage them to get drunk. ~near cause~ So when sitting with a case or fifth in a dorm room or frat house, they risk drinking to the point of injury or even death. In those circumstances, the weak constraints colleges put on them are less useful than those they put on themselves. We might avoid the worst

effects of drinking by educating students about its risks from the moment they set foot on campus. _{claim / solution}

With conceptual problems, however, we usually go a bit deeper into history: Someone studying student drinking not to control it but only to understand it might recount its centuries-long European tradition, Prohibition in the 1920s, and so on. Long historical narratives signal scholarly diligence.

How Much Detail Do Readers Need?

Once you decide where to begin the story of your problem, you have to decide how much detail readers need to understand it. We cannot give you a pat answer for this either, because it again depends on the nature of your problem and solution and your readers' knowledge. Readers need enough detail to understand the problem and to be confident that you do too. For example, in addressing the problem of helping students avoid anxieties in their first year of college, a writer might offer this as part of an argument for expanding orientation for first-year students:

> Orientation for first-year students should be expanded from one week to two to help them understand better what lies ahead. Too many first-year students become anxious and frustrated during their first semester because they misunderstand what teachers expect. They think that they can succeed in college if they just do what they did in high school. After all, high school is the only model of education we know, and few of our teachers told us what to expect here.

That account is so general that it is hard to grasp the logic of its implied causes and effects. The writer could craft a more detailed chain:

> Orientation for first-year students should be expanded to two weeks to help them understand better what lies ahead. Many first-year students are anxious and frustrated during their first semester, because they misunderstand what teachers expect. For example, most teachers want us to think and write critically about what we've read, but many first-year students think teachers just want them to report it back accurately. So they summarize their readings and their notes, but get poor grades for doing so. This happens most often with students who succeeded in high school by reporting back what they heard in class. After all, that's what many of our high school teachers told us to do, and no one warned us that our task in college would be different.

If readers needed more help, that chain could be broken into yet finer sequences.

Inexperienced writers tend to be too general rather than too specific, so as a rule of thumb, create a narrative more detailed than you think it has to be.

How Much Explanation Do Readers Need?

If you could offer a narrative that exactly matched your readers' knowledge and needs, they would need nothing more. But more likely, they look for reasons to believe that one event does not just follow another but is in fact caused by it. If so, you have to weave explanations into your narrative that explicitly establish causal relationships. You do that with analogies, warrants, and explicit analysis.

Analogies   Use an analogy when the cause and the effect in question are so much like another case that readers will quickly infer the same cause-effect relationship:

> First-year students should expect to feel anxious at first. Starting college is like taking a new job. Everything is uncertain, and it takes a while to get comfortable.

Analogies are especially useful in arguments about the future, because the only way we can predict it is by recalling the past. Analogies suggest that a proposed solution is so like another that what worked before will work again.

> We can rid our dormitories of alcohol as effectively as we did drugs with a zero-tolerance policy. Before we instituted our current policy, we did not enforce rules against drugs for fear of violating student privacy. But once we decided to suspend anyone caught using drugs, and some were, drug use virtually disappeared. _{analogy} A zero-tolerance policy can end alcohol use in the same way. _{claim}

The problem is, history is full of counter-analogies:

> We tried national Prohibition in the 1920s, but that just made alcohol more attractive and drove it underground. If we ban alcohol from university property, the same thing will happen again. _{counter-analogy}

◆ EXAMPLE

Analogy and Causation

Movie critic Michael Medved responds to those who deny that violent entertainment causes violent behavior.

Although hundreds of studies demonstrate a link between brutal media imagery and brutal behavior, skeptics argue that this reflects the tastes of violent kids rather than the influence of violent entertainment. Hollywood's most nimble apologists never tire of pointing out that our prisons are full of cold-blooded murderers who never saw *The Basketball Diaries*, whereas the overwhelming majority of children who regularly enjoy brutal movies or video games will never shoot their classmates.

Yet these reassuring arguments amount to very little, for one can say similar things about cigarettes: some people who never smoke get lung cancer, and most people who smoke never get lung cancer. But so what? Smoking still enormously increases your likelihood of getting sick. By the same token, you prove nothing with the undeniable observation that most consumers can view even the most disturbing and irresponsible products of our pop culture without discernible harm.

Consider the logic behind TV advertising: A commercial's failure to sell everybody doesn't mean it fails to sell anybody. If a Lexus ad inspires even one in a thousand viewers to take a test drive, it has dramatically improved the fortunes of the car maker. And if one of a thousand kids who watch intense violence on TV or at the movies were to try out that violence in real life, then it dramatically changes America.

Source: Michael Medved, "Hollywood Murdered Innocence," *Wall Street Journal,* June 16, 1999.

Warrants   Behind every analogy is an implicit warrant. When you articulate a warrant, you make explicit the principle that lets a reader apply a general cause-and-effect relationship to a specific one:

> Everyone feels lost when they enter a new community whose expectations seem baffling. warrant So when you start your first year here, cause you are likely to feel bewildered. effect

You rely on warrants at the risk of making doctrinaire claims. So take a fresh look at cause-and-effect relationships; don't rely on stock warrants.

Analysis   You offer analyses of cause and effect when you run through Mill's questions (pp. 280–82).

- When a cause is present, does the effect occur more often than when the cause is absent?
- When a cause is absent, does the effect occur less often than when the cause is present?
- Does the magnitude of the effect vary with the magnitude of its cause?

> We can see the contrast between students from high schools that emphasize discussion and critical writing as opposed to those from schools that emphasized rote learning. Almost 90 percent of their graduates from schools that teach critical thinking report that they feel comfortable in our first-year classes, while almost 60 percent of first-year students from schools that emphasize rote learning report anxiety, confusion, and frustration.

Weaving All Three Explanations into a Narrative   This is how you weave these explanations into your narrative:

> Orientation for first-year students should be expanded to two weeks to help them understand better what lies ahead. claim **Everyone feels lost when they enter a new community whose expectations seem baffling.** warrant **It's like moving to a new town or taking a new job. It takes a while to get comfortable.** analogy In the same way, students become anxious and frustrated during their first semester here effect because they don't know what teachers expect. cause For example, most teachers want us to think and write critically about what we've read, but many first-year students think teachers just want them to report it back accurately. cause And so they only summarize readings and their notes. effect This happens most often with students who succeeded in

high school by reporting back what they heard in class. ₍cause₎ After all, that's all that many of our high school teachers expected, and too few warned us that our task in college would be different. ₍cause₎ **We can see the contrast in students from high schools that emphasize discussion and critical thinking as opposed to rote learning. Almost 90 percent of their graduates report that they feel comfortable in our first-year classes, while almost 60 percent of first-year students from schools that emphasize rote learning report anxiety, confusion, and frustration.** ₍analysis₎

Planning an Argument Assigning Personal Responsibility

To argue that someone is responsible for an action, argue as you do in any argument about causation: use narratives, analogies, warrants, and Millsian analyses. But in an argument about personal responsibility, not only must you establish causation, you must also address the criteria for assigning responsibility.

Establish Causation

• **Did the person actually cause what you claim she did?**

Often, this is not an issue. If you claim that your school has failed to educate students about the risks of bingeing, it either did or did not, so you have to be sure of your facts.

Establish the Need to Assign Responsibility

• **Was the intended outcome good (or bad)?**

If someone saves a drowning child, the outcome is self-evidently good. But if the person jumps in to save a child's doll, the child might be grateful, but few adults would praise an action for a purpose so trivial. It may seem obvious that an action had a good effect, but do readers judge it as you do?

Address the Five Criteria for Assigning Responsibility

• **What was the person's state of mind?**

1. Did she freely choose to act?
2. Could she foresee the consequences?
3. Were her motives appropriate?

These three questions require detailed answers. To praise a heroic action, you have to show that the person chose to act (she did not act impulsively or was not forced at gunpoint), that she intended to achieve the benefit and knew the risks (she was not drunk or too excited to know what she was doing), and that she did what she did for a good purpose (not just to get a reward).

• **What was role of the context and circumstances?**

4. Was her action exceptional? Would most people have chosen *not* to do it?

5. Was her action aided or hindered by the circumstances?

If most of us would not risk our lives to rescue someone, then the few who do deserve our praise—more if they leap unaided into a swift and dangerous river, less if they wade into placid shallow pond with a life preserver. The more we think an action is extraordinary and difficult, the more strongly we praise or blame the person we hold responsible for it. Conversely, if most of us would wade into a shallow pond to save a child, then the few who do not deserve our blame.

In answering all of these questions, details matter, so make your narrative more specific than you think your readers need.

DRAFTING

The Language of Causality

You can express causality with high confidence or extreme diffidence. But careful readers know that every effect has multiple causes that interact in unpredictable ways, and rarely does anyone have all the evidence needed to make a claim with 100 percent confidence. So state your claims cautiously and modestly. These phrases move from absolute certainty to relative uncertainty:

X causes Y	X is a cause of Y	X contributes to Y
X leads to Y	X correlates with Y	X is implicated in Y
X is a factor in Y	X is linked to Y	X is associated with Y

You can use various subjects and verbs to modulate your certainty. Compare the certainty in these two:

We have *proved / established / shown / argued* that X causes Y.

Evidence *indicates / suggests / implies* that Y correlates with X.

And you can make those statements more or less certain with *may / might / could be / seems / appears:*

Some evidence *appears* to indicate that Y *may* correlate with X.

This is another example of the Goldilocks Rule—not too certain, not too cautious, but just right. (As a general principle, though, lean toward slight diffidence.)

When praising and blaming, you need language that implies knowledge, intention, and responsibility.

- **knowledge:** *know(ingly), recognize, realize, aware, foresee*
- **intention:** *intend, intentional(ly), deliberate(ly), purpose(fully), in order to, so that*
- **responsibility:** *responsible(ity), answerable, should have, could have*

Be aware of the ambiguity of *why* and *because:* Both fail to make the crucial difference between *What caused X to. . . ,* a question that encourages you to focus on external circumstances, and *What reasons did X have for. . . ,* a question that encourages you to focus on intentions. Compare:

What reasons did Oswald have for shooting President Kennedy?

What caused Oswald to shoot President Kennedy?

INQUIRIES

REFLECTIONS

1. Here is a quotation from the last few pages of Leo Tolstoy's novel *War and Peace,* written about 140 years ago. Tolstoy was trying to explain free will versus determinism. Does this have any relevance to anything discussed here?

   [T]o imagine the action of a man entirely subject to the law of inevitability without any freedom, you must assume the knowledge of an infinite number of space relations, an infinitely long period of time, and an infinite series of causes. To imagine a man perfectly free and not subject to the law of inevitability, you must imagine him all alone, beyond space, beyond time, and free from dependence on cause.

   Tolstoy, of course, knew that neither was possible. Now what?

2. Here are two stories about AIDS. Why does the second continue to circulate widely even though no evidence supports it?

   A. A virus randomly mutated in an African primate that by chance bit someone who happened to be sexually active and traveled widely enough to infect others, who unwittingly went on to infect more, eventually creating the worldwide epidemic of AIDS.

   B. A CIA lab created a virus as a weapon. As the end of the Cold War approached, they decided to use it to wipe out homosexuals and drug users, and eventually African-Americans. They enlisted drug dealers to create an epidemic of addiction to get people to infect themselves. Once this is exposed, the CIA will be revealed for the evil force it is.

3. When Princess Diana was killed in that automobile accident, just about everyone focused on the drunk driver or on the paparazzi chasing her as the cause. A few pointed out she was not wearing a seat belt and that the person in the front seat who was wearing one survived, so it was perhaps her failure to buckle-up that killed her. But after a day or two, most commentators stopped saying that, and focused on the driver and the paparazzi. Why did so few mention her not buckling up as a plausible cause of her death?

4. Imagine everyone wears seat belts all the time. How would that have changed how we understand the cause of Diana's death? Would it ever be imaginable that seat belts would make as interesting a causal story as drinking?

5. Imagine this: Every day for a month, you try to start your car; it doesn't start. You look under the hood. Someone has detached the battery wire. Then one day the car starts: the person *didn't* detach the wire. Do you say that the cause of the car starting was that the person did *not* detach the wire? Or try this: A school crossing guard does not show up one morning, and a child is hit by a car. Do you say that one of the causes of the child's being hit was that the guard did not show up? Now suppose there was never a guard at that crossing. Does that change your account of causation? Why?

TASK

6. When you fill in the details of your narrative of a problem or its solution, you do more than help your readers. You also test your own reasoning. Reread the two stories about the origin of AIDS above in Inquiry 2. Make each story more detailed by filling in possible causes for each step in the narrative. Is one story easier to fill in than the other? Does one become less plausible the more you fill it in?

IN A NUTSHELL

About Your Argument . . .

Every event has countless causes. In an argument about causes, you have to decide which ones to single out as most relevant to your solution. A cause is *practically relevant* if, by fixing it, you solve the problem. A cause is *conceptually relevant* if it allows you to understand an event in light of some special interest you and your readers bring to the question.

When you think about causes, you have to guard against cognitive biases we all share:

1. We tend to assign causality to an event that occurs immediately before an effect.

2. We tend to assign causality to events that occur rather than to events that do not.

3. We tend to assign causality to surprising events, not routine ones.

4. We tend to focus on causes that confirm our assumptions.

5. We look for causes whose magnitude is proportional to their effect.

You guard against those biases by systematically and deliberately considering as many causes as you can identify, especially those that most of us tend to miss: what we don't think of because it is absent or too routine to notice.

Use an ANOVA table to help you test your reasoning. Label each row by the presence or absence of a possible cause and each column by an alleged effect or lack of one. You can test covariation by recording the degree of the effect relative to the degree a cause is present. You can claim a plausible cause when you find a significant correlation between the possible cause and the effect, specifically if

- the effect usually occurs when the cause is present, and
- the effect usually does not occur when the cause is absent.

The greater the difference between the percentage of times when the effect is present and when it is absent, the more significant the correlation and the more confidently you can claim to have identified a cause.

. . . and About Writing It

When you plan a cause-and-effect argument about a practical problem, you have to include at least five stories that answer these questions:

1. What causes this problem?
2. How will the action you propose solve the problem?
3. How will your solution be implemented?
4. Will your solution cost more than the problem?
5. Why is your solution better than the alternatives?

When you tell the story of the problem, you have to decide how far back up the chain of causes to begin. For a practical problem, go just far enough back to give readers a sense of the context for your solution; for a conceptual one, go deeper into its history because readers generally want to see more causes when you want them to understand a question. Decompose your narrative into finer detail than you think you have to, because we all tend to be too general rather than too specific. Flesh out your narrative with explanations showing that a cause in fact produces its effect. Use analogies, warrants, and Millsian analyses.

PART IV

The Languages of Argument

Once you collect and arrange the elements of your argument, you will have invested lots of time thinking, reading, and writing. At that point, you may think that all you have left is to knock out a draft, spell-check, and print it. It is easy to grind through this last stage as a routine chore, but if you do, you pass up an opportunity to develop your argument further, because the words you choose do more than just express good ideas. As good critical thinkers know, choosing and revising your language is also an act of discovery and creativity.

- In Chapter 12, we discuss how readers respond to the language of your argument and how it makes them feel about it and even you.

- In Chapter 13, we explore how language can shape your thinking and that of your readers in ways that you may be unaware of, but that you can use to make your argument still more convincing.

CHAPTER 12

Clear Language

*In this chapter, we discuss how readers judge clarity, how you can recognize
when your own writing is unclear, and how you can revise it. We also discuss
two other qualities of prose that readers value: concision and vividness, qualities that raise the issue of the role of emotion in rational argument.*

Readers will consider your claim if you create a sound and complete argument to support it. But if they have to slog through one confusing sentence
after another to find that argument, they may never grasp it well enough to
judge it fairly. And even if they do, they are unlikely to feel well disposed
toward it—or you. Imagine that you had to read forty pages of prose like this:

1a. The Federalists' argument that destabilization of government was the
result of popular democracy was based on their belief in the tendency of
self-interested groups toward sacrificing the common good in favor of
their own narrow objectives.

You would feel friendlier toward the writer if those forty pages were closer to
this:

1b. The Federalists argued that popular democracy destabilized government
because they believed that self-interested groups tended to sacrifice the
common good for their own narrow objectives.

In fact, dense prose like (1a) risks not just your readers' good will, but their
willingness to read at all.

So once you draft your argument, you must still be sure it is written as
clearly as its substance allows. In making that judgment, however, you face two
problems:

- When you read your own prose, you always understand it more easily
than your readers do, because you remember too well what you meant
when you wrote it.

- Even when you recognize what you ought to revise, you might not
know how to change it.

We address those two problems in the first part of this chapter. In the second, we discuss how to make your writing concise and vivid. When you achieve clarity, concision, and vividness, your prose both communicates the logical force of your argument and projects an ethos that readers trust. You can't replace sound logic with clear language, but it has considerable persuasive power of its own.

Clarity and Your Ethos

Some students think their writing style is merely cosmetic: *What's important are my ideas, not my words.* But that assumes readers are willing to slog through your murky words to find your ideas. In fact, few of us have the time or patience to do that. Worse, many readers believe that the quality of your writing reflects the quality of your mind. So if you write unclearly, readers may question how clearly you think. For example, here's what one reviewer said of a book on teaching apes to communicate:

> This is fascinating stuff, but it is amazing how quickly the momentum is lost when the authors begin expounding in science-speak. You're just getting into the mind of the ape . . . when the mind of the cognitive psychologist feels compelled to elaborate: "It was expected that if apes do have language, its presence would be revealed by the animals' innate syntactical competence, a putatively genetically determined ability to order the symbols in multi-word utterances." . . . [T]here are times when the more the authors explain, the less we understand. Apes certainly seem capable of using language to communicate. Whether scientists are remains doubtful.

Your style shapes your ethos. In fact, clarity is itself an element of persuasion, because it gives readers cause to trust you.

Source: Douglas Chadwick, *New York Times Book Review,* December 11, 1994.

Some Principles of Clear and Direct Writing

Although we describe a passage as clear or unclear, simple or complex, those terms name only how we feel as we read it. We say that *writing* is confusing when *we* feel confused; that *it's* unclear when *we* feel uncertain about what it means; that *it's* convoluted when *we* feel lost in its twists and turns. Terms like that do not tell us what parts of the sentence make us feel as we do.

If you can understand why readers respond to your sentences as they do, you can then identify and revise sentences likely to give them trouble. To help you do that, we'll explain six principles of clear writing. But you can't use those principles unless you know a few common grammatical terms. Three important ones are *subject, verb,* and *noun.* It helps to know a few others: *object, preposition, active, passive, phrase, main clause,* and *subordinate clause.* We also use one technical term you probably don't know, but we'll define it when we need it. (At the end of this chapter is a glossary of grammatical terms; the first time we use a term defined there, we'll put it in all caps.)

• Principle 1: Use subjects to name your main characters.

Readers understand sentences most easily when they see in the SIMPLE SUBJECTS of VERBS the most important characters you write about. By *character* we mean not just people but whatever you can tell a story about by making it the subject of a lot of sentences. But readers judge sentences to be clearest when the characters are people or concrete objects that you can name in a word or two.

Look again at the two examples you read above. The one-word simple subjects are italicized; the WHOLE SUBJECTS that include them are underlined; verbs are boldfaced:

1a. The Federalists' *argument* that destabilization of government was the result of popular democracy **was based** on their belief in the tendency of self-interested groups toward sacrificing the common good for their own narrow objectives.

1b. The *Federalists* **argued** that popular *democracy* **destabilized** government, because *they* **believed** that self-interested *groups* **tended** to **sacrifice** the common good for their narrow objectives.

In (1a) the simple subject is *argument;* it is an abstract NOUN inside a long, abstract PHRASE constituting the whole subject:

WHOLE SUBJECT	VERB
The Federalists' *argument* that destabilization of government was the result of popular democracy	was based . . .

Moreover, inside that long abstract subject is another abstract subject:

WHOLE SUBJECT	VERB
destabilization of government	was . . .

In contrast, look at the whole subjects of (1b):

SUBJECT	VERB
The *Federalists*	argued . . .
popular *democracy*	destabilized . . .
they	believed . . .
self-interested *groups.*	tend to sacrifice . . .

In (1b), the whole subjects are short and specific. Three of them name people (*Federalists, they, groups*) and the fourth names a familiar concept (*democracy*).

That is why most of us find (1b) easier to read. So the first principle of a clear style is this:

> **Use short, concrete subjects that name your main characters.**

But now we have to qualify that principle: Sometimes, we want to tell stories not about flesh-and-blood characters but about abstractions. Look at the subjects of the following sentences (simple subjects are italicized; whole subjects are underlined; main verbs are boldfaced):

> Few *aspects* of human behavior **have been** so difficult to explain as rational thinking. *Rationality* **depends** on a range of short-term behaviors, such as not jumping to a hasty conclusion or action, having the patience to gather evidence, and the ability to bring together evidence and reasons in support of claims. But perhaps the *hallmark* of human rationality **is** the capacity to think about thinking, to reason about reasoning, to reflect on the quality of the thinking that assembles those reasons and claims into an argument.

The subjects of those sentences are abstractions:

SUBJECT	VERB
Few *aspects* of human behavior	have been . . .
Rationality	depends . . .
the *hallmark* of human rationality...................................	is . . .

In that passage we see not human characters but abstractions. But those abstract characters are familiar to anyone who has thought about the issue of rationality, so familiar that the terms *aspects of human behavior* and *rationality* seem almost as distinct as the people who behave and think. Moreover, even though those subjects are abstract, the two long ones are only five words.

To decide whether the subjects of your sentences will be clear, consider how they will look to your readers. Don't make anything the subject of a sentence if it might seem to readers like an amorphous blob, especially a long one like this:

> The Federalists' argument that destabilization of government was the result of popular democracy . . .

Few readers can easily hold in mind a subject that long and indistinct.

You can usually revise such sentences by recasting their subjects around flesh-and-blood characters. If, for example, you thought readers might find abstractions like *rationality* and *behavior* difficult, you could revise to make flesh-and-blood characters the subjects of verbs.

> <u>Psychologists</u> **have found** it difficult to explain what <u>we</u> **do** when <u>we</u> **behave** rationally. <u>We</u> **think** rationally when, in the short run, <u>we</u> **do not jump** to hasty conclusions, but instead patiently **gather** evidence, and **bring** evidence

and reasons together to support claims. But <u>we</u> **are** perhaps most rational when <u>we</u> **reason** about our reasoning, when <u>we</u> **reflect** on how well <u>we</u> **thought** when <u>we</u> **assembled** our reasons and claims into an argument.

You can't always revise stories about abstractions into stories about flesh-and-blood characters, but to the degree you can, readers will judge your prose to be clearer and more vivid. If you think flesh-and-blood characters make your sentences seem simplistic, especially to specialists, use technical terms as characters in the subjects, so long as your readers are familiar with them.

• **Principle 2: Use verbs, not nouns, to name those characters' actions.**

Once readers get past a short, concise subject, they look for a verb that expresses a specific action. The sooner they find one, the clearer they judge the sentence to be. Compare the verbs (boldfaced) in the two passages about the Federalists:

1a. The Federalists' argument that destabilization of government **was** the result of popular democracy **was based** on their belief in the tendency of self-interested groups toward sacrificing the common good for their narrow objectives.

1b. The Federalists **argued** that popular democracy **destabilized** government, because they **believed** that self-interested groups **tended** to **sacrifice** the common good for their narrow objectives.

In (1a), the only verbs, *was* and *was based,* are empty: They express no real action. In (1b), the verbs do: *argue, destabilize, believe, tend, sacrifice.*

But if the actions in (1a) are not in verbs, where are they? They are in abstract nouns (boldfaced):

1a. The Federalists' **argument** that **destabilization** of government was the result of popular democracy was based on their **belief** in the **tendency** of self-interested groups toward **sacrificing** the common good for their narrow objectives.

We have a technical term for nouns derived from verbs: *nominalization.* (When you nominalize the verb *nominalize,* you get the nominalization *nominalization.*) Writing that feels highly professional and abstract almost always has lots of these abstract nominalizations, especially in subjects. When you use nominalizations as subjects, not only do you have to use weaker verbs instead of the stronger ones you could have used, but you also have to add prepositions and articles that you don't need when you use stronger verbs:

1a. The Federalists' argument that destabilization **of** government would be **the** result **of** popular democracy was based **on** their belief **in the** tendency **of** self-interested groups **toward** sacrificing the common good **for** their narrow objectives.

So here is the second principle of clear prose:

> Use verbs to communicate actions; do not bury actions
> in abstract nominalizations, especially in subjects.

We can join these two principles: Match key elements in sentences—subjects and verbs—to key elements in your story—characters and actions.

SUBJECT	VERB
CHARACTER	ACTION

Those two principles explain why we judge some sentences to be clear and concrete, others unclear and abstract.

• **Principle 3: Get to a verb quickly.**

Contrast the following sentences (simple subjects are italicized; whole subjects are underlined; main verbs are boldfaced):

2a. <u>*Parents* who believe that school uniforms would solve most of the discipline problems in our schools</u> **argue** in favor of them, but <u>many *others* who fear that government already intrudes too much into our private lives</u> **object.**

2b. <u>Some *parents*</u> **argue** that <u>school *uniforms*</u> would **solve** most of the discipline problems in our schools, but <u>many *others*</u> **object** because <u>*they*</u> **fear** that <u>*government*</u> already intrudes too much into our private lives.

In both sentences, the simple subjects are human characters, *parents* and *others,* and familiar objects, *uniforms,* but is it fair to say that most of us find (2b) easier to read? In the first CLAUSE of (2a), we have to read 17 words to get to the verb, *argue,* and in the second clause 16 more to get to the verb *object.* In (2b), we have to read only two words before we get to the main verb in each clause:

2b. <u>Some parents</u> **argue** . . . but <u>many others</u> **object** . . .

This principle of quickly getting past a subject to a verb implies three subordinate ones:

• **Principle 3A: Avoid long introductory elements before a subject.**

Compare these sentences (the introductory elements are italicized; whole subjects are underlined; verbs are boldfaced):

3a. *In view of recent research on higher education indicating at least one change in their major on the part of most undergraduate students,* <u>first-year students</u> **should be** 100 percent certain about the program of studies they want to pursue before they load up their schedule with requirements for a particular program.

3b. *According to recent research on higher education,* <u>most students</u> **change** their majors at least once during their undergraduate careers, so <u>first-year students</u> **should be** 100 percent certain about the program of studies they want to pursue before they load up their schedule with requirements for a particular program.

3c. <u>Researchers on higher education</u> **have recently shown** that most students change their majors at least once during their undergraduate careers, so <u>first-year students</u> **should be** 100 percent certain about their program of studies before they load up their schedule with requirements for a particular program.

Most of us find (3a) less clear than (3b) or (3c). In (3a) we must work through a twenty-three-word introductory phrase before we get to the main subject (*first-year students*) and its verb (*should be*). In (3b) we have to work through only a seven-word introductory phrase, and in (3c) we start directly with the subjects of both clauses: *Researchers on higher education have recently shown. . . , first-year students should be . . .*

• **Principle 3B: Keep whole subjects short.**

This principle connects to our first one, to make subjects distinct characters, because distinct characters usually have short names. Compare these (simple subjects are italicized; whole subjects are underlined; verbs are boldfaced):

4a. A social *system* that fails to create a legal environment in which foreign investors can rely on the rule of law and on the strict enforcement of contracts **will** not **thrive.**

4b. If a social *system* **fails** to **create** a legal environment in which foreign *investors* can rely on the rule of law and on the strict enforcement of contracts, _{subordinate clause} that *system* **will** not **thrive.**

4c. A social *system* **will** not **thrive** if *it* **fails** to **create** an environment in which foreign *investors* can rely on the rule of law and on the strict enforcement of contracts. _{subordinate clause}

In (4a), we see the whole subject start at the beginning of the sentence; but we cannot see at a glance where it stops, because it goes on for 25 more words. In (4b) we quickly identify a shorter subject and its verb in a long subordinate clause. And in (4c) we see a short main subject and verb at the beginning of the sentence: *A social system* **will** not **thrive** . . .

• **Principle 3C: Avoid interrupting subjects and verbs with long phrases and clauses.**

Compare the effect of the *because*-clause in these next two sentences:

5a. Some scientists, because they write in a style that is so impersonal and objective, **do** not **communicate** with lay people easily.

5b. Some scientists **do** not **communicate** with lay people easily, because they write in a style that is so impersonal and objective.

We easily see where the two-word subject of (5a), *some scientists,* starts and stops, but just when we expect a verb, we hit that long interrupting *because*-clause. When we don't see a verb right after a subject, we usually judge a sentence to be more difficult than it has to be. So avoid interrupting the subject-verb connection: shift an interrupting element to the end or beginning of its sentence, depending on where it fits better.

The sum of these three sub-principles is this:

> Help readers quickly get past a short subject to its verb.

• **Principle 4: Begin sentences with information that is familiar to readers.**

This principle has the same effect as the first three. It lets readers build up momentum in a sentence, but it depends less on the grammar of the sentence than on the psychology of its reader: We read more easily when early in a sentence we deal with information that is simple and familiar, before we have to deal with information that is new and complex. Compare:

6a. Particular ideas toward the beginning of sentences define what sentences are "about." The cumulative effect of a series of repeated subjects indicates what a passage is about, so our sense of coherence depends on subjects of sentences. Moving through a paragraph from a consistent point of view occurs when a series of subjects seems to constitute a coherent sequence. A seeming absence of context for sentences is one consequence of making random shifts in subjects. Feelings of dislocation, disorientation, and lack of focus occur when that happens.

6b. As we read, we depend on the subject of a sentence to focus our attention on a particular idea that tells us what that sentence is "about." In a series of sentences, we depend on repeated subjects to cumulatively tell us the topic of a whole passage. If we feel that a series of subjects is coherent, then we feel we are moving through a paragraph from a coherent point of view. But if we feel its subjects shift randomly, then we have to begin each sentence out of context, from no coherent point of view. When that happens, we feel dislocated, disoriented, out of focus.

Most of us have a problem with (6a) that we do not have with (6b). As we start each sentence in (6a), we have to deal not just with long abstract subjects, but with information that *to us* is newer and less familiar than the information at the ends of those sentences:

6a. Particular ideas toward the beginning of sentences . . .

The cumulative effect of a series of subjects . . .

. . . our sense of coherence . . .

Moving through a paragraph from a consistent point of view . . .

A seeming absence of context for sentences . . .

Feelings of dislocation, disorientation, and lack of focus . . .

In (6b), however, we begin each sentence with information that seems familiar and is therefore easier to grasp (whole subjects are underlined):

6b. As <u>we</u> read, <u>we</u> depend on . . .

In a series of sentences, <u>we</u> depend on . . .

If <u>we</u> feel that <u>a series of subjects</u> is . . .

But if <u>we</u> feel <u>its subjects</u> shift . . .

Then <u>we</u> have to begin . . .

When <u>that</u> happens, <u>we</u> feel . . .

From this principle of how to begin a sentence, we can infer another about how to end it.

• **Principle 5: End a sentence with long and complex units of information.**

And from Principles 4 and 5, we can infer a sixth.

• **Principle 6: Keep your subjects consistent. Avoid beginning several sentences in a row with unrelated subjects.**

In (6a), we sense no consistency in its subjects. When sentences in a series all begin differently, we are likely to judge the passage to be unfocused, disjointed, even disorganized. In (6b), the subjects are more consistent. As a result, we read (6b) more easily. In short:

> Don't vary subjects randomly; limit them to just a few different characters.

The Principles in a Nutshell

Here are those six principles again:

1. Name the main characters in your story in the subjects of sentences.
2. Express their actions not as abstract nouns but as verbs.
3. Get to the main verb quickly.
   a. Avoid long introductory elements.
   b. Avoid long abstract subjects.
   c. Avoid interrupting subjects and verbs.
4. Begin sentences with information that is familiar to readers.
5. Push to the end of a sentence information that is newer, more complex, and therefore more difficult to understand.
6. Begin sentences consistently. Focus your subjects on a few familiar characters.

You may have to use difficult language when the substance of your ideas demands it. But you can avoid making readers work harder than they have to if you help them build up some momentum at the beginning of a sentence. When you do that, they can better deal with newer and more complex information toward the end.

Good critical thinkers know that clear writing is not just a cosmetic quality that makes readers happy. It is itself a force in an argument. Readers are more likely to assent to what they understand and to trust a writer who has taken the trouble to write clearly.

The Ethics of Deliberate Complexity

Some writers deny that clarity is important. In fact, some write complex prose deliberately, thinking that it makes them and their ideas sound impressive, and impressive means persuasive. Some writers even claim that readers benefit when they struggle to decipher complex prose, because they have to think harder. They're wrong about that. All research indicates that when readers have to struggle with a complex style, they understand not more, but less. Occasionally, complex ideas require complex sentences. And sometimes naïve readers are impressed by fancy language. But more often, complex prose is a product of self-indulgence, or at least indifference to readers.

Concision and Vividness

Readers judge sentences to be clear when they see short, specific subjects followed by verbs expressing important actions. But they look for more than that. Compare the subjects and verbs of these two passages (we underline subjects, boldface main verbs):

> The consensus of our national belief **is** the right and freedom to engage in practices reflecting the inheritance of our different cultural and historical backgrounds. Allowing widows to end their lives as sometimes happens in certain parts of the world **must** of course **be made** illegal and forbidden by law, but allowances for things like female head coverings in educational settings **should be made.** But a degree of uncertainty and unease **exists** in regard to cultural practices and traditions such as the binding force of an arranged future marriage between those not yet old or mature enough to take responsibility for the consequences of their decisions.

> We generally **believe** that Americans **should** freely practice the cultural traditions of their parents. We of course **forbid** a widow from throwing herself onto her husband's funeral pyre, as Indian women are sometimes coerced into doing, but we **allow** Islamic girls to wear head scarves in public school. But we **are** less certain about some cases: **Must** a court **recognize** as binding a contract arranging a future marriage of two eight-year-olds?

The first feels indirect and complex; the second more straightforward, partly because its subjects are shorter, clearer, more familiar, and followed by specific verbs. But the second has another virtue: Its language seems "sharper," helping us better "see" what the words refer to, and if we can vividly see their referents in our mind's eye, we are likely to respond more positively.

You create vivid prose in two ways:

- Express ideas in the fewest words your readers need.
- Use words that make readers "see" what your words refer to.

Do that, and your readers will read your argument faster, understand it better, and remember it longer. Use too many words, especially abstractions, and readers are likely to think that your argument and maybe even you are vague, fuzzy, foggy, muddy—pick your metaphor.

How to Be Concise

It is easy to tell you to write concisely, but doing it is hard, because editing for concision is labor-intensive and takes a big vocabulary. But it pays off—first for your readers, because you make their job easier, and then for you, because readers are grateful when you save them effort. If we could, we would give you rules to make editing easier, but we cannot. The best we can do is show you some common kinds of wordiness and ways to eliminate them. No shortcuts here.

Repetition and Clutter

Prose is wordy when it says the same thing twice or uses words with little meaning. For example, this next passage combines both useless repetition and empty words; the revision eliminates both:

Various improvements in productivity basically depend first and foremost on certain fundamental factors that generally involve psychology more than any kind of particular technology.

Productivity rises when we improve not just machines but the minds of those who operate them.

Here are some typical examples of clutter that you can usually cut:

certain	various	particular	specific	given
really	basically	generally	virtually	actually

Here are typical examples of redundant pairs, one of which you can always cut:

full and complete	hope and trust	any and all
true and accurate	each and every	basic and fundamental
hopes and desires	first and foremost	various and sundry

Decomposed Meaning

We most commonly befog a concept when we decompose a meaning that we could express in one word and spread it over several. When we read a word in context—*I'd like you to meet my* **brother**—the word *brother* seems to evoke a unified concept. But as we saw in Chapter 10, we can think of the meaning of *brother* as a cluster of criteria (*human, male, descended from the same parents*). So we can express a concept in one word or through several by naming all its criteria of meaning. If someone says, *I want you to meet someone who is male and descended from my parents,* we might know what that person means, but judge him to be a bit odd.

That's a silly example, but we read that kind of writing every day:

You did not read through what you wrote paying close enough attention to finding and correcting errors.

instead of

You did not edit carefully.

That longer sentence breaks unitary meanings into pieces by naming their separate criteria, smearing the meaning across many words. The shorter sentence uses a single word, which is almost always more vivid:

read through . . . errors → edit
paying close attention → carefully

Implied Meaning

Another kind of wordiness states what other words already imply. Compare:

Imagine someone trying to learn the rules and strategy for playing the game of chess.

Imagine learning chess.

Learn implies *try, strategy* and *game* both imply *play, chess* implies *game,* and *game* implies *rules and strategy.* So if we cut what readers can infer, we get something more concise and more vivid:

Imagine someone learning to play chess.

Do not, however, confuse concise with merely short. Compare:

Write directly.

Make important characters subjects and make their verbs specific actions.

The first is shorter, but too general, omitting important information.

How to Be Vivid

Once you have squeezed the wordiness from your prose, you still have to be sure that the words left convey not just the meaning you intend but the nuances of tone and feeling that support it.

Choosing the Right Feel

Words differ along so many scales that it is hard to list them all. Here are some general categories:

- **Slang vs. informal vs. formal (*wheels* vs. *car* vs. *automobile*):**

  When a fruitcake shows up in an ER too goofy to think straight, the doc has to make the call whether to shoot him up with downers.

  When someone comes to an emergency room unable to think rationally, the doctor must decide whether to calm him down with drugs.

  When a mentally incompetent individual presents in a trauma center, the attending physician must determine whether to sedate him with tranquilizing medication.

- **Neutral vs. emotional (*pregnancy termination* vs. *abortion* vs. *infanticide*):**

  Lowering taxes will raise net income.

  If we could protect some of what the tax man sucks out of our paychecks every week, we could keep more of the money we sweat for every day.

- **Native vs. borrowed (*speed* vs. *velocity*):**

  You have to show guts when the times call for it.

  It is necessary to demonstrate courage when the occasion demands it.

- **Common vs. scientific (*belly button* vs. *navel*):**

  As you go higher, the air thins out.

  As altitude increases, the atmosphere attenuates.

- **General vs. specific (*livestock* vs. *pig*):**

  A good worker plans carefully in order to do the job right the first time.

  A master carpenter measures twice to cut once.

These criteria often correlate: When a word is formal, like *abdomen*, it is likely to be less common, borrowed from French or Latin, learned in tone, and less vivid, evoking less emotion than informal words from Anglo-Saxon, like *belly* or *gut,* which are informal, more common, more vivid, and more emotionally charged.

These choices affect not just how we read, but how we judge a writer's ethos. Those three ways of describing a patient in an emergency room say something different about the writer and how she relates to readers— intimately, informally, or formally:

> When a fruitcake shows up in an ER too goofy to think straight . . .

> When someone comes to an emergency room unable to think rationally . . .

> When a mentally incompetent individual presents in a trauma center . . .

Our best advice is to choose the middle style most of the time, because that sets a neutral background that magnifies the impact of an occasional, deliberately chosen formal or informal word.

Abstract Versus Concrete

The quality most important to a vivid style is whether a word evokes an image in our mind's eye. The more easily we image the referent of a word, the more vivid the style. Contrast these:

> When someone needs emergency care, but acts so irrationally that he cannot legally consent to treatment, only the attending physician can decide whether to give that person medication without his permission before beginning treatment.

> When 16-year-old Alex White staggered into the Fairview Hospital emergency room, raving about demons under his shirt and gushing blood where he had slashed his belly with a hunting knife, trauma physician Amanda Lee's first job was to stop the bleeding. But when White grabbed a nurse by her hair and threw her to the floor, screaming that she was the Whore of Babylon, Lee had to decide in an instant whether to inject him with the tranquilizer thorazine without asking him to sign her hospital's permission form. Ohio law and hospital rules require physicians to ask for permission before administering drugs, but White could not understand Lee's raving. So as would any physician in that situation, she tranquilized him without his permission.

That second is longer but more vivid, evoking in us more feeling. (Note that its vividness does not depend on ADJECTIVES or ADVERBS, but on nouns and verbs.) Which is better? That depends on what the writer intends. If the writer wants to evoke feeling, she uses vividly specific nouns and verbs; if she wants to seem cool and objective, she chooses more abstract, general language. The biggest mistake new writers make is to depend on adjectives and adverbs:

> When a *stoned* 16-year-old Alex White staggered *crazily* into the *quiet* Fairview Hospital emergency room, *wildly* raving about *evil* and *monstrous* demons under his shirt and gushing blood where he had *brutally* slashed his *pink* belly with a *vicious* hunting knife, trauma physician Amanda Lee's first job was to *quickly* stop the *frightening* bleeding. But when White *suddenly* grabbed a *frightened* nurse . . .

What readers are able to image, of course, depends on what they know— say *drag racing* to Colomb and up pop lots of images. But to evoke those images in people who don't know the LaPlace Dragway, he would have to be specific:

Sixteen-years-old and burning rubber down Claiborne Avenue at 3 A.M. on a Sunday morning in a supercharged '57 Bel Aire, hubcap to hubcap with Don Debarbaris' four barrel GTO.

Most of us usually prefer vivid writing, because we read it faster, understand it better, and remember it longer. So what we might lose in economy measured by number of words, we gain in impact. And of course, a writer can combine the general and specific:

> When someone needs emergency care, but acts so irrationally that he cannot legally consent to treatment, . . . For example, when on the night of May 13, 1998, 16-year-old Alex White staggered into the Fairview Hospital Emergency room raving . . .

The System of Imageable Words

There is, however, more to being vivid than just being specific, because not all kinds of specificity are equal. In fact, all human languages seem to have a systematic way of making some kinds of specificity more easily imaged than others. For example, what image comes to mind when you read the word *life?* Certainly no image most of us share; nor do we get a distinct image from the more specific word *vegetation.* Now imagine a *pine tree.* For most of us, that term evokes a distinct image with more distinct feeling. But now imagine a *Joshua tree.* Unless you know desert vegetation, this more specific term probably inhibits your imagination, giving you no clear image at all. Words can get so specific that we cannot call up an image unless we happen to know the specific referent.

Speakers of every language seem to organize their vocabulary in that systematic way, on a scale from general to specific, but with a break point between words that evoke no distinct image and words that do. In this array, the break point is shaded:

life	thing	stuff	nourishment	utility
creature	object	merchandise	food	transportation
animal	device	household goods	produce	conveyance
livestock	tool	furniture	fruit	vehicle
horse	hammer	table	apple	motorcycle
palomino	ballpean	Federal drop-leaf	Fuji	Harley

Words like *horse, hammer, table, apple,* and *motorcycle* refer to things at what psychologists call the *basic level of categorization.* Words at this level evoke in us distinct mental images. Above the basic level (*livestock, tool,* etc.), we conjure up random vague images. Below it, we get a more specific image only if we happen to know what a ballpean or Fuji looks like. For the rest of us, a Fuji is just another apple (these hyper-specific terms are typical of hi-tech military novels).

Most of us prefer prose that uses words at the basic level because we read, understand, and remember such words most easily. As writers, though, we see images in our prose more distinctly than our readers will, because we know our subject so well (recall Colomb's response to *drag racing*). If you write about a *creature's right to be free from inhumane treatment,* you may see in your own mind a bunny twisting away from chemical drops burning its trusting, black button eyes. But your readers will get that specific image only if you give it to them.

We can even create a gradation of specificity:

> There have been recent decreases in weapons crimes.
>
> Recently, crimes involving inexpensive firearms have decreased.
>
> Compared to a few years ago, a person is less likely to be the victim of someone with a cheap handgun.
>
> Compared to 1995, you are half as likely to be mugged by someone shoving a twenty dollar Saturday night special in your face.

What we image more clearly, we respond to more viscerally. If it is visceral response you want from readers, use words whose referents have vivid images in their mind's eye.

Deliberate Generality

Sometimes, however, you do not want to be specific, especially when you develop general claims in a cool objective style:

> . . . whenever any Form of government becomes destructive of these ends, it is the Right of the People to alter or to abolish it, and to institute new Government, laying its foundation on such principles and organizing its powers in such form, as to them shall seem most likely to effect their Safety and Happiness.

That principle of democratic governance still resonates because it covers not just this country two centuries ago, but all countries at all times. The drafters of the Declaration of Independence would have been wrong to write:

> . . . since King George III and his Parliament have taken away our right to be free to do what makes us happy, like acquiring and owning property such as farmland and slaves, we have the right to revolt and create a new country . . .

That sentence is too specific to express a universal truth. Later in the Declaration, however, the drafters wrote more vividly and thereby evoked more emotion when they explicitly described King George's crimes against the colonies:

> He has excited domestic insurrections amongst us, and has endeavoured to bring on the inhabitants of our frontiers, the merciless Indian Savages, whose known rule of warfare, is an undistinguished destruction of all ages, sexes and conditions.

This more general version would have served less well:

> He has caused problems by encouraging some native people to act against us.

Some writers, however, use two or more general words specifically to discourage readers from seeing clearly and sharply what they are referring to, an act that can verge on dishonesty. Compare the following:

To reduce to zero-level the agricultural production of psychotropic substances derived from plants in northern South America, agencies responsible for international covert action should introduce bioactive substances entailing the permanent interruption of growth cycles in ways that avoid calling attention to that project. Such a course of action may have nontemporary deleterious biological effects on collateral agricultural production and on some of those indigenously associated with it, but the desired results are of sufficient critical importance to warrant such action.

To stop cocaine farming in Colombia and Ecuador, the CIA should kill their cocoa crop by secretly infecting it with disease. Doing this may kill other plants that farmers eat and even poison some farmers, but our goals come first.

When you use two or more words to express what one could, you soften the edges of a concept: *abortion* vs. *termination of pregnancy; cancer* vs. *malignant growth; crippled* vs. *limited ambulatory capacity.* As always, we aim at the Goldilocks Rule: not too general, not too specific, but just right. What is just right is hard to gauge, but you might hold these two principles in mind:

- When you offer examples, evidence, and illustrations, your readers are likely to prefer language that is concrete, distinct, and vivid.

- When you state general principles, values, and assumptions, readers are likely to sense the power of those statements if you express them in more general language.

Since generalities require less hard thought and critical thinking, we are all are more likely to be too general than too specific. But hard thinking is a quality of all arguments worth making, so thinking hard about the quality of your language is a way to think better about your argument and its effect on your readers.

Jargon Watch

Even book reviewers complain about opaque academic jargon. Here a *New York Times* reviewer uses visual metaphors to describe what he had to read:

> Mr. Rabinow, a professor of anthropology at the University of California at Berkeley, tells the story of the collapse of an agreement between a French institute and an American company to collaborate on genetic research . . . [His] telling of this story is brilliant but unkempt, penetrating and impenetrable at the same time. . . . [His] writing is turgid and stilted, or so it will seem to people unaccustomed to the language and the in-group devices of the American Anthropological Association. . . . [His] main idea here threatens to become lost in a fog of highfalutin lingo, but occasionally it emerges sufficiently into the clear to be understood by mere mortals. . . . It is too bad that he chose to tell this very modern tale from within a closed professional world that keeps the rest of us on the outside looking in.

When a *New York Times* reviewer struggles to understand, the problem is the writer. Don't be reluctant to make the same judgment about what you read.

[a]Richard Bernstein, *New York Times,* October 13, 1999.

WRITING PROCESS

Clear Language

REVISING

Revising for Style

Even if you are a slow and careful drafter, don't focus on style until you have completed a draft and revised its organization. Start with passages where you felt you were struggling to express yourself clearly or were uncertain about your meaning. At such moments, we all tend to write confusing prose. Then work through the draft sentence-by-sentence, following these steps:

Diagnose

Start by underlining (or skimming) the first seven or eight words in each sentence (ignore short introductory phrases). Consider revising if you find this:

- Subjects are abstractions with lots of prepositional phrases attached.
- After seven or eight words, you see no verb, or if you do, it is a vague one, such as *do, make, have, be,* and so on.
- Those first seven or eight words express information that readers would *not* recognize from previous sentences or have reason to expect.
- Several sentences in a row keep changing subjects, so that in their first few words readers see no consistent set of characters or concepts.

For example, in the sentences in this passage, notice how long it takes to get to the verb in the main clause (whole subjects are underlined; verbs are boldfaced):

> <u>*Attempts* at explanations for increases in voter participation in recent elections</u> **came** from several candidates. <u>A general *cynicism* about honesty in government</u> **was** a common claim of some conservative politicians. But <u>the public's greater *interest* in their private affairs than in national public affairs</u> **is** also a possible reason for the drop in voting.

In the first sentence, the character *voter* appears *in* the subject, but not *as* the subject, and the whole subjects are long and complex. It is a passage begging for revision.

Revise

1. Start by identifying important characters. In the above passage, they are *voters, candidates,* and *conservative politicians.*
2. Identify their actions. Voters *participate (less), are cynical,* and *are not interested;* candidates *attempt* and *explain;* conservative politicians *claim.*
3. Revise so that most clauses (not necessarily all) begin with important characters as subjects and are followed by key actions in verbs.

Several candidates **tried to explain** why <u>fewer people</u> **voted** in recent elections. <u>Some conservative politicians</u> **claimed** that <u>voters</u> **were** generally cynical about honesty in government. But perhaps so <u>few</u> **voted** because <u>they</u> **were** more interested in their private affairs than in national public affairs.

4. Your diagnosis might find a long introductory phrase:

> Despite their role in creating a sense of loyalty among students and alumni and generating financial resources that support minor sports, on balance <u>major intercollegiate sports</u> damage the aims of higher education.

If so, revise in either of two ways:

- Make the phrase an independent clause:

    > <u>Major intercollegiate sports</u> **may create** a sense of loyalty among students and alumni and generate financial resources that support minor sports, but on balance <u>they</u> **damage** the aims of higher education.

- Make the phrase a subordinate clause. Move it after the main clause, if it communicates new information. If it is old information, try to shorten it.

    > On balance, <u>major intercollegiate sports</u> **damage** the aims of higher education, *even though* <u>they</u> create a sense of loyalty among students and alumni and generate financial resources that support minor sports.

    > *Although* <u>major intercollegiate sports</u> create loyalty and generate financial resources, on balance <u>they</u> **damage** the aims of higher education.

5. Your diagnosis might find a long whole subject whose simple subject is a flesh-and-blood character:

> <u>*Athletes* who receive special academic consideration because their time is taken up with training and competition</u> are not necessarily academically ill-prepared for the rigors of a high-quality education.

If so, revise in either of two ways:

- Turn the subject into an introductory subordinate clause. Make the simple subject its whole subject, if you can:

    > Although <u>*athletes*</u> **might receive** special academic consideration because their time is taken up with training and competition, <u>they</u> **are** not necessarily academically ill-prepared for the rigors of a high-quality education.

- Or turn the subject into its own main clause:

    > <u>Some athletes</u> **may receive** special academic consideration because their time is taken up with training and competition, but <u>they</u> **are** not necessarily academically ill-prepared for the rigors of a high-quality education.

6. Your diagnosis might turn up an interrupting element:

> <u>Major intercollegiate sports,</u> because they undermine the intellectual integrity that higher education is supposed to support by lowering standards for athletes, **should be abolished.** That kind of erosion will inevitably lead to . . .

If so, move that element to the beginning or end of its sentence, depending on whether it connects more closely to the preceding or following sentence.

<u>Major intercollegiate sports</u> **should be abolished,** because they undermine the intellectual integrity that higher education is supposed to support by lowering standards for athletes. That kind of erosion will inevitably lead to . . .

A Note on Active and Passive Verbs

If you remember any advice about writing, it is probably to avoid writing in the PASSIVE voice and to use ACTIVE voice instead. Generally, that is good advice, but often not. For example, these passages vary in their second sentences: one has an active verb, the other a passive one:

> Some astonishing questions about the nature of the universe have been raised by scientists investigating black holes in space. <u>The collapse of a dead star into a point perhaps no larger than a marble</u> **creates** _{active verb} a black hole. So much matter compressed into so little space changes the fabric of space around it in surprising ways.

> Some astonishing questions about the nature of the universe have been raised by scientists investigating black holes in space. <u>A black hole</u> **is created** _{passive verb} by the collapse of a dead star into a point perhaps no larger than a marble. So much matter compressed into so little space changes the fabric of space around it in surprising ways.

In that context, the passive verb would be the better choice:

- The subject of the active verb is long and abstract: *The collapse of a dead star into a point perhaps no larger than a marble.* But the subject of the passive verb is short, simple, and easily grasped: *A black hole.*

- The passive verb puts into the subject something we just read in the previous sentence:

  . . . exploring black holes in space. A black hole is created by . . .

We don't encourage the passive voice, but neither do we say always to avoid it. *Choose* active or passive, depending on what you want as a subject. That's what the passive is for.

A Final Point on Concision

Here is a last ~~very useful and important~~ principle of ~~careful~~ editing that you can ~~always~~ rely on: Draw a line through ~~every single~~ adjective[s] ~~that appear~~ directly before a noun and through ~~all~~ adverbs, ~~regardless of exactly where they appear~~. Then for each, ~~systematically~~ ask whether you ~~really and truly~~ need it. You will ~~probably~~ keep some, but you can ~~certainly~~ get rid of ~~a great~~ many. To be ~~really~~ vivid and concise, write ~~deliberately~~ not in ~~weak and wordy descriptive~~ adjectives and adverbs, but in ~~specific~~ nouns and verbs.

INQUIRIES

REFLECTIONS

1. We have tried to persuade you that the best style is, as a rule, the clearest style, but some have claimed that the plain style is deceptive. They

argue that complex facts are never as simple as a plain style makes them seem. Clarity itself is a trick to fool readers into accepting simplistic versions of the truth. Can you think of instances when someone might use plain speaking as a trick? How about advertisers? Politicians? Can you think of instances when someone (lawyers? experts?) might use complex language as a trick? Is any style inherently more "honest" or "sincere" than another?

2. Academic writing is rarely vivid, for reasons you can imagine. But why do so many people write so blandly, even after they leave school? For example, here is an excerpt from a report written by a swine veterinarian (that is, a pig doctor) to an operations manager (farmer) with little formal education (schooling). In person, this woman's talk is as salty as any, but notice how fuzzy her language gets when she writes. (Incidentally, "PRRS"—pronounced *purrs*—is a pig's version of a cold, and a "gilt" is a young female pig, terms familiar to her readers.)

   Of greatest urgency and most immediate concern in your ongoing project for enhancing productivity, especially as measured in market weight, is to limit the effects of PRRS on the rate of growth. Elimination of the virus is impractical chiefly in terms of ROI (return on investment), although reduction is a goal worth consideration. Most efficient, however, is to maintain growth rates after infection. Limiting gilt acquisition and proper acclimation are the most efficient additional steps, although the current program of vaccination will have to be maintained.

   She could have written something like this:

   If you want to market larger pigs, you must limit the effects of PRRS on their growth. Although you'd have to spend too much to eliminate the virus entirely, you can take steps to reduce it. Most important is to maintain growth rates after your pigs are infected. To do that, continue to vaccinate pigs as you do now. The best thing to do is limit the number of gilts you buy and to acclimate those you do.

   Or this:

   To sell fat pigs, don't let PRRS stunt their growth. It costs too much to get rid of the virus, but you can keep sick pigs growing if you vaccinate them, don't buy more gilts than you need, and don't mix them with others until you've exposed them to the virus.

   Can you think of any reasons why the vet would write in such a fuzzy, academic style? Are any of them good reasons? Between the second and third version, which do you think would be more appropriate? Why?

TASKS

3. For a week, note the style of what you read. Copy passages that seem particularly easy or hard to read, particularly well or poorly written. Can you identify features *on the page* that make those pages seem better or worse? Try revising the ones you find difficult.

4. Select a passage from a past paper in which your language is bland, pallid, or otherwise indistinctive. Rewrite it to be as vivid as you can. Use words that are specific, imageable, slangy, emotional, and so on. Have you improved it?

A GUIDE TO TERMS

Clear Language

To understand how readers will judge writing, you have to know how sentences work, and to do that you need to know a few terms: *noun, subject, verb, main/independent clause, subordinate/dependent clause, active* and *passive*. The clause is the basic unit of understanding, so we'll start there.

Clauses and Phrases

A clause consists of a subject and verb and whatever attaches to them. These are clauses, because they have both a subject (underlined) and a verb (bold-faced):

> <u>dogs</u> **bark**
>
> <u>the analysis of style</u> **depends** on knowing how to tell a good story
>
> once <u>you</u> **understand** subjects and verbs
>
> although <u>few of us</u> **write** clearly

These phrases are not clauses because they do not have both a subject and verb:

a basic unit of style	subjects and verbs	is the sentence
the sentence	write a first draft	few of us

Those units are phrases, sequences of words that "hang together" as a unit. A phrase consists of a "head" word (a noun, verb, adjective, or adverb) with words and phrases attached to it. Here, for example, is a noun phrase that contains an adjective phrase, that in turn contains an adverbial phrase: (the boldfaced words are the "head-words" of each phrase):

> NOUN PHRASE: a very easily identifiable **style**
>
> ADJECTIVE PHRASE: very easily **identifiable**
>
> ADVERBIAL PHRASE: very **easily**

On the other hand, these are not phrases, because they don't hang together:

basic unit of	subjects and	is the
to tell a good	a clear first	of style depends on

Independent Versus Dependent Clauses

We have to distinguish two kinds of clauses: *dependent* and *independent*. (Some use the terms *subordinate* and *main*.)

Independent Clauses   By definition, an independent clause does not depend on anything else and so can be punctuated as a freestanding sentence. These are independent clauses with subjects underlined and verbs boldfaced:

> <u>The basic unit of style</u> **is** the sentence.
>
> <u>You</u> **should understand** subjects and verbs.
>
> <u>Readers</u> **look** for subjects to understand what a sentence is about.

We do not begin independent clauses with subordinating conjunctions such as *because, if, when, although, since, as,* and so on. But contrary to what some say, we can begin an independent clause with a coordinating conjunction: *and, or, but, yet, so, for.* We also call an independent clause the *main clause* of a sentence:

> Though I stayed, _{subordinate clause} **he left** _{main clause} because he was tired. _{subordinate clause}

Dependent (Subordinate) Clauses   A dependent clause depends on something else. You can usually identify it by an introductory word signaling its dependency. There are three kinds of dependent clauses: (1) adverb clauses, (2) adjective clauses, and (3) noun clauses.

1. Adverb Clauses:

Adverb clauses indicate time, place, manner, cause, condition, and so on: they usually begin with an adverbial conjunction such as *because, if, when, although, before, as, since,* and *unless.* In what follows, we italicize words that signal dependency, underline subjects, and boldface verbs:

> *because* <u>readers</u> **look** for the subject of a sentence
>
> *if* <u>you</u> **want** to write clearly
>
> *unless* <u>your argument</u> **addresses** a conceptual problem

Most adverbial clauses can be moved:

> *Because readers look for the subject of a sentence,* <u>the best editors</u> **start** revising by looking at subjects.
>
> The <u>best editors</u> **start** revising by looking at subjects *because readers look for the subject of a sentence.*
>
> The <u>best editors</u>, *because readers look for the subject of a sentence,* **start** revising by looking at subjects.

When you punctuate an adverbial clause as a separate sentence, you create what writing teachers call a *fragment:*

> The best editors start revising by looking at subjects. Because readers look first for the subject of your sentence. _{fragment}

2. Adjective Clauses:

Adjective clauses modify nouns. They usually begin with one of these relative pronouns: *who, whom, whose, which, that,* and *where.*

a book ~noun~ *that* **is** hard to read ~adjective clause~

a point in the story ~noun~ *where* <u>the reader</u> **stops** ~adjective clause~

Relative clauses usually occur after the noun they modify, but there are exceptions:

<u>Some people</u> *who don't deserve to succeed* **do**.

<u>Some people</u> **succeed** *who don't deserve to*.

When you punctuate an adjective clause as a separate sentence, you again create a *fragment:*

Before we could repair the engine, we had to drill out bolts. Which were so rusted that they were frozen onto the frame. ~fragment~

3. **Noun Clauses:**

Noun clauses can be subjects or objects. They typically begin with the same words that adjective clauses do: *who, what, which, that, where.*

[*That* <u>*your argument*</u> **will fail**] ~noun clause as subject~ **is** always possible.

<u>Your reader</u> wants to know [*why* <u>you</u> **have raised** the problem]. ~noun clause as object~

Subjects and Verbs

It is hard to define subjects and verbs separately, because each defines the other. There can be no subject without a verb or verb without at least an implied subject (as in commands: *[You] stop!*).

Verbs

You may remember being told that a verb is an "action" word. That definition works in this sentence:

<u>He</u> **revised** his prose carefully.

But not for this sentence:

<u>His revision of his prose</u> **was** careful.

The verb is *was,* but the real action is in the subject, *revision.*

Though we cannot define a verb easily, we can tell you how to identify one: A verb is the word whose ending you change when you change past to present, present to future, future to past, etc. Do that in two steps:

1. Decide whether the sentence refers to the past, the present, or the future. For example, this sentence refers to a past action:

   Studies of the problem **were** conducted by the staff.

2. Change the time, in this case from past to present:

   Studies of the problem **are being** conducted by the staff.

The words you change are verbs (ignore words like *today, tomorrow,* etc.).

For our purposes, we also count as verbs what follows the word *to:*

The need <u>to</u> **review** the program **caused** us <u>to</u> **hire** more staff.

We call these "infinitives."

Subjects

You may also recall being told that the subject of a sentence is the "doer" of the action expressed by the verb. That is true for many sentences:

<u>We</u> **made** mistakes when <u>we</u> **tried** to **explain** why <u>the project</u> **failed.**

But that definition of subject as "doer" doesn't work with a sentence like this:

<u>Our explanation of the failure of the project</u> **had** mistakes in it.

In the first sentence, the subjects are *we* and *the project,* and both seem to do things: *make mistakes, try to explain,* and *fail.* In the second, however, the subject is a series of actions: *explanation of the failure.* The verb, *had,* refers to no action at all.

We have asked you to notice two kinds of subjects, what we have called the *simple* subject and *whole* subject.

Simple Subjects   The simple subject is just the single word that the verb agrees with in number:

Our *need* to work toward compromise on these problems **was** obvious.

The *answers* offered in response to the question **were** not helpful.

A *problem* and its *solution* **are** at the heart of every argument.

(When a subject is compound, there are two-word simple subjects: *He and I* **left.**)

Whole Subjects   The whole subject is the simple subject and everything attached to it:

<u>Our *need* to work toward compromise on these problems</u> **was** obvious.

Here's a way to identify whole subjects and simple subjects:

1. Locate the verb as described earlier:
    Our need to work toward compromise on these problems **was** obvious.
2. Turn the sentence into a question by putting *who* or *what* before the verb:
    What **was** obvious?

The most complete answer is the whole subject:

<u>Our need to work toward compromise on these problems</u> **was** obvious.

The shortest possible answer is the simple subject:

(Our) <u>need</u> **was** obvious.

Active and Passive Voice

Grammatically, we define "active" and "passive" voice by three criteria:

1. The subject of an active verb feels like a "doer" doing something to the object of the verb:

   <u>The collapse of a dead star</u> _{subject} **creates** _{verb} a black hole. _{object}

   The subject of a passive verb, on the other hand, is the object toward which the action is directed:

   <u>A black hole in space</u> _{subject} **is created** by . . .

2. The passive verb always has a form of *be* in front of it and is in its past participle form: **is created.** (You also create a past participle when you put *have* before a verb: *has gone, has seen, has stopped.*)

3. An active verb has an object: . . . **creates** a black hole. A passive verb, on the other hand, may (or may not) be followed by a prepositional phrase beginning with *by* naming the doer of the action expressed by the verb.

   A black hole is created (**by** the collapse of a dead star).

When you talk about a passive style, you have to distinguish what is grammatically passive from what only *feels* passive. This next sentence is passive in the technical, grammatical sense:

<u>Poor people</u> **are** often **deprived** of food.

This next sentence is not passive in that grammatical sense, but it certainly feels passive because its subject is a nominalization:

<u>Deprivation of food</u> often **afflicts** poor people.

Nouns, Adjectives, Adverbs, and Prepositions

Nouns

You may recall being told that a noun refers to a person, place, or thing. To make that definition work, we would have to group under "thing" anything that we already know is a noun. In this next sentence, the nouns are boldfaced:

> The **success** of the **program** was hampered by an endless **series** of **problems** whose **solutions** were wholly beyond our **ability** to implement.

We call the boldfaced words *things* not because they are literally "things," like rocks and chairs, but because we know they are nouns and we think of nouns as things by definition. A simpler definition of a noun is anything that fits this frame:

(The) _____ is good.

To understand how we judge prose, we distinguish three kinds of nouns:

1. Nouns that are concrete: *chair, book, person, car, tree, door, sky, stairs.*
2. Nouns that are intrinsically nouns, but abstract: *law, series, motion, strategy, vision, effort, shape.*

3. Nouns that are abstract because they are derived from verbs or adjectives: *movement, investigation, resemblance, responsibility, equivalence.*

The technical term for a noun derived from a verb or adjective is *nominalization.*

Adjectives
You can identify most adjectives by trying them out in this frame:

That is very _____.

Some adjectives like *additional* and *molecular* do not fit, but it is a handy guide. Like verbs, most adjectives can be nominalized: *intelligent* → *intelligence.*

Adverbs
Some adverbs are derived from adjectives: *careful* → *carefully.* Others are intrinsically adverbs: *often, very, rather,* and so on. They modify verbs, adjectives, and other adverbs.

Prepositions
Prepositions are easier to list than to define: *of, by, with, for, in, out, over, under, beside, before, after, at, on, into, . . .*

IN A NUTSHELL

About Your Prose . . .

You cannot read your own prose as your readers will, because you know too well what you wanted it to mean when you wrote it and so it will always be clear to you. To overcome that obstacle, you need a way to diagnose your prose objectively. Here are six principles of clear writing to take not as ironclad rules for every sentence but as advice about how most of them should work:

1. Make your important characters the subjects of verbs. If they are abstractions, be sure that they are terms familiar to your readers.
2. Express the important actions not in abstract nouns but in verbs.
3. Get to the verb in the main clause quickly:

    Avoid long introductory elements.

    Keep whole subjects short.

    Don't interrupt subject + verb connections with long phrases or clauses.
4. Begin your sentences with information that seems familiar to your readers.
5. End sentences with information that seems new to them.
6. Keep your subjects consistent by using as subjects your most familiar characters. Avoid beginning successive sentences with unexpectedly different subjects.

In addition to writing sentences with distinct subjects and verbs, work to write prose that is concise and vivid. You do that in three ways:

- Avoid using words that add little or nothing to your ideas, such as *very, basically, really,* and so on.

- Avoid decomposing a meaning into several words if you can express it in a single word: *do not pay attention to* → *ignore.*

- Avoid stating what a word implies: *it was red ~~in color.~~ Future events will unexpectedly surprise us.* → *The future will surprise us.*

You are likely to write more vividly if you choose words that are common and down to earth: *belly button* rather than *navel.* Some writers, such as newspaper editorial writers, rarely use either slang or more formal words, sticking to a middle style. Other writers use a lot of slang and no formal words; still others—scientists, for example—use no slang and all formal words. And some good writers include an occasional formal or slang expression to give their prose a little kick.

Another way to create a vivid style is to choose a word that conjures up an image in the mind of your readers. Just about every word is on a scale of words that range from general to specific. But for many scales, there is a break point where one word creates no particular image in our minds, but the next more specific one does: *object – weapon – gun – pistol – Glock 19.* We might have a vague image associated with *gun,* but *pistol* has a more distinct one.

Some arguments need words that are general and abstract enough to avoid evoking feelings, to assert general philosophical principles, or to lay down warrants and assumptions that govern specific cases.

. . . and About Revising It

First, diagnose your prose: Underline the first seven or eight words in each major clause. (Ignore short introductory phrases and clauses, especially when they refer to previous sentences.) Consider revising if you see these characteristics:

- Subjects are not a specific character named in a short phrase.
- By the seventh or eighth word, you do not see a verb.
- Those first seven or eight words express new information.
- Several sentences in a row keep changing subjects.

Revise like this:

1. Start by finding the important characters.
2. Identify the key actions they perform.

3. Revise so that most of your sentences begin with important characters as subjects and are immediately followed by key actions in verbs.

4. When you find a long introductory phrase, rewrite it into a sentence or clause of its own.

When you find a long subject, consider these revisions:

1. Revise it into an introductory subordinate clause.

2. Revise it into a sentence of its own.

When you find a long interrupting element between the subject and verb, move it to the beginning or end of its sentence, depending on whether it connects more closely to the preceding sentence or to the one that follows.

CHAPTER 13

The Overt and Covert
Force of Language

*In this chapter, we look at how words express values and evoke feelings,
shaping belief in ways that are both obvious and subtle, sometimes even
dishonest—not to help you be dishonest, but to make you aware of the power
of language to lead and mislead. We discuss how the subjects of sentences
influence who or what readers see as responsible for events and how metaphors enliven prose but may also mislead readers—and writers as well.*

When we write clearly, concisely, and vividly, we help readers get through
our argument quickly, understand it easily, and remember it accurately.
But the force of language goes deeper than that. We can use words to evoke
values and feelings that not only color but shape our readers' reasoning.

Invoking Values, Evoking Feeling

Value-Laden Words

We color how readers feel about our arguments when we use words that invoke
their values. If we oppose a cut in the income tax, for example, we might claim
that the cut will

> stuff the wallets of those fat cats who already hoard most of our nation's
> wealth.

But if we support the cut, we might argue that it will

> restore to American workers some of our hard-earned wages that the IRS
> sucks out of our paychecks every week.

Both descriptions arguably refer to the same circumstance, but the words
invoke different values: *stuff the wallets, fat cats,* and *sit on our nation's wealth*
versus *restore to American workers, hard-earned wages,* and *IRS sucks out* (not to
mention the more subtle ***those*** *fat cats* versus ***our*** *paychecks*).

We see such value-laden language most often in politics and advertising. Ads are covert arguments whose unexpressed main claim is obvious enough: *Buy this product.* But they usually support their claims more with feelings than with reasons. For example, look at the language of this ad for Lady Foot Locker, in a fashion magazine for older teens:

> Sure, working out's all fabulous the first month or so. And then somehow, the treadmill is about as appealing as that ex-boyfriend of yours with the color coordination issues. Luckily, new Nike Tuned Air (with the perfect combination of cushioning and stability) can help you fall in love with your workout all over again. Which is more than we can say for your ex.

This ad wants readers to imagine the tedium of working out when they read *the treadmill is about as appealing as that ex-boyfriend of yours with the color coordination issues.* But that language relies on values (as in *color coordination issues*) that only some women share. How would readers of a woman's body-building magazine respond?

Values in Academic Writing

In academic writing, you will rarely see words as value-laden as *swell the wallets of those fat cats who already hoard most of our nation's wealth.* That kind of language in a political science paper would damage your credibility. Academic readers expect you to project an ethos of cool, objective distance. That does not mean you eliminate all signs of value in your writing. (You couldn't if you tried.) You might, for example, write in a political science paper how the tax cut would *augment the personal wealth of those who already control most of the nation's resources.* That kind of language reflects values but does not seem crudely emotional.

You Can't Avoid Values

Some argue that we betray the spirit of fair, rational argument when we use value-laden language of any kind, because it "slants" or "biases" our argument. We should appeal, they claim, not to our readers' warmest feelings but to their coolest logic. Following that principle, both sides in the tax cut debate could describe it in terms emptied of emotion:

> The tax reduction will augment the financial resources of those with the highest incomes.

> The tax cut will raise net earned income for everyone.

But even when you drain language of emotion, as those two sentences almost do, you still project a value—that of dispassionate objectivity.

You begin choosing values the moment you frame your problem. The Supreme Court, for example, will eventually decide an issue that contending parties frame in different ways, reflecting their different values:

The right to assisted suicide	vs.	The duty of the state to prevent physicians from killing their patients
The right to a dignified end of life	vs.	The duty of the state to protect the helpless
The sanctity of bodily privacy	vs.	The sanctity of life

We gain a big advantage if we can get those who have to decide an issue to accept our way of framing the discussion, because that imposes on others the burden of denying our self-evident lofty values. Who can reject the value of human dignity or, alternatively, the sanctity of life? Those who can frame an issue in their own terms usually prevail.

When those with different views frame an issue around values, they often focus on the same referents out there in the world. In that case, we are limited in what words we can choose by the nature of those referents: the phrase *massive tax cut* cannot refer to the same thing that others call *a minor adjustment in rates;* those we call *fabulously rich* cannot also be called *dirt poor*. Readers would judge one (or even both) of those contrary terms to be at least exaggerated, if not plain false.

But within those limits we do have room to choose words that support our case. For example, those different ways of framing the issue of assisted suicide refer to the *same* referent, choosing to die. But when we use the terms "the sanctity of bodily privacy" or "the sanctity of life," we frame that issue in different sets of values. That's why two people can look at exactly the same referent but disagree over how to name it:

Lee is a reckless daydreamer!	No, he is a daring visionary!
Jones is a chauvinist reactionary!	No, he is a patriotic conservative!

We could probably agree that if Jones is anything like a left-wing, flag-burning radical, he cannot arguably be called a *chauvinist reactionary*. They are just different things. But what if he waves the flag, speaks proudly of his country, is against gun control and for a constitutional amendment banning flag burning? He could arguably be called either a *chauvinist* or a *patriot*. So which is he?

In cases like this, we can't rely on common criteria of meaning or features of the referent to decide what someone or something *is* (review pp. 249–50). In fact, we ask the wrong question when we ask *What **is** Jones, a chauvinist or a patriot?*

What we *call* him depends less on what he *objectively* is than on what we think is at stake in using one term or the other—that is, on what problem we solve by getting others to agree to call him that. If we think we can solve the problem by getting people to think well of him, we call him *a conservative patriot;* if we can solve it by getting people to think badly of him, we call him *a chauvinist reactionary*. We *first* decide what problem we want to solve by naming Jones; *then* we pick the terms that support our solution. In matters like this, the debate over what to call Jones is almost certainly a surrogate argument for a larger issue (review pp. 250–51).

When Emotional Language Undermines Sound Thinking

It is fair to use value-laden words to elicit feelings in your readers, so long as your argument is otherwise sound. In fact, for some matters you would be wrong not to enlist your readers' emotional commitment. Given what's at stake in assisted suicide, those debating the issue are right to appeal to our deepest feelings, but not at the cost of our best critical thinking. The risk in emotional language is that it does just that. In this matter, everyone who makes a thoughtful argument has a duty not to invoke feelings in others that replace careful thought.

Polarizing Language

If you call your views *sincere, normal,* and *reasoned,* you imply that those who hold different views must be *cynical, abnormal,* and *irrational,* thereby demonizing them. If your reader is not *pro-choice,* then she must be *anti-choice;* if not *pro-life,* then *anti-life.* That kind of language encourages us to reason in what are called *disjunctive syllogisms:*

> You are either a conservative or a liberal.
>
> You are not conservative?
>
> Therefore, you must be a liberal.

> The answer to the drug problem is either punishment or treatment.
>
> You think that more treatment programs are the answer?
>
> Therefore, you must be against tough drug laws.

In both examples, the reasoning is formally valid but substantively false, because it offers what seem to be mutually exclusive alternatives that in fact are not:

- Maybe both choices are right. Maybe we need both tougher laws and new drug treatment programs.
- Maybe we need *slightly* tougher laws and *some* new treatment programs.
- Maybe both are wrong and a third choice is right—more education.
- Maybe both are right along with the third choice.

Reality is almost always more complex than *either-or* language allows. You owe readers a duty to avoid not only making issues more complex than they have to be, but also, as Einstein once said, no simpler than they really are.

Respecting Differences of Degree

Here is how a prominent evolutionary biologist explains our need to find opposing features that definitively distinguish us from apes:

> We have generally tried to unite our intellectual duty to accept the established fact of evolutionary continuity with our continuing psychological need to see ourselves

as separate and superior, by invoking one of our worst and oldest mental habits: dichotomization, or division into two opposite categories, usually with attributions of value expressed as good and bad or higher and lower. We therefore try to define a "golden barrier," a firm criterion to mark an unbridgeable gap between the mentality and behavior of humans and all other creatures. We may have evolved from them, but at some point in our advance, we crossed a Rubicon that brooks no passage by any other species. . . . The basic formulation of them vs. us, and the resulting search for a "golden barrier," represents a deep fallacy of human thought. We need not fear Darwin's correct conclusion that we differ from other animals only in degree. A sufficient difference in quantity translates into what we call a difference in quality *ipso facto*. A frozen pond is not the same object as a boiling pool—and New York City does not represent a mere extension of the tree nests [of chimpanzees in their native habitat] at Gombé.[a]

[a]Stephen Jay Gould, "The Human Difference," *New York Times*, July 2, 1999.

Cynical Language

If intensely value-laden language can undermine sound thinking, it can also betray the ethical duty we owe our readers. In fact, we must condemn as ethically corrupt those who cynically use words to appeal to feelings alone. In recent elections, for example, political consultants have circulated lists of words that they urged their clients to use:

- To incite animosity toward their opponents, politicians were told to call them *liberals* and *liars,* to say they were *extreme, radical, wasteful, corrupt,* and *hypocritical* and to refer to themselves as *pioneers* with *vision,* as *fair* and *moral,* dedicated to principles of *truth* and *courage.*

- To exploit voters' decency, they were advised to talk about their own *pride in America,* their *families, common sense,* and *duty,* and to accuse others of *betraying* the *common good* by their *greed* and even *treason.*

Those words convey more than different shades of meaning, because we know that the difference between *courage* and *treason* is more than political "spin." When politicians use language cynically, they corrupt our civic life by undermining the foundations of our democracy, not just because they substitute feeling for thinking, but because they teach us to distrust all political discourse. As bad money drives out good, cynical language drives out thoughtful argument.

In addition to your ethical duty to avoid dishonest language, you also have a pragmatic reason: No matter how persuasive you think strong language is, it alienates thoughtful readers, because it discredits any way of looking at an issue other than your own, and that damages your ethos. To be sure, when you use moderate language, you risk being called wishy-washy by those taking a with-us-or-against-us attitude. And in some cases, nuanced language is wrong. Many people couldn't believe that Hitler was as unqualifiedly evil as he turned out to be. But except for such rare cases, you do well to err on the side of moderation, because nuanced language encourages nuanced thinking, in both you and your reader. Strong language might make you feel good, but it can also make you look very bad.

Emotional Language and Ethos

Here a reviewer complains that a writer of an otherwise good book loses credibility because of its extreme language:

> [The author] makes his claims about Allied capabilities [to destroy German concentration camps during World War II] mostly persuasive, but does so in a style as dogmatic and vindictive as that of some of the "myth" purveyors he condemns. . . . Such invective detracts from his weighty evidence and illustrates a disturbing trend: some scholars shout as if engaged in "McLaughlin Group" combat or the exposé culture of the tabloids. Gray academic prose presents its own problems, and [the author] is not the first on this subject to shout. But his tone can cheapen his valuable scholarship.[a]

[a]Ann Finkbeiner, *New York Times Book Review,* October 12, 1999.

Subjects and Point of View

In Chapter 12, we showed you that what readers take from sentences is not the words themselves, but a story—images, scenes, a mental scenario. That is why the most readable prose is storylike, with the key elements of sentences—subjects and verbs—matching key elements of a story—characters and actions. But storytelling offers an opportunity not only to be clear but to shape how readers understand and judge by focusing them on particular characters.

Manipulating Subjects to Assign Responsibility

With every sentence you write, you have to decide who or what to make its subject and thereby its main character. But more than that, when you choose to make one character rather than another the subject of a sentence, you impose on your readers a point of view toward the story the sentence tells. For example, compare these pairs of sentences; both sentences in each pair arguably refer to the same state of affairs in the world.

  1a. Smith obtained stolen goods from Jones.

  1b. Jones provided stolen goods to Smith.

  2a. We learn from history that we need free speech to strengthen democracy.

  2b. History teaches us that a democracy grows strong from free speech.

If the first sentence in each pair is true, then arguably so is the second. But we respond to them differently because each assigns responsibility to a different character, imposing on us different points of view about who is responsible.

Subjects and the Nature of Things

We might think that subjects are somehow in the nature of things "doers" of actions:

> The dog **chased** the cat for a while before he finally **caught** her.

In the world, the dog did something to the cat; so it seems natural to make the dog the subject of *chase* and *caught*. But events do not determine subjects of sentences. We can *choose* to make the cat the center of attention:

> The cat **ran away** from the dog until it finally **got caught.**

By reshaping that sentence around the cat, we change which character seems to claim the center of our attention.

That story, of course, is a trivial one. Here is one that is more consequential:

> Reporters grilled the mayor until they finally got the admission they wanted: Companies owned by his friends who got contracts with the city contributed more than $100,000 to his campaign.

> The mayor went through a grilling from reporters until he finally admitted what he had tried not to reveal: He had taken more than $100,000 in campaign contributions from friends whose companies got contracts with the city.

The first sentence focuses on the press and the companies; the second on the mayor. Which is "truer"? Wrong question: if one is true, so arguably is the other. The right question is which better serves the aims of an argument. Who does the writer want us to focus on as the responsible character, the mayor or the press?

We tend to remember best the character that appears most often in subjects, and we tend to make that character most responsible for what happened in a story. So by managing the subjects of sentences, deft writers can get us to make judgments without consciously knowing that we have, much less why.

Managing Subjects by Managing Verbs

To manage subjects, however, you have to manage verbs. The easiest way to change subjects is to shift between active and passive verbs:

> My friend **taught** me Spanish.

> I **was taught** Spanish by my friend.

> We **recorded** the fluid velocity at thirty-second intervals.

> The fluid velocity **was recorded** at thirty-second intervals.

(Those of you in technical fields will write many sentences like that last one, because technical writers usually tell stories about things like velocity or fluids rather than about those who measure them.)

A more subtle technique is to find verbs that tell roughly the same story, but from different points of view:

<u>My friend</u> **taught** me Spanish.

<u>I</u> **learned** Spanish from my friend.

<u>George</u> **bought** a handgun from Fred.

<u>Fred</u> **sold** a handgun to George.

Sometimes, we have to think hard to find alternatives:

<u>The New York Yankees</u> **are losing** fans to the Mets.

<u>The New York Mets</u> **are attracting** fans from the Yankees.

<u>Fans</u> **are moving** from the Yankees to the Mets.

All three sentences arguably refer to the same action "out there," but lead us to assign the responsibility for that action to different characters.

When you make an argument that depends on making one character responsible for an action, make that character the subject of as many verbs as you can. When you want to downplay the role of a character, make that character anything but the subject of an action.

Treating Means as Agents

Another way to shift responsibility from flesh-and-blood actors to an object is just this side of metaphor:

I can't buy love with money.	→	Money can't buy me love.
You can conquer all with love.	→	Love conquers all.

The English language lets us make that kind of transformation systematically:

A does B to C by means of D		D does B to C
I cut my finger with the knife.	→	The knife cut my finger.
You can't buy love with money.	→	Money can't buy me love.
You can conquer all with love.	→	Love conquers all.

As common and as innocuous as this stylistic device seems, people argue over it. We've all seen or heard the slogan on this bumper sticker:

> **Guns don't kill, people do.**

Those who oppose gun control focus on the agents of shootings—people; those who support it focus on the means—guns. Thus we have a battle over two forms of the "same" concept, one a transformation of the other:

A does B to C by means of D		D does B to C
People kill people with guns.	→	Guns kill people.

This pattern also lets you attribute a claim to an objective-seeming source:

<u>We</u> **have proved** with these data that we need a raise.	→	<u>These data</u> **prove** that we need a raise.
In their recent study, <u>Smith and Yang</u> **found** evidence from which <u>they</u> **conclude** that <u>those who smoke</u> **become** prematurely senile.	→	<u>A recent study (Smith and Yang, 1997)</u> **found** <u>evidence</u> **pointing** to the conclusion that <u>smoking</u> **causes** premature senility.
	→	<u>Evidence from a recent study (Smith and Yang, 1997)</u> **points** to the conclusion that <u>premature senility</u> **results** from smoking.

Those sentences refer to the same "facts," but each slants who or what is responsible for actions and outcomes in a different way. So, think twice when you read a sentence suggesting that a "study" or "evidence" "proves" something, because such a sentence conceals an important variable: the human judgment behind the evidence.

Language and Responsibility

Shortly after 15-year-old Andrew Williams killed two classmates at Santana High School in March 2001, Daniel R. Weinberger of the National Institute of Health explained how the pre-frontal cortex controls impulsive behavior but does not fully mature until a person is close to 20 years old. He wrote this in conclusion:

> This brief lesson in brain development is not meant to absolve criminal behavior or make the horrors any less unconscionable. But the shooter at Santana High, like other adolescents, needed people or institutions to prevent him from being in a potentially deadly situation where his immature brain was left to its own devices. No matter what the town or the school, if a gun is put in the control of the prefrontal cortex of a hurt and vengeful 15-year-old, and it is pointed at a human target, it will very likely go off.[a]

Notice in the last sentence how Weinberger de-emphasizes Williams's responsibility by making *a gun* the main character: *a gun is put. . . , it is pointed. . . , it will very likely go off.*

[a]Daniel R. Weinberger, "A Brain Too Young for Good Judgment," *New York Times*, March 10, 2001, p. A27.

Abstractions as Characters

Another way to shift responsibility takes us into the realm of metaphor:

<u>Life</u> **finds** a way.

<u>Nature</u> always **tells** us <u>when</u> <u>she</u> **thinks** we have violated her laws.

<u>Duty</u> **requires** us to <u>sacrifice</u>.

We turn *Nature* into a person by making it the subject of verbs implying human action, such as *tell* and *think*. The technical term for doing that is *reification;* we also call it *personifying* or *anthropomorphizing,* which means to treat something not human as if it were. It is a kind of metaphor.

Sometimes we reify abstractions to deflect readers from a human cause:

> Science **has** the power to <u>reveal</u> nature's laws, but <u>it</u> **cannot define** our values; only <u>religious faith</u> **can guide** us down the moral path.

When we think about science and religion, we typically prefer not to focus on the fact that both are constructed through human action. So few writers would revise that sentence into this:

> <u>Scientists</u> **have** the <u>power</u> to **reveal** the patterns in the natural world, but <u>they</u> **cannot define** our values; only <u>religious leaders</u> **can guide** us down the moral path.

More commonly, however, we reify abstractions not to hide human agency but to express matters too complex for readers to picture easily. If we say,

> Your ethical <u>responsibility</u> **demands** that you resign.

we are not deflecting attention from some obvious agent:

> <u>People</u> **will think** you <u>are</u> unethical if you do not resign.

Instead, by reifying abstractions, we describe a situation in which there are no specific agents as if there were. Similarly, when the scientist in the movie *Jurassic Park* warns that the cloned dinosaurs will reproduce despite the efforts to prevent it, he says,

> <u>Life</u> **finds** a way.

He is not hiding a human agent, but using the reified abstraction to describe a situation without one.

By no means is reification always dishonest or unethical. Indeed, in our most revered political document, the drafters of the Declaration of Independence did just that. Here are just two examples, with our translations:

> *Original:*   . . . <u>a decent respect</u> to the opinions of mankind **requires** that they should declare the causes which impel them to the separation.
>
> *Revised:*   If <u>we</u> decently **respect** the opinions of mankind, <u>we</u> **should** declare why we do so.
>
> *Original:*   . . . such is now <u>the necessity</u> which **constrains** them to alter their former systems of government.
>
> *Revised:*   As a result, <u>we</u> **decided** that <u>we</u> **must** alter our former system of government.

In the first original sentence, the drafters reach past specifics to generalities. In the second, they use a metaphor that makes them not free to act, but an oppressed people forced to act by circumstances and duty: *necessity constrains them to alter.* These reifications are not just clever wordplay, because the rest of the Declaration is a model of sound reasoning. The drafters used reifications not to mislead but to support a larger and more complex argument.

Metaphorical Scenarios

The most dramatic way we use language to shape belief is by spinning out metaphorical scenarios. Metaphors can do more than reify a single abstraction. They can create a virtual world in which we play out many implications, some illuminating, some misleading. The problem is that when we create a metaphor, we may imply things we do not mean.

We earlier discussed two metaphors and some of their consequences: argument as war and communication as shipping a package of meaning. The two metaphors are easy to combine:

> I will *advance* my claims as *forcefully* as I can until you *yield* to the weight of my evidence. But if you can just *see into* my thinking about this, you'll *get* the picture.

In that sentence, we imagine two ways of coming to agreement: We force a claim on a reader, or the reader can look inside the argument to find its meaning.

We can imagine a different model for communication: guiding readers along a path that gets them from here to there:

> I will *lead* you *through* a line of reasoning that together we can *follow* to *reach* agreement.

So what if these metaphors differ? They invite us to see an event in different ways, and those differences may have consequences. For example, what if your reader fails to agree with your argument?

- If argument is war, then you lose the battle because you are too weak or your reader too strong.
- If communication is a bundle of meaning sent and received, you can blame yourself for packaging it badly or the reader for unwrapping it incorrectly.
- If communication is a path down which you lead readers, you can blame yourself for being a bad guide or your reader for being a bad follower.

A metaphor can also be so vivid that it creates networks of implications that critical thinkers know are simply wrong. Consider these metaphors:

- A school official explains why a student was suspended from school for expounding unpopular ideas:

> That kind of hate speech is a *virulence* we had to *stamp out.* We *isolated* the student because his *sick* views could have *infected* and *spread through* our community.

Beliefs are not communicable diseases, but the metaphor encourages us to think that it is in the public interest to quarantine those who might spread unpopular ideas.

- An environmentalist defends those who vandalize logging equipment:

  > A living thing has the *right* to protect itself from predators. And if it cannot *defend* itself, then those who love it have a duty to do so. The redwoods cannot *defend* themselves, so we who *love* them must *defend* them and *punish* their *attackers.* That's *nature's law.*

Trees do not have rights; only people do. But if we think in terms of "nature's law," then the metaphors of prosecution, defense, and punishment follow.

- A police officer might say this about the accidental shooting of an innocent person in a drug raid on the wrong apartment:

  > The *war* on drugs is no picnic. *Wars* have *casualties,* but that can't stop us from *fighting* an *enemy* that *attacks* innocent children. We cannot *surrender* to the *tyranny* of heroin and cocaine.

In the heat of battle, armed forces kill innocents, but should we judge police as we do soldiers? In short, metaphors can infiltrate our thinking and shape it in ways that are seriously misleading.

We do not say that you should never use value words, manipulate subjects, reify abstractions, or create metaphors. We cannot think without metaphors. Just be aware of the language you choose, because unless you think critically, it can mislead not only your readers, but yourself.

The Use and Abuse of Natural Selection

Scientists have long personified nature. When Darwin called evolution *natural selection,* he helped his readers understand a complex matter through a memorable metaphor: Nature selects those species most fit to survive. He combined an agent his readers knew well, *Mother Nature,* with a process they also knew well, *selective breeding:*

> We have seen that man by selection can produce great results, and can adapt organic beings to his own uses, through the accumulation of slight but useful variations, given to him by the hand of Nature. But Natural Selection . . . is immeasurably superior to man's feeble efforts as the works of Nature are to those of Art. (*Origin of Species,* ch. 2)

When Darwin defended natural selection against the charge that he spoke of it "as an active power of Deity," he pointed out that scientists had done the same for centuries: magnets **attract** or **repel** one another, gravity **holds** the planets in their orbits, water **finds** its own level. He claimed this was a harmless way of talking because "Every one knows what is meant and is implied by such metaphorical expressions" (*Origin*, ch. 4).

Perhaps, but Darwin could not predict how others would use his metaphor. At the end of the nineteenth century, John D. Rockefeller used *natural selection* and its rugged cousin, *the survival of the fittest,* to defend his brutal business practices:

> The growth of a large business is merely the survival of the fittest. . . . The American Beauty rose can be produced . . . only by sacrificing the early buds which grow up around it. This is not an evil tendency in business. It is merely the working-out of a law of nature and a law of God.

It's a view still current today: "Darwin was right. Only the fittest survive—especially when the creatures involved are graying commodities companies battling in the pits of a downcycle."

Source: Robert Matthews, Susan Warren, and Bernard Wysocki, Jr., "Fitness Test: Alcoa-Reynolds Union Bears Stamp of Deals Rocking Commodities," *Wall Street Journal,* August 20, 1999.

WRITING PROCESS

The Overt and Covert Force of Language

DRAFTING

When to Think About Values

It is important to pay attention to how your language evokes values and feelings, but *when* you should pay attention depends on how you write.

- If you draft slowly, decide before you start the emotional tone you want readers to respond to and then watch your words as you draft.
- If you draft quickly, look at your words as you revise. Then ask how readers will respond and look for ways to make your tone consistent.

REVISING

Subjects and Point of View

After you are sure your prose is clear and direct, check whether you have used the subjects of your sentences to focus readers on those characters that you want them to see as most responsible for the events in your story. Here is a simple test:

1. Pick out the characters that your sentences focus on:

   - Circle or boldface the subject of each main clause and subordinate clause.

   - If an important character appears in a phrase before the subject, circle or boldface it. For example,

     Thinking about **politicians,** Americans cannot help but be cynical about the future of argument as a tool of democracy.

   Then if you can, revise so that the first character is the subject of the sentence:

   <u>**Politicians**</u> make most Americans cynical about the future of argument as a tool of democracy.

2. Have you repeated a few characters or used many different ones?

   - If you find a few, do you want readers to see them as your main characters? If not, revise so that they appear elsewhere in their sentences.

   - If you find many characters, would you improve your story by focusing on fewer?

3. Are your subject-characters people or abstractions?

   - If abstractions, are they so familiar to readers that they can build a story around them? If not, revise to focus on people or familiar abstractions.

INQUIRIES

REFLECTIONS

1. Look again at the Lady Foot Locker ad (p. 332). Its appeal to younger women goes beyond its language. It also uses the structure of a problem (and a fairy tale) as part of its pitch. See if you can match each sentence to one step in a problem statement, including common ground and claim/solution. Who is the hero who steps in to solve the reader's problem? Does this structural design appeal to the same values as the language? Would the idea of being saved by a hero be attractive to women who read body-building magazines? Adult singles magazines? Would it appeal to men?

2. Recently, the Heinz company changed its advertising to appeal to teens. After surveying them, its ad agency decided that they would ignore traditional appeals, so it created a TV spot that called Heinz "the rude ketchup" for making people wait and included in its print ads lines like "Will work for food" and "Can't help broccoli." What do these slogans imply about the values that the advertisers are trying to invoke among teens? Are those your values?

3. It is almost always easier to see the emotional charge in the language of those whose opinions we reject than of those with whom we agree. Why is that? What does that tell you about the role of emotion in your relationship to your readers?

TASKS

4. An issue much in the news is the question whether states should fund only public schools or any school parents choose. Proponents call it the "voucher system" or "school choice"; opponents call it "state funding of private schools." List different ways of stating this issue that reflect different stances on the question. (You can use the rights-and-duties pattern of the assisted suicide example, pp. 332–33.) Bring out as many facets of the debate as you can. Here are other issues: same-sex marriage, immigration, affirmative action, metal detectors in schools, school uniforms, seat-belt laws.

5. Can you write without using metaphors? Is it possible to be entirely literal in every sentence? In a paper for this or another class, find a passage of at least half a page in which you use no metaphors. Remember that metaphors are part of our everyday vocabulary, so look for covert metaphors that you might not notice in casual reading. If you find a passage without metaphor, add some. If you can't find a passage, pick one and try to rewrite it free of metaphor. Ask a friend to read both passages, with and without metaphors. Which does your friend like better? How do metaphors make you seem as a writer?

6. Science has a reputation for objectivity, but scientists use metaphors when they write. We saw how Darwin treated nature as a human agent in his key term *natural selection,* but that was a long time ago. If you are taking a science class, look through your textbook to see how many metaphors you can find, especially covert metaphors. If you find any, does that mean that the writer is not being objective? Why?

7. In addition to the two refications in the Declaration of Independence we pointed out on page 340, there are a few others. Find them, then decide why the drafters used them.

IN A NUTSHELL

About Your Prose . . .

All words imply values, so you cannot write in a completely value-free way. Your problem is to figure out what values you want to invoke, because values evoke feelings, and feelings are often as powerful an element in an argument as is "pure" logic.

The most difficult issues in framing a question arise not from polar oppositions—tall versus short or rich versus poor—but when you and your readers disagree about a point of view: *filthy rich* versus *wealthy, poor* versus *impoverished.* In such debates, you waste your time if you try to match criteria to features. Instead, you have to think clearly about the problem you are trying to solve. If one term solves the problem better than the other, then that is the term you argue for.

You use value-laden words unethically when you knowingly use them to replace the rational force of an argument, rather than to augment it. When you use polarizing words, you polarize choices. You force your reader to be with you or against you, rather than somewhere in between, which is where most thoughtful people find themselves. Polarizing language squeezes out nuance, moderation, and complexity.

Every story has more than one character, so you can tell your story from different points of view. You make a character dominate a passage when you make it the subject of all or most of its sentences. Readers then focus on that character as responsible for most of the events in that part of your story.

. . . and About Writing It

- If you are a slow drafter, watch your words as you draft. Decide on an emotional tone before you begin drafting.

- If you are a fast drafter, pay attention to your words later in the revision stage.

You lead readers to focus on a character by working that character into the subjects of sentences. You do that in at least six ways:

- You can switch between active and passive verbs, which is the simplest way: *I recorded the observations* versus *The observations were recorded.*

- You can find verbs that let you move into the subject the character you want readers to focus on: *I bought a car from you* versus *You sold a car to me.*

- You can displace a feeling onto what makes you feel that way: *I had a hard time solving that problem* versus *That problem is difficult.*

- You can move the means or instrumentality of an action into a subject: *You can't buy happiness with money* versus *Money can't buy happiness.*

- You can reify abstractions by making them subjects of verbs you usually use with flesh-and-blood characters: *Love conquers all.*

- You can create metaphoric scenarios: *Racism contaminates the thinking of many people.*

Checklists for Planning and Revising

We have recommended that when you make an argument you ask yourself and your readers many questions. But if you are new to writing arguments, their number may overwhelm you. (You'll find more than ninety in the complete list below.) Not even the most experienced writers can hold them all in mind, much less systematically answer them. As you gain experience, however, you'll find that you won't need to think about them all, because you'll answer most of them without asking. But since even the most experienced writers need help to see their work objectively, we include here four checklists for looking at aspects of your paper. The first three you can run through quickly. The last is a complete list for when you have time to revise more carefully. At the end, you'll find a step-by-step procedure for storyboarding a long paper.

A Checklist for Evaluating Discussion/Paper Questions

This short checklist will help you find good questions that you can raise in class or use to formulate a conceptual problem for a paper. If you answer "No" to the first five questions, you may have to find a new topic for your argument.

1. Do you care about answering the question you have posed?
2. Will anyone else care about hearing your answer?
3. Can you imagine finding an answer?
4. Can you imagine evidence that would support your answer?
5. Can you imagine finding that evidence?

If you answer "Yes" to these next questions, you may also have to find a new topic.

6. Does the question call for a simple yes-no answer?
7. Can you answer the question in just a few words?
8. Is it a question of fact that a reader could answer just by looking something up?
9. Will your readers accept your answer without asking for reasons and evidence?
10. If they disagree, will they think the answer is just a matter of opinion?

A Checklist for Argument

This checklist will help you analyze the structure of your argument as you plan and as you revise.

1. Do your reasons/subclaims "add up" to a strong case for the main claim?
2. Can you think of any other reasons that support the main claim? If so, add them.
3. Are the reasons/subclaims in the best order? If not, reorder them.
4. Will readers recognize the principle of order for your reasons/subclaims? If not, add a transitional word or phrase to signal that order.
5. Does the evidence under each reason/subclaim in fact support it?
6. Is there enough evidence for each reason/subclaim?
7. Is there other evidence that would support a reason/subclaim?

Once you answer those questions and fill in missing information, use the diagram on the following page to guide further drafting and revising.

Ten Steps to a Coherent Paper

This checklist will help you predict whether your readers will judge your argument to be coherent. Use it for drafts that are close to finished. A "No" answer to any of the questions suggests that you have to do some revising.

1. Draw a line between the introduction and the body and between the body and conclusion.
   - Does the body begin with a new paragraph?
   - Does the conclusion begin with a new paragraph?
2. In your introduction, underline the sentences that state the problem or question.
   - Have you told your readers why it should matter to them?
   - If not, will they think it matters for the same reason you do?
3. Box the sentence that states the main claim of the paper.
   - Does it respond directly to the problem or question?
   - Does it make an arguable claim?
   - Is it at or near the end of the introduction? If not, is it in the conclusion?
   - If the claim is in the conclusion, do the last sentences of the introduction announce the key terms that appear in the main claim?
   - If your main claim is stated in both your introduction and conclusion, are the two statements similar?

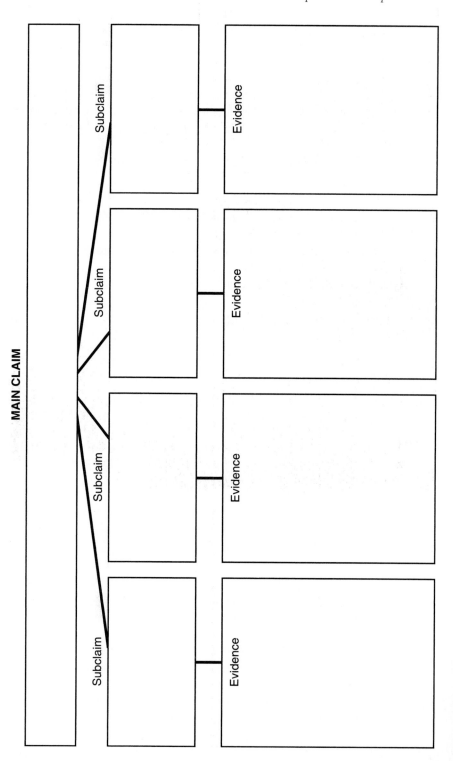

• If they are similar, is the one in the conclusion more specific, more informative?

4. Circle the key words in the last two sentences of the introduction and the most important sentence in your conclusion. Then circle those same words throughout the paper. Bracket words that refer to roughly the same concepts as the circled words or to concepts that are clearly related to them.

   • Are there three or more circled or bracketed words per paragraph?

5. Circle key words in the title.

   • Are the words that you circled the same ones that you circled in the introduction and conclusion?

   • Are they words that did not appear in your written assignment?

6. Draw a line between each major section of your paper. Box the sentence that states its main point.

   • Does it make an arguable claim?

   • Is it a reason supporting the main point/claim?

   • Do most of the main points appear at the beginning of their sections?

   • Now if you can, do the same thing for each paragraph.

7. Look at the beginning words of each section.

   • Do they begin with words that signal why the paragraphs come in the order they do, words such as *first, second; on the other hand, however; therefore, in conclusion,* and so on?

8. For each paragraph, underline every sentence that reports evidence supporting the point/claim of the paragraph.

   • Have you underlined at least half of the paragraph?

9. Underline the first half of the first sentence in each paragraph.

   • Do the words you have underlined refer back to something already mentioned earlier in the essay?

10. Underline the first six words in each sentence.

    • Do they refer to information that would be familiar to readers, or at least would not surprise them? Are they words that are mentioned earlier in the essay, obviously connected to a concept mentioned earlier, or related to concepts that readers are likely to have in mind?

A Complete List of Questions

This checklist will help you keep track of all the questions you might ask about your argument. The questions are in categories organized top down, from the most general questions about your readers and problem to the details of sentences. We have marked the most important questions with a star (★), the more important ones with an arrow (☞). If you can't cover every question, review the marked ones, and if you're *really* pressed for time, focus on the starred ones.

1. Preliminary Questions About Your Readers

★ 1. What are the general values of your readers? Liberal? Conservative? Middle of the road? Religious? Secular? Do their values reflect their race? Ethnicity? Marital status? Economic level? Profession? Expertise?

☞ 2. What kinds of arguments do your readers prefer? From lots of individual bits of evidence to a generalization? From settled principles and warrants to deductions from them? Will they expect to see the kind of argument that is common in their field of expertise?

☞ 3. What kind of evidence do they prefer? Hard statistical evidence? Field observation? Personal experience? Quotes from authorities? Primary reports of evidence? Anecdotes?

4. How much time do they have for your argument? Will they want a summary of it up front, or will they patiently read through it all?

2. Questions About Your Particular Problem

★ 1. What kind of problem are you addressing, practical or conceptual? Do you want your readers simply to believe something? Or do you want them to act, or at least support an action?

☞ 2. What costs or benefits are at stake *for your readers* in your problem? Would they agree?

3. Have your readers tried to solve this problem? Do they think they have already solved it? How committed are they to a different solution? If so, what is at stake for them in giving up their solution in favor of yours?

4. What level of agreement are you seeking: Understanding? Respect? Approval? Endorsement? Wholehearted assent?

3. Questions About Your Solution/Claim

★ 1. Is your claim significant enough to make an argument about? Is it contestable? Is it capable of being proved wrong?

↪ 2. If your claim solves a practical problem, will the solution cost less than the problem does? Will it create a bigger problem than the one it solves? Can it be implemented? Why is it better than alternative solutions?

↪ 3. Is your claim sufficiently rich in concepts to anticipate the key concepts in your argument?

4. Is it appropriately complex? Does it open with clauses introduced with *although, if,* or *when?* Does it close with clauses introduced with *because?* Would a shorter, simpler claim be more effective?

5. Is it appropriately hedged? Are there limiting conditions? Exceptions?

6. Is your solution feasible? Ethical? Prudent?

7. If your claim solves a conceptual problem, could other facts, concepts, theories, etc., contradict it?

4. Questions About Your Title

★ 1. Does your title include key words from your main claim? Are there words that someone who knew the assignment would not predict?

2. Have you taken advantage of using a two-line title?

5. Questions About Your Introduction

★ 1. If your problem is practical, have you stated the destabilizing condition clearly? Have you clearly stated the costs and/or benefits from the point of view of your readers?

↪ 2. If your problem is conceptual, have you stated clearly what is not known or not well enough understood? Have you stated the consequences in a way that shows they are more significant than the destabilizing condition?

↪ 3. Where have you located your main claim/solution? If it is in both the introduction and conclusion, do both statements harmonize? If you state it for the first time in the conclusion, did you end the introduction with language that introduces the key concepts you develop in the rest of the argument and repeat in the claim at the end?

↪ 4. Can your reader plainly see where you have ended your introduction and where you begin the body of your argument?

5. Can you find common ground to establish a context for your problem? Does it introduce key concepts about the problem?

6. Would you improve your introduction by adding a prelude, a pithy quotation, an interesting fact, or a brief anecdote that encapsulates the problem? Would a prelude suit the kind of argument you make?

6. Questions About Your Conclusion

★ 1. Have you stated your claim/solution in your conclusion?

2. Have you suggested why it is significant? Have you suggested what is still unknown, uncertain, left to be done?

3. Would you improve your conclusion by adding a coda? Would a coda suit the kind of argument you make?

7. Questions About the Body of Your Argument

★ 1. Why have you ordered the parts of your argument as you have?

↩ 2. If you have divided your argument into two or more parallel parts, can you explain their order? Is it clear to your reader? Have you introduced each part with words that signal the order?

↩ 3. If you have divided your argument into two or more sequential parts, have you ordered them from the beginning of the process to its end or from the end back to the beginning? Is that order clear to your reader?

↩ 4. Can you pick out in the body of your argument key words that you use in your title, at the end of your introduction, and in your conclusion?

5. Have you avoided laying out your argument as a history of your thinking or as a summary of your sources? Have you avoided dividing it into blocks organized around the things given to you by your topic rather than around ideas or qualities *you* discovered and choose to discuss?

6. Have you avoided opening the body of your argument with a long summary of background?

8. Questions About the Body of Your Sections and Paragraphs

★ 1. Have you organized sections as you organize a whole essay? Does each section open with its own introduction? Do you state the point of the section at the end of its introduction?

↩ 2. Do you state in the introduction to each section the key words you develop in the rest of that section?

3. If a section is longer than a couple of pages, have you concluded each section by restating the claim of the section?

4. Have you organized your longest paragraphs like your sections?

9. Questions About Your Evidence

★ 1. Have you based your reasons on reliable reports of evidence? Are your sources authoritative? Have you cited them?

★ 2. Are you sure your readers will accept what you offer as a report of evidence or will they think it is only another reason?

★ 3. Do you have sufficient evidence? Is your evidence accurate? Precise? Representative? Authoritative?

4. Have you been careful not to paraphrase your sources so closely that you have risked a charge of plagiarism?

5. Have you distinguished between quoting an authority just to restate your claims and reasons and quoting an authority as evidence?

6. Have you introduced complex quantitative evidence and long quotations with a reason that interprets the evidence for the reader?

7. Are you depending too much on your memory for evidence? Are you depending too much on a vivid anecdote?

10. Questions About Acknowledgment and Response

★ 1. Can you imagine your readers' objections and reservations? Can you respond to them? Can you support your response as if it were a subordinate claim in a subordinate argument?

2. Can you imagine a reader offering counterreasons, counterevidence, counteranalogies to your own? Can you imagine responding to them?

11. Questions About Your Warrants

★ 1. Have you made explicit what your readers must believe in general before they will consider your particular claims and reasons? Have you taken important definitions, values, assumptions for granted?

↩ 2. Should you treat your warrant as a subordinate claim that you must support in a subordinate argument?

3. Do your warrants actually cover your reasons and claims?

4. Are your warrants appropriately limited and qualified?

5. Are your warrants appropriate to your community of readers?

12. Questions About Your Reasoning

★ 1. Have you avoided becoming fixated on your first hypothesis? Have you kept your mind open to alternative ones? Can you imagine at least one hypothesis as an alternative to your own?

2. If you reasoned deductively, from a warrant and reason to a claim, are you certain of the truth of the warrant? Or have your taken it for granted?

3. If you reasoned inductively, from specifics to a generalization, are you certain that you have observed enough instances to draw a generalization?

13. Questions About Meaning and Definitions

★ 1. If your argument turns on a definition, do you want your readers simply to understand a concept in a new way, or once they understand it, do you want them to do something?

➡ 2. Are you obliged to work within the four corners of a technical definition or can you work with a common one? Are you relying on a technical definition when your readers expect a common one (and vice versa)?

➡ 3. If you rely on a common definition, can you state the criteria of meaning that best serve your purposes and then match features of the referent to those criteria?

➡ 4. If you rely on a common definition, can you describe a model member of a category that your readers will accept and then describe your referent to match that model?

5. Can you shape the criteria of meaning and the features of the referent to match each other?

6. If your problem seems to be a conceptual one, is it possible you are addressing a surrogate problem in place of a pragmatic one?

7. Have you become a prisoner of an authoritative definition, either from a standard dictionary or a specialized source?

14. Questions About Causation

★ 1. If your problem is a practical one, have you focused on those causes that you think you can fix?

★ 2. If your problem is conceptual, have you focused on those causes that are highlighted by the special interests you and your readers bring to the question?

➡ 3. Have you avoided the "One True Cause" mentality? Have you considered causes that do not immediately precede the effect? Causes that are absent? Causes that are routine rather than unusual? Causes whose magnitude is less significant than the effect? Causes that do not confirm your assumptions?

➡ 4. If your problem is a practical one, have you considered offering all five narratives that explain the causes of an effect? Have you explained the problem? How the solution will work? Why the solution will cost less than the problem? Why it won't create a bigger problem? How you can implement it? Why it is better than alternatives?

5. Have you analyzed your theory of causation using an ANOVA table?

6. Have you considered the possibility of multiple causes? Of mutual feed-back of causes?

7. Have you begun your analysis of causes far enough back in the chain of causes and effects? Or too far back?

8. Have you analyzed causes at a level of detail that suits the solution to your problem?

15. Questions About Language

★ 1. Do most of the subjects of your sentences name the main characters in your story? Do your verbs name the specific actions those characters are involved with?

★ 2. Do you begin all of your sentences with information that is familiar to your readers?

★ 3. Are your subjects relatively consistent? Are they the characters most significant to your story?

☞ 4. Do your sentences get to main verbs quickly? Do they have relatively short introductory elements? Relatively short subjects? Few interruptions between subjects and verbs?

☞ 5. Have you eliminated empty words, redundant implications of words? Have you compressed several words into one, when you can?

6. Have you tried to choose words that are specific enough to create an image in the mind's eye of your readers? Have you chosen general words for your warrants and definitions?

7. When you use words that invoke values and evoke feelings, do you do so in the context of an otherwise sound argument? Are you clear why you are using them? What problem do you think you are solving?

8. Have you avoided inappropriately trying to deflect your readers' attention away from flesh and blood characters by reifying abstractions and relying on metaphors?

Storyboarding a Long Paper

We've offered advice about organization in several Writing Process sections, and that advice should get you through most short papers. But for a longer, more complicated one, you may need help planning and managing all its parts. We recommend that you try a storyboard.

When you create a storyboard, you group related parts of your paper on separate pages, in rough outline form at first, but in greater detail as you develop your argument. A storyboard has all the advantages of an outline, but without the fussiness of indentations, having a "b" for every "a", and getting the numbering right. And unlike an outline, a storyboard reduces the complexity that you have to deal with at one time.

- You isolate the units of your paper so that you can work on each one separately without worrying about how it fits into the whole.
- You see at a glance where you have lots of information and where you have gaps.

A storyboard also helps you *see* a complex argument in its entirety, especially when you lay it out on a table or tape it to a wall.

- You take in the organization at a glance, like a physical structure with layers and sublayers all laid out before you.
- You can easily move pages around to try out different arrangements, seeing the structure of each new arrangement at a glance.
- You can easily add or delete sections.

Some people feel that they think better when they physically move around their storyboard, actually looking at it from different angles to get new perspectives on it. If you are a verbal person, better with words than shapes, think of a storyboard as a flexible, expanded outline. If you are a visual person, think of it as a picture of the structure of your paper. In either case, you'll manage a complex argument better if you use one.

1. Create templates.

To start the process, create template pages for your introduction and conclusion, with a heading for each possible element. Use whole pages.

Introduction/Problem	Conclusion
Prelude:	Main claim:
Common ground:	Significance of claim:
Destabilizing condition:	
Costs/consequences:	Work still to be done:
Solution:	Coda:

Next, create two kinds of reason templates: one for those reasons that you think you can support only with evidence (you should have few of these) and another for reasons that you have to support with a complete nuclear argument. So depending on how complex the support for your reason will be, create one or the other of the two templates below for each reason.

Reason #____
Main reason:
Reports of evidence to support main reason:

Reason #____
Main reason claim:
Reasons in support of main reason/claim:
Reports of evidence to support reasons:
Acknowledgment and response:

Finally, create templates for warrants and their supporting arguments and for acknowledgments and responses and their supporting arguments:

Warrant for Reason #____
Warrant/claim:
Reasons in support of warrants:
Reports of evidence to support reasons:
Acknowledgment and response:

Acknowledgment and Response for Reason #____
Objection/reservation/alternative:
Response/claim:
Reasons:
Reports of evidence:
Warrant/acknowledgment and response:

For the reason, warrant, and acknowledgment/response templates, make as many copies as your argument has major reasons. Save the blank template pages on your computer, but you'll start out working with them in hard copy.

2. Fill out the templates.

Fill in as many blanks as you can with what you know right now. At first, you may not have much to add, and some of it may be guesses that you have to confirm later. If you have to do some research to find something to add, do it quickly. Don't wait until the pages are full to go on to the next step.

3. Arrange the templates as they will appear in your paper.

As soon as you have enough to go on, tape the sheets to a wall or lay them out on a table, your bed, or the floor as shown below.

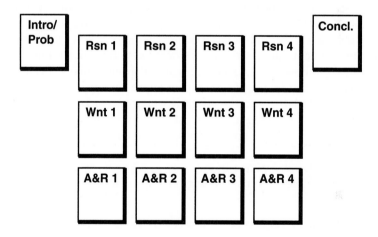

Move the pages around until you feel that you have a workable order. Add ideas as they occur to you.

If the pages get messy with notes, enter them in your computer template and print clean copies on which you can add even more notes. You can also use sticky notes that you can easily add or delete.

4. Draft, but then revisit your storyboard.

Once you have a workable plan, build your argument piece by piece. As you draft, try different arrangements. From time to time, check the skeleton of your argument by reading straight through the whole *Introduction/Problem* page, the main reasons at the top of the *Reason* pages, and the whole *Conclusion* page. If some sheets remain empty, so be it. They will remind you of opportunities. The point is to decompose your task into parts so that you are not paralyzed by the kind of complexity that even the most experienced writers cannot deal with all at once.

Avoiding Inadvertent Plagiarism Through Proper Citations

Teachers in every field have become intensely concerned about plagiarism, because they believe the Internet has made it easier than ever for students to cheat. So they are especially vigilant for signs of plagiarism in every paper they read. Honest students might think that they have no reason to worry, but they still have to be careful if they cannot anticipate how teachers identify plagiarism. Students are especially vulnerable if they don't know all the conventions for how to use and cite material from sources. Even when a teacher believes that the plagiarism is inadvertent, an honest student may still have a problem, because many teachers do not accept ignorance as an excuse. In any case, you do not help readers trust you or your argument if you fail on something as basic as signaling when you have used a source and properly citing it.

When you use any source in any way in a paper, readers expect you to follow three principles. You risk a charge of plagiarism if you ignore any one of them:

1. You must cite the source for any words, ideas, or methods that are not your own.

2. When you quote the exact words of a source, you must put those words in quotation marks or a block quotation.

3. When you paraphrase or summarize rather than quote, do not use quotation marks. But make sure that when you paraphrase, you recast the passage you are paraphrasing entirely in your own words rather than simply replacing words in the original.

Some students think that they do not have to cite all of the material freely circulated online. They are wrong. The principles of citation apply to sources of any kind—printed, recorded, oral, *and* online—but teachers are most on the lookout for plagiarism of online sources. You risk a charge of plagiarism if you fail to cite *anything* you get from a source, *especially* if it's from a Web site, a database, a Podcast, or other online source. A source is a source, and you must cite them all.

In this appendix, we outline the rules for using and citing sources. Unlike most of our principles, these are strict rules that every reader expects you to follow. For many of them, you will find fuller discussions in the Writing Process sections (see the cross references below). In some cases, you may have to ask for advice, because there are gray areas that require judgment, and some rules apply differently in different fields. But if you follow these few rules in good faith, you can guard against the suspicion that you are trying to pass off someone else's words and ideas as your own. Here, we show you how to avoid that perception by knowing first how to take good notes, then how to cite your sources.

1. Take Good Notes

You cannot use and cite source material correctly if you do not first have good notes (see "Taking Research Notes," pp. 176–77).

Take Notes that Are Accurate and Complete

Copy quotations *exactly* as they appear in the original; if the quotation is long, photocopy or download it. For every source you take notes on, record its bibliographical data, so that you will not have to look up that source again or, worse, be tempted not to cite it because you don't have its data and it's too late to find them.

Distinguish Your Words from Those of the Source

Your notes should make it impossible for you to think, weeks later, that words and ideas you found in a source are your own. Whether you take notes on a computer or longhand, *always* underline, boldface, or use a different font or type size for direct quotations, so that later you cannot mistake those quoted words for yours.

When you paraphrase rather than quote a passage, do the same: *always* identify those words in some unambiguous way so that weeks later you cannot confuse a paraphrase either with a quotation or with your own ideas.

This step may seem just busywork when you are recording page after page of information, but it will save you from a dangerous mistake. Many prominent scholars have been humiliated by accusations of plagiarism because in their notes, they failed to distinguish clearly the words they copied or paraphrased. When later they presented those words as their own, they had to claim that they "forgot" they were from a source.

Do Not Paraphrase Too Closely

When you paraphrase in your notes, don't do a word-for-word replacement of words in your source with synonyms. If you use that paraphrase in your paper, you risk a charge of plagiarism because your words will be too close to those of the original. For example, most teachers would consider the first paraphrase of the original sentence below as plagiarism, because it tracks its language almost word for word. The second paraphrase is fair use, so long as its source is cited in the text of the paper.

> **Original:** "The drama is the most social of literary forms, since it stands in so direct a relationship to its audience."
>
> **Plagiarizing paraphrase:** The theater is a very social genre because it relates so directly with its audience.
>
> **Fair-use paraphrase:** As Levin claims, we experience the theater as the most social form of literature because it takes place in front of us.

2. Cite Carefully

Every time you use words or ideas from a source, you must do this:

- Put direct quotations in quotation marks or in a block quotation.
- For any quotation, paraphrase, summary, or idea borrowed from a source, cite its bibliographical information, including page numbers, so that readers can find that source.

Those two rules, however, apply somewhat differently for different kinds of borrowings.

Direct Quotations

1. **For quotations shorter than a full sentence:**
   - The first time you quote words or phrases, enclose them in quotation marks and include a citation and page number. (For proper citation form, see "Citing Sources in the Body of Your Paper" on pp. 365–68 [MLA] or pp. 368–372 [APA].)
   - If you use those words again, you do not need either a citation or quotation marks.
   - You do not need to cite familiar words or phrases. (See "Avoiding Inadvertent Plagiarism," pp. 361–62.)

For example, read this passage:

> Because technology begets more technology, the importance of an invention's diffusion potentially exceeds the importance of the original invention. Technology's history exemplifies what is termed an autocatalytic process: that is, one that speeds up at a rate that increases with time, because the process catalyzes itself (Diamond 301).

Some phrases in that passage, such as "the importance of the original invention," are so ordinary that they require neither a citation nor quotation marks. But two phrases do, because they are so strikingly original: "technology begets more technology" and "autocatalytic process":

The power of technology goes beyond individual inventions because "technology begets more technology." It is, as Diamond puts it, an "autocatalytic process" (301).

Once you cite those words, you can use them again without quotation marks or citation:

> As one invention begets another one and that one still another, the process becomes a self-sustaining catalysis that spreads exponentially across all national boundaries.

2. **For quotations shorter than five lines:**

   - Run the quoted words into the body of your text and surround them with quotation marks. (See "Quoting and Paraphrasing," pp. 148–50.)
   - Cite the source of those words and page numbers (or other location markers in recordings, Web sites, and so on). (For proper citation form, see "Citing Sources in the Body of Your Paper" on pp. 365–68 [MLA] or pp. 368–72 [APA].)

For example:

> Posner focuses on religion not for its spirituality, but for its social functions, claiming that "a notable feature of American society is religious pluralism, and we should consider how this relates to the efficacy of governance by social norms in view of the historical importance of religion as both a source and enforcer of such norms" (Posner, 299).

   - If you quote parts of those lines again, put quotation marks around them but do not cite the source.

3. **For quotations five lines or longer:**

   - Put the quoted words into a block quotation, without quotation marks around them. (See "Quoting and Paraphrasing," pp. 148–50.)
   - Indicate where you found those words in the source by citing page numbers (or other location markers in recordings, Web sites, and so on). (For proper citation form, see "Citing Sources in the Body of Your Paper" on pp. 365–68 [MLA] or pp. 368–72 [APA].)

For example:

> Different forms of literature relate to society in different ways. Dramatic works, for example, are deeply embedded in a social framework:
>
>> The drama is the most social of literary forms, since it stands in so direct a relationship to its audience. Hence it presupposes certain fostering conditions, and its golden ages have been sporadic in finding their conjunctions of time and place: ancient Athens, classical France, baroque Spain, Zen Buddhist Japan, and Shakespeare's lifetime in England. (Levin 5)

4. **For paraphrases and summaries:**

   - Do not enclose a paraphrase in quotation marks or set it off in a block quote.

- Cite the source the first time you paraphrase, summarize, or use any ideas from it. You need not cite the source if you refer to those same ideas again.
- Include page numbers or for recordings, Web sites, and so on, some other location marker so that readers can find what you have used in the source.
- Make sure that your paraphrase is not so close to the original that it appears to be only an altered quotation.

5. **For borrowed ideas or methods:**
   - Cite the source and page numbers for any idea you use from a source, even if you had already thought of that idea on your own. You can indicate that you are not indebted to the source for your own original ideas by adding words such as *see also. . . , also discussed in . . . , for a similar/related/different/ treatment, see . . .*
   - You do not have to cite an idea or method that is common knowledge. The problem is that if you are new to a field, its common knowledge may seem to be a mystery. In that case, ask your teacher; if you can't ask, cite more than you think you have to (but not every other sentence).

The overall principle is this: Cite a source for words or ideas not your own *whenever* an informed reader might think that you are implying that they are your own. When in doubt, check with your instructor.

3. Cite Sources Properly

Your last task is to cite your sources fully, accurately, and appropriately. No one will accuse you of plagiarism if you put a comma where a period belongs, but some will think that if you cannot get these minor matters right, you are likely to get the important ones wrong. It is tedious work but worth the effort.

There are many forms of citations, so find out which style your reader expects. Two are most common:

- Modern Language Association (MLA) citations, common in the humanities.
- American Psychological Association (APA) citations, common in the social sciences.

In the next sections we explain how to cite the most common sources in those two styles. We cannot cover the citation form for every kind of source, so if you use sources beyond those covered here, buy a short guide to citation style.

MLA Citations

We first discuss listing your references in a bibliography or reference list, then we discuss how to cite them in the body of your paper.

Books (Including Collections of Articles)

General Format

The general format is as follows:

> Author. Title. Publication information.

> Last-name, First name Middle Initial. <u>Title: Subtitle</u>. City: Publisher, year.

> Meargham, Paul R. <u>The History of Wit and Practical Jokes: How Humor Coexists with Cruelty</u>. Boston: Smith, 1998.

Note that (1) titles must be either underlined or italicized, (2) there is a period after each unit of information, and (3) the second line of the entry is indented. Follow the punctuation in the models carefully; many teachers check this.

Multiple Books by the Same Author

- List each book in alphabetical order, but instead of repeating the author's name, type three dashes and a period.

> Meargham, Paul. <u>The History of Wit and Practical Jokes: How Humor Coexists with Cruelty</u>. Boston: Smith, 1998.
> ———. <u>Wit: Its Meaning</u>. Boston: Smith, 1994.

Multiple Authors

- For the first author, put the last name first; for remaining authors, start with their first names. Put a comma after each author but the last.

> Meargham, Paul, Harry Winston, and John Holt. <u>Wit: Its Tragic Meaning</u>. Boston: Smith, 1999.

- For four or more authors, give the first author's name with "et al."

> Meargham, Paul, et al. <u>Wit: Its Tragic Meaning</u>. Boston: Smith, 1999.

Multiple Volumes

- When referring to a multivolume work as a whole, indicate the number of volumes after the title (abbreviate the *volumes* and put a period after it).

> Meargham, Paul. <u>Wit: Its Meaning</u>. 2 vols. Boston: Smith, 1994.

- When referring to a particular volume, indicate which one you are using.

> Meargham, Paul. <u>Wit: Its Meaning</u>. Vol. 1. Boston: Smith, 1994.

- When referring to a particular volume in a series, indicate which one you are using and give the title of the series.

> Meargham, Paul. Wit: <u>Its Meaning</u>. Boston: Smith, 1994. Vol. 1 of <u>Wit and History</u>. 2 vols.

Multiple Editions

• When referring to any edition other than the first, indicate which one after the title but before the volumes (abbreviate the word *edition*).

Meargham, Paul. <u>Wit: Its Meaning</u>. 3rd ed. 2 vols. Boston: Smith, 1994.

Translation

Meargham, Paul. <u>Wit: Its Meaning</u>. Trans. George Playe. Boston: Smith, 1994.

Edited Book

Meargham, Paul, ed. <u>Wit: Its Meaning</u>. Boston: Smith, 1994.

Individual Item in Edited Collection

Meargham, Paul. "The History of Jokes." <u>Wit: Its Meaning</u>. Ed. George Playe. Boston: Smith, 1994. 123–46. [*Note:* The page numbers have been elided— 123–46 rather than 123–146.]

Individual Item in Reference Work

Meargham, Paul. "The History of Jokes." <u>Encyclopedia of Humor</u>. Boston: Smith, 1994. [*Note:* Do not list page numbers for dictionaries or encyclopedias.]

Articles

General Format

The general format for journal articles has the same categories as books:

Author. Article Title. Publication information.

Last name, First name Middle Initial. "Article Title." <u>Journal Title</u> vol. number (year): page numbers.

O'Connell, James. "Wit and War." <u>Theory of Humor</u> 21 (2003): 55–60.

Note that article titles are not underlined or italicized and that the publication information includes the title of the journal (underlined or italicized), data on the specific issue, and page numbers for the article.

General Circulation Magazine

O'Connell, James. "Wit and War." <u>Humor Today</u> May 2006: 45–66.

If there is no author, start with the article title.

Newspaper

O'Connell, James. "Wit and War." <u>Tulsa Clarion</u> 13 June 2003: 1B.

If there is no author, start with the title.

Scholarly Journal

O'Connell, James. "Wit and War." <u>Theory of Humor</u> 14 (1997): 335–60.

Journal that Does Not Number Pages Continuously

Most scholarly journals number pages continuously through the year. If you are citing one that starts the pages numbers over with each issue, add the issue number to the volume number.

> O'Connell, James. "Wit and War." Theory of Humor 14.2 (1997): 33–60.

Review

If the article is a review of another work, put the name of the reviewer and the title of the review (if any) first, then the name and title of the work reviewed.

> Abbot, Andrew. "I'm Not Laughing." Rev. of *Wartime Humor,* by James O'Connell. Theory of Humor 14 (1997): 401–19.

Special Formats

Film

Start with the title (italics or underlined), then name the director, the distributor, and the year of release. You can add other information (such as the screenwriter) between the title and the distributor.

> It's a Funny War. Dir. Nate Ruddle. Wri. Francis Kinahan. RKO, 1968.

Television

Include the title of the episode if appropriate, the series title, the network and/or local station that broadcast it, and the broadcast dates. You can include other information (such as the name of the director or screenwriter) after the series title.

> "The Last Laugh's on Bart." The Simpsons. FOX. 22 May 1996.

Online Print Source

If you cite a book or article that was originally printed but you obtained online, add the date of access and the URL to the end of the citation.

> O'Connell, James. "Wit and War." Theory of Humor 14.2 (1997): 33–60. 15 Nov. 2001 http://www.funnystuff.hope.edu/theory/wit.html.

If you cite a book or article that you obtained from an online database, add to the end of the citation the name of the database, your online connection, the date of access, and the URL.

> O'Connell, James. "Wit and War." Theory of Humor 14.2 (1997): 33–60. WilsonWeb. Bulwinkle College, Lake Forest, IL. 23 Oct. 2001 http://wilson-web2.hwwilson.com.

Web Page

Start with the author/owner of the page, if you can find one; otherwise, use the best identifying information you can find. Include the date of the last update, if you can find it, the date of access, and the URL.

> Center for Wartime Humor Home Page. 23 May 2004. 15 Nov. 2005 http://warjokes.org.

Citing Sources in the Body of Your Paper

The principle is to let your reader know exactly where to look in your source to find what you refer to. There are three variables you have to consider.

- If you mention your source in your text and your reader unambiguously knows to whom you are referring, you can simply insert a page number in parentheses before the final period:

  In arguing that wit is closely allied to tragedy as a way to deflect the experience of pain and death, O'Connell points to the gravedigger scene in *Hamlet* as an example of how wit and humor can relieve the oppressive weight of the unendurable (34).

- If, however, the reader cannot unambiguously find the source, you have to be more explicit. For example, if you include more than one book or article by O'Connell, you have to make clear which work you are drawing from. You do that by inserting a word from the title before the page number:

  In arguing that wit is closely allied to tragedy as a way to deflect the experience of pain and death, O'Connell points to the gravedigger scene in *Hamlet* as an example of how wit and humor can relieve the oppressive weight of the unendurable (<u>Wit</u> 34).

- If you refer to more than one writer in a passage, insert the source's name before the page number (and if necessary, a title):

  In arguing that wit is closely allied to tragedy as a way to deflect the experience of pain and death, O'Connell disagrees with Halliday, who points to the gravedigger scene in *Hamlet* as an example of how wit and humor can relieve the oppressive weight of the unendurable (O'Connell, <u>Wit</u> 34).

APA Citations

Books (Including Collections of Articles)

General Format

The general format is as follows:

Author (Date). Title. Publication information.

Last name, Initials (date). *Title: subtitle*. City, State: Publisher.

Meargham, P. (1998). *The history of wit and practical jokes: how humor coexists with cruelty*. Boston: Smith.

Note that (1) the year of publication is included in parentheses after the author, (2) titles are italicized, (3) only the first word of a title is capitalized, (4) there is a period after each unit of information, and (5) the second line of the entry is indented. Follow the punctuation in the model carefully; many teachers check this.

Special Formats

Multiple Books by the Same Author

- List each book in chronological order. If there is more than one entry for a single year, order them alphabetically and add a letter after the year.

Meargham, P. (1994). *Wit: its meaning.* Boston: Smith.
Meargham, P. (1998a). *The history of wit and practical jokes.* Boston: Smith.
Meargham, P. (1998b). *War jokes.* Boston: Smith.

Multiple Authors

- List all authors last name first followed by initials. Use an ampersand (&) in place of *and:*

  Meargham, P., Winston, H., & Holt, J. (1999). *Wit: its tragic meaning.* Boston: Smith.

For six or more authors, list only the first author followed by *et al.*

  Meargham, P., et al. (1999). *Wit: its tragic meaning.* Boston: Smith.

Multiple Volumes

- When referring to a multivolume work as a whole, indicate how many volumes in parentheses after the title (abbreviate *volumes*).

  Meargham, P. (1994). *Wit: its meaning.* (Vols. 1–2). Boston: Smith.

- When referring to a particular volume, indicate which one you use.

  Meargham, P. (1994). *Wit: its meaning.* (Vol. 1). Boston: Smith.

- When referring to a particular volume in a series, indicate the title of the series, the volume number, and then the title of the volume.

  Meargham, P. (1994). *Wit and history: Vol. 1. Wit: its meaning.* Boston: Smith.

Multiple Editions

When referring to any edition other than the first, indicate which one in parentheses after the title (abbreviate the word *edition*).

  Meargham, P. (1994). *Wit: its meaning.* (3rd ed.). Boston: Smith.

Translation

  Meargham, P. (1994). *Wit: its meaning.* (G. Playe, Trans.). Boston: Smith.

Edited Book

  Meargham, P. (Ed.). (1994). *Wit: its Meaning.* Boston: Smith.

Individual Item in Edited Collection

  Meargham, P. (1994). The history of jokes. In G. Playe (Ed.), *Wit: its meaning* (pp. 125–142). Boston: Smith. [*Note:* The page numbers have not been elided—125–142 rather than 125–42.]

Individual Item in Reference Work

  Meargham, P. (1994). The history of jokes. In *Encyclopedia of humor* (pp. 173–200). Boston: Smith.

Articles

General Format

The general format has the same categories as books:

> Author. (Date). Article title. Publication information.

> Last name, Initials. (Date). Article title. *Journal Title, vol. number,* page numbers.

> O'Connell, J. (2003). Wit and war. *Theory of Humor, 21,* 55–60.

Note that article titles are not underlined and that the publication information includes the title of the journal (italicized), data on the specific issue, and page numbers for the article.

General Circulation Magazine

> O'Connell, J. (2006, May). Wit and war. *Humor Today,* 45–66.

If there is no author, start with the title.

Newspaper

> O'Connell, J. (2003, June 13). Wit and war. *Tulsa Clarion,* p. 1B.

If there is no author, start with the title.

Scholarly Journal

> O'Connell, J. (1997). Wit and war. *Theory of Humor, 21,* 55–60.

Journal that Does Not Number Pages Continuously

Most scholarly journals number pages continuously through the year. If you are citing one that starts the pages numbers over with each issue, add the issue number to the volume number.

> O'Connell, J. (1997). Wit and war. *Theory of Humor, 14*(2), 33–60.

Review

If the article is a review of another work, put the name of the reviewer and the title of the review (if any) first, then the name and title of the work reviewed inside square brackets.

> Abbot, A. (1997). I'm not laughing. [Review of the book *Wit and war*]. *Theory of Humor 14,* 401–419.

Special Formats

Film

Start with the director and anyone else responsible for the film (such as a producer), then the year in parentheses, and the title italicized; immediately after the title, identify the work as a motion picture in brackets; add the country of origin, and the distributor.

> Ruddle, N. (Director). (1968). *It's a funny war* [Motion picture]. United States: RKO.

Television

Start with the name of the producer, director, or other significant contributors, then the date in parentheses, the title (italicized); identify the work as a television broadcast or series in brackets; add the city and the network or local station that broadcast it.

> Kinahan, F. (Writer). (1996, May 22). *The last laugh's on Bart* [Television series episode]. In J. Doe (Producer), *The Simpsons*. Reno, NV: Fox.

Online Print Source

If you cite a book or article that was originally printed but you obtained online, add the date you retrieved it and the URL to the end of the citation:

> O'Connell, James. (1997). Wit and war [Electronic version]. *Theory of Humor, 14(2)*, 33–60. Retrieved Nov. 15, 2005 from http://www.funnystuff.hope .edu/theory/ wit.html

Web Page

Start with the author/owner of the page, if you can find one; otherwise, use the best identifying information you can find. Include the date of the last update, if you can find it, and the URL:

> Center for Wartime Humor Home Page. (2003, May 23). Retrieved Nov. 15, 2005 from http://warjokes.org

Do not put a period at the end of a URL.

Citing Sources in the Body of Your Paper

The principle is to let your reader know exactly where to look in your source to find what you refer to. There are three variables you have to consider:

- If you mention your source in your text and your reader unambiguously knows to whom you are referring, you can simply insert the year.

  In arguing that wit is closely allied to tragedy as a way to deflect the experience of pain and death, O'Connell (2002) points to the gravedigger scene in *Hamlet* as an example of how wit and humor can relieve the oppressive weight of the unendurable.

- If there is more than one publication from the same year, distinguish them with a lowercase letter:

  In arguing that wit is closely allied to tragedy as a way to deflect the experience of pain and death, O'Connell points to the gravedigger scene in *Hamlet* as an example of how wit and humor can relieve the oppressive weight of the unendurable (2002a).

• If there is any chance of ambiguity, insert the source's name before the year:

In arguing that wit is closely allied to tragedy as a way to deflect the experience of pain and death, O'Connell disagrees with Halliday, who points to the gravedigger scene in Hamlet as an example of how wit and humor can relieve the oppressive weight of the unendurable (O'Connell, 2002a).

APPENDIX 2

Cognitive Biases and Fallacies

Throughout this book we have discussed both how good critical thinking can improve your argument and, no less important, how your argument can improve your critical thinking. We have shown you how to use the elements of an argument to guard against common mistakes in reasoning that can lead your thinking astray in ways that most of us do not even notice. Here we explain two common strategies for avoiding the most common errors.

Cognitive Biases

Perhaps the most serious challenge to sound critical thinking is a set of deep-seated cognitive biases that all of us share. Many of them have been uncovered by cognitive scientists in an attempt to understand why our reasoning is so often so unreliable. Here is a list of those biases and mistakes with references to where we have discussed ways to guard against them:

General Biases and Mistakes in Reasoning

1. You believe that something is true, so you distort evidence, ignore the lack of evidence, or place too much weight on the evidence you have (pp. 239–42).

2. You are too confident in your judgment, leading you to believe that you must be right (p. 242).

3. You want something to be true, so you believe that it is (pp. 239–40).

4. You seize on the first answer that occurs to you, causing you to anchor your thinking on that answer (p. 241).

5. You reason from ideological principles rather than from evidence (pp. 237–39).

6. You oversimplify an issue, thinking that there is One True Explanation for your problem (p. 278).

Linguistic Biases and Mistakes

7. You think that the meaning of a word is naturally connected to the referent of the word, so that the meaning is all you need to know about the referent (pp. 247–50).

8. You fail to respect the difference between common meanings and definitions and authorized meanings and definitions (p. 255).

9. You engage in a conceptual argument about the meaning or definition of a word but fail to recognize that your question is only a surrogate for a practical problem (p. 250).

10. You use emotional or polarizing language that distorts your thinking or that of your readers (pp. 334–35).

11. You manipulate the subject of verbs to make it seem that an instrument or abstraction is the source of an action performed by an identifiable individual or entity (pp. 336–38).

12. You create misleading metaphorical scenarios (pp. 341–43).

Causal Biases and Mistakes

13. You focus on causes that are easier to notice and ignore less obvious ones (pp. 276–77).
    - You notice causes that are immediate, present, and vivid rather than ones that are remote, absent, and obscure.
    - You notice causes that are surprising rather than ones that are routine or expected.

14. You focus on a single cause rather than multiple ones (pp. 283–84).

15. You focus on causes that match effects in kind and magnitude (pp. 277–78).

16. You confuse correlation with causation (pp. 280–84).

17. You fail to investigate whether two events that are closely correlated might be not cause and effect, but both effects of some third cause (pp. 280–84).

18. In human actions, you overemphasize personal motives and intentions and undervalue circumstances, or vice-versa (pp. 287–91).

Fallacies

There is, however, another tradition in studying flawed thinking that is almost 2,500 years old. It focuses on errors in reasoning called *fallacies*. A fallacy is not a false belief, like thinking the earth is flat. Rather, it is a bias or logical misstep in reasoning your way to a sound conclusion. In fact, you can reason validly and conclude that the earth is flat or fallaciously and conclude that it is round. There is some overlap between this classical tradition and modern studies of flawed thinking, but the classical tradition has such a long history that anyone interested in critical thinking should know about it.

Over the centuries, logicians have identified scores of fallacies and given them formidable Latin names such as *post hoc ergo propter hoc, ad verecundiam, non sequitur.* We will discuss here only the most common ones. Some of them always undermine your reasoning, while others do so only in certain circumstances. So we group them into two categories: those fallacies that you should always avoid and those that you should avoid when the circumstances require it.

Fundamental Errors in Reasoning

These fallacies are outright errors in getting from a reason to a claim. We'll introduce each of these fallacies as if you're being charged with it, and then add the technical explanation.

1. **"But what you said doesn't follow!" (Your reason is irrelevant to your claim.)**

   Cyberspace will eventually make government irrelevant _{main claim} by making all data instantly available. _{reason 1} Once we can be in instant contact with everyone else, _{reason 2} artificial national borders will wither away _{claim / reason 3} and government will have nothing to do. _{claim / reason 4}

   You might be right, but I don't see why making information available faster makes government irrelevant. Second, I don't see how being in contact with everyone will make national borders disappear. And third, I don't see why the lack of borders leaves government nothing to do. I can see some connection between governments having nothing to do and their being irrelevant, but the steps between are too much of a stretch.

   When we cannot see the logical connection between a reason and its claim, we call the claim a *non sequitur,* pronounced "nahn SE-kwi-toor," which means literally *It doesn't follow.* If your readers think you have committed a *non sequitur,* you have to think about the warrant that connects the reason to the claim: Do readers share your underlying assumptions, and have you failed to state warrants you should have? Review pages 224–25.

2. **"You're arguing in a circle and begging the question!" (Your reasons just restate your claim.)**

   To ensure our safety, we should be free to carry concealed guns _{claim 1} because we should have the right to carry a weapon to protect ourselves. _{reason 1} When criminals know that we might have a gun and would use it, _{reason 2} they'll realize that we are ready to defend ourselves. _{claim 2} Only when criminals worry about their own safety _{reason 3} will we be able to stop worrying about our own. _{claim 3}

   You are reasoning in a circle. You keep saying the same thing—we should be free to do something because we have the right to do it. That makes a kind of sense, but it's no argument. Then you say that when criminals know something they know something. That may be true, but it doesn't support the claim either.

You argue in a circle when your claim and reason mean the same thing. You can test for a circular argument by switching the claim and reason. If the sentence means the same after the switch, you are arguing in a circle:

> To ensure our safety, we should be free to carry concealed guns _{claim} because we need the right to carry one to protect ourselves. _{reason}

> We need the right to carry a weapon to protect ourselves _{claim} because we should be free to carry concealed guns to ensure our safety. _{reason}

If you cannot switch the reason and claim, your argument is not circular. Compare the last sentence in the example, which does not reason in a circle:

> Only when criminals worry about their own safety _{reason} will we be able to stop worrying about our own. _{claim}

> Only when we are able to stop worrying about our own safety _{reason} will criminals worry about theirs. _{claim}

3. **"You're assuming a fact that we haven't settled!" (Your reason is not supported with evidence or an argument.)**

   > We should reject the mere opinion _{implied claim} of a known liar like Smith. _{reason}
   > *Who says that what Smith says is "mere opinion," and who says he is a "known liar"?*

   This is cousin to begging the question. It's like *When did you stop beating your dog?* You commit this fallacy when you assume a judgment or fact that readers do not accept because it has not been proven, then use that judgment or fact as a reason for your claim.

4. **"But you can't use the lack of evidence to prove an affirmative claim!" (You rely on a false warrant: When a claim has not been proven false, we should accept it as true.)**

   > People who say they have been kidnapped by aliens from outer space should be taken seriously, _{claim} because no one has proved their stories are false. _{reason}
   > *Hold on! No one has proved that I don't have an oilfield under my back yard, but that doesn't mean that I'm going to start drilling. You can't expect me to believe something is true because I don't know for sure that it's not.*

The technical term for this fallacy is *ad ignorantiam*, pronounced "add ignore-AHN-tee-em." If you make a claim, you have to offer *affirmative* reasons for believing it. It is not up to the other person to disprove it. A claim is not true simply because no one can think of a good alternative.

A somewhat weaker strategy is to say, *Well, it could be true.* In a sense, anything could be true, even alien abductions. We can leave room for the chance that a claim could be true, but we should file such claims in a corner of our minds reserved for unsubstantiated possibilities.

5. **"You can't prove something by claiming that the consequences of not accepting it are intolerable!" (You rely on a false warrant: When it would hurt us to believe something, we should not believe it—or vice versa.)**

The Constitution protects our right to privacy, _{claim} because if it did not, then states could regulate our most intimate behavior, including our sexual lives. _{reason} That would be intolerable. _{reason}

You're right; it's intolerable that states should be able to interfere in our private lives. But that's irrelevant to what the Constitution does or doesn't say. As bad as it may seem, the Constitution gives states the power to snoop in our bedrooms.

This fallacy is called *ad baculum*, pronounced "add BACK-yu-lum." It means "with force." Those who argue like this imply that if we do not agree, something bad will happen to us.

Inappropriate Rhetorical Appeals

Unlike fundamental errors in reasoning, which are always logical blunders, these next steps may or may not be errors, depending on the circumstances of the case. The problem is relying on a warrant that applies in some cases, but not all. The trick is to know when your readers will accept these appeals and when they will not.

Inappropriate Appeals to Intellectual Consistency

6. **"But what you say now contradicts what you said before!"**

    Students should evaluate teachers every semester, because only then will they know whether they are helping students achieve their goals.

    But last month, you argued that teachers should not evaluate students because their tests do not fairly represent your strengths and abilities. How can you say that you should evaluate us when you reject our evaluations of you?

This fallacy is called *tu quoque* (pronounced "too kwo-kway"), literally "You too." It is a charge of inconsistency, at worst of dishonesty.

But this charge is tricky: It is legitimate to point out inconsistency—we distrust those who are. But what someone said in the past may have nothing to do with the merits of the case at hand: So what if someone contradicts herself? Regardless of what a person said before, we have to judge the issue before us on its own merits.

Yet so strongly do we dislike those who contradict themselves that we reject even a good argument when made by hypocrites. If readers might think that you contradict yourself, you should consider acknowledging that what you said before is not consistent with what you are saying now and show why the inconsistency is not fatal.

7. **"If you take this one step you will go all the way!"**

    We can't legalize marijuana for medical purposes _{claim} because if physicians prescribe it for dying patients, they'll prescribe it for people only in pain, then for people who just claim to be in pain. _{reason}

    You insult the intelligence of physicians, implying that they don't know the difference between taking this one step and going all the way. It's like claiming that if you drive one mile over the speed limit, you will end up driving 100 miles an hour.

This fallacy is called the *slippery slope*. It's a claim that one step must inevitably lead to the next, and the next, and the next. But we know that this is not always true.

A particular kind of slippery slope is called *reductio ad absurdum*—reduction to absurdity, pronounced "ruh-DUK-tee-o ahd ab-ZERD-um." Instead of claiming that a claim would begin a slippery slope, someone asserts that it has hit bottom.

> You want students to evaluate their teachers? I suppose you also want the criminally insane to evaluate their psychologists or criminals to evaluate their judges or children to evaluate their parents.

When a critic reduces an argument to an absurd version and then attacks it, we say the critic has built a straw man.

Appeals to Inappropriate Perspectives

8. **"You offer a false choice between only two alternatives. There are more!"**

This fallacy is related to the issue of polarizing language (p. 334).

> It's time to end the debate between "whole word" reading and phonics. The failure of "whole word" pedagogy _{reason} demands that we return to the time-tested phonics method. _{claim}
> *But most good teachers use some of both and a few other ways of teaching.*

It's misleading to insist on either-or choices when the facts of the matter allow both more-or-less or some-of-both. As you plan your argument and find yourself arguing for a choice between two exclusive alternatives, stop and think: Could you choose both, or at least some combination? Are there third, fourth, or even fifth choices? (In some cases, however, the choice really is between two and only two mutually exclusive alternatives, such as capital punishment or no capital punishment.)

9. **"That's just a metaphor! You can't act as though it's literally true."**

> Sick ideas such as gay marriage can infect those too weak to resist them _{reason} so we must isolate people who would spread their sick ideas. _{claim}
> *You may be right that the idea may spread, but ideas are not diseases. You can't stop ideas from spreading the way you stop TB.*

Metaphors may mislead us, but the fact is, we cannot communicate without them: The problem is not the metaphoric language itself; it's how it's used. So think hard about whether you are pushing the metaphors too far (see pp. 341–43).

Inappropriate Appeals to Social Solidarity

10. **"You're just appealing to the crowd! Why should we go along with everyone else?"**

> When parents pay for the education of their children, they have the right to decide what should be taught. _{warrant} Most people think intelligent

design should be taught alongside evolution, _{reason} so that's what school systems should teach. _{claim}

That caters to popular ignorance. Suppose most parents thought that the earth was flat? Should that be taught?

This fallacy is called *ad populum,* pronounced "add PAH-poo-lum." It means the arguer puts more weight on what most people believe than on the truth. The basis of an *ad populum* argument is probably our inherited human bias to conform with the thinking of the tribe.

But an appeal to popular will is not always a fallacy:

The city council must reject the plan to build a new stadium, _{claim} because the people don't want to pay for it. _{reason} This is a democracy. _{warrant}

If readers might think your appeal to popular opinion is inappropriate, acknowledge and respond to the objection:

The city council must reject the plan to build a new stadium, _{claim} because the people don't want to pay for it. _{reason} In matters of public spending, the people and not the Chamber of Commerce decides. _{response} This is a democracy. _{warrant}

Your argument will legitimately appeal to the popular will when you can legitimately use this warrant:

When most people believe / decide X, we should accept X.

11. "We don't have to accept your claim just because X says so!"

According to Senator Wise, the predicted rise in atmospheric carbon dioxide will help plant growth, _{reason} because plants take in carbon dioxide and give off oxygen. _{report of evidence} He was born on a farm, _{reason} and he knows plants. _{claimed authority} So we ought not fear greenhouse gases. _{claim}

Senator Wise may be an admirable person, but being born on a farm doesn't make him an expert on atmospheric chemistry.

This fallacy is called *ad verecundiam,* pronounced "add vare-uh-COON-dee-ahm." It literally means the "modesty" we should exhibit before authority. The psychological basis for this appeal is probably the deference we feel to power and prestige. An appeal to authority goes wrong when the authority has no reason to deserve our trust. The fact that Wise was born on a farm is irrelevant to his authority to make predictions about greenhouse gases.

But the problem is that some people are real authorities whose expertise we should respect. So when you want to use an authority, you have to weigh three questions: Is this a case where expertise matters? Is your authority truly an expert in this field? Will your readers be willing to defer ("be modest") in this case?

If readers might question an authority, anticipate their questions. You address the first two by telling them why they should accept your authority as an expert in this case and the third by reporting not just what the authority claims but the reason for claiming it.

According to Dr. Studious, we would be prudent to stockpile medication in anticipation of a new outbreak of bird flu. _{claim} As Director of Epidemiology at the National Institutes of Health, he was responsible for our being ready for the epidemic of 1987. _{basis of authority} In his research on that and twenty other epidemics, _{basis of authority} he found that the lag between the first cases and an epidemic is about two months. _{reason} Now that the first cases have begun to appear, we know that we have about two months to prepare. _{reason}

12. "You are just engaging in mud-slinging! Unfair personal attacks have nothing to do with the issues."

Senator Boomer avoided the draft during the Vietnam War, _{reason} so he is disqualified from judging the use of military power in Iraq. _{claim} No one who shirks his duty can say anything about the service he scorned. _{warrant}

Stick to the issue instead of making a personal attack! His actions as a 20-year old are irrelevant to his current analysis of the facts of the matter.

This fallacy is called *ad hominem,* pronounced "add HA-mi-nim." It literally means "against the person." It is the corollary of a fallacious appeal to authority: Just as we err when we accept an argument because we admire the person making it, so can we err when we reject an argument by someone we dislike. At times, however, we should question an argument on the basis of who makes it, if that person is regularly dishonest, unreliable, or careless.

A version of this appeal is "guilt by association," which is sometimes fair and sometimes not.

Professor Hack claims that crime drops when citizens carry concealed weapons. But his research is funded by gun manufacturers, _{reason} and he serves on a committee for the National Rifle Association. _{reason 2} He might be right, but we should look at his research skeptically. _{claim}

If readers might think you are unfairly attacking the person who makes an argument, then you have to acknowledge and respond to their objection:

. . . We should look at his research skeptically. _{claim} That doesn't mean his research is necessarily biased, _{acknowledgment} but the source of his support gives us reason to look at his methodology carefully. _{response} Even a cautious researcher can be influenced by the interests of those who support his or her work. _{warrant}

13. "Don't give me that sob story. You're just appealing to my pity!"

Teachers here at State U. are so anxious over rumors about eliminating departments _{reason} that adding a new teaching evaluation form will make them insecure and fearful. _{claim}

Our job is to improve teaching. If that makes teachers unhappy, too bad. It's irrelevant to creating a sound undergraduate education.

This technical term for this fallacy is *ad misericordiam,* pronounced "add miz-AIR-uh-CORE-dee-um." It asks us to put our sympathies ahead of reasons and evidence. The foundation of such an appeal is our sound intuition that we should respond sympathetically to the suffering of others and mitigate it when we can.

Although we can be wrong to put sympathies ahead of our reasons, we can also be right to do so:

States have released people from institutions for the mentally ill, pushing them onto the streets, where they are homeless and helpless. It's inhuman _{claim} to abandon those who cannot care for themselves. _{reason}

If readers might reject an argument based on sympathy, you have to give them reasons that go beyond it:

. . . care for themselves. _{reason} We must never put politics and economics above basic human dignity. _{warrant} That's not being a bleeding-heart. _{acknowledgment} If we knowingly refuse to help the helpless, _{reason} we become a morally callous people who will lose all sensitivity to injustice. _{claim}

There are many other so-called "fallacies," but these are the most common ones. Be alert to these fallacies in what you read, but their real value is that they help you reflect on your own thinking.

PART V

Readings

Attitudes Toward
Teaching and Learning

Obstacles to Open Discussion and Critical Thinking
The Grinnell College Study
CAROL TROSSET

*L*ike many institutions, Grinnell College hopes that one benefit of an increas-ingly diverse student body will be that students talk about their differences with each other. It sees open discussion of sensitive issues as an important part of the learning process—both in and out of the classroom. Since the college has made many attempts to foster a good climate for these discussions, recent reports that a number of students feel silenced have been disturbing news.

In an attempt to understand this problem, I undertook several semesters of ethnographic research, focusing on student assumptions about the purposes of discussion. The attitudes revealed by this study have far-reaching implications, not just for the discussion of diversity issues but for our educational mission of fostering critical-thinking skills.

Discussion as Advocacy

We presented approximately 200 students with a list of sensitive diversity-related issues (such as "whether race is an important difference between people"); for each, we asked whether it was possible to have a balanced discus-sion of that issue (involving more than one perspective, with each perspective

CAROL TROSSET *is Director of Institutional Research and lecturer in anthropology at Grinnell College. The author thanks the following people for their contributions to this project: Grinnell's former President Pamela Ferguson, anthropology Professor Douglas Caulkins, and the students who conducted the interviews, especially Gabriel Grout, Brandi Petersen, and Neelay Shah. From* Change, *September/October 1998.*

receiving about equal support and with people being civil to each other). We also asked them to explain why they did or did not want to discuss the issue. The majority of students not only thought that balanced discussion of these issues was impossible but feared that a single viewpoint would dominate—and feared reprisal if one spoke against that perspective.

The main reason students gave for wanting to discuss a particular topic was that they held strong views on the subject and wished to convince others. Likewise, not having a strong view—or finding an issue difficult—was often given as a reason for not wanting to discuss a subject. This conflict is reflected in the following student responses:

- "I want to discuss the causes of sexual orientation because I have strong views on this issue."
- "I want to discuss affirmative action because I want to educate people."
- "I like discussing gender issues because I feel knowledgeable about them."
- "I'm not sure what multiculturalism is; I don't know much about it, so I don't want to discuss it."
- "I don't want to discuss race because I never know how to approach the subject."
- "In a few cases, people cry sexual misconduct when it isn't, so I don't want to talk about it in those few cases."

Some students are so convinced of advocacy as the point of discussion that they see silence as the only way to avoid it: "I wouldn't want to discuss religion as I don't want to impose my views on others."

A few explicitly generalized this model beyond the treatment of diversity issues, saying, "Ideally, you should talk in order to make the other person realize that what they said was wrong," or, "I don't want to talk about things I'm unsure of."

Only five out of the 200 students in our sample volunteered a different, more exploratory, view of discussion, such as "I want to talk about multicultural education because I'm not sure I know enough about it," and "I want to discuss race, as it would open my mind to things I don't experience myself."

In exploratory discussion, people who are seeking more information and other view-points speak in order to learn about things. This is very different from the advocacy model, in which people who have already made up their minds about an issue speak in order to express their views and convince others.

One of our annual surveys of first-year students found 54 percent preferred to discuss a topic on which they held strong views (over a topic about which they were undecided).

Another survey, with a differently worded question, found the same preference increasing over time, rising from 25 percent of freshmen to over 50 percent of juniors. (The preference declined slightly among seniors, but the sample of seniors was not representative.) There were no ethnic or gender differences correlating with this preference in either survey.

The Search for Consensus

When we asked students why people should talk about their differences, we quite often heard about the desire to reach a consensus:

- "The best thing is when opposing views find some point of agreement."
- "Ideally, people should talk in order to mold all opinions together in a compromise."
- "People should talk in order to achieve a unified world view, the dissolution of the idea of the other, and an awareness of the oneness of all things."

Some students also told us that there's no point talking about something unless people can agree: "Discussing these things is futile; it wears you out. It seems you can never reach a consensus." Despite the discouraged tone of this last comment, many interviewees expressed great optimism about the possibility that people with different views can find common ground.

Some students spoke about issues as if a consensus already existed:

- "I don't want to discuss race because it's not an important difference between people."
- "I don't want to discuss the causes of sexual orientation because this topic is irrelevant to the nature of homosexuality."

Sometimes this assumption was combined with a preference for advocacy. One woman wants to be an advocate representing a consensus she assumes to exist: "I want to discuss sexism due to a personal interest in stating the female experience."

When we asked how likely people were to listen to and think about what someone else said under various conditions, most students said, predictably, that they would be likely to listen to someone with whom they already agreed. A majority also said that they would be unlikely to listen to someone with whom they disagreed. Their reasons included the following:

- "I have a set opinion about the causes of sexual orientation—I wouldn't want to participate in a conversation when other people have disagreeable views, but I would talk with people who have similar opinions."
- "I have strong ideas about what constitutes a multicultural education—I would have difficulty listening to those who disagree."
- "A discussion of abortion wouldn't be balanced—I would have a hard time listening to the opposite view."

Most often, it seems, students created artificial consensus groups by only discussing difficult issues when they knew it to be "safe"—that is, in carefully selected groups with homogeneous opinions, as reflected in the following comments:

- "People don't talk about race on this campus—carefully selected company might mean opposing views are not present."

- "It appears that people prefer to interact with others who verify their own views, instead of actively pursuing alternative points of view. This could cause individuals to believe there is widespread support for their own views, when in fact there may not be."

Seventy-five percent of the students we asked said that they would discuss diversity issues with people of the same views or background as themselves, but only 40 percent said they would discuss the same issues with people whose views were unknown to them.

Personal Experience as the (Only) Source of Legitimate Knowledge

As with cases in which they already agreed with a speaker, most students we surveyed said they were very likely to listen to someone they perceived as knowledgeable. Before we interpret this as traditional academic respect or expertise, however, we must examine where students think knowledge comes from.

When we asked 47 students in interviews, "How knowledgeable are you about diversity issues?" most said they were fairly to very knowledgeable. When asked where their knowledge came from, most mentioned more than one source. Forty-three percent of the respondents attributed knowledge to personal experience, and another 35 percent said knowledge came from talking to others about their experiences.

This bias in favor of personalized knowledge as opposed to knowledge accessible to all comers such as that contained in scholarly writings—a kind of knowledge stressed by only six of the 47—is also visible in the distribution of which groups claimed knowledge of which issues. Thus, students of color were more likely than whites to claim to be knowledgeable about race, women were more likely than men to claim knowledge about gender, and homosexuals more likely than heterosexuals to claim knowledge about sexual orientation.

White males in their first two years were the only group likely to say that they had little knowledge of diversity generally. Their claim to know little about gender, "because I have no personal experience," shows that these claims attribute expertise not only to experience, but to a particular kind of experience (that of belonging to a typically less powerful group).

About The Study

Grinnell is a selective, private, residential four-year college located in a small town in central Iowa. Its roughly 1,300 students come from all 50 states and some 40 countries.

This study was conducted primarily using ethnographic interviewing techniques, where individuals not only respond to questions face to face but are asked to explain their thoughts and the meaning of what they say, then to situate these things in their experiences.

Each semester for three years, I trained student interviewers through an anthropological research methods class; they then collected data from their fellow students, while I gathered additional data and guided the project design and analysis.

Several different samples, most comprising about 200 students, contributed to the data presented here. Each sample has good representation with respect to race, gender, and class year.

—Carol Trosset

This valuing of one kind of experience helps to limit what can be said in discussions. For example, the following comments on sexism came from two men and two women:

- "Guys are not able to challenge women's sexist remarks."
- "Women are unlikely to be labeled sexist no matter what they say."
- "I want to discuss gender—it's easy to say, I'm a woman; as a woman . . ."
- "Not being a woman, I don't feel my comments would be seen as valid."

This bias both forces members of less powerful groups into the role of peer instructors, and supports the impression that members of more powerful groups have nothing legitimate to say.

The Right Not to Be Challenged

Not only do people participate in discussion for the purpose of advocating views they already hold, but some of them expect to do so without anyone questioning or challenging their statements. In our most representative interview study, when asked, "As a member of a diverse community, what are your rights?" 15 percent of the sample volunteered the idea that they had the right to think or say whatever they liked without having their views challenged.

Some of the phrases used to express this position include

- "I have the right to present my views without being criticized";
- ". . . to not have people judge my views";
- ". . . to say what I believe and not have anyone tell me I'm wrong";
- ". . . to feel and think anything and not be looked down on";
- ". . . to hold my own beliefs and not feel attacked because of them"; and
- ". . . to speak my mind and not feel inhibited."

The students who claimed the right not to be challenged were nearly all women. Twenty-five percent of the women we interviewed made this claim, compared to only 6 percent of the men. (Other statements in their interviews suggest that most Grinnell men expect their views to be challenged by others.) Equal proportions of whites and students of color made this claim (which was rarely made by international students). Particularly disturbing is the fact that this claim was made evenly across the four class years, suggesting that students who arrive with this assumption do not alter it as a result of what they learn.

Implications

We hear a great deal these days about the pedagogical benefits of discussion. But the assumptions we uncovered—such as the belief that advocacy is the purpose of discussion—illustrate why this method is often not as effective as we'd hope. Cultural attitudes of this sort have a pervasive impact on behavior. These attitudes affect not only how students discuss things among themselves, but how they hear what professors say and how they read course material.

Many of us as academics share a number of expectations about the dispositions of educated people. These include exploring ideas from a variety of perspectives, learning about things outside one's own experience, evaluating the quality of evidence and arguments, and the capacity to be persuaded of new perspectives when presented with high-quality evidence and argument. In line with this, the fostering of critical-thinking skills appears in the mission statements of our institutions. But our students often do not share this common faculty agenda.

Colleagues in philosophy have told me they see students who think Socrates was a bully. One student even equated Socrates with Rush Limbaugh—this on the grounds that both of them want everyone to agree with them.

A faculty member I encountered at a conference, who clearly valued both diversity and open discussion, also claimed that Socratic academic discourse was a bad model for students. One complication here is the difference between critical and empathic thinking, both of which may be educational goals but which should not be confused with each other.

Some students to whom I presented this research told me, quite articulately, that "your identity comes from what, not how, you think." One, apparently struggling with the need to change his views on certain subjects, said he resolved this by realizing that at his age his identity was still changing. These statements were strikingly different from the typical scholar's identification with how one uses evidence and argument—something that has nothing to do with one's conclusions of the moment, since these will always change in the face of new evidence and better arguments.

Radical Relativism

Developmental and learning-style theorists may take issue with my concerns; it's all a "stage" or just their "style," they say. Their challenges, however, beg the question of how we as teachers are going to accomplish our educational missions, which are centered around the development of critical-thinking skills and which require our students to grow analytically.

What should we do, for example, with a student who says, after reading Malinowski (whose publications were based on four years of detailed field research), we still can't say anything about the Trobrianders because "it's just his opinion"? Traditional relativism, of course, is an important part of anthropology; it is based on the idea that any statement is made from a particular perspective, which must be taken into account when considering its meaning. The radical relativism of students carries this perspective beyond its original intention and argues that, therefore, everything is "just" an opinion and that no comparisons can be made between ideas or perspectives. (Indeed, people taking this position usually argue that any perspective claiming the ability to make comparative judgments is inferior.)

This orientation among students supports their claim that there is no way to learn about something outside one's own experience. This assertion, in effect, denies the methodological basis of most disciplines. It also supports students' idea that people have the right to not have their views challenged. Critical thinking itself is devalued here, since the assessment of evidence and logic is seen as just another way of doing things.

Given these orientations, we need to recognize that when we recommend "tolerance" to students, they may not hear the same message we're trying to send. Many of us think of tolerance in terms of civility, of behaving in well-mannered ways toward all members of the community, whether or not we approve of their views or behavior. Many students, on the other hand, think that being tolerant means approving of all ways of being, and believing that all ways are equally valid (except, of course, any position that openly makes value judgments and does not extend equal approval to all).

Being Comfortable

Eighty-four percent of the first-year class we surveyed chose the statement "It is important for the college community to make sure all its members feel comfortable" over the statement "People have to learn to deal with being uncomfortable." Across the student body, it is a common demand that the college as a whole, as well as its individual members, must act to ensure the comfort of all students, especially those who are members of traditionally underrepresented groups. At the same time, people insist that members of traditionally powerful groups (such as heterosexuals) should get comfortable, quickly, with previously unfamiliar groups and lifestyles.

"People are not interested in the sources of discomfort. They just want everyone to get comfortable," one student said. Of course, people should not be made to feel excluded because they belong to a minority group. But the demand for comfort often reaches much farther than this, sometimes to the point of claiming that no persons should have to learn new behaviors or ways of thinking, or indeed to do anything that might make him or her uneasy.

These e-mail messages were sent to colleagues of mine; the students clearly expect that they will be accepted as legitimate excuses:

- "You haven't received my paper because I'm not comfortable with it yet."
- "I'm not coming to class today because I haven't done the reading, and I'm not comfortable asking any of the other students if I can borrow their books."

Exploring new ideas, encountering people with different values, learning a new discipline's way of thinking, and having someone point out a flaw in one's argument—these can be uncomfortable experiences. For some people, simply finding themselves disagreeing with someone else is uncomfortable. Promising our students that we will make them comfortable may simply confirm them in their view that they have the right not to be challenged.

Ironically, typical suggestions for how to foster discussion feed into this attitude. Stressing the importance of making everyone feel "safe" often seems to result in making many people afraid to disagree with anyone, for fear of intimidating or offending them. Perhaps the teacher's solution is not ever more safety and respect (words that can be variously interpreted), but cultivating a more careful distinction between the idea and the person.

Speakers need to remember this distinction when they issue challenges, but those on the receiving end also need to remember it, so as not to overinterpret any conceptual or factual challenge as a threat to identity. With respect to sensitive issues, it might help to encourage everyone to think less, rather than more, about identity; to focus students' attention not on their differences, but on some shared interest or problem-solving task that has the potential to bring them together.

Clearly, many students hold assumptions about discussion that present difficulties for teaching critical thinking. Deeply personal issues are, of course, among the most difficult places for anyone to apply such skills. But the ability to hold just such discussions would be an acid test of whether we have indeed fostered critical thinking in our students.

On the Uses of a Liberal Education

MARK EDMUNDSON

Today is evaluation day in my Freud class, and everything has changed. The class meets twice a week, late in the afternoon, and the clientele, about fifty undergraduates, tends to drag in and slump, looking disconsolate and a little lost, waiting for a jump start. To get the discussion moving, they usually require a joke, an anecdote, an off-the-wall question—When you were a kid, were your Halloween getups ego costumes, id costumes, or superego costumes? This sort of thing. But today, as soon as I flourish the forms, a buzz rises in the room. Today they write their assessment of the course, their assessments of me, and they are without a doubt wide-awake. "What is your evaluation of the instructor?" asks question number eight, entreating them to circle a number between five (excellent) and one (poor, poor). Whatever interpretive subtlety they've acquired during the term is now out the window. Edmundson: one to five, stand and shoot.

And they do. As I retreat through the door—I never stay around for this phase of the ritual—I look over my shoulder and see them toiling away like the devil's auditors. They're pitched into high writing gear, even the ones who struggle to squeeze out their journal entries word by word, stoked on a procedure they have by now supremely mastered. They're playing the informed consumer, letting the provider know where he's come through and where he's not quite up to snuff.

But why am I so distressed, bolting like a refugee out of my own classroom, where I usually hold easy sway? Chances are the evaluations will be much like what they've been in the past—they'll be just fine. It's likely that I'll be commended for being "interesting" (and I am commended, many times over), that I'll be cited for my relaxed and tolerant ways (that happens, too), that my sense of humor and capacity to connect the arcana of the subject matter with current culture will come in for some praise (yup). I've been hassled this term, finishing a manuscript, and so haven't given their journals the attention I should have, and for that I'm called—quite civilly, though—to account. Overall, I get off pretty well.

Yet I have to admit that I do not much like the image of myself that emerges from these forms, the image of knowledgeable, humorous detachment and bland tolerance. I do not like the forms themselves, with their number ratings, reminiscent of the sheets circulated after the TV pilot has just played to its sample audience in Burbank. Most of all I dislike the attitude of calm

MARK EDMUNDSON *is professor of English at the University of Virginia and a contributing editor of* Harper's Magazine. *He is the author of* Nightmare on Main Street, *a study of the gothic in contemporary culture. From "On the Uses of a Liberal Education," by Mark Edmundson. Copyright 1997 by* Harper's Magazine. *All rights reserved. Reproduced from the September issue by special permission.*

consumer expertise that pervades the responses. I'm disturbed by the serene belief that my function—and, more important, Freud's, or Shakespeare's, or Blake's—is to divert, entertain, and interest. Observes one respondent, not at all unrepresentative: "Edmundson has done a fantastic job of presenting this difficult, important & controversial material in an enjoyable and approachable way."

Thanks but no thanks. I don't teach to amuse, to divert, or even, for that matter, to be merely interesting. When someone says she "enjoyed" the course—and that word crops up again and again in my evaluations—somewhere at the edge of my immediate complacency I feel encroaching self-dislike. That is not at all what I had in mind. The off-the-wall questions and the sidebar jokes are meant as lead-ins to stronger stuff—in the case of the Freud course, to a complexly tragic view of life. But the affability and the one-liners often seem to be all that land with the students, their journals and evaluations leave me little doubt.

I want some of them to say that they've been changed by the course. I want them to measure themselves against what they've read. It's said that some time ago a Columbia University instructor used to issue a harsh two-part question. One: What book did you most dislike in the course? Two: What intellectual or characterological flaws in you does that dislike point to? The hand that framed that question was surely heavy. But at least it compels one to see intellectual work as a confrontation between two people, student and author, where the stakes matter. Those Columbia students were being asked to relate the quality of an *encounter,* not rate the action as though it had unfolded on the big screen.

Why are my students describing the Oedipus complex and the death drive as being interesting and enjoyable to contemplate? And why am I coming across as an urbane, mildly ironic, endlessly affable guide to this intellectual territory, operating without intensity, generous, funny and loose?

Because that's what works. On evaluation day, I reap the rewards of my partial compliance with the culture of my students and, too, with the culture of the university as it now operates. It's a culture that's gotten little exploration. Current critics tend to think that liberal-arts education is in crisis because universities have been invaded by professors with peculiar ideas: deconstruction, Lacanianism, feminism, queer theory. They believe that genius and tradition are out and that P.C., multiculturalism, and identity politics are in because of an invasion by tribes of tenured radicals, the late millennial equivalents of the Visigoth hoards that cracked Rome's walls.

But mulling over my evaluations and then trying to take a hard, extended look at campus life both here at the University of Virginia and around the country eventually led me to some different conclusions. To me, liberal-arts education is as ineffective as it is now not chiefly because there are a lot of strange theories in the air. (Used well, those theories *can* be illuminating.) Rather, it's that university culture, like American culture writ large, is, to put it crudely, ever more devoted to consumption and entertainment, to the using and using up of goods and images. For someone growing up in America now, there are few available alternatives to the cool consumer worldwide. My students didn't ask for that view, much less create it, but they bring a consumer *weltanschauung* to school, where it exerts a powerful, and largely unacknowledged, influence. If we want to understand current universities, with their multiple woes, we might try leaving the realms of expert debate and fine ideas and turning to the classrooms and campuses, where a new kind of weather is gathering. [. . .]

How did my students reach this peculiar state in which all passion seems to be spent? I think that many of them have imbibed their sense of self from consumer culture in general and from the tube in particular. They're the progeny of 100 cable channels and omnipresent Blockbuster outlets. TV, Marshall McLuhan famously said, is a cool medium. Those who play best on it are low-key and nonassertive; they blend in. Enthusiasm quickly looks absurd. The form of character that's most appealing on TV is calmly self-interested though never greedy, attuned to the conventions, and ironic. Judicious timing is preferred to sudden self-assertion. The TV medium is inhospitable to inspiration, improvisation, failures, slips. All must run perfectly.

Naturally, a cool youth culture is a marketing bonanza for producers of the right products, who do all they can to enlarge that culture and keep it grinding. The Internet, TV, and magazines now teem with what I call persona ads, ads for Nikes and Reeboks and Jeeps and Blazers that don't so much endorse the capacities of the product per se as show you what sort of person you will be once you've acquired it. The Jeep ad that features hip, outdoorsy kids whipping a Frisbee from mountaintop to mountaintop isn't so much about what Jeeps can do as it is about the kind of people who own them. Buy a Jeep and be one of them. The ad is of little consequence in itself, but expand its message exponentially and you have the central thrust of current consumer culture—buy in order to be. [. . .]

What they will not generally do, though, is indict the current system. They won't talk about how the exigencies of capitalism lead to a reserve army of the unemployed and nearly inevitable misery. That would be getting too loud, too brash. For the pervading view is the cool consumer perspective, where passion and strong admiration are forbidden. "To stand in awe of nothing, Numicus, is perhaps the one and only thing that can make a man happy and keep him so," says Horace in the *Epistles,* and I fear that his lines ought to hang as a motto over the university in this era of high consumer capitalism.

It's easy to mount one's high horse and blame the students for this state of affairs. But they didn't create the present culture of consumption. (It was largely my own generation, that of the Sixties, that let the counterculture search for pleasure devolve into a quest for commodities.) And they weren't the ones responsible, when they were six and seven and eight years old, for unplugging the TV set from time to time or for hauling off and kicking a hole through it. It's my generation of parents who sheltered these students, kept them away from the hard knocks of everyday life, making them cautious and overfragile, who demanded that their teachers, from grade school on, flatter them endlessly so that the kids are shocked if their college profs don't reflexively suck up to them.

Of course, the current generational style isn't simply derived from culture and environment. It's also about dollars. Students worry that taking too many chances with their educations will sabotage their future prospects. They're aware of the fact that a drop that looks more and more like one wall of the Grand Canyon separates the top economic tenth from the rest of the population. There's a sentiment currently abroad that if you step aside for a moment, to write, to travel, to fall too hard in love, you might lose position permanently. We may be on a conveyor belt, but it's worse down there on the filth-strewn floor. So don't sound off, don't blow your chances.

But wait. I teach at the famously conservative University of Virginia. Can I extend my view from Charlottesville to encompass the whole country, a whole generation of college students? I can only say that I hear comparable stories about classroom life from colleagues everywhere in America. When I visit other schools to lecture, I see a similar scene unfolding. There are, of course, terrific students everywhere. And they're all the better for the way they've had to strive against the existing conformity. At some of the small liberal-arts colleges, the tradition of strong engagement persists. But overall, the students strike me as being sweet and sad, hovering in a nearly suspended animation.

Too often now the pedagogical challenge is to make a lot from a little. Teaching Wordsworth's "Tintern Abbey," you ask for comments. No one responds. So you call on Stephen. Stephen: "The sound, this poem really flows." You: "Stephen seems interested in the music of the poem. We might extend his comment to ask if the poem's music coheres with its argument. Are they consistent? Or is there an emotional pain submerged here that's contrary to the poem's appealing melody?" All right, it's not usually that bad. But close. One friend describes it as rebound teaching: they proffer a weightless comment, you hit it back for all you're worth, then it comes dribbling out again. Occasionally a professor will try to explain away this intellectual timidity by describing the students as perpetrators of postmodern irony, a highly sophisticated mode. Everything's a slick counterfeit, a simulacrum, so by no means should any phenomenon be taken seriously. But the students don't have the urbane, Oscar Wilde-type demeanor that should go with this view. Oscar was cheerful, funny, confident, strange. (Wilde, mortally ill, living in a Paris flophouse: "My wallpaper and I are fighting a duel to the death. One or the other of us has to go.") This generation's style is considerate, easy to please, and a touch depressed.

Granted, you might say, the kids come to school immersed in a consumer mentality—they're good Americans, after all—but then the university and the professors do everything in their power to fight that dreary mind-set in the interest of higher ideals, right? So it should be. But let us look at what is actually coming to pass.

Over the past few years, the physical layout of my university has been changing. To put it a little indecorously, the place is looking more and more like a retirement spread for the young. Our funds go to construction, into new dorms, into renovating the student union. We have a new aquatics center and ever-improving gyms, stocked with StairMasters and Nautilus machines. Engraved on the wall in the gleaming aquatics building is a line by our founder, Thomas Jefferson, declaring that everyone ought to get about two hours' exercise a day. Clearly even the author of the Declaration of Independence endorses the turning of his university into a sports-and-fitness emporium.

But such improvements shouldn't be surprising. Universities need to attract the best (that is, the smartest *and* the richest) students in order to survive in an ever more competitive market. Schools want kids whose parents can pay the full freight, not the ones who need scholarships or want to bargain down the tuition costs. If the marketing surveys say that the kids require sports centers, then, trustees willing, they shall have them. In fact, as I began looking around, I came to see that more and more of what's going on in the university is customer driven. The consumer pressures that beset me on evaluation day are only a part of an overall trend. [. . .]

How did we reach this point? In part the answer is a matter of demographics and (surprise) of money. Aided by the G.I. bill, the college-going population in America dramatically increased after the Second World War. Then came the baby boomers, and to accommodate them, schools continued to grow. Universities expand easily enough, but with tenure locking faculty in for lifetime jobs, and with the general reluctance of administrators to eliminate their own slots, it's not easy for a university to contract. So after the baby boomers had passed through—like a fat meal digested by a boa constrictor—the colleges turned to energetic promotional strategies to fill the empty chairs. And suddenly college became a buyer's market. What students and their parents wanted had to be taken more and more into account. That usually mean creating more comfortable, less challenging environments, places where almost no one failed, everything was enjoyable, and everyone was nice.

Just as universities must compete with one another for students, so must the individual departments. At a time of rank economic anxiety, the English and history majors have to contend for students against the more success-insuring branches, such as the sciences and the commerce school. In 1968, more than 21 percent of all bachelors' degrees conferred in America were in the humanities; by 1993, that number had fallen to about 13 percent. The humanities now must struggle to attract students, many of whose parents devoutly wish they would study something else.

One of the ways we've tried to stay attractive is by loosening up. We grade much more softly than our colleagues in science. In English, we don't give many Ds, or Cs for that matter. (The rigors of Chem 101 create almost as many English majors per year as do the splendors of Shakespeare.) A professor at Stanford recently explained grade inflation in the humanities by observing that the undergraduates were getting smarter every year; the higher grades simply recorded how much better they were than their predecessors. Sure.

Along with softening the grades, many humanities departments have relaxed major requirements. There are some good reasons for introducing more choice into curricula and requiring fewer standard courses. But the move, like many others in the university now, jibes with a tendency to serve—and not challenge—the students. Students can also float in and out of classes during the first two weeks of each term without making any commitment. The common name for this time span—shopping period—speaks volumes about the consumer mentality that's now in play. Usually, too, the kids can drop courses up until the last month with only an innocuous "W" on their transcripts. Does a course look too challenging? No problem. Take it pass-fail. A happy consumer is, by definition, one with multiple options, one who can always have what he wants. And since a course is something the students and their parents have bought and paid for, why can't they do with it pretty much as they please? [. . .]

Is it a surprise, then, that this generation of students—steeped in consumer culture before going off to school, treated as potent customers by the university well before their date of arrival, then pandered to from day one until the morning of the final kiss-off from Kermit or one of his kin—are inclined to see the books they read as a string of entertainments to be placidly enjoyed or languidly cast down? Given the way universities are now administered (which is more and more to say, given the way that they are currently marketed), is it a shock that the kids don't come to school hot to learn, unable to bear their own ignorance? For some measure of self-dislike, or self-discontent—which is much different than simple depression—seems to me to be a prerequisite for getting an education that matters. My students, alas, usually lack the confidence to acknowledge what would be their most precious asset for learning: their ignorance. [. . .]

Then how do those who at least occasionally promote genius and high literary ideals look to current students? How do we appear, those of us who take teaching to be something of a performance art and who imagine that if you give yourself over completely to your subject you'll be rewarded with insight beyond what you individually command?

I'm reminded of an old piece of newsreel footage I saw once. The speaker (perhaps it was Lenin, maybe Trotsky) was haranguing a large crowd. He was expostulating, arm waving, carrying on. Whether it was flawed technology or the man himself, I'm not sure, but the orator looked like an intricate mechanical device that had sprung into fast-forward. To my students, who mistrust enthusiasm in every form, that's me when I start riffing about Freud or Blake. But more and more, as my evaluations showed, I've been replacing enthusiasm and intellectual animation with stand-up routines, keeping it all at arm's length, praising under the cover of irony.

It's too bad that the idea of genius has been denigrated so far, because it actually offers a live alternative to the demoralizing culture of hip in which most of my students are mired. By embracing the works and lives of extraordinary people, you can adapt new ideals to revise those that came courtesy of your parents, your neighborhood, your clan—or the tube. The aim of a good liberal-arts education was once, to adapt an observation by the scholar, Walter Jackson Bate, to see that "we need not be the passive victims of what we deterministically call 'circumstances' (social, cultural or reductively psychological-personal), but that by linking ourselves through what Keats calls an 'immortal free-masonry' with the great, we can become freer—freer to be ourselves, to be what we most want and value."

But genius isn't just a personal standard; genius can also have political effect. To me, one of the best things about democratic thinking is the conviction that genius can spring up anywhere. Walt Whitman is born into the working class and thirty-six years later we have a poetic image of America that gives a passionate dimension to the legalistic brilliance of the Constitution. A democracy needs to constantly develop, and to do so it requires the most powerful visionary minds to interpret the present and to propose possible shapes for the future. By continuing to notice and praise genius, we create a culture in which the kind of poetic gamble that Whitman made—a gamble in which failure would have entailed rank humiliation, depression, maybe suicide—still takes place. By rebelling against established ways of seeing and saying things, genius helps us to apprehend how malleable the present is and how promising and fraught with danger is the future. If we teachers do not endorse genius and self-overcoming, can we be surprised when our students find their ideal images in TV's latest persona ads?

A world uninterested in genius is a despondent place; whose sad denizens drift from coffee bar to Prozac dispensary, unfired by ideals, by the glowing image of the self that one might become. As Northrop Frye says in a beautiful and now dramatically unfashionable sentence, "The artist who uses the same energy and genius that Homer and Isaiah had will find that he not only lives in the same palace of art as Homer and Isaiah, but lives in it at the same time." We ought not to deny the existence of such a place simply because we, or those we care for, find the demands it makes intimidating, the rent too high.

What happens if we keep trudging along this bleak course? What happens if our most intelligent students never learn to strive to overcome what they are? What if genius, and the imitation of genius, become silly, outmoded ideas? What you're likely to get are more and more one-dimensional men and women. These will be people who live for easy pleasure, for comfort and prosperity, who think of money first, then second, and third, who hug the status quo; people who believe in God as a sort of insurance policy (cover your bets); people who are never surprised. They will be people so pleased with themselves (when they're not in despair at the general pointlessness of their lives) that they cannot imagine humanity could do better. They'll think it their highest duty to clone themselves as frequently as possible. They'll claim to be happy, and they'll live a long time.

It is probably time now to offer a spate of inspiring solutions. Here ought to come a list of reforms with due notations about a core curriculum and various requirements. What the traditionalists who offer such solutions miss is that no matter what our current students are given to read, many of them will simply translate it into melodramas, with flat characters and predictable morals. (The unabated capitalist culture that conservative critics so often endorse has put students in a position to do little else.) One can't simply wave a curricular wand and reverse acculturation.

Perhaps it would be a good idea to try firing the counselors and sending half the deans back into the classrooms, dismantling the football team and making the stadium into a playground for local kids, emptying the fraternities, and boarding up the student-activities office. Such measures would convey the message that American colleges are not northern outposts of Club Med. A willingness on the part of the faculty to defy student conviction and affront them occasionally—to be usefully offensive—also might not be a bad thing. We professors talk a lot about subversion, which generally means subverting the view of people who never hear us talk or read our work. But to subvert the view of our students, our customers, that would be something else again.

Ultimately, though, it is up to individuals—and individual students in particular—to make their own way against the current sludgy tide. There's still the library, still the museum, there's still the occasional teacher who lives to find things greater than herself to admire. There are still fellow students who have not been cowed. Universities are inefficient, cluttered, archaic places, with many unguarded corners where one can open a book or gaze out onto the larger world and construe it freely. Those who do as much, trusting themselves against the weight of current opinion, will have contributed something to bringing this sad dispensation to an end. As for myself, I'm canning my low-key one-liners; when the kids' TV-based tastes come to the fore, I'll aim and shoot. And when it's time to praise genius, I'll try to do it in the right style, full-out, with faith that finer artistic spirits (maybe not Homer and Isaiah quite, but close, close), still alive somewhere in the ether, will help me out when my invention flags; the students doze, or the dean mutters into the phone. I'm getting back to a more exuberant style, I'll be expostulating and arm waving straight into the millennium, yes I will.

Has Student Consumerism Gone Too Far?

Michael Pernal

There is little doubt that college administrators are changing their methods of dealing with students because of the movement that has come to be known as "student consumerism." As a result of state and federal legislation, court rulings, and voluntary changes on the part of colleges themselves, higher education institutions are now viewed by many as *marketers* of products or services. Students, in turn, have come to be regarded as *purchasers*.

While much has happened to support such a trend, it should be kept in mind that the student consumer phenomenon actually developed as an offshoot of the general consumer movement in the United States. Although a number of similarities exist between the two, there is much about the student-college relationship that is unique to the educational environment. As a result, strict marketplace applications of this relationship occasionally miss the mark.

This article, which acknowledges the fact that many reforms were necessary to protect students from abuses at colleges, will attempt to advance the notion that further development of student-college relationships within the concept of consumerism should be undertaken only after serious study. In short, this article asks the question: Have we gone far enough to protect the interests of our students?

Where We Are Today

Few educators would claim that colleges view their students as they did 20 or 30 years ago. As a result of increasing court suits and legislation, colleges have gradually come to regard students more as adults and less as children who have been placed in the care of deans, administrators, and faculty members. The Educational Amendments of 1976, for example, adopted a federal strategy for student consumerism. Colleges which disburse federal financial aid are now required to provide prospective students, on an annual basis, complete information regarding financial aid programs, application procedures, and conditions of awards (loan requirements, etc.). In addition, institutions of higher education must be prepared to furnish, upon request, placement statistics which indicate, by major or program, the college's record in finding employment for its graduates before students are obligated to contract for loans.

As a result of passage of such legislation and other bills like the Family Educational Rights and Privacy Act of 1974 (the so-called Buckley Amendment),

Michael Pernal *is dean of personnel administration at Eastern Connecticut State College in Willimantic.* From the College Board Review, *Summer 1977.*

the federal government has declared itself to be clearly on the side of the student. While few are prepared to argue that the student consumerism movement has not sprung up for good and valid reasons, concern does exist that institutions of higher education, both traditional and proprietary, will become buried in an avalanche of red tape and mounting expenses if additional public regulations force further adjustments to administrative practices. Many students themselves complain that registration lines have become more cumbersome because of the mountains of paper work and questionnaires that greet them in response to federal and/or state regulations concerning their rights and privileges. Despite significant red tape already caused by federal regulations involved with the Buckley Amendment, Educational Amendments of 1976, Title IX, etc., consumer advocates want colleges and universities to do more. Among the many possibilities suggested as further needs are the following:

- licensing of college recruiters by states or accreditation agencies;
- written contracts between professors and students with respect to course requirements, evaluative procedures and criteria, and grading practices; and
- abolishment of mandatory student activity fees in favor of voluntary fee structures, which permit users to pay and non-users to forgo.

Have We Gone Far Enough?

Despite cries for further action on the part of student consumer advocates, my contention is that we have gone far enough for the present in protecting the rights of students, and that more attention should be paid to measuring the impact of existing safeguards on the colleges' ability to maintain their integrity as educational institutions. It certainly can be argued that students should be protected from colleges that misrepresent programs. In fact, federal dollars can be withheld from institutions which give false or misleading impressions of the success of their graduates, the types of programs offered, the costs involved, etc. Students are also presently accorded avenues on most campuses for exercising their rights to nondiscrimination, grievances, privacy, disclosure of records, challenge of information contained in records, and a fair hearing in the case of disciplinary offenses. If the facts be known, many colleges have grown overly sensitive to protecting the rights of their students. While exceptions to this trend are still to be found, a question exists concerning the good that any further pressures on colleges would accomplish.

In particular, recent federal regulations, which were actually implemented to protect students from fly-by-night institutions that promise what they cannot deliver, have had a profound impact on academically oriented institutions (i.e., liberal arts colleges) which profess few vocational implications with respect to their degrees. One major example stemmed from abuses involving the federally insured student loan programs. Certain institutions fleeced the system by encouraging students to use the program to finance tuition and fees only to cease operations leaving students indebted to lending institutions with nothing to show for their investment. Resultant legislation now requires schools to furnish placement data to prospective student borrowers and to give complete breakdowns of academic and/or vocational programs. Few can argue that steps were not necessary to curb such abuses. The question remains, however, whether the safeguards which now exist are sufficient to protect students' interests as consumers.

In my opinion, the cause of consumer protection in higher education has reached a point where most of the bases are covered, and time should now be taken to see how well things work before additional steps are taken. It may be possible that further safeguards, well-intended as they may be, could impose unnecessary burdens on institutions without taking into account the fact that colleges and universities do not strictly fall into a seller-consumer framework.

Where the Model Breaks Down

In short, the unique relationship which exists between colleges and students does not adequately lend itself enough to the seller-purchaser model to justify further commitment to the consumer concept which advocates seek. Five of the ways in which application of such a framework breaks down are listed below.

1. The Problem of Performance

In a strict seller-purchaser model, the performance requirement rests clearly with the seller. Consumers who purchase an automobile or television set expect that the machine will render reasonably trouble-free service or they can seek adjustment or replacement. In similar fashion, purchasers of a service such as legal assistance can expect certain actions or performance levels on the part of an attorney. Basically, therefore, the consumer model is premised on a certain degree of passivity on the part of the purchaser. The performance expectation rests clearly with the provider. In the college setting, however, a greater degree of responsibility rests with student consumers to maintain certain performance levels of their own. While students have a right to expect a certain level of performance on the part of the institution, the students cannot escape the fact that certain requirements are expected of them. Thus, a strict consumer framework is not entirely applicable in the college setting, and considerable gray area can exist when students make contentions that they are being shortchanged by poor teaching, administrative procedures, etc.

2.The Degree Is a Dual Creation

In the consumer marketplace, a clear distinction exists between who creates the product or service and who uses that creation. A manufacturer creates a product or service and offers it to individuals for a price. As a general rule, the purchaser has no hand in the creation of the product. Unless the user damages a manufactured product, it does not change as a result of its usage. In contrast, however, the product dispensed by colleges and universities is a mutual creation. Specifically, the college degree or licensing certificate is packaged mutually by the institution and its students. Attainment of a college degree is realized as much by the input of the student (examinations, term papers, lab experiments, class discussion, etc.) as by the role of the various instructors and administrators. As a result, it is difficult to prove that any two B.A. degrees, even if granted by the same institution, are alike. In short, colleges must not be boxed into situations that force them to advertise the value of particular programs with respect to occupational implications. Prospective employers judge the credentials of student applicants as much as, if not more than, the institutions from which they are graduated.

3.There Is No Warranty

In the general marketplace, we can think of a familiar consumer protection that is not accorded college students—the warranty. In actuality, the warranty is a protection more for the *seller* than for the *consumer.* It usually indicates that, after a specified time, the product can fall apart without any obligation forced on its manufacturer. In effect, it is the seller who is protected in the long run. After a brief period, the consumer is left powerless. In the educational setting, the college is not protected by a warranty which indicates that the result of its service need only work for a brief, specified time. Students and the general public expect colleges to provide some sort of preparation for life and tend to hold the failings of colleges accountable for a far longer period than we expect of consumer products in general. In fact, the best an educational institution can hope to do is alter its programs, when funds permit, to reflect a constantly changing occupational marketplace. Consequently, the choice of degree or program of study places as much responsibility on the student to seek information as it does on the institution to provide it.

4.The College Is not Necessarily Selling Anything

There is never any doubt in the general marketplace that the producer is selling either a product or a service. In the academic setting, the notion has arisen that colleges and universities are also placing a commodity on sale. Consumer advocates would have us believe that education is a product that is dispensed, quite simply, for a price. This argument, however, is strained at best. As long as colleges do not make such claims, education cannot be regarded as a commodity since there exists no way to measure the absolute value of a degree or certificate. Such value is dependent on a set of specifications that result from the interplay of individual students with a whole set of instructors, textbooks, outside activities, facilities, and resources. In short, students take what they choose from their educational experiences. Just what is sold can never be defined.

5. The Problem of Profit

A final way in which consumer advocates cannot reconcile the uniqueness of educational institutions centers around the question of profit. In the general community, products and services are offered to the public with the purpose of providing a profit for the producer. With the exception of proprietary institutions, the same condition simply does not hold true for colleges and universities. Consequently, decisions on how much to bill for tuition, room, board, etc. are predicated on providing educational services at the lowest possible cost. The financial records of institutions are usually available to public scrutiny in ways that are not available to the general consumer who has a complaint against a manufacturing company. Thus, the traditional decision made by colleges to bill all students for campus activities is predicated, not on reasons designed to raise income, but on the promise that such activities enhance the educational opportunities of all students, both participants and nonparticipants. While I am certain that abuses exist, it can be said that the profit motive provides a unique distinction which separates educational institutions from strict consumer comparisons.

While the major thrust of the student consumerism movement in higher education has been a much needed phenomenon, the time has come to reassess its impact in light of the nature of educational institutions. If the relationship between college and student is developed further in a strict consumer framework, we risk losing a number of important features of colleges by developing a legalistic orientation designed to satisfy external regulations. As a result, colleges could lose their uniqueness and ability to operate independently in the pursuit of knowledge. In short, the ability of institutions to educate men and women would diminish in such a framework. The pluralism among American colleges and universities would tend to disappear as institutions conform to externally invoked regulations and guidelines.

In conclusion, it is acknowledged that the consumerism movement in higher education continues to serve a useful purpose. Among other things, it has alerted colleges to assess more carefully their roles in society at large. At the same time, it should also be acknowledged that further developments toward consumerism should be advocated only after taking into consideration the perspective that we are dealing with unique institutions whose mission is not to sell, but to educate.

The Student as Consumer: The Implications and Limitations of a Metaphor

JILL J. McMILLAN AND GEORGE CHENEY

The metaphor of "Student as Consumer" appeared upon the social horizon in North America and Western Europe seemingly for all the right reasons: the responsibility of higher education to its public, the attendant accountability, an interest in practical applications of knowledge, and spiraling increases in the cost of going to college. Widespread adoption of the metaphor, however, can produce some negative educational consequences. Drawing upon the literatures of organizational studies, education, communication and rhetoric, we trace the rise of the student consumer metaphor, explore its limitations, and suggest alternatives to its use. Specifically, we argue that this metaphor (a) suggests undue distance between the student and the educational process; (b) highlights the promotional activities of professors and promotes the entertainment mode of classroom learning; (c) inappropriately compartmentalizes the educational experiences as a product rather than a process; and (d) reinforces individualism at the expense of community. We conclude with a consideration of a more embracing model of the learning process which we term "critical engagement."

We rely so heavily on metaphor that we often overlook its powerful and practical role in our discourse.[1] Euphemisms such as the currently popular organizational terms "downsizing" or "rightsizing" become so widely accepted that many users forget the old-fashioned and more brutally direct terms "firing" and "layoffs." And, every organizational member recognizes and has learned to respond appropriately (i.e., in the organizationally expected way) to such potent expressions as "We've got to destroy the competition"; "Her power rose yesterday"; and "This negotiation is just a game." Also metaphors migrate from one domain of human activity to another: for example, "blow-by-blow," "networking," and "dead wood." These and other metaphors can be compelling to users and bearers, not only in the sense of making conversation or written speech more lively, but also in winning an argument or altering a viewpoint (see Lakoff & Johnson, 1980).

JILL J. McMILLAN *is an associate professor of speech communication at Wake Forest University.* GEORGE CHENEY *is an associate professor in the Department of Communication Studies at the University of Montana. Earlier drafts of this paper were presented at the annual Macromarketing Conference in Boulder, Colorado, August 1994, the annual meeting of the International Communication Association, Albuquerque, New Mexico, May 1995, and the annual meeting of the Speech Communication Association., San Antonio, Texas, November 1995. From* Communication Education, *January 1996.*

It is now commonplace in the scholarly literature to observe that metaphors and other tropes and figures do more than simply decorate discourse (see Burke, 1945/1969). Still, we often fail to recognize how these compelling metaphors actually contribute to our knowledge of who we are, both individually and collectively. As Bellah, Madsen, Sullivan, Swindler, and Tipton (1991) observe:

> . . . While we in concert with others create institutions, they also create us: they educate us and form us—especially through the socially enacted metaphors they give us, metaphors that provide normative interpretations of situations and actions. (p. 12)

The metaphor of organization as machine, for example, arose early in this century and eventually came to dominate not only theorizing about worklife but also managerial practice. Today, as the century draws to a close, the same metaphor is prevalent in business, government, education, athletics, health care and other institutional contexts. In fact, its implications continue to be far-reaching, especially in terms of how the metaphor casts the role of the individual person, the organizational member.

The initially appealing metaphor of "student as consumer" has found its way into the vocabulary and practice of the educational institution and it suggests questionable practical and social consequences for all constituents. From a Southeastern school system which touts "School work is our work" and plasters stickers to that effect on student lunchboxes to the lofty forum of the American Association of Higher Education (AAHE), the "student as consumer" metaphor increasingly has found traction in public discourse. In fact, for the last few years, the AAHE, itself a prominent force in education and a source of national standards for many in higher education, has virtually adopted the metaphor. In the 1990s, the student/client/consumer metaphor has been especially prevalent as the AAHE has explored assessment of education outcomes. Now, for many, assessment *equals* the specific application of the student/client/consumer metaphor for program evaluation.

We argue in this essay that all of us concerned with education ought to take a closer look at the currently popular model of "student as consumer," a metaphor which appeared in the 1980s seemingly for all the right reasons—responsibility, accountability and practical relevance, to mention a few—but whose popularity and institutionalization threatens to reshape educational philosophy and process in some rather alarming ways. It may seem a bit of a stretch to lay the potential for such drastic organizational restructuring at the feet of one small metaphor. If we believe, however, that we have a certain tendency to *become* what we *say we are,* then perhaps such attribution is not so far-fetched. Our analysis is premised on just such ideas: that language is powerful, both descriptively and prescriptively; that in particular ways it can shape the way we think and act, especially in terms of the application of compelling labels and categories; that it announces what we know and how we know it, often embodying or promoting the taken-for-granted quality of our collective understandings; and that when collectively we come to share a linguistic construction, language shapes our institutions as well—in that the very distinctions and classifications we make come to affect our future thinking and behaviors in much the same way as a rule can come to "rule" its creators (see Douglas, 1986).

To advance our basic argument here, we will explore the limitations of the student-as-consumer metaphor and suggest alternatives to its use. [. . .]

Limitations of the Student-as-Consumer Metaphor

As is the case with most metaphors, there is nothing inherently wrong with the "student as consumer." With Joan Stark (1977), we believe that educational institutions should be held accountable for the goods and services that they provide: that is, they should be willing to describe their services, announce the price, specify outcomes, participate in assessment, and provide channels for complaints. Like William Massy (1989), we believe that educational institutions should adapt to the needs and interests of their constituencies. In other words, changing social and cultural trends, such as multi-culturalism and affirmative actions, should be assessed and often appropriately assimilated into the academic and social life of the institution. Along with Derek Bok (quoted in McMillen, 1991), we believe that organizations should generate and use their financial resources responsibly. While the lure of television revenues for big-time athletics or the increasing appetite for profits from scientific study may be appealing, educational institutions owe it to their constituencies to preserve their financial as well as their philosophical integrity. Like John Farago (1982), we believe that academics should not cloister themselves away from the activities and concerns of the "real world," from which their student charges come and to which most must return—hopefully with a job. Educational institutions should acknowledge the cold realities of a turbulent job market which may face students and their parents, rather than treating such concerns as superficial and shallow. Finally, we agree with Frank Riessman (1988) that we are obligated to train students "to find and raise their voices" even when what they say is disturbing. In short, our quarrel is not with the positive aspect of accountability and responsiveness that the consumer metaphor highlights; it is rather with those aspects of the educational process which the metaphor obscures or dismisses.

1. The student-as-consumer metaphor suggests undue distance between the student and the educational process. At the same time, the widespread adoption of the metaphor can undermine other organizational relationships: notably, those between faculty and administrators.
There is a rather natural temptation to treat organizations as boxes and their "environments" as everything outside. In fact, the organization-as-container metaphor went unquestioned in the writings of organizational theory until very recently (Cheney & Christensen, in press). However, the container metaphor is

limited in its suggestion that the boundaries of an organization really are fixed and perhaps even impermeable. In fact, the organization's identity, and therefore many of its activities, make sense *only in reference* to a larger environment. This is the case for any type of organization, but it is acutely relevant to *service* organizations such as schools, counseling centers, and advertising firms in which the "client" should be considered both a temporary member of the organization *and* an inhabitant of the larger environment "out there" (see Cheney, Block and Gordon, 1986). Such persons may regard themselves as *de facto* but unpaid (and often *paying*) members of the organization, especially if their association with it spans some months or even some years. In the case of student-clients, their dual status in a university, their ambiguous roles and their goals which are only partially aligned with those of the institution, are misrepresented by the metaphor which portrays students as "customers" alone. In fact, it is important for the advancement of higher education that students fulfill both roles simultaneously.

Because of students' confusing status in the organizational scheme, they are likely to have only partial commitment to the wider goals of the institution. Furthermore, they may shun the role of "co-creators" of the educational experience (Pernal, 1977). Keeping the educational process somewhat at arm's length, students may approach the university as they might a McDonald's drive-through window: selecting an option with little thought to the process that created the Big Mac or the Quarter Pounder. If students internalize the "outsider-consumer" identity, their attitude may tend toward that of a student representative to a recent faculty meeting at the first author's institution. When asked if she had any insights into why students were not signing up for advising appointments, she replied: "They are paying fifteen thousand to go here; they expect to see you whenever they want to." Even if their attitude is less consumer-oriented than that represented above, students may regard their confusing boundary status and temporary tenure as reason enough to withhold participation in the short-term planning of their school, and they and their parents may even become litigious if they believe that they have been victimized by "educational malpractice."

The consumer metaphor can adversely affect other organizational relationships as well: for example, those between administration and faculty. Keat (1990) argues that as the role of the "customer" becomes inflated, a greater degree of managerial interference may be expected. The reason for the increased control is that faculty are not viewed as having a high degree of autonomy in such a system. Thus, the cost-conscious, market-wise college president and administration may become more heavy-handed in surveillance over all aspects of academic life. [. . .]

2. The student-as-consumer metaphor excessively fosters the self-promotional activities of professors and at the same time promotes the entertainment model of learning.

Professors have recently displayed careerism and professional myopia consistent with the market imperative. A new breed of faculty has been "possessed by a vertical vision and career opportunities," in which the nebulous contract which is struck with the institution seeks to maximize income and minimize teaching responsibilities (Bledstein, 1976, p. 394). Talk of professors "marketing" themselves as commodities is now common in the academy. In fact, those who reject this strategy are often ridiculed as naïve and unrealistic. Farago (1982), himself an academic, puts the matter even more cynically. He believes that faculty members have historically prostituted themselves for student dollars in order to lead the cloistered life of autonomy and reflection: that our disappointment with our student-consumers is really anger at ourselves for having sold out.

Furthermore, when students are "consumers," teachers become vendors hawking their wares, a role which often frustrates and compromises them. In the age of rampant visual stimulation and sound bites, faculty members often identify more with Laurel and Hardy than with Aristotle or Kant. Neil Postman (1985) is one who has argued persuasively that the educational institution has been profoundly affected by the ascendancy of the televison medium, placing a new premium upon ad hoc, nonsequential learning, simplistic content, and the fast-paced visual stimulation to which television watchers have been acculturated. Postman laments:

> . . . they [students] will have learned that learning is a form of entertainment or, more precisely, that anything worth learning can take the form of entertainment, and ought to. And they will not rebel if their English teacher asks them to learn the eight parts of speech through the medium of rock music. Or if their social studies teacher sings to them the facts about the war of 1812. Or if their physics comes to them on cookies or T-shirts. Indeed, they will expect it. (p. 154)

3. The student-as-consumer metaphor inappropriately compartmentalizes the educational experience as a product as opposed to a process.

Not only does the consumer metaphor divide organizational membership over the matter of basic goals, it tends to recast those goals as well. While classical education sought to prepare an individual for citizenship, contemporary education tends to train for a job (Geiger, 1980). And those of us who have too long played the role of "deep pockets" to our children wonder what can be wrong with such pragmatism. Of course, we want our youth to be prepared for the job market, to be capable of making a good living for themselves and their families. And, we must both recognize and adapt to dramatic and sometimes brutal transformations of the U.S. workplace today (see, e.g., Rifkin, 1995). Increasingly, however, even colleges that espouse liberal learning seem only to be way stations on the way to "the job" (Riesman, 1980, pp. 312-13). In the last twenty years, business and management majors have doubled, mainly at the expense of history, philosophy, and English. In 1992, out of some 1.1 million bachelors' degrees awarded, one-quarter, or 256,000 students received B.A.'s in business and management—compared to 7,500 in philosophy and religion (Staff, 1994, *Chronicle of Higher Education,* p. 31). Jacoby argues, "We have a zillion students—new crops graduate each year—adept at spreadsheets and risk management and fewer and fewer who know something of the Middle East or even American literature" (1991, p. 291). And what are we giving up by these wholesale defections to the marketplace? Bellah et al. (1991) argue that we are trading in "morally and socially sensitive people capable of responsible interaction" (pp. 177-178) for individuals who regard their brains as mere "commodities" (Harman & Hormann, 1993; Rich, 1979).

Critics denounce the wholesale capitulation of the academy to outside forces as a loss of integrity (Jacoby, 1991). As a result, some argue that we have yielded our "expertise" in favor of student "equality" (for a discussion of the tension between these two values, see Billig, Condor, Edwards, Gane, Middleton, & Radley, 1987). Stanford's William Massy (1989) claims, "tastes have changed: people used to be interested in the classics; now they are interested in making money. . . . We need to provide an interesting menu at the university. . . . If they don't like the menu, we have an obligation of change it" (p. 2). Consistent with this interpretation, many observers suggest that the pendulum moves back and forth: that a renewed interest in a broad liberal-arts education may soon be upon us. In fact, some recent surveys of CEOs show a preference for broadly educated students. Students, however, apparently need more convincing (Butcher, 1990).

In a study of twenty-eight liberal arts institutions, Ragan and McMillan (1989) found that a predominant theme of the public discourse of the schools included equally strong appeals to both a classical and a vocational education. In a sort of "all things to all people" tone, the schools consistently tout their classical roots while promising market skills as well. Ragan and McMillan concluded that these institutions have indeed adapted to the fiercely competitive academic marketplace, while glossing over the fact that the two somewhat contradictory claims which they have woven together so artfully may not always harmoniously coexist in pedagogical practice.

Organizational theorists (e.g., Kaldor, 1971; Stampfl, 1978) warn that disturbing things happen when organizations become too preoccupied with the marketplace: namely, they no longer are able to set their own goals, they cannot capitalize on their own unique strengths, they are unable to predict and to plan, and they may strike dangerous compromises in their own activities in order to serve the whims of the public. In a poignant example, Carnegie-Mellon University's academic units, traditionally called simply "departments," are now commonly referred to as "profit centers." Jacoby (1991) warns that in search of the action, the modern university may have lost its soul (p. 292).

Thus far, we have tended to focus on the implications of the student-as-consumer metaphor for the professor and for the administrator. But, the potential problems with this model become even more apparent when we attend to what it means for the student. For example, those students who have internalized the consumer mentality are usually content to lay back and wait for the "quick information fix" (Martin, 1991, p. 35) which they believe they are due. Adrienne Rich (1979) describes the consumer mentality as one in which students expect to receive an education rather than to claim one: to be "acted upon" rather than to "act" in the pursuit of their educational goal (p. 231). Indeed student [. . .] "consumers" expect an exchange between the teacher and student which is increasingly monologic and unidirectional; in fact they may demand it. The first author received some criticisms of the portion of a recent course in which students were asked to give class reports. The complaints went something like this: "We didn't sign up to hear what our classmates have to say; we want to hear from you." Of course, the pedagogical sub-text in these comments supports the spoon-feeding approach to learning, the one-way transfer. The position is one of an "academic bystander," waiting to be presented with the most attractive academic option, rather than a co-participant in the transactional enterprise of learning (Pernal, 1977; Rich, 1979).

Riesman (1980) claims that in the numerous interviews which he has done with college students perhaps the most frequent complaint is that they are "bored"—by a professor who speaks in a monotone, reads from ancient lecture notes, and gives examinations that are farcically easy. Rarely do students cite their own inaction or lack of accountability as the problem. [. . .]

4. The student-as-consumer metaphor reinforces individualism at the expense of community.

Consumerism is self-centered (Lasch, 1979; Levine, 1980; Schmookler, 1993); being "first in line" for The Sale, getting the "best price," receiving "top dollar," "beating out the competition," and "winning the bid." Each of these consumer mantras suggests a zero-sum mentality in which individuals must compete with one another for scarce resources. Indeed, some may argue that consumerism and competition are difficult to disentangle in the happy world of supposedly free enterprise, and that young people must learn both lessons well and without question.

But have we overdone it in the halls of learning where we claim to promote social cohesion and cooperation? Have we taught "getting ahead" so early and so well that subsequent attempts at community have no chance? Alfie Kohn (1986), in his persuasive book, *No Contest: The Case Against Competition*, argues that the message that competition is "appropriate, desirable, required, and even unavoidable is drummed into us from nursery school to graduate school." It is, argues Kohn, "the subtext of every lesson" (p. 25). And especially in higher education, the connection is drawn by students again and again that it might be nice to cooperate, but that sort of behavior just will not fly in the "real world."[7] Psychologist Elliot Aronson (1976) says that such individualistic notions form early:

> If you are a student who knows the correct answer and the teacher calls on one of the other kids, it is likely that you will sit there hoping and praying that the kid will come up with the wrong answer so that you will have a chance to show the teacher how smart you are. . . . Indeed, [children's] peers are their enemies—to be beaten. (p. 153, p. 206)

Alternatives to the Student-as-Consumer Metaphor

We have sought to demonstrate how the consumer metaphor has come to the academy and has influenced the perceptions and actions of all its constituencies: administration, faculty, students, and community alike. We have applauded the responsiveness and accountability which the metaphor calls for, but have decried its distancing, fracturing effect on organizational actors; its spotlighting of professors' self-promotion and entertainment; its "packaging" of the pedagogical process itself; and its emphasis on "meism" at the expense of the wider social good. At times we have perhaps overstated our case against the student-as-consumer metaphor, but we have done so to make our point clearly and forcefully and in the interest of provoking debate and discussion.

Our answers to the dilemma which we have raised are modest and they are few. They also are confined to what we know best, rhetoric and communication. There seem to be at least three suggestions which make sense, and we direct them to academics and nonacademics alike:

1. Be alert to the power of language and deliberate about linguistic choices.

Numerous writers (Beattie, 1987; Fassel, 1990; Schaef, 1987) have suggested that distraction has virtually become an American way of life, and we have learned to do it well—with TV "channel surfing," with alcohol and drugs, with technology, with work, with gambling, and even with more positive things such as health and fitness. When we stop "paying attention," argue Bellah et al. (1991), we diminish our collective intelligence, feeling, and moral sensitivity, and our social institutions become weakened and impoverished. More directly to our point, Schmookler (1993) suggests that we should especially keep a watch out for the "invisible sleight of hand" of the Market, which may appear to give us choices, but which may in fact create a world that we would not opt for if we were truly "free to choose and if we were wise" (p. 13).

Metaphors, too, bear watching and listening. How are they behaving? What might they be hiding? And most important, do they still mean what we want them to mean? A presumably useful metaphor, such as *Student as Consumer*, when we turn our backs on it, can drag us where we really don't want to go (cf. Wendt, 1994).

2. Strike a good balance: be adaptable, but maintain integrity.

Some interesting voices in this debate are those of the organizational theorists who warn: "We don't care what sort of organization you're running; it will run into trouble if you pay too much attention to *any one* constituency" (see Stampfl, 1978). So while those of us in higher education, in the early days of the metaphor, "attended" as we should have to the interests of our student-customers and their parents and to the community at large, this gaze may now be in danger of becoming a preoccupied "stare." From a rhetorical perspective, this preoccupation with the customer may represent excessive pandering to the audience. Wayne Booth (1972) argues that in any formal communication situation, there ought to be a good balance between the rhetorical concerns of *ethos, pathos* and *logos.* In our application, to overemphasize the customer's wishes of the moment is unduly to privilege *pathos* and thereby assume what Booth calls "the advertiser's stance." (One can, of course, err in a more traditional direction, too, by indulging only the informational content of the message, featuring *logos,* and thus assuming "the pedant's stance." Consider, for example, the image of the classics or the chemistry professor who simply reads from the text, maintaining that "the material speaks for itself.") Offering some examples to illustrate the problem, Booth quips that Winston Churchill would hardly be the historical figure that he is had he offered the British people "peace in our time" with some laughs thrown in because a market analysis had shown that "blood, sweat, and tears" was not playing well to the audience (p. 223).

Perhaps the educational institution should take heed. The rhetoric of accommodation to the customer may seem to work well in the short term, but the academy cannot not afford "quick fixes" at the expense of its long-term strength and integrity.

3. Explore alternative ways of expressing who we are and what we do.

When a metaphor becomes inappropriate or counterproductive, argues Turbayne (1970), "we should choose a new one" (p. 65); that is, we should look for different words to talk about who we are and what we do in the academy. Fairclough (1993) argues that today the consumer-driven rhetoric of "promotionalism" emanates from our halls of ivy. DuGay and Salaman (1992) remind us that "for an ideology/discourse to be considered hegemonic, it is not necessary for it to be loved" (p. 630). Rather, argues Leys (1990, p. 127, as quoted in DuGay & Salaman) it is merely necessary that it have no serious rival. Perhaps it is time for those of us who know the academic experience best to submit some serious rivals: some different words, some new metaphors, some creative images.

It has been suggested that we leave the "language of the sovereign consumer" (DuGay & Salaman, 1992), which features such terms as "objectivity," "control," "utility," and "quantity" (Bellah, et al., 1991), for "replacement metaphors." (Ivie, 1987) such as schools as "learning communities" (Gamson & Associates, 1984), as "communities of inquirers" (Peirce, quoted in Bellah, et al., 1991), as "communities of interpreters" (Royce, 1916). Even a move from "customer" to "client" would be helpful for education in that the client is not always right! In that vein, Solow (1993) suggests that educators adopt a relationship to students akin to that of a physical trainer; the teacher's role is to guide and direct the exercise of the muscle of the mind: "Having a good instructor," argues Solow, "is necessary to a successful workout, but the benefit of the session also depends on how hard members [students] work . . . No pain, no gain" (p. 1).

The innovative Marketing Department at Odense University, Denmark, practices what the alternatives above are preaching: In response to their students' challenges to adopt, reflexively, a "pure" (i.e., traditional) marketing orientation, the faculty responds:

> We take to be our mission a product orientation: that is to say, the development and presentation of the highest quality product possible in the study of marketing. We invite you, the student, to learn what we have to offer and to help shape and improve that product (personal conversations with the second author, 1993).

Thus one academic department seeks to demonstrate the redefinition of a metaphor: to show us that it is indeed possible, through intention and through language, to distribute accountability more equitably across stakeholders in the educational process. (Of course, a product metaphor has its limits, too.)

To those who would promote the student as consumer, we offer the counter-proposal of a model of *critical engagement.* In the past, of course, we were content simply to call students "students." Today, however, the felt need to redefine them is an indication of widespread dissatisfaction with institutions of higher learning, just as it is a diffusion of influence of the sovereign Market. We seek a model that does not distance students from the complete educational process, but one that includes, entices and involves them. At the same time, we need to recognize and preserve the legitimate province of expertise and authority in which faculty members do their work. Students can thus be seen as "collaborators in training," emphasizing that they are co-creators of the educational experience even though they have less experience than their instructors; "citizen-specialists," stressing both the breadth and focus of an individual's education; or "apprentices in learning," suggesting an intimate and multi-faceted relationship between the student and the instructor. Clearly, we need to depart from the old-fashioned model of passive information transmission, in which the student is viewed merely as a receptor and mirror, just as we should avoid the temptation to give students' momentary reactions full governing control of the educational process. The ideal of critical engagement is a classroom of dynamic presentations of important and interesting material, lively discussion and debate, open and constructive criticism, and experiences that not only *connect* with the "real" world but also *transform* perspectives on it. Critical engagement suggests mutual respect between teachers and students, common dedication to the process of learning, and allowance for changes in and re-creating of that process. Critical engagement means that students and teachers are "stakeholders" in education—each with interests, energies and talents to contribute. Students in this way can take a certain kind of "ownership" of learning while respecting the individual and collective wisdom of teachers. Above all and regardless of any terms, metaphors, or images we may settle upon, we should engage students, while preserving their right to critique and shape the very educational process in which they participate.

Notes

[1] As Roderick Hart (1990) observes, it is as if we have admitted a sort of linguistic defeat—that "literal" or prosaic language simply is not equal to the task of expressing our complex thoughts and emotions (p. 219). And so we employ colorful metaphors to decrease the distance between fallible symbols and "what we really mean," recognizing (at least at some level) that all language is metaphorical in that we are forced always to describe one thing in terms of another (see Burke, 1945/1969).

[2-6] . . .

[7] See Deetz (1992, p. 28), for a discussion of the political implications of attributing "realness" to the work world and "abstractness" to the educational one.

References

Aronson, E. (1976). *The social animal.* 2d. ed. San Francisco: W. H. Freeman.

Associated Press. (1994, September 28). Studies: Tuition rising, and colleges spending more on public relations. *Winston-Salem Journal,* p. 22.

Beattie, M. (1987). *Codependent no more.* New York: Harper and Row.

Bellah, R. N., Madsen, R., Sullivan, W., Swidler, A., & Tipton, S. (1985). *Habits of the heart.* Berkeley and Los Angeles: University of California Press.

Bellah, R. N., Madsen, R., Sullivan, W., Swidler, A., & Tipton, S. (1991). *The good society.* New York: Knopf.

Berger, P. (1969). *A rumor of angels.* Garden City, NJ: Doubleday.

Bevilacqua, J. (1976). The changing relationship between the university and the student: Implications for the classroom and student personnel work. *Journal of College Student Personnel, 17,* 489–494.

Billig, M., Condor, S., Edwards, D., Gane, M., Middleton, D. & Radley, A. (1987). *Ideological dilemmas: A social psychology of everyday thinking.* London: Sage.

Bledstein, B. J. (1976). *The culture of professionalism.* New York: W. W. Norton.

Booth, W. (1972). The rhetorical stance. In D. Ehninger (Ed.), *Contemporary Rhetoric* (pp. 218–225). Glenview, IL: Scott Foresman.

Burke, K. (1945/1969). *A grammar of motives.* Berkeley, CA: University of California Press.

Butcher, W. C. (1990). Applied humanities. *Vital Speeches of the Day,* 623–625.

Campbell, D. N. (1974). On being number one: Competition in education. *Phi Delta Kappan,* 143–146.

Cheney, G. (in progress). Passion, pressure and paradox: Maintaining humanistic values in a competitive worker-cooperative complex. Unpublished manuscript.

Cheney, G., Block, B., & Gordon, B. (1986). Perceptions of innovativeness and communication about innovations: A study of three types of service organizations. *Communication Quarterly, 34,* 213–230.

Cheney, G., & Christensen, L. T. (in press). Identity at issue: Linkages between "internal" and "external" organizational communication. In F. M. Jablin & Linda L. Putnam (Eds.), *Handbook of Organizational Communication: An Interdisciplinary Approach.* Newbury Park, CA: Sage.

Cherry, M. L., & Miller, M. (1994, February 3). The professor: What it is and what it can be. *Old gold and black of Wake Forest University,* p. 8.

Coleman, J. S., & Hoffer, T. (1987). *Public and private high schools: The impact of community.* New York: Basic Books.

Coleman, J. S., Hoffer, T., & Kilgore, S. (1982). *High school achievement: Public, private, and Catholic high schools compared.* New York: Basic Books.

Deetz, S. A. (1992). *Democracy in an age of corporate colonization.* New York: State University of New York Press.

Douglas, M. (1986). *How institutions think.* Syracuse, NY: Syracuse University Press.

DuGay, P. & Salaman, G. (1992). The cult[ure] of the customer. *Journal of Management Studies, 29,* 615–633.

El-Khawas, E. (1975). Consumerism as an emerging issue for postsecondary education. *Educational Record, 56,* 126–131.

El-Khawas, E. (1976). Clarifying roles and purposes. *New directions for higher education, 13,* 35–48.

El-Khawas, E. (1977, November). Management implications of student consumerism. *NACUBO business officer,* 18–21.

Entman, R. M., & Wildman, S. S. (1992). Reconsidering economic and non-economic perspectives on media policy: Transcending the "marketplace of ideas." *Journal of Communication, 42,* 5–19.

Ewen, S. (1976). *Captains of consciousness: Advertising and the social roots of the consumer culture.* New York: McGraw-Hill.

Fairclough, N. (1993). Critical discourse analysis and the marketization of public discourse: The universities. *Discourse and Society, 4,* 133–168.

Farago, J. M. (1982). When they bought in, did we sell out? *Journal of Higher Education, 53,* 701–715.

Fassel, D. (1990). *Working ourselves to death: The high cost of workaholism and the rewards of recovery.* San Francisco: Harper.

Featherstone, M. (1991). *Consumer culture and postmodernism.* London: Sage.

Gamson, Z. F., & Associates. (1984). *Liberating education.* San Francisco: Jossey-Bass.

Geertz, C. (1983). *Local knowledge.* New York: Basic Books.

Geiger, R. (1980). *The college curriculum and the marketplace: Academic discipline and the trend toward vocationalism in the 1970's.* Connecticut: Institute for Social and Policy Studies, Yale University.

Harman, W., & Hormann, J. (1993). The breakdown of the old paradigm. In M. Ray & A. Rinzler (Eds.), *The new paradigm in business* (pp. 16–27). New York: Jeremy P. Tarcher/Perigree.

Hart, R. (1990). *Modern rhetorical criticism.* Glenview, IL: Scott Foresman.

Hyde, M. J. (in press). Human being and the call of technology. In J. Wood & R. Gregg (Eds.), *The future of the field: Communication in the twenty-first century.* Cresskill, NJ: Hampton Press.

Ivie, R. L. (1987). Metaphor and the rhetorical invention of cold war "idealists." *Communication Monographs, 54,* 165–182.

Jacoby, R. (1991, Spring). The greening of the university. *Dissent,* 286–292.

Jung, S., & Hamilton, J. (1977). A student information floor. In J. Stark (Ed.), *The many faces of educational consumerism* (pp. xx–xy). Lexington, MA: D. C. Heath.

Kaldor, A. G. (1971). Imbricative marketing. *Journal of Marketing, 35,* 19–25.

Keat, R. (1990). "Introduction," In R. Keat, and N. Abercrombie (Eds.), *Enterprise Culture* (pp. 3–10). London: Routledge.

Kohn, A. (1986). *No contest: The case against competition.* Boston: Houghton Mifflin.

Lakoff, G. and Johnson, M. (1980). *Metaphors we live by.* Chicago: University of Chicago Press.

Lasch, C. (1979). *The culture of narcissism.* New York: Warner.

Levine, A. (1980). *When dreams and heroes died.* San Francisco: Jossey-Bass.

Lewis. L. S. and Altbach, P. G. (1994, January–February). The true crisis on campus. *Academe,* 24–26.

Leys, C. (1990). Still a question of hegemony. *New Left Review, 180,* 119–128.

Martin, M. (1991, April). Catering to the consumer. *Wilson Library Bulletin,* 34–35, 131.

Massy, W. (1989, January). Stanford school of education, a supplement of the *Stanford Observer,* p. 2.

McKitterick, J. B. (1958). What's the marketing management concept? In F. M. Bass (Ed.), *The frontiers of marketing thought and science* (pp. 71–82). Chicago: American Marketing Association.

McMillan, J. J. (1987). In search of the organizational persona: A rationale for studying organizations rhetorically. In L. Thayer (Ed.), *Organizations–Communication: Emerging perspectives* (pp. 21–45). Norwood, NJ: Ablex.

McMillen, L. (1991, April 24). Quest for profits may damage basic values of universities, Harvard's Bok warns. *Chronicle of Higher Education, 37,* A21, A31.

Oxford Dictionary of English Etymology (1966/1979). Oxford, England: Oxford University Press.

Paglia, C., & Postman, N. (1991, March). She wants her T.V.! He wants his book! *Harper's,* 44–55.

Penn, J. R., & Franks, R. G. (1982). Student consumerism in an era of conservative politics. *National Association of Student Personnel Administrators Journal, 19*(3), 28–37.

Pernal, M. (1977, Summer). Has student consumerism gone too far? *College Board Review,* 2–5.

Postman, N. (1985). *Amusing ourselves to death.* New York: Penguin.

Ragan, S. L., & McMillan, J. J. (1989). The marketing of the liberal arts. *Journal of Higher Education, 60,* 682–703.

Rich, A. (1979). Claiming an education. In A. Rich (Ed.), *On lies, secrets, and silence: Selected prose 1966–1978* (pp. 231–235). New York: Norton.

Riesman, D. (1980). *On higher education: The academic enterprise in an era of rising student consumerism.* San Francisco: Jossey-Bass.

Riessman, F. (1988). The next stage in education reform: The student as consumer. *Social Policy, 18*(4), 2.

Rifkin, J. (1995). *The end of work.* New York: Tarcher/Putnam.

Royce, J. (1916). *The hope of the great community.* New York: MacMillan.

Schaef, A. W. (1987). *When society becomes an addict.* San Francisco: Harper and Row.

Schmookler, A. B. (1993). *The illusion of choice: how the market economy shapes our destiny.* Albany, NY: State University of New York Press.

Smith, R. C., & Eisenberg, E. M. (1987). Conflict at Disneyland: A root-metaphor analysis. *Communication Monographs, 54,* 367–380.

Solomon, R., & Solomon, J. (1993). *Up the university.* Reading, MA: Addison-Wesley.

Solow, J. (1993, February). Passive vs. active learning. Paper presented at the conference *Learning and Iowa: Transcending tradeoffs between teaching and research,* Iowa City.

Staff. (1994). The nation: Students. *Chronicle of Higher Education, 41,* (1), 31.

Stampfl, R. (1978). Structural constraints, consumerism, and the marketing concept. *Michigan State University Business Topics, 26,* 5–16.

Stark, J. S. (1977). *The many faces of educational consumerism.* Lexington, MA: D. C. Heath.

Turbayne, C. M. (1970). *The myth of the metaphor.* (rev. ed.). Columbia, SC: University of South Carolina Press.

Wendt, R. F. (1994). Learning to "walk the talk": A critical tale of the micropolitics at a total quality university. *Management Communication Quarterly, 8*(1), 5–45.

Customers and Markets

CRAIG SWENSON

Most academic conferences these days include a paper in which the presenter calls on higher education to "respond to the needs of the market" and to "treat students as customers." As you listen, you can sense the hair rising on the backs of professorial necks.

During the coffee break following one such presentation, I overheard two professors conducting a postmortem. To view students as customers, one argued, leads inevitably to pandering. Students don't know what they don't know. That's the teacher's job—to guide them. All this talk about being responsive to the market, the other suggested, is about economics pure and simple. It has little to do with education. "The market," he said, paraphrasing Charles Dickens' famous observation about the law, "is an ass."

It was, frankly, a troubling conversation—one I've thought about many times since. I don't lack some sympathy for the view of these colleagues. A nostalgic part of me wants the campus to be a cloistered walk, a retreat from the market's incessant clamor. Students should come as intent on preparing to make a life as they are to make a living. Corporations should value as "skilled" employees who have drunk deeply from the well of knowledge and have learned to think broadly and critically.

I'm also a realist. Upwards of half our college and university students are now of the age group we used to refer to as nontraditional—of those, four out of five work full-time. Most will tell you they returned to college to better their economic lot in life. It's difficult to argue that these students shouldn't be viewed as intelligent consumers of higher education, even though doing so appeals to traditional, sometimes paternalistic views of the student-faculty relationship.

As adults, they return to school because they choose to, not to satisfy some coming-of-age ritual. Presumably, their greater life experience makes them abler to participate in determining their own educational needs. They've earned that right by virtue of being grown-up.

At a different level, a profound social transformation has accompanied our shift from a manufacturing to an information economy. If society has changed, it seems naïve to expect that its institutions wouldn't adapt and evolve as well. It seems clear, for example, that our economic future requires a workforce whose members have skills that are in many ways quite different from their predecessors.

"Knowledge" workers must be at once technically skilled and broadly educated. If knowledge doubles every seven years, it no longer seems possible

---

CRAIG SWENSON *is regional vice president at the University of Phoenix.* From Change, *September/ October 1998.*

for a person to learn the "body of knowledge" of a discipline. Rather, students will need increasingly to understand the foundation of a subject as well as how to access and how to use new knowledge as it comes available. Should we be surprised to find, then, that preparing adults who already have many of these skills will require us to change some of our own traditional practices? [. . .]

Customers as Consumers of Products

To the degree—as my coffee-break colleagues noted—that students "don't know what they don't know," it would be improper to allow them to dictate the specifications of the educational product. In the long run, customers would lose respect of an organization or its product if R&D or quality control were put in the hands of amateurs with short-term agendas. That's true of the college curriculum as well. The faculty can never abdicate its responsibility to ensure that what we teach reflects the hierarchy of knowledge in our disciplines.

What customer-driven organizations know, however, is that giving voice and listening to the people you serve is always essential and pays dividends. This is especially true in fields like health care and education, where the end "product" (health, learning) depends on the customer's active participation. In classrooms, for example, it's tempting for professors to assume that they are the ultimate experts on every topic and how it should be learned. With large numbers of adult students in our classrooms, though, it's likely that on any given night someone in class knows more from direct experience about a particular subject than the professor does. At the same time, faculties dismiss at their peril what students know about their own learning styles and needs.

When creating the 777, we might note, Boeing invested heavily in consulting not only with the airlines that would buy the planes, but with passengers who would fly in it. It's difficult to imagine Boeing adopting a customer's product suggestion that would endanger anyone's safety. But the engineers who designed that plan reported surprise at all the things they hadn't thought of. Their willingness to listen resulted in a superior aircraft.

Customers as Consumers of Services

When it comes to viewing customers as consumers of a service, most of us would agree that the customer is at least usually right. That's what each of us feels, isn't it, when we are on the receiving end of a service? We're quick to condemn the discourteous, slow, or unresponsive service we receive at a bank, service station, or department store. Why shouldn't students feel the same way about the services provided by our institutions?

With this distinction in mind, it seems fair to ask what students are entitled to by virtue of being customers of higher education. Further, in what ways are the organizations that employ our graduates also our customers? Here are five ways that colleges and universities can appropriately respond to students and their employers.

1. Create a culture that focuses on student learning instead of teaching.

In college, the motto of my accounting teachers was, "cover the material." I'm not suggesting that they didn't know their stuff—quite contrary. It just seemed that getting through the text by the end of the quarter was the goal—if students learned some accounting along the way, that was nice too.

But whose goal—and what customer was thus served? The goal of postsecondary educators should be that every one of our graduates knows and is able to do what his or her degree implies. Our business, then, is learning—not offering courses or covering the material.

Happily, most college classes are taught by instructors who know their subject matter and have high expectations for student performance. These are necessary but insufficient conditions for learning, however. Students also deserve "rich" learning environments. They deserve teachers who use methods that recognize differences in learning styles, and who understand that students will learn more if they are actively involved in their own learning. Students also deserve the right to learn from one another—a process that requires a teacher who can facilitate the exchange of information, ideas, and expertise. [. . .]

Our students further deserve answers to their questions, a clear understanding of expectations, rich and ample feedback on their work, real access to their teachers, and a learning environment that encourages them to take the personal risk of challenging, questioning, and exploring without fear of ridicule. What we give, we can then expect in return.

The assumptions upon which a learning culture depends are quite different from those for a culture emphasizing teaching. In the former, the student is at the center; in the latter, the subject matter. When student learning is the focus, the yardstick is not "Did I cover the material?" but "Did they learn what they should have?" A student (or employer) expects this. It is always the student's responsibility to learn, but the good sense of that must be met by teachers who will do everything possible to facilitate it.

2. Accept the responsibility to teach more than the course content.

Numerous studies have identified the skills needed for our students to become productive as knowledge workers. Those skills include the ability to write clearly and persuasively, to articulate and present ideas to others orally, to work capably in group and team settings, and to analyze and think critically about problems. A college education should teach these abilities as well as the subject matter of a field. But the attitude of some college teachers is an adamant, "That's not my job."

It is foolhardy to expect that a lone, required course in writing, public speaking, or critical thinking will be sufficient to develop these competencies. They require a longer term process of development (and practice), which means they have to be the aim of a learning process extending across the curriculum. The objection that "we don't have time" to teach these abilities and the subject matter betrays a poverty of aims and an ignorance of the learning process. Indeed, we can use development of these competencies to teach disciplinary knowledge more effectively; as we do so, students become more involved and effective in their own learning. Because of this link, we don't have time not to teach them.

Some students, especially some of the younger ones, won't welcome these ideas—so much for the customer always being right. Teachers will need to persuade students that these activities will prepare them better for the future. Also, students aren't the only customers here. The organizations that do or will employ them, as well as the larger society, are also customers to whom we must respond and these are the very abilities they demand of our graduates.

3. Involve students in establishing the objectives for their learning.

Regardless of age, all of us are students of subjects about which we are ignorant; we have limited abilities to make decisions about what to learn because we don't know what we don't know. However, if the literature of psychology tells us anything, it is that goal setting and task performance go hand in hand. Simply handing all students the same canned task seldom brings the personal engagement necessary to learning, especially for adults. To maximize that engagement, each student should have a part in setting goals for learning and have a measure of independence and control over the doing of assignments. This doesn't mean that teachers should abdicate their responsibility for creating a coherent curriculum. It does mean that they can't hope to do so alone.

4. Make administrative services available to students at times, in places, and in ways that meet their needs.

Treating students as customers requires support services that are convenient and accessible to them. Many colleges and universities enroll increasing numbers of commuting students, many of whom are working adults. For these students, services offered between 9 A.M. and 5 P.M., Monday through Friday, present real barriers to participation.

Students often report being forced to drop out or to take much longer to graduate than hoped because classes are often available only during "normal" business hours or only during semesters when certain professors are around. They might prefer to buy books on the way home from work or, better still, by phone or on the Internet; they can't afford to take off work to meet with an academic counselor at 10 in the morning. Soon enough, an institution's commuters come to see responses to their needs taking a back seat to those they perceive to be the real customers of the institution—its faculty and administrators.

Having customers implies giving prompt, courteous, and responsive service. It suggests following through on our commitments to them, returning their phone calls, and not making them feel they are bothering us (as in "This would be a great place to work if it weren't for those—ed students"). It requires that we treat them as we expect to be treated when we are on the receiving end of a service.

5. Listen to the corporate customer.

In my interactions with colleagues who've spent most of their adult lives in higher education, I often sense condescension toward people who chose business as a career. Too many professors think they are better and smarter than those who chose the other path—that higher education is a purer, worthier pursuit.

But my executive friends are as bright, capable, well-rounded, and virtuous as my professor friends. As responsible executives, they know what they need in employees and don't think it too much to ask that higher education assume a share of the burden for preparing them. In many cases, they're footing the bill for their employees' education. They've also found educators who are arrogant and unwilling to listen when they try to make this point.

Contrary to academic belief, business people do not want narrowly educated employees. They recognize the value of people who understand more than just their own jobs. And they believe that the practical and the theoretical can indeed be married. Some give and take on both sides, then, could result in real improvement in the product of higher education.

In sum: having "customers" in higher education doesn't mean pandering. It doesn't mean the customer is always right. It doesn't mean we never say no. It does mean treating people with respect. It means listening and adapting. It means balancing the goals of a liberal education with those of a practical education without diminishing the worth of either.

I believe it is possible to treat students and their employers as customers to be responsive to markets without apology. If higher education won't do so, I'm sure others will.

SECTION 2

Bingeing, Risk, and Public Health

Health and Behavioral Consequences of Binge Drinking in College
A National Survey of Students at 140 Campuses

HENRY WECHSLER, ANDREA DAVENPORT, GEORGE DOWDALL, BARBARA MOEYKENS, AND SONIA CASTILLO

Objective.—To examine the extent of binge drinking by college students and the ensuing health and behavioral problems that binge drinkers create for themselves and others on their campus.

Design.—Self-administered survey mailed to a national representative sample of US 4-year college students.

Setting.—One hundred forty US 4-year colleges in 1993.

Participants.—A total of 17,592 college students.

Main Outcome Measures.—Self-reports of drinking behavior, alcohol-related health problems, and other problems.

Results.—Almost half (44%) of college students responding to the survey were binge drinkers, including almost one fifth (19%) of the students who were frequent binge drinkers. Frequent binge drinkers are more likely to experience serious health and other consequences of their drinking behavior than other students. Almost half (47%) of the frequent binge drinkers experienced five or more different drinking-related problems, including injuries and engaging in unplanned sex, since the beginning of the school year. Most binge drinkers do not consider themselves to be problem

From Journal of the American Medical Association, *December 7, 1994.*

drinkers and have not sought treatment for an alcohol problem. Binge drinkers create problems for classmates who are not binge drinkers. Students who are not binge drinkers at schools with higher binge rates were more likely than students at schools with lower binge rates to experience problems such as being pushed, hit, or assaulted or experiencing an unwanted sexual advance.

Conclusions.—Binge drinking is widespread on college campuses. Programs aimed at reducing this problem should focus on frequent binge drinkers, refer them to treatment or educational programs, and emphasize the harm they cause for students who are not binge drinkers.

Heavy episodic or binge drinking poses a danger of serious health and other consequences for alcohol abusers and for others in the immediate environment. Alcohol contributes to the leading causes of accidental death in the United States, such as motor vehicle crashes and falls.[1] Alcohol abuse is seen as contributing to almost half of motor vehicle fatalities, the most important cause of death among young Americans.[2] Unsafe sex—a growing threat with the spread of acquired immunodeficiency syndrome (AIDS) and other sexually transmitted diseases—and unintentional injuries have been associated with alcohol intoxication.[3-5] These findings support the view of college presidents who believe that alcohol abuse is the number 1 problem on campus.[6]

Despite the fact that alcohol is illegal for most undergraduates, alcohol continues to be widely used on most college campuses today. Since the national study of Straus and Bacon in 1949,[7] numerous subsequent surveys have documented the overwhelming use of alcohol by college students and have pointed to problem drinking among this group.[8] Most previous studies of drinking by college students have been conducted on single college campuses and have not used random sampling of students.[9-12] While these studies are in general agreement about the prevalence and consequences of binge drinking, they do not provide a national representative sample of college drinking.

A few large-scale, multicollege surveys have been conducted in recent years. However, these have not selected a representative national sample of colleges, but have used colleges in one state[3] or those participating in a federal program,[5] or have followed a sample of high school seniors through college.[13]

In general, studies of college alcohol use have consistently found higher rates of binge drinking among men than women. However, these studies used the same definition of binge drinking for men and women, without taking into account sex differences in metabolism of ethanol or in body mass.[3,5,9,12,14-17]

The consequences of binge drinking often pose serious risks for drinkers and for others in the college environment. Binge drinking has been associated with unplanned and unsafe sexual activity, physical and sexual assault, unintentional injuries, other criminal violations, interpersonal problems, physical or cognitive impairment, and poor academic performance.[3-6]

This study examines the nature and extent of binge drinking among a representative national sample of students in US 4-year colleges and details the problems such drinking causes for drinkers themselves and for others on their college campus. Binge drinking is defined through a sex-specific measure to take into account sex differences in the dosage effects of ethanol.

Methods

The Colleges

A national sample of 179 colleges was selected from the American Council on Education's list of 4-year colleges and universities accredited by one of the six regional bodies covering the United States. The sample was selected using probability proportionate to enrollment size sampling. All full-time undergraduate students at a university were eligible to be chosen for this study, regardless of the college in which they were enrolled. This sample contained few women-only colleges and few colleges with less than 1000 students. To correct for this problem, an oversample of 15 additional colleges with enrollments of less than 1000 students and 10 all-women's colleges were added to the sample. Nine colleges were subsequently dropped because they were considered inappropriate. These included seminary schools, military schools, and allied health schools.

One hundred forty (72%) of the final sample of 195 colleges agreed to participate. The primary reason stated for nonparticipation by college administrators was inability to provide a random sample of students and their addresses within the time requirements of the study. The 140 participating colleges are located in 40 states and the District of Columbia. They represent a cross-section of US higher education. Two thirds of the colleges sampled are public and one third are private. Approximately two thirds are located in a suburban or urban setting and one third in a small town/rural setting. Four percent are women-only, and 4% are predominantly black institutions.

When the 55 nonparticipating schools were compared with the 140 in the study, the only statistically significant difference found was in terms of enrollment size. Proportionately fewer small colleges (fewer than 1000 students) participated in the study. Since these were oversampled, sufficient numbers are present for statistical analysis.

Sampling Procedures

Colleges were sent a set of specific guidelines for drawing a random sample of students based on the total enrollment of full-time and undergraduates. Depending on enrollment size, every xth student was selected from the student registry using a random starting point. A sample of undergraduate students was provided by each of the 140 participating colleges: 215 students at each of the 127 colleges, and 108 at each of 13 colleges (12 of which were in the oversample). The final student sample included 28,709 students.

The Questionnaire

The 20-page survey instrument asked students a number of questions about their drinking behavior as well as other health issues. Whenever possible, the survey instrument included questions that had been used previously in other national or large-scale epidemiological studies.[13–14] A drink was defined as a 12-oz. (360-mL) can (or bottle) of beer, a 4-oz. (120-mL) glass of wine, a 12-oz. (360-mL) bottle (or can) of wine cooler, or a shot (1.25 oz. (37-mL) of liquor straight or in a mixed drink. The following four questions were used to assess binge drinking: (1) sex; (2) recency of last drink ("never," "not in past year," "within last year but more than 30 days ago," "within 30 days but more than 1 week ago," or "within week"); (3) "Think back over the last two weeks. How many times have you had five or more drinks in a row?" (The use of this question, without specification of time elapsed in a drinking episode, is consistent with standard practice in recent research on alcohol use among this population.[3,13,18]); and (4) "During the last two weeks, how many times have you had four drinks in a row (but no more than that)(for women)?" Missing responses to any of these four questions excluded the student from the bingeing analyses.

Students were also asked the extent to which they had experienced any of the following 12 problems as a consequence of their drinking since the beginning of the school year: have a hangover; miss a class; get behind in schoolwork; do something you later regretted; forget where you were or what you did; argue with friends; engage in unplanned sexual activity; not use protection when you had sex; damage property; get into trouble with campus or local police; get hurt or injured; or require medical treatment for an alcohol overdose. They were also asked if, since the beginning of the school year, they had experienced any of the following eight problems caused by other students' drinking: been insulted or humiliated; had a serious argument or quarrel; been pushed, hit, or assaulted; had your property damaged; had to "babysit" or take care of another student who drank too much; had your studying or sleep interrupted; experienced an unwanted sexual advance; or had been a victim of sexual assault or date rape.

The Mailing

The initial mailing of questionnaires to students began on February 5, 1993. By the end of March, 87% of the final group of questionnaires had been received, with another 10% in April and 2% in May and June. There are no discernible differences in bingeing rates among questionnaires received in each of the 5 months of the survey. Mailings were modified to take into account spring break. So that students would be responding about their binge drinking behavior during a 2-week time on campus. Responses were voluntary and anonymous. Four separate mailings, usually 10 days apart, were sent at each college: a questionnaire, a reminder postcard, a second questionnaire, and a second reminder postcard. To encourage students to respond, the following cash awards were offered: one $1000 award to a student whose name was drawn

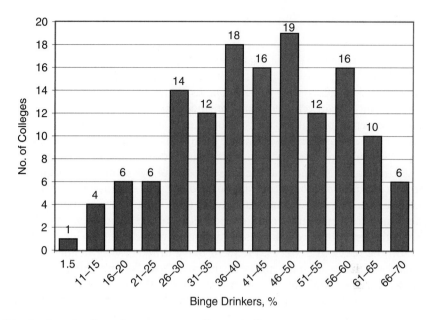

Distribution of colleges by percentage of binge drinkers.

from among students responding within 1 week, and one $500 award and ten $100 awards to students selected from all those who responded.

The Response Rate

The questionnaires were mailed to 28,709 students. Overall, 3082 students were eliminated from the sample because of school reports of incorrect addresses, withdrawal from school, or leaves of absence, reducing the sample size to 25,627. A total of 17,592 students returned questionnaires, yielding an overall student response rate of approximately 69%. The response rate is likely to be underestimated since it does not take into account all of the students who may not have received questionnaires. At 104 of the colleges, response rates were between 60% and 80%, and only six colleges had response rates less than 50%. Response rate was not associated with the bingeing rate (i.e., the Pearson correlation coefficient between the binge drinking rate the college and the response rate was 0.06 with a *P* value of .46).

When responses of early and late responders to the survey were compared, there were no significant differences in the percent of nondrinkers, nonbinge drinkers, and binge drinkers. In the case of 11,557 students who could be classified as early or late responders, there was no significant difference in terms of binge drinking (43% for the early responders vs. 42% for the late responders). An additional short form of the questionnaire was mailed to a segment of students who had failed to return the questionnaire. The rate of binge drinking of these nonresponders did not differ from that of responders to the original student survey.

Data Analysis

All statistical analyses were carried out using the current version of SAS.[19] Comparisons of unweighted and weighted sample results suggested little difference between them, so unweighted results are reported here. Chi-square analyses among students who had a drink in the past year were used to compare nonbinge drinkers, infrequent binge drinkers, and binge drinkers. Binge drinking was defined as the consumption of five or more drinks in a row for men and four or more drinks in a row for women during the 2 weeks prior to the survey. An extensive analysis showed that this sex-specific measure accurately indicates an equivalent likelihood of alcohol-related problems. In this article, the term "binge drinker" is used to refer to students who binged at least once in the previous 2 weeks. Frequent binge drinkers were defined as those who binged three or more times in the past 2 weeks and infrequent binge drinkers as those who binged one or two times in the past 2 weeks. Nonbinge drinkers were those who had consumed alcohol in the past year, but had not binged.

Logistic regression analyses were used to examine how much more likely frequent binge drinkers were to experience an alcohol-related problem or driving behavior compared with nonbinge drinkers, and to compare infrequent binge drinkers with nonbinge drinkers. Odds ratios were adjusted for age, sex, race, marital status, and parents' college education.

In examining secondary binge effects, schools were divided into three groups on the basis of the percentage of students who were binge drinkers at each school. The responses of students who had not binged in the past 2 weeks (including those who had never had a drink) and who resided in dormitories, fraternities, or sororities were compared through χ^2 analyses across the three school types. High-level binge schools (where 51% or more students were binge drinkers) included 44 schools with 6084 students; middle-level binge schools (36% to 50% of students were binge drinkers) included 53 schools with 6455 students; and low-level binge schools (35% or less of students were binge drinkers) included 43 schools with 5043 students (for 10 students, information regarding school of attendance was missing). For two of the problems that occurred primarily or almost exclusively to women (sexual assault and experiencing an unwanted sexual advance), only women were included in the analyses.

Results

Characteristics of the Student Sample

This analysis is based on data from 17,592 undergraduate students at 140 US 4-year colleges. The student sample includes more women (58%) than men (42%), due in part to the inclusion of six all-women's institutions. This compares with national 1991 data that report 51% of undergraduates at 4-year institutions are women.[20] The sample is predominantly white (81%). This coincides exactly with national 1991 data that report 81% of undergraduates at 4-year institutions are white.[20] Minority groups included Asian/Pacific Islander (7%), Spanish/Hispanic (7%), black/African American (6%), and Native American (1%). The age of the students were distributed as follows: 45% younger than 21 years, 38% aged 21 to 23 years, and 17% aged 24 years or more. There were slightly more juniors (25%) and seniors (26%) in the sample than freshmen (20%) and sophomores (19%), probably because 30% of the students were transfers from other institutions. Ten percent of the students were in their fifth undergraduate year of school or beyond. Religious affiliation was discerned by asking students in which of the following religions they were raised: Protestant (44%), Catholic (36%), Jewish (3%), Muslim (1%), other (4%), and none (12%). Religion was cited as an important to very important activity among 36% of the students. Approximately three of five students (59%) worked for pay. Approximately half (49%) of the students had a grade-point average of A, A-, or B+.

Extent of Binge Drinking

Because of missing responses, there were 496 students excluded from bingeing analyses (i.e., 17,096 were included). Most students drank alcohol during the past year. Only about one of six (16%) were nondrinkers (15% of the men and 16% of the women). About two of five students (41%) drank but were nonbinge drinkers (35% of the men and 45% of the women). Slightly fewer than half (44%) of the students were binge drinkers (50% of the men and 39% of the women). About half of this group of binge drinkers, or about one in five students (19%) overall, were frequent binge drinkers (overall 23% of the men and 17% of the women).

Binge Drinking Rates at Colleges

The figure shows that binge drinking rates vary extensively among the 140 colleges in the study. While 1% of the students were binge drinkers at the school with the lowest rate of binge drinkers, 70% of students were binge drinkers at the school with the highest rate. At 44 schools, more than half of the responding students were binge drinkers.

When the 140 colleges were divided into levels of bingeing rate, χ^2 analyses showed that several college characteristics were individually associated (at $P<.05$) with bingeing rate. Colleges located in the Northeast or North Central regions of the United States (compared with those in the West or South) or those that were residential (compared with commuter schools, where 90% or more of the students lived off campus)[21] tended to have higher rates of bingeing. In addition, traditionally black institutions and women's colleges had lower binge rates than schools that were not traditionally black or were coeducational colleges. Other characteristics, such as whether the college was public or private and its enrollment size, were not related to binge drinker rates.

Examination of whether college alcohol programs and policies have any association with binge drinking will be presented in a separate publication. There is little evidence to conclude that current policies have had strong impacts on overall drinking levels. Preliminary analyses suggest that individual binge drinking is less likely if the institution does not have any alcohol outlets within 1 mile of campus, or if it prohibits alcohol use for all persons (even those older than 21 years) on campus.

Drinking Patterns of Binge Drinkers

Table 1 indicates that our designations of binge drinker and frequent binge drinker are strongly indicative of a drinking style that involves more frequent and heavier drinking. Furthermore, intoxication (often intentional) is associated with binge drinking in men and women.

Binge drinking is related to age. Students who are in the predominant college age group (between 17 and 23 years) have much higher bingeing rates than older students. However, within the predominant college age group, students who are younger than the legal drinking age of 21 years do not differ in bingeing rates from students aged 21 to 23 years. In contrast to the modest effects of age, there is no relationship between year in school and bingeing, with rates of binge drinking virtually identical among students across the years of college attendance.

Alcohol-Related Health and Other Problems

There is a strong, positive relationship between the frequency of binge drinking and alcohol-related health and other problems reported by the students (Table 2). Among the more serious alcohol-related problems, the frequent binge drinkers were seven to 10 times more likely than the nonbinge drinkers to not use protection when having sex, to engage in unplanned sexual activity, to get into trouble with campus police, to damage property, or to get hurt or injured. A similar comparison between the infrequent binge drinkers and nonbinge drinkers also shows a strong relationship.

Men and women reported similar frequencies for most of the problems, except for damaging property or getting into trouble with the campus police. Among the frequent binge drinkers, 35% of the men and 9% of the women reported damaging property, and 16% of the men and 6% of the women reported getting into trouble with the campus police.

Drinking and Driving

There is also a positive relationship between binge drinking and driving under the influence of alcohol (Table 3). A large proportion of the student population reported driving after drinking alcohol. Binge drinkers, particularly frequent binge drinkers, reported significantly ($P<.001$) higher frequencies of dangerous driving behaviors than nonbinge drinkers.

Table I Drinking Styles of Students Who Were Nonbinge Drinkers, Infrequent Binge Drinkers, or Frequent Binge Drinkers*					
	Nonbinge Drinkers, %‡		Infrequent Binge Drinkers, %∞		Frequent Binge Drinkers, %§	
Drinking Styles	**Men**	**Women**	**Men**	**Women**	**Men**	**Women**
	(n = 2539)	(n = 4400)	(n = 1968)	(n = 2130)	(n = 1630)	(n = 1684)
Drank on 10 or more occasions in the past 30 days	3	1	11	6	61	39
Usually binges when drinks	4	4	43	45	83	82
Was drunk three or more times in the past month	2	1	17	13	70	55
Drinks to get drunk†	22	18	49	44	73	68

*Chi-square comparisons of students who were nonbinge drinkers, infrequent binge drinkers, and frequent binge drinkers and each of the four drinking styles were significant for men and women separately at $P < .001$. Sample sizes vary slightly for each question because of missing values. Bingeing is defined as four or more drinks for women and five or more drinks for men.

‡Students who consumed alcohol in the past year, but did not binge.

∞Students who binged one or two times in a 2-week period.

§Students who binged three or more times in a 2-week period.

Question asked: "On how many occasions have you had a drink of alcohol in the past 30 days?" Response categories were 1 to 2 occasions, 3 to 5 occasions, 10 to 19 occasions, 20 to 39 occasions, and 40 or more occasions.

†Says that to get drunk is an important reason for drinking.

Number of Problems

Nearly half (47%) of the frequent binge drinkers reported having experienced five or more of the 12 problems listed in Table 2 (omitting hangover and including driving after drinking) since the beginning of the school year, compared with 14% of infrequent binge drinkers and 3% of nonbinge drinkers. The adjusted odds ratios indicate that frequent binge drinkers were 25 times more likely than nonbinge drinkers to experience five or more of these problems, while the infrequent binge drinkers were five times more likely than nonbinge drinkers to experience five or more problems.

Self-Assessment of Drinking Problems

Few students describe themselves as having a drinking problem. When asked to classify themselves in terms of their current alcohol use, less than 1% of the total sample (0.2%), including only 0.6% of the frequent binge drinkers, designated themselves as problem drinkers. In addition, few students have ever sought treatment for a problem with alcohol.

Table 2 Risk of Alcohol-Related Problems Comparing Students Who Were Infrequent Binge Drinkers or Frequent Binge Drinkers with Students Who Were Nonbinge Drinkers Among College Students Who Had a Drink in the Past Year*

Reporting Problem	Nonbinge Drinkers, % (n = 6894)	Infrequent Binge Drinkers		Frequent Binge Drinkers	
		% (n = 4090)	Adjusted OR (95%)‡	% (n = 3291)	Adjusted OR (95% CI)∞
Have a hangover	30	75	6.28 (5.73–6.87)	90	17.62 (15.50–20.04)
Do something you regret	14	37	3.31 (3.00–3.64)	63	8.96 (8.11–9.95)
Miss a class	8	30	4.66 (4.15–5.24)	61	16.58 (14.73–18.65)
Forget where you were or what you did	8	26	3.62 (3.22–4.06)	54	11.23 (10.05–12.65)
Got behind in school work	6	21	3.70 (3.26–4.20)	46	11.43 (10.09–12.94)
Argue with friends	8	22	3.06 (2.72–3.46)	42	7.77 (6.90–8.74)
Engaged in unplanned sexual activity	8	20	2.78 (2.46–3.13)	41	7.17 (6.37–8.06)
Get hurt or injured	2	9	3.65 (3.01–4.43)	23	10.43 (8.70–12.52)
Damage property	2	8	3.09 (2.53–3.77)	22	9.48 (7.86–11.43)
Not use protection when having sex	4	10	2.90 (2.45–3.42)	22	7.11 (6.07–8.34)
Get into trouble with campus or local police	1	4	2.50 (1.92–3.26)	11	6.92 (5.44–8.81)
Require medical treatment of alcohol overdose	<1	<1	NS	1	2.81 (1.39–5.68)
Have five or more alcohol-related problems since the beginning of the school year§	3	14	4.95 (4.17–5.89)	47	25.10 (21.30–29.58)

*Problem occurred not at all or one or more times. Chi-square comparisons of nonbinge drinkers, infrequent binge drinkers, and frequent binge drinkers and each of the problems are significant at P<.001, except for alcohol overdose (P=.002). Sample sizes vary slightly for each problem because of missing values. OR indicates odds ratio: CI, confidence interval. See Table 1 for explanation of drinking classification.

‡Adjusted ORs of infrequent binge drinkers vs. nonbinge drinkers are significant at P<.001.

∞Adjusted ORs of frequent binge drinkers vs. nonbinge drinkers are significant at P<.001, except for alcohol overdose, P<.01.

§Excludes hangover and includes driving after drinking as one of the problems.

Table 3 Alcohol-Related Driving Behavior for a 30-Day Period Comparing Students Who Were Infrequent Binge Drinkers or Frequent Binge Drinkers with Students Who Were Nonbinge Drinkers*

Driving Behavior	Nonbinge Drinkers		Infrequent Binge Drinkers			Frequent Binge Drinkers		
	Men, % (n = 2531)	Women, % (n = 4393)	Men, % (n = 1975)	Women, % (n = 2132)	Adjusted OR (95% CI) ‡	Men, % (n = 1630)	Women, % (n = 1684)	Adjusted OR (95% CI)∞
Drove after drinking alcohol	20	13	47	33	5.13 (4.67–5.64)	62	49	10.33 (9.34–11.42)
Drove after having five or more drinks	2	1	18	7	22.23 (16.89–29.26)	40	21	74.30 (56.56–97.58)
Rode with a driver who was high or drunk	7	7	23	22	4.73 (4.20–5.32)	53	48	15.97 (14.22–17.95)

*Chi-square comparisons of nonbinge drinkers, infrequent binge drinkers, and frequent binge drinkers and each of the three driving behaviors were all significant for men and women separately at $P<.001$. Sample sizes vary slightly for each question because of missing values. OR indicates odds ratio; CI confidence interval. See Table 1 for explanation of drinking classification.

‡Adjusted OR of infrequent binge drinkers vs. nonbinge drinkers (sex combined) are significant at $P<.001$.

∞Adjusted OR of frequent binge drinkers vs. nonbinge drinkers (sex compared) are significant at $P<.001$.

Table 4 Students Experiencing Secondary Binge Effects (Based on Students Who Were Not Binge Drinkers and Living in Dormitories, Fraternities, or Sororities*)

	School's Bingeing Level				
	Low	Middle		High	
			Adjusted		Adjusted
	%	%	OR	%	OR
Secondary Binge Effect	(n = 801)	(n = 1115)	(95% CI)‡	(n = 1064)	(95% CI)∞
Been insulted or humiliated	21	30	1.6 (1.3–2.1)	34	1.9 (1.5–2.3)
Had a serious argument or quarrel	13	18	1.3 (1.0–1.7)	20	1.5 (1.1–2.0)
Been pushed, hit or assaulted	7	10	1.4 (1.0–2.1)	13	2.0 (1.4–2.8)
Had your property damaged	6	13	2.0 (1.4–2.8)	15	2.3 (1.6–3.2)
Had to take care of drunken student	31	47	1.9 (1.6–2.3)	54	2.5 (2.0–3.0)
Had your studying/sleep interrupted	42	64	2.3 (1.9–2.8)	68	2.6 (2.2–3.2)
Experienced an unwanted sexual advance§	15	21	1.7 (1.2–2.3)	26	2.1 (1.5–2.8)
Been a victim of sexual assault or date rape	2	1	NS	2	NS
Experienced at least one of the above problems	62	82	2.8 (2.3–3.5)	87	4.1 (3.2–5.2)

*OR indicates odds ratio. CI, confidence interval.
‡Adjusted ORs of students at schools with middle levels of bingeing vs. students at schools with low levels are significant at $P < .05$.
∞Adjusted ORs of students at schools with high levels of bingeing vs. students at schools with low levels are significant at $P < .05$.
§Based on women only.

A somewhat large proportion of students indicated that they had ever had a drinking problem. Slightly more than one fifth (22%) of the frequent binge drinkers thought that they ever had a drinking problem, compared with 12% of the infrequent binge drinkers and 7% of the nonbinge drinkers.

Secondary Binge Effects

Table 4 reports on the percentage of nonbingeing students who experienced "secondary binge effects," each of eight types of problems due to other students' drinking at each of the three different school types (i.e., schools with high, middle, and low binge levels). For seven of the eight problems studied, students at schools with high and middle binge levels were more likely than students at schools with low binge levels to experience problems as a result of the drinking behaviors of others. Odds ratios (adjusted for age, sex, race, marital status, and parents' college education) indicated that nonbingeing students at schools with the high binge levels were more likely than nonbingeing students at schools with low binge levels to experience secondary binge effects.

The odds of experiencing at least one of the eight problems was roughly 4:1 when students at schools with high binge levels were compared with students at schools with low binge levels.

Binge Drinking in High School

Most students reported the same drinking behavior in high school as in college. Almost half (47%) had not been binge drinkers in high school and did not binge in college, while one fifth (22%) binged in high school and in college. One fifth (22%) of the students were binge drinkers in college but not in high school, while 10% were not binge drinkers at the time of the survey in college, but reported having been binge drinkers in high school.

Comment

To our knowledge, this is the first study that has used a representative national sample, and the first large-scale study to measure binge drinking under a sex-specific definition. Forty-four percent of the college students in this study were classified as binge drinkers. This finding is consistent with the findings of other national studies such as the University of Michigan's Monitoring the Future Project, which found that 41% of college students were binge drinkers,[13] and the Core Alcohol and Drug Survey, which found that 42% of college students were binge drinkers.[5] All three studies used a definition of bingeing over a 2-week period, but the other studies used the same five-drink measure for both sexes. Binge drinking was defined in terms of the number of drinks consumed in a single episode. No attempt was made to specify the duration of time for each episode. Future research might examine whether subgroup differences exist in duration and whether such differences are linked to outcomes.

A possible limitation of surveys using self-reports of drinking behavior pertains to the validity of responses; however, a number of studies have confirmed the validity of self-reports of alcohol and substance use.[22-34] Findings indicate that if a self-report bias exists, it is largely limited to the heaviest use groups[25] and should not affect such a conservative estimate of heavy volume as five drinks.

The results confirm that binge drinking is widespread on college campuses. Overall, almost half of all students were binge drinkers. One fifth of all students were frequent binge drinkers (had three or more binge drinking occasions in the past 2 weeks) and were deeply involved in a lifestyle characterized by frequent and deliberate intoxication. Frequent binge drinkers are much more likely to experience serious health and other consequences of their drinking behavior than other students. Almost half of them have experienced five or more alcohol-related problems since the beginning of the school year, one of three report they were hurt or injured, and two in five engaged in unplanned sexual activity. Frequent binge drinkers also report drinking and driving. Three of five male frequent binge drinkers drove after drinking some alcohol in the 30 days prior to the survey, and two of five drove after having five or more drinks. A recent national report that reviewed published studies concluded that alcohol was involved in two thirds of college student suicides, in 90% of campus rapes, and in 95% of violent crime on campus.[26]

Almost a third of the colleges in the study have a majority of students who binge. Not only do these binge drinkers put themselves at risk, they also create problems for their fellow students who are not binge drinking. Students who did not binge and who reside at schools with high levels of binge drinkers were up to three times as likely to report being bothered by the drinking-related behaviors of other students than students who did not binge and who reside at schools with lower levels of binge drinkers. These problems included being pushed, hit, or assaulted and experiencing an unwanted sexual advance.

Effective interventions face a number of challenges. Drinking is not typically a behavior learned in college and often continues patterns established earlier. In fact, one of three students in the present study was already a binge drinker in the year before college.

The prominence of drinking on college campuses reflects its importance in the wider society, but drinking has traditionally occupied a unique place in campus life. Despite the overall decline in drinking in US society, recent time-trend studies have failed to show a corresponding decrease in binge drinking on college campuses.[3,13] The variation in binge drinking rates among the colleges in this study suggest that colleges may unwittingly perpetuate their own drinking cultures through selection, tradition, policy, and other strategies. On many campuses, drinking behavior that would elsewhere be classified as alcohol abuse may be socially acceptable, or even socially attractive, despite its documented implication in automobile crashes, other injury, violence, suicide, and high-risk sexual behavior.

The scope of the problem makes immediate results of any interventions highly unlikely. Colleges need to be committed to large-scale and long-term behavior change strategies, including referral of alcohol abusers to appropriate treatment. Frequent binge drinkers on college campuses are similar to other alcohol abusers elsewhere in their tendency to deny that they have a problem. Indeed, their youth, the visibility of others who drink the same way, and the shelter of the college community may make them less likely to recognize the problem. In addition to addressing the health problems of alcohol abusers, a major effort should address the large group of students who are not binge drinkers on campus who are adversely affected by the alcohol-related behavior of binge drinkers.

This study was supported by the Robert Wood Johnson Foundation. We wish to thank the following persons who assisted with the project: Lloyd Johnston, PhD, Thomas J. Mangione, PhD, Anthony M. Roman, MD, Nan Laird, PhD, Jeffrey Hansen, Avtar Khalsa, MSW and Marianne Lee, MPA.

References

1. US Dept of Health and Human Services. *Alcohol and Health.* Rockville, MD: National Institute on Alcohol Abuse and Alcoholism: 1990.

2. Robert Wood Johnson Foundation. *Substance Abuse: The Nation's Number One Health Problem, Key Indicators for Policy.* Princeton, NJ: Robert Wood Johnson Foundation: October 1993.

3. Wechsler H., Issac N. Binge drinkers at Massachusetts colleges: prevalence, drinking styles, time trends, and associated problems. *JAMA* 1992; 267: 2929–2931.

4. Hanson DJ, Engs RC. College students' drinking problems: a national study, 1982–1991. *Psychol Rep.* 1992; 71:39–42.

5. Presley CA, Meilman PW, Lyeria R. *Alcohol and Drugs on American College Campuses: Use, Consequence, and Perceptions of the Campus Environment. Volume 1: 1989–1991.* Carbondale, IL: The Core Institute: 1993.

6. The Carnegie Foundation for the Advancement of Teaching. *Campus Life: In Search of Community.* Princeton, NJ: Princeton University Press; 1990.

7. Straus R., Bacon SD. *Drinking in College.* New Haven, CT: Yale University Press: 1953.

8. Berkowitz AD, Perkins HW. Problem drinking among college students: a review of recent research. *J Am Coll Health.* 1986:35:21–28.

9. Saltz R, Elandt D. College student drinking studies: 1976–1985. *Contemp Drug Probl.* 1986:13:117–157.

10. Haworth-Hoeppner S., Globetti G., Stem J., Morasco F. The quantity and frequency of drinking among undergraduates at a southern university. *Int J Addict.* 1989:24: 829–857.

11. Liljestrand P. Quality in college student drinking research: conceptual and methodological issues. *J Alcohol Drug Educ.* 1993:38:1–36.

12. Hughes S., Dodder R. Alcohol consumption patterns among college populations. *J Coll Student Personnel.* 1983:20:257–264.

13. Johnston LD., O'Malley PM., Bachman JG. *Drug Use Among American High School Seniors, College Students, and Young Adults. 1973–1990. Volume 2.* Washington, DC: Government Printing Office: 1991. US Dept of Health and Human Services publication ADM 91–1835.

14. Wechsler H., McFadden M. Drinking among college students in New England. *J Stud Alcohol.* 1979:40:969–996.

15. O'Hare TM. Drinking in college: consumption patterns, problems, sex differences, and legal drinking age. *J Stud Alcohol.* 1990:51:536–541.

16. Engs RC, Hanson DJ. The drinking patterns and problems of college students: 1983. *J Alcohol Drug Educ.* 1985:31:65–83.

17. Brennan AF, Walfish S., AuBuchon P. Alcohol use and abuse in college students. I: a review of individual and personality correlates. *Int J Addict.* 1986:21:449–474.

18. Room R. Measuring alcohol consumption in the US: methods and rationales. In: Clark WB., Hilton ME., eds. *Alcohol in America, Drinking Practices and Problems.* Albany: State University of New York Press: 1991:26–50.

19. SAS Institute Inc. *SAS:STAT User's Guide Release 6.03 ed.* Cary, NC:SAS Institute Inc.: 1988.

20. US Dept of Education. *Digest of Educational Statistics.* Washington, DC: National Center of Educational Statistics: 1993:180–205.

21. *Barron's Profiles of American Colleges*: Hauppauge, NY: Barron's Educational Series Inc.: 1992.

22. Midanik L. Validity of self-reported alcohol use: a literature review and assessment. *Br J Addict.* 1988:83:1019–1030.

23. Cooper AM, Sobell MB, Sobell LC, Mausto SA. Validity of alcoholics' self-reports: duration data. *Int J Addict.* 1981:16:401–406

24. Reinisch OJ, Bell RM, Ellickson PL,. *How Accurate Are Adolescent Reports of Drug Use?* Santa Monica, CA: RAND: 1991. RAND publication N-3189-CHF.

25. Room P. Survey vs. sales data for the US Drink Drug Pract Surv. 1971:3:15–16.

26. CASA Commission on Substance Abuse at Colleges and Universities. *Rethinking Rites of Passage: Substance Abuse on America's Campuses.* New York: Columbia University, June 1994.

Purging Bingeing

ED CARSON

Erin and Jason don't think they drink excessively. "When I think of bingeing, I think of people drinking until they puke," says Erin, a 20-year old sophomore at the University of Oregon, adding that she usually stops at six drinks when she goes out on the weekend.

"I think drinking to get really drunk is stupid," says Jason, a 20-year-old junior. So what is a reasonable amount? "I usually have seven or eight beers," he says as he takes a gulp from his sixth glass.

But the public health establishment says both Erin and Jason are binge drinkers, defined as anyone who has had at least five drinks (sometimes four drinks for women) in one sitting during the previous two weeks. College drinking has attracted a lot of attention recently with the release of several studies reporting that some two-fifths of college students are binge drinkers. The studies say virtually all binge drinkers admit suffering some negative consequences, ranging from hangovers to sexual assaults. And they don't hurt just themselves. In a 1994 study by the Harvard School of Public Health, 82 percent of nonbinge drinkers living in dorms, fraternities, or sororities said they had experienced "secondhand binge effect." As Selena, an 18-year old Oregon freshman puts it, "You always know when they come back from the bars at 4 A.M. screaming their heads off."

So last year, when the Center on Addiction and Substance Abuse at Columbia University (CASA) claimed the percentage of college women drinking to get drunk had more than tripled during the previous 15 years, the news media were quick to hype the finding that drinking on campus had reached "epidemic proportions." But as Kathy McNamara-Meis revealed in the Winter 1995 *Forbes MediaCritic,* CASA's conclusions were based on a misleading comparison of results from a 1977 survey of all college women and a 1992 survey of freshman women. Since freshmen drink more than any other class, such a comparison would suggest an increase in drunkenness even if nothing had changed. In fact, says David Hanson, a professor of sociology at the State University of New York at Potsdam who has studied alcohol use on campus for more than 20 years, "the evidence shows that the actual trend is as flat as your little sister's chest."

As this episode suggests, the problems associated with college drinking are overstated and misunderstood. Since college students have limited responsibilities, they can usually drink heavily without serious repercussions. Drunken college students do sometimes get into trouble, of course. But this is not a drinking problem; it is a drinking *behavior* problem.

ED CARSON IS *a staff reporter for* Reason. *From* Reason, *December 1995.*

For neoprohibitionists, alcohol itself is the problem. In their eyes, college students are children—children who can vote and serve in the military, but still children—who must be shielded from the pernicious effects of drinking. According to the federal Office for Substance Abuse Prevention, "for kids under 21, there is no difference between alcohol or other drug use and abuse." Yet most college students under 21 don't think they are doing anything wrong by drinking. "I'm not hurting anyone," says Derek, a 20-year old sophomore. "I'm just having a good time." Many college administrators say the 21-year purchase age just makes drinking more attractive.

"The 21 law makes alcohol a forbidden fruit and encourages underage students to drink," says Carl Wartenburg, dean of admissions at Swarthmore College. A 1994 survey by the CORE Institute at Southern Illinois University found that students under 21 drank more, and more often, than older students.

Underage students at the University of Oregon have little trouble obtaining alcohol. Most dorms have a no-use policy, but resident assistants just try to crack down on partying and encourage students to drink off campus. Fake IDs are everywhere. If they don't have IDs, students usually can find a party off campus or get someone older to buy for them.

Students may drink to let off steam, or drink to get drunk, or boast about how much they can drink without puking. But college drinking, by and large, remains social drinking. UO students could buy a half-rack of Henry Weinhard's Ale and drink at home. But instead they pay a lot more to drink at Rennie's or Max's because they want to be around other people.

Drinking isn't only something to do—it's something everyone can do together. It's how many freshmen begin meeting people. "You don't know anybody, and then somebody hands you a beer and pretty soon you're hanging out with a bunch of guys," says Eric, a 19-year old sophomore, remembering his first days in college. Freshmen drink hard early on: A 1995 Harvard study of college freshmen found that 70 percent binge drink in their social circle (and worship once or twice at the Temple of the Porcelain God), many decide to drink infrequently or not at all.

But others choose to drink throughout college. "When people ask me why college students drink," says Hanson, the sociologist, "I say, 'Why not?'" People in the "real world" have too little time and too many responsibilities to drink heavily night after night. They have to get up early five days a week, work all day, then go home to their families. Co-workers and family members count on them to live up to their obligations. College students are usually responsible only for themselves. All they have to do is go to a few classes and study when it's convenient. Michael Haines, coordinator of Health Enhancement Services at Northern Illinois University, notes that campus life is set up for binge behavior of all kinds. Students stay up one night cramming for a test, sleep in until noon the next day, then drink all night.

Research finds that college students who drink heavily have lower grades than those who drink moderately or not at all. But these students generally aren't chemistry majors whose grades and classes will be critical for graduate school and future careers. They tend to be business or social science majors who will probably end up in jobs that have little to do with their academic studies. "The truth is that most students can go out drinking several nights a week and get by," says Wartenburg, the Swarthmore dean.

College students get into trouble not because they drink to get drunk but because they get drunk to be irresponsible. "I was drunk" is a get-out-of-jail-free card for college students who act like idiots, get into fights, climb into construction equipment, or behave in other unacceptable or embarrassing ways. It works because friends know that drinking makes people lose control and they may want to use alcohol as an excuse for their own behavior, especially sexual behavior. According to the Harvard study, 41 percent of frequent binge drinkers engage in unplanned sexual activity, as opposed to only 4 percent for nonbinge drinkers.

But unplanned does not mean unwanted. Students drink because they want to feel uninhibited. Men are less hesitant to approach women because they know that if their advances are rejected, they can laugh it off later, saying they were drunk. Women, who still face a double standard when it comes to sleeping around, can blame one-night stands on alcohol.

So men and women have a strong incentive to attribute sexual behavior to drinking, which can be dangerous. Men may be inappropriately aggressive, and willing women may later claim they did not consent. The popularity of the alcohol excuse also helps explain the higher rates of unplanned and unprotected sex while drinking, because halting "uncontrollable" sex to be responsible would destroy the illusion of chemical compulsion.

Although alcohol has consistent effects on motor skills among people of different cultures, its effects on behavior may have more to do with expectations than with pharmacology. Researchers at Washington University in Seattle have found that students who think they are drinking alcoholic beverages become more animated and aggressive, even if they've had only tonic water. Anthropologists have discovered that alcohol's behavioral effects are shaped by culture. In Europe, people grow up drinking beer or wine as a normal part of family life, so drinking is no big deal and generally doesn't cause problems. Americans, by contrast, have always been ambivalent about drinking. As Hanson notes, we "think dry and act wet": We associate drinking with negative behavior but do it anyway. In addition to a person's "set" (beliefs and expectations), the "setting" where drinking takes place has an important impact on drinking behavior. A young man having wine at a family dinner will not behave the same as he would at a bachelor party.

College drinking behavior usually resembles a bachelor party more than a family dinner, but it also varies more with the situation. When students go to a $3.00 all-you-can-drink kegger, they descend into a dimly lit, damp, smoky, and crowded basement. The beer is terrible, there's no place to sit, and everyone is pushing and shoving to get their money's worth before the keg runs out. The only thing to do is drink fast and hard. Students at keggers are mostly underage because they have nowhere else to drink, thanks to the 21 law.

Things are usually more festive at college bars and fraternity functions. The beer is flowing, so students can relax and have a good, rowdy time. Drinking takes on a party atmosphere, which means strong sexual overtones. Bars and frat parties keep the music at a throbbing volume, making it difficult to talk.

But at the East 19th Street Café, one of five microbreweries near the UO campus, the music is turned down low so people can talk without shouting and savor the premium ales, porters, and stouts. The brew pubs are probably the closest college equivalent to an adult drinking environment. Some graduate students and twenty-somethings come to 19th Street, but most patrons are undergraduates who also spend a lot of time in the campus bars. No matter how much people had to drink, I never witnessed drunken or boorish behavior by anyone at a brewery.

With an understanding of how set and setting affect drinking behavior, social norms can be used to control problems. People used to wink and laugh at drunk driving. Now it's considered reckless and stupid, and drunk-driving fatalities have fallen dramatically. Many college administrators would like to design programs to encourage responsible drinking, but they are blocked by federal law. Thanks to the Drug-Free Schools and Community Act Amendments of 1989, universities must have an official no-use alcohol policy for students under 21 or risk losing federal funds, including student financial aid. "It's hard to teach people how to do something responsibly if it's illegal to do it at all," says Swarthmore's Wartenburg.

Nevertheless, some colleges are succeeding. In the late 1980s, officials at Northern Illinois University realized that the traditional approach of controlling consumption and keeping alcohol away from underage students wasn't working. A 1988 survey found that 43 percent of NIU students were binge drinkers, but students believed 70 percent were. NIU administrators thought that misperception of the campus norm was encouraging drinking. "What people feel is the norm has a rather potent influence on behavior," Haines, the NIU administrator, observes.

So with a slim budget of $6,000 the university began taking out ads in the campus paper during the 1989-90 school year reporting actual binge-drinking rates on campus. It also hired students to dress up like the Blues Brothers and hand out dollar bills to anyone who could report this information correctly. By 1995, perceived binge drinking had fallen to 43 percent. More important, actual binge drinking fell to 28 percent, and alcohol-related problems fell proportionally.

Officials at the University of Oregon are hoping to transplant Northern Illinois's success to their campus. Oregon is also one of many colleges that has set up substance-free dorms for students who want to avoid the mayhem in the regular dorms. "It's a great way for people who don't want to drink to avoid people who do," says Hanson. But there is probably a limit to what colleges and universities can do. The days when colleges served *in loco parentis* are long gone.

The best place for students to learn responsible drinking behavior is at home. "Children follow in their parents' footsteps," says Hanson. "What they learn in the home has more impact than what they pick up from friends or at school." Instead of allowing other students to teach their children "normal" drinking behavior, parents can teach their children to drink in moderation, with food, and in the company of adults.

Unfortunately, Hanson says, many parents are reluctant to teach their children responsible drinking when underage drinking is illegal outside the home and public health campaigns warn against sending "mixed messages." But accountability is not a mixed message. The principle that people are responsible for their behavior even when drinking should be drilled into young people's heads by parents as they are growing up and reinforced in college.

Not that college students would abandon keggers, campus bars, and frat parties altogether. College is not the real world, and responsible drinking has a different meaning there. "You gotta do it [drinking] in moderation," says Craig, a 23-year-old University of Oregon senior. "I think that you should go out once a week and get wasted—that's moderation."

"Drinking Age Has Simply Got to Go," Say Campus Riots

Pamela White

(U WIRE) BOULDER, Colo.—The young are always the first to recognize hypocrisy. Unlike their elders, who've been shoveled so much manure over the years that they've grown numb to the smell, young people can tell almost immediately when society is feeding them a line. So it's no wonder that Boulder's young adults are incensed over the state's drinking laws.

Last weekend marked the first anniversary of the University Hill "beer" riots. And while the days here passed more or less without incident, riots rocked both Pullman, Wash., and East Lansing, Mich. In both cases, drinking laws were cited as one of the causes contributing to the unrest.

Old people, like me, have responded both to last year's violence and to recent events with scorn.

"They're rioting over beer?" we sniff disdainfully while shaking our graying heads, "How absurd."

Our disgust with the violence and its emotional and financial costs is well justified. Violence can only be justified in cases of self-defense, and even then, it is a tragedy. Rioting should never by condoned.

But when we casually dismiss the root of these young people's anger, we are missing the point. Their frustration has less to do with a desire to drink booze and more to do with social justice.

At age 18, Coloradans can live on their own, but they can't drink a beer.

At age 18, they can gamble, but they can't drink a beer.

At age 18, they can commit themselves to another person for the rest of their lives in marriage, but they can't drink a beer.

At age 18, they can be parents, but they can't drink a beer.

They can vote, but they can't drink a beer.

But, worst of all, males 18 and over are required to submit to the draft, through which they might be forced on pain of imprisonment to risk their lives in military combat. But they can't drink a beer. Give them a tank, but not a tankard.

This is not an inconsistency. It's a travesty. To ask someone to lay down his life defending freedoms he has yet to enjoy is both unfair and just plain stupid.

I suppose the nation could choose to remedy this by raising the age at which men are required to register with the Selective Service, or better yet, by eliminating the accursed draft altogether.

It might also be a good idea to raise the age at which people can consent to marry to 21. Or better yet, 30. Imagine how few divorces there would be if we all waited to tie the knot until we know what the heck we're doing with our lives.

From Colorado Daily, *May 8, 1998.*

Still, the best solution might be the most difficult for Coloradans to embrace, afflicted with the curse of Puritanism as most Americans are. Rather than glamorizing alcohol by setting it up as a rite of passage into full adulthood, we should abolish the drinking age completely.

I came of age in Denmark, where there is no drinking age. And, yes, I got smashed more than a few times. But I did so under the watchful eyes of my Danish parents. By the time I was 18 and living on my own in Copenhagen, the idea of drinking to become intoxicated had become passé, replaced by the notion of having a good wine with dinner.

My Danish friends, who had lived all their lives knowing that alcohol was available to them, drank less than I did, most of them needing only one hangover to convince them that bingeing on booze was a bad idea.

On the other hand, their Swedish counterparts, who back then had a legal drinking age of 18, often spent weekends in Helsingor, retching and reeking of brandy bought at the duty free shop on the Helsingor ferry. (Their behavior has given rise to the Danish stereotype of Swedes as "drunken Swedes.")

Of course, it's not really fair to compare any place in the United States with any place in Scandinavia. They've managed to achieve a level of social justice and liberty there that we can only dream about.

Yet I'm not the first person in Boulder to call for the abolition of the drinking age. The call has been sounded time and time again by sincere people across the political spectrum. But it has always fallen on reactionary ears. Instead of taking the logical step and backing off, we now have tougher drinking laws and more rigid enforcement, forgetting, I suppose, that Prohibition has never worked and never will.

Last weekend, I watched as a dozen or more police converged on a party of 40, including about 23 underage drinkers. The cops were only doing their job, enforcing a law they've been asked to enforce. But the kids, other than drinking beer, weren't behaving badly—until the police arrived. Then the whole thing degenerated, with the hosts, who'd already been ticketed for providing alcohol to underage drinkers, refusing to cooperate with the cops, even trying to barricade the doors. This was, of course, a dumb thing to do.

Not surprisingly, police were frustrated and impatient. They'd tried the kid glove approach and had found a gauntlet dropped in their laps. The students were foul mouthed and furious.

"What do they expect us to do?" asked one young woman, who was over 21 and clearly not intoxicated. "Especially on the week before finals."

I felt sorry for all of them, police and partygoers alike. The cops were only doing their job. The kids were only doing what generation upon generation of American youth have done before them. The conflict between students and police is ultimately the result of actions taken by the federal government, which forced Colorado to raise its drinking age. When I was 18, some time shortly after the Pleistocene, 18 year olds were allowed to drink 3.2 beers.

Which brings us to the only real solution to this problem—political action. Young people might consider putting aside thoughts of keggers for the moment and think about writing to their state and federal representatives instead. Because folks in the State Legislature and Congress are, generally speaking, even older than I am, it might take a while to convince them to change our drinking laws, but it is the only way to permanently effect change.

Wisdom in a Bottle

CAMILLE PAGLIA

O Auntie Mame:

I once again find myself in the spin cycle over the latest phase of screaming campus hysterics: "Binge Drinking." Though I'm the first person to call the recent death of the Louisiana State University student at the center of this episode a real tragedy, the doting uber-mothers and fathers of Clean Campus Living are now on a new warpath—probably since date rape and heterosexual AIDS have lost their novelty as crusades. Thankfully, I'm beyond their clutches, as I graduated from my university-cum-nursery school a couple of years back. My question to you, Madam Oracle, is: Do we need any more campus babysitting for "boys" and "girls" who 20 years ago, at their age, were considered very much ADULTS? Where's the common sense in these fools? Sounds like Carry Nation wields a sledge hammer, not an ax, these days! Quick— Pass me the poppers!

Shaken, Not Stirred

Dear Shaken:

The cultural savvy of Salon readers is well-demonstrated by your raffish sobriquet alluding to one of my favorite scenes in "Auntie Mame," where Mame's schoolboy nephew perkily mixes a very professional martini for the flabbergasted banker, Mr. Babcock: "Stir never shake—it bruises the gin!"

The authoritarian Big Mommy and Daddy who run the summer camps we call colleges can't decide what a student is these days: A thinking, breathing, exploring, risk-taking adult? Or a cash cow haltered and hidebound by the thick parental checkbook? I say let the herd out of the barn, and let the hooves fall where they may! Growing up means being allowed to take a tumble in your own dung.

The absurdity of the Louisiana State University case is that alcohol was banned on campus, as if the latter were in Puritan Salem rather than Xanadu Baton Rouge, La. Thus LSU students are forced to chug-to-the-max off campus to sustain their high and then endanger their lives and others' by driving home in a sodden state.

"Binge drinking" is a Dionysian response to Apollonian overcontrol of another area of life. I have always strongly opposed the draconian raising of the

CAMILLE PAGLIA *offers online advice for the culturally disgruntled at Ask Camille (available at* http://www.salon.com).

legal drinking age to 21 in this country, a highly politicized and infantilizing measure that deprived the majority of young people of their freedoms in order to constrain a tiny, careless minority responsible for traffic accidents.

Alcohol, with its ancient history and its standardized, quality-controlled modern commercial production, is far preferable to drugs or pills as a tool of youthful experimentation. Manipulation of mood and alteration of consciousness are important first stages in higher education—as long as one is not destroyed by them. Identity is developed by a temporary dissolution of the mental structure imposed by parents, teachers and other adults. Creativity in the arts especially profits from that dangerous, exciting fluidity. Teetotalers may be the spine of the nation, but drinkers are its heart and balls.

European universities would never dream of meddling in their students' private lives. But American universities have reverted to "in loco parentis" (in place of the parent)—the parietal rules and repressive oversight that my 1960s generation rebelled against and smashed. Administrators are locked in Machiavellian marriage with nosy, tuition-paying parents. Even the retiring president of Bryn Mawr College (a hotbed of p.c. feminism) recently complained to the *Philadelphia Inquirer* that today's parents won't let their children grow up and that they're overinvolved with micromanaging their Bryn Mawr daughters' lives by constant e-mail and phone calls.

It's not binge drinking that's the problem—it's the banality and mediocrity of American higher education that produces students' desperate lust for gusto. I have certainly seen many talented people destroyed by alcohol and drugs. But as William Blake said, "The road of excess leads to the palace of wisdom."

My sympathies are with the orgiasts—like Oscar Wilde, who quipped, "Work is the curse of the drinking class." And like Patsy Stone of "Absolutely Fabulous," whose Ivana-blond image, with a vodka bottle plastered to her lips, is printed on one of my favorite T-shirts. In vino veritas!

Binge Drinking as a Substitute for a "Community of Learning"

KENNETH A. BRUFFEE

The Harvard School of Public Health found in 1993 that binge drinking is widespread on American college campuses, particularly among members of fraternities and sororities. The school's most recent report documents the disturbing fact that binge drinking has not declined in the five years since that first study. Even though the proportion of students who declare themselves teetotalers is slightly larger, the effects of binge drinking continue to be widespread and severe. They range from poor grades to destruction of property, assault, drunk driving, and death (*The Chronicle,* September 18, 1998).

To stem the tide of binge drinking, colleges have tried closing fraternities and sororities, punishing heavy drinkers, enlisting the help of liquor-store owners, and banning alcohol on their campuses. So far, those efforts have largely failed. One reason may be that missing from most of them, and from most research on the subject, is an understanding of why first-year students join fraternities and sororities in the first place.

I know why I joined one, many more years ago that I care to mention. I arrived on that gracious, learned, sophisticated campus to find myself among people—professors, administrators, upperclassmen (yes, all were men in those days)—who were committed (it seemed to me) to making me feel just how green, scared, lonely, and small-town I was. They all seemed vexed that I wasn't already what they hoped I would become. Administrators told me how much I had to learn and how hard I had to work to learn it. Professors told me how little they valued what I already knew, and how trivial and misleading would be anything that I learned from anyone but themselves. I was an intrusive rube. I didn't belong.

Most of my fellow freshmen seemed committed to making me feel like a rube, too. Today I think I know why, though I certainly did not know it then. They were trying as hard as I was to conceal from everyone, including themselves, that they, too, were green, scared, lonely, and small-town.

I joined a fraternity because I wanted, desperately, to belong.

Fraternity members were the only people on the campus who seemed to know what it meant to feel like a rube, who knew the depth and overwhelming intensity of an 18-year-old's need to belong. They knew how to marshal and exploit that need because they'd been there themselves not long before. Fraternities seemed to be the only place on campus with a ready supply of friends for freshmen.

KENNETH A BRUFFEE *is a professor of English and director of the Honors Academy at Brooklyn College of the City University of New York. From the* Chronicle of Higher Education, *February 5, 1999.*

There were certainly no friends to be had where I thought I would achieve my most consequential goals as a college student—in my classes. I made no friends there until my last year in college, and then only by chance. Even today, most college students make few friends through their classes until late in their college careers, if at all.

That's one reason college students become binge drinkers.

Such a claim may sound like some kind of bad joke, so I hasten to explain.

Most of the talk about binge drinking, the research into it, and the administrative attempts to curb it assume a sharp distinction between the "academic" and the "social" connections of college students with their peers. Students also make that distinction. If you ask a cross section of college students about their friends, some may say they occasionally talk with a few of them about their course work and (if they admit at all to such eccentricities) their intellectual and aesthetic interests. With the rest of their friends, they'll say, such topics seldom come up.

It's peculiar, when you think about it, that most American colleges do not help entering students make friends through their course work. Presumably, one goal of liberal education is to enrich life with the kind of conversation that comes with substantive friendship. And when colleges actively provide students with the opportunity to make friends through their classes, they eagerly grasp the chance.

A study of 183 students who entered Brooklyn College in the fall of 1987 and took courses that were organized into "learning communities"—in which the same group of students was registered for three courses together—showed that 73 percent agreed with the statement that the experience "helps students make new friends more easily." The retention rate of the students studied was 73 per cent, compared with the college's normal average of 59 percent.

Many students who do make it to their junior and senior years are likely to concede (if only in private) that most of their friendships then tend to merge social interests with academic and aesthetic interests—from pursing genetic research to listening to Mozart concertos. By then their sense of belonging is rooted in the academic major they have chosen and in the new interests they have developed in elective courses.

Of course, some freshmen arrive on the campus in the company of old high-school friends. But those students, too—most of them similarly green, scared, lonely 18-year-olds—feel the pressing need to belong to the new world they have entered. And they, too, are willing to belong on any terms, even terms that require them to continue to keep their curiosity and thought deeply buried.

Those are the terms of membership that fraternities and sororities offer. In return, these social clubs provide companionship that is predictable, reliable, aesthetically unimaginative, and intellectually unchallenging. So-called "wild parties" and the binge drinking that fuels them are misguided attempts to breathe life into stultifying conventionality.

In contrast, many traditional college classrooms—organized around lectures and class discussions—offer surprise, change, and intellectual stimulation. But their structure emphasizes individual mastery, self-sufficiency, and exclusion of outside distractions. While encouraging individual achievement, such courses often foster little substantive social interaction among students.

Colleges can do a great deal more than they generally do to make classrooms a source of social engagement around substantive issues. One approach is collaborative learning and related ways of organizing course work, team projects, and peer tutoring.

Research can guide colleges in such efforts. We need to know whether collaborative learning actually does help students bring to the surface suppressed curiosity and thought, and, if so, how. Most of all, we need to know whether collaborative learning—especially, but not exclusively, during the first year of college—can give students opportunities to make friends in settings that are not merely social, vapid encounters, and, as a result, reduce the social desperation that drives students to binge drinking.

Granted, research is unlikely to show that collaborative learning is a universal solution to social problems in colleges. Research certainly will not demonstrate that collaborative learning alone can empty out fraternity and sorority houses.

But I am confident that research will show that collaborative learning can give entering college students a chance to experience a refreshingly new kind of social intimacy with their peers. It could help American colleges chip away at the problem of binge drinking, by helping to generate social cohesion, civil discourse, and, yes, even friendship among young people who arrive on campuses green, scared, lonely and small-town.

Smoking and the Tyranny of Public Health

Jacob Sullum

From a public health perspective, smoking is not an activity or even a habit. It is "Public Health Enemy Number One," "the greatest community health hazard," "the single most important preventable cause of death," "a pediatric disease," "the manmade plague," "the global tobacco epidemic." It is something to be stamped out, like smallpox or yellow fever. This view of smoking is part of a public health vision that encompasses all sorts of risky behavior, including not just smoking and drinking, using illegal drugs, overeating, failing to exercise, owning a gun, speeding, riding a motorcycle without a helmet—in short, anything that can be said to increase the incidence of disease or injury.

Although this sweeping approach is a relatively recent development, we can find intimations of it in the public health rhetoric of the 19th century. In the introduction to the first major American book on public health, U.S. Army surgeon John S. Billings explained the field's concerns: "Whatever can cause, or help to cause, discomfort, pain, sickness, death, vice, or crime—and whatever has a tendency to avert, destroy, or diminish such causes—are matters of interest to the sanitarian." Despite this ambitious mandate, and despite the book's impressive length (nearly 1,500 pages in two volumes), *A Treatise on Hygiene and Public Health* had little to say about the issues that occupy today's public health professionals. There were no sections on smoking, alcoholism, drug abuse, obesity, vehicular accidents, mental illness, suicide, homicide, domestic violence, or unwanted pregnancy. Published in 1879, the book was instead concerned with things like compiling vital statistics; preventing the spread of disease; abating public nuisances; and assuring wholesome food, clean drinking water, and sanitary living conditions.

A century later, public health textbooks discuss the control of communicable diseases mainly as history. The field's present and future lies elsewhere. "The entire spectrum of 'social ailments,' such as drug abuse, venereal disease, mental illness, suicide, and accidents, includes problems appropriate to public health activity," explains *Principles of Community Health.* "The greatest potential for improving the health of the American people is to be found in what they do and don't do and for themselves. Individual decisions about diet, exercise, stress, and smoking are of critical importance." Similarly, *Introduction to Public Health* notes that the field, which once "had much narrower interests," now "includes the social and behavioral aspects of life—endangered by contemporary stresses, addictive diseases, and emotional instability."

Jacob Sullum *is a syndicated columnist and senior editor at* Reason *magazine. This article is adapted from* For Your Own Good: The Anti-Smoking Crusade and the Tyranny of Public Health, *published this year by the Free Press. From* Consumers Research Magazine, *July 1998.*

The extent of the shift can be sensed by perusing a few issues of the American Public Health Association's journal. In 1911, when the journal was first published, typical articles included "Modern Methods of Controlling the Spread of Asiatic Cholera," "Sanitation of Bakeries and Restaurant Kitchens," "Water Purification Plant Notes," and "The Need of Exact Accounting for Still-Births." Issues published in 1995 offered articles like "Menthol vs. Nonmenthol Cigarettes: Effects on Smoking Behavior," "Compliance with the 1992 California Motorcycle Helmet Use Law," "Correlates of College Student Binge Drinking," and "The Association Between Leisure-Time Physical Activity and Dietary Fat in American Adults."

In a sense, the change in focus is understandable. After all, Americans are not dying the way they once did. The chapter on infant mortality in *A Treatise on Hygiene and Public Health* reports that during the late 1860s and early 1870s two-fifths to one-half of children in major American cities died before reaching the age of five. The major killers included measles, scarlet fever, smallpox, diphtheria, whooping cough, bronchitis, pneumonia, tuberculosis, and "diar-rheal diseases." Beginning in the 1870s, the discovery that infectious diseases were caused by specific microorganisms made it possible to control them through vaccination, antibiotics, better sanitation, water purification, and elim-ination of carriers such as rats and mosquitoes. At the same time, improve-ments in nutrition and living conditions increased resistance to infection.

Americans no longer live in terror of smallpox or cholera. Despite occa-sional outbreaks of infectious diseases such as rabies and tuberculosis, the fear of epidemics that was once an accepted part of life is virtually unknown. The one exception is AIDS, which is not readily transmitted and remains largely confined to a few high-risk groups. For the most part, Americans are dying of things you can't catch: cancer, heart disease, trauma. Accordingly, the public health establishment is focusing on those causes and the factors underlying them. Having vanquished most true epidemics, it has turned its attention to metaphorical epidemics of unhealthy behavior.

In 1979 Surgeon General Julius Richmond released *Healthy People: The Surgeon General's Report on Health Promotion and Disease Prevention,* which broke new ground by setting specific goals for reductions in mortality. "We are killing ourselves by our own careless habits," Secretary of Health, Education, and Welfare Joseph Califano wrote in the introduction, calling for "a second public health revolution" (the first being the triumph over infectious diseases). *Healthy People,* which estimated that "perhaps as much as half of U.S. mortality in 1976 was due to unhealthy behavior or lifestyle," advised Americans to quit smoking, drink less, exercise more, fasten their seat belts, stop driving so fast, and cut down on fat, salt, and sugar. It also recommended motorcycle helmet laws and gun control to improve public health.

Public health used to mean keeping statistics, imposing quarantines, requiring vaccination of children, providing purified water, building sewer systems, inspecting restaurants, regulating emissions from factories, and reviewing drugs of safety. Nowadays it means, among other things, banning cigarette ads, raising alcohol taxes, restricting gun ownership, forcing people to buckle their seat belts, and making illegal drug users choose between prison and "treatment." In the past, public health officials could argue that they were protecting people from external threats: carriers of contagious diseases, fumes and the local glue factory, contaminated water, food poisoning, dangerous quack remedies. By contrast, the new enemies of public health come from within; the aim is to protect people from themselves rather than each other.

Treating risky behavior like a contagious disease invites endless meddling. The same arguments that are commonly used to justify the government's efforts to discourage smoking can easily be applied to overeating, for example. If smoking is a compulsive disease, so is obesity. It carries substantial health risks, and people who are fat generally don't want to be. They find it difficult to lose weight, and when they do succeed they often relapse. When deprived of food, they suffer cravings, depression, anxiety, and other withdrawal symptoms.

Sure enough, the headline of a March 1985 article in *Science* announced, "Obesity Declared a Disease." The article summarized a report by a National Institutes of Health panel finding that "the obese are prone to a wide variety of diseases, including hypertension, adult onset diabetes, hypercholesterolemia, hypertriglyceridemia, heart disease, cancer, gall stones, arthritis, and gout." It quoted the panel's chairman, Jules Hirsch: "We found that there are multiple health hazards at what to me are surprisingly low levels of obesity. Obesity, therefore, is a disease."

More recently, the "epidemic of obesity" has been trumpeted repeatedly on the front page of the *New York Times*. The first story, which appeared in July 1994, was prompted by a study from the National Center for Health Statistics that found the share of American adults who are obese increased from a quarter to a third between 1980 and 1991. "The government is not doing enough," complained Philip R. Lee, an assistant secretary in the Department of Health and Human Services. "We don't have a coherent, across-the-board policy." The second story, published in September 1995, reported on a *New England Journal of Medicine* study that found gaining as little as 11 to 18 pounds was associated with a higher risk of heart disease—or, as the headline on the jump page put it, "Even Moderate Weight Gains Can Be Deadly." The study attributed 300,000 deaths a year to obesity, including one-third of cancer deaths and most deaths from cardiovascular disease. The lead researcher, JoAnn E. Manson, said, "It won't be long before obesity surpasses cigarette smoking as a cause of death in this country."

In his book *The Fat of the Land,* journalist Michael Fumento argues that obesity, defined as being 20% or more above one's appropriate weight, is only part of the problem. (See also "Busting the Low-Fat Dieting Myth," *Consumer Reports*, October 1997.) According to a 1996 survey, 74% of Americans exceed the weight range recommended for optimal health. "So instead of talking about a third of Americans being at risk because of being overweight," he writes, "we really should be talking about somewhere around three fourths."

If, as Philip R. Lee recommended, the government decides to do more about obesity—the second most important preventable cause of death in this country, soon to be the first—what would "a coherent, across-the-board policy" look like? As early as June 1975, in its *Forward Plan for Health,* the U.S. Public Health Service was suggesting "strong regulations to control the advertisement of food products, especially those of high sugar content or little nutritional value." But surely we can do better than that. A tax on fatty foods would help cover the cost of obesity-related illness and disability, while deterring overconsumption of ice cream and steak.

Lest you think this proposal merely facetious, it has been offered, apparently in all seriousness, by at least one economist, who wrote, in the *Orlando Sentinel:* "It is somewhat ironic that the government discourages smoking and drinking through taxation, yet when it comes to the major cause of death— heart disease—and its spiraling health-care costs, politicians let us eat with impunity . . . . It is time to rethink the extent to which we allow people to impose their negative behavior on those of us who watch our weight, exercise and try to be as healthy as possible."

Kelly Brownell, a professor of psychology at Yale University who directs the school's center for Eating and Weight Disorders, has also suggested a "junk food" tax, along with subsidies for healthy foods. "A militant attitude is warranted here," he told the *New Haven Register* last year. "We're infuriated at tobacco companies for enticing kids to smoke, so we don't want Joe Camel on billboards. Is it any different to have Ronald McDonald asking kids to eat foods that are bad for them?"

Of course, a tax on certain foods would be paid by the lean as well as the chunky. It might be more fair and efficient to tax people for every pound over their ideal weight. Such a market-based system would make the obese realize the costs they impose on society and give them an incentive to slim down.

If this idea strikes most people as ridiculous, it's not because the plan is impractical. In several states, people have to bring their cars to an approved garage for periodic emissions testing; there's no logistical reason why they could not also be required to weigh in at an approved doctor's office, say, once a year, reporting the results to the Internal Revenue Service for tax assessment. Though feasible, the fat tax is ridiculous because it's an odious intrusion by the state into matters that should remain private. Even if obesity is apt to shorten your life, most Americans would (I hope) agree, that's your business, not the government's. Yet many of the same Americans believe not only that the state should take an interest in whether people smoke but that it should apply pressure to make them stop, including fines (a.k.a. tobacco taxes), tax-supported nagging, and bans on smoking in the workplace.

In a 1977 talk show appearance, New York City lung surgeon William Cahan, a prominent critic of the tobacco industry, explained the rationale for such policies: "People who are making decisions for themselves don't always come up with the right answer." Since they believe that smoking is inherently irrational, tobacco's opponents tend to assume that smokers are stupid, ignorant, crazy, or helpless—though they rarely say so in such blunt terms. They understandably prefer to focus on the evil tobacco companies, portraying smokers as their victims.

Yet there is a palpable undercurrent of hostility toward smokers who refuse to get with the program. On two occasions in recent years, I was sitting at a (smoke-free) table with a group that included both a smoker and a busybody who took it upon himself to berate the smoker for his unhealthy habit. In both cases, the smoker, constrained by politeness, offered only the mildest of objections, and no one intervened on his behalf. Imagine what the reaction would have been if, instead of a smoker, the meddler had zeroed in on a chubby diner, warning him about the perils of overeating and lack of exercise. I suspect that the other diners would have been appalled, and the target, in turn would have been more likely to offer the appropriate response: Mind your own damned business. It seems we have special license to pick on smokers as a way of demonstrating our moral superiority.

The same sort of arrogance can be observed among public health specialists, but they are more consistent. Because the public health field developed in response to deadly threats that spread from person to person and place to place, its practitioners are used to dictating from on high. Writing in 1879, John S. Billings put it this way: "All admit that the state should extend special protection to those who are incapable of judging of their own best interests, or of taking care of themselves, such as the insane, persons of feeble intellect, or children; and we have seen that in sanitary matters the public at large are thus incompetent."

Billings was defending traditional public health measures aimed at preventing the spread of infectious diseases and controlling hazards such as toxic fumes. It's reasonable to expect that such measures will be welcomed by the intended beneficiaries, once they understand the aim. The same cannot be said of public health's new targets. Even after the public is informed about the relevant hazards (and assuming the information is accurate) many people will continue to smoke, drink, take illegal drugs, eat fatty foods, buy guns, speed, eschew seat belts and motorcycle helmets, and otherwise behave in ways frowned upon by the public health establishment. This is not because they misunderstood; it's because, for the sake of pleasure, utility, or convenience, they are prepared to accept the risks. When public health experts assume these decisions are wrong, they are indeed treating adults like incompetent children.

One such expert, writing in the *New England Journal of Medicine* two decades ago, declared "The real malpractice problem in this country today is not the one described on the front pages of daily newspapers but rather the malpractice that people are performing on themselves and each other . . . . It is a crime to commit suicide quickly. However, to kill oneself slowly by means of an unhealthy lifestyle is readily condoned and even encouraged."

The article prompted a response from Robert F. Meenan, a professor at the University of California School of Medicine in San Francisco, who observed: "Health professionals are trained to supply the individual with medical facts and opinions. However, they have no personal attributes, knowledge, or training that qualifies them to dictate the preferences of others. Nevertheless, doctors generally assume that the high priority that they place on health should be shared by others. They find it hard to accept that some people may opt for a brief, intense existence full of unhealthy practices. Such individuals are pejoratively labeled 'noncompliant' and pressures are applied on them to re-order their priorities."

The dangers of basing government policy on this attitude are clear, especially given the broad concerns of the public health movement. According to John J. Hanlon's *Public Health Administration and Practice*: "Pubic health is dedicated to the common attainment of the highest levels of physical, mental, and social well-being and longevity consistent with available knowledge and resources at a given time and place." The textbook *Principles of Community Health* tells us: "The most widely accepted definition of individual health is that of the World Health Organization: 'Health is a state of complete physical, mental, and social well being and not merely the absence of disease or infirmity.'" A government empowered to maximize health is a totalitarian government.

In response to such fears, the public health establishment argues that government intervention is justified—because individual decisions about risk affect other people. "Motorcyclists often contend that helmet laws infringe on personal liberties," noted Surgeon General Julius Richmond's 1979 report *Healthy People*, "and opponents of mandatory [helmet] laws argue that since other people usually are not endangered, the individual motorcyclist should be allowed personal responsibility for risk. But the high cost of disabling or fatal injuries, the burden on families, and the demands on medical care resources are borne by society as a whole." This line of reasoning, which is also used to justify taxes on tobacco and alcohol, implies that all resources—including not just taxpayer-funded welfare and health care but private savings, insurance coverage, and charity—are part of a common pool owned by "society as a whole" and guarded by the government.

As Meenan noted in the *New England Journal of Medicine*: "Virtually all aspects of life-style could be said to have an effect on the health or well-being of society, and the decision (could then be) reached that personal health choices should be closely regulated." Writing 18 years later in the same journal, Faith T. Fitzgerald, a professor at the University of California, Davis, Medical Center, observed: "Both health-care providers and the commonwealth now have a vested interest in certain forms of behavior, previously considered a person's private business, if the behavior impairs a person's 'health.' Certain failures of self-care have become, in a sense, crimes against society, because society has to pay for their consequences . . . . In effect, we have said that people owe it to society to stop misbehaving, and we use illness as evidence of misbehavior."

Most public health practitioners would presumably recoil at the full implications of the argument that government should override individual decisions affecting health because such decisions have an impact on "society as a whole." Former Surgeon General C. Everett Koop, for his part, seems completely untroubled. "I think that the government has a perfect right to influence personal behavior to the best of its ability if it is for the welfare of the individual and the community as a whole," he writes. This is paternalistic tyranny in its purest form, arrogating to government the authority to judge "the welfare of the individual" and elevating "the community as a whole" above mere people. Ignoring the distinction between self-regarding behavior and behavior that threatens others, Koop compares efforts to discourage smoking and other risky behavior to mandatory vaccination of school children and laws against assault.

While Koop may simply be confused, some defenders of the public health movement explicitly recognize that its aims are fundamentally collectivist and cannot be reconciled with the American tradition of limited government. In 1975 Dan E. Beauchamp, then an assistant professor of public health at the University of North Carolina, presented a paper at the annual meeting of the American Public Health Association in which he argued that "the radical individualism inherent in the market model" is the biggest obstacle to improving public health. "The historic dream of public health that preventable death and disability ought to be minimized is a dream of social justice," Beauchamp said. "We are far from recognizing the principle that death and disability are collective problems and that all persons are entitled to health protection." He rejected "the ultimately arbitrary distinction between voluntary and involuntary hazards" and complained that "the primary duty to avert disease and injury still rests with the individual." Beauchamp called upon public health practitioners to challenge "the powerful sway market-justice holds over our imagination, granting fundamental freedom to all individuals to be left alone."

Of all the risk factors for disease and injury, it seems, freedom is the most pernicious. And you thought it was smoking.

Turkey Police, Beware

RICHARD BERMAN

Food police cut more than calories by whacking feast foods. Somewhere in America, a family will eat a Thanksgiving dinner the food police would be proud of. Warm aromas of mashed tofu with fresh, creamy canola oil, baked yams with a pinch of salt-free substitute on them, boiled onions and soy-bread stuffing with low-sodium vegetable broth gravy fill the house with an air of excitement. Everyone waits for the pièce de résistance and out of it comes: A steaming, gleaming tofurky (tofu molded into a turkey), complete with fermented soy drumsticks.

In an effort to change American eating habits to conform to their puritanical vision, groups such as the Center for Science in the Public Interest, the Vegetarian Society and People for the Ethical Treatment of Animals are perverting the way Americans look at food. Nowhere is this more prevalent than in their attacks on our feast foods, those meals we eat only on special occasions. Every year the talking heads appear on the air to demonize holiday fare as unholy bastions of what CSPI calls food porn. The weeks before Thanksgiving host the now-traditional parade of health scares, tips, pranks and even outright terrorism as nanny state activists jostle for the media's attention.

Mothers against Drunk Drivers uses Thanksgiving to move almost seamlessly from its "Deadly Days of Summer" (Memorial Day to Labor Day) to its "Tie One On" (Thanksgiving to New Year's Eve) campaign. Both are intended to scare us away from even responsible drinking. As MADD's President, Karolyn Nunnallee says, "we will not tolerate drinking and driving, period." So much for any holiday cheer for those not sleeping over.

On the food front, a widely reported study—purposely released days before last Thanksgiving—claimed that just one fatty meal could induce a heart attack. (That'd sure put a damper on the giblet gravy.) Less reported was that the study surveyed only 18 men, hardly a significant medical development. That same week, other scientists released overblown warnings about malonaldehyde in turkey, arsenic in mashed potatoes, and aflatoxins in walnuts. Such arguments stretch believability. According to the American Council on Science and Health, one must eat 3.8 tons of turkey to develop cancer from malonaldehyde. A legion of chipmunks couldn't eat enough nuts to give one of them cancer.

RICHARD BERMAN *is founder of the Guest Choice Network, a nationwide coalition of restaurant and tavern operators. "Turkey Police, Beware," by Richard Berman, from* The Washington Times, *Nov. 26, 1998, p. A19. Copyright © 1998 News World Communications, Inc. Reprinted with permission of* The Washington Times (http://www.washtimes.com).

The science and the public interest group CSPI does its part for the holidays and its annual press conference warning us that "consumers need to treat every turkey as though it harbors a feast of bacteria." The group goes so far as to campaign against stuffing turkeys, for fear of salmonella or food poisoning. Isn't that why we cook our turkeys? Radical vegetarians and PETA go further, protesting everything from barbecue to the Easter ham to (again) that icon of American food, the Thanksgiving turkey. Calling the holiday "murder on turkeys," PETA suggests we eat tofurky instead.

More sinister are the antics of the Animal Avengers, which in 1996 created a scare in Vancouver, Canada, by saying the group had laced turkeys with rat poison. Another group, the Animal Rights Militia, pulled the same trick in 1994. Such relentless attacks have done more than just cut calories from our dinner plate. Thanksgiving and the winter holidays are a time for family, reunions, friends and for literally giving thanks for what we have. Food, drink, and yes, even smoking, is often part of this experience. On an even deeper level, feast foods help define who we are as an individual, as a family and as a regional or ethnic group. "There are all kinds of signposts on people's Thanksgiving table that give away who they are," *New York Times* food editor Ruth Reichl said.

Author Irene Chalmers, whose book *Food* discusses the social, psychological and emotional aspects of special meals, goes further: "The construction of the meal at holidays is a way of holding hands with past and future generations." Disrupt that, she says, and the link is broken.

The incessant (and usually bogus) health scares that emasculate our beloved family recipes do just that. They scour away the joy of cooking grandmother's stuffing or Aunt Mae's yams with brown sugar and molasses. "We are a society obsessed with the harmful effects of eating," said University of Pennsylvania Professor Paul Rozin.

Such an unhealthy obsession makes that tofurky look almost palatable. At least it's safe, so the logic goes. Few of us still go over the river and through the woods for a Thanksgiving at grandma's house. But all of us have warm memories of feasts gone by. And after the meal, the hours of conversation punctuated by coffee or brandy bind the day up into a sensation that hangs with us, sometimes forever. But those memories are being replaced by anguish over naked statistics, animal rights and cancer scares. And that's not a lot to be thankful for.

Lying

Lying
Moral Choice in Public and Private Life
SISSELA BOK

Introduction

> When regard for truth has been broken down or even slightly weakened, all things will remain doubtful. — St. Augustine, "On Lying"

> Doth any man doubt, that if there were taken out of men's minds vain opinions, flattering hopes, false valuations, imaginations as one would, and the like, but it would leave the minds of a number of men poor shrunken things, full of melancholy and indisposition, and unpleasing to themselves? —Bacon, "Of Truth"

> After prolonged research on myself, I brought out the fundamental duplicity of the human being. Then I realized that modesty helped me to shine, humility to conquer, and virtue to oppress. —Camus, *The Fall*

Should physicians lie to dying patients so as to delay the fear and anxiety which the truth might bring them? Should professors exaggerate the excellence of their students on recommendations in order to give them a better chance in a tight job market? Should parents conceal from children the fact that they were adopted? Should social scientists send investigators masquerading as patients to physicians in order to learn about racial and sexual biases in diagnosis and treatment? Should government lawyers lie to Congressmen who might otherwise oppose a much needed welfare bill? And should journalists lie to those from whom they seek information in order to expose corruption?

FROM SISSELA BOK, Lying: Moral Choice in Public and Private Life *(1978), Pantheon Books.*

We sense differences among such choices; but whether to lie, equivocate, be silent, or tell the truth in any given situation is often a hard decision. Hard because duplicity can take so many forms, be present to such different degrees, and have such different purposes and results. Hard also because we know how questions of truth and lying inevitably pervade all that is said or left unspoken within our families, our communities, our working relationships. Lines seem most difficult to draw, and a consistent policy out of reach.

I have grappled with these problems in my personal life as everyone must. But I have also seen them at close hand in my professional experience in teaching applied ethics. I have had the chance to explore particular moral quandaries encountered at work, with nurses, doctors, lawyers, civil servants, and many others. I first came to look closely at problems of professional truth-telling and deception in preparing to write about the giving of placebos. And I grew more and more puzzled by a discrepancy in perspectives: many physicians talk about such deception in a cavalier, often condescending and joking way, whereas patients often have an acute sense of injury and of loss of trust at learning that they have been duped.

I learned that this discrepancy is reflected in an odd state of affairs in medicine more generally. Honesty from health professionals matters more to patients than almost everything else that they experience when ill. Yet the requirement to be honest with patients has been left out altogether from medical oaths and codes of ethics, and is often ignored, if not actually disparaged, in the teaching of medicine.

As I widened my search, I came to realize that the same discrepancy was present in many other professional contexts as well. In law and in journalism, in government and in the social sciences, deception is taken for granted when it is felt to be excusable by those who tell the lies and who tend also to make the rules. Government officials and those who run for elections often deceive when they can get away with it and when they assume that the true state of affairs is beyond the comprehension of citizens. Social scientists condone deceptive experimentation on the ground that the knowledge gained will be worth having. Lawyers manipulate the truth in court on behalf of their clients. Those in selling, advertising, or any form of advocacy may mislead the public and their competitors in order to achieve their goals. Psychiatrists may distort information about their former patients to preserve confidentiality or to keep them out of military service. And journalists, police investigators, and so-called intelligence operators often have little compunction in using falsehoods to gain the knowledge they seek.

Yet the casual approach of professionals is wholly out of joint with the view taken by those who have to cope with the consequences of deception. For them, to be given false information about important choices in their lives is to be rendered powerless. For them, their very autonomy may be at stake.

There is little help to be found in the codes and writings on professional ethics. A number of professions and fields, such as economics, have no code of ethics in the first place. And the existing codes say little about when deception is and is not justified.*

The fact is that reasons to lie occur to most people quite often. Not many stop to examine the choices confronting them; existing deceptive practices and competitive stresses can make it difficult not to conform. Guidance is hard to come by, and few are encouraged to consider such choices in schools and colleges or in their working life.

As I thought about the many opportunities for deception and about the absence of a real debate on the subject, I came to associate these with the striking recent decline in public confidence not only in the American government, but in lawyers, bankers, businessmen, and doctors. In 1960, many Americans were genuinely astonished to learn that President Eisenhower had lied when asked about the U-2 incident, in which an American spy plane and pilot had been forced down by the Soviet Union. But only fifteen years later, battered by revelations about Vietnam and Watergate, 69 percent of the respondents to a national poll agreed that "over the last ten years, this country's leaders have consistently lied to the people."

The loss of confidence reaches far beyond government leadership. From 1966 to 1976, the proportion of the public answering yes to whether they had a great deal of confidence in people in charge of running major institutions dropped from 73 percent to 42 percent for medicine; for major companies from 55 percent to 16 percent; for law firms from 24 percent (1973) to 12 percent; and for advertising agencies from 21 percent to 7 percent.

Suspicions of widespread professional duplicity cannot alone account for the loss of trust. But surely they aggravate it. We have a great deal at stake, I believe, in becoming more clear about matters of truth-telling, both for our personal choices and for the social decisions which foster or discourage deceptive practices. And when we think about these matters, it is the reasons given for deceiving which must be examined. Sometimes there may be sufficient reason to lie—but when? Most often there is not—and why? Describing how things are is not enough. Choice requires the formulation of criteria. To lie to the dying, for example, or to tell them the truth—which is the best policy? Under what circumstances? And for what reasons? What kinds of arguments support these reasons or defeat them? [. . .] If we have all been poorly served by the dominant practices, then the most important remaining questions are: What are the alternatives, for society and for each of us individually, to merely going along with such practices? And how can we act so as to change them? What institutional and personal incentives may be needed? And what real risks might dissuade would-be liars? [. . .]

---

* Scholars in many fields have had no reason in the past to adopt a code of ethics. But some are now exerting so much influence on social choice and human welfare that they should be required to work out codes similar to those that have long existed in professions like medicine or law.

Is the "Whole Truth" Attainable?

"I was born for this, I came into the world for this: to bear witness to the truth; and all who are on the side of truth listen to my voice."
"Truth?" said Pilate, "what is that?" — John 18:37

If, like the truth, the lie had but one face, we would be on better terms. For we would accept as certain the opposite of what the liar would say. But the reverse of truth has a hundred thousand faces and an infinite field. — Montaigne, *Essays*

Like freedom, truth is a bare minimum or an illusory ideal (the truth, the whole truth, and nothing but the truth about, say, the battle of Waterloo or the *Primavera*.) — J.L. Austin, "Truth," *Philosophical Papers*

The "Whole Truth"

Is it not naïve to set forth on a general exploration of lying and truth-telling? Some will argue that the task is impossible. Life is too complex, they will say, and societies too diverse. How can one compare the bargaining in an Eastern bazaar, the white lies of everyday life, the lie for national defense, and that to spare a dying child? Is it not arrogant and myopic to conceive of doing so?

And even if these variations could somehow be encompassed, the argument continues, how can we ever attain the truth about any complex matter— the battle of Waterloo, in Austin's example—or even a single circumstance? How can one, in fact, do full justice to the words used in court: "The truth, the whole truth, and nothing but the truth"?

These words mock our clumsy efforts to remember and convey our experiences. The "whole truth" has seemed so obviously unattainable to some as to cause them to despair of human communication in general. They see so many barriers to prevent us from obtaining truthful knowledge, let alone communicating it; so many pitfalls in conveying what we mean.

How can a physician, for example, tell the "whole truth" to a patient about a set of symptoms and their causes and likely effects? He certainly does not know all there is to know himself. Even all he does know that might have a bearing—incomplete, erroneous, and tentative though it be—could not be conveyed in less than weeks or even months. Add to these difficulties the awareness that everything in life and experience connects, that all is a "seamless web" so that nothing can be said without qualifications and elaborations in infinite regress, and a sense of lassitude begins to steal over even the most intrepid.

This book is intended as a reply to such arguments. The whole truth is out of reach. But this fact has very little to do with our choices about whether to lie or to speak honestly, about what to say and what to hold back. These choices can be set forth, compared, evaluated. And when they are, even rudimentary distinctions can give guidance.

If arrogance there be, it lies rather in the immobilizing impatience with all that falls short of the "whole truth." This impatience helps explain why the contemporary debate about deception is so barren. Paradoxically, the reluctance to come to grips with deception can stem from an exalted and all-absorbing preoccupation with *truth*.

"Truth"—no concept intimidates and yet draws thinkers so powerfully. From the beginnings of human speculation about the world, the question of what truth is and whether we can attain it have loomed large. Every philosopher has had to grapple with them.* Every religion seeks to answer them.

One pre-Socratic Greek tradition saw truth—*aletheia*—as encompassing all that we remember: singled out through memory from everything that is destined for Lethe, "the river of forgetfulness." The oral tradition required that information be memorized and repeated, often in song, so as not to be forgotten. Everything thus memorized—stories about the creation of the world, genealogies of gods and heroes, advice about health—all partook of truth, even if in another sense completely fabricated or erroneous. In this early tradition, repeating the songs meant keeping the material alive and thus "true," just as creating works of art could be thought of as making an object true, bringing it to life.

Only gradually did the opposition between truth and error come to be thought central to philosophy, and the nature of verification itself spotlighted. The immense preoccupation with epistemology took hold with Plato and has never diminished since. In logic, in epistemology, in theology, and in metaphysics, the topic of "truth" has continued to absorb almost limitless energies. And since the strands from these diverse disciplines are not always disentangled, a great many references to "truth" remain of unsurpassed vagueness.

Truth and Truthfulness

In all such speculation, there is great risk of a conceptual muddle, of not seeing the crucial differences between two domains: the *moral* domain of intended truthfulness and deception, and the much vaster domain of truth and falsity in general. The moral question of whether you are lying or not is not *settled* by establishing the truth or falsity of what you say. In order to settle this question, we must know whether you *intend your statement to mislead.*

The two domains often overlap, and up to a point each is indispensable to the other. But truth and truthfulness are not identical, any more than falsity and falsehood. Until the differences are seen, and the areas of overlap and confusion spotlighted, little progress can be made in coping with the moral quandaries of lying.

---

* A glance at the Index of the recently published *Encyclopedia of Philosophy* reveals the contrast. As mentioned in the Introduction, it has no reference to "lying" or "deception." "Truth," on the other hand, receives over 100 references.

The two domains are sometimes taken to be identical. This can happen whenever some believe that they have access to a truth so complete that all else must pale by comparison. Many religious documents or revelations claim to convey what is true. Those who do not accept such a belief are thought to live in error, in ignorance, even in blindness. At times, the refusal of nonbelievers to accept the dogma or truth revealed to the faithful is called, not merely an error, but a lie. The battle is seen as one between upholders of the faith and the forces of deception and guile.* Thus Bonhoeffer writes that:

> Jesus calls Satan "the father of the lie." (John 8:44) The lie is primarily the denial of God as He has evidenced Himself to the world. "Who is a liar but he that denieth that Jesus is the Christ?" (I John 2:22)

Convinced that they know the truth—whether in religion or politics—enthusiasts often regard lies for the sake of this truth as justifiable. They may perpetrate so-called pious frauds to convert the unbelieving or strengthen the conviction of the faithful. They see nothing wrong in telling untruths for what they regard as a much "higher" truth.

In the history of human thought, we find again and again such a confusion of the two domains. It is not unrelated to the traditions which claim the truth exists, that it can be revealed, that one can hope to come face to face with it. Even Nietzsche, at war with such traditions, perpetuates the confusion:

> There is only *one* world, and that world is false, cruel, contradictory, misleading, senseless. [. . .] We need lies to vanquish this reality, this "truth," we need lies in order to live. [. . .] That lying is a necessity of life is itself a part of the terrifying and problematic character of existence.

The several meanings of the word "false" only add to the ease of confusing the two domains. For whereas "false" normally has the larger sense which includes all that is wrong or incorrect, it takes on the narrower, moral sense when applied to persons. A false person is not one merely wrong or mistaken or incorrect; it is one who is intentionally deceitful or treacherous or disloyal. Compare, to see the difference, a "false note" and a "false friend"; a "false economy" and a "false witness."*

Any number of appearances and words can mislead us; but only a fraction of them are *intended* to do so. A mirage may deceive us, through no one's fault.

---

* The confusion between "error" and "lie" underlying such a belief occasionally gives rise to the conclusion that those who are in possession of the truth—and thus not liars—are both infallible and incapable of lying. In order to sort out just what is meant by any one such claim, it is necessary to ask: Is the person believed infallible incapable of lying? of other forms of deceit? of being wrong? of being deceived? and with respect to what forms of knowledge? *Cf.* a Sufi saying: "The pious would not deceive and the intelligent man cannot be deceived." *A Sufi Rule for Novices,* ed. Menahem Wilson (Cambridge, MA: Harvard University Press, 1975), p. 41.

* To further complicate matters, there are, of course, many uses of "false" to mean "deceitful" or "treacherous" which do not apply directly to persons, but rather to what persons have intended to be misleading. A "false trail," a "false ceiling," or a "false clue" carry different overtones of deceptiveness.

Our eyes deceive us all the time. We are beset by self-delusion and bias of every kind. Yet we often know when we mean to be honest or dishonest. Whatever the essence of truth and falsity, and whatever the sources of error in our lives, *one* such source is surely the human agent, receiving and giving out information, intentionally deflecting, withholding, even distorting it at times.[†] Human beings, after all, provide for each other the most ingenious obstacles to what partial knowledge and minimal rationality they can hope to command.

We must single out, therefore, from the countless ways in which we blunder misinformed through life, that which is done with the *intention to mislead;* and from the countless partial stabs at truth, those which are intended to be truthful. Only if this distinction is clear will it be possible to ask the moral question with rigor. And it is to this question alone—the intentional manipulation of information—that the court addresses itself in its request for "the truth, the whole truth, and nothing but the truth."

But one obstacle remains. Even after the two domains of the ethical and the epistemological are set apart, some argue that the latter should have priority. It is useless to be overly concerned with truthfulness, they claim, so long as one cannot know whether human beings are capable of knowing and conveying the truth in the first place. Such a claim, if taken seriously, would obviously make the study of truth-telling and deception seem pointless and flat. Once again, the exalted and all-absorbing preoccupation with "truth" then comes to nourish the reluctance to confront falsehood.

Skeptics have questioned the certitudes of their fellows from the earliest times. The most extreme among them have held that nothing can be known at all; sometimes they have gone very far in living out such a belief. Cratylus, a contemporary of Socrates, is said to have refused discussion of any kind. He held that the speakers and the words in any conversation would be changing and uncertain. He therefore merely wiggled his finger in response to any words to show the he had heard them but that a reply would be pointless. And Pyrrho, in the third century B.C., denied that anything could be known and concluded that nothing could therefore be said to be honorable or dishonorable, just or unjust.

For these radical skeptics, just as for those who believe that complete and absolute truth can be theirs, ethical matters of truth-telling and deception melt into insignificance by comparison with the illumination of truth and the dark void of its absence. As a result, both groups largely ignore the distinctions between truthfulness and falsehood in their intense quest for certainty regarding truth.

---

† Messages between human beings can suffer from a number of unintended distortions or interferences, originating either at the source, en route, or at the reception. The speaker, for example, may be mistaken, inarticulate, or using a language unknown to the listener. En route, the message may be deflected by outside noise, by atmospheric conditions, by interruption. At the receiving end, deafness, fatigue, language problems, or mental retardation may affect the reception of the message.

But the example of Cratylus shows how difficult it is to live up to thoroughgoing skepticism. Most thinkers who confuse intentional deception and falsity nevertheless manage to distinguish between the two in their ordinary lives. And those who consider the study of "truth" to be prior to any use of information put such concerns aside in their daily routines. They make informed choices of books and libraries; of subway connections and tools and food; they take some messages to be more truthful than others, and some persons as more worthy of their trust than others. [. . .]

For all these reasons, deception commands little notice. This absence of real analysis is reflected also in teaching and in codes of professional ethics. As a result, those who confront difficult moral choices between truthfulness and deception often make up their own rules. They think up their own excuses and evaluate their own arguments . . .[O]ne deserves mention here, for it results from a misuse of skepticism by those who wish to justify their lies, giving rise to a clearly fallacious argument. It holds that since we can never know the truth or falsity of anything anyway, it does not matter whether or not we lie when we have a good reason for doing so. Some have used this argument to explain why they and their entire profession must regretfully forgo the virtue of veracity in dealing with clients. Such a view is stated, for example, by an eminent physician in an article frequently referred to in medical literature.

> Above all, remember that it is meaningless to speak of telling the truth, the whole truth, and nothing but the truth to a patient. It is meaningless because it is impossible—a sheer impossibility. [. . .] Since telling the truth is impossible, there can be no sharp distinction between what is true and what is false.
>
> [. . .] Far older than the precept, "the truth, the whole truth, and nothing but the truth," is another that originates within our profession, that has always been the guide of the best physicians, and, if I may venture a prophecy, will always remain so: So far as possible, do no harm. You can do harm by the process that is quaintly called telling the truth. You can do harm by lying. [. . .] But try to do as little harm as possible.

The same argument is often used by biomedical investigators who claim that asking subjects for their informed consent to be used in research is meaningless because it is impossible to obtain a *genuinely* informed consent. It is used by government officials who decide not to inform citizens of a planned war or emergency measure. And very often, it is then supplemented by a second argument: Since there is an infinite gradation between what is truthful and what is deceitful, no lines can be drawn and one must do what one considers best on other grounds.

Such arguments draw on our concerns with the adequacy of information to reach a completely unwarranted conclusion: one that gives *carte blanche* to what those who lie take to be well-meant lies. The difference in perspectives is striking. These arguments are made by the liar but never by those lied to. One has only to imagine how the professionals who argue in this way would respond if their dentists, their lawyers, or their insurance agents used similar arguments for deceiving *them*. As dupes we know what as liars we tend to blur—that information can be more or less adequate; that even where no clear lines are drawn, rules and distinctions may, in fact, be made; and that truthfulness can be required even where full "truth" is out of reach.

The fact that the "whole truth" can never be reached in its entirety should not, therefore, be a stumbling block in the much more limited inquiry into questions of truth-telling and falsehood. It is possible to go beyond the notion that epistemology is somehow prior to ethics. The two nourish one another, but neither can claim priority. It is equally possible to avoid the fallacies which arise from the confusion of "truth" and "truthfulness," and to draw distinctions with respect to the adequacy and relevance of the information reaching us. It is therefore legitimate to go on to define deception and to analyze the moral dilemmas it raises.

Defining Intentional Deception and Lying

When we undertake to deceive others intentionally, we communicate messages meant to mislead them, meant to make them believe what we ourselves do not believe. We can do so through gesture, through disguise, by means of action or inaction, even through silence. Which of these innumerable deceptive messages are also lies? I shall define as a lie any intentionally deceptive message which is *stated*. Such statements are most often made verbally or in writing, but can of course also be conveyed via smoke signals, Morse code, sign language, and the like. Deception, then, is the larger category, and lying forms part of it.*

This definition resembles some of those given by philosophers and theologians, but not all. For it turns out that the very choice of definition has often presented a moral dilemma all its own. Certain religious and moral traditions were vigorously opposed to all lying. Yet many adherents wanted to recognize at least a few circumstances when intentionally misleading statements could be allowed. The only way out of them was, then, to define lies in such a way that some falsehoods did not count as lies. Thus Grotius, followed by a long line of primarily Protestant thinkers, argued that speaking falsely to those—like thieves—to whom truthfulness is not owed cannot be called lying. Sometimes the rigorous tradition was felt to be so confining that a large opening to allowable misstatements was needed. In this way, casuist thinkers developed the notion of the "mental reservation," which, in some extreme formulations, can allow you to make a completely misleading statement, so long as you add something in your own mind to make it true. Thus, if you are asked whether you broke somebody's vase, you could answer "No," adding in your own mind the mental reservation "not last year" to make the statement a true one.

---

* It is perfectly possible to define "lie" so that it is identical with "deception." This is how expressions like "living a lie" can be interpreted. For the purposes of this book, however, it is best to stay with the primary distinction between deceptive *statements*—lies—and all the other forms of deception.

Such definitions serve the special purpose of allowing persons to subscribe to a strict tradition yet have the leeway in actual practice which they desire. When the strict traditions were at their strongest, as with certain forms of Catholicism and Calvinism, such "definitional" ways out often flourished. Whenever a law or rule is so strict that most people cannot live by it, efforts to find loopholes will usually ensue; the rules about lying are no exception.

I see nothing wrong with either a narrow or a wider definition of lying, so long as one retains the prerogative of morally evaluating the intentionally misleading statements, no matter whether they fall within the category of lying or outside it.* But a narrower definition often smuggles in a moral term which in itself needs evaluation. To say, for instance, that it is *not* lying to speak falsely to those with no right to your information glides over the vast question of what it means to have such a right to information. In order to avoid this difficulty, I shall use instead a more neutral, and therefore wider, definition of a lie: an intentionally deceptive message in the form of a *statement*. [. . .]

Augustine on Lying*

The first type of lie is a deadly one which should be avoided and shunned from afar, namely, that which is uttered in the teaching of religion, and to the telling of which no one should be led under any condition. The second is that which injures somebody unjustly: such a lie as helps no one and harms someone. The third is that which is beneficial to one person while it harms another, although the harm does not produce physical defilement. The fourth is the lie which is told solely for the pleasure of lying and deceiving, that is, the real lie. The fifth type is that which is told from a desire to please others in smooth discourse. When these have been avoided and rejected, a sixth kind of lie follows which harms no one and benefits some person, as, for instance, when a person, knowing that another's money is to be taken away unjustly, answers the questioner untruthfully and says that he does not know where the money is. The seventh type is that which is harmful to no one and beneficial to some person, with the exception of the case where a judge is questioning, as happens when a person lies because he is unwilling to betray a man sought for capital punishment, that is, not only a just and innocent person but even a criminal, because it belongs to Christian discipline never to despair of the conversion of anybody and never to block the opportunity for repentance. Now, I have spoken at length concerning these last two types, which are wont to evoke considerable discussion, and I have presented my opinion, namely, that by the acceptance of sufferings which are borne honorably and courageously, these lies, too, may be avoided by strong, faithful, and truthful men and women. The eighth is that

* From Augustine, "Lying," In *Treatises on Various Subjects,* ed. R.J. Deferrari, Fathers of the Church (New York: Catholic University of America Press, 1952), vol. 14, chap. 14. From Appendix to Sissela Bok, *Lying: Moral Choice in Public and Private Life.*

type of lie which is harmful to no one and beneficial to the extent that it protects someone from physical defilement, at least, from that defilement which we have mentioned above. Now, the Jews considered it defilement to eat with unwashed hands. If anyone considers that as defilement, then a lie must not be told in order to avoid it. However, we are confronted with a new problem if a lie is such that it brings injury to any person, even though it protects another person from that defilement which all men detest and abhor. Should such a lie be told if the injury resulting from it is not in the nature of the defilement of which we have been treating? The question here does not concern lying; rather, it is whether harm should be done to any person, not necessarily through a lie, so that such defilement may be warded off from another person. I am definitely inclined to oppose such a license. Even though the most trivial injuries are proposed, such as that one which I mentioned above in regard to the one lost measure of grain, they disturb me greatly in this problem as to whether we ought to do injury to one person if, by that wrong, another person may be defended, or protected against defilement. But, as I have said, that is another question.

Augustine Against Lying*

You have sent me much to read, dear brother Consentius, you have sent me much to read. [. . .] I am quite delighted with your eloquence, with your memory of sacred Scripture, with your adroitness of mind, with your distress in stinging indifferent Catholics, with your zeal in raging against even latent heretics. But I am not persuaded that they should be drawn out of hiding by our lies. For, why do we try with so much care to track them and hunt them down? Is it not so that, when they have been caught and brought into the open, we may either teach them the truth themselves or else, by convicting them of error, keep them from harming others? Is it not, in short, so that their falsehood may be blotted out or guarded against and God's truth be increased? Therefore, how can I suitably proceed against lies by lying? Or should robbery be proceeded against by means of robbery, sacrilege by sacrilege, and adultery by adultery? "But if through my lie the truth of God has abounded," are we, too, going to say, "why should we not do evil that good may come from it?" You see how much the Apostle detests this. But what is it to say: "Let us lie in order to bring lying heretics to the truth," if not the same as saying, "Why should we not do evil that good may come from it?" Or is lying sometimes a good or sometimes not an evil? Why, then, has it been written "Thou hatest all the workers of iniquity: thou wilt destroy all that speak a lie?" He has not made exception of some or said indefinitely: "Thou wilt destroy tellers of lies," so as to allow that certain ones be understood, but not every one. But he has brought forth a

---

* From Augustine, "Against Lying," in *Treatises on Various Subjects,* ed. R.J. Defarrari, Fathers of the Church (New York: Catholic University of America Press, 1952), vol. 16, chaps. 1, 2, 18. From Appendix to Sissela Bok, *Lying: Moral Choice in Public and Private Life.*

universal proposition, saying: "Thou wilt destroy all that speak a lie." Or, because it has not been said: "Thou wilt destroy all that speak any lie or that speak any lie whatsoever," are we to think, therefore, that room has been made for a certain kind of lie and that God wilt not destroy those who tell a certain kind of lie, but only those who tell unjust lies, not any lie whatsoever, because there are found just lies, too, which ought actually to be matter for praise rather than reproach? [. . .]

Often, in human affairs, human sympathy overcomes me and I am unable to resist when someone says to me: "Look, here is a patient whose life is endangered by a serious illness and whose strength will not hold out any longer if he is told of the death of his dearly beloved only son. He asks you whether the boy is still alive whose life you know is ended. What will you answer when, if you say anything except He is dead or He is alive or I don't know, the patient will believe that he is dead, because he realizes that you are afraid to say and do not want to lie? It will be the same no matter how hard you try to say nothing. Of the three convincing answers, two are false. He is alive and I don't know, and you cannot utter them without lying. But, if you make the one true answer, namely, that he is dead, and if the death of the anguished father follows hard upon it, people will cry that he was slain by you. And who can bear to hear them exaggerate the evil of avoiding a beneficial lie and of loving homicide as truth?" I am moved by these arguments—more powerfully than wisely! [. . .]

Immanuel Kant
On a Supposed Right to Lie from Altruistic Motives*

In the journal *France,* for 1797, Part VI, No. 1, page 123, in an article entitled "On Political Reactions" by Benjamin Constant, there appears the following passage:

> The moral principle, "It is a duty to tell the truth," would make any society impossible if it were taken singly and unconditionally. We have proof of this in the very direct consequences which a German philosopher has drawn from this principle. This philosopher goes so far as to assert that it would be a crime to lie to a murderer who has asked whether our friend who is pursued by him had taken refuge in our house.

The French philosopher on page 124 refutes this principle in the following manner:

> It is a duty to tell the truth. The concept of duty is inseparable from the concept of right. A duty is that which is one being corresponds to the rights of another. Where there are no rights, there are no duties. To tell the truth is thus a duty: but it is a duty only in respect to one who has a right to the truth. But no one has a right to a truth which injures others.

---

* From Immanuel Kant, *Critique of Practical Reason and Other Writings in Moral Philosophy,* ed. and trans. Lewis White Beck (Chicago: University of Chicago Press, 1949), pp. 346–50. From Appendix Sissela Bok, *Lying: Moral Choice in Public and Private Life.*

Now the first question is: Does a man, in cases where he cannot avoid answering "Yes" or "No," have a right to be untruthful? The second question is: Is he not in fact bound to tell an untruth, when he is unjustly compelled to make a statement, in order to protect himself or another from a threatened misdeed?

Truthfulness in statements which cannot be avoided is the formal duty of an individual to everyone, however great may be the disadvantage accruing to himself or to another. If, by telling an untruth, I do not wrong him who unjustly compels me to make a statement, nevertheless by this falsification, which must be called a lie (though not in a legal sense), I commit a wrong against duty generally in a most essential point. That is, so far as in me lies I cause that declarations should in general find no credence, and hence that all rights based on contract should be void and lose their force, and this is a wrong done to mankind generally.

Thus the definition of a lie as merely an intentional untruthful declaration to another person does not require the additional condition that it must harm another, as jurists think proper in their definition (*mendacium est falsiloquium in praeidicium alterius*). For a lie always harms another; if not some other particular man, still it harms mankind generally, for it vitiates the source of law itself.

This benevolent lie, however, can become punishable under civil law through an accident (*casus*), and that which escapes liability to punishment only accident can also be condemned as wrong even by external laws. For instance, if by telling a lie you have prevented murder, you have made yourself legally responsible for all the consequences; but if you have held rigorously to the truth, public justice can lay no hand on you, whatever the unforeseen consequences may be. After you have honestly answered the murderer's question as to whether this intended victim is at home, it may be that he has slipped out so that he does not come in the way of the murderer, and thus that the murder may not be committed. But if you had lied and said he was not at home when he had really gone out without your knowing it, and if the murderer had then met him as he went away and murdered him, you might justly be accused as the cause of his death. For if you had told the truth as far as you knew it, perhaps the murderer might have been apprehended by the neighbors while he searched the house and thus the deed might have been prevented. Therefore, whoever tells a lie, however well intentioned he might be, must answer for the consequences, however unforeseeable they were, and pay the penalty for them even in a civil tribunal. This is because truthfulness is a duty which must be regarded as the ground of all duties based on contract, and the laws of these duties would be rendered uncertain and useless if even the least exception to them were admitted.

To be truthful (honest) in all declarations, therefore, is a sacred and absolutely commanding decree of reason, limited by no expediency . . .

Lies, Damn Lies, and Statistics

JONATHAN RAUCH

I'm going to say this again. I did not have sexual relations with that woman, Miss Lewinsky. —President Clinton, January 26

The murder rate in Holland is double that in the United States. . . . That's drugs.—drug czar Barry McCaffrey, July 13

Which of the two quotations above is the more appalling? I suppose most people would choose President Clinton's, and I suppose, on balance, I would, too. Still, the choice isn't altogether obvious—or, at least, it shouldn't be.

The word "lie"—like the word "is" and the word "sex"—is a term that tends to be used rather loosely. Recently St. Martin's Press sent me a new book called *The 15 Biggest Lies in Politics,* by the journalist Major Garrett and the former congressman Timothy J. Penny. The 15 "lies" turn out to include "The abortion debate matters," "Medicare works," and "Democrats are compassionate."

This book, luckily, is more sophisticated than its title (this is still true of books, sometimes), and it begins usefully with what the authors call a "hierarchy in the art of political lying." At the bottom are lies of decorum, which are harmless and even useful. "Demagogic lies" and "lies meant to conceal political cowardice" are worse, but also have their uses. Most people, however, would probably agree with Garrett and Penny that the exculpatory personal lie deserves only opprobrium: "The most-damaging lies are those politicians tell about their ethical conduct, hoping the ugly truth never emerges." Now who has done that sort of lying lately?

By contrast, Barry McCaffrey's statement of July 13 seems pretty innocent. As he was about to leave for Europe, the drug czar called the Netherlands' liberal drug policies an "unmitigated disaster." When the Dutch—no doubt, looking at the non-unmitigated success of American drug policies—expressed dismay, McCaffrey fired back that in 1995 the Dutch murder rate was double America's, and that other crime was worse, too.

The claim that the Netherlands is a more murderous place than America seems roughly as plausible as the claim that oral sex is not sex; and, in fact, in 1995 the Dutch murder rate was less than a quarter of the American rate. The Netherlands, population 15.5 million, had fewer murders that year than did Houston, population 1.7 million.

What may have begun as a simple mistake, however, became more ethically complicated when, the next day, the misstatement was pointed out to

McCaffrey, not least by the flabbergasted Dutch. A mistake uncorrected is no longer just a mistake, and McCaffrey did not issue a correction. In an August interview with the *Dallas Morning News,* he seemed pleased with himself. "The other thing we did during the visit was, I started laying down other people's comparative data," he said. "God, did it annoy them."

Asked recently if the murder comment still stands, a spokesman for McCaffrey responded with a Clintonesque step to the side. "We have said if we are wrong, speak to Interpol—it's not our statistics, it's (their) reporting." But Franklin Zimring, a University of California (Berkeley) law professor who is an authority on crime, says that the Interpol numbers are raw and unaudited; and, as the Dutch pointed out right away, the numbers cited by McCaffrey for the Netherlands (though not for the US) included not only murders but attempted murders. "If you want to walk the streets safely, Amsterdam is still a good place for a vacation," Zimring says. "And, more importantly, McCaffrey knows this. Folks have been going after him on this. And the notion of hiding behind the unaudited Interpol data—they can do that if they want, but they know what they're doing."

We find ourselves, here, deep in the misty jungle between outright lying ("I did not have sexual relations," etc.) and ordinary political spin. This twilight and primeval region is the preserve of a strange but common animal, the policy lie. Actually, "lie" is not exactly the right word, since the hallmark of the policy lie is that it intends not to deceive so much as to silence or browbeat an opponent, and it aims not so much at personal gain as at keeping some policy or other alive until next week.

According to the National Association of Attorneys General, 40 states have sued the tobacco industry, demanding to be reimbursed for Medicaid and other health-program costs resulting from smoking. The only problem is that there are no such costs. In fact, the states, like the federal government, make a nice profit on smokers, even after health costs are factored in: Smokers pay high state cigarette taxes while they're alive, and then they die younger than nonsmokers, thus not living to accumulate as much in medical and nursing benefits. W. Kip Viscusi, an economist at Harvard Law School, figures that Florida, which settled with Big Tobacco for $13 billion in alleged damages, also profited by a net of 42 cents on every pack of cigarettes sold. A policy lie allows the attorneys general to strike righteous poses, when in fact they are merely greedy.

In 1996, the opponents of California's Proposition 209, which banned affirmative action in state programs, knew they had an uphill battle against public opinion. So they set out to convince the public that a vote for 209 was in fact a vote to legalize discrimination against women (there are lots of female voters). "Women could get fired if they had children or if they got pregnant," said Patricia Ireland, the head of the National Organization for Women. The chairman of the state Democratic Party said that 209 would repeal girls' athletic programs. And so on. The charge was not only false but bizarre. (The voters weren't fooled.) Or again: Instead of defending their policies of setting much lower admissions standards for blacks than for whites, elite universities and law schools have simply denied that the policies exist. Again, the lying fooled no one, though it did help discredit affirmative action.

Henry James once wrote, "The simplest division it is possible to make of the human race is into the people who take things hard and the people who take them easy." Where political lying is concerned, I'm in the easygoing camp. Stuart Taylor Jr., the proprietor of the column next door, has proposed a group called CRALP: Citizens Repelled by All Lying Politicians. I would join CRALP, but my own chapter would be called Citizens Responding with Amusement to Lying Politicians. The important thing, in my version of CRALP, is to distinguish the really loathsome or hurtful lies from the banal stretchers of everyday political and personal life.

Still, I concede that this is an issue of temperament rather than morals, and that outrage is a reasonable response to lies in public life. So, to the outraged, I propose a deal. Stay outraged, but look a little less at intentions and legality, and more at real-world harm.

Bill Clinton's lie about sex was legally wrong and morally shabby. But the lie—as distinct from the consequences of its exposure—didn't do very much real-world damage. In fact, the country would have been much better off if Clinton had gotten away with it. Personal lies and policy prevarication co-exist in a curiously transverse relationship: Shabby lies of self-preservation usually cause only retail damage, whereas even well-intentioned policy dissembling can do mischief wholesale.

On August 4, 1964, Washington got word that the North Vietnamese had launched a nighttime attack on two U.S. destroyers in the Gulf of Tonkin. The North Vietnamese had already skirmished with an American destroyer in the area two days earlier, and the Johnson administration took the second attack to Congress as justification for a broad grant of war-making powers. What the administration did not say was that reports from the scene were conflicting and confused. Owing to the dark night and the rough weather, not even the men in the gulf were sure whether they had been shooting at real enemies or phantoms. Congress gave Johnson his authority to "take all necessary measures" in Vietnam—but the attack that justified this mandate had not occurred.

The country is still living with the consequences of the Johnson administration's Gulf of Tonkin not-quite-lie. Dishonest non-defenses of affirmative action have inflamed racial resentment; the states' tobacco suits will cost smokers billions of dollars that they do not properly owe; nonsense about the Dutch murder rate fuels obsessive drug-war overkill.

So here is a suggestion: Barry McCaffrey should manfully step forward and declare, for the record, that America is a more criminally lethal country than the Netherlands. He should come clean and admit the obvious, instead of hiding behind legalisms and technical dodges. Then we can forgive him, and put this whole sorry episode behind us.

Is It Ever Right to Lie? The Philosophy of Deception

Robert C. Solomon

No matter what you think of his politics or his personality, it is hard not to sympathize with President Clinton. The economy is booming, war is on the horizon, yet the press is rabid about sex in the White House. Of course, even in this "puritan" culture, there are few who would insist that the President should be impeached because of his by now well-known sexual proclivities. Rather, the question is: Did he lie (or tell someone else to)?

The importance of this question was summarized by one Congressman who pointed out that if the president would lie about one thing, he would lie about another.

For a philosopher, that argument raises all sorts of interesting questions. Is it ever right to lie? Is a lie told to embellish an otherwise tedious narrative just as wrong as a lie told to cover up a misdeed and avoid punishment? Is a lie told in desperation any less wrong than a calculated, merely convenient lie? Is a lie told out of self-deception more or less wrong than a clearheaded, tactical lie? (Is the former even a lie?) Are all lies wrong? Or does deception serve such important functions as protecting us from harm, especially emotional harm?

Let's start with the basics: Is it ever right to lie? Common sense surely says "Yes, sometimes." But legions of philosophers and other moralists have answered "No," and then tried to make sense of this indefensible position. Insisting that lying is always wrong—as Thomas Aquinas and Immanuel Kant did, for example—appeals to our desire for absolutes. But then, of course, what about the example from freshman philosophy: The Nazis come to your door asking if you are hiding a Jewish family. You are. Should you say "No"? Or, on a mundane level, your spouse or lover walks in with an utterly silly new hairdo and asks, "Do you like it?" Does morality dictate that you ruin the evening? Or can you, in both cases, finesse the answer, not lying but not telling the truth, either, perhaps by avoiding an answer to the question?

If a person would lie about one thing, does it follow that he or she would lie about another? That depends. The demand for honesty is contextual. It depends on what the truth concerns. The Bible tells us not to bear false witness against our neighbor. Perjury, we can agree, is wrong: The consequences can be awful. In a trial, a jury's assumption that a person who lies about one thing will lie about another is perfectly justified.

But it seems to be absolutely crucial to distinguish here between public and private life. Perjury, by its very nature, is public, as is politics. Sex, with a

ROBERT C. SOLOMON *is a professor of philosophy at the University of Texas at Austin, and the author, with Kathleen M. Higgins, of* A Short History of Philosophy *(Oxford University Press, 1996). From the* Chronicle of Higher Education, *February 27, 1996.*

few obvious exceptions, is part of our private life. And just about everyone is less than forthright about sex. Lying about sex, while it may have grave significance for people in an intimate relationship, has nothing to do with one's public credibility. Indeed, when publicly asked a rudely inappropriate question about one's private (adult, consensual) sex life, it seems to me not only natural but even obligatory to lie, finesse, or refuse to answer.

Nietzsche once asked. "Why must we have truth at any cost, anyway?" It was an odd question, coming from the philosopher who prided himself, above all, on his brutal honesty, and it is an obscene question, in any case, for a profession that sees itself as seeking solely the truth. Even philosophers who challenge the very idea of truth—not just Nietzsche and Buddhist Nagarajuna, but also Jacques Derrida and Richard Rorty—are unforgiving when it comes to deception, misrepresentation, and "creative misreadings," at least of their own work. Philosophers in general insist on the truth even if they do not believe in "the Truth." They despise deception and ridicule self-deception.

The Australian philosopher Tony Coady probably speaks for most philosophers when he writes, "Dishonesty has always been perceived in our culture, and in all cultures but the most bizarre, as a central human vice." But, he adds, "we should note that this perception is consistent with a certain hesitancy about what constitutes a lie and with the more than sneaking suspicion that there might be a number of contexts in which lying is actually justified." Plato defended "the noble lie," and the English ethicist Henry Sidgwick suggested that a "high-minded lie" in the direction of humility might do us all a great deal of good.

Not all untruths are malicious. Telling the truth can complicate or destroy social relationships. It can undermine precious collective myths. Honesty can be cruel. Sometimes, deception is not a vice but a social virtue, and systematic deception is an essential part of the order of the (social) world. In many countries—Japan and Western Samoa, for example—social harmony is valued far more than truthfulness as such. To tell another person what he or she wants to hear, rather than what one might actually feel or believe, is not only permitted but expected.

Could we not begin to see our own enlightened emphasis on "seeking the truth at all costs" (as Ernst Jones wrote admiringly of Sigmund Freud) as one more ethnocentric peculiarity, another curious product of our strong sense of individualism, and a dangerously unsociable conception?

Behind the blanket prohibition on lying, we can discern the outlines of a familiar but glorious philosophical metaphor: The truth is bright, simple, the Holy Grail of Rationality, while dishonesty is dark and devious, the path to irrationality and confusion. But philosophy, one begins to suspect, has overrated those metaphors of clarity and transparency. The obvious truth is that our simplest social relationships could not exist without the opaque medium of the lie. The best answer to the question "What are you thinking?" is often "Oh, nothing." Perhaps deception, not truth, is the cement of civilization—a cement that does not so much hold us together as safely separate us and our thoughts. Some things are better left in the dark.

In contrast to Kant, for whom the rule against lying was a moral law, a "categorical imperative" never to be overridden, utilitarian philosophers insist that lying is wrong only because a lie does, in fact, cause more harm than good. There is no absolute prohibition here, rather perhaps a "rule of thumb," and there may well be many cases, such as the "white lies" described above, in which lying causes no harm and may even be commendable. The problem, as Nietzsche so wisely complains (in characteristic opposition to Kant) is "not that you lied to me, but that I no longer believe you." It is not the breach of the principle against lying that is so troublesome, nor is it the consequences of the lie or the character of the liar: It is that lying compromises and corrupts our relationships.

In other words, the wrongness of lying does not have to do primarily with breaches of principle or miscalculations of harm and good, even if these weigh heavily in particular cases—in a court of law or a Congressional hearing, for example. Lying is wrong because it constitutes a breach of trust, which is not a principle but a very particular and personal relationship between people. And in sexual relations, while personal trust is of the utmost importance, it has nothing to do with, and no necessary correlation with, public trust.

What is wrong with lying, in other words, is not exactly what philosophers have often supposed. Lying undermines relationships by undermining trust. But trust may just as often be supported by mutual myths, by religious faith, by a clear understanding of what is private and personal and what is "the public's right to know." Trust is usually violated by lies, but trust can be more deeply damaged by a violation of personal boundaries, which in turn may invite lies and deception to protect what has been violated.

What further complicates questions about lying and deception is the familiar phenomenon of self-deception. It is always easiest, the old adage tells us, to tell the truth. But next-easiest is to believe your own lie, to become so submerged in its network of details and implications that the continuation of the lie—as Aristotle argues—becomes second nature.

Discussions of lying too often focus on the straightforwardly cynical, self-interested lie and ignore the more common species of lying that includes self-deception as well. But transparency to ourselves can be just as intolerable as transparency to others, and for just the same reason. The recognition of one's own motives and the significance of one's own thoughts can be devastating to one's self-image and sense of well-being. And so we disguise, hide, distract ourselves from those facets and the self that are less than flattering. As Nietzsche puts it, "'I have done that,' says my memory. 'I cannot have done that,' says my pride, and remains inexorable. Eventually, memory yields."

Deception and self-deception are part and parcel of our engagements in the world, including, not least, the development and maintenance of our sense of ourselves. Lying can sometimes be a way of protecting our private lives, especially in the midst of a press-plagued public life. Within one's personal life, within the so-far unbreached walls of the Clintons' bedroom, for example, there is, no doubt, a continuing drama of Shakespearean proportions. But that is where this business about sex and lying about it should remain.

As for all of those inappropriate questions from otherwise distinguished journalists, special persecutors, and the curious public, they deserve no answer, or an evasion or even a lie for an answer. Clinton's sex life and what he says about it do not have anything to do with Clinton's credibility or ability to govern (which are other questions altogether). A lie or an invitation to lie that is provoked by a breach of sacred personal boundaries is in moral limbo, and no violation of a public trust.

Yes, Sometimes Lying Is Right Action to Take

Lorraine Dusky

Some years ago, I told a lie to protect one person's feelings and another's reputation. Yes, I had chopped down the cherry tree just as I had been accused, and I had not done it alone. To say that I'd done the deed would have drawn in another person who had much to lose if the truth were out, and it was clear no good could come of that. Several people would be hurt. Yes, this involved infidelity and, no, I'm not going to go further.

There are times when the cost of telling the truth is greater than the worth of honesty. It is not only that one has to stand up and take the consequences for one's misdeed, but it is also that other individuals will be irreparably harmed by the truth-telling. Then lying is the only noble course there is.

History gives us significant examples of this as recently as the '50s. Then an out-of-control, self-anointed special investigator, Joe McCarthy, wanted to get at the "truth" of the Red Menace in this country. All sorts of people were hauled before his Senate committee and the House Un-American Activities Committee and asked to be truthful about those they believed had communist leanings. Whom do we admire today? The finks who told the "truth," named names and got off with their jobs intact, or those who were blacklisted because they didn't? Early Christian history is rife with stories of martyrs who sacrificed their own lives rather than name other Christians. The same is true of the Resistance during the last World War. Certainly the Underground Railroad, which secretly transported slaves to their freedom, involved "lying" to keep it thriving.

Lying Spares Pain

Today many children in adoptive families "lie" when asked if they were searching for, or have made contact with, their first families. They want to spare their adoptive parents any pain. Doctors and parents sometimes "lie" to terminally ill children, and adult children sometimes "lie" to their terminally ill parents. In the name of truth-telling, a great many relationships have been gratuitously damaged and countless feelings hurt.

Which brings us to Bill Clinton. Let's say that when Monica Lewinsky's name surfaced in the Paula Jones suit, he did not tell the truth about his relationship with the former White House intern. Not answering would have been the same as an admission of guilt. So Clinton, responding in the only way that would protect the honor of his wife, his daughter, the young woman in question, her family and, yes, himself, perhaps was not truthful. Think, for a moment, what the truth would do.

Lorraine Dusky *is a freelance writer living in New York and is the author of* Still Unequal: The Shameful Truth about Women and Justice in America. *From* USA Today, *March 5, 1998.*

Hillary Clinton, who has had to endure some embarrassment before over Clinton's peccadilloes, would be humiliated much further. Their teenage daughter, Chelsea, would be publicly embarrassed. And Lewinsky? We've heard that she has asked: Who will ever hire me? Who will ever date me? Who, indeed? Now Lewinsky faces the threat of indictment.

Sure, Clinton Stood to Gain, But . . .

It goes nearly without saying what Clinton stood to gain by insisting that no improper relationship existed: his marriage, his dignity, perhaps even his presidency. And if it were later revealed that he was lying about it under oath, he would be in much more serious trouble than if he simply told the truth.

Considering all that has transpired since that day some six weeks ago, just possibly it would have been more self-serving to tell the "truth," if that's what it is, and confess to the nation. Judging by Clinton's popularity, he would have been pardoned by the public. His family probably would have forgiven him also. And Ken Starr, the McCarthy of our times, would have nothing to investigate. No matter what comes out about Lewinsky, legally it is of no use to the Jones team, since it's been ruled inadmissible in her trial. But Lewinsky? Ah, well she would have been trashed in the process. Would truth then have been the more honorable course? Resoundingly, no.

So, no matter what the reality of the situation, no matter what we think of our president's fatal flaws, Clinton took the high road: He said that no improper relationship existed. He responded with the sense of decency we all hope someone would draw upon if our daughter, sister or mother were named as a corespondent in such an affair. And he may have told a lie in the process.

While we might not readily compare Clinton to Antigone, the lines Sophocles gave her are relevant here: "What divine justice have I disobeyed?" she says as she is led to her death for disobeying the king. "The wise will know my choice was right."

Apparently the American public knows, too. Regardless of the consequences yet to come, Clinton made the right choice.

Response: If Lying Is OK, How Do We Determine Truth?

Free-lance writer Lorraine Dusky's assertion that sometimes lying is "the only noble course" produced a flood of letters to the editor disagreeing with her. Here are the comments of a few:

> After reading Lorraine Dusky's article, "Yes, sometimes lying is right action to take," I had to step back and ponder. Let's follow this argument to its logical conclusion. If it's all right to lie sometimes, why have a court system where we swear under oath to speak the truth? Why look for truth and try to determine justice in this society if lying "is some-

times all right"? The obvious conclusion is that there is no right or wrong, and everything is relative as long as one can justify that the reason he or she is lying is for a good purpose.

This sounds like those who believe that government should take care of society and we don't have to take personal responsibility or be accountable. What a fantastic model this would be for our children.

Dusky's logic that sometimes lying is a noble course to take fails me. Following her argument, we could hold that objective journalism would be out the window because if it's all right to lie sometimes, who knows if what is being reported is the truth or a justifiable lie? We could just live in a world of make-believe and decide "who we need to protect from the truth" by lying at will.

And when people don't have a logical argument to back up their position, it seems the tactic to take is to denigrate the other side. This sounds like name-calling from my kindergarten days or, better yet, character assassination as I have come to know it as an adult. We have an independent counsel, Kenneth Starr, who was appointed by President Clinton's attorney general, Janet Reno, and a three-judge panel to do the job he is doing. But all the pundits can do is try to undermine his character.

The truth is, if we come to the point where we justify lying and cover-up for any reason, read the history books and you will find that the moral corruption of a nation is always the pathway to destruction. It seems character may count after all.

Elaine E. Mason
Burke, Va.
From USA Today, *March 9, 1998.*

A Sign of Moral Decline

Lorraine Dusky's advocacy of lying is a shocking indication of the degree of moral degradation to which we have fallen as a nation. How dare she!

There's a sharp difference between not telling all you know and telling something you know not to be true. The former is honorable, motivated by decency, and is protective of others regardless of personal cost. The latter is dishonorable, motivated by deceit and the desire to protect oneself, at any cost, from receiving the just desserts of personal wrongdoing. Especially in sworn testimony.

It has not been proved the president lied under oath, or urged others to. If he did, only the morally bankrupt would seek to whitewash this action.

Rick Huff
Tucson, Ariz.
From USA Today, *March 9, 1998.*

The Truth

Seldom has an article almost made me physically sick the way the column by Lorraine Dusky does.

Her examples of acceptable lying involve life and death and persecution. To lump President Clinton's alleged lie with horrors like the Christian martyrs, the Underground Railroad days, war Resistance fighters and the McCarthy era is silly.

To imply that the truth can hurt Hillary Rodham Clinton suggests that she does not know her husband better than any person or that she is naïve or not too bright; these do not fit this very intelligent lady. And their daughter, Chelsea, has been hearing negatives about her father for years. She is adult enough to deal with difficult situations.

The only person who can be hurt by the truth now is the president, and his place in history. Ironically, had he admitted he had a problem and reviewed it with the American people, it probably would be over, just a footnote in history. Americans have a great capacity for forgiveness.

Is it any wonder that more people are willing to try to lie their way out of difficult situations? If it is OK for our leaders, why isn't it OK for everyone?

If children learn from what they see, their not being truthful will be a big price for the country to pay.

Barbara A. Volz
Sugarcreek, Ohio
From USA Today, *March 9, 1998.*

Credits

Index

Academic writing, xxx–xxxiv,
9–11, 200, 247; values of,
124, 161; value in, 332
Acknowledgment and response,
18, 33–34, 44–49, 117,
185–202, 264; as alternative
solution, 118; as subordinate argument, 191–93,
202; collecting alternatives,
194; dialogue, 5, 14, 17–19,
32–50, 203–06; in common
ground, 195; in previous
research, 194; language of,
196–98; locating 56, 195;
questions about, 354; restating main argument, 190–91
Alternative views, *see Others'
views*
Analogy, causation, 284, 294–5;
meaning, 266; warrant,
225–26
Anecdotes, 109; as evidence,
161, 165, 173, 183; conclusion, 92; prelude, 91, 109
Argument, about causes,
274–300; about meaning,
254–73; abuse of 3–4; academic, 9–11, 124, 161, 200,
247; as construction,
133–36, 142; as
problem–solving, xxi–xxii,
3–31, 49–50, 52–59,
72–110, 113–117, 235–45,
250–52; 275–79; 291–97;
as tool of critical thinking,
4–5, 7, 50–51; as war, 4,
117, 133, 186–87, 193;
based on alternatives,
195–6; based on warrants,
223–24, 237–39; civil, 4, 7,
9, 13, 23; conceptual, 10,
73, 75–76, 102–04 115–17,
127, 190, 250, 264, 272;
cooperation, 4, 8–9, 171,
186, 193; coherence, ten
steps. 348–50; conversation,
xxix–xxx, 4–5, 32–71,
186–87; core, 33, 36–38,
112–232, 185–86; democ-
racy, 11–12; dialogue, 5, 14,
17–19, 32–50, 203–06;

discourse community, 9–10,
115, 148–49, 161, 194,
200, 202; emotion, 3–4, 9,
14–16, 74–75, 103, 314,
331–36, 343, 345–46;
generating elements of,
32–41; hostile 3–4, 9, 27
186–87; ideology in, 78–79;
metaphor for, 4, 26, 133;
model of, 41–47; origin of
word, 4; practical, 10, 73,
74–77, 102–04, 115–17,
247, 250–51, 272; problem
posing, 94–96; questioning
stance, 5–8, 15, 39, 160,
171, 185–90, 198–99; questions about, 187–90, 348;
questions as basis of, 5,
185–90; [five] questions of,
7, 32–47, 61, 72, 185; questions of others, 5–7,
185–90; subordinate,
49–50; 191–93, 202,
208–11; surrogate, 251–54,
256, 267–68, 272; thickening, 49–50, 70, 142,
191–93, 208–11, 292; uses
of, 4–12, 27; values, 78–79,
116–17, 248, 251, 253,
272; vs. coercion, 13, 25; vs.
explanation, 13–14, 25; vs.
negotiation, 12; vs. persuasion, 12–13; vs. power, 7,
11; vs. propaganda, 13; vs.
story, 14–15; *see Elements of
argument, Levels of argument*
Aristotle, xxiii–xxiv, 180
Assumption, *see Warrant*
Authority, as evidence, 163,
165–66, 172, 183
Background information, locating, 49
Bellesiles, Michael, 158, 172
Benefit, 82, 103; as restated
cost, 82
Bernstein, Richard, 318
Berman, Richard, 116, 461–62
Best, Joel, 170
Bias, xxii, 237–42; about causation, 275–78, 300, 374;
about language, 374;

anchoring, 238–40; anticipating readers', 243,
289–90; attribution,
287–90, 300; cognitive,
xxiii, 114–15, 187, 237–44,
373–74; confirmation,
239–41; guarding against,
187, 237–44, 276–78, 288,
300; interpretation of
evidence, 238–40, 373;
jumping to conclusion,
242–43, 373; One True
Cause, 278, 290, 373; One
True Principle, 238–39;
overconfidence, 242;
personal investment, 161,
289; role of culture, 289–90;
role of ideology and politics,
78–79, 161, 189, 373; Silver
Bullet Solution, 278
Body of essay, 19–20, 47–48,
55, 58–59, 71, 86–87,
94–95, 101, 110, 195; questions about, 353
Bruffee, Kenneth A., 451–53
Carson, Ed, 164, 260, 441–45
Casement, William, 191
Castillo, Sonia, 425–40
Categories, 254, 255–268,
271–73; basic level of,
316–17
Causation, 236–37, 246,
274–300; analyzing,
280–84; ANOVA, 280–83,
300; attribution bias,
287–90; bias, 275–78, 290,
300; chains of, 274–75, 292,
300; conceptual problem,
279, 300; conditions,
disabling, 275; conditions,
enabling, 275; critical thinking about, 283–84; in ordinary thinking, 275–78;
language of, 297–98;
personal responsibility,
284–90, 296–97; personal
vs. circumstantial, 86–90,
300; practical problem, 279,
291–94, 300; questions
about, 355–56; relevant to
problem, 275–80, 300

Chadwick, Douglas, 304
Cheney, George, 148, 254,
    406–19
Character, abstractions, 339–41;
    subjects, 305–07; means as
    agents, 338–39
Citation, APA, 368–72; forms,
    148, 364–72; MLA, 364–68;
    rules for, 360–64
Claim, 5, 11, 15, 31, 32–50, 69,
    113–31, 159–62, 166–67,
    185–87, 190, 194, 199–200,
    204–13, 220–21; 227–28,
    231, 236, 246, 265, 303;
    317; articulating, 116,
    120–24, 125–6, 142–45;
    colored by reasons, 144;
    conceptual richness, 121–22;
    contestable, 118–19, 130;
    degree of acceptance,
    117–18, 161–2; discon-
    firmable, 119–20, 130;
    hypothesis, 17, 70, 114–15,
    173, 236–42; logical rich-
    ness, 121–20; locating,
    54–55, 93, 100–101; nega-
    tion test, 118–19; qualifying,
    123–24, 126–27, 130, 133;
    questions about, 187–88,
    202, 351–52; reasonable,
    120, 130; testing, 118–124;
    values, 116–17; vs. reasons
    42; *see Main claim; Main
    point; Solution*
Coda, 92, 260
Coercion, 128; vs argument 13
Collaborative writing, language
    of criticism, 23–24; ques-
    tions in, 102, 199, 227;
    value of, 23–24; writing
    group, 24
Common ground, 84, 88–90,
    92, 109–10, 260; as alterna-
    tive view, 195; academic
    writing, 89–90; conceptual
    problem, 89–90; language
    of, 100; literature review, 90;
    practical problem, 88–89
Conceptual problem, 10, 73,
    75–76, 102–04 115–17,
    127, 250, 287; as question,
    75–76, 99–100; common
    ground in, 89–90; structure
    of, 75–79, 108–10; wider
    coherence, 78–79
Conclusion, 53–54, 71, 92–93;
    critical thinking, 93; match-
    ing to introduction 59; ques-
    tions about, 353; testing,
    100–101

Condition, destabilizing, 74–76,
    79–81, 100, 108–10;
    conceptual as question,
    75–76; how to state, 82–83
Conquest, Robert, 11–12
Consequence of conceptual
    problem, 75–77, 82–84,
    100, 109–10; as question,
    75–78, how to state, 83–84;
    in applied problem, 84; vs.
    practical costs, 77–78
Conversation, as argument,
    xxix–xxx, 4, 8, 32–41,
    186–87
Cooperation, argument 4, 8–9,
    171, 186, 193; problem
    solving, 4; others' questions
    5–7
Cost of practical problem, 38,
    71, 74–76, 79–81, 100,
    103, 108–10; how to state,
    80–81; implied values,
    80–81; in applied problem,
    84; stated as benefit, 82; vs.
    conceptual consequence,
    77–78
Critic, origin of word, 6–7
Critical thinking, xxii, 4–12,
    32–33, 72–73, 79, 114–15,
    120, 123–24, 132–33, 137,
    159, 185–87, 237–42; about
    causation, 275–290; argu-
    ment as tool of, 4–7, 50–51;
    barriers to, 114–15, 237–42;
    critical imagination, 32, 39,
    185–90, 192–93, 195, 199,
    202, 203–06, 209–11,
    238–29; danger of
    emotional language,
    334–36; education, 10–11;
    how common, 8; language
    of, 242; questions,
    xxii–xxiii, 5–8, 15, 39, 160,
    171, 185–90, 198–99; ratio-
    nality, 5–7; stages, 7, 9, 14,
    37, 39, 128; testing ideas, 4,
    6–8, 33, 37, 50–51, 79,
    114–15, 123–24. 186–90,
    203–06; value of others'
    views, 6, 33, 185–90,
    203–06
Cultural diversity, 9, 210–11,
    289–90
Darnton, Robert, 87
Darwin, Charles, 256, 264,
    342–43
Data, 114, 153, 159, 172–5,
    178; as evidence, 133–4,
    142–44, 168; numerical,
    142–43, 166, 168–71, 173,

183. 221–22; visual presen-
    tation, 168–70
Davenport, Andrea, 425–40
Definition, 46–68; as warrant,
    254; authorized, 255–6,
    258–59, 262–64, 271–73;
    and common meaning,
    255–64, 267–78, 272–73;
    criteria in, 263–4; limits of,
    262–63
Democracy, 11–12
Dictionaries, 263–4, 267–68;
    criteria in definitions,
    263–4; limits of definitions,
    262–63
Discourse community, 9–11,
    115, 148–49, 161, 194,
    200, 202, 205–06, 209–10,
    279; definitions, 258–59,
    262–64; evidence, 148–49,
    161; finding problems,
    115–17; meaning, 258–59;
    prelude, 91; social contract
    with readers, 54; specialists,
    205–06, 209–10; warrant,
    209–10
Document structure, coherence,
    ten steps, 348–50; locating
    acknowledgment and
    response, 56, 195; locating
    claim, 54–55, 93, 100–101;
    locating evidence, 47–48;
    locating warrant, 57–58,
    224–25; order of elements of
    argument, 41, 43, 47–49,
    51–52, 54–58; order of
    reasons, 56; plan for argu-
    ment about responsibility,
    296–97; plan for complete
    argument, 48; plan for core
    of argument, 47–48; plan for
    practical argument, 291–94;
    plans to avoid, 51–52; *see
    Plan*
Doerner, Dietrich, 242
Dowdall, George, 425–40
Drafting, acknowledgement and
    response, 196–98; starting,
    22; styles of, 22; when to
    start, 58
Edmundson, Mark, 82, 127,
    393–400
Einstein, Albert, 264
Elements of argument, generat-
    ing, 32–41; order of, 41, 43,
    47–49, 51–52, 54–58
Elevator story, 16–17
Emotion, 14–16, 161; as moti-
    vation, 74–75, 103; hostility
    in argument, 3–4, 9, 27;

language, 314, 331–336, 343, 345–46

Ethics 12–13, 120, 190, 200; clarity, 321–22; deliberate complexity, 311; value–laden language, 331–32, 346

Ethos, xxii, 7–8, 15–16, 33, 39, 60, 80–81, 124, 160, 192; as reputation, 33, 60; implied by costs, 80–81; implied by reasons, 144; implied by style, 304, 311, 336; readers' trust, 32, 39, 44, 50, 117, 123–4, 126–27, 164–73, 178, 183, 187, 193, 195, 303–4, 311

Evidence, 11, 15, 17,32–50, 69–70, 117, 119–20, 130, 132–184, 194, 199–200; accuracy of, 162, 183, 202; anecdotes as, 161, 173, 183; as foundation, 135–36, 138–39, 142; authority, 166–67, 172, 183, 202; balancing with reasons, 151; 159; burden of, 160–62; direct, 136–39, 165; currency, 183, 202; disconfirming, 240–41; discourse community, 161, 173; documenting, 135, 159, 168, 176–77; drawings as, 176–68, 221–22; explained by reason, 142–44, 221–22; interpretation, 239–41; interviews, 174–77; kind readers expect, 161, 173; locating, 47–48; memories as, 161, 165, 168–69, 183; metaphor for, 133, 135, 142; notes, 150–151, 176–77, 184; numerical data as, 133–34, 161, 166–70, 173, 183, 221–22; origin of word, 44; photographs as, 137, 167–68, 183, 221–22; plan for finding, 162, 173–75, 239; precision of, 162–63, 183, 202; quality of, 162–64; questions about, 135–39, 160–62, 167, 172, 188, 199, 353–54; recordings as, 167–68, 183; reliability of, 162–3, 172; reports of, 37, 135–40, 160–84; representative, 162–63, 183, 202; searching, 162,

173–75; skepticism, 171; testimonial, 161, 165, 173, 178; vs. reasons, 42–43, 135–36; vs. reports of, 135–40; visual image as, 15, 137, 167–68, 183, 221–22; vividness of, 15, 166, 168;

Exhibit, 133–4, as evidence, 134

Explanation, in arguments, 49, 57–58, 293–94; in causal arguments, 293–94; vs. argument, 13–14, 25

Fact, 6, 33, 37, 133–34, 152

Fallacies, 374–81, *ad baculum*, 376–77; *ad hominem*, 380; *ad ignoratiam*, 376; *ad misericordiam* 380–81; *ad populum*, 379; *ad verecundiam*, 379–80; argue in a circle, 375–76; beg the question 375–76; false choice, 378; false metaphor, 378; guilt by association, 380; mud–slinging, 380; *non sequitur*, 375; *reductio ad absurdum*, 377–78; slippery slope, 377–78; *tu quoque*, 377; *see Bias, Logic, Reasoning*

Finkbeiner, Ann, 124, 336

Five paragraph essay, 51, 70, 140–41

Franklin, Benjamin, 124

Geertz, Clifford, 172

Google Scholar, 174

Gould, Stephen Jay, 240, 334–35

Hemings, Sally 78,102, 238

Hubbard, M., 241

Hypothesis, 17, 70, 114–15, 173, 236–42

Internet, as source of topics, 97, evidence from, 20, 168, 174, 176, need to cite, 360

Introduction, 47–49, 54–55, 71, 79–96, 104, 109–10, 115–17, 195; common ground in, 88–92; critical thinking, 93; main claim in, 54–55, 93, 100–101; matching to conclusion 59; prelude in, 90–93; problem in, 79–87; questions about, 352; solution in, 54–55; structure of, 79–92; to section, 55–56; working, 58–59

Jefferson, Thomas 73, 78, 102, 147, 152, 238

Kennedy, John F., 116–17

Kuhn, Deanna, 8

Language, abstract vs. concrete, 315–16; clarity of, 303–330; concise, 312–14; cynical, 335–36; deliberate generality, 317–18; emotion, 314, 331–336; force of, 331–46; imageable words, 265; 315–17; metaphor for argument, 4, 26, 133; metaphor for evidence, 133, 135, 142; metaphoric scenarios, 339–43; of acknowledgement and response, 196–98; of causation, 297–98; of judging prose, 304; point of view, 336–40; polarizing, 334–35, 346; questions about, 356; values, 248, 251, 253, 272, 331–33, 346; vivid, 314–16

Lepper, M. R., 241,

Library, evidence from, 174

Levels of argument, core 7, 33, 36–38, 41–44, 47; dialogic, 7, 33, 38–39; logical, 7, 33

Loftus, Elizabeth F. 165

Logic, 5, 7, 11, 14–16, 33, 39–41, 46–47, 115, 140, 142, 161, 203–31, 345–46; addressing errors in, 198; *see Fallacies; Warrant*

Logos, 15–16; *see Logic*

McMillan, Jill J., 148, 254, 406–19

Main claim, 42, 100–101, 109–110, 113–16, 178–79; delaying, 54–55; locating 54–55, 93, 100–101

Main point, 42, 113. 130; locating, 54–55; of sections, 55–56, 59, 71

Matthews, Robert, 342–43

Meaning, 246–73; analogy, 266; anticipating readers', 255, 260, 265, 272; authorized, 255–6, 258–59, 262–64, 271–73; authorized, vs. common, 255; categories, 255–268, 271–73; common, 255–64, 267–78, 272–73; criteria, 254–68, 346; definition, 246–68; dictionaries, 260–64, 267–68, 272; discourse community, 258–59; features, 254–58, 265, 346; limits on, 257–59, 332–33; matching models,

257–58; matching criteria, 254–58, 265, 346; models, 257–8, 265–66, 272–73; model, vividness, 257; questions about, 255, 356; referent, 247–50; role of history, 262, 266; specialist, 258–60; surrogate argument, 251–54, 256, 267–68, 272; term, 247–67, 271–72; values, 248, 251, 253, 272, 331–36, 346; warrants for, 234, 273

Medved, Michael, 226, 294–95

Memories, as evidence, 161, 165, 183

Metaphor, 254, 264, 341–43; fallacy, 378; for argument, 4, 26, 133; for evidence, 133, 135, 142; personification, 339–41; scenario, 341–43

Mill, John Stuart, 280, 295

Moeykens, Barbara, 425–40

Morris, Tanya, 290

Morton, Samuel, 240–41

Narrative, causal arguments, 291–96; of your thinking, 51, 70

Negotiation, 124; vs. argument 12

Notes, taking, 150–151, 176–77, 183, 194, 361–64

Organization, *see Document structure; Plan*

Others' views, 5–7, 10, 23, 45, 117, 185–90, 202, 203–06, 227; from reading, 194; imagining, 32, 39, 185–90, 192–93, 195, 199, 203–06, 209–11, 224, 238–39; from surrogate readers, xxiii, 147–48, 209; respect for, 8, 186

Outline, 21, 31, 47–48, 51–58, 194; problem posing vs solving, 94–95; *see Plan*

Paglia, Camile, 193, 449–50

Palmer, John C. 165

Paraphrase, 148–49, 151, 176, 360–64; discourse community, 148, 151

Pathos, 15–16; *see Argument, emotion; Emotion*

Patterson, Orlando, 287

Pernal, Michael, 127, 254, 401–05

Persuasion, 12–13; emotion, 14; story, 14–15; visual image, 15

Photographs, as evidence, 167–68, 183

Plagiarism, 150, 184; avoiding, 150, 176–77, 360–64; documenting sources, 135, 159, 168, 176–77, 360–72

Plan, for argument about personal responsibility, 296–97; for complete argument, 48; for core of argument, 47–48; for finding evidence, 162, 173–75; for practical problem, 291–94; to avoid, 51–52

Planning, from a topic to a problem, 96–100; outline, 21, 47–48, 51–52; problem as framework for, 20–21;

Prelude, 90–91, 109–110; discourse community, 91, 93

Premise, *see Warrant*

Practical problem, 10, 73, 74–77, 102–04, 115–17, 250–51, 287, 291–94; causation, 291–94; common ground in, 88–89; practical, structure of, 74–75, 108–110

Problem, 10, 17, 31, 36, 38, 44, 49, 70, 72–104, 113–16, 128, 130, 173, 187–88, 195, 260, 275–76, 285, 287, 291–4, 300; applied, 84; conceptual 10, 73, 75–76, 102–04 115–17, 127, 250, 287; conceptual as question, 75–76, 99–100; conceptual, structure of, 75–79, 108–10; conceptual, wider coherence, 78–79; in introduction, 79–92; practical 10, 73, 74–77, 102–04, 115–17, 250–51, 287, 291–94; practical, and causation, 291–94; practical, structure of, 74–75, 108–110; questions about, 187–88, 199, 351; solving, 4, 26, 81, 114–15; 235–45; surrogate, 251–54, 256, 267–68, 272

Professional community, 9–11

Propaganda, 128; vs argument 13

Prototypes, *see Model*

Proverb, as warrant, 206, 228–29

Qualification, 242; in science, 124; of claim, 123–24,

126–27; of warrant, 206–07, 215–16

Question, about argument, 187–90, 348, 353; about acknowledgement and response, 354; about causation, 355–56; about claim/solution, 187–88, 199, 202, 351–52; about conclusion, 353; about consistency, 189–90; about evidence 135–39, 160–62, 167, 199; 353–54; about introduction, 352; about language, 356; about logic, 213–14; about meaning, 355; about problem, 187–88, 199, 351; about readers, 351; about reasons, 199; about title, 352; about warrant, 188–89, 199, 214–17, 219–21, 354; critical thinking, 6–7, 11, 185–90, 203–06, 214–17; imagining on behalf of readers, 32, 39, 70, 185–90, 192–93, 195, 199, 203–31

Questioning stance, xxii–xxiii, 5–8, 15, 39, 160, 171, 185–90, 198–99

Quotation, 148–50, 159, 360–64; as evidence, 143–44, 166, 171, 176, 221–22; integrating, 149–50; discourse community, 149

Rationality, 5–7, 60; critical thinking, 5–7; cultural diversity, 9; subject to evidence, 119–20

Rauch, Jonathan, 44

Reader, dialogue with, 9, 14, 17–19, 23, 33, 38–39, 44–46, 185–202; anticipating questions of, 32, 39, 70, 72–73, 185–90, 192–93, 203–06, 209–11, 224; motivating, 72–92, 103–04, 115; real vs. stipulated, 18; role in argument, 85–202; surrogate, xxiii, 23, 147–48, 209; thinking about, 17–18, 72–73

Reading, for other views, 194; skimming sources, 19–20; use of problem statements, 96; web sites, 20

Research, 19–20, 173; academic, 78–79, 124, 247;

applied, 84; consequences of, 127; language of, 124, 247; notes, 150–151, 176–77; preliminary, 19–20; previous, 150–151, 176–77, 194; pure, 78, 102–03

Reasons, 5–6, 9, 11, 14–15, 17, 26–27, 31, 32–50, 69–70, 117, 132–159, 166–67, 173, 204–13, 218–19, 223, 227–28, 231; as outline of argument, 140; balancing with evidence, 151, 159; coloring claim, 144; explaining evidence, 142–44, 221–22; influence on ethos, 144; in parallel, 140–42, 145–46, 159; in series 141–42, 146–47, 159; multiple, 140–42, 145–47; order of, 56; origin of word, 44; questions about, 202, 351; relevance to claim, 33, 39–40, 46–47, 69; vs. claim 42; vs. evidence, 42–43; vs. warrant, 218

Reasoning, abductive, 235–42; deductive, 236; forms of, 235–45; inductive, 235–06; questions about, 354–44; *see Bias; Fallacies*

Recordings, as evidence, 167–68, 183

Responsibility, causal, 284–90, 296–97; subjects, 336–39

Revising, 22; for style, 319–21

Rockefeller, John D., 343

Ross, L., 241

Rothenberg, David, 95–96

Ryan, M. P., 11

Sanders, Keith R., 167

Sherry, Suzanna, 221–22

Skepticism, radical 171; *see Questioning stance*

So what?, 76–78, 92, 102, 109–10

Social contract with readers, 54–55

Solution, 10, 31, 38–39, 49, 52, 70, 78, 104, 109–110,

113–16, 128, 130, 173, 187–88, 195, 260, 285, 291–94, 300; delayed, 85–88; hypothesis, 17, 114–5, 236–42; in introduction, 52, 85–88; questions about, 187–88, 199, 202, 351–2; related to costs, 80–81; see *Claim; Main claim*

Source, primary, 161, 178; secondary, 161; tertiary, 161

Story, vs. argument,14–15

Storyboard, 52–53, 140, 194, 356–59

Style, ethics of, 311, 321–22; revising, 319–21

Subject, and verb, interrupting, 309; consistent, 311; main characters, 336–41; point of view, 336–40, 334–44, 346; responsible voice; short, 309

Sullum, Jacob, 454–60

Summary, 52, 176, 360–64

Swenson, Craig, 193, 420–24

Themes (key concepts), 55, 100–101, 121–22; in title, 101

Thesis, 42, 113

Title, 110; questions about, 352; themes in, 101

Tolstoy, Leo, 298

Topic, 96–100, 109–10, 173, 239

Toulmin, Stephen, xxiv–xxvii

Trosset, Carol, 87–88, 171, 385–92

Truth, 25, 171

Tum, Rigoberta Menchú, 161, 179–80

Values, 9, 13, 144–5, 178, 210, 343; academic writing, 78–79; claim, 78–79, 116–17; language, 248, 251, 253, 272, 331–33, 345–46

Verb, action, 307; placement of, 308

Visual Image, as evidence, 144, 167–70, 221–22; not argument, 15; persuasion, 15

Vividness, 15, 166; evidence, 15, 166; imageable words, 265; 315–17; model, 257; word choice, 312–14

Warrant, 33–34, 40–41, 46–50, 57–58, 69–70, 117, 184, 203–31, 295, 300; analogy, 225–26; applicable, 202, 208–09, 216, 219–20, 228, 231; appropriate, 202, 216–17, 231; as principle of reasoning, 9, 33, 46–47, 69, 204–11, 215, 223–24, 228–29; assumption, 204; connection of claim and reason, 39–40, 46–47, 207–11; culture, 210–11; discourse community, 204–206, 216–17; evidence, 221–22; failure of, 209–10, 214–17; for consensus, 212–13; for emphasis, 211–12, 225; limitations on, 206–07, 215–16, 227, 231, 238; locating, 57–58, 224–25; matrix, 40, 46, 206–09, 213–18; premise, 204; questions about, 188–89, 199, 202, 214–17, 219–21, 354; readers' ideas, 46–47; specialists, 204–06, 217; structure of, 40, 46, 206–09; subordinate argument, 208–011; testing, 213–18; true, 208, 214–15, 219; vs. reason, 218; when to use, 209–13

Warren, Susan, 342–43

Wechsler, Henry, 425–40

Web sites, as sources, 168, 174; need to cite, 360; reading, 20; taking notes from, 176, 361–62

Weinberger, Daniel R., 339

White, Pamela, 201, 446–48

Wikipedia, 174

Writing groups, see *Collaborative writing*

Wysocki, Bernard Jr., 342–43